Queen Victoria

A Biographical Companion

Portrait of Queen Victoria, ca. 1870. (Historical Picture Archive/CORBIS)

Queen Victoria

A Biographical Companion

Helen Rappaport

ABC-CLIO

Santa Barbara, California
Denver, Colorado
Oxford, England

Library of Congress Cataloging-in-Publication Data

Rappaport, Helen.

Queen Victoria : a biographical companion / Helen Rappaport.—1st ed.

p. cm.— (ABC-CLIO biographical companions)

Includes bibliographical references and index.

ISBN 1-85109-355-9 (hardcover : alk. paper) — ISBN 1-57607-580-X (eBook)

1. Victoria, Queen of Great Britain, 1819–1901. 2. Great Britain—History—Victoria, 1837–1901. 3. Queens—Great Britain—Biography. I. Title. II. Series: ABC-CLIO biographical companion.

DA554.R37 2003
941.081'092—dc21 2003005551

07 06 05 04 03 10 9 8 7 6 5 4 3 2 1 (cloth)

ABC-CLIO, Inc.
130 Cremona Drive, P.O. Box 1911
Santa Barbara, California 93116-1911

This book is also available on the World Wide Web as an eBook. Visit www.abc-clio.com for details.

This book is printed on acid-free paper ♾.
Manufactured in the United States of America

ABC-CLIO BIOGRAPHICAL COMPANIONS

Adolf Hitler, *by David Nicholls*

Andrew Johnson, *by Glenna R. Schroeder-Lein and Richard Zuczek*

Benjamin Franklin, *by Jennifer L. Durham*

George Washington, *by Frank E. Grizzard, Jr.*

James K. Polk, *by Mark E. Byrnes*

Queen Victoria, *by Helen Rappaport*

Susan B. Anthony, *by Judith E. Harper*

Thomas Jefferson, *by David Brown*

Winston Churchill, *by Chris Wrigley*

ABC-CLIO Biographical Companions are encyclopedic guides to the lives of men and women who have had a significant impact on the social, political, and cultural development of the Western world. Each volume presents complete biographical information in an easily accessible format. An introduction and a chronology provide an overview, while the A-to-Z entries amplify a myriad of topics related to the person. A collection of documents and extensive illustrations give the reader an acute sense of the individual's life and times.

For Liz Pride

CONTENTS

PREFACE

Queen Victoria is undoubtedly one of the most written-about women in world history, yet nothing, it would seem, can dim the enduring fascination and appeal that she holds over us—from the interested lay reader to the political historian. What is the secret of this long-standing fascination? No doubt part of it is bound up with the curiosity that the long-gone days of empire—separated from us now by a whole century—still exert. It's hard to resist the nostalgic lure of such a self-confident era that, while beset with its own fair share of political and social problems, seems, from the vantage point of the post–September 11 world, to have been more solid and secure than the one we inhabit now. As the archetypal matriarch-monarch, Queen Victoria epitomized that age and has constantly intrigued historians for the accomplished way in which, like other great female monarchs of the past—such as Maria Theresa and Catherine the Great—she not only held sway over a vast empire but had no difficulty in holding her own with, and frequently dictating to, the great and powerful male political figures of her day.

The queen did not come to the throne a well-rounded, constitutional monarch: she was young and impetuous and had to learn how to behave and rule as a queen, largely thanks to the diligent tuition of prime ministers such as Melbourne and Peel, as well as her husband, Prince Albert. She never ceased to attempt, like Albert, to meddle in British policy—both at home and abroad—and was often ungraciously hot-headed and xenophobic in her attitude to her royal and political peers such as the Russian tsars Nicholas I and Alexander II and German chancellor Otto von Bismarck. Yet her unrepentant prejudices in certain quarters did not prevent her from frequently demonstrating the most even-handed clear sightedness when it came to areas where rampant Victorian prejudices prevailed: in matters of religious practice, class, and racial prejudice. In all her many dealings—both public and private—it was primarily the queen's great strength of character and her insistence, at all times, on truthfulness—from her family, her friends, and her ministers—that would set the stamp on the largely dignified manner in which she ruled.

During the 1860s and early 1870s, Victoria's popularity suffered a serious crisis when she brought upon herself considerable public disenchantment and political antipathy by retreating into a protracted period of mourning for her dead husband and refusing to take part in all but the most necessary public affairs of state. But by the time of her 1887 Golden Jubilee, Victoria had once more emerged triumphant to enjoy the great glory days of empire and her own unchallenged role as its figurehead. She might have been queen of a vast empire but she was also, first and foremost, a wife and mother and shared the ordinary aspirations of most of her subjects: to be loved and cared for. As a queen, she was not immune to life's tragedies, and as she grew older, she learned to endure them stoically. The loss of her adored husband, Albert, in 1861 was the first to shatter her until then robust constitution, but she learned, almost perversely, to thrive on grief and went on to mourn the death of her Highland servant, John Brown, in 1883 and those of three of her children—Alice in 1878, Leopold in 1884, and Alfred in 1900. Even more tragic for Victoria was having to confront the fact that she had, unwittingly, been responsible for the transmission of hemophilia, through her female children, into most of the royal houses of Europe.

The major landmarks and achievements of the reign of Queen Victoria—military, political, social, and artistic—have all been well charted in a vast catalogue of works that would defy the energies of even the most dogged or long-lived of researchers. But despite this wealth of wonderful material, the reader seeking information on any particular or specialized aspect of the queen's life and times often faces a problem: how to cut a swathe through this great archive of material and get to the facts one is specifically looking for. Indexes alone do not always offer sufficient help to the reader, and general studies, however good, often prove disappointing when one wants to winkle out information on a particularly obscure theme—such as the queen's abhorrence of smoking.

Many fine biographies of the queen have been written, by the likes of Elizabeth Longford, Giles St. Aubyn, Cecil Woodham-Smith, Christopher Hibbert, Stanley Weintraub, and Monica Charlot—to name but six. But in covering such a long and eventful life as was Queen Victoria's, biographers often have to leave out the detail in order to convey the more important, broader themes. Hence, the reason for this book, which it is hoped will offer the interested reader or student a useful finding aid on specific aspects of the queen's life, her family, and the events that shaped her reign, each entry bearing an epigraph encapsulating the queen's view on the subject, (with the exception of two relating to her own demise!).

The primary components of *Queen Victoria: A Biographical Companion* can be identified in the thematic strands listed below. These are followed by a chronology identifying the major events of Queen Victoria's life, reign, and times. Subject areas covered by headwords arranged in an A-to-Z format range among the following:

- the queen's extended family—biographical entries on her parents, her uncles, and all her children, plus the major figures in the network of European royal families with whom she had a close relationship, such as Kaiser William II. Coverage is also given to the queen's Hanoverian and Saxe-Coburg ancestors.
- close friends, mentors, and members of the royal household, such as Jane Churchill, Lady Lyttleton, Empress Eugénie, Luigi Lablache, Baroness Lehzen, Baron Stockmar, Lady Augusta Bruce, John Brown, and the Munshi (Abdul Karim)
- private secretaries: Bigge, Ponsonby, Grey; personal physicians, Clark, Jenner, and Reid
- personal interests such as opera, art and artists, dancing; and passions—such as animals and photography
- prime ministers: Melbourne, Disraeli, Gladstone, Salisbury, and others
- favorite writers: Corelli, Scott, Dickens, Tennyson, Oliphant—and painters: Landseer and Winterhalter
- pet hates: smoking, racial and class prejudice, women's rights
- personal obsessions: the queen held very particular and stubborn view on a wide

range of things including smoking, fresh air, the paranormal, religion, sex and childbirth, class and racial prejudice
- the royal homes—at Windsor, Kensington, Balmoral, and Osborne, as well as Victoria's final resting place, the Royal Mausoleum at Frogmore
- Victorian archetypes and icons: Christmas, the Albert Memorial, the Victoria and Albert Museum, the Great Exhibition, Jack the Ripper, the Koh-i-Noor Diamond, the jubilees
- political issues: the bedchamber crisis of 1839, assassination attempts on the queen, Chartism, India, Ireland, the Crimean and Boer Wars

In addition, the book includes entries that identify how the queen was popularly perceived—through two of the most famous catch-phrases associated with her: "The Widow at Windsor" and "We Are Not Amused." There is also a group of subsections under her name that cover the particularities of Victoria's birth, accession, marriage, and death; her personality and physical appearance; and her qualities as a ruler.

Every individual headword is complemented by suggestions for further reading and research, although these lists are, by necessity, highly selective. Sadly, not all of the subjects I had originally hoped to cover could be included, owing to considerations of space, and it is with some regret that I have had to omit entries on some lesser-known ministers and ladies in waiting with whom the queen had close relationships, as well as entries on some rather more oddball themes.

To cover all the many fascinating elements of a monarch's life and times, particularly a woman whose interests ranged far and wide, such as Queen Victoria's did, would take several volumes. Even if one were to attempt a much more comprehensive review, there would still remain certain issues on which the queen would elude us. For all the regularity with which Victoria wrote her journal, filling over 100 volumes, and turned out thousands of letters and memoranda, we shall never know the whole story, because, sadly, much of the original record was edited and censored during its transcription by her daughter Beatrice after the queen's death. Many other letters and documents—particularly material relating to Victoria's controversial relationship with John Brown—were also destroyed. And so, like all great monarchs, Queen Victoria still retains that indefinable air of mystery and majesty that continues to keep us guessing. During a long and eventful reign of sixty-three years, Queen Victoria proved herself to be a woman possessed of a rich and contradictory personality. She will never cease to entertain, perplex, enrage—and often inspire us—and it is hoped that this book will make some contribution to an understanding of why, as a human being, let alone a monarch, she is never, ever boring.

This book has been inspired by the great tradition of historical and biographical writing on the queen and her reign, laid down over the last hundred years by far too many distinguished writers for me to be able to acknowledge here. But I would, in particular, like to record my enduring admiration for the late Elizabeth Longford's exemplary biography, *Victoria R.I.,* first published in 1964, which I doubt will ever be bettered, and for the continuing contribution to our knowledge of the queen and Prince Albert made by scholars such as Christopher Hibbert and Stanley Weintraub. The following friends and colleagues offered helpful advice and moral support during the writing of this book: Anne Hardy, Henry Hardy, Graham Law, Christina Malkowska Zaba, Liz Pride, Tony Sloggett, and Nicola Swash.

My thanks to Simon Mason of ABC-CLIO's Oxford office and Martha Whitt in Santa Barbara for her patience and her cool head; to my copy editor, Beth Partin, my indexer, Will Ragsdale, and proof reader,

Catherine Hope; and to Scott Horst in Denver for obtaining an excellent range of illustrations. Last but not least, my love affair with the Bodleian Library, Oxford, continues and once again I am indebted to the staff of the lower library, who, during my many months of research, delivered up endless mountains of books on Queen Victoria and her era with such good grace.

Helen Rappaport
Oxfordshire, March 2003

Queen Victoria

A Biographical Companion

A

Aberdeen, George Hamilton-Gordon, Fourth Earl (1784–1860)

So very *fair, and has served* us personally, *so kindly and truly.* (Benson and Esher 1911, 2:17)

The image of Lord Aberdeen that has come down to us from Queen Victoria is that of a kindly, elderly statesman, a father figure and "delightful companion" (Benson and Esher 1911, 2: 87) in the mold of her other much-loved prime minister, Lord Melbourne. It was tragic therefore that a man of Aberdeen's retiring and pacific disposition should have had the role of war leader thrust upon him in 1854. No one could have been less willing than he to lead a bitter campaign such as the Crimean War became.

Born George Hamilton-Gordon in Edinburgh, Scotland, Aberdeen was orphaned at the age of eleven and was brought up by guardians. He went to school at Harrow, inheriting the earldom from his grandfather in 1801. Had he not entered politics, the erudite Aberdeen might well have spent his life as an academic and traveler. A fine classical scholar, he spent time traveling in the Near East during 1803–1804. His love of Greece led him to become a member of the Athenian Society and president of the Society of Antiquaries (1812–1846). He was elected to Parliament as a Scottish representative peer for the first time in 1806 but hated the cut and thrust of parliamentary electioneering. His first government post came in 1813, as British ambassador extraordinary to Vienna, where he negotiated the Treaty of Töplitz.

In 1828 Aberdeen served as chancellor of the Duchy of Lancaster, which brought with it a seat in the cabinet; he became foreign secretary later that year (1828–1830) and served as secretary for war and the colonies under Sir Robert Peel's brief ministry of 1834–1835. Out of office during the 1835–1841 period, Aberdeen observed with increasing disapproval the close personal relationship of the prime minister, Lord Melbourne, with the young queen. Victoria, in Aberdeen's view, had become putty in Melbourne's hands. The sober Aberdeen disliked the prime minister's tendency to trivialize: "I am afraid he jokes too much with her," he observed, "and makes her treat things too lightly, which are very serious" (Ziegler 1976, 263).

Aberdeen returned to government as foreign secretary under Peel (1841–1846), fulfilling his role with a strong sense of Christian morality and attempting at all times to remain neutral. His first objective was to restore Britain's flagging entente cordiale with France; during 1842–1844 he oversaw a rapprochement that led to the queen's exchanging state visits with the French ruler, only for all his hard work to be undone by French ambitions in Spain. These resurfaced in the affair of the "Spanish Marriages," when the mother of the young Queen Isabella of Spain and her sister the Infanta Luisa proposed marrying both girls to French, Bourbon princes. The British objected to such a strong dynastic alliance, preferring their own marital candidate from Saxe-Coburg, but Aberdeen was outwitted by the wily King Louis Philippe. Aberdeen did, however, score some diplomatic successes in establishing closer links with the United States through the conclusion of the Webster-Ashburton Treaty of 1842 and the Oregon Treaty of 1846.

As a supporter of free trade, Aberdeen resigned with Peel when the long controversy over the repeal of the Corn Laws came to a head in 1846; for Queen Victoria, the loss of both men was "irreparable," for they had been a breed of politician with whom she had felt "safe." In July 1850 Aberdeen joined Peel as leader of the Peelite free traders. In 1852, after the failure of Lord Derby's brief ministry, Aberdeen took on the arduous task, even in Victoria's view, of forming a coalition government of Whigs and Peelites, serving as prime minister from 1852 to 1855. The coalition was initially popular, with both sides managing to cooperate over free trade, but Aberdeen himself was criticized as being too deferential and too anxious to serve the interests of Prince Albert—who had had a hand in the makeup of his cabinet.

By nature a pacifist and noninterventionist, Aberdeen was reluctant to adopt an aggressive policy regarding Russia's ambitions in the Middle East and its incursions on Turkish territory that began in 1853. But he could not control the mounting public demand for war in Britain and calls for the return of the belligerent Lord Palmerston, who, keen to take on Russia, impatiently dismissed Aberdeen for his reticence and his "antiquated imbecility" (Blake 1966, 257). Aberdeen remained deeply troubled at the thought of war and emphasized the forty years of relative peace that Britain had enjoyed since the end of the Napoleonic Wars, arguing that "the satisfaction which ought to be felt at this state of happiness has in too many instances given way to a very warlike spirit" (Hyde 1938, 268). The queen too had no time for his conciliatory approach, but Aberdeen was adamant: "If it comes to being safe, I fear your Majesty would not be safe with me during war, for I have such a terrible *repugnance* for it, in all its forms." The queen's response was terse: "This will never do," she told him (Longford 1998, 241).

Aberdeen soon found himself "driven into a war that he deplored and whose results he dreaded" (Bryant 1961, 151) and was profoundly disturbed by this and his own overwhelming personal sense of responsibility. Like his foreign minister, Lord Clarendon, Aberdeen remained half-hearted in the prosecution of the war and refused to take seriously Prince Albert's calls for reinforcements to the army, hoping that the war could be swiftly curtailed by negotiation. Driven by public opinion and the enthusiasm of the queen for the war, he had to contend with the looming presence of Palmerston, who constantly carped at Aberdeen's lack of resolve. Aberdeen fulfilled his duty but increasingly lost his grip over a war that brought with it disturbing reports of the state of the army, its maladministration in the Crimea, and the escalating numbers of casualties. After a year of the fighting, the public and Parliament had lost confidence in Aberdeen; and he too was preoccupied with worries at home—his three daughters were all sickly and suffered from the tuberculosis that had killed their mother. He reluctantly accepted Queen Victoria's offer of the Order of the Garter in January 1855. But at the end of the month he was defeated in a motion called by Lord Roebuck, a radical back bencher, for a committee of inquiry into the management of the army in the war. As head of the government, Aberdeen was obliged to resign.

The queen wrote to Aberdeen to express her sadness at his resignation. She regretted the loss of a "faithful friend," who "throughout his Ministry . . . has ever been the kindest and wisest adviser" (Benson and Esher 1911, 3:102). In later years she would remark that Aberdeen had been the last of her prime ministers to show real consideration for her—that is, until 1868 and the arrival of the sycophantic Disraeli. The dependable Aberdeen had represented for her the safe haven of an eighteenth-century style of statesmanship that would vanish with his death and those of Melbourne, Peel, and Wellington. Upon Aberdeen's death, Queen Victoria recorded in her journal for the 14 December 1860 that he had been "one of the few remaining experienced and truly loyal public men, who would never tolerate any dishonourable proceedings, straight-forward, high minded, the kindest of friends, so wise in his opinions."

Related entries:
Crimean War; Palmerston, Henry John Temple, Third Viscount

References and further reading:

Benson, A. C., and Viscount Esher, eds. 1911. *The Letters of Queen Victoria 1837–1861.* 1st ser., 3 vols. London: John Murray.
Blake, Robert. 1966. *Disraeli.* London: Eyre and Spottiswood.
Bryant, Arthur. 1961. *English Saga 1840–1940.* London: Fontana.
Chamberlain, Muriel E. 1983. *Lord Aberdeen: A Political Biography.* London: Longman.
Conacher, J. 1968. *The Aberdeen Coalition 1852–1855.* Cambridge: Cambridge University Press.
Hyde, H. Montgomery. 1938. *Princess Lieven.* London: George G. Harrap and Co.
Iremonger, Lucille. 1978. *Lord Aberdeen: A Biography of the Fourth Earl of Aberdeen, K. G., K. T., Prime Minister 1852–1855.* London: Collins.
Longford, Elizabeth. [1964] 1998. *Victoria R.I.* London: Weidenfeld and Nicolson.
Stanmore, Lord (Sir Arthur Gordon). 1893. *The Earl of Aberdeen.* London: Sampson Low.
Ziegler, Philip. 1976. *Melbourne.* London: Fontana.

Adelaide of Saxe-Coburg-Meiningen, Princess (1792–1849)

(Duchess of Clarence; Queen Adelaide [1830–1837])

She has ever been so maternal in her affection to me . . . (Ball 1886, 148)

In 1818, the twenty-six-year-old Princess Adelaide of Saxe-Coburg-Meiningen found herself married in haste, and without the niceties of courtship, to a man twice her age. Almost immediately she found herself propelled into an indecent race between her husband and his brothers, the other sons of George III, to produce a legitimate heir to the British throne. It is to Adelaide's enduring credit that in the face of such a mercenary arrangement, she not only made her marriage a happy one but, having failed to produce an heir herself, also demonstrated great kindness and loyalty to the new queen, Victoria.

Adelaide's husband was William, duke of Clarence. He had been obliged to desert his long-standing common-law wife, the actress Mrs. Jordan, promptly ejecting the distraught woman from his residence, Bushey House (where she had lived for many years with him and their happy brood of ten illegitimate children). Adelaide, an unsophisticated and religiously devout woman, could not have been a more dramatic contrast to the rambunctious and liberated actress; nor could Adelaide's austere background have been further removed from the libidinous theatrical world that Jordan had inhabited.

Queen Adelaide, wife of William IV, was a kind and doting mother-figure to the young Princess Victoria. (Hulton/Archive by Getty Images)

The duke's conscience was clearly troubled by the necessary and premeditated action that he had been forced to take. He was determined to do right by Adelaide, writing in a letter to his son George: "She is doomed, *poor, dear, innocent young* creature to be *my* wife. *I cannot, I will not, I must not* ill use her" (Tomalin 1994, 309). Nor did he, for he developed a genuine love for Adelaide and returned her devotion.

Adelaide, the daughter of George, duke of Saxe-Coburg-Meiningen, and his wife,

Louisa, was born on 13 August 1792. Little is recorded of her early life except that she was quiet and amiable and had no "history"—the ideal wife in fact for a British duke seeking to provide an heir to the throne. Adelaide displayed a degree of stoical acceptance of the kind that was inbred in royal princesses, trained to accept the husbands chosen for them according to dynastic, political, and financial expediency. After her marriage to the duke of Clarence, she had no alternative but to turn a blind eye to his scandalous reputation. She also had to live with her husband's mountainous debts, which prompted the newlyweds to seek refuge in Hanover for the first year of their marriage. Her behavior was exemplary: she conducted herself as a model wife and future queen, showing great kindness in particular to the duke's five illegitimate daughters by Mrs. Jordan.

Sadly, Adelaide did not follow in the steps of her fecund predecessor. She failed to produce an heir who lived into adulthood: a daughter born in Hanover in 1819 died within hours, another baby was miscarried a year later, and a daughter born in 1821 died after three months. In 1822 Adelaide was delivered of stillborn twins. The miscarriages continued until after she had become queen, thus keeping alive the hope that the aging king might yet produce an heir from his much younger wife. In anticipation of Adelaide's producing a child even after the king's death, she was nominated as regent.

It was not until the duke of York, George III's second son, died in 1827 that the once distant prospect of the duke of Clarence's becoming king became much more likely. William's older brother, George IV, looked set to die without a legitimate heir (his only child, Princess Charlotte, by his estranged wife, Queen Caroline, died in childbirth in 1817). Deeply saddened by her own inability to produce a healthy child, Adelaide, who loved children, behaved with great kindness toward her niece, the fatherless Princess Victoria, daughter of the late duke of Kent and his wife. Adelaide would have been willing to bring Victoria up as her own had not the duchess of Kent and her adviser Sir John Conroy, who had their own ambitions for a regency, blocked this.

Adelaide became queen on the duke's accession as William IV on 26 June 1830. She seemed the most unprepossessing of queens, with court diarist Charles Greville describing her as "very ugly, with a horrid complexion, but has good manners" (Fulford 1963, 31). Adelaide remained determinedly in the background as queen; she took no independent view of British affairs and would have liked nothing better than to retreat to her quiet domestic life at Bushey Park. Instead, she found herself queen during one of the most unsettled periods in British history since the Civil War. For in the 1830s Britain was in the grips of a growing movement for parliamentary reform, and the strength of the Chartist agitators raised thoughts of the unthinkable—a revolution in Britain and the overthrow of the monarchy. Like her husband, Adelaide was a staunch Tory and was fearful of reform, privately nursing fears that she and King William might go the way of Marie Antoinette and Louis XVI (who had been guillotined during the French Revolution).

After being widowed in June 1837, Adelaide adopted the honorary role of queen dowager on Victoria's accession to the throne. Victoria made over to Adelaide her home at Bushey Park and another residence, Marlborough House, together with a generous pension. Adelaide lived out the rest of her life in relative seclusion, capitulating to a succession of tiresome illnesses, which at least preoccupied her with the fruitless search for medical treatment. She wrote kind and affectionate letters to the young queen, full of religious homilies, advice, and talk about the weather, and took great comfort in the letters Victoria wrote to her. She became a godmother to Victoria and Albert's first child, the Princess Royal.

For the remaining twelve years of her life, Adelaide devoted herself to acts of benevolence, patronizing the then fashionable charity bazaars in London that raised considerable amounts for the deserving poor. She also donated much of her own money to various good causes to the tune of £20,000 per year or more. She filled her time by traveling around England and on the Continent. But it was undoubtedly her religious faith that gave meaning to her somewhat aimless existence. Such was her horror, during a cruise of the Mediterranean in 1838–1839, at finding that the island of Malta lacked a Protestant church in its capital Valetta, that she personally provided the £10,000 to build one there.

When Adelaide died on 2 December 1849, she was buried at Windsor. Victoria mourned the loss of "the kindest and dearest of friends" (Benson and Esher 1911, 2: 230); the depth of her affection for her aunt contrasted starkly with her alienation at that time from her own mother, the duchess of Kent.

Related entries:
Victoria, Queen: Birth of; William IV

References and further reading:

Ball, T. Frederick. 1886. *Queen Victoria: Scenes and Incidents of Her Life and Reign.* London: S.W. Partridge.

Benson, A. C., and Viscount Esher, eds. 1911. *The Letters of Queen Victoria: A Selection from Her Majesty's Correspondence between the Years 1837 and 1861.* 1st ser., 3 vols. London: John Murray.

Fulford, Roger. [1993] 2000. *Royal Dukes.* Harmondsworth, UK: Penguin.

Fulford, Roger, ed. 1963. *The Greville Memoirs.* London: B.T. Batsford.

Hasted, Jane Eliza. 1950. *Unsuccessful Ladies: An Intimate Account of the Aunts (Official and Unofficial) of the Late Queen Victoria.* London: Ayer Publishing.

Hopkirk, Mary. 1946. *Queen Adelaide.* London: John Murray.

Tomalin, Claire. 1994. *Mrs. Jordan's Profession: The Story of a Great Actress and a Future King.* London: Viking.

Albert Edward, Prince of Wales (1841–1910)

("Bertie"; King Edward VII, 1901–1910)

If only our dear Bertie was fit to replace me! Alas! Alas! I feel very anxious for the future
(Fulford 1976, 47)

During his brief nine-year reign as King Edward VII, the eldest son of Queen Victoria and Prince Albert set his stamp upon an age, in as definitive a manner as his mother had before him. Victoria's reign had marked the rise and consolidation of the British Empire; Edwardian England, in contrast, would bask, somewhat complacently, in the last halcyon days of empire before Europe was torn apart by a war that would see the collapse of monarchies and inaugurate a new and more troubled era.

The queen spent much of her life complaining about the Prince of Wales's many defects, yet, for all his many shortcomings, her son inherited some of her best points—her charm and her astute judgment of character, her lack of racial and class prejudice, her social tact and a natural gift for putting people at their ease. But the prince's charming and affable manner could not disguise what he patently lacked—an ability to knuckle down to the more onerous aspects of royal duty above his dedicated pursuit of pleasure. In the family, Albert Edward was always called Bertie; as king he was popular with the people, who often referred to him as Teddy. Both names convey the sense of a worldly, endearing personality who enjoyed the good things in life. A man of impeccable manners, a master of royal protocol and court etiquette, the Prince of Wales was a legendary *bon viveur.* He eschewed the intellectual pursuits of his parents and elder sister Vicky for a life replete with good food, the best champagne, fat cigars, and beautiful women. He spent an enormous amount of time indulging himself in the hedonistic life of an interna-

Queen Victoria's difficult relationship with her eldest son, Bertie (Albert Edward, prince of Wales) would cause her much anxiety; she doubted he would ever make a good king, yet he remains one of the most popular British monarchs ever. (The* **Illustrated London News** *Picture Library)

tional playboy: entertaining, partying, traveling, and pursuing the hunting-shooting-fishing lifestyle of the idle rich. He protested frequently about his political emasculation by his mother and his lack of an official role, yet one wonders how he might have found time for one.

Queen Victoria had rightly predicted that her second child would be the much-wanted son and heir. Bertie was born a big, lusty baby on 9 November 1841. The queen would have liked him to be christened just plain Albert, after his father, but was obliged to give him a traditional royal name, Edward, as well. Victoria had the highest expectations of her heir, informing her Uncle Leopold in December: "You will understand *how* fervent are my prayers, and I am [sure] *everybody's* must be, to see him resemble his angelic dearest Father in *every, every* respect, both in body and mind" (Benson and Esher 1911, 1:366).

Such impossibly high expectations of the young prince would not only create bitter disappointments for his parents but also do considerable damage to the young boy's psyche. As a child, craving parental affection and reassurance, Bertie found himself constantly struggling to live up to the high standards demanded of him. Much of his naturally cheerful and ebullient nature was suppressed by the austere regime imposed by Prince Albert, leading to outbursts of temper and frustration. The queen worried that Bertie's bad behavior made him her "caricature," dreading that, in his laziness and egocentricity, he might grow up tainted by the blood of his disreputable Hanoverian ancestors.

The queen and Prince Albert made the mistake of insisting that a rigorous education would knock Bertie into shape. But unlike his father's favorite, his brilliant elder sister Vicky, Bertie, although gifted with emotional intelligence, was no intellectual. At the age of seven and a half he was placed in the charge of a master from Eton, whom Albert, with his highly developed views on education, provided with a carefully plotted daily timetable comprising religious instruction, English, writing, French, music, calculating, German, drawing, and geography. Bertie struggled to cope but found many of his academic subjects beyond him and had serious difficulty in concentrating. A more exacting tutor, Frederick Gibbs, was appointed, who joined forces with the queen and Prince Albert in endlessly chastising Bertie for his poor academic performance, Victoria openly describing her son as weak, lazy, dull, and ignorant.

Albert's response, with advice from Baron Stockmar, was to turn the screws even tighter, demanding that Bertie study seven hours a day seven days a week, in a relentless quest for self-improvement. When Bertie was seventeen, three equerries were appointed to take turn in ensuring that he behaved like a gentleman. He was not to loll around in armchairs or stand with his hands in his pockets and was to be kept from idle gossip and frivolous pursuits such as cards. He should be encouraged instead "to devote some of his leisure time to music, to the fine arts . . . hearing poetry, amusing books or good plays read aloud, in short, to anything that whilst it amuses may gently exercise the mind" (Magnus 1964, 25). The queen dreaded Bertie's coming of age in 1858 as a terrible moment; on the day of his eighteenth birthday, he was greeted with a long pedantic letter, full of exhortations about his moral duties and a detailed enumeration of his responsibilities: it provoked floods of tears in the prince.

Prince Albert had by now reached a state of despairing resignation: "He is lively, quick and sharp when his mind is set on anything, which is seldom," he wrote, "but usually his intellect is of no more use than a pistol packed at the bottom of a trunk if one were attacked in the robber-infested Appenines" (Magnus 1964, 27). By April of the following year, Victoria wondered what on earth would happen should she die and Bertie become king. "His only safety—and the country's—is his implicit reliance in everything on dearest Papa, that perfection of human beings!" (Fulford 1964, 174). There was only one thing that might save Bertie from himself : an early marriage, and Victoria and Albert were intent on finding a bride of good stolid German stock.

As heir to the throne, Bertie was forbidden from taking up an army career, as he had wished. He was sent to study at Edinburgh University in the summer of 1859 and then entered Christ Church College, Oxford, completing his studies at Trinity College, Cambridge. But he was a poor student, and the queen carped on about his failings. All in all, Bertie was a dullard and sinfully idle; but she still held out hope, constantly scrutinizing his every action—watching for any reassuring signs of improvement.

During the long university vacation in 1860, Bertie was sent to Canada, to open a railway bridge over the St. Lawrence River in Montreal and lay the foundation stone of the new federal parliament in Ottawa. He traveled on to New York and Washington, D.C., attending balls and receptions, visiting the White House, and winning the respect of the American people for his open and friendly manner. Neither the queen nor Prince Albert grasped the significance of this successful tour and saw that here was an obvious role for their gregarious son—as a goodwill ambassador for his country. Instead, in the summer of 1861, the reluctant prince was sent for a ten-week military training course in the Grenadier Guards, based at the Curragh in Dublin. It was here that he had his first sexual encounter, with an actress, Nellie Clifden. Gossip found its way back to the royal couple. Prince Albert, already unwell, went to Cambridge to give Bertie a dressing-down. The prince fell ill shortly afterward and died on 14 December. For many years after the queen would hold Bertie responsible for his father's premature death, declaring "I never can see Bertie without a shudder" (Hibbert 1976, 111). Her primary objective now was to see him safely married, and in 1862, after rejecting several other candidates, Bertie chose the beautiful and charming Alexandra of Denmark.

As the queen's long seclusion dragged on, and life at court became increasingly monotonous, Bertie and Alexandra set up their own rival court at their London home, Marlborough House. Here, the prince entertained an eclectic mix of friends from the arts, business, and banking, as well as the aristocracy. A warm and generous friend, he was not always well served by the sycophants who surrounded him and with whom he frequented the opera, music halls, clubs, casinos, and bordellos. A night bird—he was rarely in bed before 1:30 A.M.—Bertie proceeded to live social life to the hilt. With Princess Alexandra regularly pregnant and increasingly preoccupied with her children and domestic life, he became restless and spent more and more time away from home. Every spring he would travel to Paris and from there go yachting in the south of France. He would return to England for the summer and autumn, which he would spend in an endless succession of jaunts and country house parties. A dedicated follower of the sporting season, he enjoyed the racing at Ascot, Epsom, Doncaster, Newmarket, and Goodwood, then proceeded straight to the Isle of Wight for the yacht racing at Cowes. In September it was time for the deer hunting and grouse shooting season in Scotland, after which he went to his estate at Sandringham in Norfolk. This residence became famous for the prince's lavish shooting parties, during which his guests slaughtered an average of 30,000 game birds a year. In between all these endless social engagements, Bertie made futile annual trips to European spas to take the cure and fight the flab.

In 1870 Bertie caused the queen much embarrassment and concern when he was cited as corespondent in a divorce case by one of his acquaintances, Sir Charles Mordaunt. The case came at a time when the queen was being attacked in the press for her continuing seclusion. Bertie, anxious to play some useful public role, now began trying to establish a better relationship with his mother. Slowly Victoria mellowed in her attitude toward him, warming to his attentiveness, although never ceasing to criticize his gadabout lifestyle and the dubious company he kept. Yet she resolutely refused to allow Bertie access to cabinet and state papers until 1892, nor would she let him act as her representative on state visits abroad at times of national crisis. Bertie himself turned down any suggested role in Ireland or India that would take him away from his social life in London. The queen's private secretary, Sir Henry Ponsonby, saw the crux of the problem as being Bertie's low boredom threshold, coupled with his inability to take up intellectual challenges: "Nothing can be more genial and pleasant than he is for a few minutes," he wrote, "but he does not endure. He cannot keep up the interest for any length of time and I don't think he will ever settle down to business" (Ponsonby 1942, 100).

With both Bertie's reputation and that of the monarchy under scrutiny in 1871, as republican rumblings grew louder, the situation was retrieved by an upsurge of public sympathy when, in December 1871, Bertie fell dangerously ill with typhoid. It was typhoid that had killed his father (or so it was then believed), and it looked as though Bertie might die very close to the anniversary of his father's death on the 14th. He made a nearly miraculous recovery, however, and this sobering experience prompted Bertie to take stock of his past misdemeanors. The rapprochement with his mother continued during the 1870s, with Bertie acquitting himself well during a tour of India during 1875–1876, in preparation for his mother's proclamation as empress.

But Bertie's addiction to the social whirl inevitably drew him once more into indiscretions and, in 1877, the first of several affairs—in this case with the actress Lillie Langtry. Princess Alexandra tolerated this and a string of other liaisons with the actress Sarah Bernhardt, Lady Frances Brooke, and, from 1898 on, Mrs. Alice Keppel. But in 1890 Bertie once more found himself embroiled in a scandal, the Tranby Croft affair, leading to a famous libel case in which he was exposed in the witness box as an idle profligate and gambler. In an attempt at damage limitation, the queen stood by him—as she always did when Bertie's reputation was publicly called into question—having by now come to accept that she could never change her son.

On 22 January 1901, Bertie finally became king, at the age of fifty-nine. Possessed of no real experience in statecraft, he put his natural diplomacy and his cosmopolitanism to good use as an archetypal "gentleman king" and affable figurehead. His 1903 visit to Paris promoted the entente cordiale with France, and in 1907 he fostered an Anglo-Russian agreement, thus ensuring that these two major European powers would be Britain's allies during World War I against Germany. Keenly interested in the nation's defense, Bertie gave his wholehearted support to military and naval reforms, which ensured British preparedness for war, while at the same time trying to maintain the peace as *l'Oncle de l' Europe* (the uncle of Europe). But the changing political climate made him at times gloomy and depressed about the prospects for peace and the future of monarchies, and he was convinced that his son George, the Prince of Wales, would be Britain's last king. Nevertheless, during his short reign Edward VII did much to revitalize the monarchy after sixty-three years of Victoria's rule, reviving the pageantry of royal occasions, official levees, and receptions. As a promoter of civic virtue, he earned the affection of his people, not by dint of his political achievements but simply by being one of them. During the period 1890–1910 his pride and joy was his racing stud—and his three Derby winners—a fact that endeared him to the ordinary man in the street who enjoyed a bet on the horses. As newspaper proprietor Lord Northcliffe would remark, Edward VII was "the greatest monarch we've ever had—on a race-course. Only thank God he doesn't meddle in politics like his mother!" (Pearson 2000, 6).

Bertie never abandoned his indulgent lifestyle. As well as being a heavy cigarette (twenty a day) and cigar (twelve a day) smoker, he wrecked his arteries with a lifetime's overeating, his voracious appetite enabling him to dispose of five meals a day, as his girth expanded to forty-eight inches. After only nine years as king, his worn-out body failed him, and he died after a series of heart attacks. To the end he had remained publicly loyal to his wife while privately devoted to the discreet Mrs. Keppel. Shortly after the king's death, Lord Fisher offered perhaps the most humane assessment of his life: "He wasn't clever, but he always did the right thing, which is better than brains" (letter to Reginald McKenna, 14 May 1910)

Related entries:
Albert of Saxe-Coburg-Gotha, Prince Consort; Alexandra of Denmark, Princess of Wales; Empress of India; Smoking

References and further reading:

Benson, A. C., and Viscount Esher, eds. 1911. *The Letters of Queen Victoria: A Selection from Her Majesty's Correspondence between the Years 1837 and 1861.* 1st ser., 3 vols. London: John Murray.

Brook-Shepherd, Gordon. 1975. *Uncle of Europe: The Social and Diplomatic Life of Edward VII.* London: Collins.

Cowles, Virginia. 1956. *Edward VII and His Circle.* London: Hamish Hamilton.

Fulford, Roger. 1964. *Dearest Child: Letters between Queen Victoria and the Princess Royal, 1858–61.* London: Evans Brothers.

Heffer, Simon. 1998. *Power and Place: The Political Consequences of King Edward VII.* London: Weidenfeld and Nicolson.

Hibbert, Christopher. 1976. *Edward VII: A Portrait.* London: Allen Lane.

Hough, Richard. 1992. *Edward and Alexandra: Their Private and Public Lives.* London: Hodder and Stoughton.

Lee, Sir Sidney. 1925–1927. *King Edward VII.* 2 vols. London: Smith, Elder, and Co. (the official biography).

Magnus, Philip. 1964. *King Edward the Seventh.* London: John Murray.

Pearson, Hesketh. 2000. *The Whispering Gallery, being Leaves from a Diplomat's Diary.* London: Phoenix.

Plumptre, George. 1995. *Edward VII.* London: Pavilion.

Ponsonby, Arthur. 1942. *Henry Ponsonby, Queen Victoria's Private Secretary: His Life from His Letters.* London: Macmillan.

St. Aubyn, Giles. 1979. *Edward VII, Prince and King.* London: Collins.

Weintraub, Stanley. 2000. *The Importance of Being Edward: King in Waiting 1841–1901.* London: John Murray.

Albert Memorial

really magnificent (Nevill 1997, 86)

Queen Victoria's obsessive desire, from the first days of her paralyzing grief over Prince Albert's loss in December 1861, was that his memory should be forever engraved in the hearts and minds of the nation by the erection of statues, plaques, and other monuments commemorating his life and achievements. Such was the ensuing plethora of imagery that mushroomed in every railway station, city center, and town hall across the land that there was no escaping the prince's image. Charles Dickens remarked on the fact in a letter to his friend John Leech: "If you should meet with an inaccessible cave anywhere in that neighbourhood, to which a hermit could retire from the memory of Prince Albert and testimonials to the same, pray let me know of it. We have nothing solitary and deep enough in this part of England" (Hobhouse 1983, 169).

The most grandiose memorial would be that constructed in London's Hyde Park, plans for which were set in motion soon after the prince's death. A committee was brought together under the aegis of the lord mayor of London, William Cubitt, in January 1862, and a competition was launched to find the best design. Seven eminent architects submitted designs, and the public—at home and abroad—also sent in a wide range of unsolicited ideas, often structurally unfeasible and of absurdly ambitious design. Queen Victoria herself was adamant about what she wanted: nothing less than an imposing statue of Prince Albert that would be sited out of doors where the public could come and pay homage to him as to a secular saint.

The commission was finally given to that eminent exponent of the Victorian Gothic revival—Sir George Gilbert Scott—whose design was inspired by that of a medieval shrine. Scott rejected all idea of a militaristic statue of the prince and was determined that the monument should promote the prince's passion for the arts and sciences, which he had fostered with such energy and dedication. Uncharacteristically for the times, Scott constructed a seated figure, of bronze and Italian marble and inlaid with semiprecious stones such as agate, cornelian, crystal, onyx, and jasper, to be surrounded by other free-standing statuary.

But the monument, on which construction began in 1864, would cost far more than its original budget. Public subscription—amounting to £60,000—was raised to supplement the spiraling costs, and the monument would not be completed until twelve years later, at a cost of £120,000. Work on the Albert Memorial frequently fell victim to the political disquiet of the times, to financial shortages, and to personal political rivalries. Liberal Prime Minister William Gladstone objected to the escalating costs and held up construction; his successor, the Conservative Benjamin Disraeli, speedily saw to it that the queen's mounting impatience was placated and that the construction was completed.

The site in Hyde Park, opposite to that on which the Royal Albert Hall would later be constructed, was near the original site of Albert's brainchild, the Great Exhibition. For a while it was mooted that the whole structure, with its semiprecious stones and glass mosaics, be protected by a huge glass canopy, based on the style of the glasshouse erected for the Great Exhibition. A design was produced in 1876, but the project came to nothing. Meanwhile a decision was taken not to have the seven tiers of statuary surrounding the monument made in gilded bronze. Scott decided instead that they should be sculpted from Sicilian marble, with only the four angels protecting the high canopy to be fired in bronze. The basic structure was completed in June 1868, and it was inspected by the queen, with Albert's statue not yet in position, on 1 July 1872. Two days later the public were allowed to

The newly regilded statue of Prince Albert takes center stage in the refurbished Albert Memorial in London's Kensington Gardens, designed by the master of the Victorian Gothic revival, Sir Charles Gilbert Scott. (Helen Rappaport)

view the work so far, but the central feature, the statue of Prince Albert, designed by the Italian sculptor Carlo Marochetti, was rejected, and his death before he had revised his design meant the statue commission had to be placed with another sculptor, John Foley. It was another two years before the fourteen-foot, ten-ton bronze statue, cast from recycled war cannons from the Woolwich Arsenal, was completed. It depicted Prince Albert dressed in the robes of the Order of the Garter and holding the catalog for the Great Exhibition. The statue was finally placed on its pedestal in November 1875 and unveiled the following March after it had been gilded.

Albert's statue is protected by a feat of Victorian engineering—a canopy raised on granite marble columns and topped with a 175-foot spire that many cynics thought would fall down. Surrounding his statue on the upper level are carved angels, statues of those Christian virtues by which "Albert the Good" and his queen had tried to live their lives: Humility, Justice, Prudence, Fortitude, Temperance, Faith, Hope, and Charity. Other bronze statues representing Astronomy, Chemistry, Geometry, Geology, Medicine, Philosophy, Physiology, and Rhetoric also grace these upper levels, attached to pillars. Surrounding the four corners of the base of the central platform are groups representing the Great Exhibition: Engineering, Agriculture, Manufacturing, and Commerce. The exterior, raised platform is decorated with a white marble frieze featuring representations of 169 famous figures from the arts such as Shakespeare, Mozart, and Dante. A flight of granite steps leads down to the base of the monument, which is surrounded by wrought iron gates, and just outside them, four imposing statuary groups representing the four continents of the British Empire—Europe, Asia, Africa, and America—which were finally all in position by the summer of 1872.

Within years of its construction the memorial was dismissed as vulgar and sentimental, and by the end of the nineteenth century, as modernism in art swept in and Victorian architecture was rejected wholesale, the memorial was much reviled and neglected. By the 1980s it had so deteriorated that it was in urgent need of restoration. Polluting smoke and city grime had also totally blackened Prince Albert's statue over the years. After much campaigning, led by the Victorian Society, which fought off arguments in favor of the memorial's partial demolition, a restoration project of sorts was announced in 1987. But it was not until there were a concerted press campaign and protests from many heritage groups that the government finally committed itself to funding some of the much-needed restoration work. In the 1990s the entire edifice was surrounded in scaffolding and work began, under the auspices of English Heritage. It was an ambitious project: the gilding was to be restored to its original glory, the bronze angels removed and conserved, the glass jewels polished, and all the gates and railings repainted, at an estimated cost of £11 million. On 21 October 2000, the memorial, restored in time for the millennium, was unveiled to a fireworks display spelling out the words "Albert Saved" and was once more reopened to the public.

Related entries:
Albert of Saxe-Coburg-Gotha, Prince Consort; Art and Artists; Frogmore

References and further reading:
Brooks, Chris, ed. 2000. *The Albert Memorial: The Prince Consort National Memorial: Its History, Contests and Conservation.* New Haven: Yale University Press.

Darby, Elisabeth, and Nicola Smith. 1983. *The Cult of the Prince Consort.* New Haven: Yale University Press.

Hobhouse, Hermione. 1983. *Prince Albert: His Life and Work.* London: Hamish Hamilton.

Nevill, Barry St-John. 1997. *Life at the Court of Queen Victoria: With Selections from the Journals of Queen Victoria.* Stroud, Gloucestershire: Sutton.

Albert of Saxe-Coburg-Gotha, Prince Consort (1819–1861)

Without him everything loses its interest (Aronson 1991, 86)

Till the day she died, Queen Victoria never doubted that she owed everything to her adored husband, Prince Albert. "It is *you* who have entirely formed me," she once told him (James 1983, 275–276), and she never ceased to remind her children of their debt to "dearest Papa." Albert had been all things: "my father, my protector, my guide and adviser in all and everything, my mother (I might also say), as well as my husband" (Fulford 1966, 111–112). During his twenty-one years as prince consort, he had proved himself to be a man of high moral purpose, remarkable intellect, and wide-ranging interests. There was hardly an aspect of British civic, cultural, and political life in which he did not take an active part, in addition to being a devoted and patient husband and an attentive, although frequently exacting, father.

In Prince Albert's domestic life with the queen there was not a subject on which she did not solicit his advice or approval. But even though Victoria promoted her husband as a paragon of virtue, many found it impossible to warm to his stiff and inhibited manner. He seemed so decidedly superior in his detachment from court circles and his disdain for the British aristocracy. The prudish streak in the prince's nature often made him appear more pedant than paragon, a man so formal and so circumspect that his real character was rarely divined by others and even now remains elusive. In 1900, the writer Margaret Oliphant wondered whether Albert's reserve had been "a hindrance to that true appreciation which his character deserved" (1900, 62), for during Albert's lifetime, people tended to respond to his personality as either one of two extremes—as Queen Victoria's saintly "Albert the Good" or the much-disliked foreign interloper "Albert der King" (in popular parlance).

Albert Francis Charles Augustus Emmanuel was born three months after Queen Victoria, on 26 August 1819, at the Castle Rosenau near Coburg, in present-day Germany. The second son of Ernest, duke of Saxe-Coburg-Gotha, and his wife, Louise (of the house of Saxe-Gotha-Altenburg), Albert was very close to his brother, Ernest, with whom he shared a hedonistic love of the forested countryside at this, the family's summer residence. Together they enjoyed walking, hunting, shooting, fencing, and skating, as well as sharing a fascination with science and nature and a passion for collecting specimens. Trained as an accomplished pianist and organist by his father, Albert would always be at his most self-expressive when playing the organ, and music, his greatest love, provided a conduit for the reflective and melancholic side of his nature.

Albert's young life was marred by the collapse of his parents' marriage in 1824; his mother was forced to leave her sons behind when the couple separated, and she died of cancer in 1831 without ever seeing Albert and Ernest again. Albert, a shy, earnest, and studious child, soon showed signs of an insecurity probably aggravated by the absence of his mother, which manifested itself in later life in a compulsion to be controlling over others (particularly Victoria and his children). His constitution did not appear particularly strong, and he tired easily. Almost from Albert's birth, plans had been laid that he might one day make the perfect husband for his first cousin, Princess Victoria, the architect of this scheme being their uncle, Leopold (later king of the Belgians). But on her first meeting with Albert, engineered by Leopold in 1836, Princess Victoria had failed to be engaged by Albert's embryonic charms. Further grooming was obviously required, and Albert was sent to Brussels and then Bonn University to complete his education.

This 1843 etching of Prince Albert depicts him as the incarnation of a handsome, medieval knight in armor and was one of the queen's favorites. (Hulton/Archive by Getty Images)

When he visited his cousin Victoria again in the autumn of 1839, Albert made an immediate and unexpected impact; Victoria was entranced by his beauty, and four days after his arrival exercised her royal prerogative and proposed to him. Engaged in October, Albert had only four months to adapt to the idea of leaving his beloved Coburg forever. He contemplated his future life in England with great apprehension, but he was single minded about the challenge that awaited him: "With the exception of my relations toward [the Queen] my future position will have its dark sides, and the sky will not always be blue and unclouded," he wrote to his stepmother. "But life has its thorns in every position, and the consciousness of having used one's powers and endeavours for an object so great as that of having promoted the good of so many, will surely be sufficient to support me" (Grey 1867, 238). At the end of January, Albert left Coburg in floods of tears, embarking on his self-ordained road to Calvary, anticipating marriage to Victoria rather as a trial of his personal strengths and sense of duty than as the fulfillment of any emotional aspirations. On 10 February 1840 he and Victoria were married at St. James's Palace.

Albert was right to anticipate the sense of alienation he would feel in England, made far worse by the fact that he arrived in a country already well disposed not to like him—as both a German and a foreigner. From the outset he was made fun of for his German accent and lampooned by cartoonists and the satirical press. Soon after his arrival, Parliament voted to reduce his personal allowance from £50,000 to £30,000 per annum. But what would prove far harder for Albert to reconcile himself to was being married to a wife who, while acknowledging at all times her husband's authority as head of the *household* and domestic affairs, seemed intent on excluding him from any useful role in her official duties: "In my whole life I am very happy and contented; but the difficulty in filling my place with the proper dignity is, that I am only the husband, and not the master of the house" (Bolitho 1964, 49).

Albert's emasculation during these early months, as he struggled for a modicum of independence, was both frustrating and humiliating. It took place against a backdrop of heated arguments between the queen and the government over his precedence at court and his appointment as regent (should she die in childbirth). Having accepted naturalization on his marriage to the queen, Albert expected some official recognition of his position of preeminence—perhaps a peerage and with it a seat in the House of Lords. The queen could not deny that she would have liked him to be accorded the status of king alongside her, but this was not to be. After years of argument with successive governments, Victoria used her own royal prerogative to elevate Albert to prince consort in 1857 by Royal Letters Patent.

Domestic life with Victoria, although bringing many pleasures as the children began arriving, was not sufficient to a man of Albert's intelligence and ambitions. Slowly but concertedly he began inculcating in Victoria his own lofty ideals and interests. Under her husband's tutelage, the queen's slim grasp of the arts and science was enhanced; she eagerly accepted his leadership as regards the books they read, the music they enjoyed, the paintings and sculpture they collected. She even modified her own habits by ceasing to stay up late at night and giving over less and less of her time to the frivolities of dancing and idle gossip with her ladies-in-waiting. But Albert, with his thirst for constant self-improvement, was discontented merely to sit by his wife's side, blotting her official letters as she wrote them. Determined to play some active role in the political life and culture of his adoptive country, he studied British laws and the constitution and set about asserting his influence in the only way open to him—by educating his young and impressionable wife in constitutional monarchy and impressing upon her the all-essential political impartiality of the sovereign. In so doing, he helped to soften the obstinate and shamefully partisan attitude that Victoria had displayed with such ill grace during the Bedchamber Crisis of 1839, weaning her away from her Whig bias toward an acceptance of the new Conservative government and a respect for the status of the cabinet and Parliament. The first real opportunity given to Albert to exercise his punctilious sense of order and frugality had come in 1842 with his reorganization of the royal household in a sweeping program of cost cutting and elimination of waste. By 1845 so great was Prince Albert's growing influence over the queen's political decisions that the court diarist, Charles Greville, observed that "they are one person, and as He likes and She dislikes business, it is obvious that while she has the title he is really discharging the functions of the Sovereign" (Strachey and Fulford, 1938 5:257).

Although by now set on a course of slowly winning the confidence of the British government and nation, much of Albert's time was still consumed by domesticity, providing support to his wife through her successive pregnancies and dealing with her severe headaches and her bouts of histrionics and postnatal depression. As a natural introvert, Albert hated emotional confrontations and developed a habit of writing personal notes to his wife about her behavior rather than dealing with it face to face, a practice that infuriated the headstrong and argumentative Victoria. His authoritarian attitudes and his exacting scholastic standards did not necessarily translate well in the royal nursery either. A hard taskmaster with his children, he closely supervised the nursery's day-to-day running and the health and welfare of the royal children with Teutonic precision and, having a particular interest in education, personally devised their demanding educational curriculum. Albert's great interest in education would receive a fillip in October 1847, when he was elected as chancellor of Cambridge University, against considerable opposition, in which capacity he would encourage a liberalizing and widening of the scope of its courses.

The prince's unceasing hard work in pursuit of his many noble visions and aspirations for the enhancement of British culture and industry, as well as the promotion of British prestige as an international power, all took a heavy toll on his physical and mental well-being, making him always vulnerable to the deep-seated melancholy that lay at the core of his personality. By the end of his short life, he could claim responsibility for serving as the queen's unofficial private secretary, if not minister, as well as being the impetus behind a wide range of social and political innovations and the modernization of the army. As a man with a passionate interest in art and architecture, he was a leading promoter of the Victorian Gothic revival. His collection of early Renaissance art as well as works by Cranach, Dürer, Memling, and Van Eyck, greatly enhanced both the Royal Collection and the National Gallery. In 1845 he became president of the Society of Fine Arts. In his reorganization of the incomparable print collections at Windsor and his cataloging of the royal collection of drawings by Raphael, Holbein, and Leonardo da Vinci, he left a lasting memorial to his own considerable scholarship as an art historian.

His interest in art and architecture had brought an invitation to join the royal commission set up in 1841 to supervise the interior decorations of the new Houses of Parliament, inspiring Albert to later take a hand in supervising the design and construction of the royal family's new homes, first at Osborne and then at Balmoral, where he set up model farms, as well as in Windsor Great Park, introducing modern agricultural techniques and building up herds of prize livestock. He would show an equal interest in the development of model housing for workers on the royal estates and elsewhere and was a patron of the Society for Improving the Condition of the Working Classes.

As time went on, Prince Albert was increasingly in demand to give lectures on art, science, business, and philanthropy; to sit on committees, attend exhibitions, and play a more high-profile role in the cultural life of the country. And although his significant political influence over the queen might never be publicly broadcast, British arts, commerce, and industry received an enormous boost under Albert's patronage. The prince's visionary approach to the promotion of British excellence at the Great Exhibition, masterminded by him from 1849 until its opening in 1851, in turn inspired the Dublin Exhibition of 1853 and the Manchester Art Treasures Exhibition of 1857, as well as many similar exhibitions abroad. Albert's fostering of the construction of a complex of institutions, colleges, and museums in South Kensington, later known collectively as Albertopolis, would be one of the greatest of his legacies, a lasting tribute to his pursuit of scholarship and academic excellence. On a more prosaic level, his enthusiasm for the Germanic celebration of Christmas set in place an iconography that persists to this day.

Such an impressive range of interests was further enhanced by the prince's ambitions to break down British insularity with regard to foreign affairs, and he increasingly brought his years of political study into play. His grasp of foreign policy finally found an outlet after the onset of war against Russia in the Crimea in 1854, when even the grudging Lord Palmerston was forced to admire the prince's political acumen. This was not the case, however, with the popular press, which whipped up the old hostilities toward Albert as a foreigner and called his political allegiances into question, even spreading rumors that he might be a Russian spy. Albert was an all too obvious scapegoat for British xenophobia. He stoically endured the abuse and, with the queen, was outspoken about the mismanagement of the war, repeatedly urging the organization of British militia forces, to be sent as reinforcements to the Crimea. He wrote endless memorandums on every aspect of the war, yet the only publicly acknowledged contribution he was allowed to make during this time of national crisis was the design of the newly instituted Victoria Cross.

By the end of the war Albert was showing visible signs of fatigue. Yet still he labored on, rising every morning at seven to do an hour's work in his study before breakfast; filling his every moment with letter writing and paperwork, and incessantly traveling up and down the country, making speeches, opening bridges and hospitals, laying foundation stones, and appearing as patron or chair at the many scientific, cultural, and academic organizations that he supported. Work had now become the surrogate for a life among people, with whom he had never felt at ease. The only respite from his self-imposed duties came during family holidays at Balmoral and Osborne, where he would lose himself in his great loves of hunting, shooting, fishing, and overseeing the home farms on the estates. But such holidays never restored his health and his spirits for long.

Albert never overcame his sense of isolation, exacerbated by the loss of his close friend and private secretary, George Anson, who had died suddenly in 1849. With the departure of his favorite daughter, Vicky, who married the son of the crown prince of Prussia in 1858, much of his vital spark faded. Without real friends, or his own entourage at court, or a supportive political faction in Parliament, his only consolation was his work and his love for the queen. But even Victoria's unqualified love and undying admiration could not prevent his becoming increasingly melancholic and pessimistic: "Man is a beast of burden," he remarked gloomily in November 1856, "and he is only happy if he has to drag his burden and if he has little free will. My experience teaches me every day to understand the truth of this, more and more" (Bolitho 1964, 166). Victoria might fulminate loud and often to their children about their father's virtues, but his wife's praise was no palliative for "the dragon of his dissatisfaction," which "devoured with dark relish that ever-growing tribute of laborious days and nights" (Strachey 1971, 168). Albert was lonely, "not merely with the loneliness of exile," contended Strachey, "but with the loneliness of conscious and unrecognized superiority. . . . There was something that he wanted and that he could never get. . . . Who *could* appreciate him in England?" (169).

A lifelong hypochondriac, Albert's mental strain and exhaustion accelerated during 1859 and 1860. He suffered interrmittently from many debilitating complaints, including indigestion and gastric upsets, catarrh, toothache, insomnia, headaches, neuralgia, and rheumatism. He hated the cold and damp of the English climate, but his wife never made any concessions to this need by allowing their homes to be properly heated. Albert resorted to wearing thick long johns at night and a wig at breakfast to keep his bald head warm. His poor health was made worse in his last few months by his stressful relationship with his eldest son, Bertie, Prince of Wales, and the need to support his hysterical wife after the death of her mother, the duchess of Kent, in the spring of 1861. As ever, Albert was calm, solicitous, and kind and painstakingly tolerant of the queen's excessive grief. As lady-in-waiting Lady Augusta Bruce wrote: "I never saw such tenderness, such gentleness, such tact as His—Oh! He is one in millions—well might She love Him as she did—I was so struck with His appreciation of Her. It was so true, and, for one who is supposed to place intellect and reasoning powers above all, so remarkable" (Windsor and Bolitho 1927, 200).

One of Albert's last significant acts before his death was to help defuse the threat of war between Britain and the United States over the *Trent* Affair, early in December 1861. This crisis had arisen when U.S. officials had boarded a British merchant ship, the *Trent,* and removed two Confederate commissioners en route to England to state their case to the British on the outbreak of the Civil War. This crisis exhausted the prince's depleted reserves of strength, as he struggled to rework a bellicose despatch to the U.S. government drafted by Lord John Russell, composing in its stead a far more conciliatory document that in the event averted an outbreak of hostilities. Shortly before he fell ill, Albert had ominously informed Victoria that he did not "cling to life" as she did. When the final illness came—a chill, leading to fever and total physical collapse—he seemed resigned to die; yet even in his delirium his thoughts were of the work left unfinished: "The words 'the country; oh, the country. I could perhaps bear my own misery, but the poor country' were constantly recurring," recorded Lady Bruce (Windsor and Bolitho 1927, 242). Prince Albert died on 14 December 1861, shortly after finally being diagnosed, by Sir William Jenner, as having typhoid fever. In the absence of a postmortem, that conclusion prevailed until biographers such as Daphne Bennett and Stanley Weintraub began suggesting that the cause of the prince's death was probably an accumulation of many factors and that some of his symptoms—such as the pain and swelling in his abdomen—may have indicated stomach cancer—or possibly even hepatic or renal failure.

After the prince's death, the mistress of the wardrobe, the duchess of Sutherland, asked the rhetorical question: "Will they do him justice now?" (Lee 1902, 321). The outpouring of condolences in the press and the shock and grief on the faces of people on the streets of Britain seemed, at last, to be a validation of the prince consort's life and work. But in fact much of this popular sentiment was directed at the queen—as widow and mother of nine fatherless children. The queen's plaintive and childlike response to Albert's death was like that to the loss of a father figure: "There is no one to call me Victoria now" (Charlot 1991, 425). She remained convinced for the rest of her life that Albert's death had been brought about by two things: the stress and worry he had been put to by the Prince of Wales and his own fatal lack of "pluck" in fighting his illness.

Prince Albert would have been appalled by the grotesque cult of mourning that the widowed Victoria now set in place, establishing an iconography that transformed him into "a stained-glass-window saint" (Bennett 1977, 376). She crammed her private rooms with mementoes and portraits of her dead husband until Albert's presence was inescapable throughout all the royal homes. As one of his grandchildren recorded: "There was Grandpa in full general's uniform, Grandpa in his robes of the Order of the Garter, Grandpa in kilt, Grandpa in plain clothes, Grandpa on horse-back, at his writing table, Grandpa with his dogs, with his children, in the garden, on the mountains. Grandpa with important-looking papers in his hands. Grandpa with his loving wife gazing enraptured up into his face" (Marie, Queen of Roumania 1934, 20).

Writing of the prince in 1900, the novelist Margaret Oliphant concluded that despite all that had been written about him and his achievements, he remained "a somewhat veiled and abstract character" (60), who had never revealed his true self. What might have contributed to this sense of remoteness was Albert's lack of any obvious vices. He "had one fault, if you can call it one," in the opinion of William Gladstone, and that was that "he was too free from the temptations common to other men. He seemed without them, and the standard is one that it is not fair to judge others by" (Windsor and Bolitho 1927, 263). In his personal and professional life the prince's air of austerity and critical severity often made him appear disapproving and professorial. Such dry detachment implied a lack of spontaneity and a barrenness of spirit—a "cold egotism," as Mary Ponsonby saw it (1927, 5)—that made him appear to lack compassion for the human frailties of others.

With his highly rational and analytical approach to problems, Albert was the antithesis of the instinctive and demonstrative Victoria, who always trusted to her innate common sense and her natural intuition. Albert's insistence on impartial judgment, arrived at always after a careful evaluation of the pros and cons of a situation, had an air of cold abstraction in the German philosophic tradition, which was alien to British political life, where the empirical approach was preferred. By accident of birth, temperament, and with his strictly regimented upbringing, he was never able to understand the English tendency to fudge things, and with it the resistance to his obsessive need for control and order in everything. In her grief after Albert's death, the queen failed to perceive the significance of this inherent clash of cultural attitudes, announcing that it was "*my firm* resolve, my *irrevocable decision,* viz. that *his* wishes—*his* plans—about everything, his views about *every* thing are to be *my law!*" (Benson and Esher 1911, 3:476). For the rest of her life she adhered, in the main, to what she felt Albert would have wanted—in her personal and moral life and in her political decisions. In so doing, she upheld the values of an Albertian morality—the ethics of hard work, duty, civic pride, seriousness of purpose, and moral rectitude—that we now have come to call "Victorian."

Related entries:
Albert Edward, Prince of Wales; Anson, George Edward; Art and Artists; Balmoral Castle; Christmas; Great Exhibition; Grey, General

Charles; Jenner, Sir William; Leopold I, King of the Belgians; Osborne; Phipps, Sir Charles; Photography; Royal Albert Hall; The Royal Household; Saxe-Coburg-Gotha, Royal House of; Stockmar, Christian Friedrich von; Victoria, Princess Royal; Victoria, Queen: As a Monarch; Victoria, Queen: Courtship and Marriage of; Victoria, Queen: Personality of; Victoria and Albert Museum; Victoria Cross

References and further reading:

Aronson, Theo. 1991. *The Heart of a Queen: Queen Victoria's Romantic Attachments.* London: John Murray.

Bennett, Daphne. 1977. *King without a Crown: Albert Prince Consort of England 1819–1861.* London: Heinemann.

Benson, A. C., and Viscount Esher, eds. 1911. *The Letters of Queen Victoria, 1837–1861.* 1st ser., 3 vols. London: John Murray.

Bolitho, Hector. 1964. *Albert, Prince Consort.* London: Max Parrish.

Charlot, Monica. 1991. *Victoria: The Young Queen.* Cambridge: Polity (esp. chap. 12, "Albert's Search for Power").

Darby, Elisabeth, and Nicola Smith. 1982. *The Cult of the Prince Consort.* New Haven: Yale University Press.

Fulford, Roger. 1966. *The Prince Consort.* London: Macmillan.

Grey, Lieutenant-General, The Hon. Charles. 1867. *The Early Years of H.R.H. the Prince Consort.* London: Smith, Elder and Co.

Hobhouse, Hermione. 1983. *Prince Albert: His Life and Work.* London: Hamish Hamilton.

Jagow, Kurt. 1938. *The Letters of the Prince Consort 1831–1861.* London: John Murray.

James, Robert Rhodes. 1983. *Albert Prince Consort.* London: Hamish Hamilton.

Jerrold, Clare. 1913 *The Married Life of Queen Victoria.* London: Eveleigh Nash.

Lee, Sydney. 1902. *Queen Victoria, A Biography.* London: Smith, Elder and Co.

Longford, Elizabeth. [1964] 1998. *Victoria R.I.* London: Weidenfeld and Nicolson.

Marie, Queen of Roumania. 1934. *The Story of My Life.* 3 vols. London: Cassell.

Martin, Sir Theodore. 1875–1880. *The Life of His Royal Highness the Prince Consort.* 5 vols. London: Smith, Elder and Co.

Oliphant, Margaret. 1900. *Queen Victoria: A Personal Sketch.* London: Cassell.

Ponsonby, Magdalen, ed. 1927. *Mary Ponsonby: A Memoir. Some Letters and a Journal.* London: John Murray.

Richardson, Joanna. 1977. *Victoria and Albert: A Study of a Marriage.* London: Dent.

Strachey, Lytton, and Roger Fulford, eds. 1938. *The Grenville Memoirs.* 8 vols. London: Macmillan.

Strachey, Lytton. [1921] 1971. *Queen Victoria.* Harmondsworth, UK: Penguin (esp. chap. 6, "The Last Years of the Prince Consort").

Weintraub, Stanley. 1997. *Albert, Uncrowned King.* London: John Murray.

Whittle, Tyler. 1980. *Victoria and Albert at Home.* London: Routledge and Kegan Paul.

Windsor, Dean of, and Hector Bolitho, eds. 1927. *Letters of Lady Augusta Stanley: A Young Lady at Court 1849–1863.* London: Gerald Howe.

Alexandra of Denmark, Princess of Wales (1844–1925)

("Alix"; Queen Alexandra of Great Britain, 1901–1910)

Oh! may Bertie be worthy of such a sweet wife! Does he quite deserve it? (8 November 1862; Fulford 1968, 127)

The choice of a bride for their eldest son and heir, Bertie, the Prince of Wales, greatly preoccupied the queen and Prince Albert after the prince reached the age of eighteen in November 1859. In her search for an appropriate European princess (much of it conducted after Albert's death in 1861), the queen honed the matchmaking skills that she had acquired through the earlier dynastic alliance of her daughter Vicky with the Prussian royal family. The shy and beautiful Alexandra of Denmark, who would be the queen's favorite daughter-in-law, was by no means her first choice. Coming as she did from an impoverished branch of the Danish royal family, her political allegiances placed her at odds with the dominant, German dynastic links of the royal family.

Alexandra Caroline Marie Charlotte Louise Julie was the daughter of Prince Christian of Schleswig-Holstein-Sonderburg-Glucksburg—the heir to the Danish throne. She grew up with her five brothers and sisters at the Yellow Palace in Copenhagen—a far from grand residence, her father having to earn his living as an officer in the Danish Guards. Never an intellectual, and faintly bored by the arts and literature, Alexandra was educated by governesses to

The wedding of Princess Alexandra of Denmark and Albert Edward in 1863 was marred by the queen's recent bereavement; here, she is more engrossed in a marble bust of her late lamented husband than in the happy couple. (Hulton/Archive by Getty Images)

be accomplished at drawing, singing, and playing the piano (although her musical gifts were greatly inhibited in later life by her increasing deafness) and was taught English, French, and German. She also learned to ride with her father, becoming a fearless horsewoman, and loved the Danish national sport of ice skating.

The choice of a suitable bride for the Prince of Wales was highly circumscribed by political and financial dictates; Victoria also demanded that the right candidate should be intelligent, pretty, and physically strong (for childbearing) and should have good teeth and skin. But none of the seven most obvious candidates proved acceptable: Elizabeth of Weid was not attractive; Bertie did not like the Princess of Meiningen; Marie of the Netherlands was too plain and sickly in the queen's view; Princess Alexandrine, niece of the king of Prussia, was, poor girl, neither clever nor pretty. And although Alexandra had also been suggested, she had initially appeared to be an unlikely choice because of her blood ties to the frivolous Hesse-Cassel family, of whom the queen strongly disapproved. More important, intermarriage with the Danish royal family might invite political problems, arising from the long-standing German-Danish dispute over control of the duchies of Schleswig and Holstein (see "Palmerston, Henry John Temple, Third Viscount"). The queen had rightly feared that Alexandra might be partisan over her own country's claims and drive a wedge in the royal family's loyalties. Others in the royal household, however, saw the prospect of the marriage as a very welcome dilution of the Germanization of the British court.

Queen Victoria enlisted the help of her daughter Vicky, crown princess of Prussia, in vetting the European candidates, instructing her to find out all she could about Alexandra's character. Having seen photographs of Alexandra and received reports on her good character from Vicky, the queen realized she would be hard pressed to find another as lovely as she, although her Danishness remained a distinct inconvenience. Vicky, however, was emphatic: "I should say yes—*she* is *the* one a thousand times over" (Hibbert 2000, 272). Once Alexandra had been decided upon, the queen had to move quickly in order to preempt the aspirations of the queen of Holland, who fancied Alexandra as a bride for the prince of Orange, and those also of the tsar, who viewed her as a possible bride for the tsarevich, the future Alexander III. An "accidental" meeting was contrived for Bertie and Alix, as the family now referred to her, in September 1861, at the cathedral of Speyer, Vicky acting as mediator and making the introduction. Bertie found the sixteen-year-old Alix lovely, but although she was sweet and engaging company, he seemed indifferent about proposing and asked that Alix should visit England before he made up his mind.

By November of 1861 the efforts of the queen and Prince Albert to marry Bertie safely off had acquired a new note of urgency after he had become embroiled in a sexual relationship with an actress, Nellie Clifden, while on military training at the Curragh in Dublin. It was now of paramount importance that Bertie should be settled before he further damaged his own and the family's reputation. By January 1862, and now grieving the untimely death of Prince Albert, the queen was urging a swift resolution. "The marriage is the thing and the beloved Papa was most anxious for it" (Fulford 1968, 38). That September she met Alix at the palace of Laeken near Brussels and was greatly impressed with her beauty, her graceful demeanor, and her charm. Soon afterward Bertie finally proposed. In November Alix came to England, spending several weeks with the queen at Osborne and Windsor. The queen was enchanted with her and admitted to the pride and satisfaction she felt when she first presented the shy Alix to the family. "I can't say how I and we all love her!" she wrote to Vicky. "She is so good, so simple, unaffected, frank, bright and cheerful, yet so quiet and gentle that her *umgang* [companionship] soothes me. Then *how* lovely! . . . This jewel! *She is one* of those sweet creatures who seem to come from the skies to help and bless poor mortals and lighten for a time their path!" (Fulford 1968, 127, 130)

Privately, the queen no doubt hoped that this paragon of virtue would be the wayward Bertie's salvation. The marriage took place on 10 March 1863 at St. George's Chapel, Windsor. The event brought back the most painful memories for the queen of her own wedding day with Albert. She did not throw off her mourning for the ceremony but, draped in her widow's weeds, watched it from a private box above the chapel and did not join the wedding breakfast afterward. Her sense of desolation was unremitting, for everything about the day had been an agonizing reminder of the absence of "the guardian angel of the family," Prince Albert (Hibbert 1984, 172). She was depressed for days afterward. Alix had also been greatly agitated by the emotion of the event, but afterwards remarked: "You may think that I like marrying Bertie for his position; but if he were a cowboy I would love him just the same and would marry no-one else" (Magnus 1964, 67).

Once married, Bertie and Alexandra established their own "social sovereignty" (Magnus 1964, 68) in London. They lifted the gloom of the queen's widowhood and seclusion by gathering around them a smart new social set at Marlborough House and at their country estate, Sandringham, in Norfolk—both of which they renovated and decorated to their own taste. Alix's enjoyment of social life was inevitably cut short by pregnancy. The queen had become preoccupied that her daughter-in-law was not as strong as she had thought; suddenly the lovely complexion seemed sallow and she was losing her *fraîcheur* (freshness). It was clear that Bertie was not taking sufficient care of her—going out every night and indulging as much as before in his frivolous lifestyle. Alix's first baby was born sickly and two months premature on 8 January 1864. He was named Albert Victor, at the queen's insistence, and later given the title of the duke of Clarence. Another son, with whom Alexandra was particularly close, the future King George V, was born in 1865, followed by three daughters: Louise in 1867, Victoria in 1868, and Maud in 1869. A sixth child, Alexander, died at birth in 1871. Just prior to the birth of Louise, Alix was seriously ill with rheumatic fever, which left her with a stiff knee joint and made her congenital deafness even more pronounced.

As princess of Wales, Alix was uncontroversial and much loved. Slim, graceful, and charming, with elegant fashion sense, she injected grace and glamor into the dowdy royal family. In later life, her habit of wearing high choker necklaces, such as her nine strands of pearls, to cover a scar on her neck was also much copied by society ladies, as was the limp she was left with after her illness—soon dubbed "the Alexandra limp." She spoke, all her life, with a heavy Danish accent, and her deafness made social gatherings increasingly difficult for her. Her bad points seemed few, in the main confined to a legendary unpunctuality—Alix frequently not emerging for breakfast until 11 A.M. and regularly arriving late at the dinner table, a fact that infuriated her husband. Bertie retaliated by setting all the clocks at Sandringham a half an hour fast. Alix could also be capricious and prone to bouts of temper and had a selfish streak that was motivated by her strong maternal instincts. As she grew older she kept her two youngest daughters, Victoria and Maud, with her in much the same manner as Queen Victoria had her youngest daughters, Helena and Beatrice—discouraging them from all idea of marrying.

With Alix frequently socially indisposed by pregnancy, her restless and gregarious husband Bertie spent more and more time staying out late at parties, playing cards, and clubbing. The couple spent increasing periods apart, as Bertie pursued this hedonistic lifestyle. Alix was no intellectual and took no interest in politics; her consuming passion was her children and her family in Denmark, as well as her horses and the many dogs she kept at Sandringham. In the 1870s she became greatly absorbed in a new interest—photography—receiving instruction from a Norfolk photographer, Frederick Ralph. She became one of the most accomplished photographers in the royal family and by the end of the 1880s was taking her Kodak camera everywhere. Some of Alix's photographs were exhibited in 1897; in 1908 she allowed many more to be reproduced in *Queen Alexandra's Christmas Book,* which sold 100,000 copies in twenty-four hours.

It was to Bertie's eternal good fortune—both as Prince of Wales and as king—that his wife proved exceptionally loyal and tolerant in the face of his endless affairs, notably those with Lillie Langtry, Lady Frances Brooke, and Mrs. Alice Keppel. While enjoying their own very separate spheres—his social, hers domestic—Alix and Bertie remained deeply fond of each other and shared a lifelong mutual respect. Alix knew precisely how to manage her husband, and Queen Victoria respected Alix for not making waves over his infidelities.

Alix appears to have found compensation for her less than satisfactory marriage and her social marginalization by the prince by sublimating herself in many philanthropic interests. Like her sisters-in-law she was interested in women's nursing and the care of the sick. In November 1871 she had helped nurse Bertie devotedly through a life-threatening bout of typhoid fever—her attendance in tandem with that of trained nurses probably saving his life. As both princess of Wales and later queen, she supported many good causes: in 1886 she founded the Soldiers' and Sailors' Families Association for dependents of soldiers killed in action. On the occasion of the queen's 1897 Diamond Jubilee, Alexandra laid on a dinner for 40,000 poor people; she paid for a hospital ship to be equipped and sent out to Africa during the Boer War, and she raised funds for unemployed workmen in 1906. In 1902, now as queen, she founded the Queen Alexandra's Imperial Army Nursing Corps, which is still in existence today; in 1912 the Alexandra Rose Day was established in her name as an important fund-raiser for London's hospitals.

Alix was deeply distressed by the death of her eldest son, Albert Edward (Eddy), the duke of Clarence, on 13 January 1892 from pneumonia, and it took its toll on her health, leaving her thin and delicate looking. But her beauty endured into old age. When the queen died on 22 January 1901, Alix refused to be acknowledged as the new queen until after Victoria's funeral. She once again appeared radiant and youthful at her coronation in August 1902—in recognition of which she and Bertie paid for a £30,000 coronation tea for many of London's maids-of-all-work. After proving to be a supremely popular princess of Wales for forty years, she remained in high public regard as queen and then queen mother, during which time she was, unlike Prince Albert, never looked upon as a foreigner.

Related entries:

Albert Edward, Prince of Wales; Palmerston, Henry John Temple, Third Viscount; Photography

References and further reading:

Battiscombe, Georgina. 1969. *Queen Alexandra.* London: Constable.

Dimond, Frances, and Ann Taylor. 1987. *Crown and Camera: The Royal Family and Photography.* Harmondsworth, UK: Penguin.

Duff, David. 1980. *Alexandra: Princess and Queen.* London: Collins.

Fulford, Roger. 1968. *Dearest Mama: Letters between Queen Victoria and the Crown Princess of Prussia, 1861–64.* London: Evans Brothers.

Gernsheim, Helmut, and Alison Gernsheim. 1962. *Edward VII and Queen Alexandra.* London: F. Muller.

Hibbert, Christopher. 1984. *Queen Victoria in Her Letters and Journals.* London: Viking.

———. 2000. *Victoria: A Personal History.* London: HarperCollins.
Hough, Richard. 1992. *Edward and Alexandra: Their Private and Public Lives.* London: Hodder and Stoughton.
Magnus, Philip. 1964. *King Edward the Seventh.* London: John Murray (esp. chap. 3, "Romance 1861–1862").
Tisdall, E. E. P. 1953. *Unpredictable Queen: The Intimate Life of Queen Alexandra.* London: S. Paul.

Alfred Ernest Albert, Prince (1844–1900)

("Affie"; Duke of Edinburgh and Duke of Saxe-Coburg-Gotha)

This darling boy . . . with his dear handsome, good face—and so like dear Papa (Fulford 1964, 235)

From the day he was born, on 6 August 1844 at Windsor Castle, the queen's second son was assigned a purpose—to be the future ruler of Saxe-Coburg-Gotha, the home country of his father, Prince Albert, for Prince Albert's older brother, Duke Ernest, and his wife had produced no heirs. With this in mind, Albert determined that "the little one shall, from his youth, be taught to love the dear small country to which he belongs, in every respect, as does his Papa" (Bolitho 1964, 81).

Alfred seemed an exemplary child: attractive, intelligent, and more even tempered than his volatile elder bother, Bertie, the Prince of Wales. Alfred was also naturally brave and uninhibited; he loved climbing and swimming and, as a child, constantly took physical risks leading to numerous minor accidents. This love of the outdoors and the sea made family holidays at Osborne a joy for him. In terms of his education he also seemed more malleable and willing to apply himself; the queen wrote, just before his fifth birthday, that "the Prince has very uncommon abilities; and a mind which will make the task of instructing him most smooth and delightful" (Woodham-Smith 1972, 268).

Alfred was educated with Bertie by their tutor, Frederick Gibbs, and soon pleased his father by showing that he was logical and technically minded with an aptitude for geography, natural history, and mathematics. His diligence was most gratifying in comparison with the educational failings of Bertie. But as he grew older, Affie, as he was known in the family, developed an increasingly dour and inflexible personality and demonstrated a surprising strength of will. This was first manifested in his determination, from a young age, to enter the navy—an aspiration that threatened to overturn his allotted course toward the throne of Saxe-Coburg-Gotha. Since the event of Duke Ernest's death might be many years off, Prince Albert responded sympathetically and acknowledged that "this is a passion which we, as his parents, believe not to have the right to subdue" (Bolitho 1964, 168).

Despite the protestations of Duke Ernest, who wanted Alfred to be prepared for the role of sovereign and live in Coburg, Alfred was allowed to join the navy in 1856, taking up his naval studies in October 1857, under a retired naval chaplain Rev. William Rowe Jolley at Alverbank, near the naval base at Gosport. He learned seamanship on the training vessel *Illustrious,* passing his naval exams as midshipman in August 1858. Prince Albert was filled with pride at his son's achievements; over the next few years Affie visited Malta, then North Africa—Tunis, Algiers—and then sailed on to Egypt and Syria. In 1860 he visited the Transvaal and the Orange Free State.

Queen Victoria was overjoyed to have her darling Affie back home again at the end of February 1860; he was, she wrote, "our great delight, so full of fun and conversation and so full of anxiety to learn—always at something, never an instant idle—such steam power, such energy it is such a

The young Prince Alfred, (left) duke of Edinburgh, who, after a long career in the navy, in 1893 inherited the throne of Saxe-Coburg-Gotha. (George Eastman House/Getty Images)

great pleasure to see this." (Fulford 1964, 237). But all Affie's fine qualities only heightened her sense of disappointment with Bertie: "The contrast with someone else is sad" (ibid.).

Affie was many miles away at sea when his father died in 1861. A year later he was unexpectedly offered the throne of Greece, when the despotic King Otto had been forced to abdicate. He had little inclination to accept the offer, since he was, by now, deeply committed to his naval career. In the event, the British government vetoed the offer, as it would have contravened existing political treaties with Russia and France. During the 1860s Affie spent much time away from home, as he rose through the naval ranks. In 1863 he was promoted to lieutenant, and he became a captain in 1866, the year that he was created duke of Edinburgh and earl of Ulster and Kent by the queen. Early in 1867 he was finally given his own command—of the *Galatea*—a promotion that went to his head somewhat and encouraged his at times overbearing and irascible manner. In June he set off on a round-the-world voyage and in October was the first member of the royal family to visit Australia. During the course of his five months' stay an assassination attempt was made on him in Sydney by an Irishman, James O'Farrell, apparently in revenge for the recent execution in Britain of three Fenians.

Affie's frequent long absences opened up a gap between him and his formerly adoring mother. For his own part, he found the queen's protracted grieving hard to take and began to distance himself from her emotional demands on him. As the 1860s went on the queen became increasingly frustrated by the lack of attention he paid her. Affie seemed always to keep her at arm's length, and she worried about his emotional coldness, finding the formerly warm and affectionate child now changed into a man who was "reserved, touchy, vague and wilful" (Hibbert 1984, 210). Her darling Affie had developed a brusqueness of manner that, as the queen noted with some concern, did not endear him either to those of lower or higher rank, any more than did his habit of addressing people around him, as he would those on board ship, in an often peremptory manner. By 1873 she was openly declaring that nobody liked him.

Meanwhile, in the mid-1860s the queen's marriage brokering on behalf of Alfred had begun. But it was not until 1873, after several years of discussion of prospective candidates, that he settled on marrying a Romanov, much to Queen Victoria's chagrin. Painful memories of the Crimean War against Russia still lingered, as did an ingrained hostility toward Russian Orthodoxy and a personal distaste for the arrogance and ostentation of the Romanov court. Alfred's bride was Grand Duchess Marie Alexandrovna—only daughter of Tsar Alexander II. After several hitches and prevarication on the part of the Romanovs, they were married in January 1874 in St. Petersburg. With the queen still in deep mourning, there was no question of her attending the wedding. Victoria did not actually meet her new daughter-in-law, Marie, until after she arrived in England; she pronounced the somewhat dowdy Russian princess pleasant and unaffected. Dowdy she might be, but Marie brought with her a considerable dowry and private annual income, as well as magnificent jewels to equal the queen's—including diamonds and sapphires that had come down from Catherine the Great. Once in England, however, Marie demonstrated that a strong will lurked behind the meek exterior; she became renowned for her grandness and her determination at all costs not to integrate into the English way of life. Marie remained devoutly Russian Orthodox, having brought her own personal Russian priest and icons to be hung throughout her home. She hated English food, the language, the culture and could not bear the damp English climate and the London fogs. She was bored at Osborne and at Windsor—which seemed tin-pot residences in comparison to the grand Russian palaces—and did all she could to avoid attending court. She and Alfred would have four children; the first, a son, Alfred, was born the following October, followed by three daughters. Young Alfred was educated at Coburg in preparation for his accession to the Saxe-Coburg title after his father.

Alfred returned to his naval service in February 1876, spending much of the next fourteen years abroad. His wife objected to the "impoverished" naval billets in which she was obliged to reside. For a while the family lived in Malta and then settled back in England, moving between Clarence House in London and their estate at Eastwell in Kent, where Alfred took up farming during his periods back on land. His naval promotions continued apace: rear admiral in 1878, vice admiral in 1882, and admiral in the Jubilee Year, 1887. He served as commander in chief of the Channel fleet (1883–1884), of the Mediterranean (1886–1889), and of Davenport naval base (1890–1893); at the end of that time he was promoted to admiral of the fleet. Despite his obsession with the life at sea, Alfred also was a great lover of music, a friend of the composer Arthur Sullivan, and patron of the Royal College of Music. As a child he had secretly taught himself to play the violin in order to please his parents, but Lady Lytton records that during the 1880s and early 1890s, he became renowned at Osborne and Windsor for being "a great bore, as well as an excrutiatingly bad violin player," (Lutyens 1961, 47) so much so that Prince Henry of Battenberg gave up smoking for a while because he could no longer endure listening to Alfred drone on in the gentlemen's smoking room.

Lady Lytton observed that "there was general rejoicing at court when in 1893 he [Alfred] inherited the Duchy of Coburg and went to live there" (ibid.). But it was hard for Alfred to abandon his naval career and overcome the initial opposition and hostility of his German subjects. He proved to be a conscientious ruler, however, albeit one with little real political power, remaining deeply uneasy about the ambitions of his nephew, William, the German Emperor, and his buildup of the German naval fleet. Affie never ceased to miss the navy, although his protracted absences at sea, from Marie's point of view, had made their marriage tolerable. She had always found Alfred's bad temper difficult to deal with and despised his drinking. But, out of the navy and now living in Coburg, Alfred was bored and unhappy, and the couple became increasingly alienated.

A final and irrevocable breach between them came in 1899, when their son, Alfred, who had contracted syphilis and was suffering from depression, died from a gunshot wound—the result of a botched suicide—after an argument with his mother. His death accelerated Alfred's slide into alcoholism; he spent the last year of his life living apart from Marie and died of cancer of the tongue at the Rosenau in Coburg in July 1900, six months before the death of his mother. For the queen, now in rapidly declining health, it was a terrible blow. Alfred's younger brother declined the title, which passed to Charles, the son of his youngest brother, Leopold.

Related entries:
Albert Edward, Prince of Wales; Arthur, Prince; "Grandmama of Europe"; Smoking

References and further reading:

Bennett, Daphne. 1980. *Queen Victoria's Children.* London: Gollancz.

Bolitho, Hector. 1964. *Albert, Prince Consort.* London: Max Parrish.

Eilers, Marlene A. 1997. *Queen Victoria's Descendants.* Falkoping, Sweden: Rosvall Royal Books.

Fulford, Roger. 1964. *Dearest Child: Letters between Queen Victoria and the Princess Royal.* London: Evans Brothers.

Hibbert, Christopher. 1984. *Queen Victoria in Her Letters and Journals.* London: Viking.

Lutyens, Mary, ed. 1961. *Lady Lytton's Court Diary 1895–1899.* London: Rupert Hart-Davis.

Marie, Queen of Roumania. 1934. *The Story of My Life.* Vol 1. London: Cassell.

McKinlay, Brian. 1971. *The First Royal Tour. 1867–1868.* London: Robert Hale.

St. Aubyn, Giles. 1991. *Queen Victoria: A Portrait.* London: Sinclair Stevenson.

Van der Kiste, John. 1986. *Queen Victoria's Children.* Stroud, Gloucestershire: Sutton.

Van der Kiste, John, and Bee Jordaan. 1984. *Dearest Affie: Alfred, Duke of Edinburgh, Queen Victoria's Second Son, 1844–1900.* Stroud, Gloucestershire: Sutton.

Woodham-Smith, Cecil. 1972. *Queen Victoria: Her Life and Times.* Vol. 1: *1819–1861.* London: Hamish Hamilton.

Alice Maud Mary, Princess (1843–1878)

(Princess Louis of Hesse-Darmstadt and By Rhine; from 1877, Grand Duchess)

this dear, talented, distinguished, tender hearted, noble minded, sweet child (Hibbert 1984, 254)

The tragic circumstances of the early death of Queen Victoria's second daughter, and third child, Alice—who herself nursed her father, Prince Albert, in his final illness in 1861—ensured her deification as the most sainted of all the royal children. She was the first of Victoria's three children to predecease her—the others being Leopold (in 1884) and Alfred (in 1900). The queen's grief at Alice's death, however, masked over the fact that they had, in fact, for many years been alienated from each other.

Shy, altruistic, and compassionate, the adult Alice manifested all the attributes of the doting mother, the dutiful daughter, and the caregiver. As a small child and already sensitive to the suffering of others, she had been hampered by a lack of self-assurance that she had channeled into a desire to help the sick and needy. She often visited poor cottagers on the royal estate at Balmoral and at the age of eleven accompanied her mother on visits to the war wounded returning from the Crimea—many of them terribly mutilated. She would have been well equipped for a nursing career, serious-minded as she was and inspired by Florence Nightingale, and she received plenty of experience nursing the members of her own family through various illnesses.

Alice's childhood and youth were uncontroversial, with the princess exhibiting an ebullience that deserted her in adult life. She adored Osborne and delighted in outdoor pursuits such as skating and horse riding, demonstrating an amiable temperament and sense of humor, as well as sharing with her sisters considerable talents at drawing and playing the piano. She was considered by her father to be the most beautiful of his children, although the severe features and sharp nose suggest a rather ethereal, mournful beauty, and the last photographs of her bear the signs of a lingering sense of disappointment with life. She always seemed physically frail, particularly after an attack of scarlet fever in 1855, yet like her father set herself high standards of duty that eventually wore her out. This patrician streak was reflected in a remark she once made that "life was made for work and not pleasure"—words that uncannily echoed the sentiments of her father (Bennett 1980, 63). And even though she might have seemed sweet natured and compliant, Alice could be short-tempered with and critical of those who, in her estimation, were insufficiently aware that duty always preceded pleasure.

For most of her early years, Alice lived somewhat in the shadow of her far more academically accomplished and intellectual elder sister, Vicky. But when Vicky married and went to live in Berlin, the role of helpmate, nurse, and comforter to her parents fell to Alice, as also did the care of her ailing grandmother, the duchess of Kent (who, for this reason, was in no hurry to see Victoria and Albert marry Alice off). Alice shared

A thoughtful Princess Alice, second daughter of Queen Victoria. A devoted mother, she would die young, of diphtheria, in 1878, having nursed her own family through the disease. (Hulton/Archive by Getty Images)

many personality traits with her father; she had the same thoughtful, studious nature and had also inherited his love of music and art. She was also very close to her much maligned and often misunderstood older brother, Bertie, the Prince of Wales.

In 1860, during the racing season at Royal Ascot, Alice met the brothers Louis and Henry of Hesse-Darmstadt. Queen Victoria had orchestrated the meeting, having already decided that Louis would be a suitable husband for Alice. Luckily for Alice, she fell in love with the handsome Louis, and they were engaged on 30 November 1860. But soon afterward her powers of self-sacrifice were taxed to the limit. She not only helped nurse her grandmother, the duchess of Kent, through her final illness in the spring, but in December kept vigil by Prince Albert's bedside during his fatal illness. Many commented on her dignity, courage, and strength of character at that time. For Alice had to cope not only with her own profound sense of loss but also with the nervous collapse and hysterical grieving of her mother. For many weeks Alice, Lady Augusta Bruce, and the duchess of Sutherland were virtually the only people whom the queen would admit into her rooms, with Alice now also having to liaise with the royal household and deal with her mother's correspondence. She was, averred Lady Lyttleton, "like an angel in the house" (Wyndham 1912, 422). Alice matured overnight into a graceful and self-possessed young woman. Her composure was wonderful: "She seemed indeed to have suddenly put away childish things and to be a different creature," observed Lady Bruce (Windsor and Bolitho 1927, 246).

On 1 July 1862, Alice married Prince Louis at a low-key private ceremony at Osborne, described by those who witnessed it as being gloomy and funereal. Victoria looked on, swathed in deep mourning and barely able to contain her grief; the occasion was marked by the sound of sobbing rather than celebration, and the bride's going-away trousseau was composed of nothing but black. Alice, now removed from her mother's domineering presence, proved to be less compliant than she had of old and more than capable of standing up to her mother's endless demands that the members of her family should subordinate themselves to what suited *her.* On visits to England, Alice began to question Victoria's dictatorial manner and at times resist it. When it came to her sister Helena's marriage in 1866, which Alice considered a deliberate ploy to ensure that the queen had a compliant married daughter living with her, she challenged her mother's choice of suitor. In her view, Prince Christian of Schleswig-Holstein was an unappealing boor. For her pains, Alice was condemned by the queen as "sharp and grand and wanting to have everything her own way" (Packard 1998, 114).

Alice's own sixteen-year marriage began happily enough. Compared with other European royals, the Hesse royal family lived relatively modestly—in the Neue Palais at Darmstadt, its construction funded in part by Alice's £30,000 dowry. A shortage of money would impose considerable constraints on the way Alice ran her household, and she was constantly having to make economies (as well as regularly appealing to Queen Victoria for financial help). Darmstadt, situated in the hills of the Odenwald near the River Rhine, was something of a social backwater. Alice was a devoted wife and mother and unquestioningly loyal, but there was no disguising her increasing disappointment in her husband's emotional and intellectual shortcomings, which heightened her sense of loneliness and isolation. Louis, a born soldier, never shared Alice's passionate interests in the arts, nor did he comprehend her wide-reaching philanthropic concerns. The couple became distanced from each other. Alice was not content to be consigned to a life that consisted solely in having babies to populate the minor principalities of Europe—her first child, Victoria, arriving in April 1863. She was determined, like her father, to be of service to her adopted people and do something constructive. But, like him, as Jerrold Packard has observed, she became increasingly rigid in these aspirations: "She hadn't the art to make life easy for herself" (1998, 51). She embraced an exhausting regime of hospital visiting and nursing, which was put to good use during the seven-week Austro-Prussian War of 1866 and again during the 1870–1871 Franco-Prussian War.

With her husband away at the front leading his troops during both of these campaigns in defense of the Austrian cause, Alice threw herself into war work, despite being pregnant during the war of 1866. She established nursing facilities and organized supplies of bandages for the wounded, whom she helped to nurse in Darmstadt's field hospitals. She appealed to Queen Victoria for supplies and financial support from Britain. After the war, in 1867 Alice founded the Women's Union for Nursing the Sick and Wounded in War, which carried on its work by training nurses in peacetime and by 1869 had 2,500 members. She set up the Alice Hospital in 1871 for the destitute sick, visited orphanages and lunatic asylums, attended medical lectures, and took a keen interest in issues relating to public health. She also became patroness of the Heidenreich Institution for Lying-In Women. She supported the work of the housing reformer Octavia Hill in Britain, with whom she corresponded and whose *On the Homes of the London Poor* she translated into German. She also corresponded with Florence Nightingale. As a supporter of women's work and education, much like her sister Vicky, she advocated women's rights in opposition to her deeply conservative mother.

In November 1868 Alice finally gave birth to a son, Ernst Ludwig, her fourth child. Another boy Friedrich (affectionately named Frittie) was born in 1870, and her seventh child, Alexandra, in 1872. Two of Alice's daughters, Irene and Alexandra, like Alice herself, carried with them the fatal gene for hemophilia that had been passed down from Queen Victoria. Friedrich developed hemophilia, and he tragically died at the age of three, after falling from a window of the Darmstadt palace.

In 1871 Alice visited England after an eleven-year absence and was dismayed at the queen's continuing and stubborn seclusion. She had regularly appealed to her mother by letter to once more resume some of her public duties. The queen objected to Alice's interference, as she saw it, but soon found herself having to show gratitude to her nursing skills, when she helped her sister-in-law, Princess Alexandra, nurse her brother Bertie through a serious attack of typhoid fever that nearly carried him off in December.

In order no doubt to compensate for the disappointments of her personal life with her husband, Alice insisted on committing herself to an enormous and ever more consuming workload of philanthropic work. But by 1877, when her husband succeeded his uncle as Grand Duke Ludwig IV of Hesse and By Rhine, she was worn out and dreading having to take up the even more onerous responsibilities of grand duchess. Worse was to come, in November 1878, when her daughter Victoria fell ill with diphtheria. Within eight days, four of her other children, Alix, May, Irene, and Ernest—as well as the duke—all contracted it.

Alice nursed her family devotedly, day and night, but her youngest, five-year-old daughter, May, died. Alice kept the news from her other sick children for as long as she could, before finally succumbing herself, just as the others were recovering.

Alice died on 14 December 1878—the seventeenth anniversary of her father's death—aged only thirty-five. The queen saw her passing as a sign of divine will, recording in her journal that the timing of Alice's death was "almost incredible, and most mysterious" (Longford 1998, 425). Although Alice was buried in Darmstadt, she and her dead daughter May were commemorated in a touching, recumbent effigy, executed in white marble by the court sculptor Sir Joseph Edgar Boehm, which was placed near her father's sarcophagus in the Royal Mausoleum at Frogmore.

Related entries:
Crimean War; Frogmore; "Grandmama of Europe"; Hemophilia; Jenner, Sir William; Nightingale, Florence; Palmerston, Henry John Temple, Third Viscount

References and further reading:

Alice, Grand Duchess of Hesse. 1885. *Letters to Her Majesty the Queen.* London: John Murray.
Bennett, Daphne. 1980. *Queen Victoria's Children.* London: Gollancz.
Benson, E. F. 1938. *Daughters of Queen Victoria.* London: Cassell and Co.
Carey, Rosa Nouchette. 1899. *Twelve Notable Good Women.* London: Hutchinson.
Eilers, Marlene A. 1997. *Queen Victoria's Descendants.* Falkoping, Sweden: Rosvall Royal Books.
Epton, Nina. 1971. *Victoria and Her Daughters.* London: Weidenfeld and Nicolson.
Hibbert, Christopher. 1984. *Queen Victoria in Her Letters and Journals.* London: Viking.
Kenyon, Edith C. 1887. *Scenes in the Life of Princess Alice (Grand Duchess of Hesse).* London: W. Nicholson and Sons.
Longford, Elizabeth. [1964] 1998. *Victoria R.I.* London: Weidenfeld and Nicolson.
Noel, Gerard. 1974. *Queen Victoria's Forgotten Daughter.* Norwich, Norfolk: Michael Russell.
Packard, Jerrold M. 1998. *Victoria's Daughters.* New York: St. Martin's Press.
Prole, Lozania. 1973. *The Queen's Daughters.* London: Robert Hale.
Van der Kiste, John. 1986. *Queen Victoria's Children.* Stroud, Gloucestershire: Sutton.
Windsor, Dean of, and Hector Bolitho, eds. 1927. *Letters of Lady Augusta Stanley: A Young Lady at Court 1849–1863.* London: Gerald Howe.
Wyndham, Hon. Mrs Hugh, ed. 1912. *Correspondence of Sarah Spencer, Lady Lyttleton 1787–1870.* London: John Murray.

Animals

I feel so much for animals—poor, confiding, faithful, kind things (Hibbert 1984, 239)

During the reign of Queen Victoria, largely as a result of the queen's sentimental love for her own animals and the mass-produced images circulated of them, the keeping of domestic pets became very popular. No longer looked upon as simply the servants of man, whose place was the farmyard and the kennel, dogs in particular were welcomed into the bosom of the family by Victoria and occupied a special place in her affections. She often quoted the words of the philosopher Schopenhauer: "If it were not for the honest faces of dogs, we should forget the very existence of sincerity" (Tooley 1896, 256). The queen took a great pride in the fine herds of prize dairy and beef cattle established on the model farms at Windsor by Prince Albert, as she did also of her Aylesbury ducks, Jacobin pigeons, and exotic breeds of poultry.

As a young girl, Princess Victoria had thrilled to the spectacle of Van Amburgh's famous circus lions. She saw them perform on several occasions at Drury Lane, along with his menagerie of tigers, cheetahs, and leopards. Later on she took her own children to Astley's circus and to private matinees of the American circus when it came to the Alhambra and never lost her enjoyment of animals-as-spectacle. In old age, after many years of seclusion, she returned once more to the circus, enjoying a command performance of "Lord" George Sanger's circus at the great riding school at Windsor with her grandchildren and visiting Buffalo Bill's Wild West show when it was on tour at Earl's Court.

Although there were cats in the royal household, the queen did not have a great affection for them, and dogs always took center stage. During the lonely years of her girlhood at Kensington Palace, animals were often the young Princess Victoria's

Queen Victoria's great comfort during her long widowhood were her animals, especially her many dogs, one of her favorites being the collie Sharp, seen with her here. (Hulton/Archive by Getty Images)

only companions. She lavished love on them as she might have done on other friends and siblings. Pride of place in her early journals is taken by a King Charles spaniel named Dash or, sometimes, Dashy. He had actually been a gift to her mother, the duchess of Kent, from her equerry Sir John Conroy in 1833, but the young princess had taken such a delight in the dog that they soon became inseparable and before long he was joined by others. Even when she became queen in 1837, Victoria would have Dash with her during audiences with her prime minister, Lord Melbourne. No matter how onerous the duties of state, she would always find time for her dogs; even on that most momentuous of days, her coronation in 1838, her first thought after returning to Buckingham Palace after the exhausting five-hour ceremony had been to run upstairs to give Dash his bath.

The queen began commissioning portraits of her favorite pets soon after she discovered the talent of Sir Edwin Landseer for painting animals. In 1836 Landseer had produced an endearing portrait of Dash, and the queen so liked the picture that she commissioned him in 1837 to paint a portrait, *Her Majesty's Favourite Pets,* a work that featured Dash; a greyhound, Hector; a deerhound, Nero; and her pet parrot, Lory. Soon a wide range of prints and engravings of Landseer's animal pictures was mass produced; thanks to the queen's patronage, they made him a rich man.

Just before his marriage to the queen in February 1840, Prince Albert's own favorite dog, a greyhound named Eos, had been sent over from Germany. Thereafter, the royal couple usually had at least half a dozen dogs in the family entourage. Firm family favorites, Eos and two Skye terriers—Islay and Dandie—were featured in another Landseer painting of the 1840s, *Windsor Castle in Modern Times,* although the beloved Dash was now no more. When he had died at the end of 1840 he had been buried in a special grave, surmounted with his statue in marble, bearing an inscription testifying that "His attachment was without selfishness / His playfulness without malice His fidelity without deceit . . . / If you would be beloved and die regretted / Profit by the example of / Dash" (Longford 1998, 155). When Eos died in 1842, he too was laid in a special grave at Windsor, topped with a bronze statue by the royal sculptor, Sir Joseph Edgar Boehm.

Two other dogs that featured strongly in the queen's life were the collie dogs, Noble and Sharp, that always traveled with her to and from Balmoral, whom Victoria described with great affection in her Highland journals. Sharp, however, had a reputation for being bad tempered and was always spoiling for a fight with other dogs. He frightened most of the royal entourage, except the redoubtable John Brown. Noble was far more sweet natured and had the special role of guarding the queen's gloves. He was, the queen wrote, "the most biddable dog I ever saw" (Tooley 1896, 108); he would "hold a piece of cake in his mouth without eating it" until told to do so. "If he thinks we are not pleased with him, he puts out his paws and begs in such an affectionate way" (108). The queen was heartbroken when he grew sick at the age of sixteen. She called in her own personal physician, Sir James Reid, to administer medicine to the animal, and when the dog died the queen was so distraught that Reid had to sedate her. Noble too received a ceremonial burial at Balmoral, for the queen fervently believed that the higher animals had souls and when they died would go to a future life; they should therefore, in her view, be mourned just like humans.

In the later years of her widowhood the queen took a particular delight in a German breed of dogs, called Spitzes or Pomeranians. She bred them at her kennels at Windsor Home Park and won many awards for them. The kennels were also home to other favorites: Skye terriers, pugs, and dachshunds. In her declining years she took such pleasure in watching her dogs at play that she had a small cottage built near the royal kennels where she could watch them.

Horses too had been an important part of the queen's life after she had first learned to ride in 1831. She was an extremely accomplished rider, with boundless energy, able to ride hard for many miles around Windsor Great Park, where she frequently exhausted the elder statesmen, such as Lord Melbourne, who had to accompany her. At Balmoral, too, no matter what the weather she would go out pony trekking for hours on highland ponies. The royal stables at

Buckingham Palace housed 120 fine horses, including some superb cream-colored Hanoverians in which the queen took particular pride and which had drawn her state coach on coronation day. Windsor too had room for 80 horses, with the queen preferring pairs of grays to pull the royal carriages. A donkey, Jacquot, that the queen had rescued in Nice was a favorite with the royal grandchildren, as were Flora and Alma, two Shetland ponies presented by King Victor Emmanuel. In old age, and unable to walk any more, the queen was often conveyed around the grounds of Osborne or Balmoral in a pony chair pulled by a small Sardinian pony named Picco. When they became too old for work, the queen's horses were never sent to the knacker's yard but were put out to grass in Windsor's numerous lush paddocks.

The queen was most adamantly opposed to cruelty to animals in all its many manifestations and forbade the then fashionable practice of docking of tails on any of her own horses. She also disliked the game of polo, thinking it too cruel on the horses, and tried to discourage her son Prince Arthur from playing. A less consistent picture emerges, however, in terms of the queen's attitude to hunting and blood sports when practiced by her greatly adored consort. For she undoubtedly admired the heroic figure of Albert as chivalric huntsman and harbored a particularly romantic view of him, in all his manliness, in pursuit of the noble stag. During their holidays she would spend hours happily crawling in the damp heather with him as he stalked his prey, and she saw the prince kill hundreds of deer at Balmoral, as well as at Osborne. But she seemed to draw a line between what she perceived as this "romantic" form of hunting—the noble stag at liberty in the wild stalked by her equally noble husband—and the grisly spectacle of the mass slaughter of animals that took place during a royal visit to Prince Albert's home at Coburg, in August 1845. Here, a *battue* (canvas-fenced enclosure) was specially set up for Albert's entertainment, into which small area 300 men had spent ten days driving a herd of fifty wild deer—which were then systematically slaughtered at close range by the royal party.

As early as 1840 the queen had given her official patronage to the Royal Society for the Prevention of Cruelty to Animals, which she had supported since 1835, and critics were quick to perceive the hypocrisy of this when she continued to condone Albert's love of hunting. The reformer John Bright, on reading accounts of a *battue* at Lord Salisbury's in the 1840s, which Albert had joined, had expressed the view of many: "I think the Queen, as patron of the Society for the Prevention of Cruelty to Animals, should counsel her 'subject' husband against such barbarous slaughter of defenceless animals for amusement only" (Weintraub 1997, 166). In 1900 the first petition to be raised in Britain against hunting was, according to Hilda Kean (1998, 156), directed specifically at the queen, because she kept a pack of buckhounds in Windsor Great Park for deer hunting by members of the royal household. The queen's private secretary, Sir Henry Ponsonby, was drawn into the debate over the queen's position on hunting in 1891, by a letter from the Rev. J. Stratton, honorary secretary of the Sports Department of the Humanitarian League. Ponsonby assured the reverend, in a private postscript to his response, that although he knew nothing on the subject, "I may observe, though probably you are already aware of the fact, that the Queen has been strongly opposed to stag-hunting for many years past" (*The Humanitarian,* September 1919, 170). But exactly when she adjusted her view on the matter is not known. It is assumed that the queen drew a distinction between deer *stalking* by small groups of hunters on foot and the massed charges of stag *hunters* on horseback.

The issue of cruelty to animals was one to which the queen always responded with a great outpouring of emotion. It was, she averred, "one of the worst signs of wickedness in human nature" (Fulford 1976, 185), and she frequently donated money to animal charities. During the ministries of Disraeli and Gladstone, she began lobbying her ministers to bring in legislation to control the growing practice of vivisection in medical schools—a practice that horrified her. According to St. Aubyn (1991, 432), she subjected Disraeli to "a hurricane of words" on the subject and sent many memorandums to other responsible ministers on the sufferings of dogs. She corresponded with the home secretary, Sir William Harcourt, himself a leading antivivisectionist, on "this horrible, brutalising, unchristian-like vivisection" (Gardiner 1923, 403). Referring to a recent court case involving a vivisector, she insisted: "This must be stopped. . . . It is a disgrace to a civilised country" (ibid.).

Under pressure from the queen and the antivivisection lobby, led by a powerful female advocate of the cause, Frances Power Cobbe, Disraeli was eventually forced to call a royal commission on the subject. Lord Carnarvon reported back to the queen, who gave her wholehearted support to the passing of the Cruelty to Animals Act of 1875, which laid down stricter controls on vivisection, including the compulsory anesthesia of animals being vivisected and their prompt, humane destruction as soon as the experiment was complete. Disraeli, however, continued to share the view of most Victorian medical men that the arguments against vivisection did not stand up and that scientific progress would be seriously impeded if there were further restrictions.

After Disraeli left office, the queen continued to harangue his successor, Gladstone, writing to him from Osborne on 16 April 1881 about vivisection and urging him to speak out against "a practice which is a disgrace to humanity and Christianity" (Vyvyan 1969, 162). Gladstone noted how "greatly excited" (St. Aubyn 1991, 433) the queen was by this particular subject. In 1885 she was still on the subject, writing in a memorandum that "her poor dear friends the dogs" should never be destroyed unnecessarily (ibid.) or kept muzzled unless they were known to be dangerous. She also wished to see stricter controls of abattoirs. In her view, "nothing brutalizes human beings more than cruelty to poor dumb animals, whose plaintive looks for help ought to melt the hardest heart" (Guedalla 1933, 2:152), and the queen funded school prizes for essay writing on kindness to animals.

Despite her passionate feelings on the subject, the queen was legally required to show constitutional impartiality and could not, therefore, give her patronage to any organization that lobbied for changes to the law; nor could she sign the petitions of animal rights campaigners—thus precluding her official support for the abolitionist wing of the antivivisection movement. Victoria did, however, offer her private, moral support to organizations such as Cobbe's Victoria Street Society for the Protection of Animals Liable to Vivisection (popularly known as the Victoria Street Society). She also supported the work of the Royal Society for the Protection of Birds and condemned the use of feathers for trimming ladies' hats. Similarly, she made a point of refusing to patronize the work of any medical college or hospital that endorsed vivisection. In 1879, when the board of a new medical school at Edinburgh asked if it might be named Victoria College in her honor, the queen would only allow her name to be used if an undertaking was made that no vivisection would be carried out on its premises.

In the queen's forceful opposition to vivisection there was again, as with hunting, a worrying anomaly in her attitude. For although she made much of cruelty to dumb, defenseless animals and never ceased to abhor vivisection and its practitioners, in the most purple of prose—"the subject causes her *whole nature* to boil over against these 'Butchers'" (Hibbert 1984, 2)—she sometimes appeared to be less than sensitive about man's inhumanity to man and the sufferings of her many millions of impoverished, overworked, and abused subjects. As she lay dying, in January 1901, one of the queen's last wishes was that her favorite Pomeranian dog, Turri, be allowed to lie on her bed.

Related entries:
Albert of Saxe-Coburg-Gotha, Prince Consort; Balmoral Castle; Jenner, Sir William; Women's Rights

References and further reading:

Fairholme, Edward G., and Wellesley Pain. 1934. *A Century of Work for Animals: A History of the RSPCA*. London: John Murray.

Fulford, Roger. 1976. *Darling Child: Private Correspondence of Queen Victoria and the German Crown Princess of Prussia, 1871–78*. London: Evans Brothers.

Gardiner, A. G. 1923. *The Life of Sir William Harcourt*. 2 vols. London: Constable and Co.

Guedalla, Philip, ed. 1933. *The Queen and Mr. Gladstone, 1845–1898*. 2 vols. London: Hodder and Stoughton.

Hibbert, Christopher. 1984. *Queen Victoria in Her Letters and Journals*. London: Viking.

Kean, Hilda. 1998. *Animal Rights: Political and Social Change in Britain since 1800*. London: Reaktion Books.

Longford, Elizabeth. [1964] 1998. *Victoria R.I.* London: Weidenfeld and Nicolson.

Munich, Adrienne. 1996. *Queen Victoria's Secrets*. New York: Columbia University Press (chap. 6, "Domesticity; or, Her Life as a Dog").

[One of Her Majesty's Servants]. 1901. *The Private Life of Queen Victoria*. London: C. Arthur Pearson (chaps. 7, 18).

Ponsonby, Arthur. 1942. *Henry Ponsonby, Queen Victoria's Private Secretary; His Life from His Letters*. London: Macmillan

Rappaport, Helen, ed. 2001. *Encyclopedia of Women Social Reformers*. 2 vols. Santa Barbara, CA: ABC-CLIO.

St. Aubyn, Giles. 1991. *Queen Victoria: A Portrait*. London: Sinclair Stevenson.

Tooley, Sarah. 1896. *Personal Life of Queen Victoria*. London: Hodder and Stoughton.

Vyvyan, John. 1969. *In Pity and in Anger: A Study of the Use of Animals in Science*. London: Michael Joseph.

Weintraub, Stanley. 1997. *Albert, Uncrowned King*. London: John Murray.

Anson, George Edward (1812–1849)

very modest, very honest, very steady, very well-informed (Benson and Esher 1911, 1:200)

During the ten years in which he loyally served Prince Albert as private secretary, George Anson, the son of the former dean of Chester, became one of the prince's most trusted advisers as well as a close friend also of the queen. But things had not augured well when he was first appointed by the queen on the advice of her then prime minister Lord Melbourne and against Albert's wishes.

In the months preceding her marriage to Prince Albert in February 1840, the queen busied herself with the appointment of the members of the prince's personal household, the most important functionary of which would be his private secretary. At a time when she did nothing without consulting her prime minister, Lord Melbourne, Victoria took his advice and (without showing any regard to Albert's own personal preferences) proposed making Melbourne's private secretary George Anson available to Prince Albert also. The prince was offended by this decision; he wanted to make his own valued judgment on the right candidate and also argued that Anson was an inappropriate choice, since as a servant of Melbourne he was a staunch Whig (and had once even been a Whig candidate for Parliament). The prince was adamant that the Crown should be politically neutral; if he supported Anson's appointment, he feared he would be accused of being a "party man." The queen, however, was firm, although she did make one concession—that Anson would no longer continue to work for Melbourne as well.

Prince Albert's initial view of Anson was guarded: "Certainly he is a very good looking [man]" he conceded, but "as to character, that we must always take our chance of" (Cecil 1954, 271); he also expressed his apprehension that Anson might prove inappropriate on moral grounds, since, horror of horrors, the straitlaced Albert had observed that Anson was "addicted to dancing" (Longford 1998, 138). He was therefore gratified when Anson proved to be highly sympathetic to Albert's desire to find a useful role for himself. Anson communicated the fact with candor to Melbourne: "If you required a cypher in the difficult position of Consort of the Queen you ought not to have selected the Prince; having got him you must make the most of him." Anson recognized the prince's many latent talents; "when he sees the power of being useful to the Queen he will act," Anson averred (Weintraub 1997, 101).

Anson proved to be the perfect choice for private secretary: a man of probity and high moral character. In the opinion of General Grey, he was "utterly incapable of intrigue" (Grey 1867, 323). More important, he proved to be politically disinterested, so much so that he was respected by both Whig and Tory ministers alike, in particular the Tory prime minister Sir Robert Peel, for whom he acted as a discreet intermediary. Such was the trust placed in him that Anson later also assumed the important financial role of keeper of Albert's Privy Purse and assisted the prince in his reform of the royal household and its finances in 1841. He developed a skill for negotiating between the prince and the queen in times of tension, by defusing potential differences between them, acting always with the greatest tact and diplomacy, and supporting Albert's attempts to modify the queen's sometimes dictatorial behavior. With Baron Stockmar, Anson shared a deep mistrust of the excessive influence of Baroness Lehzen over the queen, which they both believed increased the friction between the royal couple.

In his own self-effacing way, Anson helped groom Prince Albert for his future role as the queen's unofficial minister. He became increasingly indispensable to Prince Albert, defending him against unfair treatment in a critical and hostile press, so much so that in the queen's later view, he became "almost the only intimate friend" Albert had in Britain. Anson found subtle ways of trying to counter the hostile attitude toward the prince at court, by persuading Albert that his talking in German did not go down well; nor did it, for that matter, help him improve his English. Having observed Prince Albert's early "constitutional timidity" (Fulford 1966, 62), Anson encouraged him to express his views in writing and in official memorandums, noting the "important advance" (66) he had made in 1841 when Victoria gave Albert the key to her dispatch boxes. Anson's praise for the prince's impeccable character would remain unqualified: "Mr. Anson has seen much of the world, but in no Person in any Profession has he ever seen so spotless and so pure a character as the Prince" (Fulford 1966, 104).

By the time Melbourne had fallen from power, Anson had won the queen's confidence as well. In time he increasingly took over the advisory role left vacant by the prince's adviser Baron Stockmar, who had returned to Germany, and also endeared himself to Albert socially, as a country gentleman who shared with him a love of outdoor pursuits and rode well to hounds. But on 8 October 1849, at the age of only thirty-seven, Anson died suddenly, leaving a pregnant wife (who gave birth to a surviving daughter, their other children having died). For some time he had suffered from severe, debilitating headaches, which eventually had affected his ability to work to such a degree that some of his responsibilities had been shared with Col. Charles Grey (who succeeded him as private secretary) and Col. Charles Phipps (who took over Anson's financial roles). The persistent headaches may well have been the warning signs of an aneurism or possibly even a stroke that eventually killed Anson. The queen and Prince Albert were both inconsolable—Albert in particular grieving as though he had lost a brother and pacing the corridors of Osborne looking "sad and pale and grave" (Bolitho 1964, 118). "The Prince and the Queen in floods of tears and quite shut up," recorded Lady Lyttleton, head of the royal nursery. "It is to them a heavy loss indeed, irreparable—I mean that so warm a *friend* they can hardly expect to find again, in ever so trustworthy and efficient a servant and minister" (Wyndham 1912, 393).

Related entries:
Bedchamber Crisis; Grey, General Charles; Lehzen, Baroness Louise; Melbourne, William Lamb, Second Viscount; Phipps, Sir Charles; Stockmar, Christian Friedrich von

References and further reading:

Benson, A. C., and Viscount Esher, eds. 1911. *The Letters of Queen Victoria: A Selection from Her Majesty's Correspondence between the Years 1837 and 1861.* 1st ser., 3 vols. London: John Murray.
Bolitho, Hector. 1964. *Albert, Prince Consort.* London: Max Parrish.
Cecil, David. 1954. *Lord M: or, the Later Life of Lord Melbourne.* London: Constable.
Fulford, Roger. 1966. *The Prince Consort.* London: Macmillan.
Grey, Lt.-General. 1867. *The Early Years of H.R.H. the Prince Consort.* London: Smith, Elder and Co.
Longford, Elizabeth. [1964] 1998. *Victoria R.I.* London: Weidenfeld and Nicolson.
Martin, Sir Theodore. 1875–1880. *The Life of His Royal Highness the Prince Consort.* 5 vols. London: Smith, Elder and Co.
Weintraub, Stanley. 1997. *Albert, Uncrowned King.* London: John Murray.
Wyndham, Hon. Mrs. Hugh, ed. 1912. *Correspondence of Sarah Spencer, Lady Lyttleton, 1787–1870.* London: John Murray.

Art and Artists

Amateurs never can paint in oils like artists and what can one do with all one's productions? (Hibbert 1984, 111)

As a young girl, one of Princess Victoria's greatest pleasures had been sketching and painting in watercolors. In 1827, at the age of eight, she had begun taking lessons from the royal academician, Richard Westhall, and continued under his tuition for a further nine years till his death. Later in life, she requested private tuition from the limerick writer and artist Edward Lear after seeing the published watercolors of his travels in Italy. But it was, in the main, her husband who not only encouraged Queen Victoria's artistic skills but also her artistic sensibilities. Prince Albert was a connoisseur of fine art and an accomplished artist and engraver in his own right, and under his tutelage the queen extended her own natural talents. Her husband also educated her in art appreciation, again impressing upon her his own particular views. Victoria's artistic tastes remained cautious and unsophisticated; incongruously, this, the most conservative of couples, were notable in their art collecting for their unabashed appreciation for the nude—both in painting and in sculpture.

The queen and Prince Albert took great pleasure in sketching and painting, particularly at their homes at Balmoral and Osborne. But even the prince's more sophisticated artistic taste could not alter the queen's stubborn predilection for paintings that portrayed things as *she* saw them. A painting, no matter how accomplished technically, would therefore be considered a failure in her eyes if it did not reflect its subject with verisimilitude—to the point of photographic accuracy—and if it were not executed in the correct colors. As far as portraits were concerned, the queen certainly was a stickler: such was her disarming honesty that she rejected portraits of herself if she considered them to be excessively flattering, once complaining to an official artist, Caton Woodwille, who had painted her jubilee portrait, that "We are *redder* than that" (Jullian 1971, 206). As for landscapes, the queen had no time for the impressionistic work of J. W. Turner. Nor did the more approachable work of the pre-Raphaelites move her, and the queen refused to have her portrait painted by one of the movement's pioneers, Sir John Millais. She also disdained the work of leading artist George Frederic Watts and in old age dismissed the work of the Impressionists as a bad joke. As far as artists themselves were concerned—and in particular their traditional reputation for unconventional and sexually dubious lifestyles—the queen was wary of soliciting their acquaintance. She advised her daughter Vicky, crown princess of Prussia (herself a great art patron), that "I would venture to warn against too great intimacy with artists as it is very seductive and a little dangerous" (Fulford 1976, 290).

For many years the role of court portrait painter was fulfilled by Franz Xaver Winterhalter, who was replaced after his death in 1873 by Heinrich von Angeli—an artist favored also by Vicky. The queen was particularly pleased with the accurate likeness Angeli had achieved in a portrait he painted of her in 1875. Edwin Landseer also produced several paintings of members of the royal family that were more informal, particularly when the children were young. His huge popularity with both the royal family (leading to some 200 commissions from them) and the public at large, as a result of royal patronage, rested in the main on his talent for producing sentimental animal portraits, many of them of the queen's own dogs (See "Animals").

The British art critic Brian Sewell has observed that, as a patron, Victoria was "wholly unremarkable and undistinguished—perhaps even mean" (2001, 32). He argued that her "only consistent form of patronage" was "the royal portrait and the portrayal of royal occasions" (ibid.). In all respects, the representation in art of historical subjects had to be "more a matter of recall than an act of imagination" in order to win the queen's approval (Lloyd 1998, 23), and works depicting ceremonials, diplomatic milestones, and military subjects were predominant in the royal collection. Victoria's memories in particular of the sufferings of British troops in the Crimean War and the visits she had made to the wounded prompted her to buy G. H. Thomas's *Queen Victoria and Prince Albert Inspecting the Sick and Wounded Grenadier Guardsmen from the Crimean War* (1855) and Lady Butler's moving depiction of the exhausted remnants of a battalion of the Grenadier Guards after the battle of Inkerman, *The Roll Call,* in 1874. The painting caused a stir when it was exhibited at the Royal Academy—not least because it was a military scene executed by a *female* artist—and crowds flocked to see it, both there and on tour around the country. Lady Butler later executed other significant events in nineteenth-century history, such as *Scotland Forever* (1881) depicting the Battle of Waterloo and *The Defence of Rourke's Drift* (1880).

Many of the paintings purchased by the queen and Prince Albert were chosen for personal reasons, such as William Powell Frith's *Ramsgate Sands* (1851)—bought for £1,000 after it was exhibited at the Royal Academy. It served as a reminder, for the queen, of the all too rare childhood holidays that she had spent there as a young girl. Frith's vast and detailed scenes of contemporary Victorian life—such as *Derby Day* (1858) and *The Railway Station* (1862)—were equally admired by the royal couple. Other paintings that joined the royal collection recorded events in the queen's life and reign, such as Charles Robert Leslie's painting of her coronation and Frith's painting of the marriage of the Prince of Wales. In widowhood the queen's taste in painting became even more restrained, and she tended to purchase works that pandered to her own unquenchable grief—such as Frank Holl's 1870 *No Tidings from the Sea,* depicting the grieving wife and child of a seaman.

Of the royal couple, Prince Albert was the one with the wider knowledge and more adventurous tastes. He had been a connoisseur since his teens and had taken full advantage of his wide-reaching liberal education in Europe to study oil painting, lithography, and engraving. He developed a passion for the early schools of Italian, Nederlandish, and German painting and began collecting in his twenties, with many paintings obtained for him in Europe by his agent, Ludwig Grüner. The organization, cataloging, and in some cases, relocation, of not only the royal but also the national art collections was one of many unfulfilled projects cut short by the prince's premature death in 1861. But while he was alive, Albert had taken great pleasure in reorganizing the royal print and drawing collections at Windsor, which contain many fine works by Holbein and Raphael—as well as the art galleries at Hampton Court and Buckingham Palace. The prince also laid out his suggestions for the reorganization of the National Gallery collection into schools of German, Italian, and Dutch art and so on—as part of his wider drive to bring art and culture to the nation at large. Had he lived, he would have lobbied hard to have the contents of the National Gallery in Trafalgar Square rehoused in the more salubrious environs of the Victoria and Albert Museum at South Kensington. It is unlikely either, had Albert lived, that Britain would have had to wait till 1877 for the first municipal art gallery to be established (at Liverpool; others followed, at Manchester in 1882 and Leeds in 1888).

During his short life Prince Albert left a lasting artistic legacy: his private rooms at Osborne alone would contain twenty-six early works, which greatly enhanced the royal collection, notably Duccio's *Crucifixion* and paintings by Fra Angelico, Gentile de Fabriani, Lucas Cranach, and Verrochio. William Dyce's graceful *The Virgin and Child* (1845), painted very much in the style of Raphael, was snapped up by the prince, who also encouraged Dyce's interest in reviving the art of fresco painting. In 1847 the prince commissioned Dyce to paint the huge fresco *Neptune Resigning His Empire of the Sea to Britannia,* which can be seen on the main staircase at Osborne House. The Italianate frescoes in the Royal Mausoleum at Frogmore and the new ballroom at Buckingham Palace would also be a lasting tribute to the prince's great love of Raphael and sixteenth-century frescoes. In architecture too, Victoria and Albert contributed to the popularity of the Gothic revival and with it the fortunes of its most outstanding exponent—Sir George Gilbert Scott—who won the important commission from the queen to design the Albert Memorial.

Of particular interest to biographers and art commentators alike is the fact that in one respect at least Victoria and Albert confounded their posthumous reputation as the arbiters of archetypal Victorian prudishness, and this was in their unabashed delight in paintings and sculptures of the nude. They developed a habit of presenting each other with such works on birthdays and anniversaries, and one of the queen's first gifts to the prince—on their wedding—had been a nude painting of the goddess Artemis. On the occasion of his twenty-sixth birthday in 1845, the queen gave Prince Albert Thomas Uwin's painting *Cupid and Psyche.* The gift not only confirmed her admiration for the ideal of masculine beauty, as portrayed in art, but also for the tasteful nude—provided the subject was taken from mythology or classical literature.

In August 1852 the queen's birthday gift to Albert was one of the most talked-about paintings in the royal collection: Winterhalter's *Florinda*—featuring a bevy of voluptuous beauties in a woodland setting. The painting, for which the queen had paid £1,000 and which depicted a scene from Thalberg's recent opera *Florinda,* was hung in the queen's private sitting room at Osborne, facing the desks at which she and the prince consort worked. It was later moved to Buckingham Palace. In 1857 Queen Victoria presented the prince with a magnificent gilded silver statuette of Lady Godiva on horseback by Emile Jeannest (the couple had also admired Landseer's version of the same subject, despite the painting's being condemned by critics as lewd). All these subjects were destined for the couple's private apartments, most notably a large-scale, iron-framed fresco by Anton von Gegenbaur of another mythological subject—*Omphale and Hercules*—which the prince had bought in 1844 and which he could gaze upon at his leisure while in his bathtub—it took up much of one wall of his private bathroom. Nude sculptures were also favored by Victoria and Albert, and they acquired works such as John Bell's bronze *Andromeda,* William Theed's *Narcissus* (albeit with the addition of a tastefully positioned figleaf), and an original Roman sculpture in marble of *Venus Anadyomene.* Theed would execute numerous works for the royal couple, notably a statue ofVictoria and Albert in Anglo-Saxon dress completed in 1867 as a commemoration of the couple's interest in their ancient ancestry. But Theed's most enduring work would undoubtedly be the posthumous bust of the prince commissioned by the queen, which regularly took center stage in photographs of the widowed queen and her children (see page 22). During her long widowhood, a vast industry in Albertian image making sprang up—with his face and figure becoming almost as frequently seen across the empire in statues, paintings, and memorials as that of the queen herself. The dead hand of Victoria's unrelenting grief would, after 1861, contribute to a marked downturn in royal artistic taste and patronage, which had, thanks to the prince's inspiration, looked set to blossom.

Related entries:
Albert Memorial; Animals; Great Exhibition; Landseer, Sir Edwin; Photography; Victoria and Albert Museum; Winterhalter, Franz Xaver

References and further reading:

Ames, Winslow. 1968. *Prince Albert and Victorian Taste.* London: Chapman and Hall.
Barratt, Carrie Rebora. 2000. *Queen Victoria and Thomas Sully.* Princeton, NJ: Princeton University Press.
Fulford, Roger. 1976. *Darling Child: Private Correspondence of Queen Victoria and the German Crown Princess of Prussia, 1871–78.* London: Evans Brothers.
Hibbert, Christopher. 1984. *Queen Victoria in Her Letters and Journals.* London: Viking.
Hobhouse, Hermione. 1983. *Prince Albert: His Life and Work.* London: Hamish Hamilton.
Jullian, Philippe. 1971. *Oscar Wilde.* London: Paladin.
Lloyd, Christopher. 1991. *The Queen's Pictures.* London: Chancellor.
———. 1998. *The Quest for Albion: Monarchy and the Patronage of British Painting.* London: The Royal Collection.
Millar, Sir Oliver. 1992. *Victorian Pictures in the Collection of HM Queen Victoria.* Cambridge: Cambridge University Press.
Munich, Adrienne. 1996. *Queen Victoria's Secrets.* New York: Columbia University Press.
Sewell, Brian. 2001. "Glorious Rummage through Victoria's Drawers" [review of the "Victorian Visons" Exhibition at the V&A]. *Evening Standard,* 27 April, 32–33.
Warner, Marina. 1979. *Queen Victoria's Sketchbook.* London: Macmillan.
Weintraub, Sidney. 1997. *Albert: Uncrowned King.* London: John Murray (esp. chap. 8).
Wood, Christopher. 1990. *Victorian Panorama: Paintings of Victorian Life.* London: Faber and Faber.
———. 1999. *Victorian Painting.* London: Cassell.

Arthur William Patrick Albert, Prince (1850–1942)

(Duke of Connaught and Strathearn)

the dearest *and* most precious *object to* me *on Earth* (Frankland 1993, 5)

Queen Victoria's third son and seventh child was born at Buckingham Palace on 1 May, sharing his birthday with the queen's much loved friend and adviser, the duke of Wellington. Wellington was asked to be his godfather, and Arthur was therefore named after him. The queen never made any attempt to disguise the fact that, right from his birth, Arthur was her favorite son and, aside from the baby of the family, Beatrice, "the dearest most loved of my children" (Frankland 1993, 90).

Arthur inherited his mother's large, blue, slightly bulbous eyes; she herself thought he most closely resembled his father, Albert—in looks as well as in the dutiful and formal side of his personality. She was gratified that he was not afflicted, as she saw it, with the weakness of character that had so alienated her from her eldest son, the Prince of Wales. She took a very close interest in Arthur's education, in hopes that the mistakes she felt that she and Albert had made with the more temperamental and difficult Bertie and their second son, Alfred, were not repeated. Having lost his father, Prince Albert, when he was only twelve, the young Arthur naturally gravitated to his tutor, Maj. Howard Elphinstone, on whom he looked as a surrogate father; in his relationship with his mother he proved to be the model son. The queen was unequivocal in her praise; he was, she averred, "the best child I ever saw" (Bennett 1980, 109).

With Bertie heir to the throne, and Alfred having entered the navy; Arthur embraced the next, traditional option for sons of the sovereign—a career in the army. He had in fact loved playing at soldiers as a young child, and this at a time when a real war was raging—in the Crimea. Arthur's early life was thus molded by the queen's own preoccupation with her beloved troops, military parades, and medal ceremonies. He entered the Royal Military Academy at Woolwich as a cadet in 1867 and took a commission as lieutenant in the Royal Engineers in 1868. He then spent a year with his regiment, the First Battalion Rifle Brigade, in Montreal, Canada (1869–1870), during which he saw action at the Red River Rebellion of 1870. Thereafter, his was a copybook military career, rising through the ranks from major general in 1880, to general in 1893, and field marshal in 1902. After his return from Canada, in 1874 the queen invested Arthur as duke of Connaught and Strathearn. Promoted to major, he transferred to the Seventh Hussars and during 1875–1876 served on the staff of the British adjutant general in Gibraltar.

The queen was, by now, preoccupied with finding a suitable bride for Arthur, a mission accelerated after he reached twenty-one, with Arthur frequently dispatched on visits to the royal families of Europe in order to vet the candidates. He accepted the queen's controlling influence philosophically, long having come to the conclusion that nothing would change it: "Mama will always look at everything in her own light & will not allow anybody else to have *any views* of their own" (Frankland 1993, 64). Eventually he concurred with the queen's choice of Princess Louise Margaret, daughter of Prince and Princess Friedrich Karl of Prussia. It proved to be a true love match, with Louise only too glad to get away from the gloomy royal residence in Berlin as well as her father's bullying.

The organization of the wedding, over which Queen Victoria dictated, down to what the bride should wear and where the couple should go on their honeymoon, seemed to draw the queen out of her grief and occupy her in more happy and positive thoughts. A grand wedding ceremony was laid on in 1879 at St. George's Chapel, Windsor, postponed from 1878 owing to the tragic death of Arthur's sister, Princess Alice, from diphtheria. Victoria at long last seemed enlivened by this event—and appeared at the ceremony wearing the Koh-i-Noor diamond and a long white veil. Arthur returned to his military duties at Aldershot army camp, until trouble flared up in Egypt in 1882. He was put in command of the First Guards Brigade of the Egyptian Expeditionary Force. His mother, who could not bear him ever to be very far away from her, was distraught at the thought of his going into battle. Arthur subsequently served with distinction at the battle of Tel-el-Kebir on 13 September 1882, a battle in which Egyptian nationalists led by Arabi Pasha were defeated. The queen's heart swelled with pride.

Arthur was rewarded with a series of commands in India during the period 1883–1890. In 1886 he was promoted to commander in chief of the Bombay Army (1886–1890) and involved in the reorganization of the Indian armies as a response to Russian military incursions in Afghanistan. During this posting he returned home to ride in the royal procession to Westminster Abbey during the celebrations of the Queen's Golden Jubilee. Once again the queen was gratified that Arthur had done the dutiful thing: he was "so like dear papa—so dear and good and *wise* [and] such a help to me!" (Frankland 1993, 146).

After his return from India, Arthur took up commands at army bases at Portsmouth and Aldershot; he had expected to be offered the post of commander in chief of the British Army on the resignation of the queen's cousin, the duke of Cambridge in 1895. The queen had particularly wished to see Arthur appointed at the head of her army and again tried to secure the appointment for him in 1900, but on both occasions political considerations meant that Arthur was passed over. Instead, he accepted the post as commander in chief in Ireland (1900–1904). When the War Office was reorganized in 1904, he was appointed to the new post of inspector-general to the forces (1904–1907) and then served as commander in chief in the Mediterranean (1907–1909).

Meanwhile, in 1899 Arthur had unexpectedly found himself heir to the throne of the duchy of Saxe-Coburg-Gotha, after the premature death of his brother Alfred's only son. The people of Saxe-Coburg-Gotha, however, did not take kindly to the idea that Arthur, who had every intention of retaining his military career, would be an absentee monarch. The German emperor also raised objections, insisting that a German royal should take the title. In the event, the title went to Charles, the son of the hemophiliac Leopold (Arthur's brother, who had died in 1884). As Noble Frankland pointed out (1993, 212), had Arthur taken the title, he would have found himself in the invidious position of having to fight on the wrong side in World War I.

During the period 1911 to 1916, Arthur took up a new and challenging post, in succession to Earl Grey, as commander in chief and governor-general of Canada. He took his duties seriously but provoked controversy by interfering in army affairs, particularly after the outbreak of World War I when he recruited for an Expeditionary Force of Canadian volunteer troops to go out to the European front. During his time in office he traveled the country and was active in auxiliary services and various charities in support of the war effort, as was the duchess, who assisted the Red Cross. Arthur greatly regretted the end of his tenure in Canada and before returning to England laid the foundation stone for the new parliament buildings in Ottawa. In his remaining years, he regularly appeared at important state functions, as the representative of his nephew King George V; for example, on 4 November 1910 he read out the king's address to the opening of the first parliament of the Union of South Africa at Cape Town. He also was active in the Freemasons and a supporter of the Boy Scout movement.

His happy marriage to Princess Louise ended with her death in 1917; during their life together, however, Arthur had not been immune to the attractions of other women and enjoyed their company socially, most notably that of the American socialite Lady Léonie Leslie, sister of Jennie Jerome. He maintained a discreet love triangle, condoned by his devoted wife, in which Lady Leslie acted as his close confidant for over forty years. Arthur retired from public life in 1928. He outlived his three other brothers, dying at the age of ninety-one at his home in Bagshot Park, Surrey.

Related entries:
Albert Edward, Prince of Wales; Alfred Ernest Albert, Prince; Gordon, General Charles George; Louise, Princess; Saxe-Coburg-Gotha, Royal House of

References and further reading:

Aston, Sir George. 1929. *HRH The Duke of Connaught and Strathearn.* London: Harrap.

Bennett, Daphne. 1980. *Queen Victoria's Children.* London: Victor Gollancz.

Eilers, Marlene. 1997. *Queen Victoria's Descendants.* Falkoping, Sweden: Rosvall Royal Books.

Frankland, Noble. 1993. *Witness of a Century: The Life and Times of Prince Arthur, Duke of Connaught.* London: Shepheard-Walwyn.

Longford, Elizabeth. [1964] 1998. *Victoria R.I.* London: Weidenfeld and Nicolson.

McLintock, Mary Howard. 1945. *The Queen Thanks Sir Howard.* London: John Murray.

St. Aubyn, Giles. 1991. *Queen Victoria: A Portrait.* London: Sinclair Stevenson.

Van der Kiste, John. 1991. *Queen Victoria's Children.* Stroud, Gloucestershire: Sutton.

Assassination Attempts

It is worth being shot at—to see how much one is loved (Longford 1998, 446)

Within months of her accession to the throne in 1837, Queen Victoria became the target of the first of a series of assaults and assassination attempts, commited mainly by deranged individuals acting alone. Although some of them appear to have had political motives, as sympathizers of the cause of Irish independence, none of the perpetrators seem to have been directly involved in a major plot against the queen's life. The recorded attempts were numerous—seven major attackers are known of, although there may well have been other plots that never materialized. Indeed, the first three attacks came in quick succession during her early reign, at a time when Victoria was enjoying the first flush of popularity.

In October 1837 Victoria had been shocked when a man had run up to her unguarded carriage hurling a torrent of abuse, as she was approaching Buckingham Palace along Birdcage Walk. The gist of his garbled tirade was that Victoria had stolen the throne. The attacker, who turned out to have previously caused a disturbance by trying to get into the queen's home at Kensington Palace, was hauled off to a mental asylum, where he continued to claim that, as the son of George IV and Queen Caroline, he was the true heir to the British throne.

On 10 June 1840 an eighteen-year-old public house waiter, Edward Oxford, fired two shots at Victoria and Albert when they were traveling one evening in an open carriage up London's Constitution Hill. The man was quickly apprehended by the watching crowd, muttering that he did not think the country should be ruled by a queen. Constitution Hill, a lovely tree-lined road leading from Green Park to the garden entrance of Buckingham Palace, would become a favorite vantage point for attackers, probably because of the cover afforded by its many trees and the fact that it was a point of exit and entry of royal carriages to the palace grounds. Whether or not Oxford was acting alone was never established, although there was some question as to how he had obtained possession of the two, decorative (rather than functional) silver-mounted pistols he had used. At the time of his attack Victoria was four months pregnant and the courage she displayed during the incident, which was witnessed by many, greatly boosted her popularity. Oxford was tried at the Central Criminal Court in July and found guilty of high treason. He was sent to Newgate prison but after being found insane was transferred to a lunatic asylum. He was released in 1867 and emigrated.

Two years later, on two consecutive days—29 and 30 May 1842—Constitution Hill was again the setting for two attempts on the queen's life when a man stepped out and fired a pistol at her. On the first occasion he ran off, after firing at Victoria as she

One of several assassination attempts made on the queen was that by John Francis on 30 May 1842; condemned to death, Francis was later reprieved and transported to Australia. (The* Illustrated London News *Picture Library)

was traveling back to Buckingham Palace in an open carriage with Prince Albert after attending church. With the assailant still at large, the prime minister, Sir Robert Peel, decided to try and deliberately draw him out, and the following day Victoria and Albert set out once again by carriage, only this time with a close escort and numerous plain clothes police on patrol along the route. Once again, the gunman appeared on Constitution Hill and made an unsuccessful attack at close range. This time he was apprehended, but his pistol proved not to be loaded. Upon his apprehension by police officers he was apparently heard to say: "Damn the queen; why should she be such an expense to the nation" (reported in the *Illustrated London News,* 1842, Vol. 1, 67). Despite his failure to do the queen harm, her attacker, a cabinetmaker named John Francis, was sentenced to death for high treason (a sentence that Victoria herself endorsed), but he was reprieved on 1 July and his sentence commuted to transportation for life. On 8 July he was sent to the remote penal colony of Norfolk Island (800 miles east of Australia).

There was much talk in the press about the queen's security in the wake of the Francis attack. The poet Elizabeth Barrett reported in a letter to her friend, Mary Russell Mitford, that "I hear the people go now to see the poor queen leave the palace for her drive, with a disposition to be excited, with an idea of seeing her *shot at:* there is a crowd at the gates every day!" (Kelley and Hudson 1988, 25). The poet Thomas Hood published a verse in the *New Monthly Magazine* in which the suggestion was made that Constitution Hill, where the attacks had occurred, would be better changing names with a thoroughfare in south London—Shooter's Hill. The diarist Charles Greville was one of many to express their incredulity that such an attack had ever taken place; he observed that such malice toward a young queen whom none thought had any enemies was inexplicable. Comparing her with her royal prececessors, Greville opined: "George III, a very popular King, was exposed to similar attempts, but in his case the perpetrators were really insane; while George IV, a man neither beloved nor respected, and at different times very odious and unpopular, was never attacked by anyone" (Strachey and Fulford 1938, 5, 24). Following these two attempts on the queen's life, Sir Robert Peel introduced a bill in Parliament—the Queen's Person's Protection Act (July 1842)—that provided for the public or private whipping in prison of any such offenders on up to three occasions.

Only two days after the reprieve of Oxford, however, and five weeks after the two previous attempts, on 3 July 1842 a third attack on the queen occurred, when John William Bean, a deranged and deformed seventeen-year-old youth only four feet in height, lunged at the queen with a pistol as she traveled down the Mall in an open carriage with her Uncle Leopold, king of the Belgians. The pistol, which luckily misfired, was later found to be loaded with a mixture of gravel, paper, and broken clay pipes; Bean was found guilty of assault on the queen, but because his gun had not been properly loaded he received a prison sentence of only eighteen months.

It was seven years before another attack occurred, yet again on Constitution Hill. On 19 May 1849, William Hamilton, an unemployed Irish agricultural laborer from Adare, attempted to assassinate Victoria as she drove up the hill on one of her first public outings shortly after the birth of her seventh child. His pistol, like that of the other assailants, had not been properly loaded and contained mainly powder. At his trial on 14 June, Hamilton pleaded guilty and was transported for seven years.

It was not until 27 June 1850 that another madman, this time a retired army officer, Robert Pate, got near enough to the queen to be able to hit her on the head with his walking cane as she left Cambridge House in London after a private visit to her sick uncle, the duke of Cambridge. The beating left the queen with bruises and a black eye. The defense, however, failed in their claim of insanity, and Pate, who never admitted the motive for his attack, was sentenced to seven years' transportation. The queen, by now almost impervious to threats from misfiring pistols, nevertheless was greatly shaken by this attack—more so than the others—and recorded her revulsion at the physicality of the assault: "For a man to strike any woman is most brutal, and I, as well as everyone else, think this far worse than any attempt to shoot, which wicked as it is, is at least more comprehensible and more courageous" (Hibbert 1984, 81).

By the beginning of the 1870s, the political climate in Britain had become extremely tense, and Victoria herself was going through a period of mounting public antipathy toward her long retreat into widowhood, since Prince Albert's death in 1861. It was widely resented that she had seemed to cut herself off from the pressing social concerns of the day. From the end of 1867 on, the British home secretary had been receiving reports that Irish Fenians based in Manchester were plotting to either assassinate or take the queen hostage. Security around her home at Balmoral in Scotland, where she spent increasing amounts of time since being widowed, was immediately tightened. But the queen considered such measures alarmist and unnecessary. Despite her earlier experiences of attack, she stubbornly refused to listen to warnings against traveling south from the relative security of Balmoral to her home on the Isle of Wight.

But it would once again be London where the queen would prove to be most vulnerable. The next attack occurred on 29 February 1872, as she was driving in an open landau with two of her sons, Arthur and Leopold, on her way back to Buckingham Palace from St. Paul's Cathedral, after a service of thanksgiving for the Prince of Wales's recovery from typhoid fever. A young Irish Fenian, Arthur O'Connor, came dangerously close to Victoria with a pistol as her carriage drew to a halt at the garden entrance to Buckingham Palace. He was disarmed by Victoria's loyal servant, John Brown; the pistol was found to be broken and useless. It was later ascertained that O'Connor's purpose had been to beg the queen to support a petition for the release of Fenian prisoners; the queen's advisers meanwhile saw this lucky escape, combined with the outpouring of public sympathy during the prince's recent illness, as a much welcome boost to her popularity when it was at a low ebb. O'Connor was sentenced to a year in prison and twenty strokes of the birch; the queen had hoped he would be transported.

Victoria remained haunted by the possibility of an attack by Fenians and was right to do so, for the last assassination attempt came in 1882 during a period of escalating unrest in Ireland during parliamentary debates over the fraught issue of Irish Home Rule. Victoria was yet again confronted by an attacker, this time when traveling from Windsor station to the nearby castle in an open carriage. Her assailant, Roderick MacLean, fired a shot at her but was immediately apprehended by a crowd of onlookers, including two young pupils from the nearby school at Eton, who threatened him with their umbrellas. At his trial for high treason at Reading Assizes in April, Maclean was proclaimed not guilty, and the jury accepted a plea of insanity and MacLean was committed to a lunatic asylum. The queen's reaction to this verdict was blunt: "If that is the law, the law must be altered" (Strachey 1971, 221). A year later legislation was passed to allow a verdict of guilty but insane, a law that remained on the British statute books until 1964. MacLean was committed to a lunatic asylum.

Related entries:
Gladstone, William Ewart; Ireland; Peel, Sir Robert; "The Widow at Windsor"

References and further reading:

Benson, A. C., and Viscount Esher, eds. 1911. *The Letters of Queen Victoria: A Selection from Her Majesty's Correspondence between the Years 1837 and 1861.* 1st ser., 3 vols. London: John Murray.

Campbell, Christy. 2002. *Fenian Fire: The British Government Plot to Assissinate Queen Victoria.* London: HarperCollins.

Hibbert, Christopher. 1984. *Queen Victoria in Her Letters and Journals.* London: Viking.

Jagow, Dr. Kurt, ed. 1938. *Letters of the Prince Consort, 1831–1861.* London: John Murray.

Kelley, Philip, and Ronald Hudson. 1988. *The Brownings' Correspondence,* vol 6. Winfield, KS: Wedgestone Press.

Longford, Elizabeth. [1964] 1998. *Victoria R.I.* London: Weidenfeld and Nicolson.

Martin, Sir Theodore. 1875–1880. *The Life of H.R.H. The Prince Consort.* 5 vols. London: Smith, Elder and Co.

Strachey, Lytton, and Roger Fulford, eds. 1938. *The Grenville Memoirs.* 8 vols. London: Macmillan.

Strachey, Lytton. [1921] 1971. *Queen Victoria.* Harmondsworth, UK: Penguin.

B

Balmoral Castle

this dear Paradise (Victoria 1868, 158)

When Queen Victoria and Prince Albert took a holiday home at Balmoral on the River Dee in the Grampian region of the Scottish Highlands, they were, initially, mere tenants. The extensive, 17,400-acre estate was in fact owned by the earls of Fife and let by their trustees. The royal couple's taking up of the remainder of a twenty-seven-year lease was the fulfillment of a dream to have their own private family home as far away as possible from government and prying eyes.

The queen and Prince Albert had loved Scotland since they had made their first visit there in 1842, when they had sailed up to the west coast. They visited again in 1844, staying at Blair Atholl Castle, and they took a cruise up to Ardverikie on the west coast in 1847. In choosing Scotland they set a royal precedent, since no English monarchs had effectively bothered to travel north to their Scottish domains since Charles I in the seventeenth century. There was something about the majesty and solitude of the mountainous scenery that appealed to both royal natures and that was a dramatic counterpoint to the balmier atmosphere of the southernmost holiday home they had created for themselves at Osborne on the Isle of Wight. The choice had originally been therapeutic: Victoria and Albert both suffered from bouts of rheumatism, and the royal physician, Dr. James Clark, had recommended the drier and more salubrious air of the Highlands around Deeside, in preference to the rain-swept west coast of Scotland, as a suitable location for a holiday home. Lord Aberdeen had recommended they rent Balmoral upon hearing of the death of its tenant, Sir Robert Gordon.

In September 1848 the royal couple sailed to Aberdeen in their steamship, the *Victoria and Albert,* and went to inspect their new holiday home. The house, which had something of the French chateau and the German *schloss* about it, had a beautiful Gothic charm that was all its own. It had been extensively renovated by the previous tenant less than ten years before, "with mullioned windows and flamboyant tracery, and stepped and fancy gable-ends, and embattlements, and projecting turrets at angles with lancet windows, and round towers topped by cone-shaped roofs like magicians' hats" (Whittle 1980, 40–41). Victoria was overwhelmed with the castle's tranquil location and with the wild beauty of the wooded hillsides all around: "All seemed to breathe freedom and peace, and to make one forget the world and its turmoils" (Aronson 1991, 204). The air was redolent with the balsamic smell of heather and pine and birch trees. Victoria wrote to her Uncle

The interior furnishings of Balmoral Castle, built by the queen and Prince Albert at Deeside, as a holiday retreat, all catered specifically to the royal demands for a cozy family home. (Hulton/Archive by Getty Images)

Leopold: "The scenery all around is the finest almost I have seen anywhere. It is very wild and solitary, and yet cheerful and *beautifully wooded,* with the River Dee running between the two sides of the hills" (Benson and Escher 1911, 2:194). The interior, although comfortable, was by no means luxurious. Others at court were more forthright in describing its extremely cramped conditions, with Lord Malmesbury (a minister-in-attendance in the 1850s) observing that he had to sit on his bed to write his official dispatches. Charles Greville recorded in September 1849 that the royal family lived here "not merely like private gentle folks, but like very small gentlefolks, small house, small rooms, small establishment" (Strachey and Fulford 1938, 6:185).

It soon became patently clear to Prince Albert that despite the connubial bliss that he and the queen enjoyed at Balmoral, the charming old house did not serve the needs of their growing family. Lovely though it was, it was simply not big enough to accommodate them, all their retainers—both English and Scottish—and in addition, the occasional important guests and visiting government ministers. Albert's head was also full of ambitious schemes to extend the royal domain at Balmoral to lands on the nearby estate of Abergeldie in the east, taking in another 6,500 acres beyond it at Birkhall. To the west, he set his sights on gaining possession of the much-prized forest of Ballochbuie (not achieved until long after his death, in 1878).

In 1852 Albert sent for the Aberdonian architect William Smith, instructing him to draw up plans for a new Balmoral Castle. This would be built in Scottish baronial style, with romantic pepper-box turrets, only a hundred yards or so away from the existing house, in sight of the River Dee. It would comprise two distinct units—the living quarters of the royal family and the working quarters for their staff. These two rectangular blocks each enclosed a courtyard and were connected corner to corner with a square, five-story tower at this meeting point. Construction was also ordered of new stables, an office block, and—to accommodate Albert's mass slaughter of the local deer—a venison larder.

In 1852 the royal family formally acquired Balmoral when they purchased it for £30,000—thanks to a bequest made to the queen of half a million pounds by a reclusive and miserly barrister, John Camden Neild. During their stay at Balmoral that October, the queen led the royal household up to nearby Craig Gowan to supervise the building of an eight-foot-high cairn of stones to commemorate the occasion. Work on the new house began in the autumn of 1853 using local labor and locally mined Scottish white granite from Invercalder. Queen Victoria laid the foundation stone with a silver trowel and held a reception and ball afterward for the architect and his team of contractors and craftsmen. This team worked with consummate skill and amazing speed to complete most of the house within two years, with the royal family, meanwhile, staying in the old house during their holiday visits.

With seventy rooms on three floors (or two where large state rooms required higher ceiling space) and plenty of windows (180), the new house had a staff of 100 to run it. The queen and Prince Albert each had their own private suite of rooms in the west wing; there was also hot air heating supplied by furnaces, as well as open fireplaces (most of which remained unlit, on the queen's orders, however cold it was). There were also four bathrooms for the use of the royal family; visitors had to make do with jugs and wash bowls in theirs, and chamber pots were provided, although the castle boasted the unprecedented number of fourteen water closets. Private apartments were included for distinguished visitors such as royalty and prime ministers. Much to the dismay of many, the old house—a lovely and still useful building—was demolished.

Such was the confidence of the royal couple in their privacy at Balmoral that the castle had only minimal security arrangements. Charles Greville, who visited in 1849, commented that "there are no Soldiers and the whole guard of the Sovereign and of the whole Royal Family is a single Policeman who walks about the grounds to keep off impertinent intruders or improper characters" (Strachey and Fulford 1938 6:185). The issue of the royal family's privacy at Balmoral was eventually addressed by Prince Albert, when in 1857 he obtained permission to divert a main thoroughfare away from the estate. The new house was finally ready for occupation in September 1855. A bonfire was lit to celebrate the occasion, and there was much drinking of whiskey and playing of bagpipes by the castle's loyal Scottish retainers. The finished interior was homely and a far cry from the austere reception rooms and vast corridors of Buckingham Palace. As the years went on it became ever more cluttered with paintings, stags heads (Albert's hunting trophies), family photographs, knickknacks, and ephemera.

With the royal enthusiasm for all things Scottish, Balmoral was quickly infected with "tartanitis" and a superabundance of Scottish motifs—particularly thistles—enough to "rejoice the heart of a donkey," as Lord Clarendon observed (Hardy 1976, 75). These appeared everywhere: tartan curtains, tartan wallpaper, and even tartan rugs; Prince Albert even designed a new Balmoral tartan—of lilac, red, and black on a gray background, which only the members of the royal family and their household were allowed to wear. Albert and his sons regularly wore kilts; Victoria sported plaid scarves in the daytime and silk tartan sashes and dresses in the evenings. The conscientious Albert even attempted to learn Gaelic.

Once installed in the new house, Prince Albert was by no means content. Always hungry for great schemes to occupy his creative mind, he designed a new driveway up to the castle, oversaw the completion of the ballroom, and set about improving the outbuildings, including ordering the construction of a modern dairy and workers' cottages and the setting up of a plantation. He planned the gardens, planting them with rare conifers, and designed terraces leading down to the banks of the River Dee. In what little spare time remained, he indulged his favorite outdoor pursuit of hunting—enjoying especially deer stalking (in which he was sometimes joined by an indefatigable queen who thought nothing of spending hours on end lying in the wet heather). He also enjoyed shooting grouse and ptarmigan and salmon fishing, in the process filling up the royal game larders. He even found time to go in search of rare Scottish butterflies and make a study of the local geology.

Much of daily life at Balmoral revolved around healthy outdoor pursuits. In the mornings, while Victoria usually dealt with matters of state, Albert hunted or fished. After luncheon, a walk, excursion, or picnic of some kind was de rigueur, that is, if Victoria and Albert (plus some of their children as they grew old enough) had not already gone on an all-day excursion. Some of these expeditions, which were undertaken in all weathers including gales, sleet, and snow and by a combination of carriage, pony, and foot travel, took them into the wildest parts of the Highlands and involved arduous journeys fording rivers and climbing mountainsides. The queen took an almost perverse pleasure in such rigorous exercise and in inflicting it upon others. As Lord Malmesbury observed: "H[er] M[ajesty] quite accepts the idea of sitting for hours perishing on a pony going at a foot's pace and coming home frozen" (Malmesbury 1884, 1:345) At the end of trips such as those to the primeval waters of Loch-na-Gar or the top of Ben Muich Dhui, the royal party would enjoy picnics in splendid isolation, indulging Queen Victoria's favorite occupation of making tea and boiling potatoes on a portable stove. Other expeditions and excursions made over the course of two or three days by Victoria and Albert in a small entourage in the last couple of years before his death—such as a trip to the Cairngorms—were made incognito, as "Lord and Lady Churchill," during which the queen and Prince Albert greatly enjoyed the simple food and hospitality of country inns.

The royal couple were staunch advocates of the therapeutic benefits of the Highlands. The virtues of the simple Scottish people became an abiding obsession too, and throughout her life the queen would not hear a bad word spoken about them. She constantly impressed upon the members of her household her belief that "Scotch air, Scotch people, Scotch hills, Scotch rivers, Scotch woods, are all far preferable to those of any other nation in or out of this world" (Wyndham 1912, 392). The royal seal of approval brought with it welcome revenue to Scotland as a holiday venue. Gradually, high society began to discover the Highlands; spa towns, such as Strathpeffer, with their sulphorous water, were promoted as a cure-all for gout, scurvy, and other conditions and became popular tourist destinations, patronized by the queen and other European royals.

A highlight of the year at Balmoral (although it would be a bugbear to those in the household who disliked it) would be the annual gillies' ball. This would generally take place in the ballroom located next to the servant's quarters or sometimes in a tent out of doors. Queen Victoria was extremely agile in performing highland jigs and reels to the bagpipes. But these balls often turned into extremely rowdy affairs, with excessive drinking of whiskey precipitating much unruly behavior, a fact that the queen tolerated only among her Scottish servants.

Regular visits were also made by the royal family, after 1848, to the annual Braemar Gathering. This had been inaugurated in the 1820s by the Braemar Highland Society as a way of encouraging the preservation of Scottish traditions, such as hill racing, hammer throwing, and tossing the caber. Although, as they grew older, most of the royal children actively disliked going to Balmoral, the whole family nevertheless became particularly attached to their retinue of Highland servants, and the queen and her daughters regularly made private visits to the sick and poor on the Balmoral estate. After Albert's death Victoria's mainstay at Balmoral would be her Scottish manservant John Brown and her dresser Annie MacDonald—both from local families. But the increasingly domineering presence of Brown would become the source of great discord and resentment among the household. After the queen's death in 1901, her son King Edward VII saw to it that much of the memorabilia relating to Brown installed by her at Balmoral was removed from view and destroyed.

With Balmoral located so far away from London, the royal family felt secure in their isolation from official business. The queen did of course continue to deal with the regular arrival of dispatch boxes and a minister-in-residence would always be on hand to discuss affairs of state, but most of Victoria's ministers loathed the long trek north and the spartan regime when they got there. Although the royal family had the convenience of the royal train or the royal yacht, the long tedious journey for ministers in attendance and visitors was an unwanted imposition to which many grudgingly subjected themselves. After 1867 the Deeside railway took them to nearby Ballater, but the weather was often cold and wet, and in summer visitors were eaten alive by midges. Not surprisingly, many in the queen's service would do anything to get out of undertaking a tour of duty at Balmoral. Benjamin Disraeli endured the journey after he became prime minister in 1868 and again in 1874–1878, but he complained that "carrying on the Government of the Country six hundred miles from the metropolis doubles the labour" (Whittle 1980, 149). Gladstone, however, relished the fresh air and long walks and thought nothing of covering twenty-five miles in a single day when staying there. Queen Victoria's last prime minister, Lord Salisbury, absolutely loathed the place, nicknaming Balmoral Castle "Siberia." He only went there on sufferance, insisting that in advance of his arrival his rooms should be heated to a minimum of 60 degrees Fahrenheit (by our standards still quite cold). He had no stomach either for the long and arduous walks undertaken by the royal party and refused to join them.

At Balmoral, the royal family worshipped on Sundays at the nearby parish church at Crathie. Queen Victoria and Prince Albert enjoyed walking the mile and a half to service, and the queen became a particular admirer of the Rev. Norman McLeod, who frequently came from Glasgow to preach there and to whom she turned for comfort after the death of Albert. Toward the end of the century, the church was in a bad state of repair, and Victoria ordered a new one to be built to replace it in the years from 1893 to 1895, the work overseen by her son-in-law Prince Henry of Battenberg. Private donations accounted for some of the cost of the building work, but the rest of the £6,000 needed was raised by Victoria and her daughter Beatrice (Henry's wife), who organized a two-day bazaar staffed by numerous members of the royal family.

After the death of Prince Albert in 1861, life at Balmoral lost all its vivacity. Like Osborne, it became a living mausoleum to the life and achievements of the prince. His rooms there were preserved just as they had been in his lifetime. A marble statue of him in highland dress by William Theed was placed at the foot of the staircase in 1863. A memorial cairn of granite with an obelisk was built in his memory at the top of nearby Craig Lowrigan; the queen even commemorated the place where he had shot his last stag. Victoria now spent more and more time at Balmoral, going twice a year and attended always by John Brown. The castle now seemed increasingly like a prison to those royal attendants incarcerated unwillingly for weeks at a time. Life became depressing, with days spent idly standing in wait for the queen in cold, draughty rooms and sitting through silent mealtimes. At first Victoria continued the family tradition of going for excursions, in 1867 touring the Border Country. But as time went on her desire to travel far from Balmoral and stay overnight dimmed. Instead she took day-long drives out into the country, to places such as Inverlocky, Broxmouth, and Loch Maree, or went on fishing excursions to Loch Muick. In 1869 she extended her autumn holiday from mid-August till 3 November—making this her longest stay at Balmoral yet. It was fortunate that her devoted youngest daughter Beatrice also loved Balmoral, as did Beatrice's husband, Prince Henry. In old age, their daughter Alice talked with affection of the evocative smell of woodsmoke and leather at Balmoral and of her grandmother taking her breakfast out of doors in all weathers.

Sometimes the memories of past happy times overwhelmed Victoria, and she retreated, to mourn in the solitude of her simple cottage hideaways beyond Balmoral. In 1849 she and Albert had built a cozy little retreat at Alt-na-Giuthasach, at the end of Loch Muick, but she could no longer bear to visit it after his death and in 1865 rented a two-roomed bothy up Glen Gelder called the Gelder Shiel. In the summer of 1875 the queen finally fulfilled Albert's wish and acquired the long-coveted Forest of Ballochbuie, which brought with it yet another hideaway cottage called Dantzig Shiel. Eventually, she built a new fifteen-room house, Glassalt Shiel, located two and a half miles beyond Balmoral Castle at Alt-na-Giuthasach, at the other end of Loch Muick. This was her Widow's House to which, from 1868 on, she would retreat into total solitude with only Princess Beatrice for company. It was a wild and remote location famed for its midges, "a silent place, the quietness only broken by the trickle of a waterfall high above the house and the cries of water birds" (Whittle 1980, 150–151). But in 1883 the queen abandoned this place on the death of John Brown; wherever she now went the memories crowded in on her. Eventually the gloomy life at Balmoral was broken by the arrival on holiday of royal grandchildren and relatives from abroad, notably the visit in 1896 of the Russian tsar, Nicholas II, with his wife, Alexandra (Victoria's granddaughter), and their children. The Russian royal family arrived with a huge retinue, who were housed in temporary log cabins. The Russians complained that these were freezing cold, even though it was summer. If anything, the weather at Balmoral became even less congenial toward the end of the century, one lady-in-waiting observing of her years in service, "I can safely say I never remember a warm congenial day in the highlands during the many months I spent there" (Thompson 1990, 54).

Related entries:
Brown, John; Buckingham Palace; *Leaves from a Journal of Our Life in the Highlands;* Osborne; Windsor Castle

References and further reading:

Aronson, Theo. 1991. *The Heart of a Queen: Queen Victoria's Romantic Attachments.* London: John Murray.

Benson, A. C., and Viscount Esher, eds. 1911. *The Letters of Queen Victoria: A Selection from Her Majesty's Correspondence between the Years 1837 and 1861.* 1st ser., 3 vols. London: John Murray.

Clark, Ronald W. 1981. *Balmoral: Queen Victoria's Highland Home.* London: Thames and Hudson.

Duff, David, ed. 1980. *Queen Victoria's Highland Journals.* London: Webb and Bower.

Hardy, Alan. 1976. *Queen Victoria Was Amused.* London: John Murray.
Kerr, John. 1992. *Queen Victoria's Scottish Diaries.* Moffat, Scotland: Lochar.
Malmesbury, Lord. 1884. *Memoirs of an Ex-Minister.* 2 vols. London: Smith Elder.
Millar, Delia. 1985. *Queen Victoria's Life in the Scottish Highlands, Depicted by Her Watercolour Artists.* London: Philip Wilson.
Reid, Michaela. 1987. *Ask Sir James.* London: Hodder and Stoughton.
Strachey, Lytton, and Roger Fulford, eds. 1938. *The Grenville Memoirs.* 8 vols. London: Macmillan.
Thompson, Dorothy. 1990. *Queen Victoria: Gender and Power.* London: Virago.
Victoria. 1868. *Leaves from the Journal of Our Life in the Highlands from 1848–1861.* Edited by Arthur Helps. London: Smith, Elder.
Warner, Marina. 1979. *Queen Victoria's Sketchbook.* London: Macmillan.
Whittle, Tyler. 1980. *Victoria and Albert at Home.* London: Routledge and Kegan Paul.
Wyndham, Hon. Mrs. Hugh, ed. 1912. *Correspondence of Sarah Spencer, Lady Lyttleton 1787–1870.* London: John Murray.

Battenberg, Henry Maurice, Prince of (1858–1896)

("Liko")

like a bright sunbeam in my home (Lutyens 1961, 157)

The lively and endearing presence of Prince Henry of Battenberg, husband of the queen's youngest daughter, Princess Beatrice, did much to brighten the atmosphere at court during the years 1885–1896. With his engaging manner, he helped to wean the queen gradually away from her own mawkish grieving. As Tyler Whittle observed, he had "the gift of bringing a champagne quality into life" (1980, 184). But although his social skills and his infectious personality made Prince Henry popular at court, he was not popular in the country at large, despite becoming a naturalized subject.

Liko, as he became known in the royal family, was the third son of Prince Alexander of Hesse. While serving as an officer in the Prussian household, he had met and fallen in love with the shy, plain Beatrice in 1884, at a royal wedding in Darmstadt. Queen Victoria's immediate selfish reaction was that, should the couple marry, she would lose her favorite and most useful daughter to the palace at Potsdam. She was adamantly against the idea and refused to speak to Beatrice for six months, hoping to wear down her resolve. But eventually, in January 1885, she gave way, by now admitting that Liko had "completely won my heart" (Hibbert 2000, 287). She also rose to his defense when her son-in-law Fritz (the crown prince of Germany) and other European members of the royal family queried whether Liko was sufficiently "of the blood" to marry the daughter of the queen of Great Britain.

Liko and Beatrice were married in July 1885 at the small church at Whippingham near Osborne—the first royal couple to marry there—with Liko looking like a Ruritanian prince in his white uniform of an officer of the Gardes du Corps. One of the queen's stipulations on their marriage had been that the couple would relinquish their independence and live in England with her. Liko also had to agree to give up his military career and be naturalized, with the queen according him the use of the title His Royal Highness while in the country.

Liko's arrival at court was welcomed. Lively and energetic, he brightened the dull routine of Osborne and Balmoral. The ladies-in-waiting liked him, as did male members of the royal household. For he was a man's man—a soldier, who loved sports and hunting and was a good shot. He was also a keen yachtsman and engaged in several trips, sailing round the north of Scotland and to the Scillies and, in 1889, taking on a four-month yachting trip to the Greek island of Corfu.

Bertie, the Prince of Wales, liked and admired his brother-in-law and was more than a little envious of Liko's close relationship with Queen Victoria. She had given Liko token appointments upon his marriage—as governor and captain-general of the Isle of Wight, as well as governor of Carisbrooke Castle—but these brought little useful employment with them. Liko's main role continued to be a domestic one of lightening the general mood and placating the queen's bouts of querulousness. As a peacemaker he regularly smoothed over family disagreements and even managed, against the odds, to persuade the queen to relax her strict rules on smoking. By being considerate and irrepressibly good humored, Liko won the queen's trust. But the perception of him among the public at large, however, tended to be hostile—of yet another impoverished German princeling and hanger-on for the nation to sustain, and one who spent his time in idleness and playing billiards (as he was lampooned in the press).

As a professional soldier, Liko inevitably became bored with the dull routine of life at court. He found some welcome diversion, from 1888 on, in encouraging the revival of royal *tableaux vivants* (living pictures), mainly staged by adult members of the royal family and household. A year or so later he exerted his winning ways over the queen for the resumption of royal theatricals (although he himself did not take part, apparently because his thick German accent was too trying) and obtained her permission for occasional command performances by touring theatrical companies. Not everyone at court, however, enjoyed Liko's revival of amateur dramatics, and some found them tiresome and childish.

Despite his happy marriage to Beatrice, and the birth of their four children, Liko remained restless. He missed the military life and wanted "real work" serving his adoptive country. He jumped at the opportunity to do so when trouble broke out in the British Gold Coast colony in West Africa in November 1895. Queen Victoria was extremely loath to part with him, and it took a lot of persuasion from Princess Beatrice (despite her own deep apprehensions about what might happen to him) before Liko was allowed the chance to serve. In December he set sail with the British expeditionary force, as military secretary to the British commander, Sir Francis Scott. One of the ladies at court, Marie Mallet, presciently observed before his departure that "of course he is bursting with excitement" but "it is the climate I fear, *not* the enemy" (Mallet 1968, 71). And she was right—having arrived in Africa, Liko joined the march on Kumasi, during which he caught malaria. He was taken back to HMS *Blonde,* which set sail for Madeira, and he seemed to rally. But then, just as Beatrice was about to set sail to be with him, Liko suffered a relapse and died in January 1896, off the coast of Sierra Leone. His body, preserved in rum in a tank made from biscuit tins for the long journey back to England, arrived back in Portsmouth, from where he was taken to be buried, in the service uniform of the Ashanti campaign and with full military honors, at Whippingham Church.

The queen took Liko's death particularly hard. Despite their hostility toward him, the public nevertheless shared in the queen and Beatrice's inconsolable grief, so much so that Victoria published a "Letter from the Queen to the Nation" in the *London Gazette,* thanking her loyal subjects for their "warm sympathy in a fresh and grievous affliction." "This new sorrow," she declared, was "overwhelming." She had lost a surrogate son "whose presence was like a bright sunbeam in My Home" (Lutyens 1961, 157). After Liko's death, the theatricals and *tableaux vivants* ceased, and there were no command performances either for four years.

Related entries:
Beatrice Mary Victoria Feodore, Princess; Smoking; Theater

References and further reading:
Hardy, John. 1976. *Queen Victoria Was Amused.* London: John Murray.

Hibbert, Christopher. 2000. *Victoria: A Personal History.* London: HarperCollins.
Lutyens, Mary, ed. 1961. *Lady Lytton's Court Dairy 1895–1899.* London: Rupert Hart-Davis.
Mallet, Victor, ed. 1968. *Life with Queen Victoria: Marie Mallet's Letters from Court, 1887–1901.* London: John Murray.
Ponsonby, Arthur. 1942. *Henry Ponsonby: His Life from His Letters.* London: Macmillan.
Reid, Michaela. 1996. *Ask Sir James: The Life of Sir James Reid, Personal Physician to Queen Victoria.* London: Eland.
Rowell, George. 1978. *Queen Victoria Goes to the Theatre.* London: Paul Elek.
Whittle, Tyler. 1980. *Victoria and Albert at Home.* London: Routledge and Kegan Paul.

Beatrice Mary Victoria Feodore, Princess (1857–1944)

("Baby"; From 1885, Princess Henry of Battenberg)

she is the comfort and blessing of my declining years (Bennett 1980, 129)

Queen Victoria's fifth daughter and ninth and last child, Beatrice, is probably the best known of the queen's daughters, if only because of her long years of devotion to her demanding, widowed mother. As early as 1863 the queen had most vociferously demanded, when her daughter, Alice, had married and gone to live in Darmstadt: "A married daughter I *MUST* have living with me and must not be left to look about for help"(Buckle 1926–1928, 1:85). That role fell on Beatrice, accustomed from a young age to sublimating her own needs to her mother's self-serving monopoly on her time and attention. Such was Beatrice's own natural reticence that she spent the first forty-three years of her life almost continually at her mother's beck and call, in the capacity of companion, and later nurse, amanuensis, and private secretary.

Beatrice was born when Victoria was thirty-eight and, as the baby of the family, would be cosseted and spoiled by everyone, as well as being overprotected by her mother, who would persist in addressing her by her family nickname, "Baby," even when she was a mature woman. She was an exceptionally pretty, precocious, and pert child and disarmed everyone with her candor and her quirky comments. But when Victoria was widowed in 1861, it soon became clear that she would stubbornly hold on to her youngest daughter, as a way of filling the huge void left by Albert's death. Beatrice's sole role in life would be to stay at home with mother. "I live for Beatrice," the queen admitted, adding with mawkish sentiment, "the only one who needs me now" (Benson 1939, 129). From the age of four on, therefore, this pretty little girl would be dressed in mourning, her natural, childish spirit stifled by the unremitting gloom at court; she seemed to be condemned to a life of unremitting filial duty, a role fulfilled by so many of the youngest daughters of Victorian families after one or the other of their aging parents was widowed.

The queen was determined "to hold her [Beatrice] back much more—for her own good as well as for comfort" (St. Aubyn 1991, 418) and had long since concluded that "no married daughter is of any use" (Windsor and Bolitho 1929, 161). Convinced that the compliant young Beatrice was in fact perfectly happy at home, Victoria was determined to "protect" her from all thoughts of love and marriage, by keeping her away from attractive, young male company. She did not encourage Beatrice's admiration for the charming and handsome young Prince Imperial, only son of the exiled Empress Eugénie of France, when she met him at the age of sixteen.

Victoria's perception of Beatrice's future role shifted with the untimely death of her second daughter, Alice, in 1878, who left four motherless young children. For a while, Victoria seriously considered marrying Beatrice off to Alice's widower—Louis, grand duke of Hesse—in order that Beatrice might rear their children in her sister's

The plain and shy Princess Beatrice, Queen Victoria's youngest daughter, made an unexpected love match in 1885 with the handsome Prince Henry of Battenberg. (Hulton/Archive by Getty Images)

stead. She was not in the least deterred by the fact that such a marriage was then illegal under British law and enlisted the help of Prime Minister Benjamin Disraeli in 1879, in putting forward a Deceased Wife's Sister Marriage Act that would make this possible. (It would not, however, be finally passed by Parliament until after Victoria's death, in 1907.)

The queen was therefore pulled up short when the compliant Beatrice quite unexpectedly, and most determinedly, fell in love.

Now aged twenty-seven, Beatrice met the archetypal, handsome prince all Victorian girls dreamed of, when she attended a family wedding in Darmstadt in April 1884. Resplendent in his officer's uniform, Henry, the younger brother of the bridegroom—Louis of Battenberg—threw Queen Victoria's well-laid plans into chaos. Witty, engaging, and convivial, he drew the shy Beatrice out of herself—so much so that she found the courage to tell her mother that she wished to marry him. The queen's response was one of the utmost ill humor. It proved to be one of the most telling manifestations of Victoria's deeply unpleasant streak of egocentricity in regard to the marriage and personal happiness of her daughters. All she could think of was the inconvenience to her: "You . . . cannot imagine," she told her daughter Vicky, "what agonies, what despair it caused me and what a fearful shock it was to me when I first heard of her wish! It made me quite ill" (Hibbert 1984, 287).

So determined was Victoria to wear down Beatrice's desire to marry Liko, as Prince Henry was known, that she refused to speak to her and communicated with her only by written notes. This situation dragged on for months, by the end of which time Beatrice was suffering both physically and spiritually; she had lost weight and was, quite visibly, lovesick. In finally agreeing to the match, Victoria was adamant in one, major stipulation: Beatrice and her husband would live in England with *her* in order to attend to *her* needs. She never was to regret the arrival of Liko, who became the model son-in-law; his untimely death in 1896 was a bitter blow to Victoria from which she never really recovered.

Beatrice and Liko were married at Whippingham Church near Osborne, on the Isle of Wight, on 23 July 1885—the queen lending Beatrice her own wedding veil of Honiton lace for the service. She grudgingly allowed them a two-day honeymoon—six miles down the road, at Ryde. They proved to be a devoted couple (although Liko provoked Beatrice's jealousy on more than one occasion by flirting with her sister Louise). The queen meanwhile privately dreaded any dilution in Beatrice's dogged devotion to her own interests. She hoped that the marriage would bring no "results," as she euphemistically put it, but Beatrice almost immediately fell pregnant. She miscarried but was soon carrying another child, a son, Alexander, born in 1886. There would be three other children: one daughter, Victoria Eugénie, known as Ena (1887), and two sons, Leopold (1889) and Maurice (1891). Ena and Maurice were both born at Balmoral, the first royal children to be born in Scotland since 1600. These, of all the queen's many royal grandchildren, became both a great comfort and a major source of happiness to her in her old age. After their births a more relaxed, family atmosphere was renewed at court that dispelled the many years of Victoria's gloomy isolation.

But Beatrice's happiness was cut short in 1895, when Liko contracted malaria and died when on a military campaign with his regiment in Africa. Beatrice was desolate: "The life is gone out of me," she told her mother (Hibbert 1984, 333); the thought of having to deal with the queen's grief as well as her own was more than she could bear. But she lived out her long years of widowhood (from 1896 to 1944) with great resignation and fortitude. Unlike her mother, she was brave and unselfish in her grief—a fact that won the admiration of many at court. She took over her husband's roles as governor and captain-general of the Isle of Wight and governor of Carisbrooke Castle and also developed a passion for amateur photography. But she aged rapidly, bent over by severe rheumatism, while having to cope with the burden of her mother's increasing dependence on her in the last years of her life. The queen's eyesight was failing, making it increasingly difficult for her to read dispatches from her ministers or to write her own responses. Soon Beatrice was reading these to her, as she was the daily papers and the many personal letters from relatives that arrived daily. She also spent hours taking the queen's dictation of private and official correspondence as well as writing down the daily entries in her journal.

Beatrice's otherwise uncontroversial reputation has been considerably tainted by the horrific act of literary vandalism that she committed over many years to her mother's papers, completing it in 1942, not long before her own death. As an executor of Queen Victoria's will, she was determined to fulfill the queen's wishes to the letter. Despite protests from members of the royal family, notably King George V and his wife, Queen Mary, Beatrice—after copying out large portions of the 100 journals that the queen had kept since the age of thirteen and that she had bequeathed to her daughter—systematically destroyed the originals. What is more, many sections of those entries that she did copy out were also altered or bowdlerized by her—under instructions from the queen to modify or delete any passages that seemed unsuitable for preservation. Fortunately, Viscount Esher, who in 1912 and 1914 had published extracts from the queen's journals from 1832 to 1840, had privately made a typescript of this section of the unexpurgated text—about which Beatrice was not informed. This survives in the royal archives but has not been released for publication. Beatrice also consigned to the bonfire of the queen's personal papers some thirty volumes of letters written to her children Alfred and Alice.

Related entries:
Battenberg, Henry Maurice, Prince of; Hemophilia

References and further reading:

Bennett, Daphne. 1980. *Queen Victoria's Children.* London: Victor Gollancz.

Benson, E. F. 1939. *Daughters of Queen Victoria.* London: Cassell and Co.

Buckle, G. E., ed. 1926–1928. *The Letters of Queen Victoria: A Selection from Her Majesty's Correspondence and Journal between the Years 1862 and 1885.* 2d ser., 3 vols. London: John Murray.

Duff, David. 1958. *The Shy Princess: H.R.H. Beatrice. The Enthralling Life Story of a Queen's Daughter and the Mother of a Queen.* London: Evans.

Epton, Nina. 1971. *Victoria and Her Daughters.* London: Weidenfeld and Nicolson.

Hibbert, Christopher. 1984. *Queen Victoria in Her Letters and Journals.* London: Viking.

Packard, Jerrold. 1998. *Victoria's Daughters.* New York: St. Martin's Press.

Prole, Lozania. 1973. *The Queen's Daughters.* London: Robert Hale and Co.

Sara, M. E. 1945. *The Life and Times of Princess Beatrice.* London: Stanley Paul.

St. Aubyn, Giles. 1991. *Queen Victoria: A Portrait.* London: Sinclair Stevenson.

Windsor, Dean of, and Hector Bolitho. 1929. *Later Letters of Lady Augusta Stanley 1864–1876.* London: Jonathan Cape.

Bedchamber Crisis

they wished to treat me like a girl, but I will show them that I am Queen of England (Woodham-Smith 1972, 174)

Barely two years after ascending the throne, Queen Victoria was forced to face the inevitable—the loss of her adored prime minister, Lord Melbourne. A mark of her considerable political naïveté at this stage, coupled with her youthful intransigence, can be seen in Victoria's belief that by resisting the replacement of her ladies of the bedchamber as demanded by the new, Tory prime minister, Robert Peel, she could thereby not only save Melbourne's ministry and keep him by her but, more important, protect herself from the infiltration into her entourage of unwanted enemies and "spies" from the Tory camp.

The origins of this constitutional crisis, which arose in May 1839, lay in the revolt of British sugar planters in Jamaica, who had refused to institute legislation of 1834 and 1835 abolishing slavery in the British colonies. When Parliament debated Melbourne's proposal to suspend the Jamaican constitution and implement direct rule on 7 May 1839, his Whig government had come through the vote, but with a majority of only five. With such a precarious majority, Melbourne had been obliged to offer his resignation to a distraught queen, leaving her to face the prospect of a change of government. After much sobbing and hand-holding, she parted with Melbourne; she tried to enlist the support of her other long-standing wise counselor and old family friend, the duke of Wellington, in forming a new government. But he was now too old and too deaf and politely declined her invitation to take on the task. Reluctantly, the queen had to invite the leader of the Tories, Sir Robert Peel, to do so. But Sir Robert was a man she had already resolved to dislike.

Her view was unjustified, and it was one she eventually revised, for Peel, a punctilious man of honor, who took his role with a seriousness and deeper sense of integrity than did Melbourne, accepted the task, albeit with provisos. He insisted that the queen act democratically by dismissing some of her ladies of the bedchamber who were the wives of Whig members of Parliament replacing them with Tory ladies, thus underlining her support for the new government. Unwilling to part with Melbourne after only two years, and hostile to the stiff and awkward demeanor of Peel, which seemed to her so cold and alien after the avuncular charm of his predecessor, the queen flatly refused. She declared that politics was not something she discussed with her ladies-in-waiting, nor did the ladies themselves, for that matter, have any political power. Beneath this superficial justification of her action lay a deeper and very real fear—that changes to the ladies of her entourage would lead to the loss of such allies as Baroness Lehzen, Lady Portman, and Lady Tavistock—all of whom had taken her side during the unfortunate Flora Hastings affair (see "Hastings, Lady Flora") and might be dismissed from her service by the Tories. In a state of some anxiety and indignation, the queen fired off several letters to Melbourne throughout 7 May appealing for his support.

An indignant Peel, who found himself in the most invidious position, having failed to make the queen give an inch, returned to Buckingham Palace at 5 P.M. that day and announced he was therefore unable to form a government and withdrew. In what would be condemned as a highly unconstitutional act, the queen restored Melbourne to office and for a few years more was able to resist the inevitable upheaval of an old and familiar routine with which she felt safe.

On 10 May, Queen Victoria reiterated in writing to Sir Robert Peel that to dismiss her ladies would have been "repugnant to her feelings" (Benson and Escher 1911, 1:167). After the paeans of praise her queenly dignity and composure had received in the first days of her accession, such an undignified and childish obstinacy now invited the first serious criticism of the queen. Much of the crisis, however, had in fact turned upon a misunderstanding, to which Victoria in her anxiety to keep Melbourne had remained blinkered. Rushing to the conclusion that Peel was insisting that she rid herself of *all* her ladies, she had failed to register the fact that he was in reality alluding mainly to those wives of Tory ministers closest to her—in effect only six out of the total of twenty-five women in her entourage—ladies such as her mistress of the robes, the duchess of Sutherland, who was sister to the Irish secretary, or Lady Normanby, who was wife of the secretary at war.

In 1841, when Melbourne's government finally fell, and Queen Victoria, now married, had to accept the incoming Tory government for which he had been preparing her, she more readily accepted the wise advice of the democratically minded Prince Albert. She waived her right to appoint the major offices of state and agreed to advise the prime minister of the names of her ladies of the bedchamber before she appointed them. As a concession, she subsequently dismissed three of her Whig ladies in waiting and replaced them with Tories; in later years only the position of mistress of the robes, the highest in the state that could be held by a woman, would be affected by changes of government.

It has since been suggested that the whole debacle of the Bedchamber Crisis was a somewhat ambiguous one and that there had in fact been no precedent upon which Peel could have insisted that the queen dismiss her ladies. The situation had not applied to previous British sovereigns, as since the days of Queen Anne (who died in 1714), they were all male. The ladies-in-waiting who had been appointed had thus been those of the queen *consort* and not a queen regnant. The principle of political impartiality was, however, a major point upon which Prince Albert attempted to drill the queen, with varying degrees of success. She would always find it difficult to accede to the government of her day when it went against her own judgment of political affairs or her own personal prejudices. But in old age she admitted to her private secretary, Sir Arthur Bigge, that she had indeed acted impetuously at the time of the Bedchamber Crisis, putting it down to her immaturity: "I was very young then, and perhaps I should act differently if it was all to be done again" (Hibbert 1984, 50).

Related entries:
Albert of Saxe-Coburg-Gotha, Prince Consort; Hastings, Lady Flora; Melbourne, William Lamb, Second Viscount; Peel, Sir Robert; The Royal Household; Sutherland, Duchess of; Victoria, Queen: As a Monarch

References and further reading:

Benson, A. C., and Viscount Esher, eds. 1911. *The Letters of Queen Victoria, 1837–1861.* 1st ser., 3 vols. London: John Murray.
Charlot, Monica. 1991. *Victoria: The Young Queen.* Cambridge: Polity.
Creston, Dormer. 1952. *The Youthful Victoria.* London: Macmillan.
Esher, Viscount, ed. 1912. *The Girlhood of Queen Victoria: A Selection from Her Majesty's Diaries between the Years of 1832 and 1840.* 2 vols. London: John Murray.
Hibbert, Christopher. 1984. *Queen Victoria in Her Letters and Journals.* London: Viking.
———. 2000. *Queen Victoria: A Personal History.* London: HarperCollins.
Longford, Elizabeth. [1964] 1998. *Victoria R.I.* London: Weidenfeld and Nicolson.
St. Aubyn, Giles. 1992. *Queen Victoria: A Portrait.* London: Sinclair Stevenson.
Woodham-Smith, Cecil. 1972. *Queen Victoria: Her Life and Times.* Vol 1: *1819–1861.* London: Hamish Hamilton.

Bigge, Lieutenant Colonel Sir Arthur (1849–1931)

(Later Baron Stamfordham)

of the very highest character, clever, amiable and agreeable, as well as good looking (letter, 24 October 1879)

As the queen's private secretary and a senior member of the royal household, Arthur Bigge came from a relatively humble background, in comparison with the aristocratic pedigree of most of those at court. The writer E. P. Tisdall has suggested that, as "an officer with no expectations," he "owed his appointment and subsequent distinguished career entirely to the fact of having been 'the best friend in the army of the dead Prince Imperial'" (Tisdall 1961, 136). But if he lacked depth of character, Bigge proved to be the perfect private secretary: loyal and upright, a man of exemplary behavior and total discretion.

Bigge was born at Linden Hall in Northumbria, one of five sons of a country parson. He was educated at Rossall School and entered the Royal Military Academy at Woolwich, where he was a contemporary of the queen's third son, Prince Arthur, and also became friends with the Prince Imperial, only son of the exiled Napoleon III and Empress Eugénie of France. In 1869 Bigge was commissioned in the Royal Artillery and had risen to the rank of lieutenant colonel by 1892, finally relinquishing his army post in 1898.

In 1878–1879 he saw military action in Africa during the Kaffir and Zulu Wars, during the latter serving as aide-de-camp to Sir Evelyn Wood. Bigge was mentioned in dispatches for his role in the battle of Kambula. When his friend, the Prince Imperial, who had persuaded his mother to allow him to join the campaign, was killed in Zululand in 1879, Bigge escorted the body back to England for burial. He spent time consoling the bereaved Empress Eugénie at Abergeldie, near Balmoral, where she frequently spent the autumns to be near her friend, the queen. It was there that Eugénie commended Bigge's attentive and self-effacing manner to Queen Victoria, who in January 1880 appointed him as a groom-in-waiting. Later that year Bigge took on the onerous responsibility of escorting Eugénie on the long journey to Zululand—by no means an easy undertaking—when she insisted on visiting the spot where her son had died.

Eugénie's praise for Bigge upon their return, that summer, from Zululand again was passed on to the queen, who now appointed Bigge as assistant private secretary and assistant privy purse to help her own much overstretched secretary, Sir Henry Ponsonby, with his impossible workload. Bigge proved to be a loyal and devoted deputy to Sir Henry during the fifteen years he worked under him. The years till Ponsonby's retirement in 1895 were marked by the infusion of a new atmosphere of warmth and humor at court, created by the triumvirate of Ponsonby, Bigge, and the queen's personal physician, Sir James Reid. The amiable and amenable Bigge found himself dragooned into court theatricals by the effervescent Prince Henry of Battenberg (husband of the queen's youngest daughter, Beatrice).

The queen had grown to value Bigge greatly by the time he succeeded Ponsonby in 1895, remarking that "she is sure that she can rely on him in every way" (Emden 1934, 204); she confirmed her appreciation by knighting him on 24 May 1895. Bigge would remain in service to the royal family until his death in 1931.

Although possessed of the necessarily compliant personality needed to cope with the queen's dictatorial manner, Bigge was no lackey but an intelligent and brave man. He was, by nature, conservative and cautious, and this suited the queen's needs perfectly. His reputation for discretion, if not reticence, in his dealings with his monarch earned him the somewhat derogatory nickname at court of "Better NOT" (Lutyens 1961, xxi), but he could, nevertheless, speak his mind when he chose to.

When Queen Victoria developed an aversion to typewritten letters and memoranda (after the typewriter was introduced in the 1880s), Bigge labored long-sufferingly, in copying these out in longhand. The queen's failing eyesight meant that he was also obliged to write everything very large in thick black ink, and in the course of doing so he developed a fine bold script envied by many. He also learned to tolerate the queen's thoughtless slights, when she often bypassed him and used her ladies-in-waiting for passing on messages and instructions, and he put up with being sidetracked into other time-consuming and petty duties that could be irksome. But he did his duty and kept his annoyance to himself. In the final years of the queen's reign he played an important role in advising her on the arrangements for the Diamond Jubilee in 1899, liaising with the army in organizing the military parades, and was at her side throughout the difficult campaign of the Boer War (1899–1902).

After Queen Victoria's death, King Edward VII, already having his own private secretary (Sir Francis Knollys), appointed Bigge as "Extra Equerry to the new Monarch and Private Secretary to the Heir Apparent." In this capacity Bigge accompanied, George, Prince of Wales, on his tour of the British dominions in 1901 and tours of India in 1905 and 1911. In 1910 Bigge became a member of the Privy Council and was elevated to the Lords the following year, taking the title Baron Stamfordham. He served George V jointly with Knollys, continuing after Knolly's retirement in 1913 until his death in 1931. King George commended Bigge's devotion and felt his loss greatly, averring that Bigge had taught him "how to be a king" (St. Aubyn 1991, 521).

Related entries:
Battenberg, Henry Maurice, Prince of; Eugénie Marie de Montijo, Empress of France; Ponsonby, General Sir Henry; Reid, Sir James; The Royal Household; Theater; "The Widow at Windsor"

References and further reading:
Buckle, George Earl, ed. 1930–1932. *Letters of Queen Victoria 1886–1901.* 3d ser., 3 vols. London: John Murray.
Emden, Paul. 1934. *Behind the Throne.* London: Hodder and Stoughton.
Lutyens, Mary, ed. 1961. *Lady Lytton's Court Diary 1895–1899.* London: Rupert Hart Davis.
Ponsonby, Arthur. 1942. *Henry Ponsonby: His Life from His Letters.* London: Macmillan.
Reid, Michaela. 1996. *Ask Sir James: The Life of Sir James Reid, Personal Physician to Queen Victoria.* London: Eland.
St. Aubyn, Giles. 1991. *Queen Victoria, A Portrait.* London: Sinclair Stevenson.
Tisdall, E. E. P. 1961. *Queen Victoria's Private Life.* London: Jarrolds.
Weintraub, Stanley. 1996. *Victoria.* London: John Murray.

Bismarck, Prince Otto Edward Leopold von (1815–1898)

so overbearing, violent, grasping and unprincipled that no one *can stand it* (Ponsonby 1928, 139)

The wily Prince Otto von Bismarck has gone down in history as the Iron Chancellor, the political powerhouse behind the new, united Germany, created in 1871. For more than thirty years he per-

Prince Otto von Bismarck, architect and first chancellor of a new, united Germany in 1871, was long viewed as an arch enemy by Queen Victoria. (Perry-Castaneda Library)

plexed and enraged Queen Victoria in equal measure. She was firmly of the opinion that he was a "dreadful" man and an implacable enemy of Britain, but she did not actually meet him until he had been in power for twenty-six years. Although the queen's view was dictated by her loyalty to her daughter Vicky, crown princess of Prussia and later Germany, who undoubtedly suffered at Bismarck's hands, such a simplistic view was belittling of one of the great diplomatic geniuses and outstanding political figures of nineteenth-century European history. A shrewd and skillful statesman, Bismarck dominated German politics and proved the perfect foil, in their shared command of international relations, both to Prime Minister Benjamin Disraeli and also the queen.

Bismarck was born into a Junker (noble) family in Brandenburg and grew up in

made at the 1878 Congress of Berlin, called after Russia defeated Turkey in their war of 1877–1878. Here, the European powers sought to modify Russian gains in former Turkish territories in the Balkans under the Treaty of San Stefano. It would be a historic occasion, during which the British prime minister, Benjamin Disraeli, and Bismarck played a central role in the negotiations, Disraeli stealing the honors as the "lion of the Congress," whereas Bismarck would view his own role in securing a settlement that prevented Russia's plunging into another disastrous war in Europe as that of an "honest broker." The congress proved to be the highpoint of Bismarck's power as a political mediator. With Disraeli he would share the credit for engineering a twenty-six-year period of stability in Europe—almost equal to that which had marked the period between the end of the Napoleonic Wars and the Crimean War—that lasted until the outbreak of World War I in 1914.

Bismarck and Queen Victoria finally came face-to-face in 1888 when a crisis arose over the possible marriage of one of Fritz and Vicky's daughters, Princess Victoria (known as Moretta to distinguish her in the family from her mother and grandmother) to Alexander (Sandro), a prince of Battenberg. Sandro had in 1879 accepted the throne of Bulgaria. When he proved to be a conscientious and independent monarch, unwilling to take a back seat and allow the traditional Russian dominion over his country, Tsar Alexander III had engineered his abdication in 1886. Meanwhile Sandro had fallen in love with Moretta. But Bismarck had opposed the match, adamant that a member of the house of Battenberg (with strong family allegiances to Queen Victoria) should not marry into the German royal family. Queen Victoria was enraged by this intervention and concluded that "Bismarck's tyranny is unbearable" (Ponsonby 1928, 300).

With Moretta's brother, William (the future Kaiser William II), also firmly opposed to the match, Queen Victoria went to Berlin in April 1888 for a meeting with Bismarck. The occasion reduced Bismarck, for the first time in his life, to a state of visible nervousness. He sweated profusely during the interview, the queen's equerry, Sir Arthur Bigge, being of the opinion that "this great man evidently realised he was about to be received by an equally great, or even greater, woman" (Duff 1970, 279). Bismarck emerged from the meeting wiping the sweat from his brow, impressed with the queen's good sense and practical approach to the matter. "That was a woman!" he said. "One could do business with her!" (Longford 1998, 506). Their interview had turned out to be surprisingly cordial and "interesting" in the queen's opinion, and they had concurred that the marriage was indeed a bad idea. Victoria's attitude toward Bismarck dramatically softened; she professed herself to be "agreeably surprised to find him so amiable and gentle" (Duff 1970, 279). The marriage did not go ahead.

The queen's good opinion of Bismarck was, however, shortlived. Soon afterward, her son-in-law Fritz died of cancer after enjoying only ninety-nine days as the new emperor. On his deathbed Fritz had made Bismarck take Vicky's hand, in a reassuring gesture of his future support for her. But within days of Fritz's death the queen was berating Bismarck once more: "How untrue and heartless he is," she wrote, "after all he seemed to promise me" (Hibbert 1984, 312). For, with the accession of Kaiser William II, Bismarck turned his back on the widowed empress, refusing to find time to see her.

However, during the late 1880s Bismarck himself fell under attack from the new kaiser, and in 1890 he resigned as chancellor. Vicky had nothing good to say about Bismarck on his departure. The system he had created, she declared, "was intensely corrupt and bad," but in one respect at least she allowed that "the genius and prestige of Prince Bismarck might still have been useful and valuable for Germany and for the cause of peace, especially with so inexperienced and imprudent a Sovereign [i.e., her son], and I fear that he will be missed in that respect" (Ponsonby 1928, 411–412). Relations between Vicky and Bismarck therefore thawed a little after he retired from office; she even began to find some sympathy for him, by 1893 referring to him, as did many in Germany, as "the Great Man." For his part, Bismarck admitted that he had cost the empress "many tears" but that "that feeling has now somewhat subsided" (426). In reappraising Vicky, he concluded that she was a very clever woman who in her own way could be perfectly agreeable. The fault had lain in her compulsion to meddle in German politics.

Bismarck now retired to his estates as the duke of Lauenburg, where he devoted his remaining years to writing his vast *Reflections and Reminiscences.* He preempted the new kaiser's desire to accord him a grand state funeral and left strict instructions for a simple service to be conducted on his death, which came on 30 July 1898. Bismarck was buried in the mausoleum on his estate, with the words "A loyal German servant of Kaiser Wilhelm I" (Pakula 1996, 583) making clear where his real loyalties had lain.

The queen's perception of Bismarck as having had a hand in turning the crown prince, now Kaiser William II, against his beloved parents, Vicky and Fritz, never shifted. But like Vicky, she expended far too much energy in fearing the worst of Bismarck, when the real threat to Germany's stability lay, in fact, with her grandson. During his domination of European politics, Bismarck had, in fact, contributed significantly to keeping war in Europe at bay. As Hugh Massingham observed: "Old, testy, malign, and jealous as he then was, the man who had summoned up the new spirits also knew how to keep them in check. When he ceased to rule, Europe fell to pieces" (Massingham 1932, 477). Bismarck's death now made way for "three of the most inept rulers in history"(ibid.)—William II of Germany, Francis Joseph of Austria, and Nicholas II of Russia—who between them fueled the national, racial, and economic rivalries that would lead to war in 1914. After Bismarck's removal from power, a rapprochement between Russia and France, effected by the new kaiser, created precisely the political alliance Bismarck had spent his career trying to prevent. At their last meeting in 1895 he had warned William II that "the crash will come twenty years after my departure if things go on like this" (Taylor 1995, 264). In 1914 his fear that war might spring from "some damned silly thing in the Balkans" (264) was proved right.

Related entries:

Disraeli, Benjamin; Frederick William, Crown Prince of Prussia; Victoria, Princess Royal; William II, Emperor of Germany.

References and further reading:

Bismarck, Otto von. 1966. *The Memoirs: Being the Reflections and Reminiscences of Otto, Prince von Bismarck.* Edited by A. J. Butler. New York: Howard Fertig.

Crankshaw, Edward. 1981. *Bismarck.* London: Viking.

Duff, David. 1970. *Victoria Travels: Journeys of Queen Victoria between 1830 and 1900, with Extracts from Her Journal.* London: Frederick Muller.

Gall, Lothar. 1986. *Bismarck: The White Revolutionary.* 2 vols. London: Allen and Unwin.

Hardy, Alan. 1976. *Queen Victoria Was Amused.* London: John Murray.

Hibbert, Christopher. 1984. *Queen Victoria in Her Letters and Journals.* London: Viking.

Jerrold, Clare. 1916. *The Widowhood of Queen Victoria.* London: Eveleigh Nash.

Kent, George O. 1978. *Bismarck and His Times.* Carbondale: Southern Illinois University Press.

Longford, Elizabeth. [1964] 1998. *Victoria R.I.* London: Weidenfeld and Nicolson.

Massingham, H. J., and H. Massingham. 1932. *Great Victorians.* London: Ivor Nicholson and Watson.

Morrow, Ian F. D. 1970. *Bismarck.* New York: Collier Books.

Pakula, Hannay. 1996. *An Uncommon Woman: The Empress Frederick.* London: Weidenfeld and Nicolson.

Palmer, Alan. 1976. *Bismarck*. London: Weidenfeld and Nicolson.
Pflanze, Otto. 1990. *Bismarck and the Development of Modern Germany*. 2 vols. Princeton, NJ: Princeton University Press.
Ponsonby, Sir Frederick. 1928. *Letters of the Empress Frederick*. London: Macmillan.
Taylor, A. J. P. 1995. *Bismarck: The Man and the Statesman*. Harmondsworth, UK: Penguin.

Boer War, 1899–1901

(also called the South African War and the Anglo-Boer War)

We are not interested in the possibilities of defeat; they do not exist (Cecil 1921–1932, 3:191)

Britain's troubled history in southern Africa and its attempts to suppress the nationalist aspirations of the Dutch Boers (later known as Afrikaners) date back to its annexation of the Cape Colony in 1815, a territory originally colonized by Dutch, Flemish, German, and Huguenot settlers. Two breakaway republics, the Transvaal and the Orange Free State, had been established by Boer settlers after they had made the Great Trek north in 1835. Britain acknowledged their autonomy in 1852 and 1854 respectively, but the discovery of diamonds in the Orange Free State in 1867 radically changed Britain's perspective, with many British nationals flocking to the two regions in pursuit of a fortune.

In 1877, Prime Minister Benjamin Disraeli had annexed the Transvaal, fomenting a growing resentment to British domination that resulted in a brief Boer rebellion in 1880–1881 (sometimes referred to as the first Boer War), in the Transvaal, during which the Boers had annihilated a British expeditionary force at Majuba Hill. Appalled by this dreadful debacle, the queen had been adamant that any peace terms should retrieve British honor and should not be dictated by the Boers. "Even the semblance of any concessions after our recent defeats would have a deplorable effect," she wrote to Lord Kimberley on 9 March 1881 (Buckle 1926–1928, 3: 200–201) Nevertheless, under the Pretoria Convention of August 1881, William Gladstone, the Liberal prime minister, had recognized the independence of the Transvaal and granted it a degree of self-government, although it still remained under British suzerainty. The long-term effect of the conflict and its outcome had, however, convinced the Boers that, despite the odds against them, they could defeat the British in battle.

A second, protracted, and bloody conflict in southern Africa was sparked by the discovery of gold in the Transvaal in 1886 and the influx of thousands of hated Uitlanders (foreigners—in this case mainly British, American, and German nationals) eager to exploit what the Boer settlers viewed as their own. Their president, Paul Kruger, saw to it that these Uitlanders were heavily penalized, in doing so failing to endorse the political rights promised under the Pretoria Convention. He set down a fourteen-year residency stipulation for all Uitlanders before they could apply for citizenship and a vote, meanwhile hitting them with heavy taxes.

At the end of December 1895, in an attempt to overthrow Kruger's regime, Dr. Leander Starr Jameson, the administrator of territory controlled by the British South Africa Company (in what was later Rhodesia and is now modern-day Zimbabwe), led a party of approximately 500 Rhodesian police and volunteers in a covert operation to link up with discontented Uitlanders in Johannesburg and establish a pro-British regime. His so-called raid ended on 2 January in a fiasco, with Jameson's freebooters (as they were viewed) being routed at Krugersdorp and many, including Jameson, captured. This victory provoked a resurgence of Boer nationalism in southern Africa and a formal alliance of the Orange Free State and the

Transvaal, in a concerted attempt to resist any further British incursions.

The year 1897—notable for the celebrations for the queen's Diamond Jubilee—marked the high point of a renewed wave of imperialism in Britain and the popular conviction that the empire must be preserved at all costs. But in October 1899 the Orange Free State and the Transvaal declared war and began attacking British forces in Natal and Cape Colony. An atmosphere of complacency prevailed at first; the British authorities, convinced that this would be a military walkover, were soon rudely awakened when the towns of Ladysmith, Kimberley, and Mafikeng soon were under siege by the Boers.

Queen Victoria had initially been enthusiastic about the war, much as she had been at the start of the Crimean War. She was as intent in 1899 on teaching the Boers a sharp lesson as she had been in doing the same with Russia in 1854. An injection of the British bulldog spirit was always guaranteed to renew her vigor, and despite her advanced age, she once again gave over much time to supporting the war effort. She followed the events of the war closely, firing off endless letters and telegrams to her ministers and worrying about high mortality rates among the horses having to endure the long voyage to Africa. When the wounded began arriving home, she visited them in military hospitals—no matter how severe their injuries. At the end of 1899 she ordered that every British soldier serving in the war should be sent a tin box containing chocolate, bearing her portrait, and commemorating their participation with the words "South Africa 1900." Many of the soldiers resisted the temptation to eat this precious gift and kept it as a souvenir.

The British garrison at Ladysmith, in the Transvaal, during the Boer War. The conflict, which would continue until 1902, caused the queen great grief and anxiety in her final years. (The **Illustrated London News** *Picture Library)*

Hopes of a speedy resolution to the conflict were soon dashed, during the "Black Week" of 10–15 December 1899, when British forces were defeated in battle at Stormberg on the tenth, Magersfontein on the eleventh, and Colenso on the fifteenth—in the latter suffering 1,000 casualties. There was a public outcry in Britain and demands for reinforcements to be sent immediately—a move for which the queen had long been arguing. A huge expeditionary force was assembled, which would boost British and colonial troops in southern Africa to 250,000; it embarked for southern Africa under Lord Roberts of Kandahar (a hero of the Afghan War) as commander in chief and General Kitchener as his chief of staff.

The queen was alarmed by the "terrible failures" of Black Week and wept at the casualty lists. But she refused to accept the possibility of a British defeat. She canceled her annual Christmas holiday at Osborne and remained at Windsor to keep track of events. She was distressed by a lack of support for the war within Parliament, telling her prime minister, Lord Salisbury, that she was "shocked at the shameful want of patriotism of the Opposition" (Roberts 1999, 744)—an allusion to the Irish nationalists, who openly supported the Boers, and to radical liberals under Lloyd George, who criticized the pursuit of the campaign. If Victoria had had her way, British troops in southern Africa would have been bolstered with loyal nonwhite colonial troops—such as her much loved Sikhs and Gurkhas—but Salisbury rejected this idea as a political hot potato, arguing that white British troops would not fight alongside them.

The most famous engagement of the war took place at a hill named Spion Kop on 23–24 January 1900, when British troops led by Lt. Gen. Sir Charles Warren were gunned down after an attack on a fortified Boer position on a boulder-strewn ridge. After capturing the ridge, the British had attempted to dig themselves in until reinforcements arrived, but the stony ground had proved impenetrable, and the following morning, after the mist cleared, they had found themselves sitting targets for Boer marksmen on the surrounding hillsides. Two hundred men died, and 300 were wounded in a hail of shells and Maxim gun fire. A day of national intercession was called in Britain, as the country prayed for its troops in southern Africa. A month after Spion Kop, the tide began to turn, with the relief of the four-month siege of the important diamond-mining center of Kimberley in Cape Province, on 15 February, and that at Ladysmith, in the province of Natal, after a four-month siege on 28 February. The Boers' initial offer, in March, to sue for peace was rejected by the British government, as also was the kaiser's offer of mediation, Queen Victoria telling her grandson in no uncertain terms that Britain would "resist all interference" (Roberts 1999, 785). British troops now went on to capture the major Boer strongholds of Bloemfontein on 15 March and Johannesburg and Pretoria in June.

Scenes of great jubilation were witnessed in Britain after the relief of Mafikeng on 17 May. The town had held out against a large besieging Boer force for 217 days, thanks to the combined efforts of 700 troops, 300 volunteers, and another 1,700 civilians and natives under the leadership of Col. Robert Baden-Powell. The streets of Britain resounded with celebrations on Mafeking Night—18 May—with flag-waving crowds singing patriotic songs. In a tidal wave of jingoism and imperial braggadocio, special editions of the papers hailed Baden-Powell as a national hero; he would later found the Boy Scouts movement. Queen Victoria wrote to Salisbury expressing her tremendous sense of relief: "It is indeed a most blessed termination of a long and wearying anxiety" (Farwell 1999, 352).

The war was technically over, and the British public expressed their support for Salisbury's leadership by returning him to power with a landslide victory in the "khaki" election of September 1900. The queen, however, warned of the danger of a premature withdrawal of troops from southern Africa, writing to Lord Salisbury in June that to do so would open the way for fresh troubles and the need to send out reinforcements. And indeed sporadic fighting continued in southern Africa until May 1902. The conflict now took on a different character, in the form of commando-style raids, made by bands of Boers on British army bases and lines of communication. These forced the British authorities to keep a considerable force engaged in the region, which proved ineffectual in combating such guerrilla warfare with conventional methods. Although now vastly outnumbered, these small bands of Boer fighters inflicted heavy losses. Most of them were tough, weather-hardened farmers and crack rifle shots, who knew how to reconnoiter the rugged terrain of the veldt. They were used to the climate and not hampered by heavy equipment or the problems of maintaining communications, as were the British infantry. General Kitchener resorted to draconian retaliatory methods, employing a scorched earth policy, followed by a roundup of Boer women and children and their internment in a network of concentration camps, where conditions were terrible, mainly owing to problems in maintaining the supply routes. Many of the women and children were already seriously weakened and malnourished by the long months of conflict. An unofficial visit to the camps early in 1901 by the English social reformer Emily Hobhouse alerted public opinion in Britain, prompting the sending of an official British commission under Millicent Garrett Fawcett, which led to improvements in conditions. Nevertheless, by the end of the war, between 20,000 and 25,000 had died from hunger and the epidemics of disease that had raged through the camps.

Peace finally came to southern Africa with the Peace of Vereeniging on 31 May 1902, under which the British annexed the Transvaal and the Orange Free State, English was adopted as the official language, and £3 million was made over to the Boers to rebuild their destroyed farms. A promise of future self-government was fulfilled in 1907. At the end of the two-year and eight-month long campaign, the war had cost a staggering £250 million. It had involved approximately 400,000 fighting men, of which 7,774 British and colonial troops had been killed in action and 16,168 had died of their wounds and of disease, as against 7,000 Boer dead from a total Boer fighting force of 88,000.

At Osborne on 2 January 1901, the queen had welcomed Lord Roberts back from the war, investing him with the Order of the Garter and making him an earl. Twenty days later she was dead. During the war, her prime minister, Lord Salisbury, had done his best to prevent her from seeing the worst of the rabid anti-British invective in the Continental press (including many cruel caricatures of the queen herself). It had been the first mass media war, reported on by the likes of Winston Churchill, Edgar Wallace, Arthur Conan Doyle, and Rudyard Kipling, and also the first conflict to be recorded on film. The catalog of defeats and reverses and the heavy loss of life during the war had clearly depressed the queen; it had exacerbated her insomnia and had undoubtedly taken a toll on her nerves. On the day that Victoria died, the novelist Henry James wrote of how "used up, utterly sickened and humiliated" she had seemed by the war, "which she hated and deplored from the first" (Edel 1984, 4:180). James felt that it had "finished her." Salisbury was of the same mind: "The war killed her, but she never flinched" (Roberts 1999, 795). For Britain, the Boer War had marked the beginning of the end of the great imperial dream; the fact that Queen Victoria died as the conflict was finally approaching its end remains highly symbolic.

Related entries:
Salisbury, Robert Arthur Talbot Gascoigne-Cecil, Third Marquis of; William II, Emperor of Germany

References and further reading:

Buckle, G. E., ed. 1926–1928. *The Letters of Queen Victoria: A Selection from Her Majesty's Correspondence and Journal between the Years 1862 and 1885.* 2d ser., 3 vols. London: John Murray.

Buckle, George Earl, ed. 1930–1932. *Letters of Queen Victoria: A Selection from Her Majesty's Correspondence and Journal between the Years 1886 and 1901.* 3d ser., 3 vols. London: John Murray.

Cecil, Lady Gwendolen. 1921–1932. *Life of Robert, Marquis of Salisbury.* 4 vols. London: Hodder and Stoughton.

Churchill, Winston. 1900. *London to Ladysmith via Pretoria.* London: T. W. Griggs and Co.

———. 1990. *The Boer War.* London: Mandarin.

Edel, Leon, ed. 1984. *The Letters of Henry James.* Vol. 4: *1895–1916.* London: Macmillan.

Farwell, Byron. 1999. *Queen Victoria's Little Wars.* Ware, Hertfordshire: Wordsworth Editions.

Morris, James. 1992. *Pax Britannica: Farewell the Trumpets—An Imperial Retreat.* London: Folio Society.

Pakenhan, Elizabeth. 1960. *Jameson's Raid.* London: Weidenfeld and Nicolson.

Pakenham, Thomas. 1979. *The Boer War.* London: Weidenfeld and Nicolson.

———. 1991. *The Scramble for Africa.* London: Random House.

Rappaport, Helen. 2001. *An Encyclopedia of Women Social Reformers.* 2 vols. Santa Barbara, CA: ABC-CLIO.

Roberts, Andrew. 1999. *Salisbury: Victorian Titan.* London: Weidenfeld and Nicolson.

Warwick, P. 1980. *The South African War: The Anglo-Boer War.* London: Longman.

Weintraub, Stanley. 1996. *Victoria.* London: John Murray.

Brown, John (1826–1883)

so often I told him no one loved him more than I did or had a better friend than me (Cullen 1969, 225)

In the depths of her most gloomy, self-pitying despair after the death of Prince Albert, the queen often played upon her image as broken-hearted widow and mother of a brood of "orphans," abandoned to her grief without a friend in the world. What she wanted more than anything, in her abject misery, was to be taken care of, to feel the reassuring touch—both physical and metaphorical—of a "strong arm." She found such reassurance within the fiercely protective orbit of a down-to-earth, rugged Scotsman, her Highland servant John Brown.

Sydney Lee, writing one of the first biographies of the queen, published in 1902, emphasized the queen's utter contempt for sycophancy. At court she was surrounded by far too much of it—and of the kind of people who would scuttle and hide when they knew she was in a bad mood or who would be so timid as to do nothing but reiterate her own opinions when she expressed them—anything rather than invoke her wrath. John Brown would occupy a unique position in being the only person never to stand on ceremony in the queen's presence, able frequently to contradict her and make her do what *he* wanted. The queen's placid acceptance of such behavior on Brown's part frequently invoked incredulity among observers. It seemed to be a complete contradiction of everything that the monarch stood for. Yet the queen's reaction to Brown's no-nonsense manner was, in many ways, a reflection of one of the things she claimed to hold most dear: "No one can tell of what value it is to me to hear the truth" (Lee 1902, 572).

John Brown was born at Crathienaird, Aberdeenshire, the second of nine sons and eleven children of a tenant farmer on the Balmoral estate. As a young boy he worked as a farm hand and then as a stable boy at a local inn. In 1842 he became an ostler on Sir Robert Gordon's estate at Balmoral, before being promoted to the role of gillie there in the autumn of 1849. In 1851 Brown entered the queen's service permanently when he began leading her out on her pony during her annual holiday at Balmoral. In 1858 he was appointed personal gillie to Prince Albert, by which time he

Queen Victoria's devoted Highland servant, John Brown, accompanied her everywhere after he was brought to Windsor from Balmoral at the end of 1864. (Bettmann/CORBIS)

was also one of the queen's regular outdoor attendants. In October that year she wrote to her daughter Vicky, that "good J. Brown was so attentive to us and so careful—he is now my special servant; and there can't be a nicer, better or handier one" (Fulford 1964, 139). Brown quickly made himself indispensable, accompanying the queen and Prince Albert on several incognito "expeditions" in and around the Highlands that they made in 1860 and 1861.

By now the queen had already begun making allowances for Brown's hard-drinking nature, observing that at the end of a forty-mile expedition to Grantown in September 1860, he and his fellow gillie, John Grant, had both been unable to attend them at dinner, being "bashful" (Duff 1980, 92)—the queen's euphemism for dead drunk. In their last happy autumn holiday at Balmoral in October 1861, three months before the prince's death, the queen recorded her continuing delight in the services of Brown. He was, she wrote, "an *invaluable* Highland servant" who "*is my factotum here,* and takes the most wonderful care of me, combining the offices of groom, footman, page, and *maid*" (Benson and Esher 1911, 3:461–462). The ubiquitous, attentive Brown proved also to be "*so* handy about cloaks and shawls, etc." (and often reprimanded the queen if he thought she was not properly wrapped up against the cold). All in all, as she wrote enthusiastically to her Uncle Leopold in Belgium, "*such* a good, handy, *faithful,* attached servant I have nowhere," (ibid.) and it was "quite a sorrow" for her to leave him behind when she returned to Windsor.

After the prince's death in 1861, Sir Charles Phipps, the keeper of the Privy Purse, had expressed the concern of many at court about how on earth the queen would cope. He wrote to the prime minister, Lord Palmerston, asking: "What will happen—where can She look for that support and assistance upon which she had leaned in the greatest and the least questions of her life?" (Woodham-Smith 1972, 430). After three years it finally became apparent precisely where the queen would find the support that she so craved. She found it in neither a church minister, nor even, as she had done in the past (in the case of Lord Melbourne), in a prime minister. Instead she vested her trust and her total dependence on a rough diamond and her social inferior—the argumentative, brash, and ill-mannered John Brown.

It was in October 1864, on the suggestion of Phipps and the queen's physician, Dr. William Jenner, that John Brown was brought down to Osborne, from Balmoral, with a view to alleviating the queen's depression by encouraging her to take more exercise. He duly arrived, together with one of the queen's favorite ponies, and began evoking memories of her happier life at Balmoral with Albert. By the following February, the queen's mood had already lifted, and she was noting in her journal that she was now riding daily, thanks to the good offices of Brown. She ordered that he accompany her whenever she was out of doors and gave him responsibility for the organization of her horses and carriages when she wanted to drive out, as well as taking charge of her many dogs.

The decision to make Brown the most important member of her household would cost Queen Victoria's public image dear, with rumor and increasingly salacious gossip circulating over the years about the nature of their obviously close relationship, which some suspected of harboring a "sinister familiarity" (Longford 1998, 345). For the queen, however, Brown was little short of a savior, a rock on whom she could depend, and, in all his virile masculinity, the strong arm that would protect her—"a poor, broken-hearted bairn who wanted looking after and taking out of herself" (Tisdall 1961, 66).

It was not just Brown's devotion and care, but also his possession of an earthy, no-nonsense truthfulness that won the queen's enduring admiration and kept him in her service for the rest of his life. As he had once reassured her: "You"ll never have an honester servant" (Lamont-Brown 2000, 33). For the final eighteen years of his life he never left her side, seven days a week, and never took a holiday. Many in the royal household dismissed Brown out of hand as ill mannered, coarse, and dictatorial. The queen saw things differently, warming to what she described as Brown's "cheery, original way of saying things" (Hibbert 1964, 280). Her private secretary, Sir Henry Ponsonby, was one of the few sensible enough to see beyond the gruff exterior and appreciate Brown's essentially honest personality. In Ponsonby's view, Brown posed no threat; his real strength lay in his ability to understand the queen and make her do what others, Ponsonby included, could not. For her own part Victoria filled her journals with endless reiterations of Brown's simplicity, kindness, disinterest, devotion, faithfulness, attention, care, intelligence, discretion, and common sense. There was, it would seem, no limit to his fine, upstanding qualities.

Soon a regular routine, closely supervised by Brown, was established for the queen. Whenever she was at Balmoral and Osborne, Victoria would go out for carriage drives or pony rides morning and afternoon, whatever the weather, accompanied always by Brown and usually a lady-in-waiting or one of her youngest daughters. When she was in Scotland, it was Brown, rather than her secretary, who brought her each day's mail and remained alone in Victoria's study with her, ready to fold and seal her responses. He became extremely protective of the queen and defended her from anyone whom he felt was a time waster. When the queen worked on official business in her sitting room at Windsor, Brown would stand outside, barring the way in and "fending off even the highest in the land" (Lamont-Brown 2000, 69). Such peremptory behavior inevitably provoked complaints from the queen's children and inspired jealousy among other members of the royal household.

Although Victoria might be disapproving of others with a weakness for the vices of drinking and smoking—notably her own sons—with characteristic inconsistency she indulged Brown's alcoholism along with his smoking, allowing him even to light his pipe in her presence. Her relatives, meanwhile, were consigned to a specially designated room for the purpose. Tyler Whittle observed that as Brown grew older, the drinking began to have a far more deleterious effect on him: "When he was young and living an active, out-of-door life his drinking made little difference. Brought indoors, and given next to nothing to do, whisky began to affect him; in time he was on occasion found in a state of such insensibility that he was incapable of performing his duties" (1980, 134).

Sensing the resentment at court toward Brown, Victoria went to great pains to defend his position, in June 1865 even hiring a genealogist to trace his pedigree. An ancestral link with the Farquharsons of Invercauld was discovered, which entitled Brown to carry a coat of arms and brought promotion by the queen to the post of upper servant and the queen's permanent personal attendant in December 1865. Nevertheless, a year later the English satirical journals began poking fun at her extraordinary relationship with him. Cartoons began appearing in satirical magazines such as *Punch,* insinuating that Brown was now not only the power behind the throne but perhaps also had found his way into the royal bed. The queen's retreat from public view during her widowhood inflamed criticism about her neglect of royal duty, and she made no effort to defend herself from such gossip. As Stanley Weintraub suggested, if the scandalmongering had been a plot devised by members of the royal household aimed at engineering Brown's dismissal, then it failed miserably (1996, 381). The queen was adamant on the issue of Brown's innocence, as was he in his insistence, in 1866, that all he wished to do was "to take care of my dear good mistress till I die" (Lamont-Brown 2000, 33). Such was Brown's fearsome loyalty that "in an earlier, less civilized age," observed Stanley Weintraub, "he would have killed for her as readily as he carried her tea tray" (1996, 375). In return, the royal prerogative continued to be exercised in Brown's interests over the following years: in 1872 the queen made him an esquire and raised his salary to £400 a year. Three years later, she ordered his portrait to be painted by the court artist Heinrich von Angeli.

In March 1883 John Brown fell ill with a chill that turned to a fever and resulted in another attack of the erysipelas with which he had been plagued for many years. He died in his room at Windsor Castle on 27 March, his death no doubt accelerated by the ravages of a lifetime's chronic alcoholism. After a private funeral service was held in Brown's room, the coffin was sent to Scotland for burial in the churchyard at Crathie. Here the queen had Brown's tombstone inscribed with the words from St. Matthew (25: 21): "Well done, good and faithful servant; thou hast been faithful over a few things, I will make thee ruler over many things; enter thou into the joy of the Lord" (Duff 1980, 15).

John Brown was, undoubtedly, before the drink got to him, a handsome and virile man, but he never married. His personal pleasures were simple—he asked for nothing except generous supplies of tobacco and whiskey. The cottage on the Balmoral estate, given to him by Queen Victoria in 1876, which was filled with the many personal gifts he received from her over the years, was rarely used by him. Having no desire for personal gain, he merely sought preferment for his brothers—three of whom worked on the Balmoral estate. He stubbornly neglected his own well-being in his dedication to the queen—frequently suffering the ill effects from exposure to the cold and rain when out accompanying her, dressed only in his traditional kilt and jacket. Despite being highly opinionated, he had no ambitions to exert a political influence over the queen. They concurred in their reactionary views and shared a dislike of the sycophancy of courtiers and ministers alike, Brown once remarking that, when it came to the opinions of high society, "me and the Queen pays nae attention to them" (Lamont-Brown 2000, 7).

The queen's final assessment of Brown was colored very much, as it was with all her loyal retainers, by a subjective view of *his* value to *her.* In a letter to the poet laureate, Lord Tennyson, shortly after Brown's death, she poured out her woes: "He had *no* thought but for me, my welfare, my comfort, my safety, my happiness. . . . He was *part* of *my life* and quite invaluable" (Dyson and Tennyson 1969, 103–104). Once more Victoria found herself faced with the same devastating "shock—the blow, the blank, the constant missing at every turn of the one strong, powerful reliable arm and head" (Weintraub 1996, 391), as she had on the death of Albert in 1861. At the queen's request, Tennyson chose the words (by an anonymous author) to be engraved on a plaque at the base of a life-size, bronze statue of Brown in Highland costume, executed by the royal sculptor, Sir Joseph Edgar Boehm. It was erected in the grounds of Balmoral, bearing the words: "Friend more than servant, loyal, truthful, brave! / Self less than duty, even to the grave" (Dyson and Tennyson 1969, 105). A year later, Victoria overturned precedent and also had a plaque placed inside the Royal Mausoleum at Frogmore in memory of Brown—the only one inside this hallowed royal sepulchre commemorating a person not of the royal blood. In 1884 she dedicated the second published volume of her journals—*More Leaves from the Journal of a Life in the Highlands*—to Brown and her other loyal Highlanders. In it, she reiterated how Brown's loss to her had been "irreparable": "to say that he is daily, nay, hourly missed by me, whose lifelong gratitude he won by his constant care, attention and devotion, is but a feeble expression of the truth" (St. Aubyn 1991, 424).

It was not until the 1990s and the publication of the biography of the queen's doctor, Sir James Reid, that the true extent of Victoria's feeling for John Brown finally came to light. After her body had been laid out in its coffin and covered with her wedding veil, Reid had added a few, final, and secret items, about which Victoria had given him private instructions before her death. Although the coffin contained many photos and mementos relating to Prince Albert and her children, the most personal one would be that placed in Victoria's left hand—a photograph of John Brown—together with a small case containing a lock of his hair. Other small objects were added near the body: a pocket handkerchief of Brown's, his mother's wedding ring that the queen had worn since Brown's death, and a few final letters and photographs—but all of them carefully hidden by Reid, so that none of the royal family could see them before the lid of the queen's coffin was screwed down (see Lamont-Brown 2000, 162, which contains information additional to Reid's original account [1996, 216]).

The British government and the royal family were spared the embarrassment of the queen's biography of Brown, ghosted by a Scottish friend, Miss Murray MacGregor, when she was advised against its publication in a famous standoff with the dean of Winchester, Randall Davidson, in 1883. After her death in 1901, her son and heir, King Edward VII, set about systematically destroying Brown's legacy. He ordered the destruction of many commemorative busts and statues of Brown and consigned letters to the queen from him, as well as many photographs, to be burnt. He even had Brown's room in the Clarence Tower at Windsor (which the queen had kept precisely as it was on the day of his death) made over for use as a billiard room. Posterity has, sadly, also been denied the chance to assess the queen's true feelings about Brown. Much of the evidence was lost when Brown's own journal was presumed destroyed in 1884, after Randall Davidson had succeeded in persuading the queen against publishing it; her letters to him, bar one or two fragments, were also consigned to the flames. Perhaps the final assessment should rest with Randall Davidson, who concluded, as regards the speculation over the queen's relationship with Brown, that "one had only to know the queen to realise how innocent she was" (Bell 1952, 2, 31). Ingenuous, naive, trusting she undoubtedly was, but the soundest conclusion one can come to, based on the surviving evidence, is that the queen's unqualified love for Brown was never anything other than platonic and one that never breached the enormous class divide that separated Brown, the servant, from his sovereign.

Related entries:
Albert Edward, Prince of Wales; Balmoral Castle; Davidson, Randall Thomas, Dean of Windsor; *Leaves from the Journal of Our Life in the Highlands;* The Royal Household; Tennyson, Alfred, Lord

References and further reading:
Aronson, Theo. 1991. *Heart of a Queen: Queen Victoria's Romantic Attachments.* London: John Murray.

Bell, G. K. A. 1952. *Randall Davidson, Archbishop of Canterbury.* 2 vols. Oxford: Oxford University Press.

Benson, A. C., and Viscount Esher, eds. 1911. *The Letters of Queen Victoria: A Selection from Her Majesty's Correspondence between the Years 1837 and 1861.* 1st ser., 3 vols. London: John Murray.

Cullen, Tom. 1969. *The Empress Brown: The Story of a Royal Friendship.* London: Bodley Head.

Duff, David. 1980. *Queen Victoria's Highland Journals.* London: Webb and Bower (a condensed version of Victoria's accounts).

Dyson, Hope, and Charles Tennyson, eds. 1969. *Dear and Honoured Lady: The Correspondence between Queen Victoria and Alfred, Lord Tennyson.* London: Macmillan.

Fulford, Roger. 1964. *Dearest Child: Letters between Queen Victoria and the Princess Royal, 1858–1861.* London: Evans Brothers.

Hibbert, Christopher. 1964. *The Court at Windsor: A Domestic History.* London: Longman.
———. 2000. *Victoria: A Personal History.* London: HarperCollins (esp. chap. 43, footnote pp. 322–323).
Lamont-Brown, Raymond. 2000. *John Brown: Queen Victoria's Highland Servant.* Stroud, Gloucestershire: Sutton.
Lee, Sydney. 1902. *Queen Victoria, A Biography.* London: Smith, Elder and Co.
Longford, Elizabeth. [1964] 1998. *Victoria R.I.* London: Weidenfeld and Nicolson (esp. chap. 23, "Brown Eminence, the 1860s").
Reid, Michaela. 1996. *Ask Sir James: The Life of Sir James Reid, Personal Physician to Queen Victoria.* London: Eland.
St. Aubyn, Giles. 1991. *Queen Victoria, a Portrait.* London: Sinclair Stevenson.
Thompson, Dorothy. 1990. *Queen Victoria: Gender and Power.* London: Virago (chap. 4, "Victoria and John Brown").
Tisdall, E. E. P. 1961. *Queen Victoria's Private Life.* London: Jarrolds.
Weintraub, Stanley. 1996. *Victoria.* London: John Murray (esp. chap. 9, "A Brown Study [1863–1883]").
Whittle, Tyler. 1980. *Victoria and Albert at Home.* London: Routledge and Kegan Paul (chap. 22, "Almighty Indiscretions").
Woodham-Smith, Cecil. 1972. *Queen Victoria: Her Life and Times.* Vol. 1: *1819–1861.* London: Hamish Hamilton.

Bruce, Lady Augusta (1821–1876)

(From 1863, Lady Augusta Stanley)

I thought she never *would leave* me! (Buckle 1926–1928, 3:695)

One of the queen's most loyal and beloved ladies of the bedchamber, and before that a devoted lady-in-waiting to the duchess of Kent from 1846 to 1861, Lady Augusta Bruce would leave two volumes of letters, brimming with wit, sharpness of observation, and a healthy sense of humor. These entertaining letters provide a valuable account of life at court during the course of her twenty years in service to the queen and her mother, the duchess of Kent, and also relate the major upset Lady Augusta caused when, at the age of forty-one, and much to the queen's mortification, she announced her intention to marry.

Lady Augusta was the daughter of Thomas, earl of Elgin and Kincardine, a cultured man of the world who had brought the Elgin marbles back from the Parthenon in Athens. She was one of seven children of her father's second wife, Elizabeth Oswald, herself a talented classical scholar and mathematician. When Lord Elgin died in Paris, Elizabeth remained there, where she ran a famous literary salon—thus providing an unconventional early background for her children that ensured that Lady Augusta grew up equally intelligent and cultured, noted for her wit, and a gifted pianist. Many of her natural gifts would, however, be sublimated during the long hours she would spend in the company of the duchess of Kent, reading to her, driving or walking with her, and engaging in the idle tittle tattle of ladies with not enough to do all day. Tactful and dignified, she never complained about the dullness of her life with the duchess, even though she found herself increasingly surrounded by elderly women at the duchess's homes at Frogmore and Clarence House.

By all accounts, Lady Augusta seemed therefore a woman of exemplary character, the only detractor being Mary Ponsonby, wife of the queen's private secretary, who described her as being "a little affected and manierée" (Ponsonby 1927, 39). Something of this affectation comes across in the cloyingly eulogistic descriptions of the duchess of Kent—revered as "the Beloved one"—which fill Lady Augusta's letters during the duchess's final years. In 1861, after the duchess died, the queen expressed her gratitude: "I feel deeply your devotion to her and the tender, affectionate way in which you ministered to my dearest precious mama" (Buckle 1926–1928, 2:25). With one of her ladies soon due to retire, the queen saw Lady Augusta as a perfect replacement, a suggestion endorsed by Prince

Albert, although, as Tisdall suggested, "with the object of placing his wife under the control of a personality likely to be of benefit to her" (1961, 46). A special new post was created for Lady Augusta as resident woman of the bedchamber, which she took up on 1 April 1861. When Prince Albert succumbed to his fatal illness in December, Lady Augusta was in constant attendance on the queen, leaving a valuable eye-witness account of the prince's last days.

For the first two years of her widowhood, the heartbroken and desolate queen clung tenaciously to Lady Augusta, who found herself having to take on the role of almost permanent lady companion. Such exclusive access to the queen brought with it a certain amount of jealousy among other members of the royal retinue, with Lady Augusta looked upon by some as the queen's "favorite"—and also as a palace informer. The atmosphere at court was grim: "The whole house seems like Pompeii. Life suddenly seems extinguished," wrote Lady Augusta (Tisdall 1961, 55). Indeed, for many weeks after Prince Albert's death, she, Princess Alice, and the duchess of Sutherland were the only people admitted to the queen's grieving presence. Soon she was discovering the full implications of the word "resident" in her title. But with her characteristic good humor and sympathetic manner, Lady Augusta handled the situation with considerable skill, placating the queen's private secretary, General Grey, who was impatient at the queen's slowness in dealing with the mounting piles of unsigned official documents. But there was an inevitable price to be paid for such exclusive access to the queen: the queen's monopoly of her time was, Lady August admitted, "a considerable bondage" (Windsor and Bolitho 1929, 26). But her position was an exceptionally close one; she was there "all the year round, to share the inner life of the family" (Windsor and Bolitho 1927, 14), and the younger children—Prince Arthur and Princess Beatrice—became greatly attached to her, calling her by the pet name of Guska.

Yet even the devoted Lady Augusta yearned for a personal life beyond her duties to the queen. Her extremely restrained and covert courtship by the quiet and likable, forty-eight-year-old Arthur Penrhyn Stanley, professor of ecclesiastical studies at Christ Church Oxford, had failed to attract even the queen's sharp eye, probably because she was so bound up in her own grief. And so, when, shortly after the queen had elevated Stanley to the post of dean of Westminster, Lady Augusta plucked up the courage to inform the queen of her intention to marry, it came like a bombshell. The queen was almost apoplectic with outrage: "My dear Lady Augusta, at 41 . . . has most unecessarily, decided to *marry*(!!)" (Buckle 1926–1928, 3:695).

On principle, the queen felt it was unwise for someone in middle age so to disrupt their ordered life. But she had a high regard for Dean Stanley and eventually came round to the idea, although not without grumbling about the inconvenience to her. She particularly disliked any changes in her immediate retinue and was not prepared to relinquish Lady Augusta's services altogether—insisting that she remain in the queen's service, which Lady Augusta did until her death in 1876, as an extra woman of the bedchamber.

Lady Augusta married Dean Stanley at Westminster Cathedral on 22 December 1863 and thereafter absorbed herself in developing the Deanery as a social and cultural center as well as taking up philanthropic work in the diocese, especially among its slum dwellers. She supported the work of the Westminster Hospital and the building, from 1874 on, of the Westminster Training School for Nurses and an adjacent home for nurses. In 1874 she and her husband represented the queen at the marriage in St. Petersburg of her son, Alfred, duke of Edinburgh, to the Grand Duchess Marie (the only marriage of her children that the queen did not attend). Lady Augusta continually worried about the manner in which the queen so resolutely continued to shut herself away; she tried to exert gentle pressure on her to come out of seclusion. With the help of her husband, she persuaded the queen to make a rare visit to tea at the deanery, in 1869, when the couple introduced Queen Victoria to Thomas Carlyle and Robert Browning.

Always mindful of the needs of others, Lady Augusta eventually exhausted herself in her many good works. She lived by the tenet, "Work on and go to the very bottom of things and leave work that shall be imperishable" (Windsor and Bolitho 1929, 272). But in 1876 she collapsed and died, "burnt out by the fire of her own devotion to duty" (Windsor and Bolitho 1927, 16). The queen was distraught at her death: "Oh! What it means to me to lose that dear friend who was everything to me from '61 to the end of '63, being with me at those two dreadful times in '61!" she wrote. "She was such a help in so many ways, so sympathising, loving and kind, so attached to me and mine, so clever and agreeable, known to so many" (Windsor and Bolitho 1929, 274). Lady Augusta was given a grand funeral service at Westminster Abbey before burial, at the queen's specific command, in Henry VII's chapel. The queen also erected a memorial to her dear friend at Frogmore, near the duchess of Kent's mausoleum.

Related entries:
Kent, Marie Louise Victoire, Duchess of; The Royal Household

References and further reading:

Benson, A. C., and Viscount Esher, eds. 1911. *The Letters of Queen Victoria, 1837–1861.* 1st ser., 3 vols. London: John Murray.

Buckle, G. E., ed. 1926–1928. *The Letters of Queen Victoria: A Selection from Her Majesty's Correspondence and Journal between the Years 1862 and 1885.* 2d ser., 3 vols. London: John Murray.

Martin, Sir Theodore. 1875–1880. *The Life of His Royal Highness the Prince Consort.* 5 vols. London: Smith, Elder and Co.

Ponsonby, Magdalen, ed. 1927. *Mary Ponsonby: A Memoir, Some Letters and a Journal.* London: John Murray.

Tisdall, E. E. P. 1961. *Queen Victoria's Private Life.* London: Jarrolds.

Windsor, Dean of, and Hector Bolitho, eds. 1927. *Letters of Lady Augusta Stanley: A Young Lady at Court 1849–1863.* London: Gerald Howe.

———. 1929. *Later Letters of Lady Augusta Stanley 1864–1876.* London: Jonathan Cape.

Buckingham Palace

most parts of the palace are in a sad state
(Benson and Esher 1911, 2: 33)

Buckingham Palace, the current residence of the English sovereign, became the last in a succession of royal palaces established in London over the centuries. Shortly after her accession to the throne in June 1837, Queen Victoria adopted Buckingham Palace as her official royal residence. But she never found it congenial, and within ten years she and Prince Albert had virtually abandoned it.

The site of Buckingham Palace had originally been a walled garden of several acres known as the Mulberry Garden, its name coming from the large number of mulberry trees King James I had planted there in the early seventeenth century, as part of his attempt to promote silk manufacture in Britain (mulberry leaves being the staple diet of silk worms). Two houses later occupied the site: Goring House, and then Arlington House. The latter was demolished to make way for Buckingham House, a red-brick mansion built between 1703 and 1705, which King George III bought from its owner, John Sheffield, duke of Buckingham, in 1761 as a dower house for Queen Charlotte and their large family of fifteen children. St. James's Palace had, till then, been the royal residence in London; Buckingham House, during Queen Charlotte's tenure, became known as the Queen's House and was extensively renovated by Sir William Chambers during 1762.

In 1820, King George IV ordered the house to be reconstructed for use as a family home. But he later changed his mind, and in 1826 ordered extensive rebuilding at the palace, in order to transform it into a royal palace, and one that would take the place of his current residence, Carlton House. The neoclassical designs, by the architect John Nash, revamped the existing shell of Buckingham House, funded by a government budget of £150,000. The completed palace, now double in size, was, however, considered by many to be an architectural failure, for Nash had not succeeded in changing the look of what still seemed nothing more than a large country house. The succession of expensive and badly thought-out changes and additions made to Buckingham Palace escalated the costs: the north and south wings were demolished and a new centrepiece, inspired by the French Arc de Triomphe, was constructed. But George IV never actually lived in the palace himself, for he died before the alterations, now escalating to almost half a million pounds, were completed. Nor did his successor, Victoria's uncle, William IV, for he disliked the place too. Nash was dismissed for his extravagance, but William died before his own alterations, designed by Edward Blore, could be completed.

When Victoria ascended the throne in 1837, the house had been standing empty for some time; much of the recent workmanship had been poorly executed, many of the palace's facilities did not work properly, and in particular its plumbing was inadequate and unhygienic. The young queen was undaunted by the building's shortcomings and insisted that she would make the palace her home. She reveled in having such a large building entirely at her own disposal: "I rejoice to go into Buckingham Palace for many reasons. . . . My rooms are so high, pleasant and cheerful . . . the garden is large and very pretty" (Wright 1992, 51–52). She left much of the day-to-day running of things in the hands of Baroness Lehzen and a medley of palace officials, many of whom did not even reside there, consequently having little idea of the stifling, dark, windowless conditions in which her cooks and servants labored below stairs or the miserable cold and damp attic bedrooms in which they languished at nighttime.

One of the most pernicious problems at Buckingham Palace was the unsatisfactory sanitation. Although fashionable new water closets had been fitted, many of them did not work and were not properly ventilated. In addition, an old sewage conduit was later found to run directly under the kitchen floors. This, combined with piles of rotting garbage left near the exterior walls, created a stench about the palace of which many complained. But the one thing most often bewailed by Victoria's often reluctant guests was the miserable cold of the rooms in winter (a fact that never bothered Victoria, who herself became extremely parsimonious about heating and developed cold-tolerance levels that left her entourage permanently shivering). This problem was exacerbated by the fact that none of the palace's chimneys worked properly and belched smoke into any room in which fires were lit. Inevitably, there were huge problems in staffing and adequately cleaning the rambling building's 600 rooms and in keeping food and water for washing hot during its conveyance upstairs from the bowels of the kitchens. Guests frequently got lost in the palace's maze of corridors and were not helped by the inefficient and poorly trained servants who were supposed to smooth their way.

After Victoria's marriage in 1840, the prince consort took it upon himself to address some of Buckingham Palace's many problems, including the provision of nurseries for their growing family and an urgent review of the building's sanitation problems. With Parliament voting £150,000 for modifications to be made, a new east wing, designed by the architect Edward Blore, was added to the palace from 1847 to 1850 to provide extra accommodation for the family; this change transformed the palace into an enclosed quadrangle, its original colonnaded courtyard being filled in. The interiors were enlivened with articles of furniture, fittings, and fireplaces taken from the Brighton Pavilion that the queen had sold. In 1850 Nash's elaborate Marble Arch entrance was also removed and rebuilt at its present location, at the end of Oxford Street, near Hyde Park. The forecourt of Buckingham Palace was improved by the addition of a ceremonial balcony from which the royal family could thereafter acknowledge their public on high days and holidays, weddings and victory parades. Ludwig Gruner was brought in to redecorate the grand staircase in 1845. Blore had originally been hired to replace Nash in 1830, but his work on a new, fourth wing, overseen by the master builder Thomas Cubitt, was constantly interrupted by nonpayment of bills by the Treasury. Cubitt, nevertheless, managed to save money and bring in the final bill at just over £100,000, funded, in the main, by the sale of most of the contents of the Royal Pavilion at Brighton. In 1843 Prince Albert ordered the addition of a family chapel—the building has now been refurbished to serve as the Queen's Gallery, and its paintings are open to public view.

The palace, however, continued to be beleaguered by problems, many exacerbated by the inadequacy of the officials of the royal household whose duties, instead of being consolidated into one efficient unit, were divided between the lord steward, the lord chamberlain, and the master of the horse. This problem was soon addressed by Prince Albert who, with the aid of his mentor Baron Stockmar, initiated radical reforms in the household management and the hierarchy of responsibility, consolidated under a new master of the household.

There were also problems with the fabric of the palace itself: the soft French stone of the newly built east front designed by Blore did not weather well, a victim of the high levels of polluting soot in London at that time (the facade was eventually refaced in 1913). The layout of the living space also continued to be a problem, and the royal couple rapidly became disenchanted with the palace and the absence of the coziness and intimacy of a real family home. After the birth of Princess Alice in 1843, and despite regularly decamping to Windsor Castle (although this too had dire sanitation problems), Victoria and Albert craved greater privacy, cleaner air, and an escape from the enforced etiquette of court life at Buckingham Palace. Even as late as 1855, and despite all the improvements initiated by Prince Albert, the palace was still unpopular with many of the queen's household. Her dresser, Frieda Arnold, wrote home to her family in Germany that winter that she "had never been so cold in my whole life as I was for two days at the Palace" (Stoney and Weltzien 1994, 52). She complained at how the smoking atmosphere of London found its way into all the rooms and covered everything with soot and that, with the palace by now infrequently used by the royal family, "in spite of all the heating, the tomb-like atmosphere only disappeared after several days occupation" (ibid.).

After Prince Albert's death the queen avoided spending any time at all in London; during the forty years of life remaining to her, she slept at Buckingham Palace on only about twenty occasions. The palace was left totally unoccupied for the first five years of her widowhood. When protocol demanded that she be present in London for affairs of state, the queen protested that the polluted atmosphere caused her headaches; she preferred to stay at the more salubrious environs of Windsor Castle, where she received ministers on official business. Not surprisingly, the neglected and unlived-in palace was devoid of warmth and atmosphere; as Lord Clarendon recalled, after Albert's death it was "the most dreary looking of jails" (Whittle 1980, 130). The atmosphere of abandonment was, however, later retrieved by the introduction of royal garden parties by the queen in the mid-1860s and with the gradual resumption of official receptions, known as drawing-rooms. The queen eventually allowed dancing once again, taking part herself in state balls held in the ballroom designed by Prince Albert in 1856. But even after her son and heir, the Prince of Wales, married in 1863, she would not let him make use of the palace. Its function remained that of a point of departure for royal cavalcades on state occasions such as the State Opening of Parliament, her Golden and Diamond Jubilees in 1887 and 1897, and after the relief of Ladysmith and Mafikeng during the Boer War.

Related entries:
Balmoral Castle, Dancing; Kensington Palace; Osborne; The Royal Household

References and further reading:

Benson, A. C., and Viscout Esher, eds. 1911. *The Letters of Queen Victoria: A Selection from Her Majesty's Correspondence between the Years 1837 and 1861.* 1st ser., 3 vols. London: John Murray.

Harris, J., G. de Bellaigue, and O. Millar. 1968. *Buckingham Palace.* London: Nelson.

Healey, Edna. 1997. *The Queen's House: A Social History of Buckingham Palace.* London: Michael Joseph.

Plunkett, John. "Remembering Victoria." *The Victorian,* no. 1 (August 1999): 4–90.

Robinson, John Martin. 1995. *Buckingham Palace: Royal Palaces.* London: Michael Joseph.

Stoney, Benita, and Heinrich C. Weltzien, eds. 1994. *My Mistress the Queen: The Letters of Frieda Arnold, Dresser to Queen Victoria, 1854–1859.* London: Weidenfeld and Nicolson.

Whittle, Tyler. 1980. *Victoria and Albert at Home.* London: Routledge and Kegan Paul.

Woodham-Smith, Cecil. 1972. *Queen Victoria: Her Life and Times.* Vol. 1: *1819–1861.* London: Hamish Hamilton (see chap. 8).

Wright, Patricia. 1992. "Queen Victoria and Her Palace." *History Today* 2 (December).

———. 1996. *The Strange History of Buckingham Palace.* Stroud, Gloucestershire: Sutton.

C

Chartism

our little riots here (Longford 1998, 195)

When Queen Victoria came to the throne in 1837, the popularity of the British monarchy was at an all-time low. The euphoria of the post-Napoleonic years of military might and economic prosperity had been supplanted by the dislocations of rapid industrialization and with it the growth of an impoverished underclass that inhabited the factories, mines, and mills of the north of England. The discontented masses remained restive, alienated by continuing political disenfranchisement after the failure of the 1832 Reform Bill to extend suffrage further than the urban middle classes. The punitive taxation of wheat had also sent the price of their daily bread spiraling; the introduction of machinery in agriculture and the factories had led to reductions in wages and had caused widespread unemployment; and the draconian new Poor Laws of 1834 had drastically reduced outdoor relief, forcing upon the destitute the humiliation of the workhouse. The growing sense of despair and discontent was, as Benjamin Disraeli would famously declare in his 1845 novel, *Sybil,* a manifestation of the growing divide between Britain's "Two Nations"—the rich and the poor. The country seemed now to be lurching toward that social "convulsion" that the British establishment for so long had dreaded—a proletarian uprising.

Five years earlier, between August and November 1832, during a tour of the Midlands, the thirteen-year-old Princess Victoria had had a rare first-hand sight of the grim, everyday reality in which the urban classes of the coal-mining regions lived and worked. In her journal, she described how "the men, women, children, country and houses are all black" (Woodham-Smith 1972, 88). The countryside was, she observed "very desolate Every Where" and even the grass "quite blasted and black" (ibid.) The unremitting presence of soot and smoke appalled her: "The country continues black, engines flaming, coals, in abundance, everywhere smoking and burning coal heaps, intermingled with wretched huts and carts and little ragged children" (88).

It might be assumed that such an eloquent and compassionate response to the suffering of the underprivileged would signify the stirring of a social conscience in the future queen. When she came to the throne in 1837, young, inexperienced, and impressionable as she was, Victoria's attitude to popular discontent, underpinned by her own innate sense of her royal dignity and the unquestioning loyalty the masses owed to their sovereign, was reinforced by those closest to her. The reactionary ideas on authoritarian government advocated by Victoria's unofficial political adviser, Baron

The last and largest Chartist meeting, held on Kennington Common, London, in April 1848, was followed by a march to the House of Commons demanding electoral reform. (Hulton/Archive by Getty Images)

Stockmar, coupled with the rampant disinterest of her prime minister, Lord Melbourne, served only to blind her further to the aspirations of the working classes. It was Melbourne's laconic dismissal of popular protest that bolstered the queen's own increasingly inflexible attitude to the Chartist movement. She soon found herself concurring with him that the threat of popular protest, although unsettling, was grossly overexaggerated and that the masses were being led by the nose by a gaggle of radical hotheads and criminals.

The working-class movement for democratic reform in Britain had taken root with the establishment in 1836 by William Lovett and Henry Hetherington of the London Working Men's Association. In May 1838, Lovett, Hetherington, and other sympathizers drew up a charter to be put before Parliament in the form of a petition calling for universal male suffrage and the reform of electoral districts, as well as annual parliaments, payment of members of Parliament, secret ballots, and no property qualifications for members of Parliament. In July the House of Commons voted not to debate the Chartist petition. Calls among Chartists for a general strike did not materialize, although trouble sparked in various northern cities. In November 1839 troops fired on a protest march by Welsh miners and ironworkers in Newport, Monmouthshire, over the arrest of Chartist leader Henry Vincent. Brought to trial the following January, the leaders of the march were sentenced to transportation.

In July 1840 the National Charter Association, the first working-class political party of its kind, was formed to agitate for constitutional reform, with a membership claimed to be 40,000. Two years later continuing agitation culminated in a second Chartist petition, of 3,317,702 signatures and six miles long, which was carried by thirty bearers on a huge frame across London from Lincoln's Inn Fields to Parliament at Westminster, on 2 May. Again the petition was rejected by Parliament. Over the next six years the movement went into decline, with its leadership blighted by factionalism, in a conflict over strategy that pitted those for violent confrontation against those who advocated the continuation of nonviolent moral campaigning for political reform.

During 1848, the year that went down in history as the year of revolutions in Europe, Chartist ideals were revived under the charismatic leadership of Irish radical Feargus O'Connor, who mobilized support in London among unemployed, disaffected Irish refugees from the Potato Famine of 1846–1847 and other radical activists. The neuroses of both the queen and Prince Albert about popular revolt reaching England and royal heads rolling was heightened, the prince expressing concern about the nefarious signaling network maintained between Chartist strongholds by means of carrier pigeons. A huge open-air rally was now called by the Chartists for 10 April on Kennington Common, in London. It was the intention of the organizers that the gathered crowds should then march on Parliament with yet another vast petition (supposedly of 5 million signatures but later shown to contain just under 2 million, and many of these bogus). Filled with alarm, members of the aristocracy resident in London loaded their shotguns and prepared to defend their homes. The government, fearing mob violence against the palace, persuaded the queen, who had just given birth to Princess Alice, to decamp with the royal family to the safety of Osborne House on the Isle of Wight. Nine thousand troops were deployed in the streets of London by the duke of Wellington on the day of the projected march, for which around 40,000 had turned up rather than the anticipated 1 million. But after the announcement of the official banning of the march was made by the Metropolitan Police, the disconsolate crowds dispersed in pouring rain and without incident from Kennington. The Chartist movement thereafter lost its mass support although moderates in its leadership remained politically active, advocating education, temperance, and municipal reform until the late 1850s, while the radical element pinned their hopes on new, socialist directions, as outlined in the writings of Karl Marx and Friedrich Engels. It would not be until 1918 that five of the six demands of the original 1838 charter would become part of the British constitution.

Shortly after the debacle at Kennington, a gratified queen wrote to her uncle, King Leopold, to inform him that the rally had been "a complete failure" (Woodham-Smith 1972, 289), wrongly assuming that this was due to the inherent loyalty of the masses to the throne and taking comfort in her unshakable belief that the Chartist ringleaders were "wanton and worthless men" (St. Aubyn 1991, 223). She was, however, shaken enough to tentatively inquire of a minister some days later as to "what we should do in view of the state of affairs to show our interest in the working class" (224). She seemed quite content to accept the simplistic answer given her by the benevolent and reformist peer, Lord Ashley, that the working classes "only needed some comforts and some improvements to render their dwellings more healthy" (ibid.). Thus her fears were allayed, with Victoria confident in the belief that "no charter was wished for, only sympathy and kind feeling." Thus reassured, she remained impervious to manifestations of collective suffering and devoted most of her sympathies to the suffering of animals. In September 1848, on the prorogation of Parliament, Victoria was now confident that "the strength of our institutions has been tried, and has not been found wanting. . . . My people . . . feel too sensible the advantages of order and security to allow the promoters of pillage and confusions any chance of success in their wicked designs" (Martin 1875–1880, 2:106).

Related entries:
Animals; Class; Dickens, Charles; Disraeli, Benjamin

References and further reading:

Benson, A. C., and Viscount Esher, eds. 1911. *The Letters of Queen Victoria. 1837–1861.* 1st ser., 3 vols. London: John Murray.
Bryant, Arthur. 1961. *English Saga 1840–1940.* London: Fontana (chap. 2, "Dark Satanic Mills").
Charlot, Monica. 1991. *Victoria: The Young Queen.* Cambridge: Polity.
Epstein, James, and Dorothy Thompson, eds. 1982. *The Chartist Experience.* London: Macmillan.
Fulford, Roger, ed. 1963. *The Greville Memoirs.* London: B. T. Batsford.
Hibbert, Christopher. 2000. *Queen Victoria: A Personal History.* London: HarperCollins (chap. 25).
Longford, Elizabeth. [1964] 1998. *Victoria R.I.* London: Weidenfeld and Nicolson.
Martin, Sir Theodore. 1875–1880. *The Life of H.R.H. the Prince Consort.* 5 vols. London: Smith and Elder (vol. 2).
St. Aubyn, Giles. 1991. *Queen Victoria: A Portrait.* London: Sinclair Stevenson.
Thomson, Dorothy, and L. Temple Smith. 1984. *The Chartists: Popular Politics in the Industrial Revolution.* Aldershot, UK: Wildwood House.
Woodham-Smith, Cecil. 1972. *Queen Victoria: Her Life and Times.* Vol 1: *1819–1861.* London: Hamish Hamilton.

Christmas

a most dear happy time (attributed)

The celebration of Christmas has, since the 1840s, been central to the popular perception of the Victorian ideal at its most heart-warming, cozy, and convivial, a reassuring incarnation of the caring and sharing side of the human character and one that crosses the class divide. Most of our own childhood memories of Christmas will probably focus on precisely those traditions that the Victorians popularized: the sending of cards, the decorated Christmas tree, caroling, crackers, log fires, the exchange of gifts, the set-piece dinner on Christmas day, and, in Britain, the all-essential visit to the pantomime. Above all, the Victorians made Christmas a time for families, and none more so than the nation's royal family, who set the trend for large family gatherings and who popularized the all-essential centerpiece—the Christmas tree.

It was images of the royal family's own decorated Christmas trees in the *Illustrated London News* in 1848 that finally set in stone the modern-day celebration of what, of course, had for centuries been originally a pagan winter festival. Fir trees had been used by both the Romans and the Vikings in their own rituals at this time of year; they first became part of the Christian celebration when they were used in the Rhineland of Germany to represent the Paradise Tree in the story of Genesis in medieval plays about Adam and Eve. These plays were originally performed on 24 December, with the tree decorated with sweetmeats to represent the apples of the Garden of Eden. In this form, the tree became part of a wider Christian celebration across northern Europe for many centuries, being particularly widespread among the Lutheran community of western Germany. In Britain, the celebration of Christmas had been proscribed as idolatrous and papist in the seventeenth century by the Puritan regime of Oliver Cromwell.

Because Prince Albert did so much to encourage the use of traditional German festive trappings, most notably the tree itself, it has been widely assumed that he "invented" Christmas. But the German celebration of the festival had probably been brought to England with the accession to the throne of the Hanoverians in the late seventeenth century, although there is no clear record of its popularization among the royal family until King George III's wife, Charlotte of Mecklenburg-Strelitz, set up branches of yew tree decorated with candles and sweetmeats at Windsor in 1800. At this time the British celebration of Christmas, such as it was, had been in decline for many years, and although immigrant German merchants had begun importing Christmas trees to Manchester in the early 1820s for their own use, before 1835 there was very little mention of the festival in the British press or elsewhere.

The setting up of a Christmas tree, however, seems to have continued at court, under the influence of another German, Adelaide of Saxe-Coburg-Meiningen, the wife of Victoria's predecessor William IV. The young Princess Victoria recorded her own pleasure at the Christmas tree she had at her childhood home, Kensington Palace, again no doubt under the influence of her mother, the duchess of Kent, another scion of the house of Saxe-Coburg. But it was only after Queen Victoria's marriage to Prince Albert in February 1840 and the birth of their first two children, Victoria and Albert Edward, in quick succession, that, now possessed of their own family unit, Albert suggested that they adopt the German custom of setting up a tree. A suitable fir was chopped down in Windsor Great Park for the purpose and decorated with wax tapers, ribbons, and sugarplums. Prince Albert's popularization of Christmas was also prompted, it seems, by his deep sense of nostalgia for his German homeland and the Christmases he had enjoyed there with his brother, Ernest.

The royal children took such delight in the tree, as did the queen at their pleasure in it and in the warm sense of family togetherness that Christmas at Windsor engendered, that she would always value this time of year—a time when royal protocol was set aside and the family and courtiers alike joined in the celebrations. Eventually Victoria and Albert would decorate a tree for each other in their private sitting rooms, as well as in those of the queen's mother, the duchess of Kent, and other members of the royal household. All would be imported specially from Coburg, on the edge of the Thuringian forest. Before long, too, the trees would be laden with all kinds of trinkets, toys, gilded fruit and nuts, and gifts, as well as the first manufactured tree decorations to replace homemade ones. These too were imported from Germany, notably hand-blown glass baubles and icicles, as was the Nuremberg angel, its wings outstretched, without which no Christmas tree was complete.

Throughout the 1840s Prince Albert promoted the widespread use of trees and decorations in Britain, himself presenting trees to schools and army barracks across the country at Christmas time. Although most of the other modern-day trappings of Christmas, such as crackers from France, the popularization of carols (again, French in origin), and the food eaten, were drawn from many different cultures, Victoria herself did introduce one English tradition—that of adding coins (in her case sovereigns)—to the Christmas pudding, which she apparently did as a gesture of thanks to her cook. The royal family also took particular pleasure in their own Christmas dinner. As well as opting for turkey (first introduced in the reign of Henry VIII but not popularized at Christmas until the 1800s by the prince regent), they also enjoyed home-produced beef, from cattle bred at the prince's model farm in Windsor Great Park.

The final imprimatur of royal approval of the new style of festivities came with a sixteen-page Christmas supplement to the 23 December issue of the *Illustrated London News* in 1848, which featured, among other things, an illustration of the royal family standing round their Christmas tree at Windsor. After this date the tree became the essential element of every English family Christmas, no matter how humble. The 1848 Christmas image also reached the United States (where German immigrants had first introduced trees at Christmas in Pennsylvania), where it would quickly be adopted, along with all the other paraphernalia of the English Victorian Christmas.

But if the royal family popularized the *image* of Christmas as a family event, it was the novelist Charles Dickens who captured the *essence* of the Victorian Christmas spirit. In his much-loved 1843 story, *A Christmas Carol,* he created the template for many other literary celebrations of the festive season. He did so not only by presenting the festival as a distillation of the very best of Victorian bonhomie but also, and more significantly, by injecting into it a sense of social responsibility, an opportunity for even the most curmudgeonly of misanthropes, such as the story's central character Ebeneezer Scrooge, to redeem himself—both through acts of charity within the community and also with God. The first, illustrated edition of the story sold 15,000 copies in the first year of its publication. From 1859 on, when Dickens first began giving platform readings of it, *A Christmas Carol* proved to be his own and his audiences' most enduring favorite. Dickens responded to its huge popularity by writing several other supernatural tales for the Christmas market, known as the Christmas Books, as well as by producing extra Christmas issues of his journals, *Household Words* and *All the Year Round,* containing shorter seasonal stories by him.

The idealization of Christmas as a season of good will to all men would naturally enough be translated into the self-comforting belief, held by many Victorians, that the ritual acts of charity performed by them at Christmas, such as in Scrooge's case the donation of a fat turkey to the impoverished Cratchits, would secure them their place in heaven. Manifestations of royal benevolence in Britain's workhouses and almshouses also became a tradition at Christmas. In December 1842, according to the *Times,* Queen Victoria ordered that "every poor adult in Windsor town" be given "4 lbs of beef, 2 lbs of bread, 1 lb of plum pudding, a peck of potatoes and two pints of ale" (*The Times,* 24 December 1842), a tradition repeated thereafter.

Improvements to the postal service that came with Rowland Hill's introduction of the Penny Post in 1840 gave impetus to Prince Albert's encouragement of the exchange of Christmas cards, another German practice. The first card was designed in 1843 by John Calcott Horsely, a member of the prestigious Royal Academy, at the request of Henry Cole (later one of the organizers with Prince Albert of the Great Exhibition), who had no time to write personal letters. The design bore a seasonal greeting accompanied by an illustration of a family seated around a Christmas dinner table. Surplus copies of the print run of 1,000 cards were sold. But with the first cards retailing at, for that time, the staggering price of one shilling, it is not surprising that the practice was confined to the upper and middle classes, although many children, Victoria and Albert's included, were encouraged to make their own. By the end of the 1860s cards were bearing the now familiar chintzy images of snow scenes, robins, and holly, with the more sober religious images being gradually phased out. By the 1880s the sending of cards had become universally popular in Britain, creating a lucrative industry that produced 11.5 million cards in 1880 alone.

As a young girl, Princess Victoria had taken great delight in another British tradition—the Christmas pantomime, which had originated with seasonal pageants, based on the Italian *commedia dell'arte,* introduced by Edward IV in the late fifteenth century. In particular, she had greatly enjoyed *Harlequin and Jack Frost* at Drury Lane in January 1839 and took the royal children regularly to the pantomimes staged at the

Royal Lyceum at Christmas time during the 1840s and 1850s.

A first-hand account, by Lord Torrington, of the royal family's conviviality at Christmas, encapsulates what it was about the royal celebration of the season popularized by Victoria and Albert that so endeared them to the nation and made Christmas such an indelible part of British culture. In what is, retrospectively, a poignant description of what would be their last Christmas together in 1860 (Albert died not long before the following Christmas), Torrington concluded: "It was royalty putting aside its state and becoming in words, acts and deeds one of ourselves—no forms and not a vestige of ceremony. . . . I have never seen more real happiness" (Hardy 1976, 91). After the deaths of the duchess of Kent and Prince Albert within months of each other in December 1861 and, in 1878, of one of the queen's daughters, Alice, on the same date as Albert (14 December), Christmas became a sad and mournful affair for the queen, full of too many painful memories of happier times. But in her final years, as grandmother and great grandmother of a huge brood of royal children, she once more began to enjoy family Christmases—this time at Osborne House on the Isle of Wight, where, as always, the tree itself held center stage.

Related entries:
Balmoral Castle; Dickens, Charles; Osborne; Theater; Windsor Castle

References and further reading:

Dickens, Charles. [1843] 1994. *A Christmas Carol.* Ware, UK: Wordsworth Editions.

Esher, Viscount, ed. 1912. *The Girlhood of Queen Victoria: A Selection from Her Majesty's Diaries between the Years of 1832 and 1840.* 2 vols. London: John Murray.

Foley, Daniel J. 1960. *The Christmas Tree.* Philadelphia: Chilton.

Golby, J. M., and A. W. Purdue. 1986. *The Making of the Modern Christmas.* London: B.T. Batsford.

Hardy, Alan, 1976. *Queen Victoria Was Amused.* London: John Murray.

Pauli, Hertah. 1944. *The Story of the Christmas Tree.* Boston: Houghton Mifflin.

Churchill, Lady Jane (1826–1900)

as usual, thoroughly amiable, cheerful, and ready to do everything (Duff 1980, 95)

A lady of the bedchamber from 1854 until her death in 1900, Lady Jane Churchill was a devoted friend and companion to the queen, particularly during the long years of the queen's widowhood. Yet for all her forty-six years of unstinting service, much of it in the face of her own declining health, Churchill remains a shadowy figure. She left no journal or memoirs of her years with the queen and features only in passing in sources on the queen's life and times. The poignancy of her story—of a life sublimated in the service of her monarch—is encapsulated in the fact, that having lived so closely with Victoria for so long, Churchill should, most fittingly, die barely a month before her mistress—on Christmas Day 1900.

Like several of the queen's closest and longest-serving ladies-in-waiting, we know little about Lady Jane's personal life, beyond the constant demands of the royal beck and call. She was the daughter of the second marquess of Conyngham and married to the second Baron Churchill, by whom she had a son. One of the many puzzling anomalies of the queen's personality surfaces in her relationship with Churchill. For nothwithstanding her undoubted appreciation of Churchill's companionship, and her concern for her bouts of ill health, Victoria could be ruthlessly selfish when it came to subordinating Churchill and the members of her loyal retinue to the role of unquestioning factotum. Churchill proved to be adept at self-effacement; she performed her duties with a combination of dignity, good humor, and vigilance. On a state visit to France in 1855, maid of honor Mary Bulteel, was highly complimentary: "Lady Churchill is quite brilliant by her [the queen's] side," she remarked, concluding that at all events she was "a lady in every way" (Ponsonby 1927, 19).

The queen, no doubt impressed with Churchill's discretion and dependability, in 1858 entrusted her with the task of accompanying the newly married Victoria, Princess Royal, to Berlin, in order to help her settle in to life in the vast Kronprinzenpalais, as wife of the heir to the Prussian throne. More important from Victoria's point of view, Churchill's function was to send regular reports back to the queen on the minutiae of Vicky's life in Prussia: "Don't trouble us with descriptions of great things," she advised Vicky, "leave that to Jane C." (Fulford 1964, 32). "Get Jane C. to tell me all about your rooms," she intones in another letter; soon after (35); and still with an insatiable appetite for detail, the queen again commands: "Let Jane Churchill tell me when you get up and dress and breakfast etc." (39). When Churchill finally returned home, the queen seemed less concerned with expressing her pleasure at her return than at regretting the fact that she would now "know nothing of what is going on which makes me sad" (55).

Having endured the horribly overheated palace in Berlin—to which she made frequent reference in her letters to a horrified queen, who was pathologically averse to warmth of any kind—Churchill returned to England a few months later to face an even worse ordeal—the cold. Regular, mandatory exposure to the full brunt of Scottish wind and rain, during the queen's regular visits to Balmoral, was the bane of the lives of every member of the royal household who had the misfortune to draw the short straw of spending the autumns there with her. The queen was not only opposed to overheated rooms but was also obsessive about enjoying copious amounts of fresh Scottish air. Churchill in particular would find herself the regular traveling companion on the queen's Great Expeditions in Scotland. She had taken part in the most memorable one, made by the queen and Prince Albert in 1860, when the royal couple had enjoyed the pleasures of an incognito two-day trip as "Lord and Lady Churchill" (with Jane Churchill calling herself "Miss Spencer"). The small royal party had traveled by carriage, horseback, and ferry sixty miles, across Loch Inch to Grantown, where they stayed overnight at a local inn. Having to cover twenty miles of the journey on horseback would tax the loyalty of even the most devoted royal servant, but this would be the first of many such excursions that Churchill would have to endure, up hill and down dale, often at a snail's pace on ponies. Another lady-in-waiting, Lady Augusta Stanley, commiserated with Churchill one chilly morning in October: "We were all pitying Lady Churchill this morning when it was announced that ponies had been sent on for a long expedition,"—soon after, Stanley herself was also summoned to join the royal party (Windsor and Bolitho 1927, 131).

With time Churchill no doubt became inured to the misery of daily excursions in open-topped carriages—even in the most inclement weather. In her twilight years the queen meticulously recorded in her journal her daily excursions—by wagonnette, sociable, or landau—accompanied by the ever-present Churchill and the queen's youngest daughter, Beatrice. Often these would be the only daily events punctuating the deadening routine of life at Balmoral, as recorded in the *Court Circulars.* In addition to being an all-weather companion, Churchill would regularly while away the long hours at Balmoral reading to the queen (novels such as George Eliot's *Mill on the Floss* or Jane Austen's *Pride and Prejudice* were greatly enjoyed). As a royal factotum she also found herself given the less pleasurable duty, according to Sir James

Reid, of writing the queen's reprimands to members of the royal household and passing them on. "There was no mistaking the meaning in her concise messages, which were often ill-appreciated," he observed; but he added, "some at Court liked her, and all respected her" (Reid 1987, 44). For all her long years of service Churchill never ceased to fear the queen's anger, as did many members of her close family, and the demands on her patience must have been considerable as the queen became increasingly querulous in her final years, frustrated by her failing eyesight.

In December 1900 Churchill, now also widowed, spent Christmas at Osborne with the queen, whose health by this time was causing some concern. Victoria had been suffering from insomnia and loss of appetite, and her mental powers seemed to be failing. The perceptive Churchill observed that she seemed "a dying woman" (Weintraub 1996, 630). But Churchill herself had been suffering for some years from heart problems. On Christmas Day 1900, Lady Jane was found dead in her bed, probably of a heart attack in her sleep. The queen's daughter, Princess Louise, could not resist the irony of such bad timing: "The dear Lady Jane," she commiserated, "how she would *hate* causing any disturbance" (Longford 1991, 70). The queen's physician, Sir James Reid, decided that it would be too great a shock to tell the queen this sudden news. So the queen was prepared, by degrees, first being told that Churchill had had another of her attacks, and later that her condition was grave. Eventually, in the late afternoon, Reid broke the news. For the queen the death of Jane Churchill was unbearably poignant. In her journal she recorded that "the loss to me is not to be told" (Rennell 2000, 56). The two women had been friends for almost fifty years, and this bereavement undoubtedly eroded the queen's own will to carry on. On 28 December Lady Jane's body was taken to the royal yacht and conveyed to the mainland for burial. A month later the queen was dead.

Related entries:
Balmoral Castle; Fresh Air; Reid, Sir James

References and further reading:

Duff, David. 1980. *Queen Victoria's Highland Journals.* London: Webb and Bower.
Fulford, Roger, ed. 1964. *Dearest Child: Letters between Queen Victoria and the Princess Royal, 1858–61.* London: Evans Brothers.
Longford, Elizabeth, ed. 1991. *Darling Loosy: Letters to Princess Louise 1858–1939.* London: Weidenfeld and Nicolson.
Ponsonby, Mary. 1927. *Mary Ponsonby: A Memoir, Some Letters and a Journal.* London: John Murray.
Reid, Michaela. 1987. *Ask Sir James: The Life of Sir James Reid, Personal Physician to Queen Victoria.* London: Eland.
Rennell, Tony. 2000. *Last Days of Glory: The Death of Queen Victoria.* London: Viking.
Weintraub, Stanley. 1996. *Victoria.* London: John Murray.
Windsor, Dean of, and Hector Bolitho, eds. 1927. *Letters of Lady Augusta Stanley: A Young Lady at Court 1849–1863.* London: Gerald Howe.

Clark, Sir James (1788–1870)

Good kind old Sir James (Hibbert 2000, 277)

It has frequently been observed that the queen's personal physician, Sir James Clark, was lucky to enjoy as many years in service as he did, from 1837 to 1860. As a physician of limited scientific understanding, trained in an earlier, less sophisticated medical age, his diagnoses were frequently faulty and often downright incompetent. Clark's survival for so long in the royal household was as much due to his compliant and accommodating manner and his willingness to serve the queen's medical and psychological neuroses as it was to his dubious diagnostic skills. Like any faithful servant who has learned to adjust to the quixotic nature of his employer, in matters medical Clark told the queen only what he thought she wanted to hear. When finding himself medically challenged and unable to come up with a diagnosis—such as in the case of Prince Albert's final illness—his reaction tended to prevarication and the adoption of a "watch and wait" policy.

Born in Cullen in Banffshire, Clark studied at the University of Aberdeen. He originally set out to be a lawyer but did not like the legal profession and decided to study medicine. In 1809 he became a member of the College of Surgeons in Edinburgh and served as an assistant surgeon in the British navy, twice surviving shipwreck. At the end of the Napoleonic Wars he returned to his medical studies in Edinburgh, becoming an M.D. in 1817. From 1819 to 1826 he practiced as a doctor in Rome; he was made a fellow of the Royal College of Surgeons in 1832.

Clark had early taken an interest in the effects of climate on people suffering from chest complaints such as tuberculosis and phthisis. He became convinced that the best therapy lay in the intake, by his patients, of copious amounts of fresh air. He described this theory in his essay "De Frigoribus Effectis" in 1817 and elaborated on it in *The Influence of Climate in the Prevention and Cure of Chronic Diseases* (1829) and *Treatise on Pulmonary Consumption* (1835). While visiting the medical spas of Germany in the early 1820s, Clark had met and become friends with Queen Victoria's uncle Leopold, later king of the Belgians, who appointed Clark as his personal physician. On Leopold's recommendation, in 1834 Clark became physician to the queen's mother, the duchess of Kent, and in June 1837, on Victoria's accession, he was appointed her physician-in-ordinary.

In 1835 Clark had attended the young Princess Victoria at Ramsgate on the south coast, during a serious bout of illness—at the time thought to be typhoid fever, although recent commentators have suggested it was severe tonsillitis—that lasted for five weeks. His devoted care during this time no doubt went a long way later to securing the queen's trust, and this despite his notorious medical bungling during the Flora Hastings affair of 1839. Many at court were mystified as to why the queen had not censured or even dismissed Clark after he had failed to diagnose the cancerous tumor from which Lady Flora was suffering, putting it down instead to a "derangement of the bowels" (Charlot 1991, 129). What is more, the garrulous Clark had also breached his own Hippocratic Oath as a doctor and had fueled the fires of gossip at court by stating that Lady Flora was in fact pregnant. In mitigation, it should be pointed out that, as a former naval surgeon, Clark had had no experience of examining women or of treating their ailments. He had also been greatly hampered in his diagnosis by the fact that he had not initially been allowed to examine her undressed. When Lady Flora was subsequently diagnosed with terminal cancer of the liver, the queen resisted calls to dismiss Clark from her service, even though her own mother, the duchess of Kent, had promptly done so.

But the damage to Clark's reputation was already done. Gossip raged about the debacle and lost Clark not only much of the respect and popularity he had enjoyed at court but also many of his private patients. The queen's faith in him, however, remained unshakable. From time to time he would even offer her his unofficial advice on political and other matters and encouraged the queen to support the work of Florence Nightingale in establishing proper training for women nurses. Upon her marriage in 1840 Queen Victoria ordered Prince Albert to appoint Clark as his own physician-in-ordinary as well, although this was as such an honorary post. Albert never had great faith in Clark's diagnostic skills and was critical of his ineffectual management of the ailments of the royal children—particularly in the case of the Princess Royal, who during a bout of serious illness Clark had misguidedly, in Albert's opinion, dosed with calomel.

In the main, much of Clark's diagnostic technique relied heavily on the panacea of fresh air and exercise, which he advocated in copious amounts, so much so that eventually the queen became a passionate advocate. She and the prince took Clark's advice by buying a holiday home, Balmoral, in the drier environs of Deeside in Scotland, a climate in Clark's opinion guaranteed to mitigate against the collective aches and pains, headaches, stress, and depression from which both the queen and Prince Albert regularly suffered. The queen embraced this new therapy with such dedication that, as Elizabeth Longford observed, her investment in it of "divine properties" would lead her to "[sacrifice] on its altar the convenience of her less hardy husband and courtiers, establishing as its priesthood a vast array of wall thermometers" (1966, 79).

In one aspect of the queen's well-being Clark did, at least, seem to be notably vigilant, and that was in his concern for her mental health after childbirth and the bouts of recurring postnatal depression to which she was subject. After the birth of her ninth child, Princess Beatrice, in 1857, he advised Prince Albert that the queen should have no more children. A year later, the queen, anxious about what her daughter Vicky might have to endure in giving birth to her first baby, sent Clark to Berlin to assist at the delivery of this, the queen's first grandchild. The birth of Vicky's son William (the future kaiser of Germany) proved to be a particularly traumatic one, with the baby in the breech position, eventually being delivered with a damaged left arm, which did not, as Clark predicted, ever recover its strength.

Clark retired in 1860 to a home in Bagshot Park lent by the queen, but soon found himself, in his seventies, unexpectedly recalled to royal duty when in January 1861, the royal physician, Dr. William Baly, died. Clark was now asked by the queen to take over the care of the duchess of Kent in her final painful illness—from erysipelas and cancer. The year 1861 taxed Clark's energies and limited diagnostic skills, for in December Prince Albert also fell ill. Clark, already under considerable personal strain trying to nurse his own sick wife, had to commute between his two patients at Bagshot Park and Windsor Castle. Despite Prince Albert's worsening symptoms, Clark assured the queen that there was no cause for alarm. During the early stages of the prince's illness, Clark was assisted by the equally elderly Sir Henry Holland—the two of them, in the opinion of Lord Clarendon "not fit to attend a sick cat" (Fulford 1966, 269). Clark proved incapable of coming up with a diagnosis, putting the prince's illness down to a "feverish sort of influenza." As Longford argued, Clark's problem was that he was frightened of failure and so overeager to please the queen with optimistic diagnoses that he would be economical with the truth (1966, 83). His dithering over calling in other medical opinion would be debated on the pages of *The Lancet* for some time after. It would appear that Clark made the decision—for good or for ill—not to reveal the true seriousness of the prince's condition to the queen, because he was fearful that this would provoke a nervous collapse in her. Nor would he reveal its nature to the prince, who was renowned for his hypochondria and had little fighting spirit when it came to illness. In later years he would continue to assert that there was little he could have done to save the prince, whatever the true nature of his malady. As the prince's condition worsened, Clark finally had to admit he could not cope. He called in Sir William Jenner—who, despite his own medical accomplishments, took time to come to the conclusion that it was typhoid fever. In the event, recent historians such as Stanley Weintraub (1997) have suggested that neither Clark nor Jenner can really be accused of misdiagnosis, since Prince

Albert was probably suffering from a combination of long-standing maladies and may even have had cancer.

After the prince's death, Clark went back into retirement. He was knighted in 1866. From 1838 to 1865 he served in the Senate of London University; he was also a member of the General Medical Council (1858–1860).

Related entries:
Balmoral Castle; Fresh Air; Hastings, Lady Flora; Jenner, Sir William; Reid, Sir James

References and further reading:

Charlot, Monica. 1991. *Victoria: The Young Queen.* Oxford: Blackwell.

Fulford, Roger. 1966. *The Prince Consort:* London: Macmillan.

Hibbert, Christopher. 2000. *Victoria: A Personal History.* London: HarperCollins.

Longford, Elizabeth. 1966. "Queen Victoria's Doctors." In Martin Gilbert, ed., *A Century of Conflict 1850–1950,* 75–87. London: Hamish Hamilton.

Ponsonby, Arthur. 1942. *Henry Ponsonby: His Life from His Letters.* London: Macmillan.

Weintraub, Stanley. 1997. *Albert: Uncrowned King.* London: John Murray.

Whitfield, George. 1982. *Beloved Sir James: The Life of Sir James Clark, Bart, Physician to Queen Victoria, 1788–1870.* London: G. Whitfield.

Class

That division of classes is the one thing *which is most dangerous & reprehensible . . ., & which the Queen is always labouring to alter* (Longford 1998, 536)

It has often been argued that Queen Victoria was far from being characteristically Victorian in many of her attitudes and that, if anything, she held unorthodox if not highly unconventional views when it came to matters of class, religion, and ethnicity. Several contentious issues of her day made the queen's "blood boil"—as she often described it—such as cruelty to animals, vivisection, and the campaign for women's rights. But snobbery also ranked high on the list of things she abhorred. If she had one great and abiding virtue that compensated for her blatant favoritism in matters political, then it was her extraordinary lack of prejudice. One of the queen's leading biographers, Elizabeth Longford, has argued its importance, asserting that the queen's "crusade" against racialism "was part of a deeper, private revolt against discrimination of all kinds, including class" (1998, 536).

In her attitude toward the aspiration of individuals to rise above their station and hold high office, Victoria in many ways shared the egalitarian sentiment nurtured among the nation of immigrants in the United States that "any boy could become president" (the phrase coined much later, in 1952, by Adlai Stevenson). She was rather proud of telling her private secretary, Henry Ponsonby, in later years that "she ha[d] known 2 Archbishops who were sons respectively of a Butcher & a Grocer" (Ponsonby 1942, 131); whether she would so heartily have approved of the fact that, in 1979, the daughter of a Lincolnshire grocer—Margaret Thatcher—would become the first female prime minister of Britain is a moot point. Women and politics in her view simply did not mix.

The concept of class was a relatively new idea when the queen ascended the throne in 1837—the old social order in Europe having been based not on personal wealth but on land and the aristocracy's ownership of vast manorial estates. The French Revolution had swept away much of this old system and Victoria felt that the threat of revolution still lingered, serving as a salutary warning to the aristocracy to mend their ways. As late as 1872 she would still be of the opinion that "the so called immorality of the lower classes is not to be named on the same day with that of the higher and highest. This is a thing which makes my blood boil, and they will pay for it" (Fulford 1976, 51).

What particularly incensed the queen about the British aristocracy was its indolence and frivolous lifestyle, as well as its immorality. And her antipathy was accentuated when her son and heir Bertie, as he grew up, persisted in associating with the hard-drinking, hard-gambling fast set who preferred a day at the races to devoting time to more philanthropic pursuits on their country estates. The queen also had an intense dislike for the haughty manner of the upper classes and their rudeness to servants. She and Prince Albert brought their children up to be more considerate of their social inferiors, although their influence failed to have any effect on her autocratic son, Alfred, who was universally disliked for his brusque and dictatorial manner. It was, however, most effective with the much maligned Bertie, who for all his failings excelled at putting his social inferiors at their ease—learning, much to the queen's approval, to be polite to "servants, railway guards, and small functionaries" (St. Aubyn 1991, 355).

Queen Victoria's refreshing lack of class prejudice in an age so obsessed with status, power, and preferment was based on a fundamental belief in the importance of Christian humility as the keystone to living a good life. All men in her view were equal before God; she admired the honest labor of the poorer classes and viewed their simplicity and poverty as virtues, from which those superior to them could learn. For this reason she was always far more comfortable in the company of simple, honest folk than she was in high society. Even though her ladies-in-waiting, such as Lady Augusta Bruce, might have been horrified that the queen should devote excessive amounts of space in her Highland journals to the mundane details of the lives of her servants and local cottagers at Balmoral, the queen remained passionately loyal to such people. "I would as soon clasp the poorest widow in the land to my heart as I would a Queen or any other in high position," she once wrote (St. Aubyn 1991, 354).

As queen, Victoria had it in her power to elevate those she liked well above their station. Much has been written about the special privileges she granted to her Highland servant John Brown (see "Brown, John") and about how the queen set the people of the Scottish Highlands as a breed apart. In her will she had expressed the desire that after her death she would be reunited with John Brown and her long-serving Scottish dresser, "good Annie MacDonald," over and above even her own children.

By 1867, the year that the franchise in Britain was extended to 1 million more householders, the queen was full of praise for the achievements of Britain's "Lower Classes," who were now, she wrote, "becoming so well-informed—are so intelligent & earn their bread & riches so deservedly" (Longford 1998, 352). Adopting her usual high moral tone on the subject, Victoria added that "they cannot & ought not to be kept back—to be abused by the wretched ignorant Highborn beings, who live only to kill time" (ibid.).

Related entries:
Brown, John; Chartism; Racial and Religious Prejudice; Religion

References and further reading:
Arnstein, Walter L. 1986. "Queen Victoria and Religion." In Gail Malmgreen, ed., *Religion in the Lives of English Women,* 88–128. London: Croom Helm.
Disraeli, Benjamin. [1845] 1981. *Sybil, or the Two Nations.* Oxford: Oxford University Press
Fulford, Roger. 1976. *Darling Child: Private Correspondence of Queen Victoria and the German Crown Princess of Prussia, 1871–1878.* London: Evans Brothers.
Hobsbawm, Eric. 2000. *The Age of Capital, 1848–1875.* London: Phoenix.
Longford, Elizabeth. [1964] 1998. *Victoria R.I.* London: Weidenfeld and Nicolson (352–354, 373–375).
Ponsonby, Arthur. 1942. *Henry Ponsonby, Queen Victoria's Private Secretary: His Life from His Letters.* London: Macmillan.
St. Aubyn, Giles. 1991. *Queen Victoria: A Portrait.* London: Sinclair Stevenson (354–356, 506).

Conroy, Sir John (1786–1854)

the Monster and Demon Incarnate (Hibbert 1984, 42)

The influence of John Conroy, the controller of the duchess of Kent's household, has been condemned by many, Victoria included, as a pernicious one over her early life. As an aristocrat manqué, Conroy, a charming and handsome Irishman, who had romantic notions about his ancestry, was driven by his hunger to achieve the status at court that he felt he deserved. If events had been otherwise, he might have become coregent with the duchess during Victoria's minority. Fortunately, William IV, who had never disguised his own loathing of Conroy, managed to stay alive long enough for Victoria to reach her eighteenth birthday.

Victoria's view of Conroy was very much molded by her governess, Baroness Lehzen, who, during Victoria's early life, was in constant and open conflict with Conroy and the duchess of Kent. Lehzen had sowed further seeds of discord after Conroy dismissed her compatriot, the Baroness Späeth, from the duchess's service. Victoria was unrelenting and unforgiving in her opinion of Conroy as villainous, insulting, and manipulative. Her somewhat melodramatic attitude to Conroy was shared by Prince Albert, who also regarded him as an exaggerated, pantomime bogeyman, into whose evil clutches his wife had fallen as a young and impressionable girl.

John Conroy was descended from the Irish O'Mulconrys of Elphin, County Roscommon. He was one of six children of John Conry (as the name was then spelled), who had died in 1797. Educated in Dublin, he entered the army cadets at the Royal Military College in Woolwich in 1805 and obtained a commission in the Royal Horse Artillery. His subsequent rise through the ranks was much aided by a propitious marriage, above his station, to Elizabeth, daughter of Col. (and later Maj. Gen.) Benjamin Fisher. It was at this point, as Katherine Hudson (1994) has ably demonstrated, that Conroy developed his consuming obsession with his ancestry. He succumbed to a rumor then circulating that his wife, Elizabeth, was not in fact Fisher's daughter but the product of a liaison between her mother and the duke of Kent, at a time when Fisher and the duke had both been on army service in Quebec in 1790. The possibility (now disproved by Hudson) of his wife's being a half-sister to Victoria, future queen of England, unfortunately got the better of Conroy's fertile imagination. Once convinced of his royal connection, he devoted all his time and energy to pursuing what he saw as his rightful elevation into the British aristocracy.

In 1818, when the duke of Kent hastily married in the flurry of competition between the sons of George III to provide potential legitimate heirs to the now precarious British throne, Conroy, whom the duke had known for some time, was appointed his personal equerry. His undoubted organizational skills were made good use of, one of his first tasks being to arrange for the safe transportation back to England from Coburg of the pregnant duchess of Kent not long before Victoria was born. With the premature death of the duke in 1820, the duchess, and with time her daughter, became closely involved with the Conroy family, sharing the pleasures of family outings and holidays with them. As a girl Victoria visited their homes at Shooter's Hill and later Campden Hill, and Conroy's daughters Jane and Victoire often came to play at Kensington Palace.

Conroy's role in the life of Victoria and the duchess became increasingly domineering. He not only took control of the duchess's financial affairs and the drafting of her letters but with her blessing set about organizing for Princess Victoria a rigid daily round of lessons and character-building activities at Kensington Palace. Victoria was subjected to this regimen, referred to as the Kensington System, between the ages of five and eighteen in order to prepare her for the likelihood (especially after 1825) that she would become queen. Conroy had by now developed a familiarity in his behavior toward Princess Victoria and her mother that seemed to overstep the mark. He also sought deliberately to isolate them at Kensington Palace so that he could increase his control over Victoria's future. The inevitable result was gossip (much of it prompted by a jealous Baroness Lehzen) that the deep reliance of the duchess on Conroy went to dangerous levels of intimacy (historians continue to argue over whether Victoria might have been Conroy's illegitimate child). Conroy and the duchess further antagonized those hostile to them by organizing, once Victoria became heir-apparent in 1830 on the accession William IV, a series of self-promoting, royal progresses. These were staged ostensibly to market the princess to her future people but with the undoubted objective of also promoting Conroy and the duchess's own ambitions as regents. Although the tours exhausted Victoria and brought her ultimately to serious physical collapse and illness in 1835, they were undoubtedly popular. More important for Conroy, they were seen by him as the prelude to his inevitable appointment as Victoria's private secretary.

By now, courtiers such as Baron Stockmar saw Conroy's overweening self-importance as a cause for serious concern, particularly when he petitioned Victoria to be made keeper of her Privy Purse. Fortunately, she refused, but on her accession he tried again and again to have himself appointed private secretary. He had long since determined on achieving his rightful recognition (through his wife's supposed blood relationship with Victoria) as a peer of the realm. He sought elevation to the Irish peerage from Prime Minister Melbourne, having long nurtured the dream of becoming the self-styled Viscount of Elphin Co. Roscommon. Eventually, with anxiety at court about Conroy's destabilizing influence persisting, the duke of Wellington was enlisted in 1839 to persuade him into an honorable retirement on an English baronetcy and a handsome pension of £3,000 per annum. Conroy continued for many years to demand an Irish peerage, but his request was ignored by the queen.

Conroy now entered into effective exile and took his family to Europe, returning after Victoria's marriage in 1840. He settled, in 1842, at his family home, Arborfield Hall, where he took up the life of a gentleman farmer, won prizes for his pig breeding, and gained some pleasure from reliving his past military career by founding, in 1849, the Montgomeryshire Regiment of Militia. After Conroy died in February 1854, his personal accounts revealed that he was on the brink of bankruptcy, despite his lucrative pensions and ownership of other property and lead mines in Wales. Such had been Conroy's irresponsible management of his financial affairs that he had contrived to die with almost £40,000 worth of debts.

Related entries:

Kensington System; Kent, Edward Augustus, Duke of; Kent, Marie Louise Victoire, Duchess of; Lehzen, Baroness Louise; Stockmar, Christian Friedrich von

References and further reading:

Charlot, Monica. 1991. *Victoria: The Young Queen.* Cambridge: Polity.

Esher, Viscount, ed. 1912. *The Girlhood of Queen Victoria: A Selection from Her Majesty's Diaries between the Years of 1832 and 1840.* 2 vols. London: John Murray.

Hibbert, Christopher. 1984. *Queen Victoria in Her Letters and Journals.* London: Viking.

Hudson, Katherine. 1994. *A Royal Conflict: Sir John Conroy and the Young Victoria.* London: Hodder and Stoughton.

Longford, Elizabeth [1964] 1998. *Victoria R.I.* London: Weidenfeld and Nicolson.

Plowden, Alison. 1981. *The Young Victoria.* London: Weidenfeld and Nicolson.

Vallone, Lynne. 2001. *Becoming Victoria.* New Haven: Yale University Press.

Woodham-Smith, Cecil. 1972. *Queen Victoria: Her Life and Times.* Vol. 1: *1819–1861.* London: Hamish Hamilton.

Corelli, Marie (1855–1924)

(Mary / "Minnie" Mills, Later Mackay)

one of the greatest writers of the time (Ponsonby 1951, 51)

The English popular novelist Marie Corelli had an instinct for her market and knew how to write for it. A shrewd businesswoman who fought shy of making her works more readily available through cheap "sixpenny" editions (which would have also reduced her royalties), she remained doggedly impervious to critical opinion that looked upon her work as being sensationalist and in bad taste. Convinced of the wisdom of her powerful moral message—on a vast range of subjects—Corelli was gratified to receive the endorsement of her work from no less a personage than the queen, who read each of her new sagas—of which twenty-eight were best-sellers—as fast as Corelli could produce them. The queen approved of Corelli's fiercely moralizing tone and her concern at the increasingly decadent and corrupting influences at large in society. Armed with the royal endorsement, Corelli eventually turned her back on her critics, trusting only in her adoring public.

The romantic-sounding name "Marie Corelli" was, of course, not the real name of Queen Victoria's favorite novelist. Piecing together the biography of the woman who was born plain Mary Mills has been a particular challenge for all aspirants, and Teresa Ransom (1999) has at last managed to unravel some of the truth about Corelli's long-buried and deliberately obfuscated origins. She grew up under the impression that she was the adopted daughter of Charles Mackay, a Scottish songwriter and journalist, who after being widowed had married again in 1861, taking in Mary, the daughter of his new wife, Elizabeth Mary Mills. Ransom suggested that Mary Mills aka Corelli might have been the illegitimate daughter of Mackay's daughter, Rosa, who had died of a fever in Italy in 1855. The adoption of the romantic Italian name therefore might explain her choice of the Italian pseudonym Corelli.

Educated at a convent school in Paris (1866–1870), Corelli proved to have conspicuous musical talents and looked toward respectable, useful employment, perhaps teaching singing or piano. Having tried her hand at writing poetry, she launched a concerted, but unsuccessful attack on the leading London journal *Blackwood's Magazine*, to get her work published, submitting her work under the flourish of a new and illustrious-sounding name—"Signorina Marie Corelli"—complete with the spurious pedigree of direct descent from the famous Italian composer of the same name. This marked the beginning of a lifetime's flights of romantic and self-dramatizing fantasy that would be channeled into the production of a series of long, hyperbolic, and, in the main, equally fantastical stories.

Short of money, Corelli began giving piano concerts and song recitals. In 1885, at the age of thirty-one, she signed with the publisher George Bentley for her first novel—published the following year as *A Romance of Two Worlds*. The book was an instant success. The characteristics of this and her subsequent novels were exotic settings—often in remote or classical history—mystery, romance, and a substantial injection of Corelli's favorite ingredient—the "human electricity" (as one critic put it) of the mystical, unspoken empathy between humankind and the universe at large. This "electricity" was the essential component of what Corelli eccentrically preached as being humankind's own untapped spiritual hotline to the supreme being, God himself. The quasi-religious and supernatural quality of all Corelli's writing would contribute to her huge success at a time when psychic phenomena were being explored in all seriousness by many respectable figures. New religions such as theosophy were also increasing in popularity as people, the queen included, bemoaned the decline in social standards, morality, and behavior.

Corelli's third novel, *Thelma* (1887), ensured that hundreds of little Thelmas were soon christened with the name up and down the land. It was also the novel that finally turned Corelli into a household name; by 1920 it had been reprinted fifty-one times. In her private life, Corelli, who had demonstrated little interest in men and a categorical aversion to the animal side of human nature, had already for some years shared a house with her devoted childhood friend and companion, Bertha Vyver, although there is no evidence to suggest that the relationship was ever anything but platonic.

In 1891 Queen Victoria had discovered Corelli's writing after being lent a copy of *A Romance of Two Worlds* by the dowager duchess of Roxburghe; soon afterward, Victoria requested a presentation copy and made clear that she expected, in future, to be sent copies of all Corelli's books as soon as they appeared. Corelli was eager to capitalize on the royal seal of approval, and word of the queen's endorsement rapidly circulated and gave a massive fillip to sales. A succession of novels poured from Corelli's pen, pontificating on every conceivable subject, including the evils of absinthe drinking (*Wormwood,* 1890), secular education (*The Mighty Atom,* 1896), reincarnation (*Ziska,* 1897), the Roman Catholic Church (*Master Christian,* 1900), parental neglect (*Boy,* 1900), and, in her last and most prescient novel, *The Secret Power* (1921), science fiction, germ warfare, and the all-annihilating bomb.

Hypocrisy became an issue that particularly obsessed Corelli: she saw it everywhere, and her desire to see society reform itself morally remained the major impetus behind much of her writing, thus ensuring its endorsement by the queen. The undoubted high point of her moral crusade, conducted in a torrent of highly rococco and hectoring prose, was the two strongly religious novels—*Barabbas: A Dream of the World's Tragedy* (1893) and *The Sorrows of Satan* (1895)—in both of which Corelli challenged Victorian society on the genuineness of its Christian observance and moral rectitude. More particularly in the latter, she castigated society at large for its growing obsession with material greed at the expense of Christian charity.

Barabbas touched a nerve with the public. The response was unprecedented; it was reprinted fourteen times in its first year and became a best-seller in many other translated editions. *The Sorrows of Satan,* published in the new single-volume format introduced by the circulating libraries, was also a huge popular success, much quoted by the clergy in their Sunday sermons. With such an endorsement from the established church, Corelli refused, in future, to send review copies to her hostile critics.

With the death of the queen in 1901, Corelli, who saw Victoria as the guiding influence of the nation, was convinced that the moral collapse of the country was now inevitable, deprived as it was of the queen's enduring, maternal standards of duty, propriety, and family values. In her eulogy, *The Passing of the Great Queen* (1901), Corelli mourned the loss of the "the Mother-Queen of the great British people" (5). By 1907 her career was finally on the wane; her time was now taken up with fighting rearguard actions against unsanctioned stage and film adaptations of her work. She had also adopted another moral cause—temperance—berating the evils of alcohol in *Holy Orders* (1908). In *The Life Everlasting* (1911) she once again returned to the theme of spirituality, at a time when the world was edging toward the catastrophe of war, with Corelli arguing again that civilization had lost its sense of moral direction.

Corelli was a tiny pint-pot of a woman—even smaller and dumpier in later life than the queen she so much admired. One observer ungenerously described her as "a fat little dwarf" (Ransom 1999, 197). Vain and self-conscious about her appearance, she developed a clever knack of disguising her true height, which was well under five feet. She ensured that her public never saw their idol grow old, gray, and fat, refusing, as she aged, to have her photograph taken or displayed in the papers. In response to comments once made about her having remained single, Corelli responded: "I never married because there was no need. I have three pets at home, which answer the same purpose as a husband. I have a dog that growls every morning, a parrot that swears all afternoon and a cat that comes home late at night" (Ransom 1999, 167–168). Corelli's self-fulfillment came through her writing, and she lived under the unshakable conviction that readers responded to her blazing honesty and the truth of her message: "I attributed my good fortune," she said, "to the simple fact that I have always tried to write straight from the heart to the hearts of others" (ibid.); in this respect she most certainly found a way into the heart of her queen.

Related entries:
Oliphant, Margaret; Religion

References and further reading:

Bigland, Eileen. 1953. *Marie Corelli: The Woman and the Legend.* London: Jarrolds.

Corelli, Marie. 1901. *The Passing of the Great Queen.* London: Methuen and Co.

Keating, Peter. 1989. *The Haunted Study: A Social History of the English Novel 1875–1914.* London: Secker and Warburg.

Masters, Brian. 1978. *Now Barabbas Was a Rotter: The Extraordinary Life of Marie Corelli.* London: Hamilton.

Ponsonby, Sir Frederick. 1951. *Recollections of Three Reigns.* London: Eyre and Spottiswoode.

Ransom, Teresa. 1999. *The Mysterious Miss Marie Corelli: Queen of Victorian Bestsellers.* Stroud, Gloucestershire: Sutton Publishing.

Sutherland, John. 1988. *The Longman Companion to Victorian Fiction.* London: Longman.

Vyver, Bertha. 1930 *Memoirs of Marie Corelli.* London: A. Rivers.

Crimean War, 1854–1856

this great and bloody war (Benson and Esher 1911, 3:170)

On the morning of 28 February 1854, Queen Victoria was up early to watch the manly ranks of the last battalion of her "beautiful" scarlet-coated Scottish Fusiliers march out of the courtyard of Buckingham Palace, past crowds of well-wishers, as they set off for the war in the Crimea. Describing these scenes later that day in a letter to her Uncle Leopold, Victoria's admiration for her brave soldiers was tinged with apprehension at what they might have to face. In the upsurge of national sentiment that accompanied the optimistic departure of thousands of British troops for the front in the following weeks, the general consensus was that this war would be a short one. But at the end of a difficult two-year campaign, the Crimean War would go down in history, not just for the romantic, if foolhardy heroism of troops such as the Light Brigade, but also for exposing incompetence in the leadership of the British army, the diplomatic failures of the government, and the unprecedented levels of suffering endured by the British troops.

The Crimean War is generally dated 1854–1856, from the declaration of war by Britain and France, but hostilities between Russia and Turkey had actually developed in 1853, and the so-called Eastern Question from which the war sprang had been simmering for many years. The dispute between these two nations had originated in Russia's claim to defend the rights of Balkan Christians living under Turkish suzerainty within the crumbling Ottoman Empire, as well as their right of access to holy Christian shrines in Palestine. In the summer of 1853, after the Russians had occupied Moldavia and Wallachia, the Turks had declared war. The Russian tsar, Nicholas I, shared the belief of his ministers that this incursion would go unchallenged;

The mad heroics of the Charge of the Light Brigade during the Crimean War of 1854–1856 became the stuff of legend, but were the result of ill-conceived and poorly communicated orders. (Library of Congress)

instead the Turks had embarked on war with the Russian infidel with all the zealotry of a jihad. Britain was certainly extremely reluctant at first to be drawn into the quarrel, having enjoyed forty years of peace since the end of the Napoleonic Wars. But anxieties grew in Parliament about Russia's ambitions in the region and, more particularly, beyond that, in the Middle East and on the important overland and naval routes to India.

Throughout the winter of 1853–1854, British xenophobia against Russia had been running high, particularly after 4,000 Turks had been killed in the Russian naval attack on the Turkish fleet at Sinope in November. Early in January 1854 the British fleet entered the Black Sea, intent on preventing further Russian incursions. An enraged Queen Victoria now turned on her erstwhile friend Tsar Nicholas I (whom she had entertained on a state visit to Britain in June 1844) for failing to respond to the conciliatory messages she had sent to him, blaming the conflict on his ruthless ambition. She judged that the time was ripe for a war against Russian aggression; it was one that she believed would be "popular beyond belief" (Charlot 1991, 350).

The queen's prime minister, Lord Aberdeen, did not want war, but his "repugnance" at the thought of it (as he candidly admitted to Queen Victoria) was quickly overridden by public opinion and his hand forced by demands in the press for military action. By the end of February the queen was instructing him, with the encouragement of Prince Albert, on the importance of boosting the army reserve, in excess of the 10,000 that had been mooted, in order to provide adequate backup should war prevail. A British expeditionary force was now gathered together under the command of the aging veteran of Waterloo, Lord Raglan, and at the end of February British troops began embarking for the Balkans.

At the naval base of Spithead, in Portsmouth, on 11 March the queen witnessed the "wonderful, inspiriting & solemn sight" (Dimond and Taylor 1987, 81) of the British fleet setting sail for Gibraltar and Malta in the Mediterranean, and thence to camps at Varna on the northern shore of the Black Sea. By the time Britain and France formally declared war on Russia on 28 March 1854, the British public were demanding the return to government of the foreign secretary, Lord Palmerston, who had been forced out of office in 1853 and who was viewed as a more suitable wartime leader than the pacific Aberdeen.

The war began with both government and military in Britain ignoring warnings that it would be a difficult war to prosecute from such a distance, that the army was ill prepared, and that the planners had not taken sufficient account of the exigencies of a winter campaign that would soon be upon the army in the field. The British soldiers who marched off to war were poorly equipped; nor were they battle hardened, the last English experience of war having been at Waterloo in 1815. For many British soldiers, encampment at Varna, during the broiling summer of 1854, would mark the end of their war. Contaminated drinking water quickly led to an epidemic of cholera and amoebic dysentery among the allied troops, both in camps and on board ship, at the end of which 10,000 French and British servicemen were either dead or out of action.

The real war finally began in September 1854, after British troops landed at Kalamata Bay north of the fortified naval base of Sebastopol. The Russians, under the command of Prince Alexander Menshikov, in an attempt to prevent the allied march on the town, engaged 60,000 British, French, and Turkish troops in a three-hour battle at the River Alma on 20 September. The Russians were eventually repulsed and forced back to Sebastopol after sustaining heavy losses. Two thousand British soldiers were killed or wounded; the queen considered their noble sacrifice as having been made, by all accounts, "with a *courage* and *desperation* which was beautiful to behold" (Benson and Esher 1911, 3:50).

With this first victory, the queen and her people became "entirely engrossed with one idea and one anxious thought, namely the Crimea" (Benson and Esher 1911, 3:50). It was at this point that the allied military commanders made a fatal mistake that would cost both armies dear. Instead of pressing directly on to Sebastopol from the north, while the town was still relatively underfortified, they decided to attack from the south, using backup supplies from their own naval base at the port of Balaklava. During the time it took to make this circuitous six-day march south, the Russians meanwhile built huge, defensive earthworks, brought up heavy guns, and made the town impregnable against siege. The bombardment of Sebastopol was launched by the allies on 17 October.

Back in Britain, the queen and the public were engrossed by regular reports being sent back to the *Times* newspaper by a new breed of reporter—the war correspondent—notably in the figure of William Howard Russell. Ever more Churchillian in her wartime leadership of the nation, in October Victoria admitted that, had she been a man, she would have wanted to be at the front fighting alongside her beloved troops, for there was "no finer death for a man than on the battlefield" (Hibbert 1984, 126). She was soon to see the grim reality of battle for herself in the maimed bodies of the servicemen she visited when they were repatriated home. The queen developed a strange fascination for the details of how they got their wounds, keeping precise photographic and written records of the case histories of many individual soldiers.

Victoria was, however, impatient with the time news took to reach Britain from the Crimea and with how "we must live in a suspense which is indeed dreadful" (Benson and Escher 1911, 3:52) the reports she did receive were often scanty and did not satisfy her insatiable demand for detail. She pored over maps, becoming intimate with the lay of the land in the Crimea and the positioning of allied troops. She impressed her entourage with the accuracy of her knowledge of the defenses at Sebastopol, "more than anyone I found at home knew," as the war illustrator William Simpson noted on his return (Stoney and Weltzein 1994, 154). Prince Albert, too, as a great patron of the new techniques of photography, took a particular interest in the work of the photographer Roger Fenton, whom he commissioned in 1855 to go to the Crimea as official photographer and compile what would be one of the first portfolios of warfare. Many of the 360 or so photographs taken by Fenton were exhibited in London and reproduced in the popular press, such as the *Illustrated London News*. But they lacked the punch of Russell's vivid war reporting, remaining highly selective, sanitized images of what was in fact a bloody and brutal affair.

On 25 October the high point of the war was marked with the legendary Charge of the Light Brigade at the Battle of Balaklava. The day had started with a classic demonstration of British fighting spirit, when 550 Sutherland Highlanders of the Ninety-third Division had defended the head of an inlet leading directly into Balaklava Bay against a Russian cavalry charge. Hours later, the tragic debacle of the Charge of the Light Brigade came about, due to the misinterpretation of hasty and confused orders from Lord Raglan to launch an attack against Russians taking captured Turkish guns away from their artillery positions on the Vorontsov heights above the battlefield. Unfortunately the officers in charge—Lords Lucan and Cardigan—misinterpreted Raglan's directive as referring to another set of Russian guns facing them straight ahead at the end of the valley below the heights, although they questioned the military logic of such an attack. Lucan ultimately overrode Cardigan's doubts and insisted on the immediate carrying out of the order without attempting to double-check Raglan's precise orders. Thus it was that 673 cavalrymen of the Light Brigade were sent on a suicidal charge along a narrow valley straight into the Russian guns. Within twenty-five minutes 107 were killed and 196 wounded; 397 horses also lay dead. One of their Russian opponents later described the charge as being that of "valiant lunatics" (Royle 1999, 244). After the attack, Lord Cardigan, who had led from the front and miraculously survived, blandly rode back to his private yacht in Balaklava harbor, "had a bath and a bottle of champagne with his dinner, and went to his bed" (Woodham-Smith 1957, 262). Six Victoria Crosses would subsequently be awarded to participants in this battle, of 111 awarded during the course of the war.

In England, Queen Victoria, along with the nation, mourned and thrilled to accounts of this insane act of self-sacrifice. Her "whole soul and heart" was now in the Crimea (Benson and Esher 1911, 3:52). The first year of fighting was rounded off with the Battle of Inkerman of 5 November 1854. A series of savage infantry engagements, later known as the "soldiers' battle," that turned into a confused melée, it was conducted hand-to-hand in thick fog, when Russian troops emerged from Sebastopol in an attempt to break the Anglo-French siege. Again the Russians were thrown back, with heavy losses of 10,729 wounded, killed, or taken prisoner and allied casualties totaling 3,220. The queen received news "with pride and joy" of the "glorious, but alas! bloody victory of the 5th" (Benson and Esher 1911, 3:52) rather more quickly than previous military communiqués, thanks to the recent laying of telegraph cables on the seabed from Istanbul to the Crimea.

The queen felt she spoke for the entire country in honoring "every Private Soldier" for his sacrifice (Royle 1999, 292). A few days later she announced her intention of conferring a medal on her loyal servicemen. Meanwhile, Prince Albert, alarmed by the high losses, had stepped in to enlist militia and more volunteers to boost the British army by 15,000 men. Soon German, Swiss, and Italian troops were hired to reinforce the army at Sebastopol. The British public were by now supporting the war effort through various public funds raised to send military chaplains out to the troops, provide for the soldiers' and sailors' widows and orphans, and send out medical supplies. The queen and her daughters knitted ferociously, turning out scarves, mittens, and socks. The winter months also saw the production of the first home-knitted woolen cardigans and woolen balaclava helmets, the former named after Lord Cardigan, the latter in commemoration of the recent battle. Victoria herself greatly envied Florence Nightingale, now out in the Crimea with her team of nurses, and used her own money to buy provisions for Nightingale's hospital at Scutari, even purchasing wooden limbs for those returning amputees too poor to buy them. Already a prolific letter writer, the queen wrote many letters of condolence to the families of officers killed in action.

The public plaudits and the queen's very heartfelt gratitude for Britain's hard-won military successes would, by now, have been of little comfort to the vast majority of the British forces in the Crimea. Now reduced to 16,000—many of whom were sick, ailing, and underprovisioned—they were digging themselves into their trenches to face the misery of winter. Exposed to the elements, and with few tents, they were encamped on a barren plain above Sebastopol, which afforded little shelter or wood for fires. Food was short; there were not enough blankets, nor did the men have greatcoats to protect them from the cold. This alone guaranteed many unnecessary deaths, with men in their tattered uniforms and worn-out boots freezing to death overnight as they huddled together. Many lost fingers and toes, hands and feet to terrible frostbite.

Matters had been made worse after a hurricane on 14 November had smashed twenty-one British and fourteen French supply ships at anchor in Balaklava harbor before they had been unloaded. As the ships went down with most of their crew of 1,000, so too did much-needed medical supplies, beds, blankets, ammunition, and warm winter clothing. Yet there were still sufficient supplies available—had it been possible to move them from Balaklava through the quagmire that led to the front lines. But by now the pack animals too were starving and dropping dead from exhaustion. Meat from the cattle slaughtered at the port could not be transported the six miles through the mud to where it was needed. Instead it was left to rot along with other supplies and fodder, on the quayside.

By now the British public were becoming alarmed by Russell's newspaper exposés of the administrative incompetencies of the War Office and the suffering of the troops. At the Barrack Hospital, a former Turkish army barracks across the Black Sea at Scutari, Florence Nightingale, with her team of thirty-eight nurses, had initiated a major clean-up of the premises and battled to stem the rising tide of deaths from dysentery, cholera, typhoid, gangrene, and frostbite, but still the men kept dying—in alarmingly high numbers. A shadow was cast over the royal Christmas that year, with the queen preoccupied by the escalating death toll. When Lord Cardigan returned to England that winter, he was commanded to Windsor, during which visit one of the young princes, anxious about his mother's obsession with the war, urged him: "Do hurry back and take Sebastopol, or else it will kill mamma." (Tooley 1896, 184). Public disquiet at the neglect of the welfare of the troops was also now mounting; a vote of no confidence in Parliament against Lord Aberdeen's tenuous wartime administration led to the collapse of his ministry at the end of January. A dismayed Queen Victoria was eventually forced to accept the return of Lord Palmerston, a man she deeply mistrusted. But Palmerston had the vociferous backing of the British people, who, whipped up by the popular press, were convinced that he was the "pilot to weather the storm" and bring a successful conclusion to the war.

In January 1855, British fortunes revived with 10,000 reinforcements from the principality of Sardinia-Piedmont, which had now entered the war. As the bitter winter weather receded, efforts were once more revived to break the siege of Sebastopol, with civilian labor arriving from Britain to construct a crucial railway supply line from Balaklava to the front. British troops were now also supplied with new, breech-loading Minié rifles that outclassed the old flintlocks used by the Russians. Winter clothing also finally began arriving, almost too late to be of use.

On 20 February at Buckingham Palace, the queen greeted thirty-two wounded and mutilated Grenadier Guards sent home from the Crimea, speaking to each man individually and ensuring that they were given a good meal in the servants' hall before they left. Two days later she inspected another twenty-six, this time from the Coldstream Guards—many of them amputees. She was deeply moved by the sight: "*How* anxious I feel to be of use to them," she wrote, worrying that "those who are discharged will receive very small pensions but not sufficient to live upon" (Hibbert 1984, 130). She was now overwhelmed with a profound sense of personal loss at so much bloodshed. Her hunger for news from the front was insatiable; as Lord Panmure would write that year, to Lord Raglan, "You never saw anyone so entirely taken up with military affairs as she is" (Hibbert 2000, 225).

On 9 April 1855 the second bombardment of Sebastopol began. A significant naval victory secured in May by the Anglo-French naval expeditionary force brought the destruction of the strategic fort and naval base at Kerch northeast of the Black Sea, which controlled the onward dispatch to Sebastopol of Russian supplies from the mainland. The eighteenth of June, the anniversary of Britain's defeat of Napoleon at Waterloo, was chosen as a significant day for the assault on the two great earthworks defending Sebastopol: the Malakov Tower and the Great Redan. But the attack failed. Weeks of endless stalemate followed, as the encamped troops now sweltered in the summer heat of the shelterless Crimean plain under the noise of ceaseless artillery fire; but at least, by now, the British were well supplied.

In September, after several weeks of continuous bombardment, the French and British made another combined assault on the two strategic earthworks. The French managed to take the Malakov Tower, sustaining heavy losses of 7,500 killed and wounded, and held out against a heavy Russian counterattack. But raw recruits newly arrived from England were unwilling to be used as cannon fodder in a futile attack on the fortress at the Great Redan. Their inexperience and sheer terror resulted in heavy losses, with many retreating in disarray. Eventually the relentless bombardment of Sebastopol finally convinced the Russians that the situation was hopeless. On 9 September they began evacuating, but not before blowing up their forts, torching the town and its arsenals, and sinking their ships in the harbor.

The queen was at Balmoral when she heard the news of the fall of Sebastopol after 349 days of siege, an event that was promptly celebrated by the royal family with good Scots whiskey and the lighting of a bonfire. Sporadic fighting continued until the end of that year. By the time an armistice was finally declared in the Crimea on 1 February 1856, the British army was exhausted and demoralized, longing for home, having been militarily eclipsed by the better organized and more experienced French troops. If he had had his way, Palmerston would have continued to prosecute the war to secure a conclusive defeat of Russia, a fact the queen heartily endorsed, intent particularly on imposing a humiliating peace treaty at Russia's expense and one that accommodated the wishes of Britain's close ally Prussia.

The queen began personally greeting the return of her troops, many of whom marched through the streets of London, bringing with them Russian cannon captured at Sebastopol. They were greeted everywhere by displays of fireworks and huge crowds, particularly in London's parks. At a grand ceremony in Hyde Park in June 1857, Queen Victoria handed out the first Victoria Crosses. Everywhere at court, uniformed and bemedaled military men were on view; celebrations of the victory continued for months, as did the raising of many memorials.

There would be many enduring legacies—most of them positive—of this war, which had resulted in 19,584 war dead. Its conduct had sounded the death knell of the old-school commanders and with them outmoded methods of military campaigning and brought also the overhaul of army administration. In the wake of Nightingale's work at Scutari, public health reforms were initiated in Britain. Public admiration for her work also led to the wider acceptance of women into the profession of nursing. On an international level, the work of Nightingale directly inspired the establishment of the Red Cross in the late 1850s and the drafting of the 1864 Geneva Convention on the care of the wounded. In Russia the war brought the tsar face to face also with the unavoidability of major social and military reforms, and in 1861 the Russian serfs were emancipated. But the problems of the moribund Ottoman Empire—the "sick man of Europe" as Tsar Nicholas had called it—persisted until 1914 and World War I.

Related entries:
Aberdeen, George Hamilton-Gordon, fourth Earl; Nightingale, Florence; Palmerston, Henry John Temple, Third Viscount; Russell, Lord John, First Earl; Victoria Cross

References and further reading:

Adkin, Mark. 1996. *The Charge: Why the Light Brigade Was Lost.* London: Leo Cooper.

Benson, A. C., and Viscount Esher, eds. 1911. *The Letters of Queen Victoria: A Selection from Her Majesty's Correspondence between the Years 1837 and 1861.* 1st ser., 3 vols. London: John Murray.

Chapman, Caroline. 1984. *Russell of* The Times: *War Dispatches and Diaries.* London: Bell and Hynton.

Charlot, Monica. 1991. *Victoria, The Young Queen.* Oxford: Blackwell.

Dimond, Frances, and Ann Taylor. 1987. *Crown and Camera: The Royal Family and Photography.* Harmondsworth, UK: Penguin.

Ffrench, Blake R. L.V. 1972. *The Crimean War.* Hamden, CT: Archon Books.

Hibbert, Christopher. 1984. *Queen Victoria in Her Letters and Journals.* London: Viking.

———. 2000. *Queen Victoria, a Personal History.* London: HarperCollins.

Keller, Ulrich. 2001. "My Nearest and Dearest," chapter 5 of *The Ultimate Spectacle: A Visual History of the Crimean War.* Amsterdam: Gordon and Breach.

Rich, Norman. 1985. *Why the Crimean War? A Cautionary Tale.* Hanover: Brown University for University Press of New England.

Royle, Trevor. 1999. *Crimea: The Great Crimean War 1854–1856.* London: Little, Brown.

St. Aubyn, Giles. 1991. *Queen Victoria.* London: Sinclair-Stevenson.

Stoney, Benita, and Heinrich C. Weltzien, eds. 1994. *My Mistress the Queen: The Letters of Frieda Arnold, Dresser to Queen Victoria 1854–9.* London: Weidenfeld and Nicolson.

Tooley, Sarah. 1896. *Personal Life of Queen Victoria.* London: Hodder and Stoughton.

Warner, Philip. 2001. *The Crimean War: A Reappraisal.* Ware, UK: Wordsworth Editions.

Woodham-Smith, Cecil. 1957. *The Reason Why.* London: Constable.

D

Dancing

my Operatic *and* Terpsichorean *feelings are pretty strong* (Woodham-Smith 1972, 129)

The close surveillance to which Princess Victoria was subjected during her youth, particularly once her accession to the throne seemed likely, meant that her first enjoyment of dance was vicarious—watching others perform it on stage. The teenage Victoria became a passionate devotee of the ballet as well as a considerable connoisseur of technique and performance. She not only frequently described in her journals the ballets she had seen but also drew and painted scenes from her favorites in her sketchbooks. She spent time creating miniature reproductions of the costumes during the long and often lonely hours at Kensington Palace, with the help of her governess Baroness Lehzen, dressing her collection of five-inch Dutch figurines.

Victoria's enthusiasm for ballet was fostered by her abiding admiration for the leading interpreter of the European romantic ballet, who took London by storm in the 1830s—the Italian Marie Taglioni. Taglioni, born in Stockholm in 1804, was the daughter of a notable choreographer, Filippo Taglioni. After debuting in Vienna in 1822, she was much admired for her superb technique, first making a name for herself in 1831 in a dance interlude—"The Ballet of the Nuns"—in Giacomo Meyerbeer's opera *Robert le Diable.* A year later, Taglioni created a sensation when she appeared in the new diaphanous, bell-like dancing skirt (the prototype of the tutu) at the Paris Opéra, performing what would be her most famous role—*La Sylphide.* This role marked the final departure of ballet from the more sedate Baroque style of the eighteenth century and was created for Taglioni by her father. Her delicacy, spirituality, and poetic grace won the praise and admiration of many famous people, including the writers William Makepeace Thackeray and Victor Hugo and the composer Hector Berlioz.

Adopting the new stiffened ballet shoe, Taglioni was one of the first ballerinas to dance on the tips of her toes. She did so with a skill and grace that took this new balletic form beyond the mere technical and athletic to new levels of lyrical interpretation and artistic brilliance. Her performances were, for audiences of the day, quite transfixing. Victoria found her positively magical, marveling at how she "flew in the air" (Warner 1979, 51). Watching Taglioni dance the role of *La Sylphide* in 1834, Victoria felt herself drawn into a fantasy world: "When she bounds and skips along the stage, it is quite beautiful. Quite like a fawn. And she has grace in every action. The motion of her arms and beautiful hands are so graceful, and she has such a sweet expres-

Contrary to popular belief, the queen was far from being a killjoy. She greatly enjoyed dancing—well into old age—and is seen here dancing "The Waltz in Two Time" with Prince Albert. (Stapleton Collection/CORBIS)

sion in her face" (51). So captivated was Victoria by Taglioni that she copied her costume in another ballet, *La Naiade,* and dressed herself up in it. When presented with a new horse, she named it Taglioni in honor of the dancer. She would attend Taglioni's performances over and over again until the dancer retired in 1847, her swansong being the famous *Pas de Déesses* from the French choreographer Jules Perrot's *Le Jugement de Pâris.*

By the mid-century, ballet was all the rage in London—at Her Majesty's Theatre and at Drury Lane. Taglioni returned to Europe and for a while gave dance lessons in Paris, as well as instituting new ballet examinations at the Paris Opéra. But she was forced to flee Paris during the Franco-Prussian War of 1870–1871. She arrived in London having lost all her possessions and for a while taught dance and deportment to the daughters of the aristocracy, before returning to Europe, dying in poverty in Marseilles in 1884. Meanwhile, as Victoria grew up, the opportunity to herself take to the dance floor finally arrived. In May 1829, shortly after Victoria's tenth birthday, King William IV had given a juvenile ball to honor the state visit of the girl queen Dona Maria Da Gloria of Portugal. On this, her first public ball, Victoria had demonstrated confident dancing skills. She repeated them on her fourteenth birthday ball at St. James's Palace, taking considerable delight in a rare opportunity to expend her frequently repressed energies in the quadrille and the waltz, which had come into fashion after the end of the Napoleonic Wars. The state visit of Grand Duke Alexander of Russia in May 1839 provided another memorable evening's dancing for Victoria, when she found herself twirled round the ballroom by the grand duke in a mazurka, before taking delight in the quadrille, the valse, and the new German dance, the Grossvater. "We had such fun and laughter," she wrote in her journal. "I never enjoyed myself more. We were all so merry" (Esher 1914, 250).

Victoria carried on dancing after she was married and even after the babies started arriving. Despite her increasingly plump stature, she remained a dainty dancer and cleverly adapted the graceful glide of a ballerina in her own deportment. She and Prince Albert regularly enjoyed private, informal dances at their residences, in particular those staged in the Crimson Drawing-Room at Windsor, in which members of the court took part in the then-fashionable quadrilles and the queen's favorite country dances. More elaborate and ostentatious, formal balls were mounted by the royal couple at Buckingham Palace, notably three great costume balls: the Plantagenet Ball of 1842 (often referred to as the queen's *bal masqué* [masked ball]); the Georgian *bal poudré* (powdered ball) in 1845, at which the queen danced the minuet with considerable grace; and the Restoration Ball, with costumes of the period of Charles II, in 1851. The first of the three, in which Queen Victoria appeared as Queen Philippa, consort to Albert's Edward III, was the most notable and the most controversial. It was criticized for its extravagance at a time of social unrest—the Chartist riots—and economic depression. Such was the ball's success, however, that the queen and Prince Albert commissioned the construction of a new ballroom at Buckingham Palace—123 feet long and 60 feet wide—at a cost of £45,000. It would be one of the most splendid in England, with a dais for the queen's and prince's crimson thrones at one end and lit by a combination of newly invented gas lights disguised in ornate chandeliers as well as hundreds of candles. The first state ball was held here in May 1856, by which time the waltz had become extremely popular. As her children grew up, the queen also gave dances and fancy dress balls for them as birthday treats, the first being at the palace in 1854.

After 1861 and the death of Prince Albert, however, everything changed; the queen's happy smile and the frequent bursts of laughter that had punctuated her enjoyment of dancing at court became things of the past. During Victoria's widowhood, dance, like every other life-affirming celebration, became anathema at court. Yet paradoxically, one great love, inextricably linked to Scotland and the happy times she had spent at Balmoral with Prince Albert, lingered on. That was the queen's love of Scottish reels and jigs, danced to the sound of bagpipes at the annual gillies' balls at Balmoral, over which Victoria presided. This was an experience not always shared with pleasure by those ladies and gentlemen in waiting who were obliged not only to sit and shiver through such events (they were often held outside in large marquees, no matter what the weather) but also to endure the spectacle of "sweating and whiskified Highland couples in flapping tartans tumbl[ing] on top of one another on the dance floor"(Tisdall 1961, 109). Such was the aging queen's enthusiasm for Scottish dancing that she had a new ballroom constructed at Balmoral.

When she was in her seventies, and particularly after the celebrations for the Golden and Diamond Jubilees had finally revived royal receptions and drawing rooms, the queen once more began taking to the dance floor, a fact that never failed to bemuse her royal household—and to annoy her children, who were also forced to take part. When she danced, she was transformed; her energies seemed undiminished, even in old age. She could still dance the quadrille with grace, and her private secretary, Henry Ponsonby, recorded in 1891 at Windsor that the queen executed "light airy steps in the old courtly fashion; no limp or stick but every figure carefully and prettily danced" (Hardy 1976, 159).

Related entries:
Opera; Theater; "We Are Not Amused"

References and further reading:
Esher, Viscount, ed. 1912. *The Girlhood of Queen Victoria: A Selection from Her Majesty's Diaries between the Years of 1832 and 1840.* 2 vols. London: John Murray.
———. 1914. *The Training of a Sovereign.* London: John Murray.
Hardy, Alan. 1976. *Queen Victoria Was Amused.* London: John Murray.
[One of Her Majesty's Servants]. 1901. *The Private Life of Queen Victoria.* London: C. Arthur Pearson.
Plowden, Alison. 1981. *Young Victoria.* Weidenfeld and Nicolson.
Rowell, George. 1978. *Queen Victoria Goes to the Theatre.* London: Paul Elek.
Tisdall, E. E. P. 1961. *Queen Victoria's Private Life.* London: Jarrolds.
Vallone, Lynne. 2001. *Becoming Victoria.* New Haven: Yale University Press.
Warner, Marina. 1979. *Queen Victoria's Sketchbook.* London: Macmillan.
Woodham-Smith, Cecil. 1972. *Queen Victoria: Her Life and Times. Vol. 1: 1819–1861.* London: Hamish Hamilton.

Davidson, Randall Thomas, Dean of Windsor (1848–1930)

(from 1903, Archbishop of Canterbury)

I feel that Mr Davidson is a man who may be of great use to me (Cullen 1969, 220)

As a young girl, Queen Victoria developed a pathological aversion to clergymen, especially bishops, claiming that she "had a great horror" of them "on account of their wigs and aprons" (Hibbert 1964, 9). It was not just the ceremonial robes that she found disconcerting; the queen was of the opinion, from her own experience, that when churchmen were promoted they often lost their sense of humility and became infuriatingly pompous. But she made an exception in the case of her religious adviser, Randall Davidson. In later years, when she promoted him to a bishopric, Victoria insisted that "I like the man but *not* the Bishop" (Marie Louise 1961, 116).

Randall Davidson joined the queen's service when he was appointed dean of Windsor in 1883. An intelligent and straight-talking churchman, he inspired confidence not just in the queen but, as his reputation grew, in the Anglican religious community at large. With his warm, unaffected, and outgoing personality, he suffered from none of the characteristic sanctimoniousness of many senior Victorian churchmen. He became highly influential at court and along with the queen's private secretary, Sir Henry Ponsonby, would be a close friend and wise counselor to the queen into her old age.

Davidson was born in Edinburgh in 1848, the son of a merchant. He grew up at Muirhouse and attended Harrow school in Middlesex. His studies in law and modern history at Trinity College, Oxford, (1867–1871) were marred by ill health, and he spent the next three years in foreign travel and in training for the priesthood. He was ordained in 1875 and served the community at Dartford, Kent, as curate until 1877. A year after becoming resident chaplain to Archibald Tait, archbishop of Canterbury, Davidson married one of the archbishop's daughters.

Davidson first met Queen Victoria in December 1882, when, after Tait's death, he was called to Windsor to discuss his successor with her. They struck up an immediate rapport, the queen recording in her journal that she "was seldom more struck than I have been by his personality" (Cullen 1969, 220). She urged her prime minister, William Gladstone, to appoint Davidson dean of Windsor in June 1883, in order that Davidson might serve as her personal chaplain whenever she was at Windsor. As ecclesiastical appointments went, he was relatively young for such a post—being only thirty-five years old. The queen enjoyed Davidson's sermons at St. George's Chapel, Windsor, and soon began seeking his opinion on all major appointments in the Church of England. What she liked in Davidson and what made their relationship such a successful one was that he seemed always so accommodating to her wishes and opinions.

To be consulted by the queen on a wide range of issues was a considerable honor for Davidson. But, as the queen's personal chaplain, it also brought him into painfully close contact with her perpetual state of grieving, not just for Prince Albert but also now for John Brown (who died in March 1883), closely followed by the premature death of her hemophiliac son Leopold in 1884. The death of Brown brought Davidson to the point of conflict with the queen and threatened to ruin his promising career. For he took a very strong stand against Victoria's determination to publish a memoir of John Brown and extracts from his diaries. Both manuscripts testified to her devotion to him with such candor that the royal household were horrified at the scandal publication might provoke. Davidson knew only too well that there was no truth in the scurrilous rumors abounding about the queen's relationship with Brown but believed that her tender and loving remarks about Brown could very easily be misconstrued. With Ponsonby, he was aghast, thinking that the queen's interests would be ill served by publication and tried to persuade her against it. Victoria was infuriated by such interference, responding to Davidson's remarks with a stony silence that lasted for two weeks. But having thought things over, she eventually conceded that Davidson was quite right in his objections. The queen's dignified capitulation over the issue was in Davidson's view a testament to her inherently "sound common sense judgement." "My belief," he later wrote, "is that she liked and trusted best those who occasionally incurred her wrath provided that she had reason to think their motives good" (Bell 1952, 95).

Despite being most reluctant to lose his good offices, in 1890 Queen Victoria suggested that Davidson be appointed to the vacant see of Rochester. Unfortunately, Davidson became seriously ill soon after taking up the appointment and had to resign. In 1895 he returned to duty as bishop of Winchester. The appointment once again brought him into regular contact with the queen when she was at Osborne, which was within his diocese, with Davidson regularly crossing the Solent to make private visits at the queen's invitation.

When the archbishopric of Canterbury fell vacant in 1896, the queen seriously considered Davidson's appointment to this, the highest ecclesiastical position in the land. However, the conservative powers that be in the church deemed such an elevation inappropriate for a man of only forty-eight. Davidson devoted himself, instead, to work in his local diocese at Winchester, as well as taking a leading role in social reform campaigns to control the sale of alcohol and extend elementary education. On 19 January 1901, he was called to Osborne for the last time, to be at the dying queen's bedside. His ministrations during the final days of her life and his role in her laying-out and funeral have recently been well described in Tony Rennell's *Last Days of Glory* (2000). After the queen's death, Davidson once again took a hand in protecting the queen's reputation, this time by ensuring the suppression of all references in her letters and journals to her interest in spiritualism and table rapping that might have discredited her as head of the Church of England.

On 12 February 1903, Davidson was finally promoted to archbishop of Canterbury, during his tenure working toward the greater unity of the Church of England and the revision of ritual in church worship and, with it, the *Book of Common Prayer.* He frequently spoke out against religious persecution—such as of Christians in Macedonia and the Jews in tsarist Russia. After 1909, with the growing threat of war between England and Germany, he advocated reconciliation and did much to try to promote Anglo-German friendship. During World War I, he remained an influential moderate, decrying the excessive jingoism in Britain, urging clergymen everywhere to remind all the belligerent nations of the importance of mercy and compassion, and in 1916 initiating a National Mission of Repentance and Hope. He criticized what he perceived as the use of inhumane methods of warfare—such as poison gas and aerial bombardments of civilian targets—and supported the rights of prisoners of war and those foreign aliens who had been interned in Britain.

In his final years, Davidson oversaw the passing of the Church of England Assembly (Powers) Act of 1919 and promoted the rapprochement of the Church of England with the nonconformist, Orthodox, and Catholic churches—all in his objective of achieving greater Christian unity and understanding worldwide. One of his last campaigns was to support calls by the League of Nations, in 1922, for the new Soviet government in Russia to put an end to the persecution of those who wished to continue practicing their religion.

Davidson resigned as archbishop of Canterbury in 1928—having been the longest-serving one since the early sixteenth century—taking the title Baron Davidson of Lambeth. He cowrote a two-volume *Life of Archbishop Tait* with W. Benham (1891) and, among other writings, published *The Character and Call of the Church of England* (1912).

Related entries:

Brown, John; *Leaves from the Journal of Our Life in the Highlands;* The Paranormal; Ponsonby, General Sir Henry; Religion

References and further reading:

Bell, G. K. A. 1952. *Randall Davidson, Archbishop of Canterbury.* 3d ed. Oxford: Oxford University Press.

Cullen, Tom. 1969. *The Empress Brown: The Story of a Royal Friendship.* London: Bodley Head (chap. 13).

Hibbert, Christopher. 1964. *The Court at Windsor: A Domestic History.* London: Longman.

Marie Louise, Princess. 1961. *My Memories of Six Reigns.* Harmondsworth, UK: Penguin.

Reid, Michaela. 1996. *Ask Sir James: The Life of Sir James Reid, Personal Physician to Queen Victoria.* London: Eland.

Rennell, Tony. 2000. *Last Days of Glory: The Death of Queen Victoria.* London: Viking.

Derby, Edward Geoffrey Stanley, Fourteenth Earl of (1799–1869)

the most difficult and unsatisfactory minister she or indeed anyone had to deal with (letter to Lord Granville, 30 August 1880)

The fourteenth earl of Derby was for twenty years a leading Conservative politician, although his three terms as prime minister were all short-lived. He was a man born into wealth and privilege; but despite being credited by Disraeli as being the man who "abolished slavery, . . . educated Ireland . . . [and] reformed parliament" (Eccleshall and Walker 1998, 161) he was, by nature, prone to indolence. A man of fashion, he disliked the treadmill of ministerial work and was most at home at the race track or at his country house, among the rural hunting, shooting, and fishing fraternity. To his credit, he was a benevolent landowner and supported much philanthropic work among the cottagers on his own estates, as well as being a patron of the Lancashire Relief Association. During his political career Derby became renowned as an accomplished parliamentary debater, in the eighteenth-century "silver style" of oratory. Such skills, however, cut no ice with Queen Victoria, who found him, as prime minister (in 1852, 1858–1859, 1866–1868), indecisive and unsatisfactory.

Born at the family seat, Knowsley Hall in Lancashire, Derby was educated at Eton and at Christ Church, Oxford. In 1852 he succeeded the duke of Wellington as chancellor of the University of Oxford. A right-wing member of the Whig Party, he entered Parliament in 1822, representing his father's constituency at Stockbridge and in 1832 moved to a seat in Preston, North Lancashire. As a supporter of the Catholic Emancipation Bill of 1829, he accepted the post of chief secretary for Ireland, 1830–1833, under the Whig prime minister, Lord Grey. During that time he introduced the 1831 Irish Education Act, which set up a national education board to improve literacy standards in the country, and the Church Temporalities Bill in 1833, which reorganized the resources of the church in Ireland. Derby also gave some notable speeches in Parliament in support of electoral changes under the Reform Bill of 1832. He would later recognize the need for further electoral reform, no doubt born of his sympathies for the underprivileged in his own home county of Lancashire. In 1833 he took the post of secretary for war and the colonies and was instrumental in the passing of legislation that finally emancipated Britain's slaves in the West Indies, but in August that year Derby left the Whig Party and became an independent.

Derby finally aligned himself with the Tory leader, Sir Robert Peel, under whom he again entered government, taking the post of secretary for war and the colonies, 1841–1845. As a specialist on Ireland, he continued to defend the government's Irish policy in the House of Commons, until elevated to the House of Lords in 1844 as Lord Bickerstaffe. But he had by now come into open conflict with Peel over the issue of free trade, which Derby opposed, and resigned when Peel insisted on the total repeal of the Corn Laws. A year later, when Peel fell from power over this issue, Derby declined the offer of forming a government and continued to lead the protectionists within the House of Lords throughout the 1850s and 1860s, during which period he frequently demonstrated his oratorical skills, leading to his famous nickname, coined by Earl Lytton, as the "Prince Rupert of Debate."

After the resignation of prime minister Lord John Russell in 1851, Derby, now having succeeded to the earldom, tried and failed to form a ministry at the queen's request. Another attempt followed in February 1852, but Derby's brief minority government lasted only until December 1852. During the Crimean War of 1854–1856, after a vote of no confidence was called on Lord Aberdeen's government, Derby was again invited by the queen to form a government but declined, arguing that the whole country "cried out for Lord Palmerston as the only man fit for carrying on the war with success" (Hibbert 2000, 128). Now suffering bouts of ill health, he withdrew to the more restful environment of his country estate and was most reluctant to reenter government, when he was once more summoned by the queen in 1858. He formed a ministry with the support of rising Conservative star Benjamin Disraeli, but a year later once more made way for another Palmerston ministry and attempted thereafter to work with him against the radical faction in Parliament.

Derby's final term as prime minister came during 1866–1868, at a time when, despite their differences of opinion, the queen was obliged to accept him as being the only person capable of forming a government. Together with Disraeli, in January 1867 Derby exerted pressure on the reclusive Victoria to defuse the growing discontent at her withdrawal from public life by attending the state opening of Parliament, an occasion she had shunned since Albert's death in 1861. The queen was finally persuaded, but not without going to great lengths, and in the most self-pitying of tones, to make clear the distress and the inconvenience of it all. The exertion would, she declared, be too much for someone in her precarious state of health; it would cause "a shock to her nerves" (Hibbert 1984, 197). Derby's final significant political achievement in office was, at Disraeli's urging, the passing of the Second Reform Bill in 1867, intended to defuse a renewal of political unrest over the franchise that extended the property qualification in Britain's boroughs to all tax-paying householders, as well as to certain categories of lodgers and occupiers. The legislation created another 938,000 new voters, thereby doubling the electorate. The queen was unimpressed, having no time for "that stupid Reform agitation" (Hibbert 2000, 197); she remained convinced that any increase in the democratic power of the masses was extremely dangerous.

Throughout 1867 Derby was increasingly incapacitated by attacks of gout and frequently took to his bed, his regular meetings with the queen conducted, in his place, by Disraeli. In 1868 Derby retired, having succeeded, with Disraeli's help, in revitalizing the Conservative Party and paving the way for Disraeli's spectacular rise as party leader. Derby's son, Edward Henry, who would succeed him as the fifteenth earl, also entered Parliament, serving under his father as secretary for India (1858–1859) and foreign secretary (1866–1868).

Related entries:
Chartism; Crimean War; Disraeli, Benjamin

References and further reading:

Cecil, Algernon. 1953. *Queen Victoria and Her Prime Ministers.* London: Eyre and Spottiswoode.

Eccleshall, Robert, and Graham Walker. 1998. *Biographical Dictionary of British Prime Ministers.* London: Routledge.

Hibbert, Christopher. 1984. *Queen Victoria in Her Letters and Journals.* London: Viking.

———. 2000. *Queen Victoria, a Personal History.* London: HarperCollins.

Jones, Wilbur D. 1956. *Lord Derby and Victorian Conservatism.* Oxford: Blackwell.

Smith, F. 1966. *The Making of the Second Reform Bill.* Cambridge: Cambridge University Press.

Stewart, R. 1971. *The Politics of Protection: Lord Derby and the Protectionist Party, 1841–52.* Cambridge: Cambridge University Press.

Vincent, J. R., ed. 1978. *Disraeli, Derby and the Conservative Party: Journals of Lord Stanley, 1849–1869.* New York: Barnes and Noble.

Diamond Jubilee, 1897

A never-to-be-forgotten day (Nevill 1997, 173)

On 23 September 1896 the queen recorded in her journal that she had

This splendid photograph of the queen, taken for her Diamond Jubilee in 1897, perfectly conveys her iconic power and dignity as monarch of a vast empire. (Hulton-Deutsch Collection/CORBIS)

now reigned longer by a day than any previous English monarch. The culmination of her sixty years on the throne was a testament not just to her own resilience, but also to that of the empire and an affirmation of the self-confidence of the British nation. The 1897 celebrations of the queen's longevity as monarch were slightly less protracted than those for her Golden Jubilee in 1887, on account of the queen's increasing age and frailty. But they were spectacularly successful, if rather more ridden with jingoism and bombast than the previous celebrations, the organizers having learned many lessons in stage management from the Golden Jubilee ten years earlier.

Arriving at Windsor from Balmoral, on 16 June, to prepare for the celebrations, Queen Victoria was apprehensive of the toll on her physical strength that long days of receptions might take. She had instructed the government that the celebrations should be restricted to the one day—22 June. Nor were they to be, as in 1887, dominated by a family gathering of the crowned heads of Europe. This time, pride of place would go not to royalty, but to the heads of government of the queen's wider family—the dominions and colonies of the British Empire.

On Sunday, 20 June, the actual anniversary of her accession, Victoria gave thanks in a private family service held in St. George's Chapel, Windsor. Across the country similar commemorative services were conducted. For the queen the day ended on a somber note, with a visit to the Royal Mausoleum and prayers at Prince Albert's sarcophagus. The following morning, she traveled to London by train, receiving members of her family, from her wheelchair, in the Bow Room at Buckingham Palace in the afternoon and entertaining 100 of her most important guests at a magnificent dinner that evening, afterward receiving the premiers of her colonies and their wives, including many of the contingent from India.

Before embarking on the state procession across London on Monday, 21 June, the queen had enlisted the wonders of scientific invention. On the press of a button, linked to London's Central Telegraph Office, she had sent an electric impulse that had telegraphed her thanks to her "beloved people" across the empire, in so doing originating the royal tradition of an annual message to the nation and Commonwealth (which now is broadcast by Queen Elizabeth II on Christmas Day). After a hazy start, the sun shone down on Jubilee Day, enhancing the colorful street decorations that festooned London for the occasion—and upon which a quarter of a million pounds had been spent. The queen made some concessions to her perpetual state of mourning—wearing a dress of black silk with panels of grey satin and black net embroidered in silver, a chiffon cape, and a bonnet trimmed with white flowers, feathers, and lace.

At a quarter past eleven she embarked on an even more exhausting royal progression than that of 1887—a three-hour, six-mile-long drive in an open state landau drawn by six perfectly matched cream horses, the most important streets on the route having been closed off for four nights prior to the procession. The cavalcade that accompanied her contained few European royals, barring her own children and grandchildren. In fact, the only reigning monarch whom the queen allowed was her cousin, Leopold II, king of the Belgians. She had been adamant that, in particular, her pushy grandson, Kaiser William II, should not be allowed to attend. In 1887 the kaiser's father, Crown Prince Frederick, had been the star of the show, but this time the color and ostentation of the parade came from more exotic climes—with the resplendent Indian maharajahs and princes who attended boasting fine gemstones, silks, and feathers and bringing with them magnificent gifts, many of which can be seen in the Durbar Room at Osborne House.

At the head of the march past of 46,000 men—a "living gazetteer of the British Empire" (Judd 2001, 18)—was Field Marshal Lord Roberts, V.C. Every British colony had sent a detachment of troops, which included representatives of the most diverse creeds and cultures: "broad-chested lancers from New South Wales, *zaptiehs* from Cyprus in red fezes, militiamen from Malta, hussars and dragoons from Canada and artillerymen from Trinidad . . . *dyak* policemen from Borneo . . . Ceylonese light infantrymen, baggy-trousered carabiniers in Khaki from Natal and Cape Colony, frontier policemen from Sierra Leone and a Chinese detachment from Hong Kong and the Straits Settlements, who wore large, conical coolie hats" (Roberts 1999, 1). Of all these, according to historian Andrew Roberts, "the most admired . . . were the Indian cavalry regiments, in particular the Bengal Lancers" (1). The queen herself was greatly enamored with the handsome Indian Cavalry Corps, who boasted splendid beards and turbans and who formed her Guard of Honour during the Jubilee celebrations.

When Victoria drove out of the palace gates and proceeded down Constitution Hill, she was greeted by the sound of gun salutes in Hyde Park. As the procession crossed London, the cheers and shouts from the crowds, many of whom burst into the national anthem, "God Save the Queen," as she passed, became ever louder and more tumultuous. As many as 3 million people had come into London to line the streets, with large numbers sleeping overnight in London's parks to ensure a good place from which to watch the procession. Arriving in the City of London, the queen's carriage drew up along the steps of St. Paul's Cathedral, where an assembly of diplomats, members of the cabinet, senior clergyman, and military bands had gathered to pay homage. The queen remained in her carriage, her rheumatism, she now asserted, making her unable to mount the steep flight of steps into the cathedral. As the service proceeded, she sat in her carriage holding up a black lace parasol to keep away the now hot sunshine. The 500-strong choir sang a "Te Deum" and the anthem "We Praise Thee, O God," but it was the plaintive rendition of the hymn "The Old Hundredth," which brought tears to the queen's eyes.

The short service over, the queen drove off from St. Paul's to deafening cheers, on through the City of London and across London Bridge into the poorer area of Southwark, where more crowds awaited her. The queen was visibly moved, and often in tears, for the adulation that greeted her was unprecedented. It was an experience that she found gratifying, overwhelming, and exhausting. After resting during the afternoon, she entertained her guests at a grand dinner at Buckingham Palace and afterward received the congratulations of a long line of guests in the ballroom. When she retired to her bed at eleven, the cheering and singing of the crowds in nearby Hyde Park could still be heard, and beacons were once again blazing across the land, as they had in 1887.

On 15 July queen sent out a message of thanks to the nation, from Windsor. Although much had already been said, she felt that she could not "rest satisfied without personally giving utterance" to her deepest gratitude for "the spontaneous universal outburst of loyal attachment and real affection which I have experienced" (Lorne 1901, 359). Yet, privately, in her diary she had recorded her own sense of solitude in the midst of all this adulation. For her dearest departed Albert was not there to share the day with her. Thus her Diamond, like her Golden Jubilee, was remembered with mixed sentiments: "In weal and in woe I have ever had the true sympathy of all my people" (360).

The Jubilee celebrations were not, however, without their detractors. William Gladstone had hoped that the queen might mark the occasion by finally abdicating in favor of her son-in-waiting, the Prince of Wales, who was approaching his fifty-sixth birthday. The socialist Keir Hardie, in an article in the *Labour Leader,* was scathing in his denigration of the "unwholesome parasites" who basked in "the smile of royalty." They were, in his view, victims of a "diseased organism"—the monarchy—which represented "the power of caste-class rule" and of which he longed to see the end (Chapman and Raban 1977, n.p.). The Irish republican James Connolly also condemned the Diamond Jubilee—as "a Feast of Flunkeyism"—and vented his rage on the "courtly mummers who grovel at the shrine of royalty." Irish republicans, he averred, had "more respect and honour for the raggedest child of the poorest labourer in Ireland" than they did for any "of the long array of murderers, adulterers and madmen who have sat upon the throne of England" (Randall 2001).

During those years on the throne the queen had seen enormous social and historical changes—"in France, a King, an Emperor, and half a dozen Republican Presidents in succession . . . the rise of an Empire in Germany; assassination of Royal personages; the coming and passing of nearly a score of Presidents of the United States" (Perugini 1932, 279). She had followed with anxiety the sufferings of her troops in conflicts in the Crimea, Africa, Afghanistan, India, China, and Egypt, with the Boer War yet to come. She had also lived through an era of intense innovation and invention. Her reign had witnessed the advent of the electric light, the cable telegraph, the safety bicycle, motor car, electric trams, steam turbines, and the ironclad steamship. By the time Victoria died in 1901, refrigeration, the telephone, synthetic fibers and artificial dyes, the vacuum flask, and the pneumatic tire had also come into use. Ordinary people were enjoying the advent of moving pictures, and—in health care—benefiting from the adoption of vaccination techniques, the use of chloroform, and antiseptic surgery. In the year of Victoria's death, Hubert Cecil Booth would invent that most essential of modern domestic appliances—the vacuum cleaner.

One of those to record positive memories of the Diamond Jubilee was the American author Mark Twain, who observed that the splendid march past on Jubilee Day had been representative of "sixty years of progress and accumulation, moral, material, and political," with the queen "a symbol, an allegory of England's grandeur and the might of the British name" (Harlow and Carter 1999, 400). She had also revealed herself to the nation on a far more prosaic level—in all her frail humanity. In the midst of so much pageantry and so many encomiums of praise, the head of this vast empire was, in truth, just a little, old, gray-haired grandmother in a bonnet.

Related entries:
Empress of India; Golden Jubilee; Osborne; Salisbury, Robert Arthur Talbot Gascoigne-Cecil, Third Marquis of; "The Widow at Windsor"

References and further reading:

Chapman, Caroline, and Paul Raban. 1977. *Debrett's Queen Victoria's Jubilees.* London: Debrett.

Harlow, Barbara, and Mia Carter, eds. 1999. *Imperialism and Orientalism: A Documentary Sourcebook.* Oxford: Blackwell.

Hibbert, Christopher. 1984. *Queen Victoria in Her Letters and Journals.* London: Viking.

Judd, Denis. 2001. "Gilding of the Empire State." *BBC HistoryMagazine* (January): 18–21.

Lant, J. I. 1980. *Insubstantial Pageant: Ceremony and Confusion at Queen Victoria's Court.* New York: Taplinger.

Lorne, Marquis of. 1901. *VIR: Her Life and Empire.* London: Eyre and Spottiswood.

Mackenzie, J. M. 1984. *Propaganda and Empire: The Manipulation of British Public Opinion, 1880–1961.* Manchester, UK: Manchester University Press.

Nevill, Barry St. John. 1997. *Life at the Court of Queen Victoria, with Selections from the Journals of Queen Victoria.* Stroud, Gloucestershire: Sutton.

Perugini, Mark Edward. 1932. *Victorian Days and Ways.* London: Jarrolds.

Randall, David. 2001. "Off with Her Head." *Independent on Sunday,* 29 July.

Roberts, Andrew. 1999. *Salisbury: Victorian Titan.* London: Weidenfeld and Nicolson.

Walton, Peter. 2000. *A Celebration of Empire: A Centenary Souvenir of the Diamond Jubilee of Queen Victoria 1837–1937.* Staplehurst, Kent: Spellmount Publishers.

Dickens, Charles (1812–1870)

a large, loving mind (Buckle 1926–1928, 2, 21)

The two people who, in the popular consciousness, most clearly define the spirit of nineteenth-century Britain are probably Queen Victoria and the novelist Charles Dickens. As a young woman the queen had admired Dickens's *Oliver Twist* as being "excessively interesting" (Hardy 1976, 26) and spent many years trying and failing to secure a meeting with him. It was, as Gail Turley Houston has observed, a case of the distinguished male writer giving his female sovereign the runaround. For the self-regarding Dickens, if the truth be told, viewed *himself* as the celebrity and the queen as "merely a provincial devotee" (Houston 1999, 91). He made her wait twenty-two years for the pleasure of his company, and it was not until March 1870 that they finally had their first and only private meeting, shortly before Dickens died, at the age of only fifty-eight.

A popular etching, taken from the* Illustrated London News, *of the great writer and social critic Charles Dickens; he and the queen met for the first and only time a few months before his death in 1870. (The* Illustrated London News *Picture Library)

Charles Dickens was not alone in his tongue-in-cheek rapture for the pretty young queen who came to the throne in June 1837; after four generations of dissolute or eccentric Hanoverian Georges, the whole country now invested great hope in its untainted female monarch. At the time of Victoria's accession Dickens too was on the ascendant. Having developed his craft, first as a reporter at London's Inns of Court and Houses of Parliament and then through journalistic sketches under the pseudonym of Boz in the *Morning Chronicle,* he was now hugely popular. The success of his first, comic novel, the *Pickwick Papers* (published in twenty parts, April 1836–November 1837), had been closely followed by *Oliver Twist,* the novel that would establish him as the leading literary voice of Victorian Britain. The novel had begun serialization in *Bentley's Miscellany* in February 1837, but Dickens's avid readers would not know the ultimate fates of Oliver, Fagin, and Nancy until its completion fifteen months later (April 1839), after which it was published in book form.

Like her public, the queen read *Oliver Twist* during its original serialization, despite her mother's disapproval of her reading novels. In the new year of 1839, she expressed her admiration for it in conversation with her prime minister, Lord Melbourne. Melbourne, not noted for his social conscience, had responded to her enthusiasm, however, by dismissing the novel's grim realities. Under its full title, *Oliver Twist, or, the Parish Boy's Progress,* the novel had exposed the workings of the Poor Laws, passed in 1834, which had abolished outdoor relief and condemned the destitute to a life in grim institutions, picking oakum or breaking stones. In Melbourne's view, this made for decidedly unappealing reading: "It's all among Workhouses, and Coffin Makers, and Pickpockets. . . . I don't like that low debasing style" (House and Storey 1965, 27). He could not be won over, but the queen's admiration remained undimmed. Meanwhile, in 1840 at the time of the queen's marriage to Prince Albert, Dickens observed the mounting sense of public excitement at the forthcoming event and how "society is unhinged by her majesty's marriage" (23). He visited Windsor Castle and the queen's apartments there, the scene of her imminent connubial bliss, and admitted to his friend T. J. Thompson that "I have fallen hopelessly in love with the Queen" (23).

As well as being a writer, Dickens was a keen thespian and became involved in several amateur productions, both as actor and director. In 1848 the queen saw him in a charity performance of Ben Jonson's 1598 comedy *Every Man in His Humour* at the Theatre Royal, Haymarket. Three years later he acted in and directed a production by nonprofessional actors of Edward Bulwer-Lytton's now forgotten *Not So Bad As We Seem*. He had intended giving a private performance to the queen, but the death of his father and baby daughter had caused him to postpone the plans to later date. The queen commended Dickens's acting in her journal. Six years later Dickens would again prove himself to be a compelling actor in a production of *The Frozen Deep,* a three-act melodrama based on the tragic Northern Arctic Expedition of Sir John Franklin of 1845, by his friend, the novelist Wilkie Collins. It was performed at Dickens's own small theater at his London home, Tavistock House. In order to add authenticity to the role he specially grew a beard (and retained it ever after); his high-octane death scene reduced audiences to tears.

Hearing of this, the queen intimated that she would like a private performance of the play at Windsor, but Dickens felt this would be socially awkward, because his three daughters who were in the cast had not yet been officially presented at court. Eventually, accompanied by Prince Albert and her uncle King Leopold, Queen Victoria enjoyed a private performance of the play on 4 July 1857 at the Gallery of Illustration in Regent Street. Afterward, she sent a message backstage asking to meet Dickens but, drained by the intensity of the performance, he firmly declined, not wishing to appear in front of his sovereign "tired and hot, with the paint still upon my face" (Ackroyd 1990, 785) as he later explained. Notwithstanding her disappointment, the queen recorded in her journal that Dickens's performance had been "beyond all praise and not to be surpassed" (Rowell 1978, 73). He would remain one of the few people to have the temerity to refuse the royal command.

The success of Dickens's performance in *The Frozen Deep* prompted him in the late 1850s to embark on a spectacular twelve-year career with his one-man shows of readings from his own works; the demand took him all over the country and to America and back. It made him huge amounts of money, but it also fatally sapped his energies. Before long, the queen was again requesting a private performance, particularly of Dickens's acclaimed party piece—*A Christmas Carol.* This time Dickens's excuse was that he felt he could not do the reading justice outside a proper theater. Indeed, so consumed had he become by his public readings that he expressed considerable annoyance when he was obliged to cancel them during public mourning over the death of Prince Albert, decrying the "jackasses that people are at present making of themselves" over this death (House and Storey 1998, 15–16). As the cult of the dead Albert showed no signs of abating, Dickens became increasingly cynical, in 1864 writing to his friend John Leech, "If you should meet with an inaccessible cave anywhere to which a hermit could retire from the memory of Prince Albert and testimonials to the same, pray let me know of it. We have nothing solitary and deep enough in this part of England" (425).

On 9 March 1870 the now moribund author (derided as "gushy" by Disraeli and "Mr. Sentiment" by Trollope) finally met his admiring queen, herself now portly and middle aged. After waiting so long to meet the great man, Queen Victoria had even made the concession of traveling into London to receive him at Buckingham Palace when she was informed that he was not well enough to make the journey to Windsor. Protocol demanded, however, that Dickens should remain standing through an audience that would last for one and a half hours. In deference to the respect in which she held the author, the queen did not sit either. Their conversation ranged from the prosaic (the price of meat at the butcher's) to matters of national importance (U.S. support for the Fenians). With Dickens now looked upon as the social conscience of the nation, they touched also upon the class system, as well as, no doubt, the sufferings of the lower orders. Dickens was of the optimistic opinion, as the queen later observed, that in time the divisions between rich and poor would be eroded.

At the end of the audience the queen presented Dickens with a copy of her own *Leaves from the Journal of Our Life in the Highlands,* in which she had inscribed "From the humblest of writers to one of the greatest" (Hardy 1976, 97), requesting in turn a set of his works. According to Peter Ackroyd it was rumored at the time that the queen had also offered Dickens a knighthood. Once again he had turned her down. Three months later, exhausted by overwork, Dickens died at his home in Rochester, Kent.

Related entries:
Class; *Leaves from the Journal of Our Life in the Highlands;* Melbourne, William Lamb, Second Viscount

References and further reading:

Ackroyd, Peter. 1990. *Dickens.* London: Sinclair Stevenson.

Buckle, G. E., ed. 1926–1928. *The Letters of Queen Victoria: A Selection from Her Majesty's Correspondence and Journal between the Years 1862 and 1885.* 2d ser., 3 vols. London: John Murray.

Hardy, Alan. 1976. *Queen Victoria Was Amused.* London: John Murray.

House, Madelien, and Graham Storey. 1965. *The Letters of Charles Dickens.* Pilgrim Edition, vol. 2. Oxford: Clarendon Press.

———. 1998. *The Letters of Charles Dickens.* Pilgrim Edition, vol. 10. Oxford: Clarendon Press.

Houston, Gail Turley. 1999. *Royalties: The Queen and Victorian Writers.* Charlotesville: University Press ofViriginia.

Longford, Elizabeth. [1964] 1998. *Victoria R.I.* London: Weidenfeld and Nicolson.

———. 1966. "Queen Elizabeth's Doctors." In Martin Gilbert, ed., *A Century of Conflict 1850–1950.* London: Hamish Hamilton.

Pope-Hennessy, Una. 1945. *Charles Dickens, 1812–1870.* London: Chatto and Windus.

Rowell, George. 1978. *Queen Victoria Goes to the Theatre.* London: Paul Elek.

Sutherland, John. 1988. *The Longman Companion to Victorian Fiction.* London: Longman.

Tucker, Herbert F., ed. 1999. *A Companion to Victorian Literature and Culture.* Oxford: Blackwell.

Disraeli, Benjamin (1804–1881)

(from 1876, Lord Beaconsfield)

He is full of poetry, romance and chivalry (Fulford 1971, 176)

One of Britain's most flamboyant and controversial Conservative politicians, Benjamin Disraeli was a fascinating and seductive figure. As a master of self-promotion and hyperbole, he did not easily win the admiration of other men, but he won the lifelong devotion of many women. He undoubtedly had a way with them—but more particularly, he had a unique way with his queen, Victoria, knowing full well that, in her case, the personal touch was all important. The years of Disraeli's second ministry from 1874 to 1880 drew the queen out of her secluded widowhood and with it put an end to republican rumblings about her prolonged absence from public view. He did much to revive the queen's interest in government and with it her active support for a period of vigorous British imperial policy on which Disraeli set his unmistakable stamp. Yet the great majority of Disraeli's male

British prime minister Benjamin Disraeli earned the queen's undying love and admiration and was a huge comfort to her in her widowhood. (The* Illustrated London News *Picture Library)

contemporaries resolutely refused to take him seriously. It would eventually be the queen's great European adversary, Otto Bismarck, who at the Congress of Berlin in 1878 recognized Disraeli's unique skills and respectfully conceded of the wily diplomatist: "Der alte Jude, das ist der Mann" (The old Jew—there's a man; Longford 1998, 414).

Much of the enduring hostility with which Disraeli had to contend, despite his supreme oratorical gifts and his wit, stemmed from the unrepentant anti-Semitism that was rife among the old aristocracy, who during Disraeli's early years in Parliament still dominated British politics. He would spend much of his life trying to reconcile his Jewishness with his Christian upbringing, trying and failing to convince those prejudiced against him that Judaism was complementary rather than in opposition to the Christian faith. But it was his preening manner above all that provoked male disapproval, if not jealousy, and made him the favorite subject of the caricaturists. There was simply just "too much tinsel" about Dizzy (Nevill 1910, 177), too much of the poser and dandy. Disraeli made no apologies for the artful flattery he employed in wheedling the patronage of the influential political hostesses of their day such as Lady Londonderry and Lady Jersey. The approval of such high society figures was essential in his battle, against the odds, to climb to the top of what he called "the greasy pole" of politics (Blake 1966, 487).

Benjamin Disraeli was born in London, the son of Jewish essayist and literary historian Isaac D'Israeli, whose Sephardic Jewish family had settled in Italy. Isaac had converted to Christianity after a quarrel with his synagogue and had had Benjamin baptized a Christian in 1817. Disraeli had no conventional schooling but was educated in the main by his father at home. Nor did he go to university, instead in 1821 joining a firm of lawyers in Lincoln's Inn as an articled clerk. Three restless years followed; having no appetite for a career in the law, Disraeli began to dabble in financial speculation in South American mines. In 1825 he attempted running a newspaper—the *Representative*—in a foolhardy attempt to compete against the *Times.* In the meantime he had developed literary aspirations and had begun writing novels. His first, *Vivian Grey,* was serialized anonymously during 1826–1827. Written largely in an attempt to pay off his mounting debts, it drew on Disraeli's experiences in the world of high finance, and was a considerable popular success.

But the proceeds from this and a string of fashionable romantic novels that Disraeli also polished off in quick succession did little to defray the chronic debts that he continued to accumulate. The stresses of his financial problems eventually led to nervous collapse and regular escapes abroad: in 1824, 1826, and 1830–1831, during which latter trip Disraeli visited Egypt and Palestine. Returning to Britain, he now made a concerted effort to take his place at the center of the fashionable, "silver fork" society of his day. With this in mind, he began courting social and political patrons among the old aristocracy, becoming renowned for his foppish dress and his eccentricity of speech and behavior.

When he first burst upon the London social scene in early 1830s London, Disraeli was an object of popular curiosity: the "Jew d'esprit," and a man of dubious sexual reputation. Pomaded and perfumed, he paraded himself like an exotic bird in the role of dandified writer and socialite, dressed in colors of every hue. His feminized appearance was accentuated by his long black ringlets and an over-the-top penchant for satin and velvet, lace ruffles, embroidered waistcoats, white gloves, and shoes with red rosettes (his style of dress became, mercifully, far more sober in later life). He tried and failed three times to secure a seat in Parliament as an independent, his "otherness"—accentuated by his sartorial style—probably doing little to encourage voters. Finally, in 1837 Disraeli was elected Tory member of Parliament for Maidstone in Kent. His orotund maiden speech was duly shouted down in the House of Commons on 7 December. But he was not discouraged; he knew, as he told the house then, that "the time will come when you will hear me" (Blake 1966, 149).

In 1839 Disraeli aroused considerable gossip when he married Mary Anne Wyndham Lewis, the wealthy widow of a friend and benefactor. She was twelve years older than he and brought with her the security, for Disraeli, of an income of £4,000 a year. The mercenary impulse behind this match has been much argued about, although there is no doubt about Disraeli's genuine devotion to his rather unprepossessing wife. But the marriage proved something of a setback, when Disraeli found that some of his high society friends, such as the Ladies Londonderry and Jersey, now cut him from their lists. He had committed the social faux pas of marrying a woman who was, in their view, most decidedly bourgeois. Nevertheless, in 1847, when Disraeli was elected member of Parliament for Buckinghamshire, Mary Anne's money bought them the all-important status symbol of Hughenden Manor near High Wycombe.

Disraeli was disappointed in not being nominated to the cabinet when Sir Robert Peel became prime minister in 1841. By now, his growing disaffection with the diehard Toryism of the early nineteenth century prompted him to join with three fellow members of Parliament in cultivating their own brand of Romantic Conservatism (Conservatism being the term that would replace Toryism). The "Young England" group, as it was known, voiced its opposition to Peel's policies on free trade and reform in Ireland, their ideals exemplified in Disraeli's 1844 novel *Coningsby, or the New Generation*. This was the first of a famous trilogy of social-political novels, continued with *Sybil, or the Two Nations* in 1845 and completed by *Tancred* in 1847. Although they were considerable popular successes, like all Disraeli's fiction, they never garnered a great deal of critical acclaim. With his political career now on the ascendant, Disraeli's novel writing lapsed until 1870.

In 1852 Disraeli finally obtained government office as chancellor of the Exchequer under Lord Derby. He was now well placed to concentrate his energies on restoring the moribund Tory Party's fortune, identifying it with an interest in democratic reform. It was a policy that sought to unite the classes under paternalistic Conservative rule, rather than widen the traditional divide between them. In defense of this ambition, Disraeli became one of the finest debaters in the House of Commons. With Disraeli now a minister, the queen was obliged to receive him, inviting him and Mary Anne to dinner in April 1852. Her first impression was somewhat guarded; Disraeli seemed to her "most singular" (Hibbert 1984, 90) with his strongly Semitic looks and his shiny black ringlets. She observed in her journal that he "had a very bland manner" and that his language was "very flowery" (90). She would reserve her judgment for some time; Disraeli, after all, had largely been responsible for hounding her beloved Sir Robert Peel out of office over free trade.

Early in 1858 Disraeli succeeded Lord George Bentinck as leader of the Conservative Party in the House of Commons, but it was not until after the death of Prince Albert, in December 1861, that the queen began to reappraise Disraeli, after he eulogized the late prince as a sovereign manqué (the queen having been thwarted in her desire to elevate him to king) and paid tribute to Albert's "rich cultivated mind" (Blake 1966, 431). He assured the queen, in a letter of condolence, that the prince was quite simply "the only man whom Mr. Disraeli has ever known who realised the Ideal" (ibid.). His silken words had their intended effect and rapidly secured for him a special relationship with Queen Victoria that would last until his death. In March 1863 Victoria deliberately passed over leading members of the aristocracy to grant seats (which were extremely limited) to Disraeli and his wife for the wedding of the Prince of Wales and Princess Alexandra of Denmark in St. George's Chapel at Windsor Castle.

In 1867 Disraeli's great political moment finally came when, during Lord Derby's minority government of 1866–1868, he conjured up all his debating skills to push through the Second Reform Bill extending the franchise in Britain. The impetus that he gave to this important piece of legislation sprang from his fundamental belief in the vote, not as a right, but as a privilege that should be earned through the exercise of responsible citizenship. He led the debate with unflagging energy, winning the support of Liberal rebels to carry the bill, although forced to concede some radical amendments by them that he had not anticipated. The electorate in Britain was now almost doubled, creating a whole new generation of voters among the urban classes. A year later, however, they promptly rewarded Disraeli's efforts by contributing to his downfall in the general election that returned the Liberals to power.

In February 1868 Disraeli replaced Lord Derby as prime minister but was to hold office only for ten months. Queen Victoria greeted him as premier, flattered by the protestations of devotion that he offered and still fascinated by Disraeli's strangeness. Of one thing at least she was sure: as a member of the middle classes and a Jew, he was to be commended; the premiership was, she said, "a proud thing for a man risen from the people to have attained" (Blake 1966, 487). At the end of February she wrote to her daughter Vicky, confident that "the present man will do well, and will be particularly loyal and anxious to please me in every way." But she had not quite fathomed him out: his manner still seemed to her "very peculiar" (490). Such "peculiarity" was more overtly identified with his Jewishness by those among the British establishment who would make no attempt to disguise their own anti-Semitism. Lady Palmerston was not alone in remarking that "we are all dreadfully disgusted at the prospect of having a Jew for our Prime Minister" (Aronson 1977, 104). Others, like Lord Clarendon, would be jealous of Disraeli's close relationship with the queen and share Clarendon's opinion that in Disraeli's dealings with her he acted entirely out of self-interest and not out of genuine feeling. Clarendon was of the cynical opinion that "keeping himself in power will be the sole motive and guide of his conduct. I see no reason however why his triumph should not be a lasting one for success is nowadays the only divinity adored" (Kennedy 1956, 245).

As things turned out, the queen did not have much longer to get to know Disraeli better, for in May 1868 the Conservative government lost the vote over Gladstone's resolution to disestablish the Irish Protestant Church. Disraeli offered to resign; the queen, loath to lose him, instead dissolved Parliament, hoping that the Tories could go to the country and be returned in a general election. If Disraeli acted out of self-interest, then the queen most certainly did so as well, on this and many subsequent occasions during their long relationship. Disraeli, after all, had shown "more consideration for my comfort than any of the preceding Prime Ministers since Sir Robert Peel and Lord Aberdeen" (Hibbert 1984, 206).

Disraeli lost the election. His term as prime minister would have made him eligible for a peerage, but he specifically requested a somewhat reluctant Victoria to elevate his wife to Viscountess Beaconsfield instead, the award of the title to Mary Anne being made to circumvent Disraeli's obligation, otherwise, to move up to the House of Lords. He chose to stay in the House of Commons, inaugurating a new political era that would be marked by his verbal sparring with his great parliamentary adversary William Gladstone, a man whom the queen vehemently disliked. Disraeli now launched himself into a concerted attack on the Liberal prime minister's radical views—particularly those regarding Ireland and British foreign policy. For six years he stayed relentlessly on the attack, even after the death of Mary Anne in 1872; the bereavement, if anything, brought him even closer to his grieving queen.

Disraeli was returned to power as prime minister in 1874. His relationship with the queen now entered a highly ritualistic phase, with Disraeli adopting the most burlesque tones in recasting himself as a court poet in the mold of Sir Edmund Spenser, to Victoria's Queen Elizabeth I. The allusion was sustained by his unabashed referral to her as "the Faery" (Spenser had dedicated his verse epic, *The Faerie Queen,* to Elizabeth I). The queen, captivated by Disraeli's attention, sent him bunches of spring flowers—primroses, snowdrops, violets—gathered by herself and her ladies at Osborne. Soon an edition of his collected novels was presented by Disraeli to the queen, who ventured to offer her own humble authorial efforts in return.

The key to Disraeli's successful relationship with the queen lay in his acceptance that she could not be coerced or dictated to. She could only be won over through charm, good manners, patience, and—most important of all—by being treated like a lady. Enlisting his literary skills, Disraeli rose effortlessly to the challenge: he swooned, he waxed poetic, he offered his devotion and the desire to "render the transaction of affairs as easy to your Majesty as possible" (Blake 1966, 491). He made a habit of kissing the queen's hand and of by-passing Court etiquette by sending highly personal, witty, and entertaining letters direct to the queen rather than through her private secretary. (In later years Sir Henry Ponsonby would complain that "she is always at him about something that we know nothing of" [Aronson 1977, 155]).

Victoria vowed that she had never had letters such as Disraeli's in her life. They came at a time when she felt isolated and misunderstood and was regularly being urged—if not harrassed—to resume her public duties. More important, the letters restored to her that sense of being cherished that she had had not felt since the death of Albert. Such an orgy of mutual adoration brought with it much derision in court circles. Disraeli's sycophantic behavior was condemned as a cynical ploy. He set up his own protective barrier by retaining a self-deprecating good humor about his relationship with the queen. He never intended her to take him literally; and she was too sharp a judge of character not to see that his tongue was firmly planted in his cheek. For both it was a comforting ritual, and they played it to the hilt.

It was during Disraeli's historic term as prime minister during 1874–1880 that he made his major contribution both to world and to British history, secure in his harmonious relationship with the queen, in which, as Strachey observed, "she expanded to the rays of Disraeli's devotion like a flower in the sun" (1971, 206). He now inaugurated a series of progressive domestic reforms, which would not be equaled again until Sir Henry Campbell-Bannerman's Liberal government brought in sweeping social reforms during 1906–1909. Most important among them were the Employers and Workmen Act of 1875, protecting both employer and employee against breach of contract, and the Trade-Union Act of 1875, which extended the rights of unions (made legal in 1871) and allowed peaceful picketing. The Public Health Act of 1875 set up local sanitary authorities and invested greater responsibility in doctors for monitoring the spread of disease. The Artisans' and Labourers' Dwellings Improvement Act of 1875 brought in major programs of slum clearance in urban industrial areas such as Birmingham. The Factory Acts of 1874 and 1878 improved working conditions, and the Merchant Shipping Act of 1876 brought in tough controls on the overloading of the so-called coffin ships.

But undoubtedly the highlight of Disraeli's time in office, and the cornerstone of future Conservative Party policy, was his bold pursuit of an aggressive foreign policy, which set out to affirm and extend British imperial power. In 1875 Disraeli arranged the purchase of the controlling interest in the Suez Canal Company after securing a loan of £4 million from the Jewish banking firm of Rothschild. A majority stake in the canal safeguarded a shorter route to Asia for British shipping and reinforced Britain's control over India. The consolidation of empire was signified by the doggedness with which Disraeli pushed through the Royal Titles bill in 1876, under considerable pressure from the queen and against fierce opposition in both houses, in order to gratify Victoria's desire to be titled "empress of India" on a par with the other emperors of Europe. Although this was the final confirmation of the romanticized view Disraeli held of his monarch, many in government felt that it only encouraged the queen to have inflated ideas about her own status and power.

In 1876 a grateful Victoria responded by elevating Disraeli to Lord Beaconsfield. The ailing politician now entered the less taxing environment of the House of Lords. So rapidly was Disraeli's health now failing, after years of being plagued with gout, asthma, and bronchitis, that the queen also broke with precedent and invited him to sit down during official audiences. The pinnacle of political power had come too late for Disraeli—at a time when he was least physically equipped to enjoy it. Yet now, of all times, he found himself thrown into high-risk power politics with Russia, with the queen fueling anti-Russian jingoism during the Russo-Turkish war of 1877–1878.

The Russians had once more intervened in the Balkans in the supposed protection of Christian subjects of the Ottoman empire after a series of uprisings in 1875 in Bosnia and Bulgaria, at that time under Turkish rule. Declaring war on Turkey in August 1877, the Russians quickly marched on Constantinople, forcing upon the Turks the treaty of San Stefano in March 1878, which installed a king in the independent state of Bulgaria and extended the territory of Montenegro. Britain, Germany, and Austro-Hungary were extremely hostile to the creation of the large new state of Bulgaria under Russian influence and forced a rewrite of the treaty at a congress held in Berlin in 1878. Disraeli returned home triumphant that he had won "peace with honour" (*The Times* 17 July 1878) by averting another war with Russia. Victoria was determined to heap him with yet more honors, but he refused a dukedom, accepting only the Order of the Garter. By now Gladstone had launched a concerted campaign to chase Disraeli from office over his aggressive foreign policy. Disraeli's government was defeated in a Liberal landslide in the general election of 1880, an event that sounded the death knell of his Romantic political dream and, for a triumphant Gladstone, "the end of the reign of the mad Caliph" (Jerrold 1916, 242); "the downfall of Beaconsfieldism," he intoned, "is like the vanishing of some vast magnificent castle in an Italian romance" (Blake 1966, 712).

On 27 April, Disraeli had a farewell audience with the queen; four days later he dined at Windsor—the last time Queen Victoria saw him. Disraeli retired to his manor house and devoted the remaining year of his life to writing his semiautobiographical novel *Endymion* (1880). The queen continued to write and sent him gifts of spring flowers to cheer him in his illness. When Disraeli died the following April, her grief was profound. Writing to his secretary, Lord Rowton, on 19 April, Victoria ignored protocol, unable, she said, to "write in the 3rd person [the royal "we"] at this terrible moment when I can scarcely see for my fast falling tears" (Blake 1966, 749). "Never," she assured Rowton, "had I *so* kind and devoted a Minister and very few such devoted friends" (750). She would like to have given Disraeli a grand state funeral, but he had left instructions in his will to be buried in the vault at Hughenden beside his wife, after only the most simple of obsequies. On 30 April, Queen Victoria made a private visit and placed a china wreath of flowers on his coffin.

It would be hard to deny the existence of genuine affection for the queen at the heart of the mock heroics of Disraeli's devotion to her. In essence he was an incorrigible romantic, and for all his unctuousness of manner, he remained Queen Victoria's loyal servant. For her part, the queen demonstrated an acceptance of his unconventionality where many of her illustrious contemporaries were too ready to dismiss Disraeli as lacking the true gravitas of a great statesman. Benjamin Disraeli never became a respectable, establishment figure, despite his country seat, his title, and his political successes. He was always an outsider, always looked upon as strange and "oriental," and the queen was sensitive enough to respect his difference. As she herself observed on first reading *Coningsby* in 1878, "His love for and faith in the Jews is very apparent" (Buckle 1926–1928, ii:643). He in turn never ceased to value the crucial influence exercised by the queen and her sex in molding his political career: "I owe everything to women, and if, in the sunset of life, I have still a young heart; it is due to that influence" (Aronson 1977, 186).

Related entries:

Class; Empress of India; Gladstone, William Ewart; Racial and Religious Prejudice

References and further reading:

Aronson, Theo. 1977. *Victoria and Disraeli: The Making of a Romantic Partnership.* London: Macmillan.

Blake, Robert. 1966. *Disraeli.* London: Eyre and Spottiswoode.

Bradford, Sarah. 1983. *Disraeli.* London: Weidenfeld and Nicolson.

Buckle, G. E., ed. 1926–1928. *The Letters of Queen Victoria: A Selection from Her Majesty's Correspondence and Journal between the Years 1862 and 1885.* 2d ser., 3 vols. London: John Murray.

Cecil, Algernon. 1953. *Queen Victoria and Her Prime Ministers.* London: Eyre and Spottiswoode.

Davis, Richard M. 1976. *Disraeli.* London: Hutchinson.

Eccleshall, Robert, and Graham Walker, eds. 1998. *Biographical Dictionary of British Prime Ministers.* London: Routledge.

Fulford, Roger, ed. 1971. *Your Dear Letter: Private Correspondence of Queen Victoria and the Crown Princess of Prussia, 1865–71.* London: Evans Brothers.

Hardie, Frank. 1935. *The Political Influence of Queen Victoria.* London: Oxford University Press.

Hibbert, Christopher. 1984. *Queen Victoria in Her Letters and Journals.* London:Viking.
Jerrold, Clare. 1916. *The Widowhood of Queen Victoria.* London: Eveleigh Nash.
Kennedy, A. L. 1956. *My Dear Duchess: Social and Political Letters to the Duchess of Manchester.* London: John Murray.
Times (London), 17 July 1878.
Longford, Elizabeth. [1964] 1998. *Victoria R.I.:* London: Weidenfeld and Nicolson
Maurois, André. 1937. *Disraeli.* Harmondsworth, UK: Penguin.
Moneypenny, William F., and G. E. Buckle. [1910–1920] 1968. *Disraeli, Earl of Beaconsfield.* 6 vols. London: Smith, Elder and Co.
Nevill, Lady Dorothy. 1910. *Under Five Reigns.* London: Meuthen.
Pearson, Hesketh. 1951. *Dizzy: The Life and Nature of Benjamin Disraeli, Earl of Beaconsfield.* London: Methuen.
Strachey, Lytton. [1921] 1971. *Queen Victoria.* Harmondsworth, UK: Penguin (chap. 8, "Mr. Gladstone and Lord Beaconsfield").
Vincent, John. 1990. *Disraeli.* Oxford: Oxford University Press.
Vincent, John, ed. 1978. *Disraeli, Derby and the Conservative Party: The Journals and Memoirs of Edward Henry, Lord Stanley.* Hassocks, Sussex: Harvester Press.
Weibe, M. G., gen. ed. 1982–1999. *Benjamin Disraeli Letters.* 6 vols. Toronto: University of Toronto Press.
Zetland, Marquis of. 1929. *The Letters of Disraeli to Lady Chesterfield and Lady Bradford.* 2 vols. London: Ernest Benn.

E

Empress of India (1876)

that enormous Empire which is so bright a jewel of her Crown (Benson and Esher 1911, 3:304)

Queen Victoria's elevation as empress of India on New Year's Day 1877 marked the beginning of a long and very evident love affair with India and a particular admiration for the Indian people and their culture. Yet Victoria never visited the subcontinent, although it held an endless fascination for her. This might not have been the case, perhaps, had she not been widowed in 1861, thereafter dogmatically observing the rituals of prolonged mourning and refusing to appear at any public ceremonies unless they were absolutely essential.

Although the acquisition of this coveted title did much to seal the particular love for and sense of responsibility that the queen held toward her Indian subjects, in matters of more pressing self-interest, it fulfilled the queen's own aspirations with regard to her imperial status. As she observed to her secretary, Henry Ponsonby, in 1873: "I am an Empress and in common conversation am sometimes called Empress of India. Why have I never officially assumed this title?" (Longford 1998, 404). Although frequently becoming incensed by the endless petty arguments over precedence that regularly broke out among the European royals, Victoria was, ultimately, not averse to insisting on her own elevation to a higher title.

Her son Alfred's wife, Grand Duchess Marie, daughter of Alexander II of Russia, had insisted, when they married in 1874, that she be addressed as Her Imperial Highness (rather than Her Royal Highness) because her father was an emperor; it was only after heated exchanges that a compromise had been reached. The queen had also been rankled by William I of Prussia's elevation of himself to emperor in 1871, which would mean that her daughter Vicky would have higher status than Victoria herself, as Vicky would become an empress when her husband, Frederick, inherited the throne (in 1888). Victoria's hackles had risen when William I had dared to suggest to her that Frederick should now therefore have precedence over the Prince of Wales. With three European emperors—those of Austria, Russia, and Prussia—all vying for dominance, Victoria felt "handicapped in her battles over protocol by not being an Empress" (St. Aubyn 1991, 434) and was determined to outmaneuver all of them in the royal precedence stakes.

Victoria's developing interest in the Indian subcontinent had been particularly aroused in 1857–1858 by the events of the Indian Rebellion, at the conclusion of which the British government assumed direct control of Indian affairs under the India Act. Victoria wrote to the newly created

A contemporary cartoon, from **Punch,** *April 1876, depicts Benjamin Disraeli dressed as Aladdin offering the much-prized crown of India to Queen Victoria, who now becomes empress. (Hulton/Archive by Getty Images)*

viceroy of India, Viscount Canning, expressing her delight: "It is a source of great satisfaction and pride to her to feel herself in direct communication with that enormous Empire which is so bright a jewel of her Crown, and which she would wish to see happy, contented and peaceful" (Benson and Esher 1911, 3:389). Prince Albert too had his own suggestion to make: the queen might perhaps in future be referred to there not as the queen but as "the Great Mogul" (Fulford 1966, 236).

Prime Minister Benjamin Disraeli had a considerable struggle in getting the Royal Titles Bill, elevating Victoria to empress of India, through Parliament. Faced with vehement opposition from the Liberals, he had tried hard to underplay the personal dynastic rivalries that lay at the root of the queen's desire to be an empress and had emphasized her new title as an essential facet of Britain's new, grandiose imperial policy in the East. In particular, Disraeli saw the queen's role as empress of India as a most necessary definition of Britain's preeminence as a power in the face of continuing Russian imperial ambitions.

The queen was taken aback by the opposition to the bill both in Parliament and also in much of the press, seeing this as a serious manifestation of dangerous republicanism. She was shocked by this "disgraceful agitation" (Hibbert 1984, 242) and asked ministers to quash unfounded rumors that she was about to change her and her children's titles at home: "The Queen will be always called 'the Queen,' and her children 'their Royal Highnesses,' and no difference whatever is to be made except officially adding after Queen of Great Britain, 'Empress of India,' the name which is best understood in the East, but which Great Britain (which is an Empire) never has acknowledged to be higher than Queen or King" (ibid.). The second reading was eventually carried by 105 votes, but by the time the bill was finally passed by Parliament on 1 May 1876, the process had taken a serious toll on Disraeli's failing health.

In November 1876, Bertie, Prince of Wales, at his own suggestion, embarked on an extensive, five-month tour of India but strongly resisted his mother's having a hand in the organization of his itinerary. Nor had he allowed her to meddle in who was or was not to accompany him in his eighteen-strong retinue (although the queen refused to allow the princess of Wales to accompany him). The prince's mission, as Philip Magnus asserted, had been a highly personal one, aimed at redressing any bad feeling lingering since the end of the rebellion of 1857–1858 and "to show himself to princes, soldiers, peasants and workers as the incarnation of the British Raj, which had previously been no more than a remote and abstract symbol, represented by officers and officials who extorted varying degrees of love, respect, fear and, occasionally hatred" (Magnus 1964, 135). More important, Bertie was also there to prepare the ground for his mother's proclamation as empress. With his characteristic flair, he worked his way through a succession of lavish receptions and elephant processions at cities such as Poonah, Baroda, and Calcutta, before going on to the sacred city of Benares, where he was welcomed with fireworks and carried in a gold and silver chair with an escort of camels, elephants, and armed men to the maharajah's palace above the city. At Lucknow he inspected the locations of the famous siege of 1857 and then went on to Delhi, the Punjab, and the Golden Temple of Agra.

The culmination of the prince's official duties came on the day of the queen's proclamation as empress, 1 January 1877, when together with the British viceroy, Lord Lytton, he presided over a grand durbar (Indian public levee), attended by sixty-three ruling princes of India and watched by over 100,000 people, who had come to hear Lord Lytton read out the queen's message to her loyal Indian subjects. This marked the end of weeks of medal giving, statue unveiling, military reviews, and banquets, after which Bertie spent the remainder of his stay in India engaged in what he considered a far more worthwhile pursuit—big game hunting. In Nepal on 23 February 1877 he was proud to record that he had shot six tigers in a single day. At Windsor meanwhile, the queen had headed a lavish Imperial Banquet on the day of her proclamation, taking care to wear many of her celebrated Indian diamonds and emeralds as well as the Star of India. With considerable pride she had signed herself V. R. and I. (Victoria Regina et Imperatrix) for the first time that day. (In India she would also be referred to as the Kaiser-i-Hind and the Shah-in-Shah Padshah—Monarch of Monarchs.)

For the rest of her life Queen Victoria remained convinced that the title would have far more significance in India than at home—and she was right. She took her responsibilities seriously, making a firm commitment to respect and uphold Indian religious practice and customs, and was strongly opposed to the imposition of the Christian religion on the Hindus and Muslims of India. After the death of John Brown in 1883, she appointed the first two Indian servants to her royal household, and their numbers increased thereafter. She remained highly sensitive to the cultural and religious pride of India's peoples, especially its Muslims. In 1898 she offered advice to a soon-to-be-appointed viceroy, Lord Curzon, that he "must . . . not be guided by the *snobbish* and vulgar, overbearing and offensive behaviour of our Civil and Political Agents, if we are to go on peaceably and happily in India . . . not trying to trample on the people and continuously reminding them and making them feel they are a conquered people" (letter to Lord Curzon, 27 May 1898).

Related entries:
Albert Edward, Prince of Wales; Diamond Jubilee; Disraeli, Benjamin; Indian Rebellion; The Munshi; Racial and Religious Prejudice; Religion.

References and further reading:
Benson, A. C., and Viscount Esher, eds. 1911. *The Letters of Queen Victoria, 1837–1861.* 1st ser., 3 vols. London: John Murray.
Bolitho, Hector. 1964. *Albert, Prince Consort.* London: Max Parrish.
Buckle, G. E., ed. 1926–1928. *The Letters of Queen Victoria, 1862–1885.* 2d ser., 3 vols. London: John Murray.
———. 1930–1932. *The Letters of Queen Victoria, 1886–1901.* 3d ser., 3 vols. London: John Murray.
Fulford, Roger. 1966. *The Prince Consort.* London: Macmillan.
Harlow, Barbara, and Mia Carter. 1999. *Imperialism and Orientalism: A Documentary Sourcebook.* Oxford: Blackwell.
Hibbert, Christopher. 1984. *Queen Victoria in Her Letters and Journals.* London: Viking.
Longford, Elizabeth. [1964] 1998. *Victoria R.I.* London: Weidenfeld and Nicolson.
Lorne, Marquis of. 1901. *Victoria R. I.* London: Eyre and Spottiswoode.
Magnus, Philip. 1964. *King Edward VII.* London: John Murray.
St. Aubyn, Giles. 1991. *Queen Victoria, a Portrait* London: Sinclair Stevenson.

Ernest Augustus, Duke of Cumberland (1771–1851)

(King of Hanover 1837–1851)

that old wretch (Longford 1998, 137)

Few of Queen Victoria's elderly Hanoverian relatives have been more maligned than her uncle, Ernest Augustus, duke of Cumberland. Like all those frightening figures in Victorian fairy stories, whose names were so regularly invoked to teach naughty children to behave, he was constantly conjured up before the young Victoria as a demonic Hanoverian troll. In fact, he featured little in her life in real terms—for most of the period 1813–1829 living in Berlin. Yet his name was regularly invoked, along with Victoria's other "wicked uncles," by her mother, the duchess of Kent, who viewed them all as bogeymen out to deprive Princess Victoria of her position in line to the throne. The duchess's imagination ran riot: Ernest might attempt to poison Victoria, she suggested (later dismissed by the queen herself as "utterly false"); and together with her aide, Sir John Conroy, the duchess played on the young princess's fear in their strategy of keeping her isolated from the rest of court and utterly dependent upon them.

The fearsome portrait of the duke was enhanced, in real life, by the alarm that his presence inspired in most people. Tall, lean, straight-backed, and militaristic with bushy whiskers and mustache—he had been an army man all his life—his face disfigured by a severe battle scar and the loss of an eye, Ernest Augustus looked every inch an ogre. Society gossip about his autocratic, unscrupulous, duplicitous, and, dare it be said, licentious personal career ensured that the duke was one of the most hated and feared men in England. His brother, William IV, summed him up more accurately, however: "Ernest is not a bad fellow, but if any one has a corn he is sure to tread on it" (*Dictionary of National Biography* 1998, vol. 6:814).

The fifth son of George III, Ernest was, like his brothers, educated mainly in Hanover, studying at the University of Göttingen before being consigned to the rigors of a military career in the Hanoverian army, in 1793 entering the Hussars as a lieutenant colonel. He fought on the Continent, distinguishing himself at the first battle of Tournay in May 1794, where he was seriously wounded. By the time he had been promoted to lieutentant general in 1799, he had earned an enviable reputation for heroism in battle. His father now created him duke of Cumberland and earl of Armagh. He gave up his military commands in England by 1807, although as deputy elector of Hanover he commanded the Hanoverian army as a British field marshal in 1813 and 1814. By now Ernest had become preoccupied with politics and was regularly attempting to influence the political persuasions of his brother, the Prince of Wales.

In 1810 Ernest was involved in a cause célèbre when he was attacked by his valet, Joseph Sellis. Ernest managed to beat off his assailant, although severely wounded—his skull was hacked open, exposing his brain. Shortly after the attack, Sellis was found with his throat cut. The press assumed, with Ernest's reputation for brutality stacked against him, that he had in fact attacked Sellis. The libelous rumors abounded until their perpetrator was fined and imprisoned. The duke was vindicated; evidence seemed to confirm his innocence, for Sellis, a Corsican Catholic, had apparently been seeking revenge for the duke's freely and virulently expressed hatred of Catholics. Nevertheless, gossip and scandal stuck to Cumberland. Tongues had been wagging for many years about who exactly had fathered his sister Sophia's illegitimate son, and the most recent biography (Wardroper 2001) still alleged an incestuous affair, if not rape.

Cumberland failed to mitigate his unpopularity with the public by his choice of bride in 1815, for he married a "woman with a past," the widowed Princess Frederica of Solms-Braunfels; their combined bad reputations only stoked the fires of gossip and ensured that they were not welcomed at court. The couple sought happier prospects back in German territory. With irrepressible arrogance, Ernest persisted, however, in making periodic visits to England to interfere in affairs of state whenever his brothers George IV and William IV showed signs of entertaining any idea of democratic reform, such as Catholic Emancipation in 1829 and the Reform Bill of 1832. Everything about his manner invited continuing public antipathy: he was high-handed, quarrelsome, an arch Tory, and rabidly antireform. He infuriated his brother the king, by openly patronizing the Irish Protestant Orange Lodges as part of his drive to block the passing of pro-Catholic reforms. It is said that Ernest's offensively intolerant manner in Parliament alienated many Tories in his own party.

With the prospects of William IV's being succeeded by Ernest, should William have no surviving children and should his niece and heir presumptive Victoria also die, a general sense of dread was at large throughout the country at what his draconian rule might bring. Indeed the sense of relief at Victoria's birth in 1819 had been considerable. When she became queen in 1837, under Salic law, only male heirs were allowed to succeed to the Hanoverian throne, which was still ruled jointly with Britain by the British sovereign. The title thus had to pass to Ernest. Upon his arrival in Hanover, he proceeded to govern in the dictatorial, reactionary way he saw fit: he suppressed William IV's constitution of 1833 and ruled as an absolute monarch until forced grudgingly to grant a new constitution in 1840. Surprisingly, he survived the turbulent year of revolutions in Europe of 1848 by remaining at his Hanoverian post rather than becoming, like most of his forebears, an absentee monarch. Back in England, mindful that all the time Victoria remained unmarried and childless, King Ernest was also heir to the British throne, the queen's first Whig government urged her to marry sooner than she would have otherwise wished.

Queen Victoria herself ran up against Ernest's autocratic behavior when he made a rare visit to England in 1843, to attend the christening of her daughter, Princess Alice. As king of Hanover he caused several scenes by trying to assert his royal precedence over Prince Albert and even the queen herself. By now Victoria was also involved in another and long-running dispute with Ernest over the Hanoverian crown jewels. Because these had belonged to the crown of Hanover and their previous owner, Queen Charlotte (wife of George III), had bequeathed them to him—or so the king argued—they should be returned to him. The jewels included a very fine rope of pearls of which Queen Victoria was particularly fond, as well as diamond earrings, a stomacher, and other jewels. She stubbornly resisted Ernest's claim, the more so, because civil war and the profligacy of previous British sovereigns had seen most of her own hereditary royal jewels long since sold off or melted down to pay debts. A royal commission was appointed to investigate Ernest's claim, but the matter was not finally resolved until 1857, six years after Ernest's death, when the Hanoverian claim was upheld. The queen managed to hold on to the pearls; the rest of the jewels were delivered up to Ernest's son, the blind King George V of Hanover. As a teenager, George had been briefly posited as a possible bridegroom for Victoria; he proved to be the last Hanoverian king and was deposed in 1866.

Related entries:
Hanover, Royal House of; Kent, Edward Augustus, Duke of; William IV

References and further reading:
Charlot, Monica. 1991. *Victoria: The Young Queen*. Cambridge: Polity.
Dictionary of National Biography. [1885–1901]. 1998. Vol. 6. Oxford: Oxford University Press.
Fulford, Roger. [1933] 1973. *Royal Dukes.* Harmondsworth, UK: Penguin.
Longford, Elizabeth. [1964] 1998. *Victoria R.I.* London: Weidenfeld and Nicolson.
Van Thal, Herbert. 1936. *Ernest Augustus, Duke of Cumberland.* London: A. Barker.
Wardroper, John. 2001. *Wicked Ernest: An Extraordinary Life Revealed.* London: Shelfmark.
Willis, G. M. 1954. *Ernest Augustus, Duke of Cumberland and King of Hanover.* London: A. Barker.
Woodham-Smith, Cecil. 1972. *Queen Victoria: Her Life and Times.* London: Hamish Hamilton.

Eugénie Marie de Montijo, Empress of France (1826–1920)

(Maria Eugénia Ignacia Augustina de Guzmán y Palafox y Portocarrero)

there is an expression of deep sadness in her face (Buckle 1926–1928, 2: 89)

The Empress Eugénie of France, whose legendary beauty was captured by the great European court painter, Franz Winterhalter, retained her grace and elegance into old age. But there was always a hint of sadness in the fine-boned face, which spoke volumes about the tragic events that overtook her later life, after the fall of the Second Empire in 1870. In the opinion of Princess Marie Louise of

Queen Victoria was no physical or sartorial match for the exquisitely beautiful Eugénie, empress of France, with whom the queen became close friends after they were both widowed. (Library of Congress)

Schleswig-Holstein, "one realized only too well that one was in the presence of someone who had passed through the furnace of suffering to its utmost limits" (1959, 149). Such experiences brought Eugénie close to her friend the queen during both their long widowhoods, when they would often meet and commiserate on their grief.

Eugénie was born in Granada, the daughter of a Spanish aristocrat who, as an admirer of Napoleon, had fought on the French side in the Peninsular War against Britain. She inherited from her father not only an exotic ancestry but also a passionate and romantic temperament, a sense of adventure, and great depths of physical courage. As a young woman she loved the outdoors and was a consummate horsewoman, often riding out alone and with reckless speed and enjoying the company of local gypsies. Yet there was something lacking in this otherwise magical mix; despite being beautiful and highly desirable, Eugénie herself lacked sexuality and lived by strict moral standards. The English feminist Ethel Smyth would later observe, "you felt instinctively that love can never have played a great part in her life. In her case you felt that it must have been the feeblest string of the lyre from the first" (Smyth 1987, 327–328).

Eugénie was sent away to France to be educated, from 1834 to 1838 attending the Convent of the Sacré Coeur in Paris with her sister Paca, where she developed a deep and abiding Catholic faith. Her father's sudden death was accentuated by the early departure, into an arranged marriage to the duke of Alba, of her much-loved sister. By now turning into a great beauty, renowned for her lovely golden hair, Eugénie rejected a succession of suitors, continuing to prefer the masculine pursuits of hunting and driving and the exotic pleasures of gypsy music and flamenco dancing, rather than endure the ennui of society salons. When she reached the age of twenty-one, she inherited some of her father's titles and became a Spanish countess in her own right. She first met Louis Napoleon, the nephew of Napoleon Bonaparte, in 1843; by the time she next met him he had named himself Napoleon III, emperor of France, after a coup d'état in December 1851. Napoleon, who was eighteen years older than Eugénie and had had many love affairs, was captivated by her beauty and strongly attracted to her sexually when they next met in 1852. Over a period of three months he assiduously wooed Eugénie, who steadfastly refused to enter into a sexual relationship with him outside marriage. The more she resisted, the more the libidinous Napoleon was ensnared.

Although he was emperor of France, there were, in fact, surprisingly few candidates in Europe suitable for the role of empress. Most of the great royal houses had fought in the Napoleonic Wars *against* the French and were therefore not inclined to make a dynastic alliance with their old enemy's nephew. Eugénie finally accepted his proposal, after Louis Napoleon had freed himself from his English mistress Lizzie Howard, whom he placated by setting up in considerable comfort in several homes in Paris.

A ravishingly beautiful Eugénie, resplendent in diamonds and sapphires, married Napoleon in Paris's Notre Dame Cathedral on 29 January 1853, but Napoleon's affairs continued. Unafflicted by sexual jealousy, Eugénie tolerated them as a manifestation of her husband's innate, male weakness. In private she was quietly contemptuous of most of his sex and saw them as being "worth very little" (Kurtz 1964, 69), aside, that is, from her adored son, the Prince Imperial, who did not live long enough to disappoint her.

Eugénie enjoyed the lavish lifestyle that characterized the Second Empire at a succession of royal residences, including the Tuileries in Paris and a summer home at Biarritz on the Atlantic coast. During her heyday, she applied her beauty and charisma to winning over a succession of visiting royal and foreign dignitaries to a court that became renowned around the world for its culture and opulence. She became the royal fashion icon of her day, setting trends in hairstyles and in couture, transforming French fashion and reviving the silk industry that had long been in decline. She made the fortune of the Englishman Charles Frederick Worth, who had established a fashion house in Paris in 1858 and who created some of Eugénie's most exquisite gowns. On her first state visit to Britain in 1855, Eugénie brought her legendary jewels—which she later was forced to surrender before leaving France and most of which would be auctioned in 1887 along with the crown jewels. She also arrived with a wardrobe of sumptuous dresses with huge skirts, worn over the new crinoline that had been introduced in France the previous year. This fashion trend rapidly took off in Britain and would persist until 1866. The diehard snobs of the British aristocracy continued, however, to regard the French emperor and empress as parvenus and Eugénie, whose legendary fashion sense had gone before her, as a showy *femme du monde* (woman of the world).

No one in the British court could fail to observe during this visit that, physically, the two female monarchs were utterly at odds—the queen small, dumpy, plain, and with, as the French particularly deplored, no fashion sense whatsoever; Eugénie willowy, graceful, and effortlessly stylish. Queen Victoria remained oblivious to the petty backbiting about her own mismatched clothes. She was completely entranced by Eugénie: "such grace, elegance, sweetness, and *nature.* Her manners are charming; the *profile* and figure beautiful and particularly *distingués,*" she told her uncle Leopold (Benson and Esher 1911, 3:122). But perhaps the most unexpected accolade came from the highly reserved Prince Albert, for even he had fallen under Eugénie's spell. As the queen noted in her diary with considerable surprise and gratification: "Albert who is seldom much pleased with ladies or princesses, is very fond of her and her great ally" (Martin 1875–1880, 4:95).

The descriptions of Eugénie in the queen's letters typify her often ingenuous admiration of those far more sophisticated than herself. Always responsive to superficial charm—and having already been totally beguiled by the wily Napoleon—the queen was fulsome in praising Eugénie's tact, her natural manner, and her loveableness, while failing to penetrate the detachment, if not *froideur* (coldness), that lurked beneath them. But even though there was no contest between Victoria and Eugénie in the fashion stakes, Victoria nevertheless exuded a different kind of aura—and one that could not be manufactured—that of regal authority. Many observed during the state visits that for all her inelegance and shortness of stature, the queen had total command and self-possession: "True majesty was hers, and she knew it," wrote an early biographer, Lytton Strachey; "it was the woman to whom, as it seemed, nature and art had given so little, who, by the sheer force of an inherent grandeur, completely threw her adorned and beautiful companion into the shade" (Strachey 1971, 162). The state visit was a great success and set the seal on an enduring friendship between Eugénie and Victoria, despite the marked differences between them.

Napoleon and Eugénie only had one child—a son, the Prince Imperial (also named Louis Napoleon), born in March 1856. Having suffered a protracted and agonizing labor, Eugénie was warned against having any more children. Now officially nominated as regent in her husband's absences from the country, she wholeheartedly supported his absolutist rule and took a considerable interest in the country's foreign affairs. But the royal couple's fortunes crashed when the French suffered a crushing defeat at the battle of Sedan in September 1870 during the Franco-Prussian War.

The monarchy was faced with violent insurrection, resulting in Napoleon's overthrow and the collapse of the Second Empire. Eugénie fled to England with her son, where they were later joined by the emperor after his abdication. The couple leased a house, Camden Place, in Chiselhurst, Kent, where Louis died of kidney trouble two years later. Like her friend the queen, Eugénie promptly turned her back on public life. An ardent Catholic, she devoted herself to a quiet and contemplative widowhood, keeping alight the Bonapartist flame, more loyal to her husband's memory than the adulterous Napoleon probably deserved. She devoted herself to her son, whom she affectionately called "Lou-Lou," and who as he grew up was mooted as a possible husband for Queen Victoria's youngest daughter, Beatrice. In 1879 the prince begged his mother to allow him to go out to Africa to observe the British campaign against warring Zulu tribes. Eugénie unwisely gave in, only for the prince to be killed in an ambush while on a reconnaissance mission. Queen Victoria ordered a grand funeral with full military honors for the prince, whose body was brought home to rest alongside his father's at St. Mary's Chapel, Chiselhurst.

Eugénie was disraught at the loss of her "*petit garçon*" (little boy). She left Camden Place and settled in a large rambling mansion at Farnborough in Hampshire, surrounded by mementos of her past, including, in a converted outbuilding, the state carriage in which she had ridden as empress. In the grounds of her new home she had a Gothic-style Roman Catholic church, St. Michael's, built to house three large red Aberdeen granite sarcophagi (the gift of Queen Victoria) in its crypt, to which in 1888 the bodies of her husband and son were transferred and where, in due course, she herself would rest. She was held in great affection in Britain and like that other famous royal widow, the queen, lived a quiet life of self-imposed seclusion, wearing the same, perpetual widow's weeds. Unlike the queen, however, Eugénie kept no journal and had no desire to relive the painful events of her life through the writing of memoirs. The queen was one of the few people she visited; during the 1890s she frequently spent a month or so staying near Balmoral when the queen was in residence there during the autumn. Victoria made over the use of one of the houses on the estate to Eugénie, although certain concessions were expected in return: Queen Victoria insisted Eugénie don an old-fashioned widow's lace cap, which Eugénie loathed, her sense of style never quite deserting her. In spring Eugénie would depart for her Villa Cyrnos at Cap Martin on the French Riviera, from where she and the queen, who regularly stayed at nearby Cimiez, could again exchange visits.

In 1901 Eugénie was deeply stricken by the death of the queen: "It is an immense loss to me," she wrote, "she was a friend close to my heart, always good and affectionate, a support in my chequered life. I have never felt more strange or alone in this country; I am profoundly sad and dispirited" (Aronson 1972, 229). Sadly, she herself was too sick to attend the queen's funeral, but she outlived her friend by another nineteen years, developing a close friendship with Victoria's son, King Edward VII.

Throughout her life Eugénie lived up to the role of the "Tragic Empress," as she was often referred to. Reflecting on a life that had seen her survive an assassination attempt and lose her throne, her husband, and her only son, she remarked: "My legend has taken shape: at the beginning of the reign, I was the frivolous woman only interested in clothes; towards the end of the Empire, I became the *femme fatale,* responsible for everything that went wrong! And legends always get the upper hand of history" (Smyth 1987, 329). She remained fit and active into her nineties; after her sight became seriously impaired she had an eye operation and returned to her homeland,

Spain—for the first time in many years—to recuperate, which is where she died at the age of ninety-four.

Related entries:
Napoleon III, Emperor of France; Queen Victoria: Physical Appearance of; Winterhalter, Franz Xaver

References and further reading:

Aronson, Theo. 1972. *Queen Victoria and the Buonapartes.* London: Cassell.

Aubrey, Octave. 1939. *Eugénie, Empress of the French.* London: Cobden Sanderson.

Benson, A. C., and Viscount Esher, eds. 1911. *The Letters of Queen Victoria 1837–1861.* 1st ser., 3 vols. London: John Murray.

Buckle, G. E., ed. 1926–1928. *The Letters of Queen Victoria: A Selection from Her Majesty's Correspondence and Journal between the Years 1862 and 1885.* 2d ser., 3 vols. London: John Murray.

Carey, Agnes. 1922. *The Empress Eugénie in Exile.* London: John Lane.

Guest, Ivor. 1952. *Napoleon III in England.* London: British Technical and General Press.

Kurtz, Harold. 1964. *Eugénie, Empress, Consort of Napoleon III, Emperor of the French.* London: Hamish Hamilton.

Mallett, Victor. 1968. *Life with Queen Victoria: Marie Mallet's Letters from Court 1887–1901.* London: John Murray.

Martin, Sir Theodore. 1875–1880. *The Life of His Royal Highness the Prince Consort.* 5 vols. London: Smith, Elder and Co.

Princess Marie Louise. 1959. *My Memories of Six Reigns.* Harmondsworth, UK: Penguin.

Sencourt, Robert. 1931. *The Life of the Empress Eugénie.* London: Ernest Benn.

Smyth, Ethel. 1987. "Recollections of the Empress Eugénie." In *The Memoirs of Ethel Smyth.* Abridged and introduced by Ronald Crichton. London: Viking.

Strachey, Lytton. [1921] 1971. *Queen Victoria.* Harmondsworth, UK: Penguin.

F

Feodora, Princess of Hohenlohe-Langenburg (1807–1872)

(Anna Feodorovna Augusta Charlotte Wilhelmina)

friend, sister, companion all to me (Hibbert 1984, 14)

Queen Victoria's little-known but much loved half sister, "Fidi" or "Cissi," as Victoria affectionately called her, was the duchess of Kent's daughter by her first husband, Prince Emich Charles of Leiningen. She grew up on the family estate at Amorbach in Bavaria and came to England in 1819, after her mother had married the duke of Kent. She remained with Princess Victoria at Kensington Palace until her marriage in 1828 took her back to Germany. Although the two sisters spent many long periods apart, they wrote hundreds of letters to each other over the course of forty years, but in general, despite their lasting attachment to each other, Feodora remains a shadowy figure in most biographies of the queen.

Feodora, who left England when Victoria was nine, was cherished by her as one of the few friends of her isolated childhood and who, for Victoria, represented a treasured link with it. Twelve years older than Victoria, she was a strong guiding influence, their close relationship fostered by the atmosphere of watchful control that prevailed at Kensington Palace, where the two girls were subjected to a strict daily routine of lessons, rarely being allowed farther than the palace gardens for recreation. For the teenage Feodora, such restriction had been the harder to bear; she yearned for society and romance. In their later correspondence the two women would frequently reminisce on the misery of their isolation, with Victoria referring to it as a kind of imprisonment. Feodora was particularly bitter: "Not to have enjoyed the pleasures of youth is nothing, but to have been deprived of all intercourse, and not one cheerful thought in that dismal existence of ours, was very hard. My only happy time was going or driving out with you and Lehzen [Victoria's governess]; then I could speak and look as I like" (Warner 1979, 35–36). But Feodora, at least, had "escaped some years of imprisonment, which you my poor darling sister, had to endure after I was married" (ibid.).

Romance briefly entered the life of the eagerly expectant Feodora at Kensington Palace, when she fell for Augustus, the cavalry officer son of the duke of Sussex (who had apartments at the palace). The couple exchanged messages through one of the duchess's ladies in waiting, the Baroness Späth, but Feodora, fearful of censure, finally admitted the romance to her mother. Other admirers came and went, among them the duke of Nassau and the prince of Schönburg, for Feodora was pretty and outward going and a desirable match. When a young Irish furrier named Robert Stephen, besotted with Feodora, petitioned for permission to marry her and was deported back to Ireland, the duchess of Kent quickly married Feodora off to Prince Ernest of Hohenlohe-Langenburg. The high-spirited young woman soon found herself living a life of seclusion in the prince's cold and gloomy castle, in an impoverished principality that had seen greater days.

Victoria was greatly affected by the loss of Feodora. For the next six years she saw nothing of her, and between 1829 and 1839, Feodora was much preoccupied by the birth, in quick succession, of her six children. After Victoria married in 1840, the greater part of the two sisters' subsequent letters to each other would be taken up with the problems of motherhood and babies. When Feodora and her husband visited England in 1834, Victoria noted that her sister had already lost her bloom and was stouter. She wept bitterly when the time came to say goodbye to Feodora six weeks later and felt totally abandoned.

Feodora was acquainted with both of Victoria's Coburg cousins—Ernest and Albert—who were sent to England as prospective bridegrooms in 1836 and again 1839. She favored Ernest as being "so honest and good-natured" (Erickson 1997, 52). Feodora's children would later visit England and join the royal family for summer holidays at Osborne. In 1845 the two families met at Prince Albert's home, the castle Rosenau, in Coburg. During 1848—the year of revolutions across Europe—Victoria was extremely anxious about Feodora and her family; although the Hohenlohes survived that year's civil unrest in Germany, they did so in greatly reduced circumstances, supported by loans from Queen Victoria and the duchess of Kent. The prince meanwhile achieved status and respect in political circles as the president of the upper chamber of the Kingdom of Wurttemburg. In order to rescue something of their lost royal status, Feodora and Ernest gave serious consideration to the marriage of their seventeen-year-old daughter, Adelaide, to Napoleon III of France, when he first broached the subject in 1852.

Such a marriage would have been an important dynastic and political alliance for the Hohenlohes, as well as for the British royal family—although Queen Victoria was against the match. Like others, she harbored misgivings about Napoleon's age, the religious mismatch of Catholic and Lutheran that would be involved, and Napoleon's dubious sexual and moral reputation. Adelaide decided of her own accord to reject the suit, by which time Napoleon had in any event changed his mind and married Eugénie de Montijo. Adelaide went on to marry Prince Frederick of Augustenburg—and through this match found herself drawn into the tortuous Schleswig-Holstein affair of 1863, when three rival princes vied for the vacant throne of Schleswig-Holstein, Prince Frederick among them. The crisis brought Queen Victoria into open conflict with Feodora, who naturally supported her son-in-law's claim; the situation was further complicated by the fact that Frederick was Queen Victoria's grandson (by her eldest daughter, Vicky). Feodora and the queen exchanged numerous heated and emotional letters on the subject, before the crisis was resolved in 1864, with the region coming under Prussian rule.

Similar disgruntlement on Feodora's part was reiterated during the Franco-Prussian War of 1870–1871 when she criticized Queen Victoria for not sending troops to help her beleaguered German relatives in Coburg. Feodora's son Victor also incurred Queen Victoria's disapproval when, late in 1860, he announced his plans to marry a commoner, Laura Seymour, the daughter of an admiral.

Feodora's husband died in 1860, after which Victoria, herself widowed a year later, nursed hopes that her sister might join her in England in order that they might commiserate in their widowhood. Feodora visited in 1863 but found the queen's unbearable and unrelenting grief hard to deal with. She resisted pressure from Victoria to visit on a regular basis, unwilling both to give up her home in Germany or her independence and complaining that the British weather exacerbated her rheumatism. They last saw each other when Queen Victoria visited a terminally ill Feodora at Baden in 1872. Feodora died that September. It was, for Victoria, a particularly profound loss, as she recorded in her journal: "I stand so alone now, no near and dear one near my own age, or older to whom I could look up to, left! All, all gone! She was my last near relative on an equality with me, the last link with my childhood and youth" (Hibbert 1984, 229).

Among Feodora's papers a touching letter, dated 1854, was found, with instructions that it be given to Queen Victoria upon her death. In it she wrote: "I can never thank you enough for all you have done for me, for your great love and tender affection. These feelings cannot die; they must and will live on in my soul—till we meet again, never more to be separated—and you will not forget" (Albert 1967, 239).

Related entries:
"Grandmama of Europe"; Kent, Marie Louise Victoire, Duchess of; Palmerston, Henry John Temple, Third Viscount; Saxe-Coburg-Gotha, Royal House of

References and further reading:
Albert, Harold. 1967. *The Life and Letters of Princess Feodora: Queen Victoria's Sister.* London: Robert Hale.
Charlot, Monica. 1991. *Victoria: The Young Queen.* Cambridge: Polity.
Erickson, Carolly. 1997. *Her Little Majesty.* London: Robson.
Hibbert, Christopher. 1984. *Queen Victoria in Her Letters and Journals.* London: Viking.
Vallone, Lynne. 2001. *Becoming Victoria.* New Haven: Yale University Press.
Warner, Marina. 1979. *Queen Victoria's Sketchbook.* London: Macmillan.
Woodham-Smith, Cecil. 1972. *Queen Victoria: Her Life and Times.* Vol 1: *1819–1861.* London: Hamish Hamilton.

Frederick William, Crown Prince of Prussia (1831–1888)

("Fritz"; in 1888, Emperor Frederick III of Germany)

A dear, excellent, charming young man, whom we shall give our dear child to with perfect confidence (Ponsonby 1928, 6)

The throne of Germany changed hands three times in the year 1888, with the untimely death, only ninety-nine days after his accession, of Frederick William, husband of Queen Victoria's eldest daughter, Victoria the Princess Royal. The tall, handsome, and imposing emperor, with his fine mustachios, was the epitome of the handsome Wagnerian hero—appearing to considerable effect in this guise at Queen Victoria's 1887 Golden Jubilee. Although historians remain skeptical about his effectiveness as a ruler and the extent to which his liberal sentiments were inculcated in him by his far more forceful and opinionated wife, Fritz (as the family called him) never had the chance to prove his worth. After waiting long years as crown prince of Prussia (and, from 1872 on, of Germany), he was already terminally ill when he finally became emperor.

As the son of William I, emperor of Prussia, and Augusta of Saxe-Weimar-Eisenach, Fritz had been bred to believe in the imperial destiny of the Hohenzollerns. This proud and distinguished European bloodline had ruled Brandenburg-Prussia since 1415. Under Fritz's father and with the considerable statesmanship of Bismarck, Prussia had sought to extend its influence over the neighboring German states, achieved with their unification as the German Empire at the end of the Franco-Prussian War in 1871. William I was now elevated to German emperor.

Fritz was brought up in a highly authoritarian environment by his military-minded father but nevertheless had been the first Prussian prince allowed to attend university. Military service had dominated thereafter, a career that seemed at odds with the character of a man who was gentle, tolerant, and humane, although prone to bouts of depression. He had first met Vicky in 1851, when she was only ten. When he had seen her again three years later, Fritz had been captivated by her and had proposed. Because of Vicky's extreme youth, the marriage had not taken place until after her seventeenth birthday, in 1858, when Fritz was twenty-seven. Although the queen was anxious about sending so young a daughter off to the court at Berlin, she was confident that Vicky was in safe hands. She commended Fritz's amiable character and was flattered by his deferential manner: "I already regard Fritz as my own child for he has shown such child-like faith and affection towards me" (Charlot 1991, 378). Three years later, she was still impressed with her son-in-law; he was "noble, high-principled, so anxious to do what is right, and to improve in every way, and so sweet-tempered and affectionate—so, beyond everything, devoted to Vicky" (Hibbert 1984, 120).

Although he and Vicky soon had a very young family of eight children, Fritz continued to devote much time to the Prussian army, serving with conspicuous courage and distinction as a commander during Prussia's war with Denmark over the duchies of Schleswig and Holstein in 1864 and in the Seven Weeks' War against Austro-Hungary in 1866. In both cases the superbly trained, modern Prussian armies overwhelmed their opponents, as they did again in the Franco-Prussian War of 1870–1871, during which Fritz commanded the South German troops and the Prussian Army Corps. He spent long periods away at the front. As a highly sensitive person, Fritz took his duties very seriously and often found them exhausting and the responsibility onerous. The stress wore him out, with Vicky writing to Queen Victoria that "at times he is quite overwhelmed and sheds bitter tears" (Ponsonby 1928, 79). By nature a gentle, nonbelligerent man who despised violence, Fritz could not help observing with heavy-hearted irony, after leading his troops to victory at the battle of Wörth that "An extraordinary amount of praise has been lavished on me, far more than I deserve. But is it not a strange thing that I, who much preferred to earn recognition in works of peace, am called upon to win such blood-stained laurels?" (85).

In intellect, Fritz never was the equal of his clever and opinionated wife. Many at court claimed that he was too malleable and was dominated by the vociferous Vicky, who would, had he lived longer, have been the real power behind the throne. It was the opinion of Fritz's own private secretary, Lieutenant Colonel Summerfield, that he was a weak man who did not have the will to resist his domineering wife on any issue: "You have only to look at what she's made of him," Summerfield argued in 1885. "But for her, he'd be the average man, very arrogant, good-tempered, of mediocre gifts and with a great deal of common sense. But *now* he's not a man at all. . . . He's a mere cipher" (Magnus 1964, 202). Nevertheless, the couple shared a very real passion about bringing more democratic forms of government to Prussia and were united in their opposition to the policies of the Prussian premier (and later German chancellor) Otto von Bismarck. Because Fritz's loyalties were divided by his marriage to an English princess, he would become increasingly estranged from his parents during his long years as heir to the throne, and his and Vicky's liberal ideas would ensure they would be held in suspicion by Bismarck's reactionary government.

Illness would soon cut short Fritz's political ambitions. In February 1887 he began suffering with a hoarseness in the throat. A small growth was detected on his left vocal chord, but his German doctors could not agree over whether to operate or not, wasting valuable time. An operation on the larynx was a dangerous procedure in those days, and Bismarck insisted that further medical opinion should be solicited. The best throat specialist was sought out—Professor Rudolf Morell Mackenzie—who went to Berlin in May. Here he consulted with a German specialist, Dr. Virchow, with whom he concurred that the growth was not malignant. For a while Frederick's condition improved—enough for him to travel to England in June for the celebrations of Queen Victoria's Golden Jubilee, during which he was greatly admired among the ranks of European royals. The queen's physician, Sir James Reid, remarked that Fritz had cut a fine figure, "riding in the cavalcade of thirty-two princes," in the manner of a "towering Lohengrin-like figure in white uniform, silver breast plate and eagle crested helmet, of the Crown Prince of Germany"(Reid 1996, 90). Reid also noted that Fritz seemed already "a tragic figure, outwardly the embodiment of princely grace and splendour, but inwardly conscious that if it was indeed cancer that had laid its stranglehold upon him, his span of life was drawing to a close" (ibid.). During his two-month stay in England, Fritz consulted further with Dr. Mackenzie; but Reid was firmly of the opinion that the growth was cancerous and was highly critical of the optimistic prognosis offered by him.

When German doctors finally confirmed the cancer in Berlin, they recommended removal of Fritz's entire larynx. Fritz demurred, not wanting to take the risk of such a major operation when he might, at any time, finally accede to the throne. He agreed instead to undergo a tracheotomy, if and when it proved necessary. Reid attempted to persuade Fritz that the operation was essential and continued to warn against what he saw as the erroneous professional advice of Mackenzie, who even at the end of 1887 was still prevaricating in his diagnosis and in so doing fueling the false hopes of both the patient and Vicky. By the beginning of 1888, Fritz's condition was rapidly deteriorating while his seven German and English doctors quarreled over whether or not to insert a canula in his throat to alleviate his difficulty in breathing. It was in this desperate physical state—already weak, virtually bedridden, and unable to talk—that Fritz now succeeded his father on 9 March 1888, after twenty-eight years as crown prince. He faced the ordeal of his terminal illness with considerable dignity and courage, and without complaint, his only significant political act during his all too brief reign being to dismiss the ultraconservative minister of the interior, Robert von Puttkamer. Queen Victoria was able to make the journey to visit the dying Fritz in May. On 15 June he died at the Neue Palais at Potsdam, one of his last comments, made to Vicky, supposedly being "I must not die; what would become of Germany?" (Benson 1939, 231). His brother-in-law, Bertie, the Prince of Wales, mourned the loss of a friend: "He was one of the finest and noblest characters ever known. If he had a fault, he was *too* good for this world" (Magnus 1964, 202–203).

After Fritz's death bitter controversy raged over the appropriateness of his treatment, the prevarication of the doctors, and especially the professional conduct of the English specialist, Morell Mackenzie. Vicky blamed the hastening of Fritz's death on the bungling of the German surgeon, who had inserted the canula in Fritz's throat with uneccessary force, causing violent coughing and hemorrhaging. In October 1888 the newly knighted Sir Morell Mackenzie published his own account, *The Fatal Illness of Frederick the Noble,* which was promptly banned in Germany.

Queen Victoria realized only too well the significance of Fritz's death for Vicky and how, in the loss of her husband and ally, she would now be even more isolated by her callous and dictatorial son, Kaiser William II. "The tragedy for my poor child is too ghastly," she wrote, "much worse even than mine in 1861" (Fulford 1964, 13).

Related entries:
Albert Edward, Prince of Wales; Bismarck, Prince Otto Edward Leopold von; Reid, Sir James; Victoria, Princess Royal; William II, Emperor of Germany

References and further reading:

Benson, E. F. 1939. *Queen Victoria's Daughters.* London: Cassell.

Charlot, Monica. 1991. *Victoria: The Young Queen.* Cambridge: Polity.

Fulford, Roger. 1964. *Dearest Child: Letters between Queen Victoria and the Princess Royal, 1858–61.* London: Evans Brothers.

Hibbert, Christopher. 1984. *Queen Victoria in Her Letters and Journals.* London: Viking.

Kollander, Patricia. 1995. *Frederick III: Germany's Liberal Emperor.* Westport, CT: Greenwood Press.

Lin, Jain I. 1985. *Death of a Kaiser: A Medical Historical Narrative.* Dayton OH: Landfall Press.

Mackenzie, Morell. 1888. *The Fatal Illness of Frederick the Noble.* London: Sampson, Low, Marston, Searle and Rivington.

Magnus, Philip. 1964. *Edward the Seventh.* London: John Murray.

Nichols, J. Alden. 1987. *The Year of Three Kaisers.* Chicago: Univesity of Illinois Press.

Ponsonby, Sir Frederick. 1928. *Letters of the Empress Frederick.* London: Macmillan and Co. (esp. chap. 9, "The Illness of the Crown Prince Frederick").

Poschinger, Margarethe Landau, and Frances A. Welby, eds. 1902. *Diaries of the Emperor Frederick.* London: Chapman and Hall.

Poschinger, Margarethe von. 1902. *Life of the Emperor Frederick.* London: Chapman and Hall.

Reid, Michaela. 1996. *Ask Sir James: The Life of Sir James Reid, Personal Physician to Queen Victoria.* London: Eland.

Van der Kiste, John. 1981. *Frederick III: German Emperor 1888.* Stroud, Gloucestershire: Sutton.

Fresh Air

I always feel so brisk (Hardy 1976, 134)

As they shivered through the wet, dark autumns at Balmoral, the members of the royal household must often have heartily wished that their monarch had never chosen Scotland as the location for one of her holiday homes. Queen Victoria loved its fresh, bracing air and believed implicitly in the therapeutic effects of an active, outdoor life. Much of the blame, as such, for this lifelong preoccupation, which bred in the queen a violent aversion to closed windows and open fires, can be laid at the door of her personal physician, Sir James Clark.

Clark had advised regular intakes of fresh air after Princess Victoria was seriously ill (probably a severe case of tonsillitis) for several weeks in 1835. She had been staying in Ramsgate, on the south coast, at the time, and Dr. Clark had seen the location as preeminently suitable for her convalescence: "Her Royal Highness should be as much in the open air, and in a *healthy bracing* air as possible," he asserted (Woodham-Smith 1972, 107). With the onset of puberty the princess appears to have found hot weather increasingly intolerable; by her standards, anything over 60 degrees was roasting and made her feel "dissolved." Finding summertime a trial, she also took to heart Clark's admonition against overheated rooms in winter. In later years, a regular excuse for decamping as often as possible from Buckingham Palace to the more salubrious environs of Osborne and Balmoral was to escape the polluted air of central London. The therapeutic properties of clean, Scottish mountain air became the panacea around which Victoria's sense of well-being revolved. Prince Albert concurred on the undoubted benefits of fresh air, based on the advice of his patrician mentor, Baron Stockmar (another passionate advocate of self-punishing daily regimes). But he patently suffered from the cold indoors in all the royal palaces, which added rheumatism to the catalog of his many physical woes. When it came to the upbringing of her own children, in this case Prince Arthur, the queen insisted that "too much learning and not *enough* air and exercise, checks the growth and weakness of the brain" (McClintock 1945, 30). In similar vein she would write to her eldest daughter, Vicky, in Berlin, urging her to keep her circulation up by "taking 2 hours good air and exercise regularly daily" (Fulford 1968, 97).

Marie Mallet, a lady-in-waiting who joined the queen's entourage in 1887, has, among others, recorded how even in old age the queen would daily go out for drives—of twenty miles or so, often lasting three hours—utterly oblivious to the cold, seated in an open carriage or landau. Such excursions would take place in the most inclement weather—including pouring rain, heavy snow, and driving, bitter wind. After accompanying the queen on one such late afternoon drive at Balmoral, Mallet did not return until eight in the evening, by which time she was complaining that "the wind was so cold my face turned first blue and then crimson and by dinner-time I looked as if I had been drinking hard for a week"—and this was in *June* (Mallet 1968, 38).

The queen refused to entertain any idea that too much cold air was harmful. "*Good air* is *good* air, whether there be occasional disturbance and deterioration of it from unusual rain or cold or draught" (McClintock 1945, 69). She asserted that she was "a disbeliever in the effects of climate on healthy people" (ibid.). Such dogmatism meant that she showed no pity for those of her ladies who felt the cold and was oblivious to the harm that constant exposure to the elements did to her youngest daughter, Beatrice. An almost constant companion to the queen in her widowhood, Beatrice suffered from crippling rheumatism—no doubt the result of all those freezing carriage drives. The queen's own internal overheating (perhaps due to raised blood pressure that, in later years, was no doubt exacerbated by the onset of the menopause) also led her to disapprove if those who accompanied her piled on extra layers of clothing. The trick, as courtiers at Balmoral soon learned, was to add layers without the queen's noticing, for she objected to her carriage companions "crowding" her out with rugs and furs. The composer and suffragist, Ethel Smyth, describing a visit paid by the queen on the Empress Eugénie in October 1892 while at Balmoral, was incredulous at the outdoor rigors endured by ladies-in-waiting. She sardonically observed that their suffering was "evidently nullified by the glow of loyalty within their bosoms" and admired the strength of the queen's constitution. By the time Victoria took her leave, the rain was "descending like one continuous waterfall." When Smyth asked whether the carriage covers would be shut on the journey home, Victoria's lady-in-waiting wistfully replied "O dear no, I think not" (Smyth 1987, 187).

Lady Augusta Bruce and Lady Jane Churchill were but two of the long-suffering ladies-in-waiting who found themselves frequently subjected to this arduous regime. In October 1861 Bruce recorded, in a typical letter from Balmoral, how she and Lady Churchill had been forewarned of an impending expedition, by carriage and pony. "I could only occupy myself in gathering up all my hottest clothes," she wrote. "I put on endless others and toasted myself at the fire till the fatal moment," after which "off we went, wind, spitting, and a lowering sky" (Windsor and Bolitho 1927, 231). By the time they changed over to ponies two and a half hours later, "it was pouring and the Hills could hardly be seen" (ibid.). Fortunately the queen was obliged to abandon the expedition, but it was only with the greatest reluctance that she "consented to Lunch in the carriage instead of sitting on the splashing grass" (232). Bruce, like others in the royal household, learned to be philosophical. It was futile trying to make the queen appreciate how much others felt the cold or how they dreaded "the idea of sitting for hours perishing on a pony going at a foot's pace and coming home frozen" (ibid.).

After returning from such protracted, bone-chilling outings, the royal household found little to comfort them indoors. The Gothic-style castle at Balmoral might have *looked* romantic, but it did not boast the blazing log fires that went with the image. The queen was notorious for her parsimony where fires were concerned, refusing to allow them to be lit in any room where the temperature was above 56 degrees. Compare this with the present recommended minimum temperature for working environments, generally agreed at 68 degrees Fahrenheit. She installed small ivory thermometers on the mantlepiece of every room to check on this and even ensured there was one in her pew in the private chapel at Windsor Castle. Those fires that *were* lit in the rooms of the queen's residences were pitiful affairs and, on her orders, had firescreens around them. Such draconian rules might seem positively cruel. But the queen did not see things that way; they were all for people's own good. More senior members of the government did, however, balk at this ruling: Prime ministers Benjamin Disraeli and Lord Salisbury both refused to go to Balmoral unless there was a fire lit in their room, claiming that this was on doctor's orders. When Tsar Nicholas II and his entourage—well hardened by the long and bitter Russian winters—visited in the autumn of 1896, they all complained of the miserable cold at Balmoral, which they felt was worse than Siberia (born into a climate of such legendary extremes, the Russians had long since discovered how to keep their palaces efficiently well heated).

Nor were things any different at the queen's other holiday home, Osborne, on the Isle of Wight, especially given the often unpredictable British summer. The prevailing wind that came from the sea could bring with it chilly evenings, as Lord Clarendon noted in June 1860. The queen, he said, "plays at the royal game of summer worse than ever—all windows were open and all the noses blue at and after dinner last night, and today tho' people are shivering the Q:[ueen] I understand doubts whether it is not too hot to drive to *Freshwater* (as if the water would be anything else in this weather)" (Kennedy 1956, 106). When the temperature did rise at Osborne during the summer, Victoria had herself surrounded by buckets of ice (as she also did when traveling on the royal train when the weather became oppressive).

Because Victoria was so much a creature of habit, her daily drives came to be a regular reassurance to her public that the aging queen was still alive. Considerable anxiety was aroused when, in January 1901, the queen's drives from Windsor Castle suddenly stopped. The *Daily News* saw this as an ominous sign: "As all her Majesty's subjects know, her love of fresh air has taken her out of doors in the most inclement weather. It cannot be doubted that the health of her Majesty is precarious" (20 January). The incredulous leader writer, who shared the sentiments of most of the British public that the queen was indestructible, had like them been lulled into thinking that their queen was immortal and was "exempt from sickness and decay" (Rennell 2000, 85). Two days later the queen died.

Related entries:
Balmoral Castle; Bruce, Lady Augusta; Churchill, Lady Jane; Clark, Sir James; Queen Victoria: Physical Appearance of; Smoking

References and further reading:
Fulford, Roger, ed. 1968. *Dearest Mamma: Letters between Queen Victoria and the Crown Princess of Prussia, 1861–64.* London: Evans Brothers.
Hardy, Alan. 1976. *Queen Victoria Was Amused.* London: John Murray (pp. 133–134).
Kennedy, A. L. 1956. *My Dear Duchess: Social and Political Letters of the Duchess of Manchester 1858–1869.* London: John Murray.
Longford, Elizabeth. 1966. "Queen Victoria's Daughters." In Martin Gilbert, ed., *A Century of Conflict 1850–1950.* London: Hamish Hamilton.
Mallet, Victor, ed. 1968. *Life with Queen Victoria: Marie Mallet's Letters from Court 1887–1901.* London: John Murray.
McClintock, Mary Howard. 1945. *The Queen Thanks Sir Howard: The Life of Major General Sir Howard Elphinstone.* London: John Murray.
Rennell, Tony. 2000. *Last Days of Glory: The Death of Queen Victoria.* London: Viking.

Smyth, Ethel. 1987. *The Memoirs of Ethel Smyth.* Abridged and introduced by Ronald Crichton. London: Viking.
St. Aubyn, Giles. 1991. *Victoria: A Portrait.* London: Sinclair Stevenson (pp. 197–198).
Windsor, Dean of, and Hector Bolitho, eds. 1927. *Letters of Lady Augusta Stanley: A Young Lady at Court 1849–1863.* London: Gerald Howe.
Woodham-Smith, Cecil. 1972. *Diaries of the Emperor Frederick during the Campaigns of 1866 and 1870–1871.* London: Chapman and Hall.

Frogmore

the beloved shrine (Longford 1998, 321)

Although the name of Frogmore would, after 1861, be forever associated with the Royal Mausoleum, it had since 1841 also been the location of the duchess of Kent's residence, Frogmore House. Bought in 1792 by George III as a country retreat for his wife, Queen Caroline, the house was inherited by their daughter, Princess Augusta, in 1818. Upon Augusta's death in 1841, the estate was bought by Queen Victoria and the use of Frogmore House made over to her mother in May of that year. This came at a time, a year after her marriage to Prince Albert, when the queen was seeking to distance herself from her mother's interfering presence. At Frogmore, ministered to by her adoring ladies-in-waiting, the duchess mellowed in old age, from a shrewish and manipulative mother into the archetypal sweet old grandmother, and one who suffered her various illnesses with Christian forebearance. Now reconciled with Victoria, the duchess was frequently visited by her from the castle, across Windsor Home Park.

Two mausoleums would be built by Queen Victoria in the grounds of the Frogmore Estate, one as the resting place of the Duchess of Kent, the other for herself and Prince Albert. The former, a small circular temple, built on a grassy mound, with pink granite columns and a copper covered rotunda placed over a burial shaft, was built by Albert Jenkins Humbert, from a design by Ludwig Grüner. Its construction, based on the design of a much-admired mausoleum built at Castle Howard in Yorkshire by the architect Nicholas Hawksmoor, was supervised by Prince Albert shortly before his death, with the intention being that in the duchess's lifetime the rotunda would serve as a summer house. When the duchess died in March 1861, the queen was too prostrated by grief and the onset of a deep depression to attend her mother's funeral. Work had begun on the mausoleum in 1860 but was not completed till July 1861—four months after the duchess's death. Her coffin was finally interred there, in a granite sarcophagus, in August 1861, after resting temporarily at St. George's Chapel, Windsor. The queen, who continued to find solace in the house and gardens at Frogmore after her mother's death, was impressed with the finished mausoleum, which she described as "so pretty—so airy—so grand and simple" (Hibbert 1984, 120). But Prince Albert himself died only nine months after his mother-in-law and it would be Victoria's eldest daughter, Crown Princess Frederick of Prussia (Vicky), who would advise on the construction of the larger mausoleum.

The inspiration for the grand, Romanesque resting place built at Frogmore between 1862 and 1871 for the queen and Prince Albert was the mausoleum of the prince's family, built in Coburg in 1844 upon the death of his father, Duke Ernest. In opting for their own, private mausoleum, the royal couple went against centuries of English tradition, under which sovereigns and their consorts were interred either at Westminster Abbey or St. George's Chapel, Windsor. Within a week of the prince's death on 14 December 1861, an octagonal copper dome of Romanesque design over a cruciform base was chosen by the queen, to be constructed in pink granite and Portland stone. This, too, was executed by Grüner and Humbert. Work

The Royal Mausoleum at Frogmore, located within the grounds of Windsor Great Park, was built by Queen Victoria as the resting place of Prince Albert; she was buried there with him in 1901. (Helen Rappaport)

began in January 1862, and the queen laid the foundation stone on 15 March, but it would take a quarter of a million pounds and nine years before the mausoleum was finally completed.

After his death Prince Albert had been temporarily laid to rest in St. George's Chapel, Windsor, until the new mausoleum was ready for his reburial. The queen was much criticized by church dignitaries for not having him buried in the chapel. Peers, such as Lord Clarendon, observed how misguided it was to create "insignificant tombs in that morass at Frogmore which is constantly flooded" (St. Aubyn 1991, 349). Nevertheless, on a mournful wet day in November 1862, the prince consort's coffin was finally reinterred under a temporary wooden sarcophagus at the new mausoleum at Frogmore. It would take some time yet for the splendid granite sarcophagus (designed to take both Prince Albert's and the queen's coffins) to be constructed, from a single enormous, flawless slab of Scottish granite.

The Italian sculptor Baron Carlo Marochetti, whom the royal couple had regularly patronized, was commissioned to sculpt the plaster model of the prince's effigy, as well as the queen's (although the latter would languish, gathering dust in a wall cavity at Windsor for another thirty-nine years before being needed). In November 1864 the finished effigy was transported from Aberdeen, but Marochetti himself died in 1867, before completing the four bronze angels that would eventually kneel at each of its corners (these would be cast in Paris). At long last, on 26 November 1868, the recumbent marble effigy of Albert was placed in position on top of the sarcophagus of Aberdeen granite, with a base of Belgian marble, although it would be August 1871 before all the interior decorations of the mausoleum were finally finished.

The rich interior, of marble from Belgium, Portugal, and other countries, boasts statuary of the Hebrew kings and prophets that was made in Dresden, as well as frescos based on the High Renaissance style of Raphael, a specific request of the queen in recognition of the prince's great love for Renaissance art. The inlaid floor and altar were also of marble, with the intricate bronze moldings on the latter arousing some concern that the interior might be too elaborately Romish for Church of England tastes. Leading off the central octagon containing the royal sarcophagus were four small recesses, each with its own chapel. Around the walls, memorials and commemorative plaques to other members of the royal family who predeceased the queen would be added over the years, including one to her hemophiliac son Leopold (who died in 1884) and her son-in-law Prince Henry of Battenberg (1896). Although Victoria and Albert would remain the sole occupants of the mausoleum, it contains two additional, commemorative sarcophagi, both the work of the sculptor Sir Joseph Edgar Boehm. These are of the queen's father, the duke of Kent (who died in 1820 and is interred in St. George's Chapel), and a most beautiful and touching representation of her daughter Princess Alice, grand duchess of Hesse, cradling in her arms her dead daughter May. (The princess had died of diptheria in 1878 after contracting it from May; they are both buried at the royal mausoleum in Darmstadt, Germany.)

After the prince consort's death the queen often took drives down to her mother's house at Frogmore, visiting the mausoleum nearby, where she would sit and pray and contemplate Albert's effigy, often for hours at a time. She even had her own set of keys to enable access whenever she wished and, in summer, often took picnic meals under a nearby cedar tree, where she had enjoyed taking tea with her mother when she was alive. A solemn ceremony was enacted in the mausoleum every 14 December by Victoria and her family, on the anniversary of Albert's death. And for the rest of her life, in times of trouble, national emergency, and even moments of gratitude, such as when her son, the Prince of Wales, recovered from typhoid fever in 1872, Victoria would repair to the chapel to give thanks before Albert's marble effigy.

Above the entrance to the mausoleum the queen had had inscribed the words: "Farewell best beloved, here at last I shall rest with thee, with thee in Christ I shall rise again." The body of the queen was reunited with Prince Albert there on a bitterly cold 4 February 1901. In years to come, her children would return to Frogmore to pay their respects in the mausoleum on the anniversary of her death. On one such occasion, a sparrow entered the inner sanctum and fluttered overhead, at which point several of the family wondered whether this might be mama's spirit returning, to watch over them. Victoria's daughter-in-law Queen Alexandra was, however, adamant that it was not, "because it would not have made a mess on Beatrice's bonnet" (Rennell 2000, 293).

Related entries:
Albert Memorial; Bruce, Lady Augusta; Queen Victoria: Death and Funeral of

References and further reading:

Curl, James Stevens. 2000. *The Victorian Celebration of Death*. Stroud, Gloucestershire: Sutton.

Darby, Elisabeth, and Nicola Smith. 1983. *The Cult of the Prince Consort*. New Haven: Yale University Press.

Frogmore House and the Royal Mausoleum. 2000. Official Guide. London: St. James's Palace.

Hibbert, Christopher. 1984. *Queen Victoria in Her Letters and Journals*. London: Viking.

Hobhouse, Hermione. 1983. *Prince Albert: His Life and Work*. London: Hamish Hamilton.

Packard, Jerrold M. 1995. *Farewell in Splendour: The Passing of Queen Victoria and Her Age*. Stroud, Gloucestershire: Sutton.

Rennell, Tony. 2000. *Last Days of Glory*. London: Viking.

St. Aubyn, Giles. 1991. *Queen Victoria: A Portrait*. London: Sinclair Stevenson.

G

Gladstone, William Ewart (1809–1898)

the abominable old G. man (Ponsonby 1942, 217)

The figure of the Grand Old Man of British politics, Willam Ewart Gladstone, four times Liberal prime minister of Great Britain, stands as a great monolith in nineteenth-century politics. He is famous for having exhausted himself in his self-imposed mission "to pacify Ireland" by disestablishing the Irish Church and fighting for Irish Home Rule. He succeeded in bringing in a national education system for children aged five to thirteen and also carried parliamentary reform that would bring the vote to nearly all male members of the population. Yet for all his tenacity and dedication to British political life, Gladstone was, for most of his career, the man the queen most loved to hate.

As someone who, by temperament, political beliefs, and aspirations, was so diametrically opposed to his arch political rival Benjamin Disraeli, Gladstone has been extensively compared with the Conservative leader, not just in political terms but also in relation to their very different, personal dealings with Queen Victoria. Although the bitter if not "black" hatred that grew up between these too political adversaries added an often thrilling dynamic to parliamentary debate and neither made any attempt to hide his contempt for the other, their personal antipathies directly influenced the queen's attitudes.

Gladstone—sober, earnest, moralistic, and down to earth, a man accused of always being "so damnably right" (Hardie 1935, 109)—could not have been more different from the flashy, witty, cynical man of the world, Disraeli. Whereas Disraeli had haunted the social and political salons of London soliciting the patronage of high-born women, the evangelizing Gladstone had sought, in his spare time, to rescue their downtrodden sisters from sin and prostitution. And while Disraeli effortlessly conjured up the most rococo language in which he made extravagant promises to the queen and seemed ever ready to accommodate her slightest wish, Gladstone's doggedly hectoring tone alienated her and did nothing to break through the wall of the queen's obduracy over any reforms that whiffed of radicalism. Disraeli, although admiring Gladstone's rhetoric, nevertheless regularly referred to him as the "Arch Villain" (Blake 1966, 726); the queen likewise became convinced that Gladstone was unbalanced as well as dangerous. Over the years, Disraeli would do much to inflame what became an "almost pathological animus" on her part against Gladstone (Blake 1966, 605).

Gladstone was born into a family of Scottish ancestry. The son of a Liverpool

Queen Victoria's enduring antipathy towards the Liberal politician William Gladstone never waned, although she finally, grudgingly came to acknowledge his gifts as a minister. (Library of Congress)

merchant who had had slave plantations in the West Indies, he was educated at Eton and Christ Church, Oxford, where, in 1831, he obtained a first in classics and mathematics, thereafter retaining a lifelong passion for translating Homer. His strongly evangelical upbringing created in him a religious sense of mission about all the many causes he pursued. His original intention had been to become a clergyman, but this was abandoned for the wider world of politics, which Gladstone entered in 1832 as Tory member of Parliament for Newark. Apart from one year out of office (1846), he would remain there until 1895.

Tall and imposing, Gladstone was an omnivorous reader and physically active (the only one of Queen Victoria's ministers to actually enjoy taking long vigorous walks in the bracing air of Balmoral). His physique, combined with his intense mental powers, his sense of high moral purpose, and his command of rhetoric, gave him a commanding if not intimidating presence in Parliament. In the late 1840s he entered into a vigorous social campaign, reclaiming prostitutes through the offices of the Church Penitentiary Association for the Reclamation of Fallen Women and helping to establish a refuge for them—the House of St. Barnabas-in-Soho—opened in 1847. Gladstone's mission to reclaim prostitutes became the subject of much gossip after he began openly accosting them on his way home from Parliament, offering them shelter and, he hoped, rehabilitation.

Gladstone served in a succession of junior posts before being appointed president of the Board of Trade during Sir Robert Peel's second ministry of 1843–1845. As a Peelite (reformist Tory—precursor to the Conservatives), Gladstone's political sympathies lay closer to the old Whig Party (precursor of the Liberals). He came to the fore politically after the death of Peel in 1850, remaining committed to Peelite aspirations. The most important cabinet post he held in his early career was as chancellor of the Exchequer (1852–1855) during Lord Aberdeen's coalition government, in which capacity he cut excise duties and would have liked to cut income tax also. His masterly command of oratory was demonstrated in his long speeches, such as a five-hour defense of his 1853 budget. Most of his financial plans were forestalled, however, by the outbreak of the Crimean War in 1854 and the channeling of government funds into the war effort.

Gladstone twice turned down the chance of being a member of Lord Derby's Conservative government. In 1859 he accepted the post of chancellor of the Exchequer in Lord Palmerston's Whig cabinet of 1859–1865, during which Gladstone protested the high level of defense spending in support of Palmerston's aggressive foreign policy. When Palmerston died in 1865, Gladstone became leader of the House of Commons and a year later introduced a bill for moderate franchise reform. This foundered and the government resigned. Ironically for the reformist Gladstone, it was his rival, Benjamin Disraeli, who took up the cause of franchise reform and pushed through a more radical bill in 1867, the year that Gladstone succeeded Lord John Russell as leader of the Liberal Party. In the general election of 1868, Gladstone was returned to Parliament in a Liberal landslide, as member of Parliament for Greenwich.

Gladstone had had his first official audience with Queen Victoria, as chancellor of the Exchequer, in March 1862, on which occasion he had seemed to her extremely cordial, kind, and consoling over the recent death of Prince Albert, about whom he spoke to Victoria "with such unbounded admiration and appreciation" (Hibbert 1984, 163). By 1866, Mary Ponsonby, the wife of the queen's future private secretary, was remarking that "Mr. Gladstone has no possible understanding of a joke—that, I am sure, is the hitch and the cause of his failing to reap all the benefit he might from his immense talents" (Ponsonby 1927, 59). By now Gladstone had many pressing reforms on his mind—not the least of them measures to counter growing unrest in Ireland, an issue over which he soon found himself at odds with the queen. Gladstone intended a major attempt at reconciliation with Ireland through the disestablishment of the Irish Church. Such a measure, which would release Roman Catholics from the obligation to pledge allegiance to the Church of England, horrified Victoria. She saw it as a direct assault on her God-given role as defender of the Protestant faith in Britain. The bill was passed in 1869, but it did little to placate the Irish, nor did the first Irish Land Act, brought in by Gladstone in 1870 in an attempt to protect tenant farmers from oppressive landlords.

In his personal relationships—with fellow members of Parliament as well as his queen—Gladstone's overriding problem remained his humorlessness and intolerance of frivolity. The naturally hectoring tone and clumsiness of manner with which he addressed the queen offended and alienated her. She disliked anyone who adopted the "God and my right" approach with her on any topic; for much the same reason Disraeli nicknamed Gladstone a "Tartuffe," after the pious hypocrite of Moliere's play. His other political opponents had the same problem with Gladstone's egotism and his refusal to enter into conversation on any topic that did not interest him. Nor would he indulge the queen: "When not holding forth on his own subjects, he withdrew into himself; when not haranguing he was mute. Queen Victoria could chat away gaily about her paintings and her distant German cousins with the sympathetic and courteous Disraeli; but she had to listen while Gladstone lectured her on the Hittites or Homer or the Athanasian Creed" (Pearson 1951, 175).

With or without the queen's support, Gladstone battled on with a series of major army reforms that abolished flogging in the army in peacetime, reduced the term of enlistment to six years' active duty and six in the reserves, and in a highly controversial move in 1871, abolished the purchase of officer's commissions. Other major reforms came with William Forster's Elementary Education Act of 1870, which established free education for all children aged five to thirteen; the Licensing Bills of 1871 and 1872; the legalization of trade unions in 1871; and a move to further extend voting rights through the introduction of the secret vote in the Ballot Act of 1872.

Such an extensive program of reform brought with it the need for considerable consultation with the monarch, throwing the spotlight on the queen's frequent absences from Windsor and her continuing seclusion for much of the year at her homes at Balmoral and Osborne. Gladstone was infuriated by the way in which this hampered the business of government and played into the hands of republican elements in Parliament. By 1872 the levels of antagonism between the queen and her prime minister had escalated. Gladstone was now making a determined assault on the queen's resistance to undertaking public duties; too often, it seemed she fell back on repeated excuses about the state of her health. Gladstone's lack of sympathy provoked further antipathy, with Victoria now referring to him as "a very dangerous Minister—and so wonderfully unsympathetic" (Fulford 1976, 29).

He had been warned that his direct approach would backfire on him, and it most certainly did. The queen responded hysterically to Gladstone's accusations of dereliction of duty, claiming that the overwork and worry that had carried off Albert would do the same for her. Gladstone read gloom and doom into such protestations: "*Worse* things may be imagined but smaller and meaner causes for the decay of Thrones cannot be conceived" (Guedalla 1933, 1:299–300). The institution of monarchy, to which he himself was unquestionably devoted (although the queen never seemed able to appreciate this), was in his estimation moribund: "It is like the worm which bores the bark of a noble oak tree and so breaks the channel of its life" (ibid.).

As the 1870s wore on, Gladstone felt himself inceasingly at the receiving end of a "repellent power which she so well knows how to use" and which he felt had been deliberately "put in action towards me" (Aronson 1977, 117). The queen's pen continued to scribble out invective against him. He was violent, mischievous, dangerous, impetuous, "and so very arrogant, tyrannical and obstinate with no knowledge of the world or human nature" (Blake 1966, 546)—or at least, this was what Prince Albert had told her, and he of course was always right. Victoria strongly disapproved of Gladstone's predilection for High Church ritual, making him positively a "Jesuit" and religious fanatic in her view. But his most telling shortcoming for the queen was his "want of *égard* [regard] towards my feelings" (Fulford 1976, 130). All in all he was an "unsatisfactory Premier" and a "bad leader of the House of Commons" (ibid.).

When Gladstone's government fell early in 1874, the queen was relieved; for her it was, as Blake suggested, "a wholseome sign that the nation had recovered its senses" (Blake 1966, 545). Gladstone retreated to his country estate, where he devoted time to translating Homer and wrote antipapist tracts. During his years in political opposition he fulfilled a crucial role as an outstanding political antagonist of Disraeli. No one, argued Lord Frederick Ponsonby, "could have been found better than Disraeli to draw his fire, to rouse his indignation, to be a target for his invective"(Ponsonby 1932, 216). Thus it was, that despite being out of office "in this way Gladstone was of as great a service to Disraeli as Disraeli was to Gladstone" (ibid.).

In the summer of 1876 Gladstone was greatly taken up with the so-called Bulgarian atrocities, when around 25,000 Bulgarian peasants were murdered by Turkish troops after a political insurrection against Ottoman rule. He published a pamphlet, "Bulgarian Horrors and the Question of the East," in which he denounced the Turkish nation wholesale for this act of genocide. The pamphlet provoked considerable public outcry in Britain, but it infuriated both Disraeli and the queen who, seeing Russian ambitions in the East as far more dangerous, were determined to remain allies with the Turks. Gladstone's actions in their view were dangerous, impetuous, and unprincipled and could plunge Britain back into war with Russia. Gladstone was adamant; he resigned his seat at Greenwich and, determined to defend his position, stood for reelection in the Scottish constituency of Midlothian in 1879, producing some outstanding campaign speeches. The queen found it all too distasteful: "Mr. Gladstone is going about Scotland, like an American stumping orator" (Longford 1998, 427). But it was a tactic that proved highly popular and won support for Gladstone as "the People's William." They returned him to power as prime minister in March 1880.

Gladstone's return to government during 1880–1885 brought with it the high noon of the long-simmering antipathy between himself and the queen. Her reaction to the fall from power of her beloved Disraeli was almost hysterical. As Auchincloss observed, she now found herself "being hauled out of the warm and fragrant bath of Disraeli's premiership and plunged again into the icy waters of Gladstone's" (1979, 113). She refused point-blank to cooperate with a man whom she was convinced was intent on undermining her authority and set upon ruining the country. She was ready to do anything rather than accept Gladstone. As she was not technically obliged to have him as prime minister, because he was no longer leader of the Liberal Party, she tried to enlist the new Liberal Party leader Lord Granville or the leader in the House of Commons, Lord Hartington, to take the post. But the country, it appeared, would accept nobody but Gladstone, and no new ministry had any chance of succeeding without him. Victoria was enraged: on 4 April she told Ponsonby that she would "sooner abdicate than send for or have any *communication* with that half-mad fire-brand who would soon ruin everything and be a *Dictator*" (Ponsonby 1942, 184) Full of self-righteous indignation, she sent a strong memorandum to Ponsonby making it clear that, should she concede, she would tolerate "no democratic leaning, no attempt to change foreign policy, no change in India, and *no* cutting down of estimates. In short, *no lowering* of the *high position* this Country holds, and *ought always* to hold" (St. Aubyn 1991, 445).

During this ministry, despite his advancing age (the queen kept rather hopefully observing that he always looked unwell), he was as vigorous and unsparing in pressing the queen on a succession of crucial issues as of old. His rhetoric might be powerful, but his method with Victoria still utterly failed him. The more he lectured, the more she resisted and "held him at arm's length" (Longford 1998, 445). The uncontrolled torrent of words, theological conundrums, and abstractions with which Gladstone assailed her were mind-numbing. There was too much "sound and fury" in them, as Ponsonby observed (1932, 215), and the queen had a particular aversion for such sermonizing. She protested loud and long about Gladstone's murderous intentions of ruining the country with his dangerous radicalism, most manifest in his clearly stated mission to bring about major social and political upheaval in Ireland (see "Ireland").

Gladstone's Irish policies would prove to be his greatest strength and also cause him the greatest disappointments. His second Irish Land Act (1881) set out to improve the lot of the tenant farmer, but his two attempts at introducing bills for Home Rule in Ireland were fiercely resisted and defeated in Parliament. A modicum of improvement to the franchise in Britain came with the third Reform Act in 1884—giving agricultural laborers the vote—but much of the 1880s was taken up with foreign rather than domestic affairs, including the British occupation of Egypt and the fiasco of the attempt to rescue General Gordon at Khartoum during the war in the Sudan. Gladstone's time was consumed by the writing of hundreds of letters and memorandums to the queen on a vast range of political subjects, only to find himself constantly rebuked; "The Queen alone is enough to kill any man," he remarked (Hardie 1935, 73). By June 1885, when his budget was defeated in the House of Commons, Gladstone seemed almost glad to take a breather from political life, declining the queen's offer of an earldom (a formality to an outgoing prime minister). The taste for the fight soon returned, however, when Lord Salisbury's minority government collapsed after only a few months.

After another spate of rousing election speeches, Gladstone returned for a third term in February 1886, utterly committed to a radical reformist policy in Ireland and the introduction of Home Rule. The queen was seriously alarmed at where his radical policies were taking the country; in a speech at Liverpool, Gladstone openly promised that "all the world over, I will back the masses against the classes" (*The Times,* 29 June 1886). Such words smacked dangerously of the ideals of socialism, and in Victoria's view, the road from socialism led straight to revolution. But in July Gladstone was once more ousted from power over his pursuit of a Home Rule bill for Ireland; the following six years were spent drumming up support for this cause until he was returned, by a narrow margin, for his fourth and final ministry in 1892.

By now Gladstone's sight and hearing were visibly failing, much to the queen's horror, who despaired that her government would be left "in the shaking hand of an old, wild, incomprehensible man of 82½" (Hibbert 2000, 375). She dreaded having to endure yet more of what her secretary Ponsonby had called Gladstone's "terrible earnestness" (Ponsonby 1942, 244). But the feeling was mutual: Gladstone did not look forward to their official audience, which was, he wrote, "such as took place between Marie Antionette and her executioner" (Buckle 1930–1932, 2:45). This final ministry was held together in the main by longstanding party loyalty to the old campaigner, whom many referred to as the Grand Old Man. Even the queen's daughter Vicky tried to persuade her mother to soften toward Gladstone in his twilight years, reminding her that he had always been loyal to the Crown. The queen's response was ungenerous, and as usual she overlooked her own legendary obstinacy: "It is quite idle to attempt to have any influence with him. He listens to no one and won't hear any contradiction in discussion. He is really half crazy, half silly and it is better not to provoke discussion" (Ramm 1990, 146–147). It was, she averred "awful to have such a man at the head" (ibid.).

Gladstone's infirmities did not prevent him surviving the eighty-five highly contested sittings held in the House of Commons in pursuit of the Home Rule Bill, which was eventually passed, at long last giving the Irish control of some of their domestic affairs. As expected, it was thrown out by the landed interests of those in the House of Lords. Gladstone resigned on 3 March 1894. The queen made no concessions during their final, frosty interview. When Gladstone died of cancer on 19 May 1898, she managed to summon up some words of appreciation in her journal, admitting that "he was very clever and full of ideas for the bettering and advancement of the country" (Hibbert 1984, 337). Victoria now no longer denied his loyalty to her and her family. But although she could not help feeling that he had sometimes done the country harm, she could not dismiss his undoubted popular appeal: "He had a wonderful power of speaking and carrying the masses with him" (337). But when it came to writing to Mrs. Gladstone, she had difficulty finding the appropriate words. Her "absolute love of truth," Victoria privately admitted, prevented her: "I did not like the man. How can I say I am sorry when I am not?" (Longford 1998, 550). Within three days of Gladstone's funeral and his laying to rest in Westminster Abbey, the queen was back on track again, writing to Vicky and reminding her that Gladstone for all his talents had "never *tried* to keep up the *honour* and *prestige* of Great Britain. He gave away the Transvaal, he abandoned Gordon, he destroyed the Irish Church and tried to separate England from Ireland and to set class against class. The harm he did cannot easily be undone" (Ramm 1990, 215). And then, almost as an afterthought, "But he was a good and very religious man" (ibid.).

Just before his death, Gladstone had likened his service of the queen to that of a "Sicilian mule" that had struggled under his own weight during a visit to Sicily (Guedalla 1933, 2:75–76). Having borne his own metaphorical burden of the queen's ill grace for so many years, Gladstone was deeply dismayed by her ingratitude and also by the fact that she should ever have doubted his veneration of the monarchy and the constitution that it upheld. He certainly does not deserve the reputation, born of the queen's hostility and the bad feeling of his own political opponents, that he was nothing but "a humourless humbug, a sanctimonious hypocrite claiming the authority of the Almighty when producing the ace of trumps from his sleeve" (Blake 1966, 761). He was one of the nineteenth century's great parliamentarians and a true man of his times. A financial genius at the Exchequer, a scholar, and a great speech-maker, he combined the instincts of preacher, social reformer, champion of the underclasses, and humanitarian. He served the British Parliament with unstinting energy for sixty-three years.

Gladstone's old adversary Disraeli would always pride himself on the fact that, whereas Gladstone treated the queen "like a public department," Disraeli himself treated her "like a woman" (Longford 1998, 402). It is the opinion of Disraeli's biographer, Robert Blake (1966, 765), however, that the stolid, hard-working Gladstone was undoubtedly the moral and intellectual superior of that great, gaudy political showman.

Related entries:
Boer War; Disraeli, Benjamin; Gordon, General Charles George; Ireland; Peel, Sir Robert

References and further reading:

Aronson, Theo. 1977. *Victoria and Disraeli: The Making of a Romantic Partnership.* London: Macmillan.

Auchinloss, Louis. 1979. *Persons of Consequence: Queen Victoria and Her Circle.* London: Weidenfeld and Nicolson.

Blake, Robert. 1966. *Disraeli.* London: Eyre and Spottiswoode.

Buckle, George Earl, ed. 1926–1928. *Letters of Queen Victoria 1862–85.* 2d ser. London: John Murray.

———. 1930–1932. *Letters of Queen Victoria 1886–1901.* 3d ser. London: John Murray.

Cecil, Algernon. 1953. *Queen Victoria and Her Prime Ministers.* London: Eyre and Spottiswoode.

Eccleshall, Robert, and Graham Walker, eds. 1998. *Biographical Dictionary of British Prime Ministers.* London: Routledge.

Feuchtwanger, E. J. 1975. *Gladstone.* London: Allen Lane.

Foot, M. R. D., and H. C. G. Matthew, eds. 1968–1994. *The Gladstone Diaries.* 14 vols. Oxford: Clarendon Press.

Fulford, Roger, ed. 1976. *Darling Child: Private Correspondence of Queen Victoria and the Crown Princess of Prussia, 1871–1878.* London: Evans Brothers.

Guedalla, Philip. 1933. *The Queen and Mr. Gladstone, 1845–1898.* 2 vols. London: Hodder and Stoughton.

Hardie, Frank. 1935. *The Political Influence of Queen Victoria.* London: Oxford University Press.

Hibbert, Christopher. 1984. *Queen Victoria in Her Letters and Journals.* London: Viking.

———. 2000. *Victoria: A Personal History.* London: HarperCollins.

Jenkins, Roy. 1995. *Gladstone.* London: Macmillan.

Longford, Elizabeth. [1964] 1998. *Victoria R.I.* London: Weidenfeld and Nicolson.

Magnus, Philip M. 1954. *Gladstone: A Biography.* London: John Murray.

Matthew, H. C. G. 1986. *Gladstone 1809–1874.* Oxford: Clarendon Press.

Morley, John. 1905–1906. *The Life of William Ewart Gladstone.* 3 vols. London: Macmillan.

Pearson, Hesketh. 1951. *Dizzy: The Life and Nature of Benjamin Disraeli, Earl of Beaconsfield.* London: Methuen.

Posonby, Arthur. 1942. *Henry Posonby, Queen Victoria's Private Secetary: His Life from His Letters.* London: Macmillan.

Ponsonby, Lord. 1932. "William Ewart Gladstone." In H. J. and H. Massingham, eds., *The Great Victorians.* London: Ivor Nicholson and Watson.

Ponsonby, Magadalen. 1927. *Mary Ponsonby: A Memoir, Some Letters and a Journal.* London: John Murray.

Ramm, Agatha, ed. 1990. *Beloved and Darling Child: Last Letters between Queen Victoria and Her Eldest Daughter, 1886–1901.* Stroud, Gloucestershire: Sutton.

Shannon, Richard. 1982. *Gladstone, Peel's Inheritor: 1809–1865,* vol. 1: *Gladstone, Heroic Minister: 1865–1898,* vol. 2. London: Hamish Hamilton.

St. Aubyn, Giles. 1991. *Queen Victoria, a Portrait.* London: Sinclair Stevenson.

Golden Jubilee, 1887

this never-to-be-forgotten day will always leave the most gratifying and heart-stirring memories behind (Aronson 1973, 6)

The year 1862 should have seen celebrations for the queen's Silver Jubilee, but coming so soon after the death of Prince Albert (who had died in December 1861), there was absolutely no question of the queen's appearing in public to celebrate at a time when she was still prostrate with grief. Between then and her Golden Jubilee twenty-five years later, the queen had resisted appearing in public on all but the most essential state occasions. Such a withdrawal from public view had done Victoria considerable damage in the eyes of the nation and in terms of national prestige abroad. There had been regular and often serious rumblings of discontent about her absence, with

London street decorations during Queen Victoria's Golden Jubilee of 1887. Here, her carriage is en route for Buckingham Palace after a service of thanksgiving at Westminster Abbey. (Hulton/Archive by Getty Images)

a marked rise in republicanism, particularly at the beginning of the 1870s. However, by the end of 1887, the Jubilee Year, Queen Victoria would have been restored to the bosom of the British public, whose show of affection for her would once more make her happy—insofar as she ever would be during her widowhood. The pageantry of the Golden Jubilee would also reaffirm the queen's status as an international symbol of benign, constitutional rule. As a spectacular public relations exercise in nation building, it would celebrate the years of stability since the end of the Crimean War in 1856, which had stimulated the expansion of the empire (now covering one-quarter of the earth's land surface) and with it the growth of overseas investment.

The celebrations and public declarations of loyalty to the queen began months before in many parts of the empire—with street parties and parades in Australia, firework displays in India in the shape of the queen's head, and even the doling out of extra rice to the inmates of leper hospitals in Singapore. In Britain, bells were rung, medals were struck, statues were commissioned, and a steady stream of memorabilia filled the shops: Jubilee mugs, cups, plates, flags, brooches, and pins as well as more prosaic commodities such as Royal Anniversary Soap and the cure-all Jubilicon digestive preparation. On 18 June a general amnesty was granted to British soldiers who had deserted, and many inmates of British prisons were also released. In Sind, in India, the Jubilee was celebrated, in somewhat unorthodox fashion, with the opening of the Queen Victoria Jubilee Burial and Burning Ground.

For weeks in advance of the ceremony, people in London began seeking out the best viewpoints. The press carried enticing advertisements from people with houses along the route. In *Punch* one such unnamed "Nobleman's Mansion" offered "a few excellent seats . . . on the chimney-pots" at the extortionate price of five guineas and offered a concessionary rate of three guineas for a seat on the kitchen chimney, on account of the fact that "there will be necessarily a fire lighted below"! (Harlow and Carter 1999, 394). The whole of the country was gripped with Jubilee fever by the time June began, with endless street parties and parades. The queen, too, had been on an exhausting round of public engagements for weeks beforehand: attending "soirées, symposia, balls, garden parties, commemoration services, presentations of testimonials, royal progresses, dinners with interminable toasts and droning addresses, dedications of buildings and statues, naval reviews, openings of exhibitions" (Weintraub 1996, 6), as well as receiving spectacular gifts of gold, silver, and jewels from around the empire. On the nineteenth the queen spent some time in quiet contemplation beside Prince Albert's sarcophagus in the Royal Mausoleum at Frogmore. Her sense of solitude amid all the activity going on around her still prevailed the following morning: "The day has come, & I am alone" (Nevill 1997, 127). That day, she traveled by train from Windsor to Paddington. From there she rode in an open landau to Buckingham Palace, to find it bursting with guests, many of whom she later received in the Picture Gallery. The rest of the day was filled with a luncheon party and a formal dinner in the Supper Room—with the gathered male royals resplendent in their respective uniforms.

As 20 June, the anniversary of her accession, was also the anniversary of the death of the queen's predecessor, William IV, in strict deference to the rituals of mourning the queen refused to allow her Jubilee to be celebrated on that day. It was a day for Christian worship and reflection and one on which she recorded in her journal that "God has mercifully sustained me through many great trials and sorrows" (Longford 1998, 499); as yet the queen's sense of celebration was entirely absent and apprehension prevailed. Meanwhile, throughout the churches of Britain voices were raised to sing the "Hymn for the Jubilee," in which the queen was lauded for the "stainless honour" with which she had upheld the state, despite having also to grasp "the chalice of deep sorrow" (Bullock 1887, 201).

The procession from Buckingham Palace took place in fine weather on the morning of 21 June, along Piccadilly and Pall Mall, across Trafalgar Square, down Whitehall, and to Westminster Cathedral. The queen had refused point-blank to wear her cumbersome state robes, nor would she wear a crown, which apart from being far too ostentatious, in her opinion, would have made her much too hot. She did, however, make a minor concession in her dress, by not appearing completely swathed in black and instead wearing "a dress and bonnet trimmed with white point d'Alençon [lace], diamond ornaments in my bonnet, and pearls round my neck, with all my orders" (Hibbert 1984, 305). She was accompanied in her carriage by her eldest daughter, Vicky, crown princess of Prussia, and by Alexandra, princess of Wales. The cavalcade of forty-seven carriages bearing many of the crowned and putative heads of Europe and their families would be—along with the queen's funeral in 1901—the last great state gathering of so many monarchs—a large number of whom would have lost their crowns by the end of World War I in 1918. The male members of Victoria's vast family followed the state carriages on horseback and in uniform, prominent among them the queen's now middle-aged heir, Albert Edward, Prince of Wales, wearing the red tunic of a British field marshal.

But, by common consensus, the star of the show was the distinguished, ramrod figure of Frederick William, the German crown prince, dressed as a Pomeranian Cuirassier and wearing the Order of the Garter, which Victoria had awarded him. "Nothing could exceed the splendour of his presence in a uniform wholly white, and having on his burnished steel helmet the great silver crest of an eagle with outspread wings," remarked the marquis of Lorne in his account (Lorne 1901, 346). It was a brave and loyal gesture, for Frederick was already seriously ill with cancer. He died the following year, upon which Victoria, grieving for a much-loved son-in-law, sent to Prussia for the horse that Frederick had ridden in the Jubilee parade and had it stabled at Windsor "with orders that no one was ever to cross its back again" (Bullock 1887, 67).

At the thanksgiving service, held at 3 P.M. at Westminster Abbey, the queen took center stage, seated in the coronation chair of Edward III. It was a testing moment for her, the emotion welling up inside: "I sat alone (oh! without my beloved husband, for whom this would have been such a proud day)" (Bolitho 1949, 304). Soon she heard the choir of 300 voices sing the "Te Deum" composed by Prince Albert. The religious ceremony was a relatively short one, the queen having informed her prime minister, Lord Salisbury, the previous December that "there should be no discourse or sermon: because at that time of year the weather is likely to be hot; and in hot weather, her strength fails her almost entirely" (Roberts 1999, 460).

The queen returned to Buckingham Palace, drained by the heat of the day, to take a late luncheon at 4 P.M. By the time she had got through this and another march past of the Blue Jackets, which she watched from a balcony, she was "half dead with fatigue" (Hibbert 1984, 306). After resting in her room, where she attempted vainly to read through a deluge of telegrams, she returned to take head of table at a late dinner, and then watched fireworks displays. Bonfires were lit across the land. The queen retired for the night, still hearing the sound of the crowds outside. "I am very tired, but very happy" she remarked (Lee 1902, 487). Next day the papers around the empire, as well as in New York, carried extensive coverage of the celebrations. The queen drove to Hyde Park that afternoon to witness a huge party laid on for 26,000 (although the queen claimed 30,000 in her journal) of London's poor children, who were fed with buns and milk and given a Jubilee mug and who watched as a huge hot-air balloon inscribed "Victoria" was launched over London. She returned to Windsor Castle that evening; her carriage ascended the hill to the sound of cheers, the singing of the national anthem, and music from military bands.

The queen would write in her journal that the two days of her Jubilee celebrations would "remain indelibly impressed on my mind" (Hibbert 1984, 307). On 24 June she sent her own personal message to the British people, thanking them for the warmth of her reception. While acknowledging how hard it had been for her to continue since the loss of Albert, she felt buoyed up by the love and affection in which she was held by the nation. "This feeling and the sense of duty towards my dear country and subjects, who are so inseparably bound up with my life, will encourage me in my task, often a very difficult and arduous one, during the remainder of my life" (Lorne 1901, 346).

On 21 July the queen sent her thanks to her prime minister, Lord Rosebery. The celebrations had been, she felt, a vindication of "fifty years' hard work, anxiety, and care" (Hibbert 1984, 307). Before they ended, the queen presided over a Jubilee Garden Party at Buckingham Palace, which brought to a close the London season. A military review of 58,000 troops at Aldershot was followed by a naval review of 135 vessels and 20,000 officers and men at Spithead.

During Jubilee Year the queen was deluged with telegrams and loyal addresses, as well as letters of goodwill, from many of her poorest subjects, "often written on cheap paper in painfully formed handwriting" (Chapman and Raban 1977, n.p.). She received hundreds of lavish and unusual gifts: the thakore of Morvi brought over his favorite horse from western India and offered it to her. The queen of Hawaii, who had made a long and tiring journey from the other side of the world and who had been one of those much remarked upon during the Jubilee parade, presented Victoria with a somewhat puzzling artifact composed of "very rare feathers, but very strangely arranged as a wreath round my monogram, also in feathers on a black ground, framed" (Aronson 1973, 3). By far the most significant gift was a subscription by 3 million women of England that raised a total of £75,000 as a Women's Jubilee Gift; the queen made most of it over to founding an institution, the Queen's Jubilee Nurses, to train nurses for the care of the poor sick in their homes.

In Jubilee Year the queen's image was commemorated on many memorials, notably a Jubilee statue by the royal sculptor Sir Joseph Edgar Boehm that was raised at Windsor. Her sculptress daughter Louise also began work on a statue, which she did not complete until six years later. The queen attended the statue's unveiling, in 1893, in Kensington Gardens, to the sound of cheering crowds. Returning to Windsor by carriage, her granddaughter, Princess Marie Louise, remarked that such demonstrations of public affection no doubt made the queen very proud, to which she had replied: "No, dear child, very humble" (Marie Louise 1961, 124).

Related entries:
Diamond Jubilee; Empress of India; Fresh Air; Salisbury, Robert Arthur Talbot Gascoigne-Cecil, Third Marquis of; "The Widow at Windsor"

References and further reading:

Aronson, Theo. 1973. *Grandmama of Europe: The Crowned Descendants of Queen Victoria.* London: Cassell.

Bolitho, Hector. 1949. *The Reign of Queen Victoria.* London: Collins.

Bullock, Rev. Charles. 1887. *The Queen's Resolve: A Jubilee Memorial.* London: "Home Words" Publishing Office (chap. 10).

Chapman, Caroline, and Paul Raban. 1977. *Debrett's Queen Victoria's Jubilees.* London: Debrett.

Craik, D. M. M. 1887. *Fifty Golden Years: Incidents in the Queen's Reign.* London: R. Tuck and Sons.
Harlow, Barbara, and Mai Carter, eds. 1999. *Imperialism and Orientalism: A Documentary Sourcebook.* Oxford: Blackwell.
Hibbert, Christopher. 1984. *Queen Victoria in Her Letters and Journals.* London: Viking.
Lant, J. I. 1980. *Insubstantial Pageant: Ceremony and Confusion at Queen Victoria's Court.* New York: Taplinger.
Lee, Sir Sidney. 1902. *Queen Victoria, A Biography.* London: Smith, Elder and Co.
Longford, Elizabeth. [1964] 1998. *Victoria R.I.* London: Weidenfeld and Nicolson (chap. 33).
Lorne, Marquis of. 1901. *V.R. I.: Her Life and Empire.* London: Eyre and Spottiswoode.
Mackenzie, J. M. 1984. *Propaganda and Empire: The Manipulation of British Public Opinion, 1880–1961.* Manchester, UK: Manchester University Press.
Marie Louise, Princess. 1961. *My Memories of Six Reigns.* Harmondsworth, UK: Penguin.
Nevill, Barry St. John. 1997. *Life at the Court of Queen Victoria, with Selections from the Journals of Queen Victoria.* Stroud, Gloucestershire: Sutton.
Perugini, Mark Edward. 1932. *Victorian Days and Ways.* London: Jarrolds.
Richards, T. 1987. "The Image of Victoria in the Years of Jubilee." *Victorian Studies* 3 (1): 7–32.
Roberts, Andrew. 1999. *Salisbury: Victorian Titan.* London: Weidenfeld and Nicolson.
Weintraub, Stanley. 1996. *Victoria.* London: John Murray (chap. 1, "Jubilee [1887]").

Gordon, General Charles George (1833–1885)

("Chinese Gordon")

Mr. Gladstone and the Government have . . . Gordon's innocent, noble, heroic blood on their consciences (Hardie 1935, 83)

The charismatic soldier Gen. Charles Gordon, who earned the sobriquet of Chinese Gordon for his fearless leadership during the second Opium War in China, is undoubtedly one of the most fascinating figures in the pantheon of Victorian military heroes. He was enshrined as a Victorian icon after his death at the siege of Khartoum, during an uprising in the Sudan. But few knew the real man, for he lived a life of rigorous self-denial and material austerity. He never married and spent much time alone, in religious contemplation and an almost obsessional study of the Bible. Indeed, in different circumstances Gordon might have lived the life of an ascetic or hermit. Victoria, for her part, deeply admired the public man; according to her biographer Sidney Lee, "no disaster of her reign caused the Queen more pain and indignation" (1904, 479) than Gordon's murder in 1885.

Gordon followed his father into the army, in 1852 being commissioned as a second lieutenant in the Royal Engineers. He first attracted attention for his reckless bravery during the Crimean War, at the siege of Sebastopol. Promoted to captain in 1859, he volunteered the following year to join British forces fighting in China during the second Opium War of 1856–1860 (also known as the Arrow War) and took part in the occupation of Peking and the burning of the Chinese emperor's summer palace in

The archetypal Victorian military hero, General Charles Gordon, who was greatly admired by the queen, died a violent death at Khartoum in 1885. (Library of Congress)

1860. Two years later he took charge of engineering work to fortify the defenses of the European port at Shanghai during the Taiping Rebellion. He was put in command of 3,500 peasant forces, which, through sheer strength of character and military genius, he drilled from a mismatched rabble into an effective fighting force that was nicknamed the Ever Victorious Army. In military engagements during this eighteen-month campaign, Gordon was always to be seen leading from the front, brandishing only a cane that his troops dubbed his "magic wand." After the rebellion was quashed, the grateful Chinese emperor offered Gordon a huge financial reward. Having no interest in personal gain, he declined it, accepting instead the honorary title of a mandarin of the first class—the highest military rank in China.

Gordon was promoted to lieutenant colonel and in 1865 returned to England, to be greeted everywhere as Chinese Gordon. He retreated from the limelight, however, to take command of the Royal Engineers at Gravesend in Kent, an area of considerable poverty and deprivation. Here he devoted much time to Bible study and to philanthropic work among destitute boys in the local ragged schools as well as caring for the indigent sick in the workhouse infirmaries. Gordon took many of the boys he rescued from the streets into his own home and arranged a career for them at sea.

In 1873 the British government delegated Gordon to serve the Egyptian khedive, Ismail Pasha, as governor of the province of Equatoria in the Sudan, which was then under Egyptian control. While based there he spent the years 1874–1876 exploring and mapping the upper Nile and setting up British outposts along it as far as the border with present-day Uganda. After a brief return to England, Gordon returned to Africa to take up the post of governor-general of the Sudan, where the khedive had asked him to try to put a stop to the domestic and Arab slave trade.

The harsh climate in Africa and the relentlessness with which Gordon continually drove himself took their toll on his health, and he resigned his post and returned to England in 1880. For the next two years he continued in army service in India, China, and Mauritius—in which latter command he was promoted to major general—before being sent to the Cape Colony in South Africa to lead forces attempting to quell trouble among the Basutos. In 1883 Gordon visited many religious sites in the Holy Land while awaiting a posting to the Congo, in the service of King Leopold II of Belgium. When the posting was vetoed by the British war department, he contemplated resigning his commission; but at the end of 1883 he was asked to returned to Sudan as the khedive's governor-general in Khartoum.

Upon his arrival early in 1884, Gordon had been instructed to organize the evacuation of 2,500 officials from the Egyptian garrison, which was now being threatened by rebel forces led by the religious leader Muhammad Ahmed. Claiming to be the Mahdi—"the divinely guided one"—he had announced his mission to purge the Sudan of all corruption and sinful behavior and lead the true followers of Islam into virtuous living. The Mahdi called for a jihad against the occupying Egyptian forces and rapidly drove most of them out before laying siege to Khartoum.

It was during the ensuing ten months of siege that the legend of General Gordon as mystical hero was born. The British authorities had, however, chosen the wrong man for the job: retreat was not in Gordon's nature, and he was now trapped in a no-win situation from which he would die rather than capitulate. Back home, Queen Victoria had been following the events with escalating anxiety. On 9 February, in a letter to her prime minister, William Gladstone, she wrote: "The Queen trembles for Gen. Gordon's safety. If anything befalls *him,* the result will be awful" (Hardie 1935, 83). She urged Gladstone to authorize a show of British military strength, thoughtfully suggesting that loyal Indian troops might be sent from Aden as a relief force, because "they could bear the climate" (Hibbert 1984, 285).

Gladstone procrastinated over mounting demands to send out a force to relieve Gordon, fearful of the carnage that might ensue on both sides. Such an invasion force would, he told the House of Commons, effectively be mounting a war of conquest over a people fighting for their own nationhood. Queen Victoria refused to accept his assurances that Gordon was under no immediate threat (due in part, no doubt, to the misinformation coming intermittently by telegraph from Gordon himself, to the effect that he could hold out indefinitely and that his lines of retreat were, in any case, still open). With Gladstone stubbornly resisting, Victoria fired off a heated telegram to Lord Hartington, secretary for war, on 25 March, demanding help for Gordon. She reiterated her feelings to her private secretary, Henry Ponsonby: "If not only for humanity's sake, for the honour of the Government and the nation, he must not be abandoned" (Farwell 1999, 280). This was a blatant, unconstitutional act on Victoria's part since it undermined Gladstone's authority as prime minister. But public opinion against him was mounting, and the queen was, by May, brimming over with outrage at the government's "miserable" conduct of "this Egyptian business" (280). Quite apart from the fact that she was furious at not being listened to, when, in matters political "*all* she foretold *invariably* happened" (ibid.), Victoria was preoccupied too by the damage such lack of government resolve was doing to British prestige. It was, she insisted "dreadful for her to see how we are going downhill and . . . unable to prevent the humiliation of this country" (280).

In August 1884, after months of lobbying from the press, the army, and the queen, Gladstone finally capitulated and sent a relief force under Sir Garnet Wolseley. But further delays in organizing and transporting this force meant that the advance guard did not reach the vicinity of Khartoum until the following January. Meanwhile, it would appear that Gordon deliberately chose not to try to evacuate his forces to safety, even though supplies were now almost exhausted. He believed it his duty to act out the will of God; he considered it utterly ignoble to be rescued: "I altogether *decline* the imputation that the projected expedition has come to *relieve me.* It has *come to SAVE OUR NATIONAL HONOUR.* . . . I am not the *rescued lamb,* and I will not be" (Harlow and Carter 1999, 302–303).

On 26 January 1885, the Mahdi's rebels, hearing of the approaching relief force, finally stormed Khartoum. Gordon was stabbed to death in a hail of spears. His head was cut off and sent to the Mahdi, who displayed it on the public highway. The Desert Column under Sir Charles Wilson arrived two days afterward. But, as the telegraph messages sent back to England baldly stated, it was "Too late!" (Farwell 1999, 290). Gordon's final days rapidly became the stuff of legend back in England, his derring-do entering the mythology of the great days of empire. The queen was deeply affected by this "frightful" news. On 17 February she wrote a distraught letter to Gordon's sister Mary, commending the heroism and self-sacrifice of her brother as being "so edifying to the World" (Harlow and Carter 1999, 304). She offered the condolences of her family for what she described as "the *stain* left upon England for your dear Brother's cruel, though heroic, fate!" (304). In response, Mary Gordon sent the queen the Bible that her brother had taken everywhere with him, including his first tour of duty in the Sudan, and which he had given to her when it became worn out. The queen gratefully accepted it and had a special display case of enamel and crystal—the St. George's Casket—made for it, in which the Bible was placed on a white satin cushion. This case stood in the South Corridor of the royal apartments at Windsor, alongside it a marble bust of the general, commissioned by Victoria.

A day of national mourning for Gordon was set on 13 March 1885, and services were held in churches throughout Britain. Statues and monuments were raised in his memory, including one in Trafalgar Square, unveiled in 1888, and another by the royal sculptor, Sir Joseph Edgar Boehm, which was placed in St. Paul's Cathedral. The Gordon Boys' Home was opened for homeless boys in his memory.

Queen Victoria never ceased to lay the blame for Gordon's murder at the door of Gladstone—for his dilatoriness in getting relief forces to Khartoum. This, and the continuing idolization in the press of Gordon as a martyr, contributed to the downfall of Gladstone's government that year, its majority falling to only fourteen after a vote of censure over the Gordon affair.

The Mahdi did not enjoy his moment of triumph for long; he died a few months after Gordon. But his Mahdist state in Sudan continued until 4 September 1898, when it was decisively defeated by British forces led by Gen. Horatio Kitchener at the battle of Omdurman, after which British colonial rule was reestablished.

Related entries:
Crimean War; Gladstone, William Ewart

References and further reading:
Allen, Bernard. M. 1931. *Gordon and the Sudan.* London: Macmillan.
Buchan, John. *Gordon at Khartoum.* London: P. Davies.
Farwell, Byron. 1999 ed. *Queen Victoria's Little Wars.* Ware, Hertfordshire: Wordsworth Editions.
Guedalla, Philip. 1933. *The Queen and Mr. Gladstone, 1845–1898.* 2 vols. London: Hodder and Stoughton.
Hardie, Frank. 1935. *The Political Influence of Queen Victoria.* London: Oxford University Press.
Harlow, Barbara, and Mai Carter, eds. 1999. *Imperialism and Orientalism: A Documentary Sourcebook.* Oxford: Blackwell.
Hibbert, Christopher. 1984. *Queen Victoria in Her Letters and Journals.* London: Viking.
Lee, Sidney. 1904. *Queen Victoria: A Biography.* London: Smith, Elder and Co.
Morley, John. [1903] 1971. *The Life of William Ewart Gladstone.* 3 vols. London: Macmillan.
Nutting, Anthony. 1966. *Gordon of Khartoum: Martyr and Misfit.* London: Reprint Society.
Shannon, Richard. *Gladstone, Heroic Minister: 1865–1898.* Harmondsworth, UK: Penguin.
St. Aubyn, Giles. 1991. *Queen Victoria: A Portrait.* London: Sinclair Stevenson.
Strachey, Lytton. 1971. *Eminent Victorians.* Harmondsworth, UK: Penguin.
Waller, John H. 1988. *Gordon of Khartoum: The Saga of a Victorian Hero.* New York: Atheneum.

"Grandmama of Europe"

A morganatic marriage is something we would never wish to discuss (Hamilton 1964, xiii)

When Queen Victoria died in 1901, she left thirty-six grandchildren and thirty-seven great-grandchildren, who between them ruled many of the royal houses of Europe. Thirteen years later, when war broke out in the summer of 1914, her descendants still occupied the thrones of Britain, Germany, Spain, Russia, Norway, Greece, and Romania as well as those of the German states of Hesse-by-Rhine, Saxe-Meiningen, and Saxe-Coburg. Many of these thrones were to tumble by the end of the war in 1918—notably those of Germany and Russia.

In 1899, in the final years of the queen's long reign, it was with some sense of justification, therefore, that her grandson Kaiser William II of Germany, on showing members of his retinue around Windsor Castle, remarked, in the queen's apartments, "From this Tower the World is ruled" (St. Aubyn 1991, 608). But if Victoria did indeed hold sway over her vast European family, it was now in the matriarchal rather than the political sense—as its great unifying figure. The process had been set in motion by the union of two German duchies—those of

Queen Victoria is here (1894) surrounded by just a few of her huge European family of children and grandchildren: on her left sits her eldest daughter, Victoria, dowager empress of Germany, and on her right, her nephew, Kaiser William II. (Bettmann/CORBIS)

Saxe-Coburg-Gotha and Saxe-Gotha-Altenburg—when Queen Victoria had married Prince Albert in 1840. As their own children began being born, Victoria and Albert would consult the oracle—*The Almanac de Gotha,* the indispensable guidebook to the royal houses of Europe—with the intention of singling out suitable dynastic marriages for them.

Uppermost in their minds was the avoidance of a misalliance or worse, a morganatic marriage, the latter being beyond contemplation. The queen had the support of Prince Albert in arranging the marriages of her first three children, the process being initiated with enviable success when Vicky, the Princess Royal, had fulfilled her parents' desire for dynastic union with Prussia (and later a unified Germany), by marrying into this, one of the mightiest and most distinguished royal houses of Europe. This union would in turn establish links with the throne of Greece, through Vicky's daughter Sophie's marriage to King Constantine. The marriage of the queen's eldest son, the Prince of Wales, would bring later union with the kings of Norway through Bertie's daughter Maud. Through Alice's daughter, Alix, links were established with the Romanov house of Russia, as they were also through the queen's son Alfred's marriage to Grand Duchess Marie of Russia. A daughter of this union, Marie, in turn married into the royal family of Romania. A daughter (Margaret) of Victoria's son Arthur married into the Swedish royal family, and one of Victoria's daughter Beatrice's children (Ena) made a dynastic union with Spain. In the following generation of great-grandchildren, the British royal family would further unite with the thrones of Sweden, Yugoslavia, and Denmark.

Throughout her life, Queen Victoria had frequently voiced her doubt about the success of marriage; all too often it was a "lottery" for women—even more so for the daughters and granddaughters in her own family whose choice was severely limited to partners who were of the right royal blood. Love matches were fortuitous if they happened. When her eldest daughter, Vicky, left home in 1858 for her new life in Prussia as wife of the son of the crown prince, Frederick William (to whom she would remain happily married until his death in 1888), the queen was consumed by a sense of guilt at sending an innocent seventeen-year-old away from home. It was, she wrote, "like taking a poor lamb to be sacrificed" (Fulford 1964, 182). "It really makes me shudder when I look around at all your sweet, happy unconscious sisters," she wrote to Vicky, "and think that I must give them up too—one by one!" (ibid.).

After Prince Albert's death in 1861 the queen had been faced with the responsibility of ensuring that the remaining six of her children were suitably married off, a preoccupation that provided a welcome diversion from the misery of her protracted state of mourning. Much of the initial vetting of prospective candidates was done for the queen in Europe, by Vicky. But Victoria herself kept tight control over the final choice and could be ruthlessly dictatorial and interfering. She liked to inspect all prospective brides and grooms personally before agreeing to a match and was careful to obtain detailed descriptions of their physique and health—including the state of their teeth and skin and their deportment—as well as their personal qualities.

The establishment of such a network of close interfamilial relationships is extraordinary, not just in the impressive bloodlines that were united by means of Victoria's exhaustive stage management but simply by dint of the fact that it was exceptional, in Victorian times, for any family to see all nine of its children live into adulthood. Queen Victoria never seems to have remarked on her own exceptionally robust constitution in producing nine healthy babies, without any of the modern-day medical aids to ease the agonies of childbirth except chloroform and without succumbing herself during labor. A far more tragic price was paid, however, in that through Victoria, the royal families of Europe were fatally tainted with the disease of hemophilia, which is transmitted through the female line and affects male children (see "Hemophilia").

Victoria was somewhat amused by the rapidity with which her international family multiplied. In 1868, she remarked on the latest arrival that, "I fear the seventh granddaughter and fourteenth grand-child becomes a very uninteresting thing—for it seems to me to go on like the rabbits in Windsor Park" (Fulford 1971, 200–201). As she grew older, she found the process of overseeing first her children's, then her grandchildren's, and finally even her great-grandchildren's marriages increasingly stressful. By 1871 she was already of the opinion that "times have changed; great foreign alliances are looked upon as causes of trouble and anxiety, and are no good" (Eilers 1997, 94). It was not just the physical shortcomings of potential candidates that concerned her but also the complex, political ramifications of such dynastic unions, which often further complicated internal family rivalries and provoked squabbles over royal precedence. The queen was accused in later years of too much favoritism toward the Battenberg family (her son-in-law Henry of Battenberg being her great favorite) and criticized for too often seeking marriages with German houses.

Victoria had had great doubts over her son Alfred's marriage to a Romanov in 1874. Russia had been held in deep suspicion both by herself and the prince consort since the Crimean War of 1854–1856. Her apprehensions about such a political alliance resurfaced with her granddaughter Alix's marriage to the future Tsar Nicholas II in 1894, about which she felt deeply uneasy. "The position is an anxiety," she remarked, and she talked presciently about the marriage as sealing Alix's "fate" (Longford 1998, 532).

The marriage of her daughter Louise in 1871 had posed a different kind of problem; with no suitable royal candidates available, the queen had agreed to Louise's choice of a commoner—the duke of Argyll (not a prince of the blood and therefore, technically, a subject of the sovereign). Once again she bewailed the fact that "there is nothing so horrid as a daughter's engagement & marriage. One never knows how it will all turn out" (Longford 1998, 511). By 1881 she was admitting to not being enthusiastic about any marriage, even more so when her hemophiliac son Leopold, over whom she had watched so closely even into adulthood, insisted on getting married, in an attempt to lead a normal life. Left with only Helena and Beatrice at home, the queen, as she grew older and more rheumatic and as her sight began to fail, stubbornly resisted giving up her last two unmarried daughters to husbands who might take them out of the country and away from their many daily duties to her. She only agreed to the marriage of Princess Beatrice to Henry of Battenberg in 1885, when the couple promised to live with her.

The queen's death in 1901 seems, retrospectively, most fitting in its timing, for it not only brought a close to the long Victorian era but also spared Victoria from having to witness the worsening relationship between the two royal houses of Britain and Germany, in which for so long she and Prince Albert had invested such hopes for constitutional monarchy in Europe. She did not live to see her grandson, King George V, having to declare war on another grandson, Kaiser William II, in 1914, nor the latter's ignominious defeat and flight into exile in 1918, with the collapse of the German Empire after only thirty-seven years. She would have been equally horrified by the demise of the Russian Empire, torn apart by a socialist revolution, as she would that of Austro-Hungary, which also collapsed in disarray. By the end of World War II in 1945, only seven monarchies would still be surviving in Europe: those of Belgium, Britain, Denmark, the Netherlands, Norway, Spain, and Sweden—of which the current members of all but those of Belgium and the Netherlands are directly descended from Queen Victoria.

Related entries:
Albert Edward, Prince of Wales; Alfred Ernest Albert, Prince; Alice Maud Mary, Princess; Arthur, Prince; Beatrice Mary Victoria Feodore, Princess; Bismarck, Prince Otto Edward Leopold von; Helena Augusta Victoria, Princess; Hemophilia; Leopold I, King of the Belgians; Louise Caroline Alberta, Princess; Victoria, Princess Royal.

References and further reading:

Aronson, Theo. 1973. *Grandmama of Europe: The Crowned Descendants of Queen Victoria.* London: Cassell.

Ashdown, Dulcie. 1975. *Queen Victoria's Family.* London: Hale.

Buchanan, Meriel. 1954. *Queen Victoria's Relations.* London: Cassell.

Duff, David. 1967. *Hessian Tapestry.* London: Macmillan.

Eilers, Marlene A. 1997. *Queen Victoria's Descendants.* Falkoping, Sweden: Rosvall Royal Books.

Fulford, Roger. 1971. *Your Dear Letter: Private Correspondence of Queen Victoria and the Crown Princess of Prussia, 1863–71.* London: Evans Brothers.

———, ed. 1964. *Dearest Child: Letters between Queen Victoria and the Princess Royal, 1858–61.* London: Evans Brothers.

Hamilton, Gerald. 1964. *Blood Royal.* London: A. Gibbs and Phillips.

Longford, Elizabeth. [1964] 1998. *Victoria R.I.* London: Weidenfeld and Nicolson (esp. 477–481, 510–513, 531–532).

St. Aubyn, Giles. 1991. *Queen Victoria: A Portrait.* London: Sinclair Stevenson.

Great Exhibition (1851)

the triumph of my beloved Albert (Benson and Esher 1911, 3:317)

When Queen Victoria opened the Great Exhibition on 1 May 1851, she was quite right to feel a deep sense of personal pride at this, the apogee of Prince Albert's civilizing and cultural aspirations for his adopted country. In a letter to King Leopold, she designated it as the "*greatest* day in our history, the *most beautiful* and *imposing* and *touching* spectacle ever seen. . . . It was the *happiest, proudest* day in my life" (Benson and Esher 1911, 3:317). Although the Great Exhibition would forever after be associated with Prince Albert, for it was he who had brought the project to fruition, its enduring symbol, the Crystal Palace itself, was also the work of a man of great vision, the landscape gardener and architect Sir Joseph Paxton.

The idea for an exhibition of British industrial and manufacturing achievement had first been mooted in 1849 by the prince and a group of supporters at the Royal Society of Arts (of which the prince had been president since 1847). They had concurred that an international exhibition, to serve as a showcase for British industry, should be organized at a time when British exports were increasing, in order further to encourage the development of British arts, crafts, and manufacturing expertise. As such the idea was not a new one—similar, albeit much smaller, exhibitions had been staged in the northern cities of Leeds, Liverpool, and Sheffield at the end of the 1830s and during the early 1840s, as well as in Paris at the exposition of 1849. But Prince Albert's desire to stimulate public interest in aesthetic beauty and the ennobling powers of science and industry prompted him to envision a much more ambitious plan. At a speech at the Mansion House he had described his own objective for the exhibition as being "to give us a true test and a living picture of the point of development at which the whole of mankind has arrived . . . and a new starting-point from which all nations will be able to direct their further exertions" (Hobhouse 1983, 98). Fund-raising and the enlistment of guarantors for a Royal Commission to be established to lay down plans quickly got under way. But the first and most pressing problem was to decide on a site.

When London's Hyde Park, the suggestion of Prince Albert's close adviser, Henry Cole, became the favorite candidate, alarm was raised among the wealthy inhabitants of this upmarket area. Such an undertaking, with its inevitable noise, disruption, and the influx of large work gangs, would lower the tone. Worse, once the exhibition was up and running, it would invite all kinds of riffraff from the lower classes to invade a relatively small area, turning it into "something between Wolverhampton and Greenwich Fair" (Hardy 1976, 80) and no doubt leaving behind them piles of detritus. Householders in the surroundings areas of Mayfair and Knightsbridge began to express their anxiety for the safety of their wives and daughters as well as their homes, and a petition was got up by Lord Brougham and other residents. The gathering of such large crowds also prompted critics to warn of the dangers of thieves and pickpockets or the incitement of such large numbers by socialist or Fenian subversives into riots and stampedes. There was even hysteria about the possible spread of plague or venereal disease by foreign visitors. In the end, a compromise was reached, when it was decided that the building containing the Great Exhibition would only remain on the Hyde Park site for the summer. Heed was taken, however, at protests about the prospect of trees along the park's famous riding route being torn down to make way for the building.

Prince Albert was chairman of the committee set up by the Society of Arts to choose a design for the venue. A competition was launched, but the judges liked

The Crystal Palace, designed by Joseph Paxton and specially constructed in London's Hyde Park to house the Great Exhibition of 1851, was a feat of Victorian engineering. (Library of Congress)

none of the 245 proposed designs put before them. It was not until July 1850 that they accepted the design of Joseph Paxton and the tender to construct it of the contractors Fox and Henderson, who would transport the manufactured sections in by rail from Birmingham. As superintendent of the gardens of the duke of Devonshire, Paxton had constructed a large glass conservatory at the duke's residence, Chatsworth House, and also at Kew Gardens. He now proposed a design that was, in effect, a giant greenhouse made of iron and glass, which, while enabling the display of all kinds of exotic plants, would be well ventilated to avoid the buildup of condensation. Three times the size of St. Paul's Cathedral and over 1,848 feet long, Paxton's cruciform building would cover twenty-two acres. Again, the critics came out in full force: local residents were dismayed at having "a big conservatory placed between themselves and their view of the Serpentine water" (Lorne 1901, 214). Others argued that such a vast edifice might come crashing down on everyone. It seemed a preposterous undertaking; the noted art critic John Ruskin dismissed the design with withering contempt as a "cucumber frame between two chimneys" (Fulford 1966, 221).

Nevertheless, in August 1850 construction began. At an estimated cost of £79,800, the building would take 2,000 workmen four months to erect. Prince Albert was able to monitor daily progress from an upstairs room in nearby Buckingham Palace and watch as the giant framework of 2,300 cast-iron girders painted cobalt blue was erected and fitted with 1 million square feet (293,655 panes) of glass, its roof tops displaying the many-colored flags of the thirty-four participating nations. The strain of the project, particularly control of its spiraling costs, upon the thirty-one-year-old prince's nervous system and physique was enormous. The total figure eventually reached £169,998. Throughout the construction of the building, the prince was worn down by unrelenting criticism.

The queen was consumed with pride at what her husband had achieved, as too were those who assembled for the magnificent opening ceremony of this, The Great Exhibition of the Works of Industry of All Nations (to give the exhibition its full title). The entrance to the Crystal Palace, as the building had now been nicknamed by the popular magazine *Punch,* was guarded by two massive bronze equestrian statues of the mythological twins, Castor and Pollux. As visitors entered, they would see magnificent scarlet wall drapes and multicolored banners, and beyond them a veritable hanging garden of exotic plants—as well as the fully grown elm trees, which had been preserved within the building's framework. At either end of the nave, fountains gushed and musicians played as the visitors traversed the central walkway of pine floorboards, passing rows of statuary and busts of the great and good. It would take several miles of concerted walking for a visitor to view all of the palace's 100,000 exhibits. Laid on by 13,000 exhibitors, these were displayed in the eastern nave—which contained foreign (particularly American, French, and German) and British colonial exhibits; the western nave was dominated by British exhibits, which themselves made up half the exhibition. Some of the most alluring set pieces of the exhibition were the recreation of the famous Alhambra palace of the Moorish kings of Spain in Fine Arts Court no. 16, the Egyptian court in Fine Arts Court no. 13, the fabled halls of ancient Nineveh and Byzantium, and a reproduction of the entrance to the Cathedral of Mainz.

As for the smaller exhibits, these were classified in eight categories and exhibited in four main sections: Raw Materials and Produce; Machinery; Manufactures; and Fine Arts. Exhibits ranged from the industrial might of the five-ton Nasymth steam-hammer to the priceless beauty of the Koh-i-Noor diamond (see "Koh-i-Noor Diamond"). Visitors could marvel also at the exquisite workmanship of jewelers, clock makers, piano makers, and the finest china produced by the Sèvres, Copeland, Minton, and Wedgewood companies. Sculpture and furniture of every description vied with colorful silks from Genoa, Brussels lace, Gobelins tapestries, mosaics and cameos from Rome, jewels from the East India Company, and oriental carpets. There was also much to see from Britain's colonies: malachite and gold from Australia, iron from New Zealand, and iron ore, coal, black lead, wheat, and fur from Canada. Invention and innovation also took center stage, represented by exhibits such as envelope-making machines, microscopes, the Colt revolver, and the McCormick reaper. But amid all these cultural riches, only one black exhibitor was present—former U.S. slave Josiah Henson, who, after escaping into Canada, had become a British citizen. There was also much to see that was eccentric if not totally bizarre, such as a silver nose (possibly a prosthetic device for syphilitics), a "silent alarm bedstead" that tipped its sleeping occupant into a bath of cold water, "a pulpit connected by gutta-percha tubes to the pews of the deaf, a doctor's walking stick which contained an enema . . . and a group of stuffed frogs, one holding up an umbrella, from Wurtemberg" (Fulford 1966, 223).

For the opening ceremony on 1 May 1851, which had been declared a public holiday, troops were deployed all over London, and extra police had been brought into the capital. The whole city was gridlocked by traffic jams of carriages as everybody tried to make their way to Hyde Park, although only 25,000 guests, including bigwigs and foreign dignitaries and season ticket holders, were allowed in for the ceremony. A cortège of nine carriages conveyed the royal party and their guests to the site. The queen, in pink watered silk, and Prince Albert, in field marshal's uniform, accompanied by their two eldest children, Vicky and Bertie, mounted a dais near the central crystal fountain in the main transept. Here an Indian chair, covered in scarlet cloth and canopied with blue and silver fabric, was placed as a throne, surrounded by the assembled ambassadors and ministers and peers of the realm. The prince read out his official report of the proceedings of the commission and outlined the building's construction, followed by the queen's response and a prayer led by the archbishop of Canterbury. To a burst of the "Hallelujah Chorus" by a 600-strong choir, followed by gun salutes in the park, the exhibition was officially opened.

Many were visibly moved by the occasion; the critics of the Crystal Palace were silenced virtually overnight. The press reviews the following day concurred not only on the triumph of the exhibition and its fairy-tale venue but also on its boost to national pride. As for the portentous warnings about the problems of crowd control—those who thronged Hyde Park and would do so, day in day out, for the next six months had behaved in an exemplary manner. The novelist Charlotte Brontë herself was a witness: "Amongst the thirty thousand souls that peopled it the day I was there, not one loud noise was to be heard, not one irregular movement seen—the living tide rolls on quietly, with a deep hum like the sea heard from a distance" (Weintraub 1997, 253). The only moment of anxiety about crowd control had come when the old and tottering duke of Wellington was mobbed by his adoring public—but this was not until he visited the exhibition in October.

Daily attendance at the Crystal Palace was often more than 60,000; within 140 days over 6 million visitors (equivalent to one-third of the British population) had visited it. So successful was the exhibition that after three weeks, the five-shilling cost of admission was reduced to one shilling on four days of the week. Public conveniences were provided in the form of new water closets specially installed for the purpose. Catering and refreshments were offered by the drinks company Schweppes, although alcohol was strictly forbidden. The public demand to see the exhibition gave a great boost to Britain's burgeoning railways, which found themselves catering to the demands of day trippers from the industrial north, who in their thousands took advantage of the lower-cost shilling days. London benefited too, from new pavements and streets as well as housing developments around the main railway terminals and near the exhibition site. Cheap overnight accommodation in the area mushroomed, to cater to the demands of so many extra visitors to London. By bringing together the most beautiful manufactured goods from France, Germany, Italy, and elsewhere, the exhibition also prompted improvements in British standards in arts and crafts, and a spate of similar exhibitions followed in its wake. Museums too grew in popularity, prompting bequests of private collections—such as that made by Sir Hans Soane to the British Museum. Queen Victoria and Prince Albert themselves spent money at the exhibition, buying paintings, sculpture, and furniture. The profits from the Great Exhibition of £186,000 also served to set up a fund for the construction of Prince Albert's other great architectural dream—the museum complex in South Kensington, later nicknamed Albertopolis—most of which would not, however, be completed until long after his own death.

For Queen Victoria the Crystal Palace was little short of a miracle—"one of the wonders of the world, which we English may indeed be proud of" (Charlot 1991, 331). She averred that opening day had been "the *greatest* day in our history" and "a fairy scene" (Benson and Esher 1911, 2:317–318). It had been equal only to the day of her coronation, and in her diary entry for that day she overflowed with national and personal pride: "God bless my dearest country, which has shown itself so great to-day!" (Lorne 1901, 220). By the time the exhibition closed in October 1851, 6,063,986 visitors (many coming several times) had made their way to London to worship contemporary industrial and economic achievement and innovation in this great secular glass cathedral. The queen felt decidedly melancholy on the occasion of the exhibition's closing, having, it is said, visited the exhibition forty times herself, including spending her thirty-second birthday there.

It took four months for the whole edifice to be carefully dismantled, packed up and transported to Sydenham Hill, two hours' drive away in south London, from which vantage point the reconstructed Crystal Palace could be seen for many miles. Once again the queen attended the ceremonials to mark the building's reopening—on 10 June 1854. Indeed, the new building, set in 200 acres of parkland, was half as big again as the original and had lost none of its appeal. One of the queen's dressers, Frieda Arnold, remarking in a letter that it was "the most beautiful fairy palace that ever a child's fantasy could create" (Arnold 1994, 71). For another thirty years or so the palace retained its national and cultural significance, with 2 million or so visitors annually, but by the end of the century and Victoria's death it had gone into decline and was in a poor state of repair. An attempt to restore its fortunes was made with the staging there of the 1905 Colonial and Indian Exhibition and the 1911 Festival of Empire. But by the 1930s the building "presented a most woe-begone picture, peeling and sunblistered paintwork, the glass grimy, ironwork encrusted with rust and stonework suffering from erosion" (Auerbach 1999, 211), and there was talk of pulling the whole thing down.

The sense of euphoria inspired by the Great Exhibiton during its six months fueled British self-assertion in the international arena. As Roger Fulford has argued, "The awe-inspiring majesty of the Crystal Palace in 1851 was the first step along the road of imperialist expansion—from Rotten Row to Majuba Hill, Omdurman and Mafikeng" (1966, 224). But Prince Albert's loftier ambition that, through the exhibition, Britain would unite the civilized world on a higher spiritual plane of brotherly love and international cooperation did not bear fruit. Three years later most of Europe would find itself embroiled in the Crimean War. And, tragically, the Crystal Palace itself, that great monument to high Victorian art, industrial achievement, and commerce, was totally destroyed by fire on the night of 30 November 1936. The red glow in the sky could be seen forty miles away at Brighton on the south coast.

Related entries:
Art and Artists; Koh-i-Noor Diamond; Racial and Religious Prejudice; Victoria and Albert Museum

References and further reading:

Arnold, Frieda. 1994. *My Mistress the Queen: The Letters of Frieda Arnold, Dresser to Queen Victoria 1854–9.* London: Weidenfeld and Nicolson.

Auerbach, Jeffrey A. 1999. *The Great Exhibition of 1851: A Nation on Display.* New Haven: Yale University Press.

Benson, A. C., and Viscount Esher, eds. 1911. *The Letters of Queen Victoria 1837–1861.* 1st ser., 3 vols. London: John Murray.

Charlot, Monica. 1991. *Victoria, the Young Queen.* Cambridge: Polity.

Fay, Charles Ryle. 1951. *Palace of Industry 1851: A Study of the Great Exhibition and Its Fruits.* Cambridge: Cambridge University Press.

Fulford, Roger. 1966. *The Prince Consort.* London: Macmillan.

Greenhalgh, Paul. 1988. *Ephemeral Vistas: The Expositions Universelles, Great Exhibitions and World's Fairs, 1851–1939.* Manchester, UK: Manchester University Press.

Hardy, Alan. 1976. *Queen Victoria Was Amused.* London: John Murray.

Hobhouse, Hermione. 1983. *Prince Albert: His Life and Work.* London: Hamish Hamilton.

Leapman, Michael. 2001. *The World for a Shilling: How the Great Exhibition of 1851 Shaped a Nation.* London: Headline.

Lorne, Marquis of. 1901. *VRI: Her Life and Empire.* London: Eyre and Spottiswood.

Priestley, J. B. 1972. *Victoria's Heyday.* London: Heinemann.

Weintraub, Stanley. 1997. *Albert, Uncrowned King.* London: John Murray.

Grey, General Charles (1804–1870)

(Later Colonel)

most truly devoted and faithful and had such a kind heart (Hibbert 1984, 219)

Gen. Charles Grey, the queen's private secretary in the years immediately following the death of the prince consort, took office at the most difficult of times. He found his patience and loyalty stretched to their limit by the queen's retreat from public life but nevertheless fulfilled his duties conscientiously. But at court, he was a man more respected than loved.

Grey was the second surviving son of the British statesman Charles, second Earl Grey, Whig prime minister 1831–1834, who had introduced the Reform Bill of 1832. Born in Northumberland, Charles joined the army when he was sixteen and began his career as a second lieutenant in the rifle brigade. He rose through the ranks, becoming a colonel of the Third Buffs in 1860, and during 1830–1834 acted also as his father's private secretary. He served as Liberal member of Parliament for High Wycombe from 1831 to 1837, giving up his seat when the queen came to the throne, upon which he became an equerry in the royal household. In January 1840 Grey was entrusted, along with Lord Torrington, with making the journey to Coburg to invest Prince Albert with the Order of the Garter before accompanying him to England for his marriage to the queen. When the prince's private secretary, George Anson, began suffering bouts of the illness that would kill him in 1849, Grey took over some of his responsibilities. After Anson's death, Grey moved up a rank, taking over the work of Col. Charles Phipps as private secretary, with Phipps taking charge of the prince's Privy Purse.

The queen had become greatly attached to Grey during his service to the prince, and in Scotland in 1860 he had accompanied the royal couple on one of their Great Expeditions, traveling incognito as Dr. Grey. Upon the death of Prince Albert in 1861, Grey was asked to transfer his secretarial role to Queen Victoria. The actual post of private secretary to the queen was not officially created until 1866, when the prime minister, Lord Derby, in recognition of Grey's service, created the post for him and added to it joint control of the queen's Privy Purse after 1866. Although by now being highly experienced in the job, Grey was unprepared for the demands of the queen's very different personality and found the emotional extremes to which she descended during the early days of her widowhood extremely difficult to deal with. Privately, he seriously wondered whether she was losing her sanity.

Grey's personality was very much that of the military man: bluff, gruff, stolid, and formal. Although appearing outwardly kindly and accommodating, he was not ingratiating. He had a strong sense of his own independence and could, on occasion, stubbornly resist the queen's wishes if he did not agree with them. In 1861 he had published a biography of his father, *Some Account of the Life and Opinions of Charles, Second Earl Grey,* which is no doubt what prompted the queen to ask him to take over the writing of a biography of Prince Albert, which she herself had begun preparing. Grey's subsequent work, *The Early Years of his Royal Highness the Prince Consort,* was published using private papers, and translations of the prince consort's journals and letters, provided by the queen and Princess Helena. Having had much highly personal material put at his disposal, Grey soon suggested to the queen that some of its candor should be modified and that the work itself should be kept for private circulation within the family. During its preparation he had to suffer the queen's regular guidance if not interference; as such the work remained predominantly hers, including the footnotes, with Grey fulfilling the role of compiler. This eulogistic work did not remain a private document; the queen insisted on its publication, in 1867, and it was later translated into French, German, and Italian.

One of the more onerous tasks that Grey found himself having to perform as the queen's private secretary was to make her many and frequent excuses about appearing in public. He became exasperated with her constant claims of incapacitation—through grief, ill health, or both—and referred to her as the "royal malingerer" (Longford 1998, 380). He could not abide the queen's histrionics and disapproved of her doctor, the indulgent Sir William Jenner, whom he felt pandered to her self-pity and her hypochondria and helped the queen find far too many excuses for avoiding her public duties. For his own part, Grey averred that the queen's endless petty physical complaints "have simply no effect whatever on me" (Longford 1998, 380), and he said as much in his correspondence with William Gladstone.

Grey continued to discharge his duties with efficiency, but he frequently spoke his mind with a bluntness that could offend. He could be stubborn if commanded to do something by the queen of which he disapproved or that he "did not regard as his proper business" (Hibbert 1979, 31). On one occasion, having noted that a lady-in-waiting was wearing too much rouge on her cheeks, the queen had remarked that "Dear General Grey will tell her." When he received this missive, Grey's response was terse: "Dear General Grey will do nothing of the kind" (Ponsonby 1942, 360). As time went on, he became less and less tolerant of the queen's dereliction of her duty and often seemed moody and disgruntled. Frustrated by the difficulties that Victoria's perpetual state of mourning created for the day-to-day running of her affairs, he greatly reduced his contact with her during his final years at court. The queen in any event had become irritated by Grey's increasing deafness, so much so that she frequently communicated with him by notes rather than discussion. He continued to attempt (although not hard enough in the view of his critics) to persuade the queen to reappear in public and encouraged her decision to build the Royal Albert Hall as a lasting memorial to her dead husband. But he did not live to see it open (in March 1871). Grey died in March 1870 after a series of seizures. Queen Victoria, as was her wont on the occasion of any deaths in her entourage, went to view his corpse, laid out on his deathbed, and commiserated with Grey's widow about "our dear General" (Hibbert 1984, 219). Grey was succeeded by the supremely tactful Col. Henry Ponsonby—the husband of Grey's niece Mary.

Related entries:
Ponsonby, General Sir Henry; The Royal Household

References and further reading:

Grey, Hon. Charles. 1867. *The Early Years of His Royal Highness the Prince Consort.* London: Smith, Elder and Co.

Hibbert, Christopher. 1979. *The Court of St. James: The Monarch at Work from Victoria to Elizabeth II.* London: Weidenfeld and Nicolson.

———. 1984. *Queen Victoria in Her Letters and Journals.* London: Viking.

Longford, Elizabeth. [1964] 1998. *Victoria R.I.* London: Weidenfeld and Nicolson.

Ponsonby, Arthur. 1942. *Henry Ponsonby.* London: Macmillan.

Tisdall, E. E. P. 1961. *Queen Victoria's Private Life.* London: Jarrolds.

H

Hanover, Royal House of

I am far more proud of my Stuart than of my Hanoverian ancestors (Creston 1952, 24)

By the time William IV, last of the sons of George III, died in 1837, the nation had become thoroughly disenchanted with the German dynasty, which had reigned over it since the early eighteenth century. The situation had worsened during the reigns of George IV and his brother William IV, so much so that, as J. H. Plumb argued, "the Royal Family was held in almost universal contempt" (1966, 148). Such was the sense of relief when the country made a peaceful transition in 1837 to the rule of a young, untested, and uncontroversial queen that many historians have argued that had the rule of William IV lasted for much longer, the Hanoverians might have proved to be the last British monarchs.

Hanoverian rule lasted from 1714, when the elector of Hanover, George I, assumed the throne of Great Britain, until the death of Queen Victoria in 1901. The reputations of the queen's colorful Georgian predecessors frequently unnerved Victoria, who saw the worst aspects of her own behavior as being the product of her "passionate" (that is, hot-tempered) nature and what she termed the "bad blood" of the Hanoverians. In the previous reign of the queen's uncle, William IV, the diarist Charles Greville had rued the dismal record of the various members of that family: "Good God, what a set they are! . . . the three kingdoms cannot furnish such a brood, so many and so bad, rogues, blackguards, fools and whores" (Strachey and Fulford 1938). Victoria's elder statesman, the duke of Wellington, similarly looked upon the reprobate sons of George III as "the damnedest millstones about the neck of any Government that can be imagined" (Plumb 1966, 148). Collectively, the four Georges and their various offspring—legitimate and illegitimate—did not appear therefore to have much to recommend them. And yet they were not by any means as consistently reprehensible as popular opinion, and in particular the contemporary press of the day, persisted in painting them.

The state of Hanover had originally been created in 1638 as the principality of Brunswick-Calenberg-Gottingen and had eventually become known after its major town, Hanover. It was ruled by the Guelph (or Welf) dynasty of German nobles, who were promoted to the status of electors in 1692. In the eighteenth century the elector of Hanover became monarch of Great Britain when the childless Queen Anne died in 1714. This came about because, thirteen years earlier, an Act of Settlement had been passed, designating that the British throne should pass to Electress Sophia of Hanover (a granddaughter of

James I and the nearest Protestant heir), or her descendants, should the British monarch die without issue. In the event, Sophia died two months before Queen Anne, and so her son George Louis, succeeded to the British throne as George I.

There was much division in Britain between those who accepted the Hanoverian succession, and the Jacobites, who supported the heirs of King James II, who had been deposed in 1688. The Hanoverian monarch would be obliged to divide his time between Britain and Hanover, a situation that raised apprehensions in political circles that this would divide that monarch's loyalties and weaken the throne. Hanover came to be looked upon as Britain's "Achilles' heel" in continental Europe, for it was frequently invaded. Finally, in 1806 it fell to the French. Part of its territory was incorporated into the French empire; the remainder became part of the Kingdom of Wesphalia.

The court of Hanover at Herrenhausen under Electress Sophia (1630–1714) had acquired a reputation for etiquette, culture, and learning (with Handel and the philosopher Leibniz being two of its luminaries). Yet there was much hostility among the British people at being ruled by someone they disdained as a petty monarch of a provincial kingdom—and one best known until then for its wholesome beer. Sophia's son, George Louis (George I) (1660–1727), arrived in England with a German entourage (including two fat and much-disliked German mistresses), lived an indolent lifestyle, and remained steadfastly attached to German ways. He spoke poor, ungrammatical English and made regular visits to Hanover, where he had left his wife, Sophia, languishing as a virtual prisoner after he had accused her of adultery. George's embattled relationship with his heir, the Prince of Wales, served only to alienate the British people and foster a resurgence of Jacobitism (there were rebellions in 1715 and 1719). By the time of his death, however, and despite his unpopularity, George I had at least established a strong government, thanks to the good offices of his ministers Horace Walpole and Charles Townshend.

George II (1683–1760), who succeeded in 1727, although undoubtedly a courageous soldier (he was the last British monarch to lead troops into battle—at Dettingen in 1743), was rigidly militaristic and unbending in matters of court etiquette. He exercised his military muscle in condoning the brutal suppression of the Jacobite Rebellion of 1745–1746 by his son the duke of Cumberland. George II had hated his father yet emulated him by also being a dictatorial parent. He developed a violent dislike for his own son and heir, Frederick (sympathetically nicknamed "Poor Fred" by the public), who died before him, in 1751. The luckless George remained without friends, consoled only by his love of money, by Handel's music, and by a succession of mistresses. He remained parsimonious in the use of his wealth among his own subjects, his only redeeming feature being his witty and intelligent wife, Caroline of Ansbach, who had some considerable influence over his political decision making until her early death in 1737.

The reign of George III (1738–1820), the grandson of George II, would last for a long sixty years (1760–1820), with the obstinate king determined to lead in matters of government and becoming, in Walter Bagehot's words, "a kind of consecrated obstruction" (Bagehot 1867). A dullard and a slow learner, despite his interest in and patronage of the arts and sciences, George III was not really up to the enormous task of being king. His erratic rule, which witnessed the loss of the American colonies at the end of a disastrous war (1775–1783) and prompted him to contemplate abdication, has led to his being unfairly accused of being despotic. In his personal life he was religiously devout, a faithful husband to a dull and ugly wife, and father of fifteen, for once, legitimate children. As John Clarke argued: "The plain fact is that George III was the only Hanoverian who could be called a genuinely decent and good man" (1977, 232). George's tragedy as a monarch is that his good intentions were overtaken by the onset of insanity. But as a father, he proved to be yet another in the Hanoverian line of bad parents. His rigid insistence on his sons having occupations—generally in the military, to which not all of them took with alacrity—combined with his propensity for leaving his six daughters locked away in obscurity, eroded any sense either of family unity or loyalty.

During the second half of his reign, George III's behavior became increasingly unpredictable. He rapidly lost his hold on domestic politics, as he succumbed to what doctors then saw as inexplicable bouts of madness (now generally thought to be the result of the condition porphyria, which affects the nervous system). Sadly, the king's mental derangement did isolate him, at a time when little was understood about the nature of madness. Meanwhile, George III quarreled endlessly with his heir, the Prince of Wales (particularly after the latter's secret marriage to a Roman Catholic and a commoner, Mrs. Fitzherbert, in 1785). A regency was established in 1788–1789 when George was first incapacitated; he was ill again in 1801 and 1804. The last years of his reign, from 1811 to 1820, by which time George had also gone blind, saw his son again become regent. It was in George III's last pathetic, demented state, at a time when the French Revolution had dispatched its own monarchy, that the British public discovered a degree of affection for the old king. The sad irony of his final days, as Plumb (1966) observed, was that he had, in his dotage, finally earned the love of the nation and a degree of respect for his honesty, in the face of public apprehension at the approaching reign of his profligate son.

The self-regarding George IV (1762–1830), who devoted more time to his personal appearance than he did to affairs of state and who lived up to the Hanoverian reputation for extravagance by running up vast debts in the pursuit of his expensive tastes, was not without his redeeming features. In the words of Viscount Esher, he was "the first Sovereign since Charles I who showed a blundering reverence for Beautiful things" (1914, 7). As a man of wit, intelligence, and immaculate good taste, he was an important patron of the arts in Britain at that time and lent his support to the building up of the great collections at the National Gallery and the British Library. He also loved good architecture (the apotheosis of his artistic taste being the new Royal Pavilion that he built at Brighton) and sought to civilize the rather stodgy British court that had been lulled into apathy by sixty years of his father's rule. But George's charm and political acumen were sadly overshadowed by his indulgent lifestyle, by his bouts of disabling inertia, and by his bitter feuding with his estranged wife, Caroline, whom he had abandoned almost as soon as he had married in 1795, objecting, among other things, to her lack of personal hygiene.

George tried famously and unsuccessfully, after many years of separation from Caroline, to divorce her in 1820. But public opinion, in the face of his unrepentant profligacy, had by the 1820s swelled behind the much-maligned queen. The most memorable moment in George IV's ten-year reign (1820–1830), which earned him a brief respite from continuing public antipathy, was the elaborate and overblown coronation ceremony that he stage managed in July 1821, at which he appeared, now grossly overweight, "buried in satin, feathers and diamonds" (Aldington 1948, 46). The lavish ceremonial robes alone had cost the nation the staggering sum of £24,704.8s.10d.

To the young Princess Victoria, George IV was a kind if somewhat frightening figure in the background of her childhood, to whom she affectionately referred as "Uncle

King." She visited him at his preferred residence, the Royal Lodge at Windsor, in 1826, during his final sad, reclusive years as king. Victoria found his literally huge (325-pound) presence somewhat daunting but took "great pleasure" in riding out with him in his fine phaeton with its liveried footmen. Notwithstanding the king's affability toward her personally (and this despite his undisguised loathing for her mother, the duchess of Kent), Victoria's later opinion of George IV, and all her Hanoverian ancestors for that matter, was to a large degree colored by the prejudices of her prime minister, Lord Melbourne, who guided her through her first years as queen. It was Melbourne's opinion, which she carefully recorded in her journal, that George IV's failing had been not to take good advice; in a characteristic oversimplification of a complex personality, Victoria observed that " if he [George IV] had been properly talked to he might have listened" (Esher 1914, 161). When in 1874, the diaries of the politician, Charles Greville, were published with their unflattering revelations about her Hanoverian uncles, particularly George IV, Queen Victoria was, however, quick to rise to his defense. "Of George IV he speaks in such shocking language; language not fit for any gentleman to use of any other gentleman or human being, still less of his Sovereign" (Hibbert 1984, 238). Similarly, the queen was so offended by the satirical portraits painted of her predecessors by William Makepeace Thackeray in *The Four Georges* that when Thackeray died in 1863 she refused permission for him to be buried in Poet's Corner at Westminster Abbey.

The reign of Queen Victoria's uncle, William IV (see "William IV") saw the rise of a powerful political challenge to the monarchy in the movement for parliamentary reform. This brought with it the serious threat of popular revolt, prompting Princess Victoria in 1836 to wail to her Uncle Leopold (in reference to their own German ancestry): "I should like to know what harm the Coburg family has done to England" (Benson and Esher 1911, 1:53). When she became queen in 1837, Victoria was prohibited, under Salic law, from taking the Hanoverian throne, which could only pass to a male heir. Her uncle, Ernest Augustus, duke of Cumberland, succeeded to the title instead.

For Victoria, there was no escaping the distinctive features of her Hanoverian ancestry. She displayed them all too obviously in the slightly bulging blue eyes, the round face prone to chubbiness, and the receding chin—the "irascible expression of the Guelphs," as J. H. Plumb described it (1966, 40). She also worried about another German physical characteristic—the long and slightly hooked "Coburg nose." She had inherited this from her mother's Saxe-Coburg side and passed it on to her children, particularly the Prince of Wales. It was the Hanoverian propensity for apathy, idleness, and self-indulgence that found its true inheritor in her son and heir, Bertie. And even though the queen demonstrated the Hanoverian qualities of obstinacy and wilfulness in considerable measure, in which regard she seemed a natural descendant of George III, there was also a positive side to her "Hanoverian" nature, reflected in a surprisingly broad-minded sense of humor, which although never exhibited in public was reflected in an enjoyment of rather risqué jokes among her close entourage, even into old age.

Queen Victoria would be the last of Britain's Hanoverian monarchs; her heir, the Prince of Wales, was, by his father Prince Albert, of the house of Saxe-Coburg. Hanover itself, which had grown considerably in size as it absorbed more territory, eventually became the fourth-largest German state after Austria, Prussia, and Bavaria. In 1866, George V of Hanover was deposed, and Hanover was annexed by Prussia. Until the end of World War II, it remained a province of Prussia; in 1946 it became part of Lower Saxony (now part of the Federal Republic of Germany).

Related entries:
Albert of Saxe-Coburg-Gotha, Prince Consort; Hemophilia; Saxe-Coburg-Gotha, Royal House of; Victoria, Queen: Birth of; William IV

References and further reading:

Aldington, Richard. 1948. "The Grand World of 'Prinney.'" In Richard Aldington, *Four English Portraits 1801–1851*. London: Evans Brothers.

Bagehot, Walter. 1867. *The English Constitution*. London: Chapman and Hall.

Benson, A. C., and Viscount Esher, eds. 1911. *The Letters of Queen Victoria, 1837–1861*. 1st ser., 3 vols. London: John Murray.

Clarke, John. 1977. "The House of Hanover." In Antonia Fraser, ed., *The Lives of the Kings and Queens of England*. London: Futura.

Creston, Dormer. 1952. *The Youthful Victoria*. London: Macmillan.

Esher, Viscount, ed. 1914. *The Training of a Sovereign*. London: John Murray.

Fulford, Roger. 1975. *From Hanover to Windsor*. London: Fontana.

Green, Vivian H. H. 1963. *The Hanoverians 1714–1815*. London: Arnold.

Hibbert, Christopher. 1972–1973. *George IV*. 2 vols. London: Longmans.

———. 1984. *Queen Victoria in Her Letters and Journals*. London: Viking.

Parissien, Steven. 2001. *George IV: The Grand Entertainment*. London: John Murray.

Plumb, J. H. 1966. *The First Four Georges*. London: Fontana.

Smith, E. A. 1999. *George IV*. New Haven: Yale University Press.

Strachey, Lytton, and Roger Fulford, eds. 1938. *The Grenville Memoirs*. 8 vols. London: Macmillan.

Hastings, Lady Flora (1806–1839)

that wretched Ly. Flo (Longford 1998, 104)

Throughout the first six months of 1839 the court of Queen Victoria was divided over the true cause of the suspicious "illness" of one of the duchess of Kent's ladies-in-waiting, Lady Flora Hastings. As rumor and gossip proliferated and the press was inevitably drawn in, Queen Victoria would have to confront her own often peremptory and highly partisan judgment of those who did not sit on her social or political side of the fence.

Lady Flora Hastings had first entered the royal household at the age of twenty-eight in 1834 as a lady of the bedchamber to the duchess of Kent. The daughter of a former Tory governor-general of India, the first marquess of Hastings, she was a gifted and intelligent woman who wrote poetry and was soon noticed for her sharp, acerbic wit. Her talent for scathing remarks would soon make her the bête noir of many at court—notably Princess Victoria's governess, the Baroness Lehzen. In pandering to the duchess's rampant jealousy of Queen Victoria's close friendship with the quirky German, Hastings took delight in making Lehzen the butt of many jokes, in particular her odd habit of constantly chewing caraway seeds.

When Victoria became queen and moved into Buckingham Palace in July 1837, as an unmarried woman she was obliged to take her mother with her, installing her with her entourage. In April 1838, and much to the queen's disgruntlement, the duchess promoted Hastings, whom the queen already had no liking for, to lady-in-waiting when a post became vacant. At a time when Victoria was engaged in intermittent verbal war with her mother and was desperate to be rid of the malevolent influence of the comptroller of the duchess's household, Sir John Conroy, it was all too easy for Victoria to allow her suspicious mind to get the better of her. She soon became convinced that among the duchess's coterie, the arch gossip Lady Flora had been enlisted as a spy and was reporting back to Sir John Conroy on her every movement.

After passing the Christmas holidays of 1838 with her family in Scotland, Lady Flora made the overnight journey back to London, unchaperoned, by post chaise in the company only of Sir John Conroy (a personal friend). Upon her arrival, on 10 January, Hastings visited the royal doctor, James Clark, complaining of sickness and pain in her side, from which she had been suffering for some weeks. Prevented by the strict codes of propriety that prevailed at that time, and also hampered (as events would soon prove) by a lack of diagnostic skill, Clark had not been able to make any kind of physical examination of Lady Flora. He did, however, notice that her abdomen was distended. Having prescribed the (ineffectual) palliatives of rhubarb and ipecacuanha pills and the use of a liniment, Clark erroneously concluded that Lady Flora must be pregnant. Rumor soon reached the queen, and by early February she and Lehzen could hardly contain themselves, scandalized that if this were the case, then Lady Flora's pregnancy was indubitably the work of their favourite bogeyman—Sir John Conroy. Here, at last, seemed a perfect opportunity for engineering Conroy's removal. Queen Victoria instructed her own ladies-in-waiting—Ladies Tavistock and Portman—to keep watch on Lady Flora's expanding middle.

Historians have long assumed that it was Lehzen who fomented the gossip at court and orchestrated the vilification of Lady Flora, that it was she who poisoned the young queen's mind. Monica Charlot, however, contended that much of the tragedy that unfolded was the result of Dr. Clark's own medical incompetence and his continuing insistence (despite Lady Flora's till then untainted and pious reputation) that she was pregnant. In the doctor's defense, one should perhaps remember that at this stage he had not been permitted, as he later stated, so much as to "lay my hand upon her abdomen with her stays removed" (Charlot 1991, 130), thus making diagnosis difficult. Rumors were such that the embattled Lady Flora had no alternative but to seek further medical opinion to vindicate herself or leave the court in ignominy. A specialist in women's ailments, Sir Charles Clarke (no relation to Dr. James Clark) was brought in, and on 17 February pronounced Lady Flora to be a virgin. The queen was naturally aghast and sent her deep regrets to Lady Flora, asking to see her. Lady Flora, still unwell, met with the queen on 23 February and graciously agreed to let the matter rest, out of loyalty to the duchess, who was of course still living under Queen Victoria's roof.

Despite the provision to Lady Flora of a medical certificate upholding her innocence, the gossip continued. She was still showing signs of a swelling in her abdomen (although its size was constantly fluctuating). Dr. James Clark still suspected a pregnancy—which was, technically, possible, even in a virgin, if the hymen had not been ruptured during intercourse. He suggested that Lady Flora had perhaps made a "secret marriage." By now the situation had been complicated by the involvement of Lady Flora's family, who collectively rose to her defense, writing letters to the papers, to the queen, and to Prime Minister Melbourne. The appalled duchess of Kent had summarily dismissed Dr. Clark as her physician; the Hastings family demanded that the queen should do the same and that she should make reparation to Lady Flora for the defamation of her good name. Eventually, still demonized at court and increasingly unwell, Lady Flora resorted to the press in her own defense, at the end of March, publishing an account in the *Examiner* in which she alluded to the prime mover behind the gossip against her as being "a certain foreign lady" (that is, Lehzen). The queen and Melbourne were now openly attacked in the press. With Melbourne's majority in Parliament now extremely fragile, his Whig government was also in jeopardy. The queen was booed when she drove out of Buckingham Palace and hissed at Ascot Races.

By April, the liberating euphoria of Victoria's first months as queen had been replaced by physical exhaustion, stress, the never-ceasing war with her mother, and now this most unpleasant affair. By May, Victoria was dealing with her first constitutional crisis—precipitated by her refusal to relinquish her Whig ladies of the bedchamber under Peel's new government—and with a sense of abandonment at the temporary loss of Melbourne. In all this Lady Flora was, for a while, forgotten. The queen, temporarily distracted by the charms of Grand Duke Alexander of Russia on a state visit in early May, could only think of one thing—how to get rid of the constant, carping presence of the duchess of Kent.

By June, although she had bravely continued her duties at court, it was clear that Lady Flora Hastings was dying. On 27 June a contrite Victoria visited her in the duchess of Kent's apartments and was shocked to find Hastings now skeletally thin and without hair. On 5 July Lady Flora died. A postmortem, which she herself had specifically requested before her death in order to finally vindicate her, revealed she had been suffering from a tumor of the liver. Five thousand people attended Lady Flora's funeral at her family home at Loudon in Scotland; the press meanwhile went to war, with the *Times* taking the queen's side against the *Morning Post,* which had been supplied by Lady Flora's family with all the documents relating to the sad affair and now launched a vituperative attack.

Several historians have taken Queen Victoria to task for the callous way, they feel, in which she treated Lady Flora. Elizabeth Longford, however, has revealed that the queen was haunted by the affair, which gave her nightmares for many years afterward (Longford 1998, 446). It also taught the young queen a most necessary and salutary lesson—never again to listen to gossip, nor to demean herself by acting, in public at least, in such an inexcusably partisan fashion. As for Dr. Clark: in the September issue of the medical journal *The Lancet,* an article by John Fisher Murray, M.D., entitled "The Court Doctor Dissected" listed the many, and obvious, other possible medical conditions that might have caused Lady Flora's distended abdomen—all of which Clark had failed to consider. The good doctor would, however, thanks to the queen's stubborn regard for him, remain in her service until his retirement in 1866. Posterity has been less kind; condemning Clark, in the words of one commentator, as being "perhaps the most incompetent royal doctor of all time" (Pearsall 1969, 5).

Related entries:
Bedchamber Crisis; Clark, Sir James; Kent, Marie Louise Victoire, Duchess of; Lehzen, Baroness Louise; Melbourne, William Lamb, Second Viscount; The Rroyal Household

References and further reading:

Charlot, Monica. 1991. *Victoria: The Young Queen.* Cambridge: Polity.
Creston, Dormer. 1952. *The Youthful Queen Victoria: A Discursive Account.* London: Macmillan and Co.
Longford, Elizabeth. [1964] 1998. *Victoria R.I.* London: Weidenfeld and Nicolson.
Pearsall, Ronald. 1969. *The Worm in the Bud: The World of Victorian Sexuality.* London: Weidenfeld and Nicolson.
Woodham-Smith, Cecil. 1972. *Queen Victoria: Her Life and Times.* Vol 1: *1819–1861.* London: Hamish Hamilton.

Helena Augusta Victoria, Princess (1846–1923)

(*"Lenchen"; from 1866, Princess Christian of Schleswig-Holstein-Sonderburg-Augustenburg*)

Lenchen is so useful . . .that I could not give her up, without sinking under the weight of my desolation (Buckle 1926–1928, 1: 85)

The queen's early observations on her third daughter and fifth child did not augur well: "Poor dear Lenchen, though most useful and active and clever and amiable, does not improve with looks and has great difficulties with her figure"

Princess Helena, Queen Victoria's third daughter (on the left) and her sister Louise wear matching tartan skirts, a reflection of the royal passion for Scotland. (Hulton/Archive by Getty Images)

(Packard 1998, 84). Victoria always struggled to find original ways of describing her children's limited virtues. Helena in particular suffered under a shower of pedestrian epithets that poured from the queen's pen: she was by turn noble, amiable, pleasing, agreeable, sensible, generous, useful. But nothing could disguise the fact that she was also decidedly dull. Victoria's patronizing tone became even more overt when she expressed her pity for Helena's lack of beauty, her poor figure, and her equally poor marriage prospects. "Nature certainly divides her gifts strangely," she observed with some dismay (Bennett 1980, 89). She never took time to seek out Helena's several, hidden virtues. Of all the royal daughters, she is the one least credited for her many charitable works, in particular her work in the setting of higher standards of nurses' training.

As an obsessive matchmaker, Victoria feared that such all-round dullness would conspire against Helena's ever marrying. But even poor, plain Lenchen did find herself a husband. And what is more, she managed to remain happily married to a man who equaled her in dullness. She had enough backbone, however, to balk at the idea of living with her mother after she was married. As time went on, the queen found that her erstwhile malleable daughter could be difficult when she chose to be.

Helena was born at Buckingham Palace on 25 May 1846. As a child she was sturdy, physically active, and tomboyish. She loved the outdoor life at Balmoral and became a passionate and accomplished horsewoman. Queen Victoria's dependency upon Helena greatly increased after Victoria was widowed in 1861. With her other remaining daughter, Beatrice, still a child, the queen was adamant that Helena remain close at hand: "A married daughter I must have living with me, and must not be left constantly to look about for help," she insisted in a letter to her Uncle Leopold in 1863. "I intend," the queen wrote, insisting that Beatrice herself wished it, "to look out in a year or two (for till nineteen or twenty I don't intend she should marry) for a young, sensible Prince, for Lenchen to marry, who can during my lifetime make my house his principal home" (Buckle 1926–1928, 18, 85).

But suitable candidates of good reputation were thin on the ground. Eventually, Prince Frederick Christian of Schleswig-Holstein-Sonderburg-Augustenburg was suggested. Fifteen years Helena's senior, he was penniless, balding, and a heavy smoker; many thought he looked like her elderly uncle. But he was also kind and docile and would be eternally grateful that Helena liked him enough to marry him, which she did, despite objections from her brothers the Prince of Wales and Prince Alfred, who both opposed the marriage for political and financial reasons. The wedding, which took place at St. George's Chapel, Windsor, in July 1866, turned out to be a happy and uncontroversial one that produced four more grandchildren for the queen.

Nevertheless, Victoria soon found cause for complaint: Christian indulged the frequently pregnant and sickly Helena far too much, in her opinion. He did nothing but sit and smoke, was unambitious and idle. He had to be found something useful to do and was given the sinecure of ranger of Windsor Park. The post brought with it a residence, Frogmore House (the duchess of Kent's former home) and later Cumberland Lodge, where Helena determinedly kept her distance from the castle and her mother—a fact for which the queen was never quite able to forgive her. At Windsor Helena occupied herself in mundane royal engagements and undertook philanthropic work in the local community. Victoria patronizingly commended her altruism: "So good, such an example to all" (Hibbert 1984, 287). Helena, she wrote, always had "a kind, sweet smile on her poor, sad face" and was "always thinking of others and not of herself" (ibid.).

Perhaps too sensible and too ordinary, Helena has been of little interest to royal biographers until recently. With her mother and her sister Vicky, she shared a passionate interest in politics and was never reticent about expressing her opinion in this regard, in particular her admiration of Benjamin Disraeli. She played the piano well; was good at painting and sketching, like all the female members of the family; and spoke excellent French. But her real strong points were her practicality, her loyalty, and the genuineness of her social concerns. She shared with her other sister, Alice, a devotion to good works and a compassion that she channeled into much unsung work for charity. She was an early member of the Red Cross (founded in 1870) and an admirer, with her sisters, of Florence Nightingale. At Nightingale's request Helena accepted the presidency of the British Nurses Association in 1889, an organization that set new training standards for nurses in hospitals and that in 1892, as a result of Helena's request to the queen, received a royal charter. During the years 1890–1914, Helena devoted a considerable amount of time and energy to the development of nurses' training in Britain and was equally supportive of the movement for better standards of nursing care in workhouse infirmaries, initiated by the reformer Louisa Twining. Helena was instrumental also in the establishment of a children's home and infant nursery at Windsor and encouraged the work of the Society for the Prevention of Cruelty to Children and the Young Women's Christian Association. At Windsor, in 1894, Helena established the Princess Christian District Nurses. By 1902 four houses had been built to accommodate them, which, in 1904, were converted into the Princess Christian Nursing Home. In 1917 this was enlarged, and in later years Helena's daughter, Marie Louise, initiated the addition of a maternity wing. It is now known as the HRH Princess Christian's Hospital and still serves the local community.

Princess Helena never ceased to be grateful for her good fortune in marrying Christian, although her domestic happiness was irrevocably blighted by the tragic death of her son Christian Victor, an army officer who, during service in the Boer War, contracted malaria and died in southern Africa in 1900. She showed great fortitude in dealing with her grief, but her health was always poor in later life. Difficulties during pregnancy and childbirth (she lost two babies) had left her with nervous problems, which manifested themselves in psychosomatic complaints, such as a bout of eye trouble in 1888 and an increasing dependency on laudanum.

Related entries:
Alice Maud Mary, Princess; Louise Caroline Alberta, Princess; Nightingale, Florence; Victoria, Princess Royal; Women's Rights.

References and further reading:

Baird, Diana, ed. 1958. *Victorian Days and a Royal Friendship.* Worcester, UK: Littlebury.

Bennett, Daphne. 1980. *Queen Victoria's Children.* London: Victor Gollancz.

Benson, E. F. 1939. *Daughters of Queen Victoria.* London: Cassell.

Buckle, G. E., ed. 1926–1928. *The Letters of Queen Victoria: A Selection from Her Majesty's Correspondence and Journal between the Years 1862 and 1885.* 2d ser., 3 vols. London: John Murray.

Chomet, Seweryn. 1999. *Helena, Princess Reclaimed: The Life and Times of Queen Victoria's Third Daughter.* New York: Begell House.

Eilers, Marlene A. 1997. *Queen Victoria's Descendants.* Falkoping, Sweden: Rosvall Royal Books.

Epton, Nina. 1971. *Victoria and Her Daughters.* London: Weidenfeld and Nicolson.

Hibbert, Christopher. 1984. *Queen Victoria in Her Letters and Journals.* London: Viking.

Marie Louise, Princess. 1956. *My Memories of Six Reigns.* London: Evans Brothers.

Packard, Jerrold M. 1998. *Victoria's Daughters.* New York: St. Martin's Press.

Prole, Lozania. 1973. *The Queen's Daughters.* London: Robert Hale.

Van der Kiste, John. 1986. *Queen Victoria's Children.* Stroud, Gloucestershire: Sutton.

Hemophilia

Our poor family seems persecuted by this awful disease, the worst I know (Aronson 1973, 172)

Toward the end of her reign, Queen Victoria had come to realize that the splendid dynastic marriages that she had made for many of her children and grandchildren had also brought with them unseen perils, by setting them at the head of nations wracked with political strife. But the royal families of Europe would also be fatally flawed in a far more insidious way—by the unwitting transmission, by Queen Victoria, of the faulty gene of hemophilia. The close intermarriage of Victoria's extended family ensured the disease's proliferation; at a time when hemophilia was so little understood, most of them turned a willful blind eye to it. But, as babies continued to be born displaying the indisputable signs of the disease, rumors abounded that this was yet another manifestation of the "curse of the Coburgs"—a probably apocryphal story originating in a supposed curse made on their house by a Hungarian Prince in the early nineteenth century.

Hemophilia is a disease of the blood characterized by attacks of uncontrollable bleeding; it is carried by females, who do not suffer from the disease but who pass it on to their male children (while their daughters in turn become unknowing carriers). Because the blood plasma of sufferers lacks the essential clotting agent normally present in healthy people, the slightest knock, cut, or fall can provoke excessive bruising and bleeding, frequently leading to death. The life of any sufferer, in the days before an effective treatment had been developed, was thus highly circumscribed; every move would be closely monitored, and all activities involving any kind of physical risk would be forbidden. It was often the case, however, that despite the most scrupulous precautions, hemophiliacs succumbed and died as a result of the most trivial accidents long before even reaching adulthood; very few were lucky enough to survive into middle, let alone old age.

To this day opinion remains divided over how the fatal gene of hemophilia was passed on to Queen Victoria—herself a carrier—or whether it actually was passed on at all by either of her parents. Her father, the duke of Kent, could not have inherited it since he was free of the disease, and without DNA (deoxyribonucleic acid) testing ofVictoria's mother's remains, it will never be known whether the duchess of

The tragic young Russian tsarevich, Alexis, probably the best-known victim of the hereditary disease of hemophilia, which Queen Victoria passed on through her female children. (Hulton-Deutsch Collection/ CORBIS)

Kent was a carrier, although this seems unlikely. What was perplexing for the doctors—then and now—is that there was no known history of the disease, either on Victoria's Hanoverian side or in the Saxe-Coburg family of her husband, Prince Albert. Hemophilia is transmitted through the female X chromosome, but it is a recessive gene and does not necessarily appear in every generation; it can be passed down through several generations before finally manifesting itself. The study of modern genetics was still in its infancy when Victoria's children were being born; in fact, its pioneer, Gregor Mendel, did not publish his findings until 1866, and it was the turn of the century before any of them were taken seriously. As for the disease itself, hemophilia, which was first recognized in 1803 by the Philadelphian physician John

Otto, was little understood during the nineteenth century and often treated in the worst way possible—by bleeding. It would not be until the 1930s that blood transfusions would come into use as an effective treatment of the condition. In 1936 a clotting agent, Factor VIII, was finally identified by A. J. Patek Jr. and R. H. Stetson and extracted from the blood plasma of healthy donors. By the 1960s, it had become widely available in the treatment of hemophilia.

The best and most logical explanation offered to date, although this was something never posited in Victoria's lifetime, is that the disease originated with Victoria herself—as the result of a mutant X chromosome in her own genetic makeup. Alternatively it may have come from a spontaneous mutation in her mother's ovum, which is more likely than one in her father's sperm. It has been suggested by Potts and Potts—who rate the chance of a mutation at 1 in 50,000—that the duke of Kent may in fact have been infertile and not the father of Victoria at all (see Potts and Potts 1995, chap. 6, "Mutation or Bastard?"). The highly contentious suggestion that Victoria might have been illegitimate would also imply that she had inherited the gene from a hemophiliac father. The possibility of Victoria's illegitimacy is not a new argument, and it has often been suggested that her mother may have had an extramarital affair with Sir John Conroy, with her husband's encouragement (he being infertile), in the race to produce an heir to the British throne.

In Queen Victoria's case, the hemophilia she carried fortunately only manifested itself in one of her four sons—Leopold, born in 1857. He grew up a chronic invalid, his childhood blighted by regular bouts of bruising and hemorrhaging that left his joints stiff and affected his posture. The queen endlessly found fault with his awkwardness and his unattractiveness. But Leopold surprised her: he was highly intelligent and determined to live as normal a life as possible, taking particular pleasure in practical jokes. But he was constantly prone to minor accidents that exacerbated one of the characteristic problems endured by many hemophiliacs—frequent hemorrhages in the knee joints—causing him severe pain and lameness and requiring long periods of bed rest. Leopold, who according to the queen had been "four or five times at death's door during his life" (Dewhurst 1980, 185), bravely fought his mother's endless proscriptions on his lifestyle. He lived long enough to marry and produce two children. The second, a son, Charles, who was born after Leopold's death from a brain hemorrhage, fortunately did not have the disease; his sister, Alice, passed hemophilia on to her son.

The proliferation of hemophilia through the royal houses of Europe came mainly through two of Victoria's five daughters—Alice and Beatrice—both of whom were carriers of the disease and who in turn passed it on to several of their children. But although it is certain that the queen's eldest daughter, Vicky, was not a carrier—as none of her children were affected—it is possible that the gene might have been present in Victoria's third daughter Louise (who had no children). It is equally likely that Helena—whose daughters appeared healthy but who did not produce male grandchildren in whom the gene might have reappeared—might also have been a carrier.

Princess Alice, who died of diphtheria in 1878, married into the royal house of Hesse-Darmstadt. She had seven children, passing hemophilia to her second son, Frederick, who died from internal bleeding after falling from a window when he was three. Of her five daughters, Irene and Alix (Alexandra) were carriers, Irene marrying her first cousin Henry of Prussia (the son of her aunt Vicky) and taking the disease into the German royal family. Their son, Waldemar, lived with the disease until the age of fifty-six; the hemophilia of Irene's other son, Henry, killed him at the age of four.

It is the story of Alice's other daughter, Alix, that would be the most tragic. When, in 1894, Tsar Alexander III of Russia had agreed to his son's marriage to Queen Victoria's granddaughter, he had been oblivious to the fatal gene that she carried and with it the threat it posed to the continuance of the Romanov blood line. The subject in any event had been one that European royal families had avoided discussing, let alone attempting to comprehend, since it appeared to strike at random. Tragically, after bearing four daughters, Alix finally passed hemophilia on to her youngest child and much adored only son, Alexis, when he was born in 1904 (we shall never know, of course, whether any of his sisters were carriers).

It has often been said that the Tsarevich Alexis's hemophilia contributed directly to the fall of the Russian Empire, as a result of the tsarina's utter dependency on the monk Grigori Rasputin, who demonstrated an unexplained ability to control the life-threatening attacks of bleeding. Alix had suffered agonies of guilt when she discovered that she had passed on hemophilia to the son for whom she had so longed. A deeply pious and emotional woman, she had converted to Russian Orthodoxy on her marriage and fervently believed in the power of prayer in protecting him. In 1913, when Alexis suffered his worst-ever attack and would most likely have died, Alix, having heard of Rasputin's reputation as a holy man and healer, sent for him. Rasputin quickly effected a miraculous recovery in the tsarevich, achieved, it has been suggested, through the powers of some kind of hypnosis. Alix from then on looked upon Rasputin as little short of divine. She would brook no criticism of him, calling him in whenever her son suffered attacks. The closeness of their relationship led to rumors that Rasputin had the tsarina, as well as the tsar, in thrall, and even to gossip that he had a sexual hold over Alix and her daughters, who also revered him.

The short life and violent death of Tsarevich Alexis, who was murdered in 1918 by the Bolsheviks at the age of fourteen, along with the rest of his family, has become the stuff of legend. It has fueled the unending appetite for stories of miraculous survival from the hail of bullets by a succession of claimants, including the most famous—Anna Manahan, who claimed to be Anastasia. Her highly plausible story was finally quashed by DNA testing in the 1990s, with members of the British royal family cooperating in the donation of their own DNA samples for comparison. Similar tests on the remains of Queen Victoria and her parents would, of course, settle once and for all any talk of her illegitimacy and also perhaps throw light on the origins of the royal hemophilia. But this has been firmly vetoed by the royal family.

It was Princess Beatrice of Battenberg's family who suffered most from the inheritance of hemophilia; of her four children, two of her three sons were sufferers and her daughter, Victoria Eugénie (known as Ena), was a carrier. The marriage in 1905 of Ena to King Alfonso XIII of Spain went ahead despite Alfonso's knowing the history of hemophilia in the British royal family, and two of his and Ena's five sons inherited the disease. Don Gonzalo died aged twenty in 1934 from uncontrollable bleeding brought on after a minor car collision. His brother, the prince of the Asturias, died in 1938 aged thirty-one, after breaking his leg in another minor car accident. Their sisters, Beatrice and Maria Cristina, did not, however, pass on hemophilia to their children. King Alfonso was deeply embittered and blamed Ena for this catastrophe. Gerald Hamilton has suggested that hemophilia was as significant in the collapse of the Spanish throne as it was that of Russia: "the bleeding of the Prince of the Asturias was one more contributory cause of the Revolution of 1931." "The Spanish people," he asserted, "interpreted his bleeding as a sign from Heaven that the mandate of the House of Bourbon had departed" (1964, 110).

It now seems likely that the "royal disease" of hemophilia has died out in most of the royal families that inherited it, although the suggestion has been made that it is still present in descendants of the Spanish royal family, via possible female carriers descended from Queen Ena. In 1998, however, the publication of a medical study by Röhl, Warren, and Hunt (1998) brought to the surface a longstanding speculation over the existence of another serious hereditary disease in the British royal family, which also might well have been passed on by Queen Victoria. As a young woman, she had often expressed her fear of inheriting the "madness" of her grandfather George III, a condition that has since been diagnosed as the rare disease of porphyria. This affects the metabolism and provokes bodily overheating, severe headaches, nervous excitement, and erratic behavior suggesting mental breakdown and even madness. It is the contention of Röhl, Warren, and Hunt that Victoria, who throughout her life was affected by her "nerves" and sick headaches—enough to make Prince Albert seriously worry about her mental instability—had inherited the gene and passed the disease on to her eldest daughter, Vicky. The queen described her bouts of illness in great detail in her letters to Vicky in Prussia, who responded by confiding that she too suffered many similar symptoms. Porphyria is notoriously difficult to diagnose, as it is very variable in its severity and can in some cases be so mild as to be unidentifiable as anything more than an intermittent malaise. In Vicky's case, however, the symptoms were far more pronounced and wide ranging (see Röhl, Warren, and Hunt 1998, chap. 6). Throughout her life, she endured long periods of ill health and agonizing pain. Not least among them were severe pains in her arms, legs, and back; digestive trouble; weight loss; lumbago; wracking headaches; a raised pulse and palpitations; dark red rashes on her face; abdominal pains; and, like her mother, an intolerance of heat. Röhl, Warren, and Hunt contended that the details of Vicky's medical history are sufficient to argue a strong case for her having suffered from variegate porphyria.

Related entries:
Conroy, Sir John; Hanover, Royal House of; Leopold I, King of the Belgians; Sex, Pregnancy, and Childbirth; Victoria, Princess Royal; Victoria, Queen: Birth of; Victoria, Queen: Physical Appearance of

References and further reading:

Aronson, Theo. *Grandmama of Europe: The Crowned Descendants of Queen Victoria.* London: Cassell (chap. 18, "The Royal Disease").

Dewhurst, Jack. 1980. *Royal Confinements.* London: Weidenfeld and Nicolson (esp. chap. 10, 183–188).

Duff, David. 1967. *Hessian Tapestry.* London: Macmillan.

Hamilton, Gerald. 1964. *Blood Royal.* London: A. Gibbs and Phillips.

MacAlpine, I., and R. Hunter. 1969. *George III and the Mad Business.* Harmonsworth, UK: Penguin.

Massie, Robert K. 1968. *Nicholas and Alexandra.* London: Victor Gollancz.

Noel, G. 1999. *Ena, Spain's English Queen.* London: Constable.

Potts, D. M., and W. T. W. Potts. 1995. *Queen Victoria's Gene: Haemophilia and the Royal Family.* Stroud, Gloucestershire: Sutton.

Radzinsky, Eduard. 1992. *The Last Tsar.* New York: Doubleday.

Röhl, John C. G., Martin Warren, and David Hunt. 1998. *Purple Secret: Genes, Madness and the Royal Houses of Europe.* London: Bantam (esp. chaps. 5 and 6).

I

Indian Rebellion, 1857–1858

(also called the Indian Mutiny and the Sepoy Rebellion/Mutiny)

so much more distressing than the Crimea—where there was glory *and honourable warfare*
(Benson and Esher 1911, 3:247)

The outbreak of rebellion in India in 1857, which came hard on the heels of two years of war in the Crimea, exceeded even that conflict in the frenzy of outrage that it provoked in the British press. Lurid and often unreliable accounts of atrocities, passed on at second- and thirdhand and separated from real events by the many weeks that it took letters to reach England, contributed to a long-standing view of the events of 1857–1858 as being a major uprising against British rule. Stories of the murder of innocent women, children, and wounded centered around the siege at Lucknow and the massacre at Cawnpore. The perpetrators—a combination of rebel troops nursing genuine grievances and maverick, criminal elements who opportunistically exploited the situation—were countered by a series of heroic British acts of derring-do that long served to cast a smokescreen over the fact that a good two-thirds of the Indians in the British Army in India had remained loyal to the Crown and had played no part in the rebellion. Nor had events ever been likely to escalate into a nationalist uprising that would have seriously threatened British rule in India. The rebellion was, at all a times, a regional rather than a national affair; confined in the main to the military population of northwestern India, it brought to an end the 250-year domination of the British East India Company.

British influence in India had been steadily growing since the seventeenth century, particularly after the disintegration of the Mughal empire in the mid-eighteenth century. After a succession of wars with France and with Indian princes, the British had gained supremacy through the offices of the East India Company, which had administered the region under a governor-general based in Calcutta. The government became increasingly concerned, however, about the company's commercial and political monopoly and assumed greater Crown control. By 1834 the East Indian Company's role had been emasculated and was now mainly managerial.

Further British territorial gains in India had come with the annexation of the provinces of the Sind (1843) and the Punjab (1849), followed in 1856 by the takeover of the Kingdom of Oudh in the Upper Ganges Valley. Those independent states in India that remained were feudal, ruled over mainly by despotic native princes. But by the 1840s it was clear that the disempowered East India Company

The storming of Delhi by British troops during the Indian Rebellion of 1857–1858. (The* Illustrated London News *Picture Library)

could no longer manage such a vast colonial interest, which had doubled in size in twenty years. Corruption and dishonest practice were on the increase and discontent was clearly brewing, particularly among dispossessed Indian princes who had had their hereditary rights to land revenues taken from them. Resentment was also mounting, in the Upper Ganges Valley, to the enforcement of the Doctrine of Lapse. Under the traditional, native system of heredity, a prince without an heir had been allowed to adopt one to inherit his wealth. This practice was now outlawed, with the East India Company annexing the territories where princely thrones had no heir, placing them under company control.

The erosion, by British rule, of other Indian traditions relating to religious practice were also seen as a direct challenge to orthodox religion, with many Muslims and Hindus fearing that the activities of Christian mission stations would lead to the imposition of the Christian religion and enforced conversion. The British had certainly introduced changes—such as banning suttee (the traditional practice of a widow's throwing herself upon her husband's funeral pyre)—and had attempted to stop child marriage and female infanticide, as well as trying to outlaw the Hindu rule that widows could not remarry. Among native troops in the British Army in India there was also hostility to the refusal of the authorities to respect religious practice (such as ritual washing by Muslims).

The rebellion began in 1857 in the heavily populated area of Oudh, incited by native troops in the British Army in Bengal. Local landowners, hostile to the region's recent annexation by Britain, also gave their support to what they perceived as the increasing imposition of Western culture and economic systems on Indian rural society.

The catalyst for rebellion was the introduction of the new Enfield rifle to replace old standard-issue muskets. As part of the loading process, the ends of the Enfield paper cartridges had to be bitten off, to release the gunpowder, before being rammed down the gun barrel. Rumors began circulating that the paper was greased with a mixture of unrefined beef and pork fat. Such a directive was deeply offensive to the culture of both Muslims and Hindus, who observed strict dietary rules (Hindus did not eat beef; Muslims did not eat pork). The troops objected, saying that this practice made them unclean and was a contravention of religious belief. By the time rumor had spread panic among these troops, the threat had in fact disappeared. At the end of January 1857, having been apprised of this error, army headquarters in England had sent orders that vegetable fat be used to grease the cartridges. Instructions were also issued that the cartridges could, in any event, be opened with the fingers.

Despite this attempt to defuse the situation, on 10 May 1857 a rebellion broke out in Meerut, where sepoys of the Bengal Native Cavalry refused to use the cartridges. The men were tried by court martial and sentenced to ten years. Three native regiments mutinied in sympathy; they murdered their British officers and burned their barracks, before embarking on an orgy of violence, killing every European in sight, as they proceeded through the villages of the Ganges valley on the forty-mile march on Delhi. Entering the city on 11 May, the rebels devastated much of the city and again murdered all the Europeans they could find, after which they marched on other strategically important military depots at Cawnpore and Lucknow. British resistance at first was minimal: at this time native troops (sepoys) in India numbered 230,000, as against 40,000 British and European. The British detachments were widely scattered, and a great logistical problem presented itself in getting them to the Delhi area, at a time when the railway did not extend that far north from the main administrative center of Calcutta.

With violence having spread across the northwestern provinces of India, some civilian populations in upper and central India joined the rebellion, as did bands of roving criminals. But much of the fighting was localized and disorganized, lacking military leadership—often degenerating to mob violence. The atmosphere of terror among the increasingly embattled white Europeans in the area was heightened in the terrible heat—with temperatures over 100 degrees—and the drenching summer rains. By the end of June, Cawnpore, a garrison comprising four native regiments and a European battery of artillery, had surrendered to the rebels, and Lucknow was under siege.

At Cawnpore, in Oudh province—270 miles from Delhi on the road to Calcutta—four native regiments had mutinied. About 600 fighting men had been besieged by rebels for about eighteen days in open trenches, exposed to the blazing heat and enduring terrible thirst, while another 300 or so of their wives and children as well as some sick and a few civilians had been holed up inside the garrison in a disused ammunition store. Eventually, on 25 June, the leader of the rebels, local princeling Nana Sahib, offered the survivors a safe passage by boat down the Ganges to Allahabad. Two days later, as the group of mainly wounded, women, and children was about to set off from the shore, firing broke out and most of the men were killed. The remainder—125 women and children—were taken back to Cawnpore. When Sahib heard that a British relief force was on its way, he ordered the systematic massacre of the women and children. This was carried out by rogue elements (the sepoy troops having refused to shoot them). On 17 July Cawnpore was relieved by troops led by Sir Henry Havelock who, after awaiting reinforcements, then went on to relieve Lucknow.

In England, sensationalist accounts of the gruesome details of the massacre at Cawnpore had provoked unprecedented public fury and calls for revenge. Queen Victoria had found the long delay in obtaining news of events in India intolerable; the state of hysteria in Britain was exacerbated by the much greater distance from home and the time it would take for relief forces to arrive in India. Nor was this a campaign where the traditional rules of engagement were being observed. It was perceived as a "dirty" war and one without honor because of the attacks on innocent civilians. The queen's primary concern was for the innocent victims: "The horrors committed on the poor ladies—women and children—are unknown in these ages, and make one's blood run cold" (Benson and Esher, 1911, 3:247). By September she was, she confessed "in sad anxiety about India, which engrosses all our attention" (247). She admitted to Lady Canning (a former lady-in-waiting, whose husband had been appointed governor-general of India in 1855) to being perplexed as to what had prompted "people once so gentle" as the Indians to commit such atrocities (Hibbert 1984, 137). She was particularly grieved, too, "to think of all this blood shed in a country which seemed so prosperous—so improving and for which, as well as its inhabitants, I felt so great an interest" (ibid.). She urged Lady Canning to let her have details of those who had escaped as soon as she could, but letters at that time took six to seven weeks to reach England.

The tide turned against the rebels when the fort they held at Delhi was captured and the city retaken on 20 September. Meanwhile, Lucknow continued to be besieged. At the governor's residence, where about 600 European women and children had taken refuge, along with a few sick, wounded, and noncombatants, Sir Henry Lawrence was holding out as best he could with the help of loyal native troops and a handful of civilian volunteers. Together they had built makeshift defenses against besieging rebel forces (estimated at around 6,000). But Lawrence was killed by a shell on 4 July, and the defenders' numbers and their morale were reduced by the ravages of cholera, smallpox, and dysentery and by constant shelling and repeated attempts by the rebels to storm the stockades and tunnel into their entrenchments. Supplies had begun to run out after two and a half months of siege, when on 25 September Sir Henry Havelock attempted to relieve the garrison. After losing over 500 dead and wounded, he could do little more than reinforce those already there and with them endure another seven weeks of disease, hunger, and thirst while native forces continued to encircle the city.

The queen was greatly relieved to hear of this improvement to the situation at Lucknow and by this time, as more accurate reports reached Britain, was now more sanguine about some of the exaggerated accounts of atrocities that she had heard. Together with the rest of the country she celebrated the final relief of Lucknow (1 March 1858), several months after troops, commanded by Sir Colin Campbell and led by the Ninety-Third Highlanders playing "The Campbells are Coming" on their bagpipes, had relieved the governor's residence there on 16 November. By March, when the whole city was back in British hands after a siege of five months, Campbell had been further reinforced with 10,000 Gurkhas from Nepal.

Remaining pockets of resistance were crushed by British troops, and peace was declared on 8 July 1858, much of its successful conclusion owing to the fact that 40,000 native troops in the Punjab—especially Sikhs—had remained loyal to the Crown. But the aftermath for those who had rebelled was a grisly one. The savage murder of white women and children provoked equally savage reprisals against the rebels, involving torture and summary execution. Lynch law prevailed for a while, with 400 rebels hanged in one mass execution while British officers watched the proceedings to the sound of regimental bands. Whole villages suspected of supporting rebels were destroyed, along with their livestock and crops. Particularly notorious was the execution of hundreds of rebels, who were tied to the mouth of a cannon and blown to bits—(although this did not pass without protests from some British officers).

Such reprisals were precisely what the queen had dreaded back in September 1857, when she had told Lady Canning, after the massacre at Cawnpore, of her apprehension that "the retribution will be a fearful one" (Hibbert 1984, 137). But she had hoped that "our Officers and Men will show the difference between Christian and Mussulmen and Hindoo—by sparing the old men, women and children" (ibid.). Victoria had been greatly comforted by stories of the loyalty of most of the native troops; she saw it as a vindication of her insistence on religious and racial tolerance in India, "for then indeed how could we expect any respect or esteem for us in future?" (ibid.). Controversy in Britain raged over the true nature of the rebellion and the government's response to it. The queen, like the governor-general Lord Canning, was a conciliator and argued for moderation. She had found the excessive "blood thirsting" in the British press "shameful" (138) and was now strongly critical of those who had not waited for reliable explanations of events, instead "judging things from a distance" (ibid.) without weighing up all the facts.

Canning found himself the butt of much criticism for his efforts at reconciliation, including being nicknamed "Clemency" Canning. In his view, "The reputation of England's power . . . has had a rude shake" (Benson and Esher 1911, 3: 237). He had warned the queen of the "violent rancour of a very large proportion of the English community against every native Indian of every class" (251) and had told her that many Indians who had remained loyal would suffer. He was particularly concerned about armchair politicians back in England, who understood little of the true situation in India. By December 1857 his tone had become increasingly anxious, but he took a brave stand. Determined to curb reprisals and stabilize British rule, Canning insisted, in a letter to Lord Granville, that "as long as I have breath in my body, I will pursue no other policy than that I have been following; I will not govern in anger. . . . I will never allow an angry or undiscriminating act or word to proceed from the Government of India, as long as I am responsible for it" (Bolitho 1964, 180). In the event, both Lord Canning and his wife would pay dearly for their love of India—Charlotte, worn down by the climate, died of fever in 1861, and Lord Canning died a year later, a broken man.

Britain's inability to control—either administratively or militarily—its interests in India resulted in the passing of the Government of India Act in November 1858. The East India Company was abolished and its holdings in India transferred to the British Crown, which also assumed control of its administrative responsibilities and vested them in a viceroy at the head of a Council of India, composed of paid officials. The Doctrine of Lapse and other British-imposed social measures offensive to religious practice were abolished, and the territories of the remaining Indian princes guaranteed. The queen had been anxious to ensure that, when drawing up the act, the prime minister, Lord Derby, "should breathe feelings of generosity, benevolence and religious feeling, pointing out the privileges which the Indians will receive in being placed on an equality with the subjects of the British Crown and the prosperity following in the train of civilisation" (Benson and Esher 1911, 3:379).

During the rebellion, Chancellor of the Exchequer Benjamin Disraeli had urged the House of Commons that "their real

Ruler and Sovereign, Queen Victoria" should play a closer role in India (Blake 1966, 376). Over the next thirty years, the British Raj in India would become the jewel in Britain's crown—and it was widely celebrated as such in Queen Victoria's Diamond Jubilee 1897 when Indian troops took a prominent place in the cavalcades. These years also marked a period of rapid economic growth in India and with it the entrenchment of a wide-reaching civil service and the growth of an Indian middle class who were crucial to India's ruling elite. Reforms brought improvements in English-language education and literacy standards, as well as the development of roads, the railway network, and the telegraph. Improved communications led also to the rise of the major cities of Calcutta, Madras, and Bombay.

Related entries:
Diamond Jubilee; Empress of India; Racial and Religious Prejudice; Religion; Women's Rights

References and further reading:

Allen, Charles. 1986. *A Glimpse of the Burning Plain: Leaves from the Indian Journals of Charlotte Canning.* London: Michael Joseph.

Benson, A. C., and Viscount Esher, eds. 1911. *The Letters of Queen Victoria, 1837–1861.* 1st ser., 3 vols. London: John Murray.

Blake, Robert. 1966. *Disraeli.* London: Eyre and Spottiswoode.

Bolitho, Hector. 1964. *Albert, Prince Consort.* London: Max Parrish.

Chaudhuri, Sashi Bhusan. 1979. *English Historical Writings on the Indian Mutiny, 1857–59.* Calcutta: World Press.

Chick, Alfred Noah. 1974. *Annals of the Indian Rebellion.* London: Charles Knight and Co.

David, Saul. 2002. *The Indian Mutiny 1857.* London: Viking.

Harlow, Barbara, and Mia Carter. 1999. *Imperialism and Orientalism.* Oxford: Blackwell.

Hibbert, Christopher. 1980. *The Great Mutiny, India 1857.* Harmondsworth, UK: Penguin.

———. 1984. *Queen Victoria in Her Letters and Journals.* London: Viking.

Hilton, Richard. 1957. *The Indian Mutiny: A Centenary History.* London: Hollis and Carter.

Priestley, J. B. *Queen Victoria's Heyday.* Harmondsworth, UK: Penguin (chap. "1857").

Ward, Andrew. 1996. *Our Bones Are Scattered: The Cawnpore Massacres and the Indian Mutiny of 1857.* London: John Murray.

Woodham-Smith, Cecil. 1972. *Queen Victoria: Her Life and Her Times.* Vol. 1: *1819–1861.* London: Hamish Hamilton.

Woodruff, Philip. 1985. *The Men Who Ruled India.* 2 vols. London: Jonathan Cape.

Ireland

You see more ragged and wretched people here than I ever saw anywhere else (Woodham-Smith 1962, 397)

In a speech to the House of Commons on 16 February 1844, the British Conservative politician Benjamin Disraeli warned of a looming domestic crisis, to which many in government had turned a blind eye for too long: the Irish question. It was a problem that had, in his view, been created on four fronts: "a starving population, an absentee aristocracy, and an alien Church, and in addition the weakest executive in the world." (*Hansard,* 16, February 1844) In this, at least, Disraeli would concur with his great political rival, the Liberal leader William Gladstone, who only a year later gloomily warned: "Ireland, Ireland! That cloud in the west, that coming storm" (Bassett 1986, 64). Throughout the nineteenth century parliamentarians would be continually confronted with the urgent need to grapple with Ireland's unresolvable problems and avert violence. But whenever it came to granting the country a degree of independence, a measure that might have gone a long way to avert continuing unrest, the British Parliament would be bitterly divided.

One of the unquantifiable elements of the Irish question is the extent to which Queen Victoria's persistent absence from that country contributed to the alienation of its population and the growth of nationalist resentment. Sydney Lee, in one of the first biographies of the queen, estimated that during her sixty-three-year reign, the queen had spent an equivalent of barely five weeks in Ireland, as opposed to *seven years* on her estate at Balmoral (Lee 1902, 565). This fact did not go unnoticed among the queen's own entourage. In 1868, Lady Augusta Stanley, one of her most loyal ladies-in-waiting, observed that "if it had been Ireland she had visited and settled on, instead of Aberdeenshire—the ecstasies and interests that would have grown up would have been just as great—and Fenianism would never have existed" (Windsor and Bolitho 1929, 65).

Many of the problems then facing Ireland were the accumulated results of the ill-fated Irish Rebellion of 1798, when the United Irishmen, with the support of a French expeditionary fleet, had failed to ignite a widescale revolution across Ireland. The British had responded with harsh repression and the 1801 Act of Union, dissolving the Irish parliament and bringing Irish affairs under direct rule. Thereafter, regular petitions for Irish Catholics to be granted the right to hold senior government offices were presented to the British government, in an atmosphere of increasing unrest. In 1829 the home secretary, Robert Peel, and the prime minister, the duke of Wellington, finally pushed through the Catholic Emancipation Act, which granted civil rights to Irish Catholics, by extending the franchise and allowing them to hold all government offices except those of regent, lord chancellor, and lord lieutenant of Ireland.

The young Princess Victoria had studied Irish history with her governess, Baroness Lehzen, her natural compassion aroused by the sufferings of the people: "How ill treated that poor country and nation has been" (St. Aubyn 1991, 119). But her attitude toward Ireland hardened under the influence of her Whig prime minister, Lord Melbourne, whose contempt for the rebellious Irish underclasses was equaled only by his indifference to the suffering of Ireland's tenant farmers, many of whom paid excessively high rents to absentee English landlords. In addition, even though they were Catholics, the Irish peasantry had to pay tithes to the English, Anglican church. This anomalous situation created bitter resentment, its absurdities encapsulated by the writer Sydney Smith: "the bell of a neat parish church often summons to worship only the parson, and an occasional conforming clerk, whilst two hundred yards off, a thousand Catholics are huddled together in a miserable hovel, and pelted by all the storms of heaven" (Ziegler 1976, 91).

Elizabeth Longford argued that it was Lord Melbourne who was largely responsible for molding Princess Victoria's impressionable young mind at a time when she demonstrated a natural compassion toward the oppressed. It was under his "callous tuition" that Victoria "gradually came to believe that every rebellious Irishman was 'a low Irishman'" (Longford 1998, 68–69). Melbourne planted the seeds of fear in her that poverty bred discontent and that this was but a short step from revolution. The Irish underclasses were thus dangerous and should be mistrusted. With unrest in Ireland continuing throughout the agricultural depression of the 1830s, Melbourne introduced a series of coercive measures and martial law. All talk of a visit to Ireland by the queen was quashed; an invitation, made in 1844, by the lord mayor of Dublin was entertained but rejected after renewed economic crisis made any such visit an impossibility.

In 1845 one-third of the Irish potato crop—the staple diet of the peasantry—was lost, owing to blight. The following year's crop also failed, and few potatoes could be sown because seed potatoes were still in very short supply. The country faced a catastrophe: people were starving, relying on hand-outs from churches, charities, and the local gentry. For Robert Peel, this was final proof that the protectionist Corn Laws must be repealed to allow cheap imports of grain to relieve the suffering. Queen Victoria urged him to do so, in order to save her Irish subjects from imminent starvation, fearful that their hunger might raise the specter of rebellion of which Melbourne had warned. By 1846 she was discussing the expediency of a state visit to Ireland with her new prime minister, Lord John Russell (Peel's government having fallen over the repeal of the Corn Laws). It was, she agreed "a journey which must one day or other be undertaken, and which the Queen would be glad to have accomplished," for she would not countenance accusations of cowardice and speculation about "whether she *dare* visit one part of her dominions" (Benson and Esher 1911, 2:93).

By 1847, economic recession was now gripping England as well as Ireland. The new relief measures inaugurated by Lord John Russell's government, which had set up soup kitchens to provide as many as 3 million meals a day, had come too late. Many Irish peasants had by now died of starvation, succumbed to typhus, or emigrated to the United States and Australia. An analysis of census records suggests that up to 1.5 million people died of starvation and a million more emigrated during the famine years of 1845–1849. Victoria was appalled by stories of landlords appropriating the corn of hungry peasants but equally alarmed when these starving people, driven to desperation, turned to violence and began murdering their rapacious landlords. The "insubordination of the poor" (Longford 1998, 191) frightened her. When its ugly face was made manifest to monarchies across Europe during the 1848 year of revolutions, and agitation was once more sparked, this time by the Young Ireland group, the British government postponed a trip to Ireland planned for the queen that year. The following August, when the danger seemed to have past, Victoria finally made her first state visit—twelve years after her accession. The country was still suffering the very visible effects of four years of crop failure and famine; yet the British government hoped that this malnourished and dispirited nation would respond patriotically to the "magical effect of the royal presence" (Woodham-Smith 1972, 294).

The royal couple, accompanied by their four eldest children, arrived at Cove harbor on the royal yacht *Victoria and Albert* on 2 August and proceeded on into Cork on the first leg of a ten-day visit. The streets were decorated with bunting and banners proclaiming "Hail Victoria, Ireland's hope and England's glory" (Woodham-Smith 1962, 395). Military bands played, and huge crowds waving their hats and handkerchiefs gave the family a rapturous welcome. The queen was gratified that "the enthusiasm and excitement shown by the Irish people was extreme" (Charlot 1991, 282–283), noting in her journal that "the beauty of the women is very remarkable . . . such beautiful dark eyes and hair, and such fine teeth." "Almost every third woman was pretty," she remarked, "and some remarkably so" (Woodham-Smith 1962, 395). Renaming Cove as Queenstown, to commemorate her visit, the queen then sailed to Dublin, entering the city on the evening of the sixth to find its buildings spectacularly illuminated to greet her. The royal family stayed at the viceroy's lodge in Phoenix Park for a week, from whence they took several drives along the streets of the capital, refusing an official escort and enjoying the noisy welcome of cheering crowds, many of whom ran after their carriage. Before leaving, the queen held an evening reception at Dublin Castle on 8 August, making a point of supporting the Irish textile trade by wearing a dress of Irish poplin, decorated with shamrocks. The following day a grand military levee was held in her presence in Phoenix Park.

Prince Albert was very taken with "the brilliant bustle of our Irish tour" (Martin 1875–1880, 2: 214); he considered it an unqualified triumph—and a vindication of Irish loyalty. The queen was captivated by the warmth and affection shown by the Irish to herself and in particular to her children, who, according to Theodore Martin, "were objects of universal attention and admiration" (2:207). It is a pity that the queen did not take to heart the words of one enthusiastic old lady, who shouted after her carriage in Dublin: "Oh! Queen, dear! . . . make one of them Prince Patrick and all Ireland will die for you" (ibid.).

In her classic study, *The Great Hunger,* Cecil Woodham-Smith observed that for a few heady days, the queen's visit had revitalized Dublin (a city of the empire then only second in importance to London) so that it had seemed "like a city risen from the dead" (1962, 403). Victoria sincerely believed that she had conquered Irish hearts and would continue to cling to the idea that she was loved by the Irish, despite the fact that she did not make another state visit for fifty-three years. In political terms her visit did not work the expected miracle of appeasing Ireland: "The affection was brief, the participants unsuited, the episode soon forgotten and the course of history uninfluenced," remarked Woodham-Smith, "but for a few days in August, 1849, the attraction was a reality" (394).

For the remainder of the queen's reign, successive British governments would discover, to their cost, that there was no quick fix as far as Ireland was concerned, for it was "past the point where the Irish could be made governable with a few kind words' (Woodham-Smith 1962, 297). A brief, private visit was made to Dublin by Victoria and Albert in 1853, to see an exhibition of Irish industries, and another in 1861 to visit the prince of Wales, when he was attached to a regiment at the Curragh Camp near Dublin. Meanwhile, in New York in 1858, a group of republican Irish exiles had founded a secret society—the Fenians—bent on the liberation of Ireland from British rule.

After Prince Albert's death in 1861, the queen's affection for the Irish soured considerably when Irish nationalists boycotted his funeral and the statue of Prince Albert that she had presented to the city of Dublin was refused by the mayor and city corporation and returned. Such an insult to the sainted Albert's memory was never forgiven by Victoria; it may well have thrown cold water on any inclination she had to return there, as did the failure of the authorities in Dublin to send loyal addresses to the queen on the occasion of her jubilees in 1887 and 1897. The growth of Fenianism provoked regular rumors of kidnap and assassination plots against the queen, such as those circulating in October 1867. She dismissed the rumors with her usual sangfroid, remarking: "Poor things, if they were so silly as to run away with me, they would find me a very inconvenient charge" (Gosse 1901, 318). A couple of months earlier a bungled attempt by five Irishmen to rescue Fenian prisoners from a police van in Manchester had resulted in the death of a policeman. The queen regretfully admitted that "we shall have to hang some" (Longford 1998, 360). The execution of the three ringleaders in November aroused calls for revenge. At Christmas that year, the government got wind of a supposed plot by Fenians, on their way to the Isle of Wight by sea, to murder the queen at Osborne House. She was entreated to return to the mainland but refused to be intimidated by what turned out to be an absurd rumor. But Queen Victoria had to revise her views when her son, Prince Alfred, on a visit to Australia the following year, was shot and wounded by a Fenian. A sixth botched attempt on her own life followed in 1872 when an Irish youth, Arthur O'Connor, threatened her with a pistol, in an attempt to win the release of Fenians held in jail in England.

In 1868, the new Liberal prime minister, William Gladstone, had announced: "My mission is to pacify Ireland" (Matthew 1986, 147). The "Anglican Establishment in Ireland had become an indefensible anomaly," he argued, and "its removal was the essential first step towards the reconciliation of the Irish to English rule" (Blake 1966, 497). The British public now had to accept the inevitability of the disestablishment of the Anglican church in Ireland. A bill was introduced by Gladstone, in an attempt to defuse the deep resentment of Catholics forced to pay tithes to the Anglican Church; the church in Ireland was now partially disendowed and promptly lost half of its Irish revenues. Queen Victoria was very opposed to the move; as Defender of the faith she saw this as a threat to the security of Anglicanism, not just in Ireland but also in England. Disraeli agreed with her, remarking that such an act was divisive, more presciently observing that "its tendency is to civil war" (Feiling 1966, 938).

In 1869 Gladstone urged Queen Victoria to show a greater interest in Ireland by establishing a royal residence there, as she had done in Scotland. But the widowed queen, now spending long periods at Balmoral, strongly resisted the idea. She also refused to entertain his suggestion, made in December 1870, that the prince of Wales be given a role in Irish affairs, as viceroy of Ireland. Victoria was extremely defensive over the issue. Anxious to deflect any unwelcome suggestion that she or her family had neglected Ireland, she responded with a host of objections. She was, she assured Gladstone, perfectly willing for members of the royal family to make visits there from time to time, but their cost should not be borne by the royal purse. Excessive amounts of time spent in Ireland in the pursuit of public duties would, in her view, be a waste of time and money "when Scotland and England deserved it much more" (Hibbert 1984, 212). From a constitutional point of view, Victoria argued that the prince of Wales should not take any kind of official role in Ireland that would identify him with that country at the expense of England. And although she would be more than glad to see him being deprived of the hedonistic pleasures of London society, the last thing the queen wanted was for her heir to be too far away from her controlling influence. Her impulses were entirely selfish: in essence, she would brook no ascendancy of Ireland over her beloved Scotland. She offered the lame excuse that the damp Irish climate would be bad for Bertie's health. She had said as much to Disraeli when he had raised the matter in 1868: "For health and relaxation, no one would go to Ireland, and people only go who have their estates to attend to" (204).

Throughout the 1870s and into the 1880s Irish nationalism grew, with the Home Rule Association leading the fight for a devolved government in a country whose population was hemorrhaging away through emigration. Three million had now left: three-fifths of them going to the United States, many more arriving on the British mainland seeking work. Gladstone, by now recognizing that the resolution of Ireland's troubles hinged on the removal of the injustices of its system of land tenure, brought in the first of a series of land acts in 1870 (others followed in 1881, 1885, and 1903). These attempted to help pauperized Irish tenants by setting strict controls on rents and protecting them from eviction.

Militant groups, such as Charles Parnell's National Land League, continued to fight the malpractices of Irish landlords in the early 1880s in the form of mass boycotts. The evictions of thousands of tenants led to an orgy of violence, during which landlords were murdered, their homes torched, and their cattle killed. In April 1882 the new Irish chief secretary, Lord Frederick Cavendish, and his undersecretary, Frederick Burke, were stabbed to death by Fenians as they walked across Phoneix Park in Dublin.

Queen Victoria was greatly alarmed at the increasing lawlessness in Ireland; the people seemed to her incorrigible and their intransigence should, she argued, be returned with even greater coercion by the government. By 1885 Gladstone had come to the conclusion that there was only one solution to the Irish problem: Home Rule.

He initiated a long campaign in Parliament, that was fraught with tension, to give the Irish responsibility for some of their own domestic affairs in a subordinate parliament based in Dublin. The debate would last through successive governments until 1923, during which time the House of Commons twice passed a bill for Home Rule (1886 and 1889), only for it to be rejected by the landed interests of the aristocracy in the House of Lords. Victoria remained bitterly opposed to the idea, seeing it as a betrayal of Protestant Ulster. She was relieved when the bills were thrown out. Gladstone never gave up on his mission, warning that "we are bound to lose Ireland in consequence of years of cruelty, stupidity and misgovernment and I would rather lose her as a friend than as a foe" (Asquith 1933, 213)—but it was a faint hope.

It was the conduct of her loyal Irish troops in the Boer War, and particularly at the siege of Ladysmith, that finally prompted Queen Victoria to make a belated state visit to Ireland in 1900. She had been so taken by the courage of these volunteers that she took the unprecedented step of allowing them to "wear the green" (the national emblem—the shamrock) on St. Patrick's Day and founded a new regiment in their honor—the Irish Guards. Claiming that her visit to Dublin was "entirely my own idea" (Longford 1998, 555), Victoria sailed across the Irish Channel for the first time in thirty-nine years. Irish officialdom, notwithstanding the widespread poverty that still prevailed, went to considerable expense to stage a show of mock loyalty for its aging monarch. But throughout the queen's hectic three-week visit, from 4 to 25 April, the government remained paranoid about Fenian attacks on her. Ministers begged her to have an escort of cavalry for her carriage drives around Dublin. Having survived seven assassination attempts during her reign, Victoria was not now about to display fear of an unseen enemy: "Why, if I were to show the least distrust of the Irish, they would think I deserved to be afraid of them," she remarked (Gosse 1901, 318). In private, she was desperate to win the approval of the Irish and to rekindle the displays of loyalty and affection that had been shown her in 1849.

But Irish nationalists such as Maud Gonne, who viewed the visit for what many thought it was—a thinly disguised publicity stunt to win further Irish volunteers for the Boer War—roundly condemned Victoria. In an article entitled "The Famine Queen," published in a nationalist journal in France, Gonne intoned: "Queen, return to your own land: you will find no more Irishmen ready to wear the red shame of your livery" (Cardozo 1979, 185–186). In the past, Irishmen had pledged their loyalty out of ignorance and poverty, she argued, but three weeks of public carriage rides and a huge party in Phoenix Park for 52,000 Irish schoolchildren could not repair the damage of forty years of royal neglect. The queen's 1902 biographer, Sydney Lee, concurred, attempting to present a more balanced view among the welter of hagiography that had followed the queen's death. Although observing that the 1900 visit was "a triumph of robust old age and a proof of [Victoria's] alertness of sympathy" (Lee 1902, 565), he argued that it "brought into broad relief the neglect of Ireland that preceded it." It had emphasized "the errors of feeling and of judgement which had made her almost a complete stranger to her Irish subjects in their own land" (565).

In 1912 a bill for Irish Home Rule was finally passed. It went onto the statute book in 1914, but its enactment was held up by the outbreak of World War I in that year. Ireland did not achieve independence until 1923. A guerrilla war by Irish nationalists began in 1919 and ended in a 1921 Anglo-Irish treaty establishing the Irish Free State. This act of partition, separating the Protestant North from the largely Catholic South, provoked a six-month civil war (1922–1923) over the acceptance of the treaty. But factionalism in Ireland could not be contained; a resurgence of the Protestant-Irish conflict during the so-called Troubles of the late 1960s brought many hundreds more sectarian killings. It was once sardonically observed that Gladstone had "spent his declining years trying to guess the answer to the Irish Question; unfortunately whenever he was getting warm, the Irish secretly changed the question" (Sellar and Yeatman 1930, 108). That question remains unresolved to this day.

Related entries:
Assassination Attempts; Boer War; Gladstone, William Ewart; Melbourne; Peel, Sir Robert; Religion; Russell, Lord John, First Earl

References and further reading:

Asquith, Margot. 1933. *More Memories.* London: Cassell.

Bassett, A. Tilney, ed. 1986. *Gladstone to His Wife.* London: Methuen and Co.

Benson, A. C., amd Viscount Esher, eds. 1911. *Letters of Queen Victoria 1837–1861.* 1st ser., 3 vols. London: John Murray.

Blake, Robert. 1966. *Disraeli.* London: Eyre and Spottiswoode.

Campbell, Christy. 2002. *Fenian Fire: The British Government Plot to Assassinate Queen Victoria.* London: HarperCollins.

Cardozo, Nancy. 1979. *Maud Gonne: Lucky Eyes and a High Heart.* London: Gollancz.

Charlot, Monica. 1991. *Victoria, the Young Queen.* Cambridge: Polity.

Feiling, Keith. 1966. *A History of England: From the Coming of the English to 1918.* London: Macmillan.

Foster, R. F. 1988. *Modern Ireland 1600–1972.* Harmondsworth, UK: Penguin.

Gosse, Edmund. 1901. "The Character of Queen Victoria." *Quarterly Review* (January–April): 301–307

Hammond, J. L. 1964. *Gladstone and the Irish Nation.* London: Cass.

Hibbert, Christopher. 1984. *Queen Victoria: In Her Letters and Journals.* London: Viking.

Lee, Sir Sidney. 1902. *Queen Victoria, A Biography.* London: Smith, Elder and Co.

Longford, Elizabeth. [1964] 1998. *Victoria R.I.* London: Weidenfeld and Nicolson (esp. chap. 32).

Loughlin, James. 1986. *Gladstone, Home Rule, and the Ulster Question, 1882–93.* Atlantic Highlands, NJ: Humanities Press International.

Martin, Sir Theodore. 1875–1880. *The Life of His Royal Highness the Prince Consort.* 5 vols. London: Smith, Elder and Co.

Matthew, H. C. G. 1986. *Gladstone: 1809–1874.* Oxford: Clarendon Press.

O'Brien, Conor Cruise, ed. 1960. *The Shaping of Modern Ireland.* London: Routledge and Kegan Paul.

Sellar, W. C., and Yeatman, R. J. 1930. *1066 and All That.* London: Magnet.

St. Aubyn, Giles. 1991. *Queen Victoria, A Portrait.* London: Sinclair Stevenson.

Windsor, Dean of, and Hector Bolitho. 1929. *Later Letters of Lady Augusta Stanley 1864–1876.* London: Jonathan Cape.

Woodham-Smith, Cecil. 1962. *The Great Hunger: Ireland 1845–9.* London: Hamish Hamilton (esp. chap. 18).

———. 1972. *Queen Victoria: Her Life and Times.* Vol. 1: *1819–1861.* London: Hamish Hamilton.

Ziegler, Philip. 1976. *Melbourne: A Biography of William Lamb 2nd Viscount Melbourne.* London: Fontana.

J

Jack the Ripper

the Queen fears that the detective department is not so efficient as it might be (Buckle 1930–1932 1:449)

In the autumn of 1888 the back alleys and drinking dives of the East End of London were caught in the grip of a terrifying and grisly catalog of murders of prostitutes. Queen Victoria, like the mass of her subjects, was fascinated by the story, departing for once from her characteristic disinterest in the fate of the denizens of London's low-life districts. By the time two more victims were murdered on the same day in September, she was being petitioned by the women of Whitechapel to order the government to close down the brothels that lured criminal elements to the area. Although the man who became notorious as Jack the Ripper would never be apprehended, Queen Victoria herself would unwittingly be closely linked with one of the most fanciful theories about his true identity.

The queen had been quick to express her dismay that the victims of the Whitechapel murderer were "unfortunate women of a bad class' (Longford 1998, 336), but she nevertheless felt compelled to voice her concern. She complained to her prime minister, Lord Salisbury, about the incompetence of the home secretary, Henry Matthews (responsible for the police force), for failing to find the killer. In October, she wrote to Salisbury, alarmed at the continuing mismanagement of the investigation and complaining also about Matthews's "want of sympathy" for the victims.

Public fascination with these sadistic murders had been fueled by gory waxwork representations of the victims, displayed in a traveling show even before the final and fifth victim, Mary Jane Kelly, was murdered on the night of 8–9 November. The queen now upbraided Salisbury for not seeing to it that the street lighting in Whitechapel had been improved, presumably in the naive belief that this would make a difference. Desperate to compensate for the patently deficient detective work on the case and the failure to arrest the perpetrator, on 10 November Salisbury's cabinet agreed to offer a free pardon to anyone who would give evidence leading to a conviction, after the queen, in a state of escalating outrage, had telegraphed him urging "some very decided action" (Buckle 1930–1932 1:447). On 13 November she wrote to Matthews questioning the efficiency of his detectives and offered up one or two amateur-detective suggestions of her own, regarding a search for the killer's blood-stained clothes and a check of the ports for likely suspects trying to flee.

Debate still continues as to exactly how many victims were claimed by Jack the Ripper, although the general consensus is that it was five: Mary Ann Nicholls (31 August 1888), Annie Chapman (8 September 1888), Elizabeth Stride and Catherine Eddowes (both on 30 September 1888), and Mary Jane Kelly (the night of 8–9 November 1888). The murders of several other women in the Whitechapel area between April 1888 and February 1891 have led theorists to offer up several other possible victims. The sobriquet of Jack the Ripper—forever identified with the murderer—first appeared as the signature to a letter and then a postcard claiming to be from the murderer, sent to the Central News Agency in London in September and October 1888.

Eighty-two years after the murders had consumed public interest for month after month and sales of the *Illustrated London News* featuring gruesome drawings of the mutilated victims had never been greater, interest was renewed, this time through an unlikely royal connection. The ongoing debate over this, the greatest unsolved mystery in British criminology, was rekindled by an article and, close on its heels, a book, offering a theory that would directly link Queen Victoria herself with Jack the Ripper. For the suggestion was now made that Jack the Ripper had been none other than Victoria's grandson, Albert Edward Victor, duke of Clarence (1864–1892) and son of the Prince of Wales (later Edward VII).

The theory might be new but it was based on old gossip, drawn from rumors, in circulation since the time of the murders, about Eddy, the duke of Clarence, and his sexual proclivities. The duke was not known for his intelligence. His inability to concentrate on anything for more than a few minutes at a time had been noted by his tutor, the Rev. John Neale Dalton, who had commented that Eddy's intellect was in an "abnormally dormant condition" (Hibbert 1976, 181). Incorrigibly lazy and perpetually bored, Eddy flunked out of the naval cadets (where he shared a mistress with his brother George), dropped out of Trinity College, Cambridge, and had an equally short-lived career in the army. He led an aimless, dissolute existence, "constitutionally incapable of concentration, except on whist, which he played quite well, and on polo, at which he was adept" (183).

It is thought that Eddy was probably a bisexual; he was known as Collar and Cuffs and nicknamed Victoria in gay circles, for his dandified style of dress. Along with other members of the aristocracy, he visited brothels, including a notorious male brothel at 19 Cleveland Street. The premises were raided by the police in August 1889, and the names of several of its aristocratic frequenters who had consorted with rent boys were traced, including that of Eddy. The Home Office swiftly intervened to hush up the potential scandal involving an heir presumptive to the throne (Eddy being the eldest son of the Prince of Wales). It was the common consensus that the country was spared a throughly disreputable future monarch when Eddy died of pneumonia in 1892. "It is one of God's mercies to us that that horrible young man died," remarked Lord Godard (Souhami 1996, 44). Soon after Eddy's death, his correspondence and private papers were consigned to the flames on his father's orders.

Although a stream of theories on the identity of Jack the Ripper had been published from the beginning of the twentieth century on, it was the "Royal Ripper" theory that caused a sensation when it finally emerged in the 1970s (although a passing suggestion about Eddy's involvement had been made in a 1962 biography of Edward VII by the French writer Philippe Julien). It was now suggested by Dr. Thomas Stowell, in an article in the *Criminologist,* that an unnamed "heir to power and wealth" had been responsible for the murders. Privately, Stowell had confided to the Ripperologist Colin Wilson that he thought the duke of Clarence was the Ripper. His theory was that, suffering from final-stage syphilis of the brain, contracted from prostitutes, the prince had set about murdering them in the East End as an act of revenge. Stowell further claimed that the queen's physician-in-ordinary, Sir William Gull, had been involved in a cover-up of the crimes and that he, Stowell, had learned all this after being allowed to examine Sir William's private papers. Substantiation of this theory was offered by the fact that Eddy had been used to hunting and disemboweling deer at Balmoral and had acquired an erotic pleasure from the experience. The *Criminologist* article contained plenty of pointers to the identity of the unnamed suspect; within days the allegation that Queen Victoria's grandson had been the Ripper was splashed over newspapers around the world. Two years later Stowell's claim was quashed, when a check of Eddy's movements at the times when the five known victims were murdered showed he had been nowhere near London. For example, on 30 September, when Stride and Eddowes were murdered, Eddy was, in fact, at Abergeldie in Scotland, on which occasion the queen recorded in her diary having lunch with him.

The cast of Ripper suspects now gained another player: the painter Walter Sickert, in a new story that again linked the duke of Clarence to the murders. Sickert's son, Joseph, emerged in the 1970s to claim that his maternal grandmother—one Annie Elizabeth Crook, an artist's model—had had an affair with and secretly married Eddy after meeting him at Sickert's studio. In 1885 Annie had given birth to an illegitimate daughter, Alice (who, in a bizarre twist, later ended up living with Walter Sickert and became Joseph's mother). Annie Elizabeth Crook, it transpired, had been a friend of the Ripper's last victim, Mary Jane Kelly, and had hired her as a nursemaid for her and Eddy's child, Alice. Crook, however, had told her East End drinking cronies, including Kelly, about the affair. The murders had therefore been undertaken to destroy all the women who knew about Annie Elizabeth Crook, Eddy, and the baby. They had been perpetrated with the connivance and knowledge of Sir William Gull and even, it was claimed, Lord Randolph Churchill. A freelance reporter, Stephen Knight, who had interviewed Joseph Sickert about the story and was convinced of its veracity, turned the Sickert story into a best-seller: *Jack the Ripper: The Final Solution*. Published in 1976, the book alleged that Walter Sickert, who had a known obsession with the Whitechapel murders, himself may have taken part in them and that he had left clues to his involvement in his paintings. This argument resurfaced in 2002 when the eminent U.S. crime writer Patricia Cornwell expended more than a million dollars of her considerable fortune in buying up and examining paintings by Sickert, in an exhaustive attempt to secure samples of his DNA (deoxyribonucleic acid) to compare with letters written to the press by the Ripper. So convinced is she that Sickert is the real Ripper that she has publicly staked her reputation on it (see Cornwell 2002).

Steven Knight's book remains the most widely debated one on the Ripper murders to date (although Cornwell's theories are yet to be analyzed in detail). It was Knight's controversial contention that Sir William Gull himself (a man, after all, possessed of the necessary anatomical knowledge) who had undertaken the murder of Kelly and her associates, utilizing bizarre Masonic rituals, in response to the blackmail demands made by the women that they would reveal the truth about Eddy's secret marriage and child. Further, Gull's fellow Freemasons had closed ranks to protect him from possible detection by the police. Annie Elizabeth Crook, the putative wife of Eddy, after years of moving from one workhouse to another, eventually died in the lunacy ward of the workhouse on London's Fulham Road. The duke of Clarence/Annie Elizabeth Crook story was the basis for two films, *Murder by Decree* (1978) and *From Hell* (2002).

The accusation that Eddy, duke of Clarence, was Jack the Ripper would appear to have been disproved by Harrison in 1972, with his verification of the duke's movements in contemporary Court Circulars at the times of the murders. Theories linking Eddy with the Ripper murders, possibly through his sexual activities among London's low life, refuse, however, to die down. The author of another contentious theory—Paul H. Feldman in *Jack the Ripper: The Final Chapter* (1997)—is convinced, on the evidence of supposed diaries kept by a Liverpool businessman, James Maybrick, that Maybrick was the real Ripper. Maybrick's wife, Florence, was tried in 1889 for allegedly poisoning him (Feldman's argument being that she did so when she discovered the terrible truth of her husband's murderous identity), and only a huge public outcry at the death sentence saved her from being executed. It is unlikely, however, that Feldman's book will be the "final chapter," any more than Cornwell's has proved that the case is "closed." The mystery steadfastly refuses to be solved. Feldman remains convinced that there is an element of truth in the duke of Clarence story and that an as yet undiscovered link between Eddy and James Maybrick is yet to emerge.

Related entries:
Salisbury, Robert Arthur Talbot Gascoigne-Cecil, Third Marquis of

References and further reading:

Aronson, Theo. 1994. *Prince Eddy and the Homosexual Underworld.* London: John Murray.

Begg, Paul, Martin Fido, and Keith Skinner. 1991. *The Jack the Ripper A to Z.* London: Headline.

Buckle, George Earl, ed. 1930–1932. *Letters of Queen Victoria: A Selection from Her Majesty's Correspondence and Journal between the Years 1886 and 1901.* 3d ser., 3 vols. London: John Murray. Fairclough, Melvin. 1992. *The Ripper and the Royals.* London: Gerald Duckworth and Co.

Cornwell, Patricia. 2002. *Portrait of a Killer: Jack the Ripper—Case Closed.* London: Little, Brown.

Feldman, Paul H. 1997. *Jack the Ripper: The Final Chapter.*. London: Virgin.

Fisher, Trevor. 1995. *Scandal: The Sexual Politics of Late Victorian Britain.* Stroud, Gloucestershire: Sutton.

Harrison, Michael. 1965. *Clarence: The Life of the Duke of Clarence and Avondale KG 1864–1892.* London: W. H. Allen.

Hibbert, Christopher. 1976. *Edward VII: A Portrait.* London: Allen Lane.

Knight, Stephen. 1976. *Jack the Ripper: The Final Solution.* London: Harrap and Co.

Longford, Elizabeth. [1964] 1998. *Victoria R.I.* London: Weidenfeld and Nicolson.

Souhami, Diana. 1996. *Mrs. Keppel and Her Daughter.* London: Flamingo.

Trow, M. J. 1998. *The Many Faces of Jack the Ripper.* London: Summerdale Publications.

Jenner, Sir William (1815–1898)

I cannot sufficiently praise the skill, attention, and devotion of Dr Jenner, who is the first fever Doctor in Europe (Benson and Esher 1911, 3:473)

Sir William Jenner was already a practitioner of some distinction when he was called in by the queen's personal physician, Dr. James Clark, in December 1861 to offer his medical opinion on the nature of Prince Albert's serious illness. Over several years of dedicated medical research, Jenner had studied and described the distinguishing features of typhus and typhoid fever, two diseases that had, till then, often been confused as one and the same.

Jenner was born in Chatham, Kent, and studied medicine at University College, London. After becoming a member of the Royal College of Surgeons in 1837, he set himself up in private practice, becoming an M.D. in 1844. In 1847 he conducted research into the identities of typhus and typhoid fever through his observation of patients at the London Fever Hospital. Taking bacteriological samples, he made a clinical and pathological study of thirty-six cases, which he described in 1850 in *On the Identity and Non-Identity of Typhoid Fever.* Typhoid fever, he concluded, was transmitted by contaminated food or water and was characterized by fever, severe headache, nausea, and loss of appetite, combined with constipation and sometimes diarrhea. Typhus, on the other hand, is a disease transmitted by mites or ticks that live mainly on the skin of rats and mice and can be transferred to humans, living in their hair and clothes.

Jenner was subsequently appointed physician to the London Fever Hospital (1853–1861) while also serving University College, from 1849 on, as professor of pathological anatomy and as professor of the principles and practice of medicine (1863–1872). From 1854 to 1876 he worked in the college as a physician (as well as at the Great Ormond Street Hospital for Sick Children [1852–1862]). In 1879 he accepted the post of consulting physician at University College.

Jenner was appointed a physician-extraordinary to Queen Victoria in January 1861 after the death of one of the queen's doctors, William Baly. In December of that year, the queen and Prince Albert's personal physician, Dr. James Clark, called Jenner in when Clark had encountered difficulty in identifying the cause of the prince's serious illness. Despite his own considerable clinical experience in the study of typhoid fever, Jenner was cautious and did not make a conclusive diagnosis straightaway, other than recognizing the feverish nature of the symptoms. In any event, he was obliged to defer to Clark as the queen's personal physician, and Clark was characteristically dilatory in coming to any conclusions. The prince presented such a plethora of symptoms that it was difficult to pinpoint precisely what lay at the root of his suffering, which manifested itself variously as insomnia, fever, shivering, stomach pain, and bouts of nausea and vomiting. It was not until 7 December (a week before the prince's death) that the telltale rash signifying typhoid fever appeared. Jenner himself would later confide to the queen that "*no one* can diagnose typhoid at first" (Longford 1998, 81). Even when he finally dreaded the worst, he did not want to raise the alarm, thinking that, if the prince received the correct nursing, the illness would run itself through in a month. (It has since been suggested by both Bennett [1983] and Weintraub [1997] that the prince's condition was more complex and that he was probably also suffering from some kind of terminal disease, such as stomach cancer.)

The queen found Jenner's presence, backing up the now septuagenarian Dr. Clark, very reassuring. Jenner himself had long been an admirer of Prince Albert and was deeply impressed with his work. He later left a touching postscript to his own account of the prince's dying days. "You can have no idea of the excellence of the man," he wrote. "He was the finest specimen of intellectual and moral greatness and religious excellence I have ever known—so great, so good did I think him that when sitting at his bedhead in the stillness of the night, fearing the result, I have longed and longed that I might die in his place" (Fulford 1966, 269).

After Prince Albert's death and the return of Dr. Clark to retirement, Jenner took over as the queen's personal physician; a year later he was also appointed to the Prince of Wales. In 1871 he attended the prince at Sandringham, during a serious bout of typhoid fever (although Prime Minister William Gladstone had reservations about Jenner's skills as a physician and said he himself would have dismissed him). It has been suggested that the prince's recovery was as much a testament to the skillful nursing he received throughout his illness from his sister Alice, who fortuitously had been visiting from Darmstadt, as it was to Jenner and the other royal physicians. Nevertheless, Jenner's services were rewarded with a baronetcy in 1868, and he was made knight commander of the Order of the Bath (KCB) in 1872. The queen came to rely greatly on Jenner's professional skills, and it was thanks to him that, in 1871, the pioneer of antiseptic surgery, Joseph Lister, was called in on Jenner's recommendation to lance a severe, inflamed abscess on the queen's arm, which had resisted treatment. In December 1878 the queen sent her trusted Jenner to Darmstadt in Germany when her daughter Alice's children fell sick with diphtheria; sadly, he was unable to save the princess when she herself succumbed to the disease. She died on the anniversary of her father's death—14 December. Victoria again turned to Jenner in 1879, when her Highland servant, John Brown, suffered a severe bout of erisypelas and again in 1883. But on the latter occasion, complications set in, and Brown died.

A bluff, good-humored, and kind-hearted man, Jenner could at times be autocratic and always spoke his mind—often with considerable wit. He had the booming voice of a military man and was noted at court for being an entertaining raconteur, a fact that also endeared him to the queen, as did his affable bedside manner, which she found calming. As an old-school, establishment figure, he was an arch Tory and as reactionary as the queen, who concurred with Jenner in his opposition to women's training as doctors. As a medical man Jenner often found himself subjected to the queen's very passionate views on vivisection, which he found extreme and tried to modulate. He attempted to persuade her of the logic of some carefully controlled and scientifically necessary animal experimentation and persuaded her that the most effective way forward, rather than outlawing vivisection altogether, was to uphold animal experimentation, but by strictly humane methods.

Without doubt, Jenner's insistence that the grieving queen should not be overtaxed in her widowhood bolstered her stubborn refusal to come out of seclusion for state occasions. Jenner was often accused of pandering to the queen's many ailments and to the state of heightened nervousness and irritability that often manifested itself in supposedly agonizing headaches. He patiently listened to her endless complaints about the stress she was under with official paperwork and the cruel and insensitive way in which her ministers constantly badgered her to show herself in public. He came to the conclusion that such pressures were counterproductive and only exacerbated the queen's already agitated response to any suggestion that she might not be fulfilling her regal duties. He was prepared to defend his position on this, particularly when republican rumblings appeared in the press, criticizing the queen's withdrawal from public life. Such pressures, he warned, might provoke a complete nervous breakdown; the fragile state of the queen's nerves, he averred, was a "species of madness" against which it was "hopeless to contend" (Longford 1998, 387), and he blamed Gladstone for aggravating these neuroses. Gladstone, for his part, pooh-poohed such a defense of the queen's state of mind, arguing that Jenner was a "feeble-minded doctor" who indulged the "fanciful ideas of a woman about her own health" to the point where she almost believed them (Hardie 1935, 197).

Because of his own numerous professional commitments, Jenner did not, like other members of the royal household, reside at court. He was therefore able to evade long exposure to much of the queen's more trying behavior; her doctors James Clark, and later James Reid, would take the brunt of her unending, and often trivial, medical complaints as she grew older. Jenner had become mentor to his successor, James Reid, at the end of the 1880s, retiring in 1889 when his health began to fail. He gave up his lucrative medical practice in 1890 (the royal endorsement of his medical skills having made him a rich man). Such was his poor state of health that he felt unable to take up the majority of the queen's frequent invitations to Windsor and Osborne. In 1893 his visits to the queen ceased. When

Jenner died at his home in Hampshire in December 1898, the queen lamented him as "a most devoted and faithful servant, a most able doctor, and a truly kind friend to whom I could always speak frankly and confidentially" (St. Aubyn 1991, 337).

Related entries:
Albert Edward, Prince of Wales; Albert of Saxe-Coburg-Gotha, Prince Consort; Animals; Clark, Sir James; Reid, Sir James

References and further reading:
Bennett, Daphne. 1983. *King without a Crown.* London: Heinemann.
Benson, A. C., and Viscount Esher, eds. 1911. *The Letters of Queen Victoria, 1837–1861.* 1st ser., 3 vols. London: John Murray
Fulford, Roger. 1966. *The Prince Consort:* London: Macmillan.
Hardie, Frank. 1935. *The Political Influence of Queen Victoria.* Oxford: Oxford University Press.
Hibbert, Christopher. 2000. *Victoria: A Personal History.* London: HarperCollins (esp. chaps. 40–43).
Longford, Elizabeth. [1964] 1998. *Victoria R.I.* London: Weidenfeld and Nicolson (esp. chap. 26).
Ponsonby, Arthur. 1942. *Henry Ponsonby, Queen Victoria's Private Secretary: His Life from His Letters.* London: Macmillan.
St. Aubyn, Giles. 1991. *Queen Victoria: A Portrait.* London: Sinclair Stevenson.
Tisdall, Sarah. 1961. *Queen Victoria's Private Life.* London: Jarrolds.
Weintraub, Stanley. 1997. *Albert: Uncrowned King.* London: John Murray (esp. chap. 18).

K

Kensington Palace

our poor old Palace (Woodham-Smith 1972, 109)

Situated on the western perimeter of London's Hyde Park, the elegant and beautifully proportioned, redbrick house that became Kensington Palace was bought by the royal family in its original, Jacobean form in 1689. Known as Nottingham House, it was purchased by William III for £18,000 from his secretary of state because he had so disliked his official residence, the damp, riverside palace at Whitehall, which had aggravated his asthma. Four English monarchs died here: Mary II, William III, Queen Anne, and George II.

The house had been built in 1661 as a country home, and during his reign (1688–1702) William III ordered a series of additions to the main structure and also the development of its gardens; he commissioned Sir Christopher Wren to revamp the interiors of the house so that the king and his household were able to occupy it around 1690. The work was overseen by William's clerk of works, Nicholas Hawksmoor, and new facades were added to the south and east. The famous King's Gallery was added in 1695–1696 by Sir Christopher Wren.

Queen Anne (1702–1714) loved the house and spent much time there, ordering a grand orangery to be built around 1704–1705, probably designed by Hawksmoor. George I, who also held the house in great affection because it reminded him of his home in Hanover, ordered further renovations to the interior, as well as initiating the laying out of Kensington Gardens by the notable landscape gardener and designer William Kent between 1723 and 1727. Over time the external fabric of the building had been persistently neglected, however, and no money was spent on maintaining it. The later Hanoverian monarchs made less and less use of the palace. George III preferred Buckingham House, as it then was, and Kensington Palace was allowed to fall into further disrepair. Its only long-term occupant was one of George III's younger sons, the duke of Sussex (1773–1843)—that same eccentric "Uncle Sussex" at whom the young Victoria would frequently scream in terror whenever she encountered him.

In 1798, Queen Victoria's father the duke of Kent was given apartments here, although he lived most of the time abroad to avoid his debtors, returning in 1819 with his wife to await the birth of their child, Victoria. From the time of her birth here on 24 May 1819, Victoria lived a secluded life till she became queen in 1837. At that time Kensington was a quiet, rural part of west London. The Kents' apartments were furnished at the duke's behest with new upholstery, curtains, and bed hangings, at considerable expense. A north-facing room was adapted to serve as a nursery. But the accommodation was not ideal; located on the ground floor, it could often be dark and gloomy. It had also been long infested with black beetles and other insects. Beyond, and facing east, stretched the peace and tranquility of the chestnut and beech trees of Kensington Gardens and bucolic views of grazing sheep farther away in Hyde Park. What few houses there were in the surrounding area did not intrude upon the unspoiled views.

In 1832 the widowed duchess of Kent, excessively preoccupied with her role as mother to a future queen, took it upon herself to commandeer seventeen more rooms on the upper floors of the palace without seeking the permission of William IV. She commissioned Sir Jeffrey Wyatville, the architect who had remodeled Windsor Castle, to redesign the layout of these rooms and provide suitably grand surroundings for the entertainment of important guests. The famous grand staircase with its trompe l'oeil murals leading to state rooms, including the King's Gallery, was restored. In January 1836 the duchess installed herself and her entourage in these new surroundings, with the princess's doctor, James Clark, endorsing the far more healthy environment of the new light and airy rooms.

The public were first allowed in to view the state apartments at Kensington Palace in 1889, when the queen celebrated her seventieth birthday. For most of her reign, however, the apartments were allowed to fall into disuse, with only a brief occupation by troops, who were quartered there during the time of the 1851 Great Exhibition. In 1897 the palace was restored and the state rooms reopened to the public on the occasion of the queen's Diamond Jubilee, when the queen had given up some of her lesser properties in exchange for a parliamentary grant of £36,000 for Kensington Palace's maintenance. But it was not until 1923 that the public was again admitted. Over the years, several royal descendants of Queen Victoria have had apartments at Kensington, including her daughter Princess Louise; the present queen's sister, Princess Margaret; and Diana, princess of Wales, after her divorce from Prince Charles. The public gardens at the front of the palace were engulfed in a sea of flowers and tributes when Diana died in 1997.

Related entries:
Balmoral Castle; Buckingham Palace; Frogmore; Windsor Castle.

References and further reading:

Hayes, John T. 1985. *Kensington Palace.* London: Department of the Environment.

Hedley, Olwen. 1974. *Kensington Palace: The State Apartments.* London: Pitkin Pictorials.

Hudson, Derek. 1968. *Kensington Palace.* London: Davies.

Morton, Andrew. 1988. *Inside Kensington Palace.* Bath, UK: Chivers.

Lorne, Marquis of. 1901. *V.R.I.: Her Life and Empire.* London: Eyre and Spottiswoode.

Woodham-Smith, Cecil. 1972. *Queen Victoria: Her Life and Times. Vol. 1: 1819–1861.* London: Hamish Hamilton.

Kensington System

my otherwise rather melancholy childhood (Benson and Esher 1911, 1, 10)

When the eighteen-year-old Princess Victoria succeeded to the British throne in 1837, such had been the isolation of her upbringing that her public knew very little of her character or the details of her early life. A considerable amount of detail on the carefully controlled regime under which Princess Victoria was brought up at Kensington Palace has come down to us, thanks to the dutiful daily record she kept of the minutiae of her life in her journals starting at the age of thirteen. Here Victoria painstakingly recorded the daily routine of both lessons and recreation, upheld by the duchess of Kent under guidance from her comptroller, Sir John Conroy, which became known as the Kensington System. It was a system deliberately designed to exclude any outside influence that might distract Victoria's undivided loyalty to her mother and her mother's ambitions.

The early years of Princess Victoria's education provide one of the few glimpses of her shadowy half-brother, Charles, prince of Leiningen (1804–1856), who had a considerable say in Victoria's upbringing. Because he enjoyed the close companionship of Sir John Conroy whenever he was in England visiting his mother, the duchess of Kent, Charles tried to smooth over the young Victoria's growing hostility toward Conroy. Charles supported the duchess's aspirations for a regency, should Victoria accede to the throne before she was eighteen, and endorsed the Kensington System under which Victoria was brought up. In 1841 Charles would produce "A Complete History of the Policy Followed at Kensington, under Sir John Conroy's Guidance," in which he would justify his support for this regime (see Longford 1998, 55, footnote).

Under the supervision of the Rev. George Davys, dean of Chester, Princess Victoria was instructed in the scriptures from the age of five on. The duchess, who placed religious knowledge high on her list of accomplishments, herself drilled Victoria in religious matters and often questioned her on the content of Sunday sermons that she had heard in church. Victoria's German governess, Louise Lehzen, attended to matters of good behavior and general instruction, teaching Victoria to read and spell before her formal education began at age eight. In 1831 the duchess of Northumberland was appointed state governess in a figurehead role deemed necessary to reflect Victoria's status, but her presence was largely ignored by the princess, for no one could supplant Lehzen in her loyalty and affections.

In later life the queen asserted: "I was not fond of learning as a little child" (Woodham-Smith 1972, 73). This was not the case after she reached the age of eight, for she proved a conscientious pupil once she embarked on serious study and had several eminent teachers, some enlisted as a result of her own enthusiasms. Rev. Davys oversaw her growing list of accomplishments, inculcated in morning lessons from 9:30 to 11:30 and in the afternoon from 3:00 to 5:00. He himself taught Victoria geography and history and ensured that she was versed in the rites of the Church of England. Mr. Steward from Westminster School taught Victoria writing and arithmetic. She also studied Latin and Greek and later learned Italian, but her major languages were French, with Monsieur Grandineau, and German, with Rev. Henry Barez. Although she might have been tempted to converse in that language with her German mother and governess, Victoria did not in fact begin speaking German regularly until her courtship by Prince Albert in 1839.

More pleasurable pursuits, such as dancing lessons, were given by Madame Bourdin, and on one special occasion, Victoria's idol, the ballerina Marie Taglioni, was invited to give her a lesson. Singing tuition with Mr. J. B. Sale from the choir of the Chapel Royal was eventually supplanted in 1836 with lessons from the great Italian opera star Luigi Lablache, who subsequently taught Victoria whenever he was in London for the season. Lessons in sketching were given by Mr. G. Westall, a member of the Royal Academy. Although Victoria's intellectual studies were not on a par with those undertaken by a previous and most accomplished English queen, Elizabeth I, she enjoyed most subjects and was a diligent pupil.

During her childhood Victoria was obliged to ingest an excessive amount of devotional literature, moral tales, and sermons. She purported to enjoy edifying matter, such as the bishop of Chester's "Exposition of the Gospel of St. Matthew" or the Rev. Leigh Richmond's evangelical tract *The Dairyman's Daughter,* in preference to novels, which she was not allowed to read. She also read and discussed with Lehzen the letters of Madame de Sévigné and Racine's tragedies. For fiction she ventured no further than the tales of Harriet Martineau or Maria Edgeworth. Not surpisingly, on the rare occasion when Victoria was allowed to savor something less conventional, she deemed actress-turned-novelist Fanny Kemble's memoirs "full of trash and nonsense" (Strachey 1971, 34). She read much poetry—Pope, Gray, Cowper, and Sir Walter Scott—and later revered the verse of Tennyson. Although, in later life, the queen would enjoy the novels of Charles Dickens, Marie Corelli, Margaret Oliphant, and George Eliot, she would remain intellectually challenged by most of the serious literature she attempted and had little time for Shakespeare.

Although history was not her strongest subject, Princess Victoria was determined to become versed in the subject. She struggled through William Russell's *The History of Modern Europe* in five volumes, the Earl of Clarendon's *History of the Rebellion,* Washington Irving's *The Conquest of Granada,* John Malcom's *Life of Lord Clive,* and other dusty tomes. On the recommendation of her Uncle Leopold, she made a particular point of studying French history and memoirs, such as those of the duc de Sully, to gain an insight into the workings of kingship, politics, and government. The occasional moments spent perusing a copy of her mother's French periodical *La Belle Assemblée,* devoted to fashion plates and society gossip, were a rare departure from so much sober study.

A detailed report to Parliament on the princess's education was made in 1830 by the bishops of London and Lincoln. The two churchmen questioned Victoria on her studies and assessed both her moral and intellectual attributes. The duchess of Kent, who had found inspiration in the education theories of Matthew Arnold, was commended for her conscientious supervision of her daughter's education and for inculcating in her those qualities of modesty, virtue, and sense of duty appropriate to a future queen. Victoria took the occasion of her confirmation at the Chapel Royal, St. James's, on 30 July 1835 extremely seriously, determined to "become a true Christian" (Strachey 1971, 35).

Between lessons, Victoria was allowed to walk or play in Kensington Gardens. A donkey given to her by her uncle, the duke of York, was a great favorite, and she often rode it, led by an old soldier who had served her father. Fresh air was encouraged; Victoria often took her breakfast in the open air, a habit she continued all the year round and throughout her life. But she had no real playmates of her own age except Conroy's daughter Victoire and her older half-sister Feodora, who left England when she married in 1828. Victoria's childhood playmates were mainly her much-loved dolls that she would sit and dress with Lehzen. Occasional visits to her Uncle Leopold at his home—Claremont—in Surrey provided some of Victoria's happiest moments in 1824 and 1825, but he too departed England—to become king of the Belgians in 1831. There were, however, seaside holidays in the autumn, Broadstairs and Ramsgate being favorite places where Victoria enjoyed the sands. In August 1831 she made her first visit to the Isle of Wight and stayed at Norris Castle. A second visit in 1833 provided her first glimpse of Osborne Lodge, the holiday home that she and Prince Albert would later replace with a fine new building.

In the early 1830s the duchess of Kent deemed that the time had finally come to put Princess Victoria on public view. Together with Sir John Conroy, she orchestrated a series of "royal progresses" (as King William sarcastically dubbed them) around England, to introduce the young princess to the people and bolster political support for her own Whig sympathies. A tour of the West Midlands from a base in the Malvern Hills in 1830 took Princess Victoria to stately homes such as Blenheim Palace but also past Birmingham's factories, bringing with them the princess's first experience of dirt and poverty. The novelty and excitement of such a release into the outside world were countered by the exhausting itinerary she endured on other tours—of the south and west of England in 1831 and the Midlands, east of England, and Wales in 1832. An ambitious tour of the north in 1835, against the expressed wishes of King William and despite the warm welcome she received from crowds wherever she went, reduced the exhausted Victoria to the brink of emotional and physical collapse. By September, when she arrived in Ramsgate on the south coast for the annual family holiday, she was so ill that she did not emerge for the next five weeks.

Related entries:
Dancing; Dickens, Charles; Feodora, Princess of Hohenlohe-Langenburg; Fresh Air; Lablache, Luigi; Lehzen, Baroness Louise; Opera; Scott, Sir Walter; Tennyson, Alfred Lord; Theater

References and further reading:

Charlot, Monica. 1991. *Victoria: The Young Queen.* Cambridge: Polity.

Creston, Dormer. 1952. *The Youthful Victoria.* London: Macmillan.

Esher, Viscount, ed. 1912. *The Girlhood of Queen Victoria: A Selection from Her Majesty's Diaries between the Years of 1832 and 1840.* 2 vols. London: John Murray.

Hibbert, Christopher. 1984. *Queen Victoria in Her Letters and Journals.* London: Viking.

Hudson, Katherine. 1994. *A Royal Conflict: Sir John Conroy and the Young Victoria.* London: Hodder and Stoughton.

Longford, Elizabeth. [1964] 1998. *Victoria R.I.* London: Weidenfeld and Nicolson.

Plowden, Alison. 1981. *The Young Victoria.* London: Weidenfeld and Nicolson.

Strachey, Lytton. 1971. *Queen Victoria.* Harmondsworth, UK: Penguin.

Vallone, Lynne. 2001. *Becoming Victoria.* New Haven: Yale University Press.

Warner, Marina. 1979. *Queen Victoria's Sketchbook.* London: Macmillan.

Woodham-Smith, Cecil. 1972. *Queen Victoria: Her Life and Times.* Vol. 1: *1819–1861.* London: Hamish Hamilton.

Kent, Edward Augustus, Duke of (1767–1820)

I was always taught to consider myself a soldier's child (Benson and Esher 1911, 1:8)

Queen Victoria was a baby of only eight months when her father Edward, duke of Kent, died unexpectedly on 23 January 1820. The romanticized image of her soldier father that she would cherish throughout her life was considerably removed from reality. For the doting parent who made much of showing his baby daughter off as a future queen of England had a professional reputation as one of the most despised men in the British army. As a hard-nosed and rigid authoritarian, the duke was renowned for his extreme brutality and his fondness for draconian punishment, so much so that the soldiers under him eventually threatened to mutiny.

Large, bland, and with dyed whiskers, the duke expended much time in talking and moralizing. His daily life was conducted with military-style precision, by the clock. Beneath the superficial veneer of charm and congeniality there was a pomposity and false piety that led even his sisters to refer to him as "Joseph Surface"—in an allusion to the devious and self-important character in Richard Brinsley Sheridan's play, *School for Scandal.* The duke of Wellington, in blunt contempt for the duke's soldiering, dismissed him as "the corporal."

Born the fourth son of George III, the duke had, after completing his education and military training in Hanover, begun to accumulate debts. As a cadet in Hanover he experienced at firsthand the iron discipline

Edward Augustus, duke of Kent, was the fourth son of George III and the only one of his seven sons to produce a surviving legitimate heir to the throne, when his daughter Princess Victoria was born in 1819. (Hulton/Archive by Getty Images)

of army life and would put it into practice himself after he was given a commission in the army in command of the Seventh regiment of the Royal Fusiliers at Gibraltar in 1790. His predilection for flogging his soldiers for the most trivial offense was well established before the regiment was sent to Canada. In one notorious incident he punished a Frenchman who had deserted in the face of his harshness to 999 lashes—an ordeal the man miraculously survived.

While serving in Canada, the duke took as his mistress a French widow, Madame Julie de St. Laurent (in fact, Therese-Bernardine Mongenet, an actress from Besançon who kept from him the fact that she was seven years his senior). Stanley Weintraub (1996) has revealed that prior to his relationship with St. Laurent the duke had an affair with a French actress in Geneva that produced an illegitimate daughter, Adelaide Victoire Auguste, born in 1789.

The duke saw further army service in the West Indies and in Nova Scotia. In 1799 Parliament voted him an annual income of £12,000, and he was raised to the peerage as duke of Kent and Strathern and earl of Dublin. An inevitable elevation of his military rank followed—to commander in chief of British forces in Canada. After serving another year in Halifax, Nova Scotia, he engineered his return with pleas of ill health and in 1802 was sent as governor-general and commandant of the British post at Gibraltar. Here with his usual enthusiasm for discipline the duke proceeded to bring the riotous garrison under his thumb. He quickly alienated his soldiers with his obsession with the punctilious discharge of duties and the minutiae of uniform, going so far as to tell them on which side they should part their hair. His ban on the sale of liquor to troops, as punishment for their supposed "slovenliness," led to mutiny and the execution of the ringleaders. The duke's severity by now had made him a liability the army could no longer continue to carry. In 1803 he was recalled to London and in 1805 quietly removed from service, with a token promotion to marshal.

After his return, the duke lived briefly and extravagantly with Madame de St. Laurent, at his home near Ealing, where he continued to observe a strictly regimented routine involving close daily checks on the domestic bills and the conduct of his servants. His daily habits were punctuated by the constant chiming of his many clocks and the whirring of numerous mechanical fountains and automatons. In an unlikely contradiction of his army reputation as a martinet, the duke publicly professed liberal, Whig sentiments and embraced suitably philanthropic causes such as the Anti-Slavery Society, the Society for Promoting Christianity among the Jews, and the Bible Society. He also developed a friendship with the industrialist and social reformer Robert Owen, supporting his scheme for improving the living and working conditions of cotton mill workers. Having won Owen's friendship, the duke would later have absolutely no qualms about pressurizing him for substantial loans, which were never repaid.

The debts had continued to accumulate and forced the duke to leave the country again in 1815. He removed to Brussels where, failing to make any economies, he set himself up in a mansion in the Place Royale. Two years later he was back in England, when his fortunes unexpectedly changed. For some time, and like the other financially embarrassed sons of George III, the duke had been contemplating a practical solution to his problems by finding a rich bride. This mission became even more urgent when Princess Charlotte, the Prince Regent's only child and his heir apparent, died in childbirth in 1817. The chances of one of the Prince Regent's brothers possibly becoming king after his demise were thus greatly enhanced, as, by association, were those of their children.

Princess Charlotte's widower, Leopold of Saxe-Coburg, was keen to see the duke of Kent marry his widowed sister, Victoire, who had been left with two children, Feodora and Charles, at the age of twenty-eight. As dowager princess of Leiningen, she was acting regent for Charles, but as such the titles and properties she brought with her were minor. The duke acknowledged that the match was second best, pontificating about his duty to his family and his country to become a married man. Madame de St. Laurent did the honorable thing and made a discreet retreat to Paris, accepting a pension from a relieved duke, and content in his solemn assurances to her that his marriage to Victoire was "*not* from the least diminution in an attachment which had stood the test of twenty-eight years" (Weintraub 1996, 31).

The duke of Kent traveled to his bride's family castle at Amorbach. Now temporarily buoyed up by a loan of £3,000 from Coutts's bank, he married Victoire in Coburg on 29 May 1818; on 13 July they went through a Church of England ceremony at Kew Palace. By November, the duchess was pregnant. The match itself seemed a happy enough one; the duke brought his pregnant wife on the arduous 427-mile journey back to England for the birth, and Princess Victoria arrived on 24 May 1819. The duke took genuine delight in his baby daughter, making sure that all who saw her were aware that a gypsy on Gibraltar had told him that he would have a daughter who would one day become a "great queen."

Sadly for the duke, his much-prized asset (who was now fifth in line to the throne) brought no amelioration in his precipitous financial affairs. Parliament refused to allow him to sell his house at Ealing by lottery and, after enjoying the charity of his brother-in-law Leopold at his home, Claremont, in Surrey, the duke resolved that a return to Amorbach was inevitable. Meanwhile he decided to spend the winter modestly in Devonshire, leasing Woolbrook Cottage at Sidmouth. Not long after arriving there in dismal winter weather, the duke got soaking wet while out walking, caught a cold, and developed pneumonia. Even his formerly robust health (he had always expected to outlive all his brothers) could not sustain the bleeding and the use of strong purgatives by the duke's doctors, who between them ensured his untimely death at the age of fifty-two, six days before that of his father, King George III.

The court gossip, Princess Lieven, expressed the reaction of many to the duke's demise: "No one in England will mourn the Duke. He was false, hard, and greedy. His so-called good qualities were only for show" (Weintraub 1996, 49–50). Others such as the diarist Croker were more conciliatory: "You will be surprised at the Duke of Kent's death," he wrote to Lord Lowther. "He was the strongest of the strong. Never before ill in all his life, and now to die of a cold when half the kingdom have colds with impunity. It was very bad luck indeed" (Croker 1884–1885 1:155).

Related entries:
Conroy, Sir John; Hanover, Royal House of; Kent, Marie Louise Victoire, Duchess of; Leopold I, King of the Belgians

References and further reading:

Ashdown, Dulcie. 1974. *Queen Victoria's Mother.* London: Robert Hale.

Benson, A. C., and Viscount Esher, eds. 1911. *The Letters of Queen Victoria 1837–1861.* 1st ser., 3 vols. London: John Murray.

Charlot, Monica. 1991. *Victoria: The Young Queen.* Cambridge: Polity.

Creston, Dormer. 1952. *The Youthful Queen Victoria.* London: Macmillan.

Croker, John Wilson. 1884–1885. *The Croker Pages.* 3 vols. London: John Murray.

Duff, David. 1938. *Edward of Kent.* London: S. Paul and Co.

Esher, Viscount, ed. 1912. *The Girlhood of Queen Victoria: A Selection from Her Majesty's Diaries between the Years of 1832 and 1840.* 2 vols. London: John Murray.

Fulford, Roger. [1933] 2000. *Royal Dukes.* Harmondsworth, UK: Penguin.

Gillen, Mollie. 1970. *The Prince and His Lady.* Toronto: Griffin House.

Hasted, Jane Eliza. 1950. *Unsuccessful Ladies: An Account of the Aunts (Official and Unofficial) of the Late Queen Victoria.* London: Ayer.

Weintraub, Stanley. 1996. *Victoria.* London: John Murray.

Windsor, Dean of, and Hector Bolitho, eds. 1927. *Letters of Lady Augusta Stanley: A Young Lady at Court 1849–1863.* London: Gerald Howe.

Woodham-Smith, Cecil. 1972. *Queen Victoria: Her Life and Times.* Vol. 1: *1819–1861.* London: Hamish Hamilton.

Kent, Marie Louise Victoire, Duchess of (1786–1861)

her love for me—*it is* too *touching!* (Benson and Esher 1911, 3:439)

There are two conflicting portraits of Queen Victoria's mother, the duchess of Kent, that have come down to us: one is of a sweet old lady, surrounded by adoring daughter and grandchildren and devoted retainers, uncomplainingly enduring the pain of terminal illness with fortitude and Christian piety. The other is of a self-obsessed, histrionic, and impetuous virago, forever making unreasonable demands about her own status and income and in the process alienating most of the British royal family into which she had married. Some of the duchess's demanding behavior can no doubt be ascribed to her having twice entered upon dynastic marriages of convenience to men considerably older than herself, only to be quickly widowed and left in straitened circumstances.

The daughter of Francis Frederic Antony, duke of Saxe-Saalfeld-Coburg, and his wife, Augusta Carolina Sophia of Reuss-Eberstadt, Marie Louise Victoire (as she was christened) was a pretty and amiable woman with a penchant for silk, Brussels lace, and expensive feathered hats. She was born in Coburg on 17 August 1786 and at the age of seventeen was married (1803) to Emich Charles, prince of Leiningen-Dachsburg-Hardenburg (twenty-three years her senior). Their eleven-year marriage produced two children: Charles Frederick William Ernest (1804) and Anna Feodorovna Augusta Charlotte Wilhelmina (known as Feodora) (1807).

Victoire was plucked, somewhat reluctantly, from what might have been a long widowhood by the duke of Kent, for she had become regent for her son, Charles, on her husband's death and wanted to keep an eye on his safe succession to the Leiningen title. Despite his bride's being not quite from the top drawer of the European aristocracy, the duke of Kent, anxious to produce an heir, married Victoire in May 1818 in a Lutheran ceremony at Coburg and again, in a Church of England service, at Kew in July. When she was eight months pregnant, acceding to her husband's desire that their baby should be born in England, the duchess agreed to an exhausting 427-mile road journey back to England, in a rattling coach from her home in Amorbach.

The widowed Marie Louise Victoire, duchess of Kent, with her young daughter, Princess Victoria, c. 1821 (Hulton/Archive by Getty Images)

Throughout her two-year marriage to the duke of Kent the duchess knew no financial security, and the couple were considering returning to the Continent to live at the time of his death in 1820. Victoire was left penniless and socially isolated in a country whose language she barely spoke. Her British relatives found her an unwanted financial encumbrance: the duchess had no money to pay for her return to Amorbach, although George IV would certainly have been happy to see the back of her. The "poor widow and her fatherless girl," as Victoria later sentimentally referred to herself and her mother, were rescued by an annuity of £2,000 (later increased to £3,000) from the duchess's brother Leopold, which augmented her jointure of £6,000 awarded on her marriage.

But no money she received was ever enough to clear her dead husband's long-accumulated debts, which amounted to £70,000 (these were eventually paid off by Queen Victoria from her own Privy Purse when she came to the throne). The duchess therefore had no choice but to throw herself on the mercy of her English brothers-in-law, whom she patently disliked. George IV and his heir, the duke of Clarence, later King William IV, made no attempt to disguise their own contempt for the duchess. She stubbornly resolved to honor her husband's wishes of bringing Victoria up in England and proceeded to do so with the help of her German retainers, the Baroness Späth and Louise Lehzen. Disapproving of William IV's vulgarity and bad language, the duchess immured herself and Victoria in their apartments at Kensington Palace. Here she assiduously devoted herself to a single mission: that of nurturing (literally—for she did that very rare thing and breastfed her infant) her poor little fatherless "Vickelchen." She fiercely protected the child from her supposedly predatory uncles. From now until she ascended the throne, Victoria slept in her mother's room, and her every waking moment was closely monitored. The duchess made the mistake, however, of succumbing to the folly of putting her trust in the comptroller of her household, Sir John Conroy, who proceeded to bring out the worst in her by encouraging her ambitions to become regent. Sir John, who looked to his own advancement should this happen, took advantage of the duchess's ingenuousness. He fed her obsession that Victoria's wicked uncles, particularly the duke of Cumberland, were out to harm her and also encouraged in her an overblown sense of her own importance.

Willam IV's hatred of his sister-in-law's brazen impertinence was made manifest in his frequent refusals to accede to her demands over precedence—occasions that often resulted in tantrums by the duchess. On being told, for example, at William's coronation in 1831 that Princess Victoria could not have her own procession to the abbey, the duchess had promptly refused to let her daughter attend at all. The bickering continued, culminating in William IV's famous tirade against the duchess at his 1836 birthday banquet, when he declared that he hoped he would live another nine months—long enough to see Victoria achieve her majority so that her scheming mother would be denied the longed-for regency.

The duchess refused to abandon her excessive demands, even after Victoria became queen in 1837. She expected to be accorded the title of Queen Mother—a request rejected by Victoria, who talked openly with her prime minister, Lord Melbourne, about her mother's undignified behavior. The eighteen-year-old and her minister sagely concurred that Mamma was not only a fool but "a liar and a hypocrite" (St. Aubyn 1991, 72). The ruthlessness with which the eighteen-year-old Victoria relegated her mother to obscurity after becoming queen is astonishing. She promptly had her bed removed from her mother's room and reveled in being able both to eat and to sleep on her own for the first time in her life; for advice on matters of government Victoria turned to Melbourne or her Uncle Leopold, the duchess's brother. For maternal comfort, Victoria threw herself into the reassuring bosom of her governess and protector, Baroness Lehzen. The latter, herself no stranger to the art of machination, had for long exploited the growing alienation between mother and daughter. For most of her young life, therefore, Victoria viewed her mother at secondhand, through the distorted lens of Lehzen's own hostility; in return the duchess became obsessively jealous of those who came between her and Victoria, most particularly Lehzen and Melbourne.

Bereft of a purpose, and allowed to see her daughter only by appointment and at formal dinners and receptions, the duchess was abandoned to her suite of rooms at Buckingham Palace. After Conroy's death in 1854, she was forced to come to terms with the fact that in the course of controlling her affairs, he had systematically defrauded her of £60,000. The duchesss bewailed Conroy's betrayal and her own folly. Reduced to a tedious round of gossip, cards, embroidery, and playing the piano with her few remaining cronies, at Victoria's wedding to Prince Albert in 1840 the duchess was relegated to a minor role—eclipsed by Lehzen, who received a warm embrace from the queen, who merely shook her mother's hand. As for the duchess's suggestion that she should live with the royal couple: this was flatly vetoed—by both Victoria and Melbourne. The duchess had to give up her suite of rooms at Buckingham Palace for the use of Prince Albert and eventually took over the royal residence at Clarence House in St. James, as well as having a home, Frogmore Lodge, at Windsor.

It was Prince Albert who took it upon himself to reconcile mother and daughter. The duchess was, after all, his aunt. He had been her first choice all along as husband for Victoria, and there was an affection between them that Albert carefully built on, effecting the rapprochement of Victoria and the duchess after the birth of the couple's first child in November 1840. Readmitted to the royal fold, the duchess reciprocated by committing herself with utter devotion to her adored nephew. As the grandchildren arrived, she found a new and dignified role as grandmother and softened in her intemperate behavior. As her relationship with Victoria warmed, the duchess began accompanying the royal family on their trips to Osborne and Balmoral; eventually mother and daughter were exchanging letters and visits on an almost daily basis.

The duchess's devoted lady-in-waiting in her final years, Lady Augusta Stanley, wrote many letters to her family, which provide a poignant portrait of the duchess at this time. Now suffering from numerous unspecified but debilitating physical complaints (including severe erysipelas and a cancerous tumor on her arm), she was a model of unselfishness and patient endurance. When the duchess died on 16 March 1861 (just nine months before Albert's death), the long-suppressed and contradictory emotions provoked by their difficult relationship overwhelmed the queen. She was prostrate with grief and remorse. In a subsequent outpouring of bathos in which she eulogized the dear departed, her exemplary personality, and her years of uncomplaining devotion, Victoria exorcised her own sense of guilt at having neglected her mother during the early years of her reign. A letter to King Leopold of 16 March 1861 is typical: "*She* is gone! That *precious, dearly beloved tender* Mother—whom I never was parted from but for a few months—without whom *I* can't *imagine life*—has been take away from us! It is *too* dreadful!" (Benson and Esher 1911, 3:435); considering the early history of her fraught relationship with the duchess, Victoria's hypocrisy is breathtaking.

In penance, Queen Victoria ensured that the duchess enjoyed the long sleep of the dead in a purpose-built mausoleum at Frogmore. The duchess's body was reburied there from St. George's Chapel, Windsor, in August. Victoria now indulged herself in a further torrent of *faux sentiment* as she went through her mother's things and found "touching relics" of her "poor Father" (Benson and Esher 1911, 3:439)—the duke and duchess's letters to each other, the duchess's diaries, the scrapbooks in which she had pasted locks of baby Victoria's hair and noted down her every stage of development. The loss of her mother, which was her first close experience of death, was "the most dreadful day of my life" for Victoria (Benson and Esher 1911, 3: 435). Nine months later she transcended this orgy of unbridled grief in an even greater bereavement—the death of Prince Albert.

Related entries:
Bruce, Lady Augusta; Conroy, Sir John; Feodora, Princess of Hohenlohe-Langenburg; Kensington System; Kent, Edward Augustus, Duke of; Leopold I, King of the Belgians; Melbourne, William Lamb, Second Viscount; Saxe-Coburg-Gotha, Royal House of; William IV

References and further reading:

Ashdown, Dulcie. 1974. *Queen Victoria's Mother.* London: Robert Hale.

Benson, A. C., and Viscount Esher, eds. 1911. *The Letters of Queen Victoria 1837–1861.* 1st ser., 3 vols. London: John Murray.

Creston, Dormer. 1952. *The Youthful Queen Victoria.* London: Macmillan.

Charlot, Monica. 1991. *Victoria: The Young Queen.* Cambridge: Polity.

Esher, Viscount, ed. 1912. *The Girlhood of Queen Victoria: A Selection from Her Majesty's Diaries between the Years of 1832 and 1840.* 2 vols. London: John Murray.

Hudson, Katherine. 1994. *A Royal Conflict: Sir John Conroy and the Young Victoria.* London: Hodder and Stoughton.

Stuart, Dorothy. 1941. *The Mother of Victoria: A Period Piece.* London: Macmillan.

St. Aubyn, Giles. 1991. *Queen Victoria: A Portrait.* London: Sinclair Stevenson.

Windsor, Dean of, and Hector Bolitho, eds. 1927. *Letters of Lady Augusta Stanley: A Young Lady at Court 1849–1863.* London: Gerald Howe.

Woodham-Smith, Cecil. 1972. *Queen Victoria: Her Life and Times.* Vol. 1: *1819–1861.* London: Hamish Hamilton.

Koh-i-Noor Diamond

You know how I dislike wearing the Koh-i-noor (Fulford 1976, 111)

The historic Koh-i-Noor diamond, its name meaning "mountain of light" in Persian, is supposedly possessed of supernatural qualities. In Indian legend, it is said to bring victory over their enemies to whoever is in possession of it; in addition, it brings good luck to any woman who owns it and bad luck to any man. In 1849 the diamond was confiscated by the British government from the deposed ruler of the Punjab and eventually ceremonially presented to Queen Victoria in 1876 on the occasion of her declaration as empress of India. It has in present times acquired a national significance for the Sikhs, the nation to whom it once belonged. During its long and often obscure 700-year history the diamond has changed hands several times.

The stone is thought to have been found in the ancient diamond mining area between Hyderabad and Madras but exactly when is unknown. According to legend, it once hung around the neck of the sun god himself. It was claimed to have been in the possession of the family of the raja of Malwa in India for some time before it was seized from him by Sultan Ala-ud-Din Khalji in 1304. Others argue that it was given to the son of Babur, the founder of the Mughal dynasty, by the raja of Gawlio, after the 1526 battle of Panipat. The diamond may possibly have been set in the famous peacock throne of the Mughal emperor Aurangzeb, who died in 1707. What is certain is that it was captured by the Persian ruler Nadir Shah, when he invaded the Mughal empire in 1739, raided Delhi, and took away many precious objects including the peacock throne and the Koh-i-Noor diamond. After the death of Nadir Shah, the stone's history is uncertain. It was purportedly brought back to the Punjab by a fugitive Afghan prince, from whom the dia-

THE CELEBRATED KOH-I-NOOR DIAMOND.

Within a reinforced display case the legendary Koh-i-Noor diamond, ceded to the British crown in 1849 by the Maharajah Duleep Singh, was exhibited at the Great Exhibition of 1851. (CORBIS)

mond was confiscated by the Sikh warrior ruler Ranjit Singh. Singh ordered the diamond to be cut and set in an armlet. But such was its lack of brilliance that he had the workman beheaded for his failure; the diamond was subsequently kept in a treasury at Lahore.

With the death in 1843 of Ranjit Singh, fighting broke out among his heirs. The new British governor-general of the British East India Company, Lord Dalhousie, set out to take control of the Punjab, and in 1849, when the British defeated the Sikhs and Afghans at Gujerat, the state was annexed. Ranjit Singh's nine-year-old successor, Duleep Singh, was forced by the treaty of Lahore to abdicate and hand over the contents of the treasury, including the Koh-i-Noor diamond, to the British Crown.

The roughly faceted stone of 186.10 carats, set in an armlet, with smaller diamonds on either side, was lodged in the Tower of London with the other crown jewels. It was put on show at the Great Exhibition on 1 May 1851 in a gilded cage, with the gas lighting turned up in an attempt to accentuate its brightness. It was, however, something of a disappointment to the vast crowds that jostled to see it, and more so the queen herself, who deemed it to be insufficiently brilliant. As the diamond also still had some natural flaws, the following year it was recut to 108.93 carats, in an oval brilliant, by Dutch glypticians at the famous London jewelers Garrards—in the process losing 40 percent of its bulk.

The story of Duleep Singh, the boy-king of the Sikhs, who had surrendered the diamond to the British crown, was a poignant one that touched the heart of Queen Victoria. In 1854, having converted to Christianity, he settled in England, where he was provided with a generous pension by the state. He met the queen, who was quite captivated, as she always was by masculine beauty. She thought him "so handsome, so charming" (Campbell 2000, 426) and was greatly taken with his sensitive personality and his impeccable manners. She was moved by the upheavals Duleep had suffered in his early life and was not without a twinge of guilt about his dispossession. She took the exotic young maharajah under her maternal wing, developing a strong attachment to him. She felt she had a mission to protect him from his former "heathen" nature. Duleep was feted at court, where he aroused great curiosity with his exquisite Indian costumes. The queen and Prince Albert invited him to stay at Windsor, Balmoral, and Osborne, where he played with the royal children and spent hours with Prince Albert in the dark room developing photographs of the royal family.

In 1855 Queen Victoria commissioned the court painter, Franz Winterhalter, to paint Duleep Singh's portrait and also sketched him herself. Now a loyal and devoted subject, in return Duleep wore a miniature of the queen. When Queen Victoria discovered that the maharajah nursed a deep desire to see the Koh-i-Noor diamond once again, she duly summoned a detachment of yeoman to bring the diamond from the Tower and allowed him to hold it in his hands for a few minutes before, with great deference, he symbolically placed it back in her hands. In later years the queen claimed that she disliked flaunting the Koh-i-Noor, as a symbol of Indian subjugation to Britain. "As regards India I am bound to say that no one feels more strongly than I do about India or how much I opposed our taking those countries" (Fulford 1976, 111). Nevertheless, she enjoyed the title Empress of India.

At the age of twenty-five Duleep married a Coptic Christian and had six children by her. His Anglicization continued at his estate—Elvedon Hall, in Suffolk—where he wore plus fours, went hunting and shooting like any other English country gentleman, and invited the Prince of Wales to regular house parties. In one year alone his royal shooting parties massacred 10,000 rabbits and 20,000 partridges. The hall's interior, however, displayed many traditional trappings of Indian cutlure—rich carpets, tapestries, and other artifacts. Duleep also kept exotic animals, such as cheetahs, as well as sparrowhawks.

During the 1880s, Duleep Singh began suffering from mental illness. Fueled by a burning desire to regain his lost empire and lead a revolt against British rule in the Punjab, he began studying state papers in the British Museum, renounced his Christianity, and tried to set sail for India. Turned back by the authorities, he went to Paris, where he took up with Russian anarchists and Irish Fenians. He traveled to St. Petersburg and entered into bizarre negotiations to win Russian support for his claim and foment an Anglo-Russian war. Queen Victoria was incensed by what she saw as an act of personal betrayal and for several years broke off contact with him. In July 1890 the maharajah, in failing mental and physical health, suffered a stoke in Paris. Sensing his imminent death, he wrote a contrite letter to the queen asking her to pardon him so that he could return to England. The matter was discussed by the British cabinet, with the queen urging them to be merciful. A chastised Duleep was given permission to return, but in the event he was too sick to travel and remained in France.

At the Grand Hotel, Grasse, in April 1891, a now fat and balding Duleep Singh visited the queen, who was enjoying her annual holiday on the Riviera. Left partially paralyzed by a stroke, he apologized for being unable to kneel and beg her forgiveness. In a torrent of tears, Duleep bewailed his misfortunes; the queen found the interview uncomfortable but was relieved that she had had the opportunity to forgive him. Two years later, Duleep Singh died suddenly in a Paris hotel, at the age of only fifty-three. His body was returned to England, and he was given a Christian burial at his estate at Elvedon.

When the queen was named empress of India on 1 May 1876, the British prime minister, Benjamin Disraeli, formally presented the Koh-i-Noor diamond to her, to affirm, by her possession of the jewel, her sovereignty over India. Now the queen's personal property, the diamond was worn by her on state occasions, such as the 1879 wedding of her son Arthur to Princess Louise of Prussia. In 1887, during the celebrations of her Golden Jubilee, the queen sat for her portrait wearing the Koh-i-Noor. After her death, the diamond became the centerpiece of the state crown worn by Queen Mary, wife of George V, at their 1911 coronation and by Elizabeth the Queen Mother at hers in 1937.

A statue to Duleep Singh was erected by the Sikh community at Thetford, near his old home at Elvedon Manor, in the 1990s. Although the legendary diamond that symbolized so much for Duleep Singh in his doomed enterprise to regain his lost kingdom is now closely guarded at the Tower of London, his statue at Thetford has become a rallying point for Sikhs, who are now demanding the diamond's return to its rightful home in India. This campaign gathered pace in 1999 in the wake of the setting up of a British committee to examine the possible return of the Elgin marbles to Greece. It is claimed, however, that the diamond's return would be likely only to provoke a dispute between India and Pakistan as to which country had the greater claim to it, since the Punjab from which it was originally taken is now part of eastern Pakistan.

Related entries:
Empress of India; Great Exhibition; Indian Rebellion

References and further reading:

Alexander, Michael, and Sushila Anand. 2001. *Queen Victoria's Maharajah.* London: Phoenix.

Campbell, Christy. 2000. *The Maharaja's Box.* London: HarperCollins.

Howarth, Stephen. 1980. *The Koh-i-Noor Diamond: The History and the Legend.* London: Quartet Books.

Rushby, Kevin. 1999. *Chasing the Mountain of Light: Across India on the Trail of the Koh-i-Noor Diamond.* London: Flamingo.

L

Lablache, Luigi (1794–1858)

il mio buon e caro Maestro [my good and kind master] (Esher 1912, 1:165)

One of many contradictions to the dour image of Queen Victoria that has been so relentlessly perpetuated is the fact of the queen's great passion for singing and the Italian opera. She was possessed of a fine, sweet singing voice and during Prince Albert's lifetime took enormous pleasure in performing duets with him. Her lovely voice was perfected, over a period of twenty years, under tuition from one of the great nineteenth-century Italian bass baritones, Luigi Lablache.

Born in Naples of mixed Irish and Italian blood, Lablache was a leading dramatic singer of his time, admired by the composers Schubert and Wagner. Lablache studied singing in Naples from the age of twelve on, where he made his debut in 1812. After an acclaimed first appearance at La Scala in Milan in 1817, as Dandini in Rossini's *La Cenerentola,* he built up a varied repertoire in operas by Rossini, Donizetti, Verdi, and many others. He was particularly noted for his ability to handle both comic and tragic roles—his most famous being Giorgio in Bellini's *Il Puritani* (one of the queen's favorite operas), Don Pasquale in the opera of the same name by Donizetti, and Leporello in Mozart's *Don Giovanni*. Lablache notably sang in Mozart's *Requiem* at Beethoven's funeral in 1827.

After several years of singing in Italy and Vienna, Lablache made his first appearance in London in 1830, at the King's Theatre in the Haymarket (from 1837 on known as Her Majesty's Theatre), where he would subsequently appear regularly until 1852. On the occasion of Princess Victoria's sixteenth birthday in 1835, her mother, the duchess of Kent, arranged a concert at which Lablache performed with other leading singers of the day whom Victoria idolized—Giulia Grisi, Giovanni Rubini, and Antonio Tamburini. Such was Victoria's admiration of Lablache that he was prevailed upon to give her singing lessons, which he took up in April the following year, continued until the end of his London season in August, and resumed every year thereafter until 1856.

After overcoming her extreme nervousness during her first lesson, at which she ambitiously sang the difficult aria "Or che in cielo" from Donizetti's *Marino Faliero,* Victoria was completely smitten by Lablache's patience and his "gentlemanlike" behavior. She would, if she could, have had lessons every day instead of every week. In August 1836, at the end of Lablache's season, during which she had received twenty-six lessons, she wrote that "I shall count the weeks and months eagerly till next April when I shall resume my delightful lessons with him" (Esher 1914, 60–61).

Under Lablache's tuition Victoria learned many Italian arias, which she preferred to French ones and which he adapted to suit her vocal range. Lablache himself often joined her in duets, as did her mother and her cousin Prince Albert of Saxe-Coburg, when he was visiting in May 1836. But it was not just the singing instruction that Victoria so looked forward to; it was also the never-ending fund of entertaining stories with which Lablache regaled her, in a mixture of French and Italian (the queen spoke both languages), and the romantic vision of Naples and Italy that he conjured up for her. They also shared a passionate admiration for the Swedish singer Jenny Lind and often discussed her performances.

When William IV died in June 1837, Victoria was dismayed that her lessons with Lablache had to be curtailed, now that the court was in official mourning. Now queen, she was impatient for her singing lessons to resume, which they did in August. Eager to introduce music and opera at Buckingham Palace, on 17 August 1837 the queen held the first of many concerts there, with the composer and conductor Signor Michael Costa directing an array of leading performers of the day, including Lablache. After Victoria's marriage, she and Prince Albert would themselves sing at concerts at Buckingham Palace, such as that held on 12 June 1840, again directed by Costa, at which they sang a duet by Ricci and the queen sang a trio with Lablache and Rubini from *The Magic Flute*. Lablache, meanwhile, went on to establish a reputation for himself in Paris and in St. Petersburg. He was still in good voice at the age of sixty—although by now grossly overweight—and finally retired in 1856. Of his thirteen children, his eldest son, Federico, became an opera singer.

Related entries:
Albert of Saxe-Coburg-Gotha, Prince Consort; Dance; Kensington System; Opera; Theater

References and further reading:

Charlot, Monica. 1991. *Victoria: The Young Queen*. Cambridge: Polity.

Creston, Dormer. 1952. *The Youthful Victoria*. London: Macmillan.

Esher, Viscount, ed. 1912. *The Girlhood of Queen Victoria: A Selection from Her Majesty's Diaries between the Years of 1832 and 1840*. London: John Murray.

Esher, Viscount, ed. 1914. *The Training of a Sovereign*. London: John Murray.

Plowden, Alison. 1981. *The Young Victoria*. London: Weidenfeld and Nicolson.

Rowell, George. 1978. *Queen Victoria Goes to the Theatre*. London: Paul Elek.

Warner, Marina. 1979. *Queen Victoria's Sketchbook*. London: Macmillan.

Woodham-Smith, Cecil. 1972. *Queen Victoria: Her Life and Times*. Vol. 1: *1819–1861*. London: Hamish Hamilton.

Landseer, Sir Edwin (1802–1873)

Such a loss! He and Winterhalter—our old friends—and two such unrivalled artists both gone within three months of each other (Fulford 1976, 111)

By the time he died in 1873, there was hardly a front parlor—rich or poor—in England that did not boast a popular engraving of one of Sir Edwin Landseer's celebrated animal pictures. Thanks to his patronage by Queen Victoria and Prince Albert, he died a very rich man, having indelibly inscribed the popular art of his day with a style of sentimentalized animal portraiture that helped promote the embryonic animal rights movement in Britain and the cause of antivivisection.

Landseer came from a family of London engravers, his father, John Landseer, having taught him and his brother Thomas the craft. As a young boy his artistic skills in chalk, watercolors, and pencil were mainly self-taught. He had a lifelong fascination for animals and loved to go out sketching them—especially the lions and tigers at Edward Cross's menagerie—as well as learning their anatomy by dissecting the carcasses of lions and cows.

At the age of ten, Landseer sold his first animal picture—of a brown mastiff—for the then exceptional price for such a young artist of seventy guineas. His talent was spotted by the Society of Arts, and Landseer exhibited his first picture—of a dog and puppies—at the Royal Academy and entered its school in 1816. In 1824 Landseer fell in love with Scotland, when he visited the novelist Sir Walter Scott at Abbotsford and made drawings of his dogs, which were later used as the basis for the illustrations to Scott's series of "Waverly" novels (published from 1831 to 1841). Landseer's career went from strength to strength; in 1826 he was the youngest person to be made an associate of the Royal Academy, at the age of twenty-four. He rapidly gained himself an enviable list of society patrons who snapped up his pictures of their family dogs, horses, and other animals and made him a frequent and welcome guest in their homes.

Landseer's first and one of his most emotive paintings was *The Old Shepherd's Chief Mourner* (1837)—portraying a sheepdog with its head raised up onto the coffin of its dead master. It was a powerful image of loss that would have its later parallels in a photograh of the queen in mourning gazing up, in similar longing, at a bust of the dead Albert. In 1837 Landseer set the seal on the romantic image of the young queen, by painting an unusual (for then) equestrian portrait of her on her horse Comus. Landseer had been painting portraits since 1823, although these never achieved the same popularity as his animal pictures. But in 1839, after the queen commissioned him to paint her portrait as a wedding gift for Prince Albert, he would produce many paintings and drawings of the royal family, their gamekeepers, and, of course, their pets. During the 1840s he became a frequent guest at Buckingham Palace, Osborne, and sometimes Balmoral, where he entertained the queen and Prince Albert with his humorous anecdotes about animals. He sketched and painted the royal children as they were born and gave lessons in painting and etching to the queen and prince—both of them keen artists.

Landseer received many commissions to paint royal family portraits as birthday gifts—for example, the portrait of the Princess Royal with Prince Albert's greyhound Eos that the queen commissioned in 1842 as a birthday gift for the prince. Undoubtedly, Landseer's most famous royal work, and one that perpetuated the rose-tinted image of domestic harmony that Queen Victoria so cherished, was *Windsor Castle in Modern Times,* (1841). Another famous image, which depicted a romanticized view of royalty, was Landseer's portrait to commemorate the medieval costume ball held in May 1842 at Buckingham Palace, showing Queen Victoria dressed as Queen Phillippa and Albert as Edward III. The queen offered Landseer a knighthood shortly afterward. With admirable modesty, he politely declined it, stating that "he had scarcely done enough to entitle him to the honour which it was contemplated to bestow upon him" (Benson and Esher 1911, 1:397). He asked the queen to postpone the honor until he had completed some "works of a more important character," (ibid.) finally accepting the knighthood in 1850. The following year his reputation was sealed, when his most familiar painting, depicting a triumphant stag and entitled *Monarch of the Glen,* was unveiled. Prince Albert, at that time involved in the redecoration of the House of Lords, suggested that the painting should be purchased for the peers' refreshment room. Parliament, however, declined to stump up the money.

By the mid-1860s, only the rich could afford Landseer's paintings, which were selling for as much as £6,000 or £7,000 each. And his patrons were not only the privileged few of the aristocracy, but, increasingly, self-made men and rich industrialists. Landseer's final and most visible works are the sculptures he made for the casting of the bronze lions that today stand at the foot of Nelson's column in Trafalgar Square. Commissioned in 1859, these were unveiled in 1867.

In 1867 Landseer found himself drawn into controversy over one of his most famous paintings—*Her Majesty at Osborne*—which depicted the queen in full mourning seated on a black pony and reading a dispatch, with John Brown, her Scottish servant, standing holding the pony's bridle. Exhibited at the Royal Academy in May, the painting attracted huge crowds and was soon circulated in cheap engravings. Public curiosity was aroused because it seemed to endorse the gossip about the queen's "relationship" with Brown, who had served her so devotedly since the death of Prince Albert. Such a composition was deemed imprudent, if not positively scandalous by some, for it featured a servant in a prominent position alongside the queen. It was criticized for suggesting an equality of status that was demeaning to the queen and suggestive (to those with suspicious minds) of something "improper." A cartoon version of the painting that soon appeared in the magazine *Tomahawk* under the catchphrase "All is black that is not Brown" would launch a spate of parody in the popular press.

Throughout his life Lanseer's mental health had been unstable. He had collapsed completely in 1862–1863, suffering a bout of severe depression. His eyesight was also rapidly failing—affecting his ability to work—and this, aggravated by his inability to sleep, led to fits of alcoholism. His sad physical decline was noted with regret by the queen, who recorded in her journal at the time of his death that Landseer had spent the last three years of his life "half out of his mind" (Hibbert 1984, 233).

When Landseer died he left £200,000—an enormous sum for its time, and much of it accumulated from the mass reproduction of prints from engravings of his work, of which 434 had been made by 1875. With typical attention to detail, the queen would record that she herself owned "39 oil paintings of his, 16 chalk drawings, two frescos and many sketches" (Buckle 1926–1928, 2, 282–283). In the days before the advent of the paparazzi and the photo opportunity, which have done so much to demolish the sanctified image of royalty, the paintings that Landseer left, as well as those of his contemporary Winterhalter (they died within months of each other), performed an important public relations role for the monarchy. In their depiction of Victoria, Albert, and their children, they promoted a public image of unsullied domestic bliss, moral propriety, and solicitude for dumb animals that idealized the royal couple and underlined their rejection of worldly vices—a stringent new morality that would underpin the Victorian age.

Related entries:
Animals; Balmoral Castle; Scott, Sir Walter; Winterhalter, Franz Xaver

References and further reading:

Batty, J. 1990. *Landseer's Animal Illustrations.* Alton, UK: Nimrod.

Benson, A. C., and Viscount Esher, eds. 1911. *The Letters of Queen Victoria 1837–1861.* 1st ser., 3 vols. London: John Murray.

Buckle, G. E., ed. 1926–1928. *The Letters of Queen Victoria: A Selection from Her Majesty's Correspondence and Journal between the Years 1862 and 1885.* 2d ser., 3 vols. London: John Murray.

Hibbert, Christopher. 1984. *Queen Victoria in Her Letters and Journals.* London: Viking.

Lennie, Campbell. 1976. *Landseer: The Victorian Paragon*. London: Hamish Hamilton.

Longford, Elizabeth. [1964] 1998. *Victoria R.I.* London: Weidenfeld and Nicolson.

Munich, Adrienne. 1996. *Queen Victoria's Secrets.* New York: Columbia University Press.

Ormond, Richard. 1982. *Sir Edwin Landseer.* New York: Rizzoli.

Leaves from the Journal of Our Life in the Highlands

my poor little Highland book (Fulford 1971, 51)

The publication, in 1868, of extracts from the queen's journals, in which described her happy family holidays at Balmoral with her beloved Albert, did much to restore her to her public, at a time when her protracted and deep mourning for her late husband had been coming under increasing attack. But although the British people might have warmed to the queen's paeans of praise for Scotland's wild romantic beauty—its hills, lakes, heather, mountains, and forests—and for the simplicity of its people, many in the royal household had long since come to find the queen's love affair with Scotland tedious in the extreme.

When Queen Victoria and Prince Albert first visited the Highlands of Scotland in September 1842, they had been instantly captivated by them, particularly as the scenery reminded Albert of the Thuringian forest of his homeland, as well as the Swiss Alps, which he knew and loved so well. The couple returned to Scotland in 1844 and again in 1847. By the end of the 1840s, their visits there became ever more frequent. They were particularly fond of Perthshire and made six visits to it between 1842 and 1866, staying at the castle at Blair Atholl. With each visit the queen found it harder and harder to leave Scotland; in later years she would openly admit that she feared that she loved "the dear Highlands . . . more than matter-of-fact, unpoetical England" (Hibbert 1984, 223). It was her belief that England had never acknowledged its debt to Scotland and the Scots, a people characterized by "energy, courage, worth, inimitable perseverance, determination and self-respect" (ibid.). By October 1848, the superintendent of the nursery, Lady Lyttleton, noted that the queen had returned from a recent visit "in her usual devoted, passionate admiration for the Highlands. Leaving them is always a case of actual *red eyes*" (Wyndham 1912, 386). A year later, she would wearily observe that the queen's obsession continued unabated, with her continually lauding "Scotch air, Scotch people, Scotch hills, Scotch rivers, Scotch woods" as all being "far preferable to those of any other nation in or out of this world" (393).

After the death of Prince Albert in December 1861, the queen would associate many of their happy times together with family holidays at the home they built in Scotland at Balmoral. She had extracts from her Scottish journals privately printed in 1865 and circulated at court. The reaction to this was mixed; the queen's otherwise devoted lady-in-waiting Lady Augusta Bruce was, like Lady Lyttleton, less than impressed with the queen's uncritical admiration for all things Scottish. Although Bruce admitted that the queen's journal was enjoyable enough and that it evoked many memories of her own years in the queen's service, she also was highly critical. She felt that the public frenzy of overpraise for the queen's rather guileless book when it was published was a case of the emperor's new clothes; her criticisms of the queen's follow-up volume, published in 1884, would be even more acerbic, with Bruce objecting most strongly, as did others in the royal household, to the queen's devoting endless footnotes to details of the lives of the lowliest of household servants at Balmoral.

While being utterly convinced of the importance of her message on the virtues of Scottish life and ways, the queen was under no illusions about her creative gifts. It took considerable persuasion by Arthur Helps, clerk to the Privy Council, to get her to agree to the editing of her journals for publication, with Victoria modestly protesting that her journals were mere "homely" descriptions of her outings in and around Balmoral. It was, however, precisely this mundane quality that would make the work so endearing to the public. As unobtrusively as possible, Helps eradicated some of the queen's lapses in grammar, her repetition, and use of colloquialisms and slang, as well as expunging some of her more excessive underlining. The published edition of the Scottish journals was illustrated with some of Victoria's own watercolors of Scotland, in January 1868. Entitled *Leaves from the Journal of Our Life in the Highlands, from 1848 to 1861,* it was dedicated "To the dear memory of him who made the life of the writer bright and happy" (Kerr 1992, 8), her husband, Albert.

The British press responded in the main with excessive, if not outlandish praise, some commending the journals as being the best thing ever written. The writer Margaret Oliphant specifically requested by the queen to review the book, admired its artlessness, spontaneity, and simplicity while keeping to herself her judgment on its literary merits. In a study "Queen Victoria: A Personal Sketch" published posthumously in 1900, Oliphant was less equivocal. In literary matters, the queen was, she argued, "no student of style, nor does she ever, we imagine, ponder and wait for the best word" (Houston 1999, 158). The *London Quarterly Review* emphasized the book's more significant, long-term value as an important, historic document: "Our descendants will have the great figures of the historical portrait set before them with a minuteness of description, a completeness of detail, and a delicacy of touch, which will, after any lapse of time reproduce before them the real life of the present century in its best proportions" (Munich 1996, 41). In some respects the comment proved correct, for *Leaves* has since became an essential source in all studies of the queen's life and times.

The queen was thrilled with the response to her book but determined not to let it go to her head. She was, she told Sir Theodore Martin, "much moved—deeply so—but not uplifted or 'puffed up' by so much kindness, so much praise" (Gernsheim and Gernsheim 1954, 148). In her view, its popularity was a vindication of hers and Albert's own deeply held values; she hoped that "the kind and proper feeling toward the poor and the servants will I hope do good, for it is very much needed in England among the higher classes". The book's success signified that the public too had appreciated that the journals went to the heart of "what is simple and right" (Fulford 1981, 171)

Victoria avidly collected her reviews, which came thick and fast. "Newspapers shower in," she wrote to Vicky on 22 January (ibid.). She knew full well that the work had no great literary pretensions, yet what made it so appealing was its candor and the engaging spontaneity of the queen's thought, despite her grammatical lapses. The diarist Alfred Munby made the shrewd observation that *Leaves* "may turn out to have been, by its very artlessness, a masterstroke of art" (Hudson 1972, 249). However, the Prince of Wales viewed his mother's books as "twaddle." He was not the only member of the royal family who winced at the queen's revelation of what, in their opinion, were far too many personal details. Ministers worred that it painted a false picture of the queen's life. With its endless descriptions of picnics, drives, expeditions, and pony treks, it seemed to suggest that Victoria spent most of her life on holiday and at leisure, whereas, in fact, even when at Balmoral she kept in touch with the affairs of state and got through a prodigious amount of official paperwork.

Nevertheless, the book was a huge financial succes and quickly became a best seller (during the first three months it sold 80,000 copies). It was so in demand, that according to Tooley, "the circulating libraries ordered it by the ton" (Tooley 1896, 236). Most of the £4,000 profits were given to charity, in the form of educational bursaries for pupils of parish schools, including the local one at Crathie near Balmoral. The book turned out to be an even greater publishing success in the United States; it was translated into many languages, including Hindustani and, at the shah's specific request, Persian. In all, it is estimated that the royalties on *Leaves* totaled around £30,000. In the wake of this success, the queen commissioned a two-volume illustrated history of the Highlanders in 1868. In 1870, when she finally came to meet her hero, Charles Dickens, she presented him with a copy inscribed "from the humblest of writers to one of the greatest" (St. Aubyn 1991, 365). Tennyson too was prevailed upon to accept one, from "a very humble and pretending author, the only merit of whose writing was its simplicity and truth" (Dyson and Tennyson 1969, 85).

The controversy over the queen's incursions into authorship was revived when, in 1884, she published a second volume of Highland journals. Coming a year after the death of John Brown, *More Leaves from the Journal of a Life in the Highlands, from 1862 to 1882* was dedicated by the queen "To My Loyal Highlanders and especially to the Memory of my Devoted Personal Attendant and Faithful Friend John Brown" (Kerr 1992, 8). Here once more was a celebration of the lofty feelings and proud independence of the Highland people—down to the lowliest of cottagers. Victoria, convinced that this second volume would, like the first, be a good exercise in public relations, delighted in reporting to Vicky in Prussia that "the enthusiasm and affectionate sympathy with which my book has been received is most touching and gratifying" (20 February 1884, Fulford 1981). There had, she said, "been some 30 or 40 different articles—really beautifully written"(ibid.). Vicky for her part was horrified that *More Leaves* contained endless references to John Brown and laid the queen ever more open to ridicule and to spurious rumor about her relationship with him. The Prince of Wales found the book nothing less than an act of "insanity." Having seen an advance copy, he had written to his mother, informing her quite bluntly about the "grave doubts" he held over whether the confidential details of her "private life . . . should be, as it were, exposed to the world" (Magnus 1964, 178). He had begged her only to circulate it privately. After publication, he complained that he was not mentioned, only to be sent away with a flea in his ear, when the queen brusquely pointed out that "had he been kind enough to read the book carefully," he would have found that he was mentioned on pages "1, 5, 331, and 378" (178).

The British upper classes also turned their noses up at the queen's book; they found the work irredeemably bourgeois, its language trite and its sentiments vulgar, as did the popular journal *Punch,* whose reviewer made the snide pun, "the trait that seems to be the most prominent in her Majesty's book is the Tea-tray" (Jerrold 1916, 87). The publication of *More Leaves from the Journal of a Life in the Highlands* prompted yet more satirical comment, such as the anonymous seventy-seven-page parody "John Brown's Legs, or Leaves from a Journal in the Lowlands," which appeared in New York, bowdlerizing the queen's heartfelt original dedication as "To the memory of those extraordinary legs, poor bruised and scratched darlings"—an allusion to the exposure of the kilted Brown's legs to the elements during pony treks at Balmoral (Jay 1999, 197).

The publication of her two volumes of Scottish journals fostered an erroneous assumption that Queen Victoria was hiding other, as yet undiscovered, literary gifts. In 1888, when Oscar Wilde was editing the journal *Woman's World,* he wrote to the queen soliciting some verses by her for publication. Victoria was greatly annoyed by this; her response was disarmingly honest and categorical: "Really, what will people not say and invent. Never could the Queen in her whole life write *one line* of *poetry* serious or comic or make a *rhyme* ever. This is therefore all *invention* and *myth*" (Jullian 1971, 134). A more stern critic of Victoria's failings as a writer would be the novelist Virginia Woolf, who, in a perceptive if somewhat unforgiving review article of the queen's letters in 1934, wrote that "between the old Queen and the English language lay an abyss which no depth of passion and no strength of character could cross"(Woolf 1992, 155). Criticizing the queen's limited vocabulary, with its "few poverty stricken words . . . bruised and battered; now hooked together with hyphens, now desperately distended with italics and capital letters," Woolf drew attention to the tragic failing of the queen as a writer. "This primitive machine," she concluded, "is all that she has with which to register some of the most extraordinary experiences that ever fell to a woman's lot" (ibid.).

Related entries:
Balmoral Castle; Brown, John; Bruce, Lady Augusta; Churchill, Lady Jane; Fresh Air; Lyttleton, Lady; Scott, Sir Walter

References and further reading:
Dyson, Hope, and Charles Tennyson, eds. 1969. *Dear and Honoured Lady: The Correspondence between Queen Victoria and Alfred, Lord Tennyson.* London: Macmillan.
Fulford, Roger. 1981. *Beloved Mama: Private Correspondence of Queen Victoria and the German Crown Princess, 1878–85.* London: Evans Brothers.
Gernsheim, Helmut, and Alison Gernsheim. 1954. *Victoria R: A Biography in Word and Picture.* London: Longman's Green and Co.
Hibbert, Christopher. 1984. *Queen Victoria in Her Letters and Journals.* London: Viking.
Houston, Gail Turley. 1999. *Royalties: Queen Victoria and Victorian Writers.* Charlottesville: University Press ofVirginia.
Hudson, Derek. 1972. *Munby, Man of Two Worlds: The Life and Diaries of Arthur J. Munby.* London: Abacus.
Jay, Elisabeth. 1999. "'Mrs Brown' by Windsor's Other Widow." *Women's History Review* 6., no.2: 191–200.
Jerrold, Clare. 1916. *The Widowhood of Queen Victoria.* London: Eveleigh Nash.
Jullian, Philippe. 1971. *Oscar Wilde.* London: Paladin.
Kerr, John. 1992. *Queen Victoria's Scottish Diaries: Her Dream Days.* Moffat, Scotland: Lochar Publishing.
Magnus, Philip. 1964. *King Edward the Seventh.* London: Murray.
Martin, Sir Theodore. 1908. *Queen Victoria as I Knew Her.* Edinburgh: William Blackwood and Sons.
Millar, Delia. 1985. *Queen Victoria's Life in the Scottish Highlands.* London: Philip Wilson.
Munich, Adrienne. 1996. *Queen Victoria's Secrets.* New York: Columbia University Press.
Oliphant, Margaret. 1900. *Queen Victoria: A Personal Sketch.* London: Cassell.
St. Aubyn, Giles. 1991. *Victoria, A Portrait.* London: Sinclair Stevenson.
Tooley, Sarah. 1896. *Personal Life of Queen Victoria.* London: Hodder and Stoughton.
Victoria, Queen. 1868. *Leaves from a Journal of our Life in the Highlands, from 1848 to 1861.* Edited by Arthur Helps. London: Smith Elder and Co.
———. 1884. *More Leaves from the Journal of a Life in the Highlands, from 1862 to 1882.* London: Smith, Elder and Co.
Whittle, Tyler. 1980. *Victoria and Albert at Home.* London: Routledge and Kegan Paul
Woolf, Virginia. 1992. *A Woman's Essays.* Harmondsworth, UK: Penguin.
Wyndham, Hon. Mrs. Hugh, ed. 1912. *The Correspondence of Sarah Spencer, Lady Lyttleton, 1787–1870.* London: John Murray.

Lehzen, Baroness Louise (1784–1870)

I owed her much and she adored me (Fulford 1971, 301)

One of the most influential figures in the early life of Princess Victoria, from the age of five until after her marriage to Prince Albert in 1840, was her German governess, Louise Lehzen. To Victoria, who remained in awe—if not in fear—of her, Lehzen was little short of a saint, "my *precious* Lehzen . . . my best and truest friend" (Esher 1912, 1:175). To Prince Albert, however, she was "the old hag" (Charlot 1991, 193) and "a crazy stupid intriguer, obsessed with the lust for power" (Hough 1996, 84). Lehzen was accused by others hostile to her in the royal household of being a highly manipulative personality who was dangerously overfond of gossip.

The woman who graduated from governess to friend and adviser, lady of the bedchamber, and effective domestic secretary to Victoria was born at Langenhagen, near Hanover, one of nine children of a Lutheran clergyman. At the age of thirty-five, on the recommendation of Dr. Kuper, of the German Lutheran Chapel at St.

James's Palace, she was engaged by the duke and duchess of Kent as governess to Victoria's half-sister, Feodora (by her mother's first marriage). She was brought to England to take up her appointment in 1819, just before Victoria was born.

In April 1824, when Victoria was five, Lehzen was promoted to the position of subgoverness to the Princess Victoria. She found herself confronted with a child who had a reputation for being unmanageable but who also impressed her with her most extraordinary candor. A strong personality in her own right, Lehzen resisted the controling influences of the duchess of Kent and her comptroller, Sir John Conroy, instead imposing her own. She could be quite inflexible: not only was Victoria never left on her own at any time, but the books she read, the hobbies she pursued, her every thought, both written and spoken, was scrutinized by Lehzen, as it was also by her mother. But although the duchess's role in her daughter's life might be confined to trivialities such as pinning a sprig of holly on the neck of her dress to make her sit up straight at dinner, it was Lehzen who was the real influence in Victoria's life. In 1827 George IV had conferred the honorary title of Hanoverian baroness on the humble fraülein, in appreciation of Lehzen's services, but also, and more important, in order to provide her with a social standing equivalent to the significance of her role. Such an act of overpromotion rather went to her head, and her overweening manner antagonized other members of the royal household already hostile to her. Lehzen's natural eccentricities would make her a prime target for jokes at her expense, but she was no passive victim of anti-German feeling at court. She responded to the gossips in kind, in later years fueling the queen's unfounded suspicions over the moral conduct of Lady Flora Hastings (see "Hastings, Lady Flora").

From her early childhood on, Victoria had been at the center of intense rivalry for control of her young life, with her mother and Conroy coming into conflict with William IV. They now increasingly also ran up against the fiercely partisan Lehzen, who, having once been passionately defensive of her employer, grew to loathe the duchess for allowing herself to be manipulated by Conroy. Lehzen's self-importance received a knock in 1830, when Victoria's uncle succeeded to the throne as William IV. As it now became even more likely that Victoria would succeed him as monarch, a member of the British aristocracy, the duchess of Northumberland was appointed as Princess Victoria's official governess. But such was the affection in which Victoria held her dear "Daisy," as she called Lehzen, that she was kept on as a lady-in-waiting. Her influence did not diminish; if anything it increased in the face of the duchess's and Sir John Conroy's continuing machinations to gain control as regents.

In 1835, on the occasion of Victoria's sixteenth birthday, when she was to be confirmed in the Church of England, the duchess and Conroy had planned to sack Lehzen. But Victoria fell seriously ill. Lehzen nursed her devotedly through five weeks of recuperation (often as her sole attendant for long hours at a time), making her own position now almost inviolable. After Victoria became queen in 1837, Lehzen, having enjoyed preferential seating at the coronation ceremony, stayed on at court. Although she was not given any official position, she retained considerable influence over the queen's mind and her correspondence, as well as holding sway over her private spending (the Privy Purse). At this stage, the court diarist Charles Greville observed that Lehzen was "the person in the world She [Victoria] loves best" (Strachey and Fulford 1938, 3:394). This was not the case among the ladies at court, whose opinion of Lehzen plummeted after her involvement in the Lady Flora Hastings affair of 1839; Lehzen's involvement in the affair prompted mocking broadsheets and pamphlets, in which she was referred to as "a rouged old woman" and "the Palace washerwoman" (Hudson 1994, 165).

By the time the queen married Prince Albert in February 1840, Lehzen was popularly perceived as the power behind the throne. But everything soon changed with the arrival of the punctilious Albert, who had his own equally controlling and character-building plans for his wife's intellectual improvement. As far as he was concerned, Lehzen was persona non grata. He would not countenance her having direct access into the couple's private suite at Buckingham Palace and was supported in his mistrust of her by his adviser, Baron Stockmar, who found the baroness equally meddlesome and manipulative. Albert viewed Lehzen's ill temper and interfering nature as corrosive—"a house dragon spitting fire" (Gernsheim and Gernsheim 1959, 46). Her predilection for palace gossip and tittle-tattle only reinforced his view of her as a malevolent influence. Albert did his best to drive Lehzen out, but she would have none of it.

With the arrival of her first child and the new preoccupations and strains of motherhood, even Victoria eventually tired of the frequent quarrels with her husband that were sparked by her old governess. And with Prince Albert now initiating a rapprochement between herself and her mother, Victoria realized that the two women would only renew old animosities and provoke more conflict. She had for long indulged Lehzen's interference out of a sense of affection, but now ever more in awe of the gifts and wisdom of her husband, Victoria viewed Lehzen's role as increasingly superfluous. Regretfully she released Lehzen from service, a polite excuse having been found (by Baron Stockmar) to retire her back to Germany in order to recover her "declining health." On 30 September 1842, the fifty-six-year-old Lehzen returned to Hanover, to live on her memories and an £800 a year pension. She shared a small house in Bückeberg with her sister, who soon died, leaving Lehzen, surrounded with photographs and portraits of the royal family. She spent time reminiscing to local professional men, whom she invited for coffee and the finest Havana cigars, the wafting smoke of which reminded her of days gone by. Victoria dutifully wrote to Lehzen every week; with time it became once a month (at Lehzen's request). When the royal train passed through Bückeberg on a visit to Germany in 1842, Lehzen appeared on the platform to wave; but the royal train did not stop for Victoria to greet her. When Lehzen died, the queen expressed her gratitude for her old governess's devotion but nevertheless admitted that "after I came to the throne she got to be rather trying, and especially so after my marriage"(Hibbert 1984, 221). This was not "from any evil intention," she added, "only from a mistaken idea of duty and affection for me" (ibid.).

Related entries:
Conroy, Sir John; Hastings, Lady Flora; Kensington System; Kent, Edward Augustus, Duke of; Kent, Marie Louise Victoire, Duchess of; Stockmar, Christian Friedrich von

References and further reading:

Charlot, Monica. 1991. *Victoria: The Young Queen.* Cambridge: Polity.

Creston, Dormer. 1952. *The Youthful Victoria.* London: Macmillan.

Esher, Viscount, ed. 1912. *The Girlhood of Queen Victoria: A Selection from Her Majesty's Diaries between the Years of 1832 and 1840.* 2 vols. London: John Murray.

Gernsheim, Helmut, and A. Gernsheim. 1959. *Victoria R: A Biography in Word and Picture.* London: Longman's Green and Co.

Hibbert, Christopher. 1984. *Queen Victoria in Her Letters and Journals.* London: Viking.

Hough, Richard. 1996. *Victoria and Albert: Their Love and Their Tragedies.* London: Richard Cohen.

Longford, Elizabeth. [1964] 1998. *Victoria R.I.* London: Weidenfeld and Nicolson.

Hudson, Katherine. 1994. *A Royal Conflict: Sir John Conroy and the Young Victoria.* London: Hodder and Stoughton.

Pearsall, Ronald. 1969. *The Worm in the Bud.* London: Weidenfeld and Nicolson.

Plowden, Alison. 1981. *The Young Victoria.* London: Weidenfeld and Nicolson.

Strachey, Lytton, and Roger Fulford, eds. 1938. *The Grenville Memoirs.* 8 vols. London: Macmillan.

Vallone, Lynne. 2001. *Becoming Victoria.* New Haven: Yale University Press.
Wilson, Philip Whitwell, ed. 1927. *The Greville Diary.* 2 vols. Garden City, NY: Doubleday.
Woodham-Smith, Cecil. 1972. *Queen Victoria: Her Life and Times.* Vol. 1: *1819–1861.* London: Hamish Hamilton.

Leopold I, King of the Belgians (1790–1865)

(Leopold George Christian Frederik of Saxe-Coburg-Saalfeld)

he is indeed like my real father, as I have none (Esher 1912, 1:166)

When, Princess Charlotte, the sole legitimate heir of the Prince Regent (later King George IV) died in childbirth in 1817, her ambitious husband, Leopold of Saxe-Coburg-Saalfeld, was denied the role of consort to a queen that he had so coveted. After his niece Victoria was born in 1819, Leopold was able to vicariously fulfill some of his thwarted ambition, not only by tutoring her for her possible future role as queen but also by quietly grooming her cousin, Albert of Saxe-Coburg-Gotha (his nephew), for the important role of her consort.

Leopold was the youngest son of Francis, duke of Saxe-Coburg-Saalfeld. After serving with the allied armies against Napoleon, he became a figure of note at military assemblies in Paris in 1815, where he sought a dynastic marriage that would best promote his own interests. In 1816 he succeeded in persuading the Prince Regent to accept him as a husband for his only daughter. But the prince disliked his son-in-law, finding his manner irritatingly ingratiating. Disdaining Leopold's cautiousness and indecision, he nicknamed him the Marquis Peu-a-Peu ("the marquis little-by-little"). Others could not conceal their animosity, either; the diarist Creevy called Leopold a "humbug" and the society hostess Princess Lieven found him tiresome.

Leopold presented an exceedingly dull and patrician figure at court. His undoubted political shrewdness and his later talents in diplomacy could not disguise a pedantic, opinionated, and prissy nature, of which Queen Victoria would remain largely uncritical, if not reverential. He remained for her a paragon: a wise counselor, surrogate father, and, until 1831 when he left England to take up the throne of Belgium, one of the few people she could trust.

Leopold's brief marriage to the bright and impetuous Princess Charlotte bore many of the hallmarks of Prince Albert's later reeducation of the young Queen Victoria. He set about taming Charlotte's naturally boisterous nature and no doubt, had she lived, he would, little by little, have drained the vivacity and spirit out of her. When Charlotte died after a protracted labor during which her baby was stillborn and she herself suffered at the hands of incompetent doctors, Leopold had been prostrated by her loss. Having only a string of petty German titles, a generalship in the British army, and the Order of the Garter, he consoled himself with a generous pension from the British government of £50,000 per annum. (When he later became king of the Belgians, he retained £20,000 of it to fund his personal establishment and expenses in England.)

Eventually Leopold found himself a German mistress, the actress Karoline Bauer—a respectable woman and cousin of his adviser, Baron Stockmar. Leopold persuaded Bauer to give up her career and come to live in England. Her mother came too, to add the prerequisite false air of propriety, and the two women were discreetly installed in a villa at Regent's Park. Here Leopold kept Karoline closeted in stultifying boredom, and on a tight budget (he was notoriously penny-pinching), refusing to go out in public with her. The couple's sole recreation consisted in Karoline's reading aloud to Leopold while he cranked away at a "drizzling box"—a then popular device for extracting from tassels, epaulettes, and lace the gold and silver dust that, thus recycled, could then be sold. When Leopold stayed at his other home at Claremont in Surrey, Bauer was kept in strict seclusion in a small house nearby, forbidden contact with the untainted young Princess Victoria, when she came on visits. In 1830, unable to bear it any longer, Bauer escaped back to Germany, where she later published two volumes of memoirs.

It was inevitable that, being brother and adviser to the duchess of Kent and on numerous occasions during her widowhood coming to her financial assistance, Leopold would extend this role to her daughter, Victoria. In some ways Victoria was a substitute for the child he had lost. She also presented him with a challenge similar to the one he had embraced in schooling his headstrong young wife. Leopold was welcomed by Victoria as parental adviser during her years of incarceration at Kensington Palace. She was a receptive audience to his endless homilies on a wealth of topics, remarking that "to hear dear uncle speak on any subject is like reading a highly instructive book" (Hibbert 1984, 19).

In 1829 Leopold's personal fortunes changed when he was offered the vacant throne of a newly independent Greece. On evaluating the political situation, however, he declined. Six months later he had the good fortune to be offered the throne of Belgium. This was a more difficult prospect, in terms of internal religious rivalries between Catholics and Protestants, but one in which he acquitted himself well, from 1831 establishing a stable monarchy and ensuring Belgian neutrality during later periods of turmoil in Europe. For four years after Leopold left England for Belgium, Princess Victoria did not see her uncle. They would maintain a regular and lengthy correspondence until his death in 1865, in which Leopold instructed Victoria on all things European, offering his often lengthy and frequently didactic prognostications on diplomacy, politics, and the art of government. He also found a new role for himself as an international diplomat and, as the queen's children grew up, dynastic marriage broker.

In the latter capacity, Leopold engineered his own second marriage, in 1832, to another prize bride—the vivacious and lovable twenty-year-old Princess Marie Louise, daughter of Louis Philippe of France. It was a cold-blooded and calculating act, seen by Leopold as a way of reconciling Catholic and Protestant factions in Belgium (he was a Lutheran, his wife a devout Catholic). Queen Victoria had a particular and deep affection for Queen Louise, for whose company and many kindnesses Victoria was deeply grateful when the royal couple visited her in England in 1835 and 1837. With Leopold's tight-lipped disapproval of all frivolity and a sober and serious attitude to the burdens of royal duty, the court at Brussels became a somber place. Queen Louise meekly submitted to her duty and devotedly produced four children before dying at the age of thirty-eight in 1850.

Leopold's flair for royal matchmaking was spectacularly successful: in 1836 he negotiated the marriage of one nephew, Ferdinand of Saxe-Coburg, to Dona Maria da Gloria, queen of Portugal; in 1840, that of another, Albert of Saxe-Coburg-Gotha, to his niece Victoria; and in 1864, that of his daughter, Charlotte, to Archduke Maximilian of Austria, later emperor of Mexico. This final sacrificial act of his only daughter to dynastic ambitions ended in tragedy when Maximilian was executed in 1867; Empress Carlotta (as she had become) was unhinged by the event and became a recluse for the rest of her life.

Related entries:
Albert of Saxe-Coburg-Gotha, Prince Consort; "Grandmama of Europe"; Hanover, Royal House of; Kent, Marie Louise Victoire, Duchess of; Saxe-Coburg-Gotha, Royal House of

References and further reading:
Benson, A. C., and Viscount Esher, eds. 1911. *The Letters of Queen Victoria 1837–1861.* 1st ser., 3 vols. London: John Murray.
Charlot, Monica. 1991. *Victoria: The Young Queen.* Cambridge: Polity.
Corti, Count E. 1923. *Leopold of Belgium.* London: Unwin.
Creston, Dormer. 1952. *The Youthful Victoria.* London: Macmillan.
Esher, Viscount, ed. 1912. *The Girlhood of Queen Victoria: A Selection from Her Majesty's Diaries between the Years of 1832 and 1840.* 2 vols. London: John Murray.
Hibbert, Christopher. 1984. *Queen Victoria in Her Letters and Journals.* London: Viking.
Longford, Elizabeth. [1964] 1998. *Victoria R.I.* London: Weidenfeld and Nicolson.
Plowden, Alison. 1981. *The Young Victoria.* London: Weidenfeld and Nicolson.
Richardson, Joanna. 1961. *My Dearest Uncle.* London: Jonathan Cape.
Strachey, Lytton. 1971. *Queen Victoria.* Harmondsworth, UK: Penguin.
Stuart, Dorothy Margaret. 1951. *Daughter of England: A New Study of Princess Charlotte and Her Family.* London: Macmillan.
Vallone, Lynne. 2001. *Becoming Victoria.* New Haven: Yale University Press.
Woodham-Smith, Cecil. 1972. *Queen Victoria: Her Life and Times.* Vol. 1: *1819–1861.* London: Hamish Hamilton.

Leopold George Duncan Albert, Duke of Albany (1853–1884)

the illness of a good child is so far less trying than the sinfulness of one's sons (Zeepvat 2000, 39)

Queen Victoria's fourth son and eighth child, Leopold George Duncan Albert, who was named after her favorite uncle, Leopold, king of the Belgians, lived for only thirty years. He is probably most famous for the circumstances of his birth, for at his delivery on 7 April 1853 Queen Victoria had, for the first time, been administered chloroform by the anesthetist Dr. John Snow, in order to relieve her suffering.

A thin, ugly, and sickly baby, Leopold was not baptized until three months later. He did not take well to his wet nurse and seemed always to be crying. By the time he had begun to crawl and then walk, the child's all too apparent malaise was confirmed as being provoked by a serious disorder. He was constantly bruising himself, and these dark disfigurements were identified by the royal doctors as confirmation that he suffered from the hereditary and little-understood blood disorder of hemophilia.

In the days before the disease could be controlled medically, the prospects for a hemophiliac were extremely poor. And even though the retinue of royal nursemaids and servants could give Leopold the very best chance a few years of life by keeping watch on his every move, it could take only the most insignificant wound or slight knock to provoke internal bleeding that even the finest doctors would not be able to control. Leopold's young life therefore inevitably became "a very tried one"(Longford 1998, 367), as Victoria later described it, blighted by a catalog of life-threatening illnesses and crises—including one in 1868 when he "came back from the brink of the grave" (ibid.).

Queen Victoria was naturally angry at being so cruelly visited upon by fate; all of her other children having been robust, her attitude to her sickly son betrayed a degree of annoyance at his frail condition. Notwithstanding the sense of responsibility she bore, as his mother, for having unwittingly passed on the disease to him, she was patently disappointed at Leopold's poor posture and awkward way of holding himself. In her letters to her daughter Vicky, Victoria was constantly critical of his ugliness, his lisp, his poor French, his "despairing" manners. Leopold's physical shortcomings were extremely vexatious to her. Such was her disappointment in his and his brother Bertie's undistinguished looks that both boys were looked upon as "too frightful" compared to her other, prettier children.

Because of his illness, Leopold became Victoria's "child of anxiety" (Erickson 1997, 140) who would always betray a

Prince Leopold, duke of Albany, Queen Victoria's hemophiliac son, who died at the age of 30 in 1884. (Hulton/Archive by Getty Images)

"restless longing" (Longford 1998, 461) for the things he could never hope to do, a longing that was at times difficult to contain. Unable to join in any sports or games, and not even allowed to take up a normal education, he was forced to live the life of a semi-invalid. His overprotective mother ensured that he was kept constantly in the background, away from excitement, as well as possible royal embarrassment (as some historians have suggested—Victoria's letters to her daughter Vicky certainly endorse this). Leopold was often left behind at Balmoral or Osborne after the family had departed at the end of their annual holiday, or alternatively was packed off to the warmth of the French Riviera in wintertime to avoid succumbing to colds and chills. His sense of isolation and rejection led to a loathing of Balmoral—"that *most vile* and *most abominable* of places" (Zeepvat 2000, 70). In all this, Leopold's one great consolation was books and reading.

The stress and irritability that constant fretting over Leopold's condition induced would spark off numerous passionate rows between the queen and Prince Albert, as they argued over the best way of protecting him against accident and injury. Leopold rebelled against their strict controls over his every waking activity. Despite long periods of being bedridden after attacks of bleeding, he tried hard to live a normal life but inevitably succumbed to bouts of despair and depression, dreading in particular the possibility of a long and painful death. He was keen on the military and wanted to take up his elder brother Bertie's suggestion of commanding a corps of volunteers at Balmoral. Victoria naturally quashed such a suggestion immediately. It took a considerable amount of persuasion before the queen finally allowed Leopold to study at Oxford, albeit with a long list of provisos. Here, despite interruptions of illness and the constant vigilance of his mother's hirelings, he attended lectures in history, languages, and the arts as well as political economy and science. But the constant surveillance exasperated him: "even here . . . I receive bullying *letters* and *telegrams* from 'Home Sweet Home'" (Zeepvat 2000, 90).

At Oxford Leopold demonstrated that he had an agile mind and considerable intellectual gifts. Eventually, the queen recognized that he, of all her sons, had inherited his father's brains as well as his grasp of politics. With time, therefore, Leopold won his mother's approval, by being clever if nothing else. After leaving Oxford he balked at returning once more to a life of inactivity, closely controlled by the queen. He found making himself useful to her as her unofficial private secretary from 1877 onward insufficiently challenging. If given any choice in the matter, he would have liked a peerage and elevation to the House of Lords, which would have enabled him to attend Parliament. But the queen remained adamant; not only did she not wish Leopold to enter public life, but she still resisted his attempts to engage in many social and sporting events.

Leopold finally took his seat in the House of Lords after the queen made him duke of Albany in 1881. He was now anxious to marry, seeing this as his only chance of escaping from the stultifying routine as his mother's factotum. A wife was found for him among the lesser European royalty. He married Princess Helen of the German house of Waldeck-Pyrmont in St. George's Chapel, Windsor, on 27 April 1882. The queen was still reluctant to relinquish her control over Leopold. She was apprehensive that his marriage was "a risk and experiment" (Hibbert 2000, 271) but nevertheless made a gift to the couple of the royal estate at Claremont in Surrey and was surprised and gratified when the couple produced a daughter, Alice, only ten months later.

In March 1884, while on holiday in Cannes, Leopold suffered a fall that resulted in a series of seizures and a brain hemorrhage from which he died on the twenty-eighth, a few days before his thirty-first birthday. The queen wanted to have him laid to rest with his father in the royal mausoleum at Frogmore but nevertheless acceded to his wish that he be buried in military uniform at St. George's Chapel, Windsor. Leopold's widow and children (a son was born posthumously in 1884) spent a good deal of time with the queen and were the source of much happiness to her in her final years. Leopold and Helen's daughter, Princess Alice of Albany, later Countess of Athlone, lived until 1981—the last to die of the great European dynasty of forty grandchildren descended from Queen Victoria.

Related entries:
Hemophilia; Sex, Pregnancy, and Childbirth

References and further reading:
Bennett, Daphne. 1980. *Queen Victoria's Children.* London: Gollancz.
Erickson, Carolly. 1997. *Her Little Majesty.* London: Robson.
Fulford, Roger. 1964. *Dearest Child: Letters between Queen Victoria and the Princess Royal 1858–1861.* London: Evans Brothers.
Hibbert, Christopher. 2000. *Victoria: A Personal History.* London: HarperCollins.
Jones, Steve. 1996. *In the Blood.* London: HarperCollins.
Longford, Elizabeth. [1964] 1998. *Victoria R.I.* London: Weidenfeld and Nicolson.
Potts, D. M., and W. T. W. Potts. 1995. *Queen Victoria's Gene: Haemophilia and the Royal Family.* Stroud, Gloucestershire: Sutton.
Reid, Michaela. 1996. *Ask Sir James: The Life of Sir James Reid, Personal Physician to Queen Victoria.* London: Eland.
Van Der Kiste, John. 1986. *Queen Victoria's Children.* Stroud, Gloucestershire: Sutton.
Zeepvat, Charlotte. 2000. *Prince Leopold: The Untold Story of Queen Victoria's Youngest Son.* Stroud, Gloucestershire: Sutton.

Louise Caroline Alberta, Princess (1848–1939)

(Marchioness of Lorne; from 1900, Duchess of Argyll)

so very difficile (Packard 1998, 134)

Born in 1848, the year of revolutions in Europe, Princess Louise (she was christened Louisa), the queen's fourth daughter and sixth child, proved to be the most difficult and troubled of all the royal princesses. Without doubt the most beautiful, artistic, and fashionable of the five girls, she exceeded even her gifted elder sister Vicky in her considerable artistic skills, becoming a talented sculptress. Like Vicky also, Louise could be temperamental and headstrong. As a determined individualist, she did all she could to avoid having to put up with the stuffy routine at court, which she so despised. She had a knack of self-concealment and, because she was childless, she remained far more independent of her mother than her other sisters, whose own ties of motherhood bound them naturally more closely to the queen. As she grew older, Louise became notable for her waspish manner and her sharp tongue. Her spiteful remarks and verbal indiscretions infuriated the queen, as did Louise's often moody behavior, so much so that her mother at one point came to the conclusion that Louise was "very odd, dreadfully contradictory, very indiscreet" (Fulford 1971, 114).

The queen was delighted with Louise when she was born and pronounced her the most "delicious" baby. As a small child she continued to please by being easy and amiable and conforming to the behavior expected of her. But there were always occasional displays of naughtiness that testified to a rebellious spirit. The queen responded to such tantrums, as she did with all her children, by trying to stifle such unruly manifestations of independence. Louise knuckled under and learned to be polite and ladylike to please her mother, but the queen never eradicated her individuality, which shone out in Louise's artistic gifts. These were nurtured by her drawing teacher, Edward Corbould, from a very early age, although there was no question of Louise's being allowed to follow an artistic career. The map of her life, as a daughter, was already defined: to marry, and to marry well.

But first it fell to Louise's lot, in 1866, to take the place as her mother's companion when her third sister, Helena, married. Forced to endure the monotonous pilgrimages to Balmoral and Osborne, and isolation from the intellectual and artistic world she longed to be part of, she was even denied the pleasure by her mother—who still was in deep mourning—of her own coming-out ball at Buckingham Palace when she reached the age of eighteen in 1865. Louise managed to contain her frustrations and remain amiable and companionate, until her twentieth birthday, upon which, longing to further her interests in art—particularly sculpture—she begged the queen to at least allow her to study part-time at the National Art Training School in Kensington (later the Royal College of Art). Here, she came under the tutelage of the queen's sculptor-in-ordinary, Sir Joseph Edgar Boehm, who also became a close friend until his death in 1890 (in later years there were rumors that the relationship went beyond friendship). Marble busts executed by Louise of her brother Arthur and her mother were both exhibited at the Royal Academy in the late 1860s and commended for their skill.

By now the queen had begun planning Louise's marriage in earnest. She was certainly most attractive—always immaculately dressed and with a slender figure—unlike her dumpy sisters Victoria, Helena, and Beatrice, who had all inherited their mother's physique. Her sister Vicky from Berlin eagerly put forward her own preferences. Princes from Prussia, Denmark, and the Netherlands all were taken into consideration but rejected because none of them would be prepared to accede to Victoria's demand that they live in Britain with her after their marriage. Victoria eventually surprised everyone by agreeing to Louise's own choice, John Douglas Sutherland Campbell, marquess of Lorne, heir to the duke of Argyll. Goodlooking and boasting a mop of blond hair and blue eyes, Lorne shared an interest in the arts and literature with Louise and was an aspiring poet. As a grandson of the queen's late mistress of the robes, the duchess of Sutherland, he came of proud Scottish lineage; but he was not a prince of the blood.

Queen Victoria thought Lorne eminently suitable, even though he was a commoner, although she disliked his affected Etonian drawl. With the supply of solvent princes in Europe almost exhausted and the British public in any event hostile to the idea of yet another German marrying into the royal family, she agreed to the match, which proved to be popular—until the queen applied to Parliament for a £30,000 dowry for Louise provoking considerable opposition, before it was agreed. Louise was thus the first royal daughter to marry a subject of the sovereign (rather than a foreign prince) since the reign of Henry VII in 1515.

Louise and Lorne were married just after her twenty-first birthday in 1871. The couple initially had a home in London's select district of Belgravia, and later a country residence in Tunbridge Wells, Kent, as well as spending time in Scotland at the family seat, Inverary Castle. But financial constraints led to them to accept the queen's offer of apartments at Kensington Palace in 1875, which remained their main home thereafter. Lorne had been elected as a Liberal member of Parliament in 1868 (to 1878) and had a varied and liberal mix of friends from the world of politics and art. With her elder sisters Vicky and Alice, Louise shared an interest in women's rights, philanthropy, and nursing, although her political views remained generally conservative, and she never became involved in the women's suffrage campaign. She did, however, correspond with social reformers such as Elizabeth Garrett Anderson and Josephine Butler and was a devoted fan of the writer George Eliot. She was a patron of the uncontroversial Ladies' Work Society—which provided poor women with a living from dressmaking and ornamental needlework. In the main, however, Louise channeled her energies into fervent support for women's education, and in particular the teaching of art, not just in schools but also through the Home Arts and Industries Association as a "recreational hobby" (Anderson 2002, 10). In 1872 she encouraged the establishment of the National Union for the Higher Education of Women and served as its first president. She promoted the work of girls' secondary schools through her many public speeches and articles and, with her husband, in 1875 was a founder of the Girls' Public Day School Company. In 1887 Louise accepted the vice presidency of the newly founded Kyrle Society, established to "disseminate a love of beauty by decorating public spaces" and became its president in 1900 (ibid.).

In 1878 Lorne was appointed governor-general of Canada, the idea coming from Benjamin Disraeli, eager to please the queen and to extend the parameters of royal statecraft by assigning a member of her family to a role in the colonies that would bring kudos to the British crown. At their residence, Rideau Hall, in Ottawa, Louise soon put her artistic talents and good taste to work improving the interior decorations. Summer months were spent in Quebec city, where Louise also did much painting and sketching in the vicinity. But in February 1880 she was involved in a serious accident, when her sleigh overturned, and she was dragged for a hundred yards. This left her with serious head injuries, and she was plagued by severe headaches for the rest of her life.

Louise had quickly tired of the narrowness of colonial life in Canada and the tedious round of official receptions. Her natural reserve had always made her fight shy of being in the public eye, and she disliked being photographed. The injuries she received in the accident now gave her an excuse to flee the bleak, freezing winter in Ottawa. She left to recuperate in Bermuda, and from there returned to England. There may also have been deeper personal reasons for her desire to get away from a marriage that probably was not sexually fulfilling. She contrived to stay away for almost two years, finally returning to Canada in October 1883, shortly before Lorne completed his five-year tenure.

Meanwhile, in 1882 when the Northwest territories of Canada were given new, official names, Lorne named the Province of Alberta after Louise—at her specific request honoring her late father by using her second name. Lorne fulfilled his duties in Canada in an honorable but uninspired manner. He established, with Louise, the Royal Canadian Academy of the Arts, the Canadian National Gallery, and a Royal Society. But by the time they returned to England, it was clear that the couple had become estranged from each other. They established an acceptable modus vivendi in their private apartments at Kensington Palace that allowed them to lead separate lives while remaining married, but they gave few parties. Eschewing the social round, Louise found renewed satisfaction in her art and sculpture, her home at Kensington Palace becoming a venue for her artistic and bohemian friends, including the painter Sir Lawrence Alma-Tadema and her mentor, Sir Joseph Edgar Boehm.

Louise continued to fulfill her public duties, as well as engaging in much philanthropic work relating to the care of army veterans and convalescents. She also undertook welfare work for women and children—such as through her support for the National Society for the Protection of Young Girls. The Princess Louise Home for Girls and the Princess Louise Nurses for Children both resulted from her interests in this regard. She often traveled to the Continent (using aliases such as Mrs. Campbell or Lady Sundridge) and continued to stay determinedly out of the public eye, in a desire perhaps to avoid gossip about the true nature of her relationship with her husband. The subject remained a thorny one, on which Louise remained tight lipped, although she did come to confide some of her unhappiness to her friend, the queen's physician Sir James Reid. On family gatherings at Balmoral and Osborne, her boredom and restlessness led her into flirtations with male members of the royal household, such as the queen's assistant private secretary, Arthur Bigge, and her brother-in-law Henry of Battenberg (although Louise privately complained that he had made advances to her). The impression Reid leaves of Louise in his memoirs is of a life tinged with unaccountable bitterness that turned at times to spite. She undoubtedly had a dangerous sexual edge that had aroused the jealousy of her sisters Helena and Beatrice and provoked quarrels with the latter, who ran and told tales to the queen.

When Louise sanctioned an official biography, published in 1940, she ensured that its author, David Duff, produced a sanitized work that papered over the cracks and evaded any discussion of the persistent rumors about her marriage and the duke's homosexuality (which apparently had been the reason why the Prince of Wales had opposed the match). Despite their physical estrangement from each other, the couple became reconciled in their final years. When Lorne died of pneumonia in 1914, Louise genuinely mourned his loss. Outliving him by twenty-five years, she became reclusive, much in the manner of her own mother before her, retreating to her Scottish home, Roseneath House in Dumbartonshire. Here she took great pride in the Argyll and Sutherland Highlanders of whom she was appointed colonel in chief in 1919. When she died at the age of ninety-one at the outbreak of World War II, Louise was cremated and her ashes interred in the Frogmore Royal Burial Ground. She left behind some commendable sculptures, including a fine marble statue of her mother in her coronation robes, which was erected overlooking the round pond in Kensington Gardens, and another statue of the queen that was sent to Montreal, Quebec. Of Queen Victoria's nine children, Louise was the only one not to have children. She had sought cures in European spas for this and menstrual problems in the 1870s, but it is probable that she had been left infertile by an attack of tubercular meningitis in 1864.

Related entries:
Alice Maud Mary, Princess; Arthur, Prince; Battenberg, Henry Maurice, Prince of; Beatrice Mary Victoria Feodore, Princess; Bigge, Lieutenant Colonel Sir Arthur; Frogmore; Helena Augusta Victoria, Princess; Sutherland, Duchess of; Women's Rights; Victoria Adelaide Mary Louise, Princess Royal

References and further reading:
Anderson, Anne. 2002. "Queen Victoria's Daughters and 'The Tide of Fashionable Philanthropy.'" *Women's History Magazine* 41 (June): 10–15.
Bennett, Daphne. 1980. *Queen Victoria's Children.* London: Gollancz.
Benson, E. F. 1938. *Queen Victoria's Daughters.* London: Cassell.
Duff, David. 1940. *The Life Story of HRH Princess Louise, Duchess of Argyll.* Bath, UK: Cedric Chivers.
Eilers, Marlene A. 1997. *Queen Victoria's Descendants.* Falkoping, Sweden: Rosvall Royal Books.
Epton, Nina. 1971. *Victoria and Her Daughters.* London: Weidenfeld and Nicolson.
Fulford, Roger, ed. 1971. *Your Dear Letter: Private Correspondence of Queen Victoria and the Crown Princess of Prussia, 1865–71.* London: Evans Brothers.
Longford, Elizabeth, ed. 1991. *Darling Loosy: Letters to Princess Louise 1858–1939.* London: Weidenfeld and Nicolson.
Packard, Jerrold M. 1998. *Victoria's Daughters.* New York: St. Martin's Press.
Prole, Lozania. 1973. *The Queen's Daughters.* London: Robert Hale.
Stamp, Robert M. 1988. *Royal Rebels: Princess Louise and the Marquis of Lorne.* Toronto: Dundurn Press.
Van der Kiste, John. 1986. *Queen Victoria's Children.* Stroud, Gloucestershire: Sutton.
Wake, Jehanne. 1988. *Princess Louise: Queen Victoria's Unconventional Daughter.* London: Collins.

Lyttleton, Lady (1787–1870)

(Lady Sarah Spencer)

Lady Lyttleton is of course perfection (Charlot 1991, 218)

Appointed in 1838, not long after the queen's accession, as one of the eight ladies of the bedchamber, Lady Sarah Lyttleton was placed in charge of Queen Victoria's maids of honor. In 1842 she was promoted to lady superintendent of the royal nursery shortly after the birth of the Prince of Wales. From this position she had a guiding influence on the formative years of the first royal children, as their much-loved "Laddle," developing a particular affection for the Prince of Wales.

Lyttleton's appointment came at a time when Prince Albert had been reorganizing the royal household. He and the queen had been dissatisfied with the then nursery superintendent, Mrs. Southey, who proved unable to cope, and Lyttleton had been suggested for the post by Prince Albert's adviser Baron Stockmar, who deemed her of sufficient rank and maturity to undertake the role. And indeed Lyttleton's pedigree was impeccable: daughter of the second Earl Spencer, she came from one of England's leading aristocratic families and had grown up on the family estate at Althorp. She was related to the prime minister, Lord Melbourne (a cousin of his wife), and had married the third Lord Lyttleton in 1813, by whom she had five children. More important, she was also a Whig lady, and thus her political loyalties would not be in question. Widowed in 1837, and with the Lyttleton estate now about to pass to her eldest son, the post with the royal household came at an opportune time for her, for it provided a salary of £500 per annum. Although grateful and flattered to be asked to take on such an important role, Lyttleton had the self-possession to set out a detailed job description that was agreed upon jointly by her and the royal couple. This upheld her sole authority regarding matters to do with the nursery, down to selecting the clothes that the children wore, and it also underlined her requirement of full and regular consultation with the queen and Prince Albert over any problems that might arise.

The royal couple, although at first apprehensive as to whether they had made the right choice, quickly concurred that Lyttleton was perfect for the job. They would take her advice on many decisions regarding the children, although they later modified their unqualified admiration in light of Lady Lyttleton's observance of High Church ritual, such as taking communion. Although the royal children's education, as they passed from babyhood, was the province of their various tutors and governesses, Lady Lyttleton oversaw their diet, health, and day-to-day well-being. It soon became apparent that the lively and intelligent eldest child, Vicky the Princess Royal, was the apple of her father's eye and shared his intellect and that both parents despaired of their eldest son, the Prince of Wales. Lyttleton took pity on the young prince and would pay particular attention to his emotional needs at a time when his exacting parents did nothing but criticize. Where Victoria and Albert saw only weakness of character, an inability to concentrate, and lack of academic achievement, the more compassionate Lyttleton looked always for the Prince of Wales's good points. Like him, she disliked the harsh, Germanic discipline imposed by Prince Albert. She warmed to Bertie's natural affability and gregariousness; she had the intuition to observe that although he was a slow learner, he was nevertheless "passionate and determined enough for an autocrat" (Charlot 1991, 279). An exasperated Victoria, however, did nothing but reiterate her son's shortcomings in her daily journal entries.

In the spring of 1849 Lyttleton's protective influence over the prince was removed, when a personal tutor, Henry Birch, was appointed to drill him for his future role as king. Lyttleton witnessed with dismay Bertie's painful struggle to absorb an unforgiving daily curriculum. A year later, she regretfully handed in her notice, when, on the death of her daughter Lavinia in childbirth, Lyttleton felt she must leave to go and care for Lavinia's four children. Lyttleton's rich observations of life at court were recorded in her witty letters, which provide some valuable insights into the royal family in the 1840s. She came to greatly admire Prince Albert and was one of the first to record the melancholy side to his personality, observing his love of music and how, when he played the organ, it afforded him an escape from the stresses of family and official life: "Nobody but the organ knows what is in him, except, indeed [*sic*] by the look of his eyes sometimes" (Wyndham 1912, 348) As regards the queen, it was the perceptive Lyttleton who made the classic observation that "a vein of iron runs through her most extraordinary character" (348).

Related entries:
Albert Edward, Prince of Wales; The Royal Household; Sex, Pregnancy, and Childbirth

References and further reading:

Askwith, Betty. 1975. *The Lyttletons: A Family Chronicle of the Nineteenth Century.* London: Chatto & Windus.
Charlot, Monica. 1991. *Victoria: The Young Queen.* Cambridge: Polity.
Longford, Elizabeth. [1964] 1998. *Victoria R.I.* London: Weidenfeld and Nicolson.
St. Aubyn, Giles. 1991. *Queen Victoria: A Portrait.* London: Sinclair Stevenson.
Van Der Kiste, John. 1986. *Queen Victoria's Children.* Stroud, Gloucestershire: Sutton.
Woodham-Smith, Cecil. 1972. *Queen Victoria: Her Life and Times.* Vol. 1: *1819–1861.* London: Hamish Hamilton.
Wyndham, Hon. Mrs. H., ed. 1912. *The Correspondence of Sarah Spencer, Lady Lyttleton.* London: Longmans.

M

Melbourne, William Lamb, Second Viscount (1779–1848)

I feel so safe when he speaks to me and is with me (Esher 1912, 1:254)

In June 1837, the charming and worldly elder statesman Lord Melbourne, now aged fifty-eight, had no doubt been entertaining the prospect of a tranquil and uncontroversial last few years of political life. He had never been one to relish its stresses and strains, which, with his sardonic humor, he admitted as being "a damned bore" (Wyndham Lewis 1948, 63). With the accession of Queen Victoria in 1837, however, he found himself, as prime minister, entrusted with a unique and challenging new duty, defined by Charles Greville as "to educate, instruct and form the most interesting mind and character in the world" (Strachey and Fulford 1938, 4: 93). During the first four years of the queen's reign, the aging Melbourne would find his energies drained in his fulfillment of the roles of surrogate father, mentor, and romantic admirer; he did so with consummate skill, tact, and tolerance.

That he managed to overcome his own at times incapacitating inertia and disinterest to take on the political indoctrination of an untrained eighteen-year-old queen is all the more commendable in a melancholy skeptic such as Melbourne. For he was a product of the Regency—an era in which indolence and self-indulgence had been transmuted into a fine art by his society associates such as the dandy Beau Brummell and the Prince Regent. Never needing to work, and entering Parliament almost by default in 1806 (his mother employed her social connections to obtain the seat for him through her friend Charles James Fox), Melbourne developed a penchant for wasting time in the most pleasant and effortless manner. He disdained nepotism and displays of self-seeking and only reluctantly accepted the Order of the Garter when offered it by the queen. One of his greatest pleasures was to lounge or pleasantly drowse in one of his clubs—Brooks or the Reform—or indulge in gossip at such social watering holes as Holland House and Devonshire House. But now, hauled out of his time and his milieu, he found his attentions commandeered by a bright, eager, and questioning young mind that constantly demanded the answers to the most wide-ranging questions.

Educated at Eton and Cambridge University, Melbourne had briefly toyed with a career at the bar before entering Parliament. Had he had ambitions, he might have been a classical scholar or a theologian, such was his passion for reading and his fine intellect. But his natural indolence drew him instead into the aimless life of a socialite. In 1805 he married the highly strung Lady

An unusual early image of the young Queen Victoria, soon after her accession in 1837, out riding with her prime minister, Lord Melbourne on her right, and another, earlier, prime minister, Lord Grey, on her left. (Hulton/Archive by Getty Images)

Caroline Ponsonby, the daughter of the earl of Bessborough, and in 1812–1813 suffered the gossip and humiliation of her very public and histrionic affair with Lord Byron. Despite his own reputation for lax morals and an eye for the ladies, Melbourne endured twenty years of misery, refusing to separate from his mentally unstable wife until 1825. His life would be forever blighted by the fact that of their three children, two died in infancy and the third—Augustus—was a mentally handicapped and epileptic who died at the age of nineteen.

In Parliament, Melbourne served as chief secretary for Ireland, 1827–1828, under George Canning and his successor, Earl Grey, but Melbourne's Whig loyalties were in fact conservative in the extreme. In 1828, unexpectedly inheriting the title of Second Viscount Melbourne (his elder brother had died), his financial future was secured, and he continued in government as home secretary (1830–1834) under Grey. During this ministry Melbourne demonstrated the limits to his sense of democracy, responding to civil upheaval in the only way he knew how—by sending in the military. He abhorred political reform and liked "what is tranquil and stable" (Aronson 1991, 17); he rode out these difficult years by applying his own form of minimalist government, which was to preserve the status quo. He dealt harshly with radical discontent among farm laborers protesting the introduction of mechanization in 1830 and was equally repressive during the unstable period that witnessed the rise of Chartism and the escalation in agitation against the unpopular Corn Laws. He passed on his belief that political unrest was incited by a handful of radicals to the impressionable young Queen Victoria. Supremely indifferent to the fate of the socially underprivileged, he also believed that the sufferings of the poor were overstated. But although his own sense of social justice was beyond redemption and was a reflection of his detached and sardonic view of life, the unquestioning way in which the queen absorbed these views has been seen as probably the most damaging legacy of Melbourne's otherwise exemplary tutelage.

During the first months of her reign, and for an average of six hours a day in his company, Queen Victoria hung on Melbourne's every word. She admired many things in her handsome "Lord M," as she came to call him, especially his affectionate nature, his fine intellect, his moral guidance, and his honesty. In her own cloistered life till then, without a father and constrained by a domineering mother, she had known no real affection, except from her governess, Baroness Lehzen. When she had done with her daily interrogations on matters of government, the energetic, young Victoria would expect the weary Melbourne to join her on long rides—often for three hours at a time and mostly at an exhilarating gallop. For the urbane Melbourne, used to his club and sophisticated society, evenings spent in the drawing room of Buckingham Palace were a crippling bore. Forbidden absolutely from lingering, after dinner, over the port with male members of the household, he found himself obliged to indulge the queen's childish interests. Forced to sit up in straight chairs, he looked at picture albums, listened to the queen sing, or played cards, charades, or draughts—even, heaven help him at his age—exerting himself in a game of shuttlecock. When Melbourne was finally allowed home to his bed, the queen would record in meticulous detail his every observation on subjects such as politics, constitutional government, religion, education, slavery, social welfare, and even the queen's Hanoverian forebears. She noted his likes and dislikes in reading matter and music, as well as his abhorrence of boiled mutton and rice pudding, and reveled in his humorous anecdotes, his effortless aphorisms, and his perceptive observations on social behavior and good manners. Melbourne, with his vast experience, his sophistication, and his powers of observation, channeled through Victoria's receptive mind the accumulated wisdom and observations of a lifetime. Those who witnessed them in conversation together complained that his responses to the queen's questions were too often rather flippant—that he spent too much time joking and relating anecdotes instead of opining on more serious matters of state—but it was clear that he had a unique influence over the queen, like that of a royal protector or regent.

Their close working relationship finally came to an end in August 1841, when Melbourne's weak ministry finally fell over the repeal of the Corn Laws. A year later Melbourne suffered a stroke, and during the last six years of his life he became increasingly disconsolate and physically frail. The queen's marriage to Prince Albert in 1840 had done a great deal to dilute his influence, with Albert now not only supplanting Melbourne in the queen's affections but also taking over her continuing indoctrination in the principles of good government. For a while Melbourne and the queen corresponded regularly, but by 1845 this came to an end when the queen's adviser, Baron Stockmar, deemed such intimate contact with her former minister as being politically "irregular" and persuaded her of its undesirability. By this time, in any event, the queen had distanced herself from her former frivolous life of dancing, staying up late, and indulging in gossip—such as she had enjoyed with Melbourne. With a new-found air of seriousness and moral piety, she now frowned on Melbourne and the dissipations of his generation. Melbourne himself genuinely missed the queen's presence, as he might that of a much-loved daughter. He had never considered his task in tutoring her an onerous one and later admitted to the queen that during their four-year association he had come to like their daily meetings better with each day that passed. In 1848 Melbourne suffered a final, crippling stroke and retreated to the solitude of his country home, Brocket Hall in Hertfordshire. It was the court diarist Charles Greville who most compassionately summed up the fundamental sadness in Melbourne's character: "He is a man with a capacity for loving without anything to love" (Strachey and Fulford 1938, 4: 93). For her part, the queen, now consumed with the preoccupations of husband and family, although commending Melbourne's attachment to *her* and his nobility of character, observed that he had been "not a firm Minister" (Hibbert 1984, 79).

Related entries:
Bedchamber Crisis; Class; Chartism; Peel, Sir Robert; Stockmar, Christian Friedrich von

References and further reading:

Aronson, Theo. 1991. *Heart of a Queen: Queen Victoria's Romantic Attachments.* London: John Murray.

Cecil, Algernon. 1953. *Queen Victoria and Her Prime Ministers.* London: Eyre and Spottiswoode.

Cecil, David. 1954. *Lord M.: Or the Later Life of Lord Melbourne.* London: Constable.

Eccleshall, Robert, and Graham Walker. 1998. *Biographical Dictionary of British Prime Ministers.* London: Routledge.

Esher, Viscount, ed. 1912. *The Girlhood of Queen Victoria: A Selection from Her Majesty's Diaries between the Years of 1832 and 1840.* 2 vols. London: John Murray.

Hibbert, Christopher. 1984. *Queen Victoria in Her Letters and Journals.* London: Viking.

Kreigel, A., ed. 1977. *The Holland House Diaries.* London: Routledge.

Mandler, Peter. 1990. *Aristocratic Government in the Age of Reform.* Oxford: Clarendon Press.

Marshall, D. 1975. *Lord Melbourne.* London: Weidenfeld and Nicolson.

Mitchell, L. G. 1997. *Lord Melbourne, 1779–1848.* Oxford: Oxford University Press.

St. Aubyn, Giles. 1991. *Queen Victoria: A Portrait.* London: Sinclair Stevenson.

Strachey, Lytton. 1971. *Queen Victoria.* Harmondsworth, UK: Penguin.

Strachey, Lytton, and Roger Fulford, eds. 1938. *The Greville Memoirs.* London: Macmillan.

Wyndham Lewis, D. B. 1948. *Four Favourites.* London: Evans Brothers.

Ziegler, Philip. 1976. *Melbourne.* London: Collins.

The Munshi (1863–1909)

(Hafiz Abdul Karim)

to make out that he is so low *is really outrageous* (Ponsonby 1942, 131)

After the death of her loyal Scottish servant John Brown in 1883, no one, it seemed, would ever be able to replace him as Queen Victoria's trusted confidant and adviser. The role of secretary-cum-general factotum for several years devolved to her youngest daughter, Beatrice, who now seemed condemned to becoming her widowed mother's spinsterly companion. But eventually even the dutiful Beatrice found herself a husband. The aging Victoria, with all her children now grown up and married, and feeling herself lost and rudderless, despaired of finding a reliable helpmate. But her Golden Jubilee in 1887 brought with it much celebration in her Indian empire and the arrival at court of two new Indian servants—Mahomet Baksh and Abdul Karim.

The queen enjoyed being waited on by these tall, handsome, and exotically turbaned manservants, and before long they were enjoying special privileges, such as attending her during drives in her carriage (a role usually performed by immediate members of the family or ladies-in-waiting). Of the two, the queen's favorite, Karim, seemed to her to be rather too dignified for the role of mere servant, and he soon ceased to undertake the menial tasks of waiting on the queen at mealtimes. Desirous of learning more about the Indian subcontinent over which she reigned, the queen enlisted him, as her personal Indian clerk, with the task of teaching her Hindustani and educating her in Indian culture.

Now referred to by her as "the Munshi" (teacher), Karim found himself at the head of a growing retinue of his own countrymen. One of his earliest roles had been to bring Victoria her letters and dispatch boxes every morning; soon he was assisting the queen in dealing with correspondence relating to Indian affairs. Those surrounding Victoria at court soon became alarmed at the degree of trust and confidentiality she invested in the Munshi; the obvious parallels with her former close relationship with John Brown set alarm bells ringing in many people's minds. But although the basic integrity of Brown had never been in doubt despite his love of whiskey and his frequent outbursts of bullish bad temper, many suspected the Munshi of being a manipulative, if not sinister, influence over the queen. Aspersions were cast on the Munshi's claim to being the son of an Indian surgeon general from Agra. The queen rejected these doubts, seeing to it personally that his father, and indeed several female "relatives' (the Munshi probably had more than one wife), were afforded every hospitality on visits to England.

The Munshi was eventually granted the use of private cottages on the queen's estates at Windsor, Osborne, and Balmoral. She preempted numerous subversive attempts by her staff to sideline the Munshi at formal occasions, but resentment if not open hostility toward him grew, to the point where Victoria's own doctor admitted that she was "quite off her head" about him (Aronson, 1991, 234). Rumors abounded that the Munshi had glossed over the truth of his humble origins, and when this was investigated, it turned out that his father was merely an unqualified hospital assistant in a prison. When the evidence was presented to her, Victoria insisted it was false. She appeared to be oblivious to the insidious personality at work behind the Munshi's ingratiating manner. Now comfortably fat and excessively self-important, the Munshi was almost universally loathed. Much of the antipathy toward him was undoubtedly bound up in the racial attitudes of the times, but nothing could disguise the fact that he was taking increasing liberties in his insistence on special treatment as the queen's right-hand man. He pushed this insistence to its limits on the occasion of the wedding of her granddaughter, Victoria of Saxe-Coburg, in 1894. After protracted negotiations, at the queen's insistence and much to the bride's father's dismay, the Munshi was given a seat at the wedding ceremony. Affronted to find, however, that he had not been seated with the most important guests in accordance with his own inflated sense of status, but in the gallery with other servants, the Munshi departed in a rage. Victoria later wrote a groveling apology to him.

As the century drew to a close the Munshi had assumed an almost godlike, ubiquitous presence, forever hovering around the queen, resplendent in his Indian robes. His access to confidential documents pertaining to Indian affairs was now shared by his close friend, Rafiuddin Ahmed, whose integrity Victoria accepted without question and whom she even suggested for a post at the British embassy in Constantinople. The slow-burning fuse of resentment against the Munshi finally touched off a major confrontation when, in 1897, he was due to accompany Queen Victoria on a holiday to Cimiez in the south of France. The male members of the royal household, on discovering that the Munshi would take his meals with them, protested; the queen was forced to relent. By now hostility toward the Munshi was such that even her son, the Prince of Wales, was bent on securing his downfall. Intelligence reports from India were secured, confirming the Munshi's less than genteel background and possible links with the subversive Muslim Patriotic League through his friend Ahmed. The queen dug her heels in and refused to acknowledge any blot on his character. After years of repeated accusations made against him, one wonders whether, privately, she might have begun to doubt her own judgment of the Munshi's character. As she became older and more frail, Victoria seemed to cling increasingly to the sense of security provided by his domineering presence. She remained unshakable—a reflection of her long love affair with India—in her obstinate refusal to tolerate racial hatred of any kind manifested toward the Munshi and her other Indian servants.

When Victoria finally died in 1901, the Munshi was allowed to pay his last respects at her open coffin, before being commanded by Victoria's heir, Edward VII, to burn all letters he had received from the queen. He was swiftly removed from his comfortable sinecure in the royal household and pensioned off to a cottage back in India, where he died in 1909.

Related entries:
Brown, John; Empress of India; Racial and Religious Prejudice

References and further reading:
Ansand, Sushila. 1996. *Indian Sahib: Queen Victoria's Dear Abdul.* London: Duckworth.
Aronson, Theo. 1991. *The Heart of a Queen.* London: John Murray.
Erickson, Carolly. 1997. *Her Little Majesty.* London: Robson.
Hibbert, Christopher. 2000. *Queen Victoria: A Personal History.* London: HarperCollins.
Lutyens, Mary, ed. 1961. *Lady Lytton's Court Diary.* London: Rupert Hart-Davis.
Ponsonby, Arthur. 1942. *Henry Ponsonby.* London: Macmillan.
Reid, Michaela. 1996. *Ask Sir James: The Life of Sir James Reid, Personal Physician to the Queen.* London: Eland.
St. Aubyn, Giles. 1991. *Queen Victoria: A Portrait.* London: Sinclair Stevenson.

N

Napoleon III, Emperor of France (1808–1873)

(Charles-Louis-Napoleon Bonaparte)

my dearest and most intimate ally (Bresler 1999, 283)

harles-Louis-Napoleon Bonaparte, who, as president of the Second Republic of France promoted himself to Emperor Napoleon III in 1852, attempted to repeat history by emulating the ambitious foreign policy and military campaigning of his illustrious uncle Napoleon Bonaparte. This small man, with his large nose and legs too short for his upper torso, was a somewhat prissy, dandified figure. Yet, with his exaggerated, waxed moustaches and rouged cheeks, he won himself many lovers—and admirers, including the queen. He had a reputation for a strong sexual appetite throughout his life and produced numerous illegitimate children. His skills as a ladies' man were employed with great success when he came to England on a state visit in 1855, during which, despite the queen's inbred Francophobia and her initial mistrust, he established a close and affectionate relationship with her that would greatly perplex her ministers.

The debonair ladies' man Napoleon III, emperor of France, beguiled the impressionable young Queen Victoria on his state visit to England in 1855. (Library of Congress)

It is not difficult to fathom the nature of Napoleon's attraction for Queen Victoria. There was about the emperor a grand and romantic sense of his own destiny that appealed to the impressionable Victoria. His persuasive cosmopolitan charm was a quality the more dour Albert lacked. Born in Paris, the third son of Napoleon's brother, Louis, he grew up in exile in Switzerland after the entire Bonaparte family were banished from France at the end of the Napoleonic Wars. Longing to be restored to his patrimony, he nursed a romantic sense of mission to restore Bonapartism in France and once more lead a great nation. When Napoleon Bonaparte's only son died in 1832, Louis Napoleon considered himself to be the rightful heir to the French throne. In 1836, he attempted to stage a coup d'état with troops from the French army garrison at Strasbourg. This inevitably doomed act of insurgency resulted in a second period of exile—well out of the way this time, in the United States. In 1838 Louis Napoleon turned up in England, where he published his own version of benevolent despotism in his political manifesto—*Idées Napoleoniques*—in 1839.

In 1840 Napoleon made a second ill-judged and abortive attempt to capture the French throne by trying to stage a coup at Boulogne. Captured and imprisoned for the next six years in the fortress of Ham near Amiens, he was now a figure of ridicule among European politicians. But his vision of restoring a Napoleonic state in France remained undimmed. In May 1846 he escaped and fled to England, where he lived incognito, disguised as a workman. In 1848 he acted as a special constable during the Chartist riots. That same year France suffered upheaval and civil unrest as revolutionary activity swept across Europe. Napoleon knew that his moment had come. A group of supporters rallied to nominate him to the new Constituent Assembly, and on returning to Paris in September he stood for the presidency. The public responded to the prospect of a return to the old days of Napoleonic glory that he offered, and, on his promise of restoring economic prosperity and political stability, Louis Napoleon was duly elected. With some in the Constituent Assembly firmly opposed to his usurping of power, however, he set out to secure his position by taking command of the army and positioning his own men in places of importance.

Louis Napoleon was a shrewd ruler, who always tried to stay one step ahead of public opinion. He traveled the country and in so doing constantly tested the political waters, offering firm leadership as a counter to any possible threat of unrest. But his term as president was for four years only and was not renewable. Determined to preempt this, he staged a coup against the only effective opposition—the Republicans—in December 1851 and then brought in a new constitution, imprisoning or deporting his opponents and censoring the press. He was declared emperor in November 1852. The following January he found himself an empress, marrying the countess Eugénie de Montijo (something of a second-best choice after his failure to find a willing candidate of high royal blood).

French culture flourished during Louis Napoleon's twenty-year rule, during which he set himself the goal of restoring France as a great international power. The country's alliance with Britain against Russia during the Crimean War provided the ideal opportunity for a reassertion of French military might. By the summer of 1855 Napoleon, impatient to bring the war in the Crimea to a conclusion, announced he would go to the front to rally the French Expeditionary Force. The British government were greatly alarmed by this decision, mindful that Louis Napoleon would not get a friendly reception from British troops should he try to take over command. In an attempt to defuse the situation, Louis Napoleon was invited on an official state visit to England. Victoria, already alarmed at the exercise of French military might in the Crimea and disapproving of Louis Napoleon's unlawful seizure of power, prepared herself to be intimidated and endure an official duty occasioned by political necessity.

But Louis Napoleon was not the man she had envisaged. She got on well with him from the start, finding him quiet, low voiced, well mannered and altogether seductive and mysterious. She was intrigued by his colorful early life, which had taken him through revolution and imprisonment. A little harmless flirtation and well-informed flattery were enlisted by Louis Napoleon in winning the queen's confidence. Despite being a married woman, there was still something of the sexual innocent about Victoria, for she had never as such experienced the subtle art of wooing, her own courtship of Albert having been perfunctory. Louis Napoleon was a master at putting women at their ease; Victoria relaxed in his company and reveled in his quiet, solicitous manner. She was soon confiding to her journal that "he is a most extraordinary, mysterious man, whom one feels excessively interested in watching and knowing" (Aronson 1991, 102). On 2 May 1855, having said goodbye to her new-found royal friends amid much hugging and tears, Victoria wrote a long and perceptive memorandum of her impressions of Louis Napoleon's character. At the end of it, she concluded that she would be "curious to see if, after the lapse of time, my opinion and estimate of him has been the right one" (Benson and Esher 1911, 3:26).

A nine-day return visit to the French monarchs in Paris took place in August. The whole occasion quite went to Victoria's head, her reaction that of a young provincial girl's first visit to the big city. She waxed lyrical in her letters about the vast crowds on the streets of Paris that greeted the royal procession and described the splendors of Versailles and the French Exposition, gurgling with false modesty that "they have asked to call a new street, which we opened *after me!*" (Benson and Esher 1911, 3:136). She did not, however, miss the irony in the fact that she, the granddaughter of George III, the king who had fought against Napoleon Bonaparte, should be dancing at Versailles in the arms of the new French emperor. In a somber moment, amid the pleasures of a truly enjoyable visit, Victoria sealed Britain's rapprochement with her old adversary, France, by sharing a moment of quiet contemplation with the emperor at Napoleon Bonaparte's tomb.

By the end of her visit, and despite her disapproval of the showy and libertine French court that she dubbed "Sodom and Gomorrah," the queen was once again excitedly listing all of Napoleon's many virtues. He had engaged her in intimate discourse on a number of often profound topics, and Victoria was convinced of the depth of their reciprocal affection. "He is so simple, so *naïf,* never making *des phrases,* or paying compliments—so full of tact, good taste, high breeding" (Benson and Esher 1911, 3:122). Albert, however, was more circumspect. He had many worrying doubts about Louis Napoleon and the true objectives of his increasingly militaristic regime. By the late 1850s, Victoria's belief in Louis Napoleon's moral probity had also been shaken by rumors about his mistresses, of whom there were several; when she met him that year the atmosphere was restrained. She and Prince Albert sensed a change in Louis Napoleon's behavior toward them and were now anxious at the burgeoning of the French fleet and with it France's capacity for war.

And indeed France soon was at war—with Austria—over its control of northern Italy. Louis Napoleon's attempt to help wrest the state of Piedment-Sardinia from Austrian rule was inspired by his romantic desire to liberate oppressed minorities, but it aroused considerable antipathy both from the papacy and from Britain and added further fuel to the gathering atmosphere of mistrust and suspicion between the two countries. Having seen him liberate northern Italy and annex Savoy and Nice at the end of the war in 1860, Queen Victoria feared that this might inspire further French ambitions. She was incensed that Louis Napoleon, of all people, might precipitate a major European crisis and, worse, that he might even harbor secret designs on England. As a safeguard, the royal couple called for the enlisting of a large volunteer force in Britain.

By the end of the 1860s, however, Louis Napoleon's political position was under threat from mounting opposition in the French government; his removal from power now seemed inevitable. In 1869 he dismissed his prime minister and instituted reforms to the constitution in an attempt to hold back the threat of revolution. But dissident elements in the army were growing, and he finally resorted to the distraction of war with Prussia in July 1870, as an opportunity to defuse the situation. In entering this war, Louis Napoleon made one last attempt to salvage his position, but after French troops were defeated in September at Sedan, he was captured and imprisoned at Wilhelmshole by the Prussians. French Republicans seized the moment and deposed him; a Third Republic was proclaimed.

Thirteen years had passed by the time Queen Victoria met Louis Napoleon again. In the interim, the empress had fled to England with the couple's only child, the Prince Imperial. In March 1871, Louis Napoleon finally joined them at their modest, rented home in Chiselhurst in Kent. He was now in considerable physical decline, and the queen was greatly moved by the dramatic change in his appearance. The dapper charm of earlier years had now been supplanted by an air of melancholy; she noted that he was now "very stout and grey and his moustaches are no longer curled and waxed as formerly" (Aronson 1991, 164). He nevertheless had lost nothing of the gracious art of conversation and politesse. She found him courageous and uncomplaining about his lot. Once again she was forced to change her opinion of him, resolving that he had all along been a "faithful ally to England." She was mortified by his reduced status to that of a "poor, insignificant exile" and went out of her way to help the couple, inviting them to Windsor and to state occasions such as the official opening of the Royal Albert Hall.

The former emperor and empress continued to live in Chiselhurst, surrounded by a court in exile. They adopted the lifestyle of English gentry, supporting local cricket matches and bazaars. Louis Napoleon, however, only enjoyed two more years of life. Plagued with a kidney stone since the 1850s, he consulted with numerous fashionable doctors and eventually agreed, in 1878, to an operation. The surgeon, Sir Henry Thompson, attempted three times to crush and remove the large kidney stone that was blocking the emperor's bladder, but Louis Napoleon died suddenly not long afterward, probably of septicemia. Six years later his only (legitimate) son died while on a reconnaisance mission, while observing the Zulu Wars in southern Africa and was laid to rest beside him. Eugénie outlived him for forty-seven years.

To Victoria, Louis Napoleon had been a tragic, charismatic figure who bravely attempted to fulfill his destiny; others were more circumspect in their estimation of the ill-fated emperor's ultimate ignominious fall from power. To Bismarck, he was "the sphinx without a riddle" (Bresler 1999, 418); and even though the royal family, and the Prince of Wales in particular, had reason to pity how the mighty emperor had fallen, the queen's private secretary, Sir Henry Ponsonby, considered that "he had dragged down his nation to ruin, plunged them into an awful war when it was his duty to have known they were unfit for it" (333).

Related entries:
Crimean War; Eugénie Marie de Montijo, Empress of France

References and further reading:
Aronson, Theo. 1972. *Queen Victoria and the Buonapartes.* London: Cassell.
———. 1991. *Heart of a Queen: Queen Victoria's Romantic Attachments.* London: John Murray.
Benson, A. C., and Viscount Esher, eds. 1911. *The Letters of Queen Victoria 1837–1861.* London: John Murray.
Bresler, Fenton. 1999. *Napoleon III: A Life.* London: HarperCollins.
Bury, J. P. T. 1964. *Napoleon III and the Second Empire.* London: Hodder and Stoughton.

Guedalla, Philip. 1932. *The Second Empire.* London: Hodder and Stoughton.
Guest, Ivor. 1952. *Napoleon III in England.* London: British Technical and General Press.
Hibbert, Christopher. 2000. *Queen Victoria: A Personal History.* London: HarperCollins.

Nightingale, Florence (1820–1910)

Such a head. *I wish we had her at the War Office* (Strachey 1971a, 217)

In the pantheon of eminent Victorians, few ranked higher than Florence Nightingale, who was lauded as the pioneer of modern nursing and immortalized as a latter-day saint and the "Lady of the Lamp." At a time when it was considered immodest for any woman to take up public work, the outbreak of the Crimean War in 1854 had brought her an unprecedented opportunity not only for overcoming public prejudice but also for winning the unqualified support in her work of the queen herself. In this respect Nightingale occupies a unique position as a woman, for she won the approval of a queen who was otherwise notoriously and fervently opposed to women's emancipation.

Florence Nightingale was named after the Italian city where she was born during her parents' extended honeymoon touring Europe. Returning to England, her early life was spent between two family homes, Lea Hurst in Derbyshire and Embley Park in Hampshire, interspersed with regular visits to London for the social season. She received an exceptional, liberal education for her time; her father, a Whig and a Unitarian, tutored her at home in Latin, Greek, French, German, and Italian. Together they also studied philosophy and history as well as mathematics, a subject at that time considered unsuitable for young women. At the age of seventeen, the religiously devout Nightingale experienced a revelation that God had a particular mission for her—as yet unrevealed. It took years of escalating discontent, playing the role of the dutiful daughter and being slowly suffocated by the quiet domestic round, before she finally found her vocation. Breaking the monotony of her life with occasional charitable visits to the poor and the sick in workhouse hospitals and trips to nurse sick relatives, she set her sights on taking up nursing.

In the meantime, Nighingale had determinedly put up barriers to any idea of marriage, in 1849 finally rejecting the prolonged courtship (since 1842) of Richard Monckton Milnes. In a discourse on women's dependency and purposelessness, entitled *Cassandra,* she expressed her rage at the inadequacy of domestic life for women like herself of "passion, intellect, moral activity" (Strachey 1970, 396). There was only one solution, in her view, for a woman such as herself—work. In 1844 Nightingale announced her desire to study nursing for three months at Salisbury Infirmary. Her family were horrified. Despairing at their response, Nightingale went into a deep depression. She resolved to continue visiting hospitals whenever the family were in London and buried herself in the private study of Blue Books on public health and social conditions—becoming an exceptional statistician, thanks to her mathematical skills.

In 1850, Nightingale's parents, keen to dispel all idea of nursing once and for all, sent her on a trip to Greece. On her way back to England she made a detour to spend time observing the work of the nursing sisters at the Institution of Protestant Deaconesses, at Kaiserwerth in Germany. In July 1851, she persuaded her family to allow her to return there, to train as a nurse. The regime was spartan, the hours long. Operations and amputations were performed without anesthetic. The training as such, she admitted much later in 1897, had been "nil," the standards of hygiene "horrible." These deficiencies were, however, compensated for by the institution's high

The image that gave birth to a legend: Florence Nightingale famously depicted in the **Illustrated London News** *as the "lady with the lamp," making her rounds of the wounded at the British hospital at Scutari during the Crimean War of 1854–1856. (The* **Illustrated London News** *Picture Library)*

moral tone and frequent calls to prayer, of which Nightingale, as a devout Christian, heartily approved.

After three months at Kaiserwerth she returned home, her mind irrevocably set on a nursing career. The offer of the post of superintendent (without salary) of the Institute for the Care of Sick Gentlewomen in Harley Street, London, finally released Nightingale from parental control. Given a private allowance of £500 a year by her father, she took up her post in August 1853. But for a woman of her vision and ambition, the institute soon seemed far too limited a sphere of activity, and she began looking for a new arena in which she could fulfill her sense of vocation. It came when war broke out in the Crimea in March 1854. Reports of the sufferings of British troops prompted Nightingale to volunteer her services. She was asked by her friend, Sidney Herbert, secretary of state for war, to head a party of thirty-eight nurses being sent to the military hospital established in old army barracks at Scutari, a suburb of the capital, Constantinople. The situation that greeted her on her arrival on 4 November was one of imminent catastrophe; and the stink was overwhelming. "I have been well acquainted with the dwellings of the worst parts of most of the great cities in Europe," she wrote, " but have never been in any atmosphere which I could compare with that of the Barrack Hospital at night" (Strachey 1971b, 119).

The wounded, who were being transported from the front lines, 300 miles away, across the Black Sea to the hospital at Scutari, were dying at an alarming rate. Mortality rates from postoperative trauma, after the amputation of limbs without anesthetic, were particularly high, but many other patients with relatively minor wounds were picking up infections and fevers once they were hospitalized. A great many suffered from malnutrition and scurvy and, during the winter months, from frostbite. The wards in which they were housed were filthy, without proper plumbing and infested with vermin. And soon they were overflowing with hundreds of additional wounded from the battle of Inkerman, which took place the day after Nightingale's arrival. Medical supplies of the most basic kind were lacking: there were insufficient bandages and dressings, basins, towels, and soap and even a shortage of operating tables. Food and water, clothing for the wounded—who often arrived half-naked—and clean linen were also in very short supply. The nonexistent sanitation and lack of proper heating all contributed to the spread of diseases such as dysentery and cholera.

With ruthless efficiency, Nightingale set about cleaning up the hospital and purchasing supplies and clothing for the wounded. Floors were scrubbed, walls repainted, corridors repaved, and the straw-strewn wards properly floored; laundries were set up where soldiers' wives took on the washing. Yet, despite their dedication, Nightingale remained circumspect in her view of the nurses serving under her, many of whom she felt did not come up to her own high standards. Some, proving unsuitable, were sent home; others tired of Nightingale's harsh and dictatorial manner and went elsewhere in the Crimea to nurse. Having banned her nurses from the wards after 8:30 P.M. (fearful that they might succumb to improper advances from the soldiers), Nightingale patrolled the hospital corridors on her own. Thus was born the image of the "Lady with the Lamp," first publicized in the February 1855 edition of the *Illustrated London News* and later immortalized in an 1857 poem by Longfellow, "Santa Filomena."

Thanks to the publicity surrounding Nightingale's nursing achievements in the Crimea, the war became popular at home, led by that great enthusiast, Queen Victoria. For some time the queen and Nightingale had nursed a mutual admiration for each other from afar. Nightingale observed that, as a child, she had never been able to pray for George IV or William IV, "but when Victoria came to the throne, I prayed for her in a rapture of feeling, and my thoughts never wandered" (Housman 1932, 35). The queen, deeply troubled by the sufferings of the ordinary troops during the terrible Crimean winter of 1854–1855, frequently complained that she heard "*no details of the wounded,* though I see so many from officers etc., about the battlefield" (Woodham-Smith 1950, 154–155). She had kept a close eye on accounts of Nightingale's work in the Crimea, demanding to see any reports sent by her to the War Office. Nightingale was touched by the queen's concern, particularly when in December that year she sent Nightingale a personal message accompanied by gifts to distribute to the wounded, observing that "your goodness and self devotion in giving yourself up to the soothing attendance upon these wounded and sick soldiers has been observed by the Queen with sentiments of the highest approval and admiration"(155).

In November 1855, in recognition of the dedicated work of Nightingale and her nurses in the Crimea, a fund was set up to provide money with which she would be able to establish a program of nursing training after the war. Soon after, in January 1856, Queen Victoria sent her a letter of grateful thanks, asking her to accept a small gift—a brooch, specially designed by Prince Albert—"as a mark of esteem and gratitude for her devotion toward the Queen's brave soldiers" (Woodham-Smith 1950, 193). Nightingale remained at her post at Scutari until the last troops had left in July 1856. The queen was most anxious to meet the reluctant heroine of the Crimea, as soon as she returned to Britain in August. Cecil Woodham-Smith described the insatiable public appetite for public statements and appearances that greeted Nightingale. "Unknown admirers showered gifts, poems, songs, illuminated addresses and proposals of marriage" (ibid.); although she doggedly rejected the limelight, by now her mythologization was out of control, ensuring her "visible march to heaven," as her contemporary, the novelist Elizabeth Gaskell, described it (Uglow 1993, 365).

The British nation now very rightly looked upon their Lady of the Lamp as public property, but Nightingale steadfastly refused all requests for public appearances and interviews. She could not, however, refuse the command of an official interview with the queen, at Balmoral on 21 September 1856. Nightingale was invited to stay with her old family friend, Dr. James Clark, the queen's personal physician, who had a home nearby. Her first meeting with the queen and Prince Albert turned into a discussion of the ills of the British military hospital system, which Nightingale cataloged with characteristic efficiency during the course of an intense two-hour audience. The royal couple were impressed both with her modesty and her no-nonsense approach.

The queen commanded Nightingale's presence again on several occasions during her stay in Scotland, sometimes driving over to visit her privately. The two women commiserated over the suffering of the British army in the Crimea, with the queen showing Nightingale her carefully compiled album of photographs of wounded war heroes and her notes on each soldier's history. Nightingale in turn regaled the queen with tales of her work at Scutari and the shortcomings of army administration there, no doubt priming royal support for the radical reforms that Nightingale was now advocating. The queen's support in this was an essential prerequisite, for she, as monarch, would have to issue a warrant for a royal commission to investigate the conduct of the war. Such were Nightingale's persuasive powers that she eventually wore down the resistance of the secretary of state for war, Lord Panmure, and in May 1856 was invited to prepare a confidential report.

Although her popular, public career had now effectively ended, Florence Nightingale's work as a reformer was only just beginning. The remaining years of her long life would be spent in determined isolation from the public gaze, at a house in Mayfair, broken only occasionally by trips to the family homes in the country. Now physically frail, Nightingale's intellect was, however, far from impaired, and she would exert a significant influence on social reform, often from her sickbed, where she also received government ministers and other eminent visitors. It was here that, after making a careful study of the high death rate at the Barrack Hospital at Scutari during the winter of 1854–1855, Nightingale was finally forced to recognize that bad hygiene, caused by overcrowding in the poorly laid out and unventilated barracks, compounded by bad sanitation as the result of blocked sewers, had been responsible for thousands of unnecessary deaths. For all her assiduous reorganizing of supplies, her scrubbing, her night patrols, and nourishing soups, her hospital had been, in her own view, little more than a death camp. She wrote up her conclusions in a report entitled "Notes on Matters Affecting the Health, Efficiency, and Hospital Administration of the British Army, Founded Chiefly on the Experience of the late War," with the damning statistics contained in a new section—"Causes of Disaster at Scutari"—which she intended as an appendix. The Royal Commission into the Health of the Army sat during May, June, and July 1857, but the government was reluctant to publish Nighingale's findings, in order to "protect the new public enthusiasm for nursing" (Small 1998, 114) and with it, no doubt, Nightingale's reputation.

The perception that hygiene was the essential factor in hospital care, over and above good administration and improved nursing training, shifted Nightingale's perspective on nursing thereafter. Her interest in the medical training of nurses was supplanted by a mission to improve the nursing of the destitute sick in the workhouses of Britain, as well as standards of public health, with Nightingale drawing parallels between her findings at Scutari and the high mortality rates among Britain's population from tuberculosis and whooping cough. She began to argue for greater consideration of the wider social aspects of deprivation—poor housing, lack of sanitation, clean water supplies, poor diet—and supported legislation put to Parliament in 1867 by the eminent reformer Edwin Chadwick. Nightingale next turned to examining the high peacetime mortality rates among soldiers posted to India, writing endless letters and gathering evidence in support of the calling of the 1859 Royal Commission on the Health of the British Army in India.

Despite her continuing physical infirmity, her appetite for work was prodigious. Lytton Strachey has remarked on the paradox of Nightingale's long life as a valetudinarian, observing that she was "an invalid of curious character . . . who was too weak to walk downstairs" but yet who "worked harder than most Cabinet Ministers" (1971b, 151–152). Although male officialdom never ceased to balk at being told what to do by an interfering woman, Nightingale would persist, over the next thirty years, in offering her unpaid advice on a wide range of reforms—at home and in India. She had long since lost interest in the training of nurses, although the many hagiographies that lauded her work over the years would persist in placing an undue emphasis on her as a pioneer of nursing, to the detriment of Nightingale's other much more important contributions to public health reform. Indeed, after realizing the dangers of hospital nursing in the spread of infectious disease, Nightingale turned violently against hospitals and was decidedly reluctant to become involved in hospital work again, by now convinced that the sick were better off being nursed at home.

There was, however, the matter of the £45,000 proceeds from the Nightingale Fund established during the Crimean War to finance further nursing reforms by her. She therefore endorsed the money's use in the building of the Nightingale School for Nurses but took little active interest in it thereafter. The school trained up new generations of midwives and nurses who in turn promoted the "Nightingale Model of nursing in Britain and abroad, thus perpetuating the myth of Nightingale as the guiding light of nursing practice. The method she inaugurated would, however, in later years, come under attack for its authoritarian attitudes, its close surveillance of trainees, and the undue emphasis on strict, military-style order. The regime imposed at St. Thomas's would prove daunting to all but the most determined probationer nurses, with Nightingale as ever remaining excessively critical of the caliber of most of the women who entered nursing training.

Nightingale's influence throughout Victoria's reign was ever present, even among the royal family. Victoria's daughters Alice, Vicky, and Helena all in one way or another were inspired by Nightingale's work. As a young woman, Alice took up the visiting of the sick and poor and nursed various members of the royal family through illness, including Prince Albert on his deathbed. In 1866, and now living in Darmstadt, she took a personal interest in the plight of war wounded and advocated the establishment of field hospitals during the six-weeks Austro-Prussian war. In 1878, after nursing her own children devotedly through diphtheria, she too succumbed and died of the disease. During the Franco-Prussian War of

1870–1871, Alice's older sister, Vicky, the crown princess of Prussia, oversaw the provision of supplies to the hospitals for the wounded and attempted to improve the German hospital system, facing the same kind of bureaucratic obstacles as had Nightingale in the Crimea. Princess Helena too would become noted for her philanthropy and interest in nursing and involved herself in the early activities of the Red Cross during the Franco-Prussian War. As for the queen herself, at the time of the Golden Jubilee of 1887, she decided to devote the major part of the money that had been presented to her by the women of England as the Women's Jubilee Gift to setting up a training schemes for nurses to provide care for the sick poor in their own homes.

From the privacy of her home in Mayfair, Nightingale remained an influential voice in moral and social reform in Britain until the 1890s. She began going blind in 1895 and by 1901 had lost her sight altogether. Her mental powers, too, had begun to fail. She lived on for another nine years, in 1907 becoming the first woman to be awarded a new honor, inaugurated by King Edward VII, the Order of Merit. She left strict instructions to have no memorial and no state funeral and was buried, not in Westminster Abbey as the authorities wished, but in her family grave.

Related entries:
Alice Maud Mary, Princess; Crimean War; Helena Augusta Victoria, Princess; Victoria, Princess Royal; Women's Rights

References and further reading:
Bostridge, Mark. (Forthcoming). *Florence Nightingale: The Making of an Icon.* Harmondsworth, UK: Penguin.
Boyd, Nancy. 1982. *Three Victorian Women Who Changed Their World.* London: Macmillan.
Forster, Margaret. 1984. *Significant Sisters: The Grassroots of Active Feminism 1839–1939.* Harmondsworth, UK: Penguin Books.
Goldie, Sue M. 1987. *I Have Done My Duty: Florence Nightingale in the Crimean War 1854–1856.* Manchester, UK: Manchester University Press.
Housman, Laurence. 1932. "Florence Nightingale." In H. J. Massingham and Hugh Massingham, eds., *The Great Victorians.* London: Ivor Nicholson and Watson.
Small, Hugh. 1998. *Florence Nightingale: Avenging Angel.* London: Constable.
Smith, F. B. 1982. *Florence Nightingale: Reputation and Power.* London: Croom Helm.
Strachey, Lytton. [1918] 1971a. *Eminent Victorians.* Harmondsworth, UK: Penguin.
———. [1921] 1971b. *Queen Victoria.* Harmondsworth, UK: Penguin.
Strachey, Ray. 1970. *The Cause: A Short History of the Women's Movement in Great Britain.* London: Virago.
Uglow, Lynn Jenny. 1993. *Elizabeth Gaskell: A Habit of Stories.* London: Faber and Faber.
Vicinus, Martha, and Bea Nergaard, eds. 1989. *Ever Yours, Florence Nightingale.* London: Virago.
Woodham-Smith, Cecil. 1950. *Florence Nightingale, 1820–1910.* Edinburgh: Constable.

O

Oliphant, Margaret (1828–1897)

(popularly known as "Mrs. Oliphant")

So distinguished a Writer as yourself (Houston 1999, 151)

Like Queen Victoria's other favorite author, Marie Corelli (who would supplant Oliphant in the best-seller lists), the prodigiously hard-working and prolific Margaret Oliphant was able to produce one novel after another, year in, year out. In all, over 100 books (98 of them novels) and more than 267 journal articles for *Blackwood's Magazine* alone poured from her pen during her fifty-year writing career. Some have argued that, in pursuing her craft with the ruthless efficiency of a trade rather than of a calling, Oliphant sacrificed her true artistic talents. Oliphant herself refused to ascribe any mystique to writing. The queen was one of her many eminent admirers, acquiring Oliphant's novels for her own Royal Library. She is said to have had every one of them read aloud to her.

Oliphant was born in Wallyford, near Edinburgh, Scotland, the daughter of a customs and excise official. Her family, who moved to Liverpool, were members of a dissenting group—the Free Church of Scotland. The controversial circumstances in which it broke away from the Church of Scotland in 1843 provided much material for Oliphant's first novel, *Passages in the Life of Mrs Margaret Maitland,* a moving portrait of Scottish life that was well received, and praised by Charlotte Brontë. *Caleb Field,* a historical novel, followed in 1851, as did others drawing on the Scottish setting, such as *Merkland* (1851) and *Katie Stewart* (1853), set in the Jacobite Rebellion of 1745–1746. The queen by now had become an avid reader of Oliphant's domestic romances, with their engaging mix of humor and pathos. *The Athelings* (1857) was one of her biggest successes, and by the time she published *Orphans* and *The Laird of Norlaw* in 1858, Oliphant was receiving an average of £400 for each novel.

In about 1850, Oliphant settled in London and two years later married a cousin, Francis Wilson Oliphant. Despite spending most of her life in London, where she became something of a celebrity on the literary circuit, Oliphant would never lose the strong cadences of a broad East Lothian Scottish accent; such Scottishness would appeal to the queen's own love affair with things Scottish, and she saw Oliphant as a kindred spirit. As well as writing novels, Oliphant began contributing regular articles and reviews to *Blackwood's Magazine.* But her career was interrupted when her husband contracted consumption; he died a few months later (1859), leaving Margaret with two children, pregnant with a third, and £1,000 in debt. She lived for a while in Edinburgh before returning to London, by now also supporting her alcoholic brother William and taking in her widowed brother Frank and his three children.

Oliphant's most enduring and best-known works would be her five novels known collectively as the *Chronicles of Carlingford,* which she published from 1863 to 1876. These revived her flagging popularity at a time when the market was awash with a glut of lesser novels by her. The Chronicles augment the vivid picture of the mid-Victorian rural community that was so brilliantly captured in George Eliot's *Middlemarch* (with whose work the *Chronicles* were often compared) and also crystallize the religious debates fictionalized so successfully by Anthony Trollope in his Barsetshire novels. Indeed, Oliphant and Trollope would dominate the genre of the domestic story by the end of the 1860s.

Oliphant's unceasing literary labors and considerable income from them never seemed to stem the tide of her financial obligations. She struggled to put her sons through public school at Eton, but they both would prove a great disappointment to her and would never be able to adequately support themselves. In 1865, Oliphant bought a house in Windsor; there she remained until her death, four years before the queen, in 1897. She thus found herself living a stone's throw from Britain's most famous and reclusive widow. It was Oliphant's work as a literary critic that finally brought her into close contact with the queen, when, in 1868, Victoria published *Leaves from the Journal of Our Life in the Highlands.* The queen was particularly hopeful that Oliphant, as a Scot, would be well disposed to giving her opus a sympathetic review. Oliphant, shrewdly mindful of the financial value of the royal seal of approval, had already favorably reviewed *The Early Years of His Royal Highness the Prince Consort,* which Sir Charles Grey had ghosted for the queen in 1867. Although Oliphant could admire *Leaves* for its simplicity and lack of guile, she reserved judgment on the amateurishness of its writing. Having already appealed for and failed to secure a pension from the queen in 1860, Oliphant agreed to write the review "on condition that I am not asked to tackle the holy Albert again" (Houston 1999, 148). Privately, she had scant regard for the queen's literary endeavors and warned of the danger of her conceiving literary ambitions above her most limited station. But, as Gail Turley Houston pointed out in her perceptive study, Oliphant "was very interested in what the queen could do for her" (143), and this dictated the tenor of Oliphant's review, which appeared in *Blackwood's Magazine* in February 1868. A month later, she met the queen for the first time, and in June the queen awarded Oliphant a civil list pension of £100 a year. Pragmatic considerations aside, Oliphant was genuinely admiring of many of the queen's qualities, in particular her strength of will, her independence of mind, and the industriousness with which she pursued her own particular trade as monarch.

Although she displayed undoubted gifts as a biographer, Margaret Oliphant never properly exploited this talent, evading suggestions from on high that the queen would be more than gratified if Oliphant wrote hers—albeit under the strictest of controls. Oliphant did, however, produce several sympathetic and intuitive biographies of her own contemporaries. She also wrote travel books, critical essays, reviews, and a *Literary History of England, 1790–1825* (1882). In later years her fiction writing took a more serious tone, with a series of novels exploring the plight of strong women trapped in marriages to weak men: *The Greatest Heiress in England* (1879), *Hester* (1883), *The Ladies Lindores* (1883), *Kirsteen* (1890), and *Sir Robert's Fortune* (1895). The most interesting and fashionable of her later novels, *A Beleaguered City* (1880), *A Little Pilgrim in the Unseen* (1882), and *Stories of the Seen and Unseen* (1885), all tapped into the same genre that would be extensively exploited by Marie Corelli—death, the soul, and the afterlife—in an amalgam of Christian allegory, mysticism, and the supernatural that no doubt appealed to the queen's own morbid fascination with death and the paranormal.

But the closest parallels in the lives of Oliphant and the queen are to be found in Oliphant's posthumously published *Autobiography,* in which she attempted to reconcile a career divided between the demands of motherhood and those of writing for a living. It proved to be a most affecting account of life on the authorial treadmill, imbued with a melancholy for all that she had lost, where even the sardonic Oliphant at times succumbed to the queen's propensity for mawkish "poor-me-ism and an off-putting fondness for locutions like 'my poor little unappreciated self'" (Peltason 1999, 369). Most of this was prompted by her attempts to console herself for the disappointments meted out to her by men—husband, brothers, and sons—in her life. It is a work redolent with sickness and death—of her mother, her two newborn sons, and infant daughter, followed by her husband and her ten-year-old daughter, Maggie (who died in 1864). The queen too had suffered similar losses—beginning with the death of her mother and husband in 1861; like Oliphant—who outlived both her remaining, feckless sons (Cyril who died in 1890 and Francis in 1894)—the queen also saw three of her own children predecease her (Alice, Alfred, and Leopold).

Oliphant's despair, registered in the words with which she ended her autobiography—"And now here I am all alone/ I cannot write any more"—echoes the sentiments frequently uttered by Queen Victoria on her own solitude after the loss of Albert. In her essay, Oliphant delineated the close parallels between her own and the queen's losses and widowhood. But, although admiring of the queen's consummate professionalism as monarch (which Oliphant equated with her own professionalism as a writer), Oliphant privately disapproved most strongly of Victoria's continuing seclusion. The writer doubted "whether *nous autres* poor women who have had to fight with the world all alone without much sympathy from anybody, can quite enter into the 'unprecedented' character of the Queen's sufferings" (Jay 1999, 194). The queen, she felt, had much to console her: "A woman is surely a poor creature if with a large, happy affectionate family of children around her she can't take heart to do her duty whether she likes it or not. *We* have to do it, with very little solace, and I don't see that there is anybody particularly sorry for us" (ibid.).

When asked to contribute some chapters on Queen Victoria's family life to Robert Wilson's *Life and Times of Queen Victoria* (eventually published in 1900), Oliphant discovered the extent to which the queen insisted on tight control. Although their relationship had now become a personal one—by letter and through meetings at Windsor—the queen refused point-blank to allow Oliphant any access to personal documents. Undaunted, Oliphant went ahead and wrote the chapters. Another biographical piece, "Queen Victoria: A Personal Sketch," was published after Oliphant's death, in 1900. At the end of her long career, and despite her considerable successes now in North America and throughout Europe in translation, Margaret Oliphant considered herself a creative failure. When Oliphant died in 1897, the queen rued the loss of the woman she would have most liked to have had as a biographer and whose novels, according to the *Star,* were "believed to have given more pleasure to the Queen than those of any lady writer of fiction of her reign" (Houston 1999, 151).

Related entries:
Corelli, Marie; Dickens, Charles; *Leaves from the Journal of Our Life in the Highlands;* The

Paranormal; Scott, Sir Walter; Tennyson, Alfred, Lord; "The Widow at Windsor"

References and further reading:

Colby, Vineta, and Robert A. Colby. 1966. *The Equivocal Virtue: Margaret Oliphant and the Victorian Literary Market Place.* Hamden, CT: Archon.

Houston, Gail Turley. 1999. "'The Grandest Trade of All': Professional Exchanges between the Queen and Margaret Oliphant." In Gail Turley Houston, *Royalties: The Queen and Victorian Writers,* chap 5. Charlottesville: University Press of Virginia.

Jay, Elisabeth. 1999. "'Mrs. Brown' by Windsor's Other Widow." *Women's History Review* 6, no. 2: 191–200.

Jay, Elisabeth, and Francis O'Gorman, guest eds. 1999. *Women's History Review* 6, no. 2. A special issue devoted to articles on Oliphant.

Oliphant, Margaret. [1899] 1990. *The Autobiography of Margaret Oliphant: The Complete Text.* Edited by Elisabeth Jay. Oxford: Oxford University Press.

———. 1900. *Queen Victoria: A Personal Sketch.* London: Cassell.

Peltason, Timothy. 1999. "Life Writing." In Herbert F. Tucker, ed., *A Companion to Victorian Literature and Culture,* 356–372. Oxford: Blackwell.

Peterson, Linda. 1986. *Victorian Autobiography.* New Haven: Yale University Press.

Sanders, Valerie. 1989. *The Private Lives of Victorian Women: Autobiography in Nineteenth-Century England.* New York: St. Martin's Press.

Sutherland, John. 1988. *The Longman Companion to Victorian Fiction.* London: Longman.

Williams, Merryn. 1986. *Margaret Oliphant: A Critical Biography.* London: Macmillan.

Opera

I was VERY MUCH AMUSED INDEED
(Esher 1912, 1:194)

On the many regular excursions she made to the theater during its summer seasons in the 1830s, the young Princess Victoria would enjoy mixed programs at the Drury Lane and King's theaters. These offered a showcase for the new and rapidly rising female sopranos of popular opera, who were now replacing the male castratos who had traditionally sung the female roles. As she grew older, and particularly after her marriage to Prince Albert, Victoria would develop with him a great passion for the opera. She loved this above all other musical genres (hating the long, and in her view, tiresome oratorios of Handel); in particular she relished operas containing elements of high drama and romance—most notably the works of the three great Italians Vincenzo Bellini, Gaetano Donizetti, and Gioachino Rossini. Her adoration of Italian opera, in preference to the tried and trusted Mozart, also prompted Victoria to learn to speak the language, in which she became highly proficient. It also inevitably led to a strong desire in the princess to study singing herself.

In terms of her personal musical skills, Princess Victoria was an accomplished pianist and good sight reader, and, as with any well-brought-up young woman of her day, singing tuition was part of the curriculum. She was naturally gifted as a singer and first studied singing with John Sale, a music master at St. Margaret's, Westminster. But such was her love for Italian opera, that in 1836 she persuaded the duchess of Kent to invite the Italian tenor, Luigi Lablache, to give her private lessons whenever he was in London for the season. The relationship would last for twenty years; Victoria adored Lablache as a father figure and greatly enjoyed his performances in comic opera as well as his more dramatic roles such as the title role of Rossini's *Otello* and the doge in *Marino Faliero.* The prince consort proved to be a fine singer himself, and one of his and the queen's favorite pastimes in the evenings was to play and sing duets together.

Of the new and exciting generation of female singers, the one who first caught Princess Victoria's imagination was the legendary Maria Malibran. Born María Felicitá García in Paris in 1808, she was the daughter of the Spanish tenor Manuel García and sister of the equally famous mezzo-soprano Pauline Viardot-García. Malibran was possessed of a fine contralto voice and had been trained by her father to cover an ambitious vocal range, right up to soprano. She had become a dominating force in European opera after making her debut in London in 1825 and was noted for the high passion of her performances, such as in Donizetti's *Maria Stuarda*.

When Malibran died at the age of twenty-eight, in Manchester after a sudden illness, the princess mourned her loss (as did several poets who celebrated her as a legendary figure). But by now Malibran was already being supplanted in Victoria's estimation by a new Italian singer, Giulia Grisi, whom she had first seen in her London debut in 1834 performing in Donizetti's *Anna Bolena*. Much to Victoria's joy, Grisi was invited to join Malibran and three male Italian opera stars—Lablache, the baritone Antonio Tamburini, and the tenor Battista Rubini—in singing at a special sixteenth birthday concert organized for Victoria in 1835 by her mother. The highlight for Victoria was to hear Grisi and the three men perform the thrilling quartet "A te o Caro" from *I Puritani*. At the end of the evening, Victoria recorded her new-found adoration of Grisi. Although Malibran's rich, low notes were undoubtedly "*beautiful*," she found her high notes "thick and not clear" and now admitted "I like *Grisi by far better* than her" (Warner 1979, 66). Although Malibran was a far more consummate artist, the princess was beguiled by Grisi's physical beauty, her beautiful dark eyes and hair, and her fragility and paleness, which lent a haunting vulnerability to her performances.

Victoria remained entranced by Grisi, who, in her expressiveness, proved to be a wonderful actress as well as singer. Victoria later saw Grisi sing the title role in Bellini's *Norma*—in Victoria's estimation it was Grisi's greatest role—and as Elena in Donizetti's *Marino Faliero*. But the opera Victoria loved most of all, in which Grisi took the role of Polacca, was Bellini's *I Puritani*. This had been the first opera she had seen in the company of Prince Albert before their marriage, and it would hold a special place in the queen's affection as "dear *Puritani*." The couple so came to love Bellini's work that they would revisit their three favorite Bellini operas (*Norma, I Puritani,* and *La Sonnambula*) twenty times during the course of twenty-five years.

The queen's favorite composer after Bellini was undoubtedly Donizetti. As well as enjoying his comic operas such as *La Fille du Regiment* and *L'Elisir d'Amore,* she thrilled to the high passion of the tragedies *Lucia di Lammermoor* and *Lucrezia Borgia*. She also found Rossini's comic operas *La Gazza Ladra* and *Il Barbiere de Sevilla* greatly entertaining and had a soft spot for his version of the Cinderella story—*La Cenerentola*. She had also admired his version of *Otello,* although this was soon eclipsed by Verdi's much more popular version (1887). Verdi rose to fame after Queen Victoria's retreat into widowhood, thus denying her the experience of his magnificent later works, although she was familiar with his earlier work, *Il Trovatore* (1853). Victoria made no apologies for the fact that Mozart came well down in the list of her operatic favorites. She admired his technical brilliance but found some of his operas over long; in her mature years, however, she developed a deep admiration for *Don Giovanni*.

By 1847, such was the popularity of the Italian opera that the Covent Garden Theatre was renamed the Royal Italian Opera. That year the queen and Prince Albert indulged themselves in an exceptional period of opera-going during the London season debut at Her Majesty's theater of the magical soprano Jenny Lind—the "Swedish Nightingale"—attending all sixteen of her performances. They proved loyal fans, too, during Lind's London seasons of 1848 and her farewell one of 1849. By now Grisi was a distant memory, with the queen admitting that Jenny Lind was finer, in fact "quite a remarkable phenomenon," the purity of whose singing and acting was "indescribable" (One of Her Majesty's Servants 1901, 190). Lind, who would later be invited to sing for the royal couple at

Windsor, encouraged the queen and Prince Albert toward an appreciation of the work of Giacomo Meyerbeer. His *Robert le Diable* (in which Lind had made the role of Alice her own) and *Les Huguenots* were popular successes in the 1850s. Long after Lind's death, the operatic prima donna who most captivated the queen in her final years was Emma Calvé, whose role as Carmen in the 1890s she particularly enjoyed. By the end of the queen's reign, the operettas of Gilbert and Sullivan had become firm favorites in the royal household; during her long widowhood Victoria's enjoyment of opera and operetta was rekindled in several private performances at Windsor.

Related entries:
Dancing; Lablache, Luigi; Windsor Castle

References and further reading

Esher, Viscount, ed. 1912. *The Girlhood of Queen Victoria: A Selection from Her Majesty's Diaries between the Years of 1832 and 1840.* 2 vols. London: John Murray.

———. 1914. *The Training of a Sovereign.* London: John Murray.

Hardy, Alan. 1976. *Queen Victoria Was Amused.* London: John Murray.

Lorne, Marquis of, C. 1901. *V.R.I.: Her Life and Empire.* London: Eyre and Spottiswood.

[One of Her Majesty's Servants.] 1901. *The Private Life of Queen Victoria.* London: C. Arthur Pearson.

Plowden, Alison. 1981. *Young Victoria.* London: Weidenfeld and Nicolson.

Rowell, George. 1978. *Queen Victoria Goes to the Theatre.* London: Paul Elek.

Vallone, Lynne. 2001. *Becoming Victoria.* New Haven: Yale University Press.

Warner, Marina. 1979. *Queen Victoria's Sketchbook.* London: Macmillan.

Osborne

It sounds so snug and nice to have a place of one's own, *quiet and retired* (Benson and Esher 1911, 2:35)

When Queen Victoria and Prince Albert took up a summer residence at Osborne on the Isle of Wight, in 1845, they set in motion the popularization of a middle-class trend in Britain—the annual seaside holiday. Although during her widowhood the queen took to staying at Osborne during the winter as well, the house was, essentially, a summer home. Winter guests and members of the royal household would find themselves compelled to endure chilly conditions—with all the windows of the north-facing house opened daily to admit healthy doses of invigorating ozone.

Victoria had first visited the island at the ages of twelve and fourteen, staying at Norris Castle, and had enjoyed its unspoiled beauty. But it was not till her marriage that she discovered its real pleasures, after taking possession of a new paddle steamer, the *Victoria and Albert,* in the spring of 1843. She and Prince Albert were both lovers of fresh air and the outdoors but previously had followed the royal tradition of spending time at the Regency seaside resort of Brighton. They disliked the gaudiness of the Royal Pavilion where they stayed, however, and hated the crowds that pursued them wherever they went. With the queen now pregnant with her fourth child, they both craved greater privacy and a cozy family home that they could make their very own. The prime minister, Sir Robert Peel, was therefore enlisted to seek out a suitable residence; he suggested the Osborne estate, the lease of which had come on to the market for £30,000. The government made it absolutely clear that there was no question of public money being used for the purpose, so the royal couple initially offered to pay the lease for a year, from their own Privy Purse, with the option to purchase the house and its contents later. The rest of the money would be raised through the stripping and selling off of the contents of the Brighton Pavilion, which Victoria and Albert had found so uncongenial to their tastes. Remaining items of furniture found their way to their other royal homes, including Osborne's breakfast room.

Osborne House, the summer holiday home built on the Isle of Wight, off the south coast of England, by Queen Victoria and Prince Albert; the construction by Thomas Cubitt was from designs made by the prince himself. (Hulton/Archive by Getty Images)

The queen was delighted with Osborne: "It is impossible to imagine a prettier spot—valleys and woods which would be beautiful anywhere; but all this near the sea (the woods grow into the sea) is quite perfection; we have a charming beach quite to ourselves. The sea was so blue and calm that the Prince said it was like Naples" (Benson and Esher 1911, 2:36). The original three-story Georgian mansion—which the royal couple would replace with a new residence—was located on the northernmost tip of the island, near the sailing village of East Cowes. It had its own private landing stage and beach, which gave it much-valued privacy, so that "we can walk about anywhere by ourselves without being followed and mobbed" (2:36).

Prince Albert, eager to set his own imprint on the place, immediately set about planning extensive repairs and alterations in order to accommodate the royal household. He also had plans, on a wider scale, to improve Osborne's farms. But it soon became apparent that the facilities of the existing house, with its sixteen bedrooms, were so inadequate that it would have to be demolished and a new one built. The queen's agents entered into negotiations to reduce the asking price of the house and contents—eventually agreed upon at £27,814. 18s. 5d.—but Prince Albert insisted that more land was needed to accommodate the various outbuildings he had in mind for other relatives and retainers. Winchester College was prevailed upon to lease the adjacent land and with it an Elizabethan residence at Barton Manor.

The royal couple took formal possession of the Osborne Estate in May 1845. Prince

Albert commissioned the master builder Thomas Cubitt to come up with a design for a flat-roofed, stuccoed Italianate villa with two differently styled towers. Construction of the primary, central wing of the new house (known as the Pavilion) began first. It was built facing out on to the Solent and was temporarily linked to the existing Osborne House by a covered walkway. From the inception of building work, Albert ensured that the new home had the best in modern facilities, including a system of warm-air heating, en suite bathrooms for his and the queen's own apartments, and several water closets. Osborne would become the template for many similar homes built by the upper classes on the Isle of Wight, as a spate of villa building broke out across the island.

Cubitt's team carried out the building work with exemplary efficiency, using stone from nearby Portland in Dorset and prefabricated girders and joinery brought from Cubitt's yard on the Thames. On 23 June the queen laid the foundation stone; by the autumn of that year the manor house at Barton had been renovated and was accommodating members of the household. The royal family, who had meanwhile been squeezed into the old Osborne house, were now installed in the new Pavilion when it was completed in September 1846. This was now filled with hand-picked furniture and drapery, pictures by Winterhalter, and numerous judiciously chosen old masters—Mantegna, Bellini, and Giorgione—as well as statues of classical figures and of the royal children.

Prince Albert then engrossed himself in the design and planting out of symmetrical, decorated terraces and patios with fountains, statues, and walkways with their view taking the eye down to the sea. He threw himself into planting out rare conifers and flowering shrubs in the gardens. "It does one's heart good to see how my beloved Albert enjoys it all, and is so full of all the plans and improvements he means to carry out," observed the queen. "He is hardly to be kept at home a moment" (Aronson 1991, 162). Eventually, the grounds at Osborne would also boast new stables and coach houses, as well as a new servants' barracks with its own sick room and model workers' cottages—all built to Prince Albert's instructions. In December 1847 Cubitt's men gutted the old house of anything recyclable and swiftly demolished it.

By 1848, Osborne House was complete (at an eventual total cost of £200,000). It boasted a grand entrance hall and elaborate main staircase with a marble corridor leading off it. There was also a library, a billiards room, and a room with furniture inlaid with or made from antler horn—known as the Horn Room—as well as a large council chamber for official business and an audience room to receive important guests. At a discreet distance from the family apartments was a suite of rooms on the ground floor to accommodate the queen's mother, the duchess of Kent. The furnishings at Osborne, like those of Balmoral later, would be an eclectic mix of the refined and the homely; as lady-in-waiting, Mary Ponsonby, recorded in 1865: "You cannot think . . . how some of the atrocities here strike me. It certainly is the oddest combination of upholstery; hideous presents they have received, and as ill-arranged rooms as I ever saw, yet sprinkled also with beautiful things—pictures by Landseer, De la Roche, Scheffer, in this very room, and a certain kind of *luxe* which exists nowhere else" (Ponsonby 1927, 56).

Life at Osborne was made up of a combination of indoor recreation and healthy outdoor activity, with the royal family enjoying the summer pleasures of walking, fishing, picnicking, strawberry picking, kite flying, boating, and bathing; during harvest time the children enthusiastically helped with the haymaking. At all times the house was ventilated with copious amounts of bracing sea air, and everybody in the royal household had to subject themselves to all-the-year-round ventilation in their rooms. Prince Albert himself spent much time out of doors supervising the model farm or the various building works that were always going on. The queen meanwhile took every opportunity to sit outside and work on her official dispatches. As for recreation, she took her first sea bathe in July 1847. The experience would become a regular ritual, although in the queen's case it never amounted to more than some genteel splashing in shallow water. Later, both she and Albert would enjoy their own covered, floating swimming bath moored near their private beach, which also provided safe swimming for the children and, eventually, hordes of grandchildren who would visit.

In the summer of 1855 a prefabricated Swiss chalet was imported from Germany and erected as a play house for the children, ordered, it is said, by Prince Albert in a bout of nostalgia for the alpine architecture of his German homeland. The children took great delight in this play house, where they made cakes and tea and entertained their parents. They even had their own allotments nearby and were provided with small-scale garden tools and wheelbarrows to play at gardening, all of which proved enormously popular. Later a miniature fort appeared as a practice ground for the more military minded boys to play at soldiers.

During the summer when the royal family was in residence, the island would hum with activity, and this despite the fact that the queen had hoped the sea journey would discourage an influx of curious visitors. The yachting season at Cowes became a highlight on the social calendar; in later years, the actress Lillie Langtry would recall how for nine months of the year Cowes would be deserted—"empty, forlorn and forgotten"(Langtry 1978, 69)—but that the minute the royal family were in residence by the beginning of August, "everyone who owned a yacht, or who could, by hook or crook, manage to get on board one, went to Cowes" (ibid.); within days every hotel and polite boarding house would be full.

After the death of Prince Albert in 1861, Queen Victoria retired from public view, spending virtually the whole year at her private residences. Winters, from December to February, were passed at Osborne, with the queen returning there for the summer months of July and August. In the spring she took a holiday in the south of France or Switzerland, and autumns were spent at Balmoral. After Albert's death the court came to Osborne for Christmas rather than spending the festive season at Windsor, a place that held too many painful memories for the queen (Albert had died there just before Christmas, on 14 December). Four months after Albert's death, Princess Alice was married at Osborne, in front of a temporary altar in the dining room, in a subdued ceremony, watched over by the queen in full mourning. In more happy circumstances, Alice's younger sister, Beatrice, married Prince Henry of Battenberg, at the little parish church at Whippingham near Osborne, where the royal family had regularly attended Sunday services. The little local church was, however, used less and less by the queen in old age; she resorted instead to the plain little chapel she had had built on the east end of the main wing of Osborne House in 1880.

In 1887 the queen took a surprising initiative at Osborne and commissioned the construction of a new west wing, probably sparked by the celebrations of her Golden Jubilee that year. Built during 1890–1891, this would provide resplendent accommodation for visiting dignitaries, with its focal point an oriental-style banqueting hall—known as the Durbar Room—in which Victoria would impress her guests with the wealth and diversity of her much loved Indian subcontinent. The interior design, executed by an Indian architect and designer, Bhai Ram Singh, incorporated both Indian and Saracen motifs in symmetrical designs in stone, wood, and plaster. It featured exotic creatures such as peacocks, orioles, and elephants, and an abundance of gilding and bright colors gave the room the look of an oriental palace. In 1897 it was crammed, like an Aladdin's cave, with many of the beautiful gifts that the queen received from royal relatives on the occasion of her Diamond Jubilee.

It was at Osborne that the queen died, on 22 January 1901, surrounded by her family. For fifty years after her death it remained closed up, a time capsule of Victoria and Albert's domestic life, filled with mementos and touchingly personal items, which many found morbid. Never having liked the place, King Edward VII gave the main and household wings and most of the estate at Osborne to the nation in 1902; the remainder became the Edward VII Convalescent Home for Serving and Retired Officers in 1904. Although the public were allowed in to view the state apartments and part of the gardens, it was not until the reign of Queen Elizabeth II that Queen Victoria's private apartments, including the room in which she died, were at last opened to the public (1954).

Related entries:
Balmoral Castle; Buckingham Palace; Fresh Air; Victoria, Queen: Death and Funeral of; Smoking; Windsor Castle

References and further reading:

Aronson, Theo. 1991. *Heart of a Queen: Queen Victoria's Romantic Attachments.* London: John Murray.

Benson, A. C., and Viscount Esher, eds. 1911. *The Letters of Queen Victoria: A Selection from Her Majesty's Correspondence between the Years 1837 and 1861.* 1st ser., 3 vols. London: John Murray.

Langtry, Lillie. 1978. *The Days That I Knew.* London: Futura.

Matson, John. 1975. *Dear Osborne.* London: Hamish Hamilton.

[One of Her Majesty's Servants.] 1901. *The Private Life of Queen Victoria.* London: C. Arthur Pearson.

Ponsonby, Magadalen. 1927. *Mary Ponsonby: A Memoir, Some Letters and a Journal.* London: John Murray.

Turner, Michael. 1999. *Osborne House.* Official Guide. London: English Heritage.

Whittle, Tyler. 1980. *Victoria and Albert at Home.* London: Routledge and Kegan Paul.

York, HRH Duchess of, and Benita Stoney. 1991. *Victoria and Albert: Life at Osborne House.* London: Weidenfeld and Nicolson.

P

Palmerston, Henry John Temple, Third Viscount (1784–1865)

We had, God knows! terrible trouble with him about Foreign Affairs (Buckle 1926–1928, 1:279)

Lord Palmerston was one of the great professional politicians of the Victorian era, along with William Gladstone and Benjamin Disraeli. He defended British nationalist interests in Europe in a career in the House of Commons that lasted (with one brief break), from 1807 until his death, serving in every ministry except those of Peel and Derby. His political decisions, often made without sufficient deference to the queen, were frequently controversial and often showed little or no regard for party politics. In his parliamentary career Palmerston worked to his own agenda, particularly in matters relating to foreign affairs; on occasion he acted with such notorious high-handedness and independence that he infuriated the queen as well as his colleagues in government.

Self-assertive, brusque, and interfering, Palmerston was viewed as a political firebrand by his detractors. But the newspaper-reading public in Britain, who referred to him as "Pam," loved him, particularly after he returned to power during the Crimean War. They respected the commitment with which he defended the interests of the country and his total lack of fear at having to carry the consequences of his actions. It was the public who kept Palmerston in power at times when most of those in the House of Commons, and certainly the queen and Prince Albert, would have liked to have been well rid of him.

Born in Broadlands, Hampshire, Henry John Temple was educated at Harrow and Edinburgh and studied at St. John's College, Cambridge University (1803–1806). He was elevated to the Irish peerage in 1802, succeeding his father as viscount and taking possession of the family's estates in County Sligo and Hampshire, and with them a pile of debts. His life as a career politician was thus in part necessitated by financial problems and began in 1807 when he became Tory member of Parliament for Newport, Isle of Wight. Almost immediately, he was invited to serve as lord of the Admiralty (1807–1809). Offered the plum but demanding job of chancellor of the Exchequer when he was still a political novice, Palmerston turned it down in favor of the less demanding role of secretary at war, with much of his work involving the financial administration of the army. He dutifully served in this post without controversy for nineteen years (1809–1828), in 1835 becoming member of Parliament for Tiverton, which he served until his death.

The British foreign secretary and later prime minister, Henry Temple, Lord Palmerston, often provoked rage and dismay in both the queen and Prince Albert for his breaches of protocol and his refusal to accede to their political wishes. (The **Illustrated London News** *Picture Library)*

Palmerston enjoyed the life of a nobleman and took pride in being a thoroughly English country gentleman. He was a fine shot and a fearless rider, and he had a string of fine race horses. He also enjoyed the high life in London, as a frequenter of Almack's Club, and became well known as a roué; his sybaritic lifestyle, his amorality, and sexual adventures led to the nickname "Lord Cupid." The social hostesses Lady Jersey, Princess Lieven, and Lady Cowper were said to have all been, at one time or another, his mistresses, along with a string of others. But it was Lady Cowper, the sister of Lord Melbourne, who won his heart and who also bore several of his children (while still married to Lord Cowper). Palmerston eventually married her in 1839 after she was widowed.

During his early career Palmerston had supported the policies of the progressive Tory George Canning, but after Canning's death in 1827 Palmerston joined the Whigs, as a supporter of parliamentary reform. He took the post of foreign secretary in 1830 under Earl Grey, remaining until the Whigs under Lord Melbourne fell from power in 1841. One of Palmerston's first important acts as foreign secretary, during 1830–1831, was to secure the independence of Belgium—a country strategically important to British security. After intense diplomatic activity, Palmerston managed to secure the establishment of a constitutional monarchy under Leopold I (the queen's uncle) and with it the maintenance thereafter of Belgian neutrality.

Although accusations of moral turpitude would regularly be laid at Palmerston's door during his career in domestic politics, in 1832 he gave his support to the Reform Bill. Foreign affairs would remain his preference, however, and his métier. In 1834 Palmerston secured the quadruple alliance of Britain and France with Spain and Portugal through his support for the independence of the thrones of Queen Isabella II of Spain and Maria of Portugal against the ambitions of French pretenders. In so doing, he created an alliance to counter that of Russia, Austria, and Prussia. This would be but one example of his habit, as foreign minister, of playing France off against Russia. In 1840 Palmerston's belligerent defense of British economic interests led to war with China, the so-called Opium Wars being triggered when the Chinese authorities attempted to put an end to the highly lucrative opium trade, in which many British merchants were heavily involved.

During the 1840s the queen's relations with Palmerston were extremely strained and bitter. But they had not always been so. When Victoria first ascended the throne in 1837, Palmerston, like Lord Melbourne, had been viewed by the queen as an elder statesman of gravitas whose advice on foreign affairs she valued. But as she became more self-confident in her position as monarch, particularly after her marriage, Victoria found Palmerston less and less the "agreeable" man he had first seemed to her. He regularly overstepped the mark in his conduct of foreign affairs, and she grew to dislike him intensely, finding him rude, unprincipled, and impetuous; however, she had little success in exerting greater control over him. No small part of this change in attitude had come under the strong moral influence of Prince Albert, who had serious objections to Palmerston's jaunty, irreverent manner, to his libidinous nature and his indiscretions. The two men could not have been more different: Palmerston the unrepentant man of the world whose political actions were guided by instinct; Albert the sober man of principle, patience, and balance who made no decisions without beforehand making the most carefully valued judgments.

After her marriage, the queen would see Palmerston very much through Albert's eyes and shared with him their own private nickname for him—Pilgerstein (*pilger* being German for "palmer"). Much to their joint horror, Palmerston increasingly took to issuing dispatches and memorandums before allowing sufficient time for the queen to make her own amendments. Sometimes he ignored her changes, even when he did receive them; often he sent them without consulting her at all, or only sending the obligatory copies after it was too late. Such behavior was not just mischievous; in the queen and Prince Albert's view, it was downright dangerous. It laid the British monarchy open to criticism and to insults from other nations. They attempted to rein in Palmerston by censure, as they would their own children when naughty, but by now his unbridled opportunism was beyond their control.

After a period out of office during the government of Sir Robert Peel, Palmerston returned to the Foreign Office in 1846, under Lord John Russell. He again infuriated the royal couple by taking a strong noninterventionist line during the year of revolutions of 1848. Unlike them, he sympathized in large part with the aspirations for independence in France, Italy, Germany, and the Austrian empire—so long as they did not affect British interests in Europe. Palmerston believed that enlightened, responsible government was sorely needed there, whereas the queen and Prince Albert were anxious to prop up its threatened monarchies (particularly the Germanic ones into which Albert's family, the Saxe-Coburgs, had intermarried).

Lord John Russell had a hard time trying to exert his authority over this renegade in the Foreign Office; attempts made during 1848–1850 to shunt Palmerston off into the relative backwater of Irish affairs, as lord lieutenant of Ireland, also failed. Things came to a head in 1850 with the Don Pacifico affair, a British quarrel with Greece. It rose when a Portuguese Jew from Gibraltar living in Athens, had claimed rights of British citizenship and protection when his property was destroyed by a Greek mob during an anti-Semitic riot in 1847. With his characteristic arrogance, Palmerston had responded with gunboat diplomacy, sending a fleet to blockade the port of Piraeus in January 1850 in support of Pacifico's inflated claim. This action took Britain to the brink of war, not just with Greece but also with France, which rose to the defense of Greek independence. Eventually a compromise settlement was reached, but for the queen this was the last straw: she demanded Palmerston's dismissal. Forced to defend his reckless brinkmanship, Palmerston did so with consummate skill during an exhausting four and a half hour speech in the House of Commons on 8 July 1850. This jingoistic speech, which was hugely popular with the public, silenced his detractors, including the queen, who herself recognized its brilliance. It defeated the conspiracy to oust Palmerston from power. The queen was furious that the unrepentant old reprobate Palmerston could be neither reformed, at the age of sixty-six, nor controlled: "There is no question of delicacy and danger in which Lord Palmerston will not arbitrarily and without reference to his colleagues or sovereign engage this country," she complained (Hibbert 1984, 82). But both she and Russell, who also wished to be rid of Palmerston, were powerless. A vote of censure against him was defeated. Palmerston triumphed—but not for long.

His fall from power came after he once again seriously overreached himself, this time through his support, in December 1851, for Louis Napoleon's coup d'état in France. Palmerston sent his congratulations before consulting either the queen or Parliament, an action that was not only unconstitutional but that also further antagonized his prime minister and the queen as well as many radicals in the government. Russell sacked him. Six weeks later Palmerston helped bring down Russell's weak government over its proposed Militia Bill.

In 1852 Palmerston bounced back, now serving in Lord Aberdeen's Whig-Peelite coalition ministry as home secretary (both the queen and Prince Albert having put their collective foot down over his return to the Foreign Office). He now, for once, promoted important domestic legislation, including the Penal Service Act that replaced transportation to Australia with imprisonment; the establishment of reform schools for young offenders; and measures to improve factory conditions and public health. But a year later he resigned when the government introduced another Reform Bill to extend the franchise. When the Crimean War broke out in 1854, the pacifist Aberdeen vacillated over committing Britain; the public and press were soon baying for the return of "Pam," as the only leader capable of securing military victory, a demand that filled the queen with horror. But after Aberdeen resigned in January 1855, she was forced to accept that Palmerston was, in the current crisis, the only man for the job. Despite now being over seventy, short sighted, and very hard of hearing, he became prime minister for the first time. He was derided for assuming the highest office at such an advanced age, Disraeli being of the opinion that Palmerston was "really an imposter, utterly exhausted, and at the best only ginger beer and not champaign [champagne], and now an old painted Pantaloon, very deaf, very blind, and with false teeth, which would fall out of his mouth when speaking, if he did not hesitate and halt so in his talk" (Londonderry 1938, 145–146). Disraeli was, however, forced to concede that "he is a name which the country resolves to associate with energy, wisdom, and eloquence, and will until he has tried and failed" (ibid.).

Queen Victoria and Prince Albert dreaded what new "trials" Palmerston would put them through; yet soon, by degrees, their relationship began to improve. Palmerston's former rudeness began to wane, and he proved to be more accommodating of the queen's views. They now found themselves concurring more and more over the promotion of Britain's interests abroad and in the maintaining of stability in the outreaches of the British empire, such as India, where Palmerston took strong measures to suppress the Indian Rebellion of 1857–1858. Long after Palmerston's death, the queen would admit that "with all his many faults" Palmerston had nevertheless "had the honour and power of this country strongly at heart" (Hibbert 2000, 283). She and Prince Albert now agreed "that of all the Prime Ministers we have had, Lord Palmerston is the one who gives the least trouble, and is most amenable to reason and most ready to adopt suggestions" (Charlot 1991, 367). They concluded that he was actually an "able, sensible & impartial man" (ibid.).

In 1856, Queen Victoria awarded Palmerston the Order of the Garter in recognition of his leadership during the Crimean War. He was out of power again during the brief Tory ministry of Lord Derby in 1858 but returned for a second term as prime minister with a greatly increased majority, at the age of seventy-five. However, after the death of Prince Albert in 1861, Palmerston found his own patience stretched by the queen's stubborn retreat into mourning and frequently was obliged to conduct his dealings with her by proxy, through her private secretary, General Grey. In 1863–1864 they were drawn into another clash of wills over British policy, this time over the Schleswig-Holstein crisis. Since the 1840s there had been controversy over the rights of Denmark and Germany over the mixed German- and Danish-speaking peoples living in these two duchies. In 1863 the Danish crown had attempted to unite Schleswig more closely with itself. Prussia and Austria intervened, forcing the Danes to cede Schleswig and Holstein to them. Palmerston supported Denmark's claim, whereas the queen and, while he was alive, Prince Albert wanted to see the territories united under Prussia. It was a controversy that divided even the royal family. In 1864 Prussian troops invaded on orders from Bismarck and defeated Denmark, but it remained a vexed and complicated issue that taxed the political skills of many. Palmerston himself is said to have observed that "only three men in Europe had ever understood [the Schleswig-Holstein affair] and of these the Prince Consort was dead, a Danish statesman (unnamed) was in an asylum, and he himself had forgotten it" (Seton-Watson 1937, 438).

Palmerston was returned to power for a final time in the elections of 1865 when he was past eighty, but in the event his health failed and he could not take up office. He died at his country estate, Brocket Hall, stubborn to the last, his parting words supposedly being "Die, my dear doctor! That's the *last* thing I shall do!" (Latham 1904, 2). The queen recorded his death in her journal. She had to admit to never really *liking* Palmerston, but she readily admitted his skills as a politician, remarking in a letter to her Uncle Leopold that "in many ways he is a great loss"; in conclusion, she observed that "he had many valuable qualities though many bad ones" (Hibbert 1984, 191).

Related entries:
Aberdeen, George Hamilton Gordon, Fourth Earl; Crimean War; Disraeli, Benjamin; Gladstone, William Ewart; Peel, Sir Robert; Russell, Lord John, First Earl

References and further reading:

Bourne, Kenneth. 1982. *Palmerston: The Early Years, 1781 to 1841.* London: Allen Lane.
Cecil, Algernon. 1953. *Queen Victoria and Her Prime Ministers.* London: Eyre and Spottiswoode.
Chamberlain, Muriel. 1987. *Lord Palmerston.* Cardiff: University of Wales Press.
Charlot, Monica. 1991. *Victoria, the Young Queen.* Cambridge: Polity.
Connell, Brian, ed. 1926. *Regina vs. Palmerston: The Correspondence between Queen Victoria and Her Foreign and Prime Minister, 1837–1865.* London: Evans Brothers.
Eccleshall, Robert, and Graham Walker. 1998. *Biographical Dictionary of British Prime Ministers.* London: Routledge.
Guedalla, Philip. 1926. *Palmerston.* London: Ernest Benn.
Hibbert, Christopher. 1984. *Queen Victoria in Her Letters and Journals.* London: Viking.
———. 2000. *Queen Victoria: A Personal History.* London: HarperCollins.
Latham, E. 1904. *Famous Sayings and Their Authors.* London: Sonneschein.
Londonderry, Marchioness of, ed. 1938. *Letters from Benjamin Disraeli to Frances Anne, Marchioness of Londonderry.* London: Macmillan.
Longford, Elizabeth. [1964] 1998. *Victoria R.I.* London: Weidenfeld and Nicolson (chap. 15).
Ridley, Jasper. 1970. *Lord Palmerston.* London: Constable.
Seton-Watson, R. W. 1937. *Britain in Europe 1789–1914.* Cambridge: Cambridge University Press.
Strachey, Lytton. [1921] 1971. *Queen Victoria.* Harmondsworth, UK: Penguin Books.

The Paranormal

that unseen world (Fulford 1964, 356)

Of all the many aspects of the queen's private life, the most speculated upon have undoubtedly been her relationship with John Brown and her supposed interest in the paranormal. The two subjects have in fact been closely linked, owing to persistent and unsubstantiated rumors that circulated during the queen's lifetime and continued after her death that Brown had been possessed of extrasensory gifts and had served her as a spiritual conduit for messages to and from the dead Albert. Biographers disagree on the extent to which the queen may or may not have dabbled in spiritualism and clairvoyance—namely through séances and table rapping. But, in general, they concur that the queen had a passing interest in all manner of such phenomena, including other fashionable pseudosciences of the Victorian era such as phrenology and "animal magnetism"—the inducement of trancelike states through mesmerism.

If the queen, and the highly rational Prince Albert for that matter, dabbled in such practices, then their activities need to be placed in the context of a cult of curiosity about the paranormal that was embraced across the whole Victorian social spectrum, with even prime ministers such as William Gladstone taking an almost unhealthy interest. Many writers of the day, including respected figures such as George Eliot (in the short story "The Lifted Veil"), turned their hands to tales of the occult. Others, such as Harriet Martineau, openly patronized mesmerism, and the philosopher Herbert Spencer wrote sober articles on phrenology. A great many otherwise respectable and well-educated people similarly gave serious attention to phenomena—spurious and otherwise—such as automatic writing, telepathy, levitation, and even manifestations of ectoplasm.

The spiritualist movement from which so much of this pseudoscience emanated had begun with the activities of the American mediums Margaret and Kate Fox in New York State in 1848. They had claimed to be able to communicate with the dead via messages conveyed by rapping noises on a table top. The cult rapidly spread at a time when, with high mortality rates—particularly of children—still prevailing, Victorian society was in the sway of a powerful cult of the dead and all its overblown funerary rituals. Many, the queen among them, sought consolation in the hope of the spirit's survival after the death of the body. Inspired by the Fox sisters, other practitioners had gone on the performance circuit claiming similar "gifts" for communicating with the other side. The spiritualist movement had tried in vain to rebut the accusations of fraudulence made by the religious establishment. It attempted to apply scientific method in proving its claims, but its reputation was tarnished by the increasing number of phony mediums and con artists who began cashing in on the gullibility of the grief stricken. The movement reached its nadir when the Ouija board (its name derived from the French *oui* and German *ja*) was patented in Baltimore in the United States in 1892—by a firm of toy makers, William and Isaac Fuld—to facilitate the speedier spelling out of words during séances.

Like many other Victorian families, the royal family experimented with table rapping when it first became fashionable in the 1850s—although very little reference to this is extant in published royal sources. Certainly, at Osborne in 1854, one of the queen's ladies-in-waiting, Mary Ponsonby, recorded that "the night before last the Queen sent me to know whether the tables had been made to go round in the Princess Royal's room" (Ponsonby 1927, 17). Having informed the queen that "there was a table going round in the dresser's room," she and other members of the royal household had gone up to the lady's maid's room, "and there we practised and succeeded" (17). Later on, the queen and Prince Albert joined in and "the entire evening was spent whirling tables around" (17). But it is clear that the table rapping that did take place was conducted more as a party game—and one that may well have been regularly engaged in for the amusement of the royal household during holidays at Osborne and Balmoral. It certainly persisted into the 1880s, for the queen's resident physician at Balmoral, Sir James Reid, observed the preoccupation of several of the royal household with séances—no doubt as a means of passing the tedious daily round. According to Reid, the queen and her youngest daughter, Princess Beatrice, conducted séances with Princess Irene (a granddaughter) and a lady-in-waiting. Even a reluctant Reid was dragooned into taking part—but again the emphasis was on the practice as a harmless diversion.

It was Prince Albert, who, interested in the rationalization of human behavior through scientific study, had taken a keen interest in phrenology (which as such marked a preliminary to the development of psychology). Its practitioners claimed that the distinctive topography of each human cranium could be charted and used as a guide to analyzing the configurations of the brain beneath—which determined the workings of that particular individual's personality. Like clairvoyance, phrenology became a popular pastime in Victorian England between 1820 and 1850—with demonstrations even taking place in working men's clubs and music halls. In 1842 the prince had requested that an eminent Edinburgh phrenologist, George Combe, analyze the bumps on the head of the Princess Royal and the Prince of Wales. Similarly, it has been suggested that the queen and Prince Albert may well, like many of their contemporaries, have attended spiritualist demonstrations by Daniel Dunglass Home, a famous medium patronized by their friend Emperor Napoleon III of France, their patronage of whom would have given cachet to the cult of the paranormal.

The rumors about the queen's interest in the paranormal gathered ground after the death of Prince Albert in December 1861, so much so that, in the opinion of Cullen, the endless perpetuation of "threadbare fabrications" (1969, 98) had turned the queen into "a prize exhibit of the spiritualists over the years" (97). Several of these apocryphal stories persist to this day. The most contentious is that relating to a boy medium, the thirteen-year-old James Lees. Apparently, during a mediumistic trance Lees had claimed to have received a message from Prince Albert in the spirit world, asking him to advise the queen to summon a gillie possessed of second sight, who had attended her in the Highlands, and through whom he would communicate with her. That gillie was, it is alleged, John Brown, and the boy's claim was substantiated supposedly by a séance with the queen at Windsor and a series of psychic tests, "during which he identified people from the Court who approached him under false names"(Compton 1977, 164). He also supposedly "gave the Queen a sealed envelope containing a pseudonym, unknown to anyone else, that the Prince had sometimes used when writing to her" (164). Lees apparently rejected the queen's request to appoint him her resident medium (Cullen 1969, 98) but would go on to become one of the most famous mediums of the Victorian era, patronized, among others, by both Benjamin Disraeli and William Gladstone.

But the overriding problem remains that no mention of this or any other occult practices survives in the queen's journals, nor in any of her extant letters. Elizabeth Longford, Tom Cullen, and Raymond Lamont-Brown have dismissed all claims that the queen indulged in secret séances with either Lees or Brown in attempts to contact her dead husband, whereas Underwood alleged (1982, 99) that the queen "certainly had sittings and seances with John Brown acting as a medium." He cites a story that, many years after the queen's death, King George VI came across detailed records of her séances—supposedly contained in one of Brown's diaries—"and spent a long time reading it" (110). (The séances by Brown were, it was rumored, conducted in the Blue Room at Windsor in which Prince

Albert had died.) As a counter to the continuing rumors, the weight of argument offered by detractors draws attention to the fact that the huge archive of Victoria's most important and *unedited* letters to her daughter Vicky in Berlin, with whom she was utterly candid over a forty-year correspondence on a vast range of subjects, contains no references to séances and spiritualism. Elizabeth Longford, considered by many to be Queen Victoria's most authoritative biographer, asserted that there is, purely and simply, no case to be made.

There might, however, have been one, had the one most important documentary source not been extensively censored by the queen's youngest daughter and literary executor, Princess Beatrice. She went through her mother's vast private archive after her death and systematically edited, transcribed, and then destroyed her journals and with them anything that she considered to be distasteful or in any way compromising. Underwood and the like-minded argued that the answer may very well have lain in the original unexpurgated text of her journals, or in the queen's letters to John Brown, which were destroyed after her death. Such destruction may well have been undertaken with the connivance of influential clerical figures at court, such as the queen's religious adviser, Randall Davidson, dean of Winchester. He was determined, like other establishment figures and members of the royal family, to ensure that Victoria's reputation both personally and as head of the Church of England should not be sullied by the survival of any reference to fringe religious practices in her writings. Twenty years after Brown's death, the queen's doctor, Sir James Reid, found himself having to mediate in a blackmail case when a cache of 300 letters written by Queen Victoria to a Dr. Profeit, in which she purportedly discussed her interest in communicating with the other world through Brown, was offered to the king. Reid was involved in the negotiations to buy the letters and oversaw their prompt destruction (see Reid 1996, 56). Recent commentators, such as Lamont-Brown (2000) have confirmed that "none of these matters, from spiritualism to Second Sight, is reflected in any documents or artefacts held in the royal collection at Windsor" (160). This is not, of course, to say that the queen had no interest in the subject. For, as Benjamin Disraeli remarked, when on his deathbed he was asked if he would receive a visit from the queen, "No it is better not. She would only ask me to take a message to Albert" (Blake 1966, 747).

Related entries:
Brown, John; Religion; Victoria, Queen: Personality of

References and further reading:

Blake, Robert. 1966. *Disraeli.* London: Eyre and Spottiswood.

Compton, Piers. 1977. *Victorian Vortex: Pleasures and Pecadilloes of an Age.* London: Robert Hale.

Cullen, Tom. 1969. *The Empress Brown: The Story of a Royal Friendship.* London: Bodley Head (esp. 96–99).

Lamont-Brown, Raymond. 2000. *John Brown: Queen Victoria's Highland Servant.* Stroud, Gloucestershire: Sutton.

Longford, Elizabeth. 1998. *Victoria R.I.* London: Weidenfeld and Nicolson (esp. 334–339, 341–342).

Pearsall, Ronald. 1972. *The Table Rappers.* London: Michael Joseph.

Ponsonby, Magadalen. 1927. *Mary Ponsonby: A Memoir, Some Letters and a Journal.* London: John Murray.

Reid, Michaela. 1996. *Ask Sir James: The Life of Sir James Reid, Personal Physician to Queen Victoria.* London: Eland.

Tisdall, E. E. P. 1961. *Queen Victoria's Private Life.* London: Jarrolds.

Underwood, Peter. 1982. *Queen Victoria's Other World.* London: Harrap.

Peel, Sir Robert (1788–1850)

a man of unbounded loyalty, courage, patriotism and high-mindedness (Hibbert 1984, 75)

The man who supplanted Lord Melbourne as Queen Victoria's second prime minister in 1841 (having tried and failed to form a ministry in 1839) had a very hard act to follow. Such had been the close, father-daughter relationship between Victoria and the sophisticated and relaxed Melbourne that the stiff and formal Peel was a decidedly marked contrast. The awkward, if not socially uncouth, Peel came from a different generation—the new self-made northern industrialists who had grown rich from textile manufacturing during the boom years of the industrial revolution. As social and political opposites, Peel and Melbourne could not have been more dissimilar, representing as they did the two poles of British political life—one vigorous, hard-working, and reformist, the other entrenched in idleness, tradition, and the patronage of the old aristocracy. Having none of the small talk or aristocratic finesse of his predecessor, Peel was greeted by the frostiest of welcomes by the queen when he first took office. By the time he tendered his resignation five years later, in 1846, Queen Victoria would have come to radically revise her original, hostile opinion.

The young Queen Victoria loathed Sir Robert Peel when he first replaced her beloved Lord Melbourne in 1841, but both she and Prince Albert grew to respect and value his supreme gifts as a statesman. (Library of Congress)

The son of a Lancashire cotton manufacturer, Peel was educated at Harrow and Oxford. His father bought him a pocket borough in 1809 so that he could enter Parliament, and a year later he received his first cabinet appointment, as undersecretary for war and the colonies (1810–1812) during Lord Liverpool's government. He moved from this post to that of chief secretary for Ireland (1812–1818). It was during his period as home secretary (1822–1827 and 1828–1830) that he established his reputation as a reformer, introducing changes in British criminal law and the prisons system and, most famously, setting up the Metropolitan Police Force, whose officers would be popularly nicknamed "peelers." During Wellington's ministry of 1828–1830, Peel carried the Catholic Emancipation Bill of 1829 despite his own personal doubts on the subject, but left government with Wellington's defeat. He returned to government as prime minister, also serving as first lord of the Treasury and then chancellor of the Exchequer during the reign of William IV (1834–1835), thereafter remaining in opposition effectively until 1841.

In 1834 at a political rally prior to elections in 1835, Peel delivered his classic Tamworth Manifesto, in which he immortalized the principles of Conservatism, based on a belief in the maintenance of a constitutional state committed to moderate reform. He briefly tried and failed to form a ministry in 1839 during the time of the Bedchamber Crisis (see "Bedchamber Crisis"), when a stubborn Queen Victoria refused to accede to his request to demonstrate her lack of political bias by divesting herself of some of her Whig ladies-in-waiting. The queen's response to Peel's awkward, reserved manner had been to describe him as "such a cold, odd man" (Esher 1912, 2:166). His predecessor, Melbourne, concurred, thinking Peel worthy but dull. It seemed unlikely therefore that the queen and Peel would get on when he was returned as prime minister after the fall of Melbourne, in August 1841.

Over the next five years, Peel repeatedly found himself forced by circumstance to dismantle the old political system of which the Tories had been the traditional defenders. He introduced a program of wide-ranging, and in many cases long-overdue, reform that would lead ultimately to his own political downfall. He began by reducing indirect taxation, replacing it with income tax (which even the queen was grudgingly obliged to pay), and introducing a series of budgets based on free trade. He reformed the Bank of England (Bank Charter Act 1844), improved working conditions in the factories (Factory Act 1844), improved standards of public health, and liberalized the British government in Ireland. Finally, after many years of intense debate in Parliament, Peel secured the repeal of the much-hated Corn Laws, a source of rural discontent since 1815, which had kept the price of British grain artificially high and had put money only in the pockets of the land-owning classes. The timely repeal of these laws came in 1845 during the Irish potato famine and a bad grain harvest in Britain. In his decision, Peel had the backing of the queen, who also had come to agree with him that "a removal of the restrictions upon the importation of food cannot be successfully resisted" (Charlot 1991, 260). At this high point in his career, however, Peel simultaneously lost the vote on the Irish Coercion Bill and, with his party irrevocably split over the issue after his alliance with moderate Catholics to ensure its passage, was forced to resign.

Elizabeth Longford has suggested that the key to Peel's later successful and harmonious relationship with Queen Victoria lay in the fact that he shared some of his personal qualities—integrity, diligence, incorruptibility—with Prince Albert. The prince had entered into regular correspondence with Peel and became a staunch supporter of his reformist program. Albert did a great deal to influence the queen's change of heart in her dealings with Peel and taught her to appreciate his political gifts and the wisdom of his political thinking. And in Peel, Prince Albert found a rare ally. For it was he who had gently encouraged the queen to allow the prince to sit in on their ministerial audiences from 1842 on, thus mitigating Albert's frustration at having no official role.

When his government fell in 1846, Peel seemed almost relieved to leave behind him the stresses and strains of political life. The five-month battle to get the repeal of the Corn Laws through Parliament had been debilitating. He could leave office, however, confident that his had been one of the strongest governments of that century and that it had brought the cost of living back to pre–Napoleonic War levels. Although he remained a member of Parliament, Peel was now able to spend more time at his home, Drayton Manor, in Staffordshire. He refused Queen Victoria's offer of the Order of the Garter. On 29 June 1850, when he was riding on Constitution Hill (near Buckingham Palace), he was thrown from his horse and badly injured; he died after several days in agony. Queen Victoria was greatly saddened by his death, having come to respect Peel's humility, his disinterest in personal preferment, and his talents as a servant of constitutional government. For here was a man who had sought to rise above the often sordid bickering of party politicking and who had laid the foundations for an epoch of stability in British government.

Related entries:
Bedchamber Crisis; Melbourne, William Lamb, Second Viscount; Palmerston, Henry John Temple, Third Viscount

References and further reading:

Benson, A. C., and Viscount Esher, eds. 1911. *The Letters of Queen Victoria 1837–1861.* 1st ser., 3 vols. London: John Murray.

Cecil, Algernon. 1953. *Queen Victoria and Her Prime Ministers.* London: Eyre and Spottiswoode.
Charlot, Monica. 1991. *Victoria: The Young Queen.* Cambridge: Polity.
Eccleshall, Robert, and Graham Walker. 1998. *Biographical Dictionary of British Prime Ministers.* London: Routledge.
Esher, Viscount, ed. 1912. *The Girlhood of Queen Victoria: A Selection from Her Majesty's Diaries between the Years of 1832 and 1840.* 2 vols. London: John Murray.
Fulford, Roger, ed. 1963. *The Greville Memoirs.* London: B. T. Batsford.
Gash, Norman. 1961. *Mr. Secretary Peel: The Life of Sir Robert Peel to 1830.* London: Longman.
———. 1972. *Sir Robert Peel: The Life of Sir Robert after 1830.* London: Longman.
Hibbert, Christopher. 1984. *Queen Victoria in Her Letters and Journals.* London: Viking.
Longford, Elizabeth. [1964] 1998. *Victoria R.I.* London: Weidenfeld and Nicolson.
Reed, D. 1987. *Peel and the Victorians.* Oxford: Blackwells.

Phipps, Sir Charles (1801–1866)

Phipps spoke to me with such pride & joy, at my beloved one's success (Woodham-Smith 1972, 316)

Sir Charles Phipps held an important position of trust in service to Prince Albert for fifteen years and was keeper of the queen's Privy Purse until he died in 1866. He shared with Gen. Charles Grey, the queen's private secretary, the unenviable task of persuading the reclusive monarch to attend to affairs of state at times when she felt that, as a distraught widow whose nerves were in a state of collapse, she was being excessively browbeaten by unsympathetic ministers.

The son of Sir Henry Phipps, first earl of Mulgrave, Phipps was, like Grey, an army man. He was born in Yorkshire and educated at Harrow, after which he entered the army in 1820. Between 1832 and 1834 he acted as private secretary to his brother, George Augustus, second Lord Normanby, when he was made governor of Jamaica, at a time when all slaves in the British empire were being emancipated. Phipps returned to army life during 1835–1839, rising to the rank of lieutenant colonel (1837) and serving his brother again during this period, when George was appointed lord lieutenant of Ireland. In 1846 he was appointed an equerry to the queen, and in 1847, while remaining on army half-pay, entered the service of Prince Albert, as his treasurer. Phipps shared his varied tasks with George Anson, the prince's private secretary, and General Grey. But by 1848, Phipps and Grey had taken over much of the work of Anson, who had become ill. Upon Anson's death in 1849, Phipps was made keeper of the queen's Privy Purse and treasurer to the Prince of Wales.

Little has been said or written about Phipps's quiet and unobtrusive character; his loyalty to the prince was born of a deep and mutual admiration and respect. According to Roger Fulford, Phipps acquitted himself well in his work; he was "judicious, unruffled and loath[ed] frothy exaggeration" (1966, 279). By 1851 the prince's workload had become considerable with the planning for that year's Great Exhibition, and Phipps resigned from his army post in order to assist the prince in its management. He believed that the success of the Great Exhibition would be a huge boost to the prince's public image and one that should finally silence his critics. He told the queen that the exhibition was, in his view, a vindication of the prince's work "after so much opposition & such difficulties" (Woodham-Smith 1972, 316). In 1855 Phipps attempted again to communicate to the queen his respect for Prince Albert but felt inadequate at doing him justice: "Colonel Phipps believes, not from his heart merely, but from more sober experience and matured judgement, that it is perfectly impossible to estimate the value of His Royal Highness as Consort to Your Majesty" (Emden 1934, 111).

Phipps was knighted for his devoted service in 1858. In the few years remaining to

Prince Albert, Phipps took a close, personal concern in his health and his increasing workload and tried to help reduce it. When the prince became seriously ill in early December 1861, Phipps tried to minimize the queen's anxiety and sustain the prince's own depressed and waning spirits, by playing down the seriousness of his condition, meanwhile remaining in close communication throughout with the prime minister, Lord Palmerston. Phipps was one of several members of the inner circle of the royal household who were called to Prince Albert's deathbed to make their final farewells. With the passing of the prince, Phipps felt that he had lost "the best man that I ever met with in my life" (Fulford 1966, 279). The British nation, he felt, "does not know . . . one tenth of what he did for them" (Weinbtraub 1997, 441). He admired also the queen's "quite wonderful" self-control in the first days of her widowhood and her "submissive resignation to the will of God in view of this stunning affliction" (St. Aubyn 1991, 328). The whole routine of her daily attention to government business was now disrupted by her refusal to see ministers and to deal with an increasing backlog of papers. Nor was a private secretary immediately appointed to help her and take over the huge workload that had formerly been the domain of the prince.

Phipps was only too aware of how bereft the queen was without the prince's guiding hand and regularly confided his apprehensions to Prime Minister Palmerston. In May 1862 Phipps took over the administration of the royal Duchy of Cornwall as receiver-general. But his energies were stretched by now having to deal with an extremely difficult and often histrionic monarch. By 1866 Phipps was worn out; he died of bronchitis at the age of sixty-five. In recognition of his devotion to her late husband, the queen ordered a funeral service be held for him at Westminster Cathedral and burial in the catacombs of St. George's Chapel at Windsor.

Related entries:
Albert of Saxe-Coburg-Gotha, Prince Consort; Anson, George Edward; Grey, General Charles; Ponsonby, General Sir Henry; Royal Household

References and further reading:

Bennett, Daphne. 1983. *King without A Crown.* London: Heinemann.

Emden, Paul. 1934. *Behind the Throne.* London: Hodder and Stoughton.

Fulford, Roger. 1966. *The Prince Consort.* London: Macmillan.

Martin, Sir Theodore. 1875–1880. *The Life of H. R. H. the Prince Consort.* 5 vols. London: Smith, Elder and Co.

St. Aubyn, Giles. 1991. *Queen Victoria, A Portrait.* London: Sinclair Stevenson.

Weintraub, Stanley. 1997. *Albert, Uncrowned King.* London: John Murray.

Woodham-Smith, Cecil. 1972. *Queen Victoria: Her Life and Times.* Vol. 1: *1819–1861.* London: Hamish Hamilton.

Photography

We were photographed with all the children, an instantaneous picture, which is very curious, as it even seizes & fixes emotion (Dimond and Taylor 1987, 79)

The sixty-three-year reign of Queen Victoria brought with it much invention and innovation, but nothing has probably been more significant in defining the mental picture we have of her than the photograph. Its advent allowed the wide dissemination of images of the queen throughout the empire, after photographs of her were first mass produced in the 1860s. Prince Albert and several members of the royal family embraced the new medium with enthusiasm; with the queen he built up a superlative collection of some 50,000 photographs that now form an important part of the Royal Archives at Windsor Castle.

In England, William Henry Fox Talbot had developed his own negative-positive photographic processes on silver chloride paper in the late 1830s, independently of the experiments in France at the same time made by Louis Daguerre, who invented the single-plate technique utilizing copper plates treated with silver. By 1839 the first daguerreotypes were being imported from France, but it was not until March 1841 that the photographic portrait—then still a rarity—was made available to the public, when Richard Beard set up a daguerreotype studio in London. Soon after, one of Daguerre's pupils, Antoine Claudet, established his own studio in London, having already presented the queen and Prince Albert with a selection of his images of European cities a couple of years earlier. But although a daguerreotype was made of Prince Albert as early as 1842, probably by William Constable, it is thought that the first photographer to capture the queen was Henry Collen, using the Calotype technique, some time in 1844.

As a notable patron of both science and the arts in Britain, it was inevitable that the prince consort would take great interest in the exciting new technique of photography. For her part, the queen, who embraced with enthusiasm any cultural pursuit approved of by her spouse, found that the photograph catered to her own insistence on a high degree of verisimilitude in all portraits of the royal family. In April 1847, the English daguerreotypist William Edward Kilburn, who had set up in London's fashionable Regent Street, was commanded by the queen to make the first daguerreotype portraits of herself, Prince Albert, and their children. Such a sought-after commission and Kilburn's almost immediate appointment as Photographist to Her Majesty and His Royal Highness Prince Albert led to his rise as a leading daguerreotypist of the day. Of particular significance in the history of photography is Kilburn's photograph of one of the earliest crowd scenes—the huge Chartist rally at Kennington Common in London in April 1848. Long presumed to have been lost, the photograph was rediscovered in the Royal Collection in the 1980s, a testament to the fine judgment of the royal couple as collectors.

Gernsheim and Gernsheim have pointed out that many of the first domestic photographs of the royal family were in fact not taken by professionals but by Prince Albert's librarian, Dr. Ernst Becker, and one of his equerries, Captain Dudley (1954, 258). The queen and Prince Albert both learned the early Calotype and Talbotype techniques of printing—known as the "black art" because of the staining this produced on the hands—and certainly produced some of their own photographs, although none of these seem to have survived. In the main, however, they would confine themselves to collecting rather than taking photographs, leaving the passion for photography as a hobby to be embraced by their children—in particular the Prince of Wales, Prince Alfred, Prince Leopold, and Princess Beatrice. At the end of the century, Alexandra, princess of Wales, would become one of the most gifted photographers in the royal family.

The Great Exhibition of 1851 would mark a turning point in the history of photography. Antoine Claudet, who now had premises in Regent Street, was much praised there for his work and won the highest award for portraiture. His new stereoscopic views, as well as those by Jules Duboscq, attracted much interest from the queen and Prince Albert, who were probably the first to buy one of the special, twin-lensed devices, designed by the firm of Duboscq-Soleil, on which to view them. Thanks to Victoria and Albert's patronage and the success of photographic exhibits at the Great Exhibition, sales of stereoscopic photographs became extremely popular. In 1853 Claudet was invited to take various portraits of the royal family and was appointed a royal-photographer-in-ordinary—the photographic equivalent of the queen's court painter Winterhalter—in this the year when the queen and Prince Albert were also invited to become patrons of the Photographic Society of London.

Through their patronage of this society, to which they donated money for the development of new photographic techniques, the queen and the prince met the pioneer photographer Roger Fenton, who was invited by them to set up a darkroom at Windsor in 1854. Prince Albert greatly admired Fenton's work and encouraged him to travel to the Crimea during the war of 1854–1856 to take what would be some of the first photographic experiments in photojournalism. With an eye to posterity, Albert had astutely commissioned Fenton to take 300 or more portraits of British soldiers and officers—many of them mutilated by their wounds—as a documentary record. He also commissioned several carefully composed and rather sanitized views of the battlefields, which were exhibited at the Royal Photographic Society's first exhibition in London in 1855. The Crimean War collection would be but one example of the prince's keen interest in photography as an important means of recording and teaching history. The scrupulous and systematic method that he adopted in mounting and cataloging his collection ensured that it would be preserved for posterity, the Crimean photographs constituting the first of nine volumes of photographs of British military campaigns that would be collected by the queen during her reign.

As photographic techniques became more sophisticated, the queen and Prince Albert extended their interests in photography to the serious and systematic collections of photography-as-art. And indeed Victoria and Albert proved to be as bold in their photographic collecting as they were in their unconventional penchant for the nude in art and sculpture. In 1857 they purchased an allegorical photograph—a collage of thirty separate negatives of seminude figures—executed by the London-based Swede Oscar G. Rejlander, entitled *Two Ways of Life.* It set out to mimic narrative painting on the same grand scale and, although it provoked considerable controversy in the art world, was purchased by the queen for ten guineas as a gift for Prince Albert. It is also noteworthy that from the early 1850s on Prince Albert utilized photography in his ambitious project to make photographic reproductions of the priceless drawings by the artist Raphael that were held in the Royal Collection and other repositories, the end result being published in 1876.

The success of the Great Exhibition and the advent in that year of the wet-collodion process using glass plates inaugurated a new and exciting era in the history of photography. Used in conjunction with the larger, more stable camera, the process finally made portrait photography commercially viable on a wider scale, although it would not be until the 1880s that the whole photographic process would become substantially more efficient. By the end of the 1850s, however, the *carte de visite* (visiting card) designed by André Disderi had become a popular novelty in polite society. He had refined the use of glass plates, making the process cheaper and therefore more accessible to ordinary people who wished to have a photograph taken for a special occasion. In 1859 the *carte de visite* had been given the royal seal of approval after Disderi's work was patronized by Emperor Napoleon III. A year later, the queen had *cartes de visite* made of her own family, who sat for the U.S. photographer John Mayall. These portraits were subsequently published in 1860 as a royal album—the first authorized royal collection of its kind—that sold extremely well, particularly after the prince consort's death in December 1861, when the entire stock of 70,000 copies of his own *carte de visite* by Marion and Co. was sold out in a single week—a landmark in the history of photography and one that led to black market copies being put on sale.

It was as much the rise of the photograph as the queen's retreat into mourning at the end of 1861 that brought an end to her till then lifelong pleasure in drawing and sketching people. By now she had become an avid collector of photographs of her ever-growing European family as well as of the members of her royal household and some of her long-serving servants. After Victoria was widowed, the photographic medium showed what a potent force it could be in the creation of an iconography of the dead. The queen began collecting photographs (or drawings) of friends, relatives, and even favorite servants on their deathbeds. She specifically requested such images whenever there was a death in her entourage and also took advantage of the invention of the microphotograph (1859) to have pendants, rings, and bracelets containing the dead Albert's photograph made up for herself, the royal family, and her ladies-in-waiting. A hand-colored photograph of Albert on his deathbed was hung above his now vacant side of the royal bed; and the queen regularly had herself and her children photographed in poses of quiet and doleful adoration, seated around Albert's marble bust.

As photographic techniques became more sophisticated and exposure times shortened with the introduction of fast gelatine dry plates in the 1880s, the camera was at last able to accommodate some movement in its subject. With it, more informal snapshots of the queen emerged—and at long last, the queen's all too elusive smile was at last captured. It was, nevertheless, a shock to many to see their sober little queen displaying her gums and a row of small mouselike teeth. The image of an unsmiling queen had been the bedrock of the iconography of her reign, although it had led to frequent criticism, such as from her eldest daughter Vicky in 1896. Photographs of her mother never did her justice, Vicky complained, to which the queen tartly retorted: "I fear I do not think . . . much of artistic arrangements in photographs and God knows there is nothing to admire in my ugly old person" (Dimond and Taylor 1987, 69).

The introduction of the lightweight, portable Kodak camera in 1888 finally brought photography to the masses, as well as to many younger members of the royal family. The princess of Wales took up photography in 1890, and the queen's youngest daughter, Princess Beatrice, also became an enthusiast after the premature death of her husband, Prince Henry of Battenberg, in 1896. Indeed, Beatrice spent so much time in the darkroom at Osborne that the queen's secretary, Sir Henry Ponsonby, would complain that she frequently neglected her duties of reading dispatches and letters to the queen because she was always "in a hurry to develop a photograph" (Hardy 1976, 189). The queen herself had continued to issue her royal warrant, now enjoyed by twenty-eight London photographers. Her favorite, and the most fashionable, was the Bassano Studio, again located in upmarket Regent Street and noted for the quality of the props it used—real furniture rather than pâpier-maché and cheap backdrops. By now the queen had become so completely enamored of the photographic art that one of her courtiers observed that "it is quite a weakness of hers to be photographed in every possible condition of her daily life" and that during family gatherings "the Queen's photographer is always to be sent for and ordered to 'fix the picture'" (One of Her Majesty's Servants 1901, 69–70).

Victoria found another important, functional use for the photograph—in the detailed photographing of every article of furniture, piece of plate or china, and even the smallest of decorative ornaments at each of her royal residences. After Prince Albert's death in the Blue Room at Windsor, it was carefully photographed from every angle on the queen's instructions, in order that it should be maintained precisely as it had been during his lifetime. Victoria's own private photographer, Mr. Cleave, was regularly dispatched either to Osborne, Balmoral, Windsor, or Buckingham Palace to ensure that this documentary record of all her homes was kept up to date. After approval by the queen, the photographs of all these objects, together with detailed descriptions and measurements, were bound in catalogs and regularly consulted in ensuring that all the royal palaces were maintained in precisely the same layout and decor as they had been during Prince Albert's lifetime. In old age, one of the queen's greatest pleasures was to sit for hours leafing through these vast catalogs or reliving her life with Albert through the forty-four volumes of family photographs and thirty-six volumes of *cartes-de-visite* that she had so carefully accumulated.

Related entries:
Alexandra of Denmark, Princess of Wales; Art and Artists; Beatrice Mary Victoria Feodore, Princess

References and further reading:

Dimond, Frances, and Ann Taylor. 1987. *Crown and Camera: The Royal Family and Photography.* Harmondsworth, UK: Penguin.

Gernsheim, Helmut, and Alison Gernsheim. 1954. *Queen Victoria: A Biography in Word and Picture.* London: Longman's Green and Co.

———. 1969. *The History of Photography.* Rev. ed. London: Thames and Hudson.

Hardy, Alan. 1976. *Queen Victoria Was Amused.* London: John Murray.

Lorne, Marquis of. 1901. *V.R. I.: Her Life and Empire.* London: Eyre and Spottiswoode.

Macdonald, Gus. 1979. *A Victorian Eyewitness.* London: Batsford.

[One of Her Majesty's Servants.] 1901. *The Private Life of Queen Victoria.* London: C. Arthur Pearson.

Stamp, Gavin. 1984. *The Changing Metropolis: Earliest Photographs of London 1839–1879.* Harmondsworth, UK: Penguin.

Ponsonby, General Sir Henry (1825–1895)

so universally beloved by all, high and low
(Ponsonby 1942, 406)

In her widowhood Queen Victoria was exceptionally well served by her private secretary, Sir Henry Ponsonby, a man of exemplary good humor and tolerance who sacrificed his own health to an impossible workload. If all the many and flattering epithets applied to Ponsonby are true, then he was not only a paragon of patience, hard work, fair mindedness, discretion, and tolerance but also one of Britain's most underrated, unofficial statesmen. And what is more, he managed to be so at a time when the queen, in her self-imposed seclusion, was often at her most querulous and dictatorial.

Ponsonby had the perfect background for royal duties: he came from a respected Anglo-Irish family with a tradition of service to the Crown in the army, navy, and diplomatic service. He was related to the queen's previous private secretary, Earl Grey, through his marriage in 1861 to one of Grey's granddaughters, Mary Bulteel—herself a childhood friend of the queen's eldest daughter, Vicky, and a lady-in-waiting to the queen. Ponsonby had entered the army in 1842; from 1847 to 1858 he served as private secretary and aide-de-camp to his uncle, Lord Bessborough, the lord lieutenant of Ireland and to two of his successors. He requested permission to rejoin his regiment of the Grenadier Guards to serve during 1855–1856 in the Crimean War, after which he was appointed equerry to Prince Albert (he still remained attached to his regiment). Ponsonby was promoted, after service in Canada (1862–1864), to major general (1868) and appointed equerry to Queen Victoria in 1864. On 8 April 1870, on the death of the queen's private secretary, General Grey, Ponsonby seemed the most obvious successor. His life thereafter would be so consumed by his duties to the queen that he would have to endure frequent separations from his wife and family in order to be in constant attendance upon the queen at all her royal residences. And indeed, Ponsonby found himself having to undertake a dual role—that of private secretary as well as, from 1878 on, keeper of the Privy Purse (the two functions had originally been separate).

Eventually two assistant secretaries—Sir Arthur Bigge and Sir Fleetwood Edwards—were appointed to help him, but Ponsonby's workload remained prodigious.

The appointment as private secretary brought Ponsonby one the most important roles within the royal household (and one that had not been created until 1805 under George III). With the queen still stubbornly resisting calls from the press and her ministers to show herself in public, the conscientious Ponsonby was seriously concerned at the damage to her public image this was causing. It was certainly fueling republican discontent, and he feared that "if . . . she is neither the head of the Executive nor the fountain of honour, nor the centre of display, the royal dignity will sink to nothing at all" (Ponsonby 1942, 71). When he felt the "royal dignity" was even more seriously threatened by the queen's decision to publish a biography of John Brown after his death in 1883, Ponsonby was swift to find subtle but firm ways of persuading her against such a step. He wrote to her, asking the "Queen's forgiveness if he expresses a doubt whether this record of Your Majesty's innermost and most sacred feelings should be made public to the world" (Auchincloss 1979, 11). The queen eventually recognized the wisdom of this; she relented in her stubborn insistence and did not go ahead with the biography, although, true to character, she made absolutely no admission that Ponsonby had drawn such a concession from her.

It required similar diplomatic skills on Ponsonby's part to juggle the legitimate demands made on the queen as monarch with her frequently overblown reaction to the pressure placed upon her, a pressure that the queen frequently threatened was taking her to the brink of physical and nervous collapse. Ponsonby fielded such outbursts with great aplomb, remaining highly sensitive to the queen's occasional lapses into unconstitutional behavior. These were most manifest in regard to her favoritism of Benjamin Disraeli over and above William Gladstone, whose ministry she was obliged to accept in 1880 after Disraeli's fall from power. As a convinced Liberal and admirer of Gladstone, Ponsonby did not allow his own political sentiments to color his good judgment and impartiality when advising the queen. It is regrettable that his political acumen was never usefully exploited in a wider political arena, although he played an invaluable role as a moderating force, guiding the queen through the minefield of some of the most contentious issues of her reign, such as Home Rule in Ireland, Cardwell's reforms of the army, and the extension of the franchise. As Disraeli observed of Ponsonby's even-handedness in all such affairs: "I can only say that I could not wish my case better stated to the Queen than the Private Secretary does it" (Reid 1996, 41).

The writer A. C. Benson has described Ponsonby as being the "most perfectly and beautifully courteous man . . . so resourceful, so entirely natural that for a time one hardly realised what triumph of art, in a sense, his manner was, how singularly trained, adjusted, and applied to bring about the complete ease and security of any circle in which he found himself" (Emden 1934, 402). Tall, somewhat gangly, and with a natural stoop, Ponsonby set no store by his personal appearance. He wore his trouser legs too long and often looked crumpled, but he exuded such natural charm and kindliness that he had an innate talent for putting people at their ease. If anyone made life bearable at court during the long dull days at Windsor and Osborne, it was he, certainly until the vivacious Henry of Battenberg married into the family in 1885. The two men, both good conversationalists and possessed of a strong sense of humor, immediately established a great rapport; Battenberg soon dragooned Ponsonby into amateur theatricals to relieve what Ponsonby himself had described in 1878 as the "uneventful stagnant atmosphere of Balmoral" and the "severe dreariness of its palatial rooms" (Ponsonby 1942, 75, 116).

As a man of absolute discretion, Ponsonby was looked upon by those in service to the queen as a wise owl in whom they could confide. He always made time for people seeking his advice, no matter how busy he was, and was a good listener. If any single facet of his personality kept him on an even keel during some very trying times in the queen's service, it was probably his broad sense of humor. Ponsonby had an ability to preserve a healthy, but discreet irreverence for the queen's sometimes unreasonable demands. Although appreciating her basic good sense, he learned never to take her too seriously when she overindulged in cataloging her many woes. He knew precisely when to climb down gracefully whenever the queen, against his good advice, stubbornly stuck to her views, however misguided. He knew how much she hated having to concede that she was in the wrong and so did his best, wherever possible, to modify her extremely autocratic behavior and, as Emden observed, "to lead the sometimes overflowing temperament into smoother waters" (1934, 164). The secret of his skill was to get the queen to compromise without knowing that she had. And if the queen's sometimes absurd irrationality could not be countered, then so be it. "When she insists that two and two make five I say that I cannot help thinking they make four. She replies that there may be some truth in what I say, but she knows they make five. I drop the discussion" (Ponsonby 1942, 151).

Ponsonby's onerous daily duties involved him in the reading and digesting of all incoming official documents and preparing clearer copies in thick black ink of many of them. He also had to keep tabs on everything that was going on in Parliament and on events of any public significance. On a more trivial, but hugely time-consuming level, he also suffered under the queen's directive that every communication, no matter how brief, between himself and the many members of the royal household, should be made in writing, and, for that matter, with the ponderous formality of being written in the third person. In addition to all these duties, Ponsonby's son, Arthur, noted that both his father's and the queen's time and patience were exercised in listening to "the grievances, complaints, poverty, debts and most especially desire for rank and promotion of the many minor royalties who hovered at a distance round the Court" (Ponsonby 1942, 94).

The queen never publicly acknowledged the huge burdens placed on Ponsonby, if anything, finding fault even more in their last years together, especially when his handwriting became, as she claimed, increasingly difficult to read. Unfortunately, Ponsonby's eyesight, like hers, was failing, as too were his energies and his powers of recall. He was rapidly outliving his usefulness, and the queen complained that he was far too passive and compliant and seemed to have no opinions of his own. Although she might remain grudging in her appreciation of Ponsonby's skills, there were others in high places who went out of their way to communicate their appreciation of them. Not the least of these was William Gladstone, who on his retirement in 1894, commended Ponsonby as being a true gentleman, "to the manner born," observing that "such a combination of tact and temper with loyalty, intelligence and truth I cannot expect to see again" (Auchincloss 1979, 117).

On 6 January 1895, all the stresses and strains of his work finally took their toll; Ponsonby suffered an attack of paralysis and lost his power of speech. The queen visited him regularly, but he remained partially paralyzed in his right arm and leg. By May it was clear that he would never recover; in any event, his mental faculties were irretrievably impaired, as the queen's resident physician, Sir James Reid, regretfully informed Victoria. Ponsonby's wife composed a letter of resignation on his behalf; seven months later he died and was buried in the small parish church at Whippingham on the Isle of Wight. Ponsonby's successor, Sir Arthur Bigge, shared the view of many that overwork had killed him—as it had done Prince Albert in 1861.

To lose Ponsonby after thirty-eight years of loyal service in the royal household was, for the queen, a major inconvenience. Although she assured his widow that "his memory will ever be gratefully remembered by me and mine" (Ponsonby 1942, 406), she had only once in their long association stepped over the very formal boundaries that divided them as monarch and servant and written to him in the first person—on the occasion of the death of his mother. Ponsonby's wife, Mary, herself a strong personality of decidedly radical views that had often alarmed the queen, defined the most important quality in her husband's "strong, generous, loveable character" as being his ability for "self-effacement." "The absence of egotism and vanity was simply a second nature" to him, she wrote, and "it was above all the absence of effort and the unconsciousness with which he put himself always last which was astonishing" (Ponsonby 1927, 192–193).

It is the opinion of Louis Auchincloss that Ponsonby raised the role of private secretary to a "great art" (1979, 106), but the man himself never showed the least concern with receiving praise or credit where due, although he eventually accepted a knighthood in 1879. His crucial role in the management of the queen's day-to-day duties as monarch is often, for this reason, underestimated. The ultimate sign of Ponsonby's warm heart, informality, and accommodating manner could be seen in the sign he had posted on his study door: "Don't knock; come in" (106).

Related entries:
Battenberg, Henry Maurice, Prince of; Bigge, Lieutenant Colonel Sir Arthur; Grey, General Charles; Phipps, Sir Charles; Reid, Sir James; Royal Household; Victoria, Queen: As a Monarch

References and further reading:

Auchinloss, Louis. 1979. *Persons of Consequence: Queen Victoria and Her Circle.* London: Weidenfeld and Nicolson.

Emden, Paul. 1934. *Behind the Throne.* London: Hodder and Stoughton.

Hibbert, Christopher. 1979. *The Court of St. James: The Monarch at Work from Victoria to Elizabeth II.* London: Weidenfeld and Nicolson.

———. 1984. *Queen Victoria in Her Letters and Journals.* London: Viking.

———. 2000. *Victoria: A Personal History.* London: HarperCollins.

Kuhn, William M. 2002. *Henry and Mary Ponsonby: Life at the Court of Queen Victoria.* London: Duckworth.

Lutyens, Mary, ed. 1961. *Lady Lytton's Court Diary 1895–1899.* London: Rupert Hart-Davis.

Ponsonby, Arthur. 1942. *Henry Ponsonby: His Life from His Letters.* London: Macmillan.

Ponsonby, Magadalen. 1927. *Mary Ponsonby: A Memoir, Some Letters and a Journal.* London: John Murray.

Reid, Michaela. 1996. *Ask Sir James: The Life of Sir James Reid, Personal Physician to Queen Victoria.* London: Eland.

Watson, Vera. 1952. *The Queen at Home: An Intimate Account of the Social and Domestic Life of Queen Victoria's Court.* London: W. H. Allen.

Q

Queen Victoria Memorial

I devoted myself entirely to those qualities which made our great Queen so beloved [Sir Thomas Brock] (Plunkett 1999, 8)

Within days of the queen's death in January 1901, plans were laid throughout the empire to erect a series of statues and memorials to her—as had been the case after the death of Prince Albert in 1861. In London it was decided to erect a permanent memorial outside Buckingham Palace (rather than Westminster Cathedral, which was also suggested), as part of wider-reaching plans to transform the whole frontage and thoroughfare leading to the palace. A committee was formed to discuss various designs submitted in a small-scale competition among five architects. It settled on one of suitable imperial grandeur by Sir Aston Webb, at the center of which would be a statue of the queen in white Sicilian marble, by the sculptor Thomas Brock. In the twentieth century, the Queen Victoria Memorial would become the focal point of a remodeled and enlarged Mall leading from the newly constructed Admiralty Arch at the Charing Cross corner of Trafalgar Square, to Buckingham Palace. Designed by Webb, this was undertaken over a ten-year period, 1901–1911. The Mall was also considerably widened at this time to become the grand processional route that for the last century has served as the conduit between the palace and St. Paul's Cathedral and Westminster Abbey on all royal state occasions—such as the state opening of Parliament, coronations, and state funerals.

The eighty-two-foot-high Queen Victoria Memorial, comprising 2,300 tons of marble and surrounded by two semicircular fountains, has as its perimeter the nearby Memorial Gardens and their lamplit, ornamental gateways with emblems representing the far corners of the empire. The memorial itself was envisaged to symbolize the achievements of the queen's life, reign, and empire and is composed of a white marble platform, surrounded by solid granite paving and topped with a statue of Victory, covered in gold leaf, together with her handmaidens Courage and Constancy. The statue of Queen Victoria enthroned, which sits at the base of this group, depicts the queen dressed in her robes of state and holding the orb and scepter. She gazes straight ahead of her, down the wide, leafy thoroughfare of the Mall, although, as Mee pointed out (1960, 177), during the queen's reign this thoroughfare was little more than an unmade country lane.

At the base of the marble platform on which the queen's statue rests are representations of Truth, Justice, and Motherhood. Weinreb and Hibbert observed that

The Queen Victoria Memorial, constructed opposite the gates of Buckingham Palace after the queen's death as a lasting tribute to the great days of empire. (Hulton/Archive by Getty Images)

the writer Sir Osbert Sitwell described these sentimental representations in less than flattering tones—as "tons of allegorical females in white wedding cake marble, with whole litters of their cretinous children" (1983, 630). Like the Albert Memorial, the monument is approached by flights of steps, at the four corners of which are plinths mounted with bronze representations of Manufacture and Agriculture, Progress and Peace, Painting and Architecture, and the Army and Navy. Other statuary and emblems on the central monument denote various aspects and products of the empire. Lower down, at ground level, and continuing Brock's chosen emphasis on Britain's maritime power, the monument is encircled with a wall containing friezes of legendary sea gods and water nymphs.

The new Queen Victoria Memorial and its nearby formal gardens (also created by Webb) were officially unveiled by Queen Victoria's grandson Kaiser William II, on Empire Day, 24 May 1911. By this time, the German Empire over which he reigned was engaged in building a massive fleet and mounting a serious maritime challenge to British supremacy. As Plunkett observed, the monument already represented "an acute contrast between its grandiloquent pretensions and the imperial world order it had been originally intended to self-evidently embody" (1999, 9). Three years later, Britain and Germany would be at war.

Most of the construction of the Queen Victoria Memorial, Admiralty Arch, and the Mall was completed in time for the coronation procession of King George V in 1911.

Related entries:
Albert Memorial; Art and Artists; Royal Albert Hall; Victoria and Albert Museum

References and further reading:

Darby, Elizabeth, and Nicola Smith. 1983. *The Cult of the Prince Consort.* New Haven: Yale University Press.

Jones, Edward, and Christopher Woodward. 1983. *A Guide to the Architecture of London.* London: Weidenfeld and Nicolson.

Mee, Arthur. [1937] 1960. *The King's England: London, Heart of the Empire and Wonder of the World.* London: Hodder and Stoughton.

Plunkett, John. 1999. "Remembering Victoria: The National Memorial to the 'Great Queen.'" *The Victorian,* no. 1 (August): 4–9.

Service, A. 1977. *Edwardian Architecture: A Handbook to Building Design in Britain.* London: Thames and Hudson.

Weinreb, Ben, and Christopher Hibbert, eds. 1983. *The London Encyclopedia.* London: Macmillan.

R

Racial and Religious Prejudice

natives and coloured races should be treated with every kindness and affection as brothers (Buckle 1926–1928, 2:361)

With regard to issues of racial and religious intolerance, the queen developed very determined and unconventional views, as she did on class, from an early age. As young as seventeen, when staying at her Uncle Leopold's home in Sussex, she had noted that the arrival of gypsies in the neighborhood had brought with it unfounded accusations of crime, with any misdemeanors being laid at their door. She found this "shocking" and asked "if they are always looked upon as vagabonds, how *can* they become good people?" (Esher 1912 1:182). In later life she applied the same attitude to her perception of other minority groups and races. Immune to the preconceived ideas of her times about racial inferiority, she judged individuals not by their color but by their merits.

When the Conservative politician Benjamin Disraeli rose through Parliament to become leader of his party, and prime minister for the first time in 1868, the queen gave her approval to a man who had not just risen above his social station (his father having been a writer rather than an aristocrat) but who had also done so as a Jew. The fact that he had been baptized a Christian in 1817 could do nothing to counter the prejudice meted out to Disraeli for his unmistakably Semitic features. Eventually he succeeded in becoming an establishment figure against the odds, by marrying above him and achieving a title. The manner in which he fought his way to the top made him, in the queen's eyes, forever a man of the people.

Queen Victoria's lack of prejudice toward Jews had also manifested itself soon after her accession when she had knighted Sir Moses Montefiore, a sheriff of the City of London—the first Jew in Britain to be so honored. Victoria viewed Montefiore as "an excellent man, charitable to the highest degree & universally respected" (Arnstein 1986, 115), and later made him a baron. But in 1869 she refused to grant a knighthood to another Jew, Nathaniel Rothschild, the son of the famous Jewish banking family; in his case, she felt the family had achieved its wealth and status by usury—rather than through philanthropic work as in the case of Montefiore. (She finally relented in 1885 and granted the knighthood to Rothschild.) During the last twenty years of her reign Victoria was outraged by the rise of anti-Semitism and the pogroms carried out against Jews in eastern Europe. She was a passionate supporter of the French Jew, Capt. Alfred Dreyfus, the victim of rampant anti-Semitism in the French army. When, in 1899, Dreyfus was imprisoned after a retrial at which he had been expected to be acquitted, Victoria thought the verdict "monstrous." "I am quite *boulversée* by the news of poor martyred Dreyfus's new condemnation," she wrote. "It is the greatest disgrace to France and the army which could take place" (Ramm 1990, 235). She fired off a telegram to her prime minister, Lord Salisbury, expressing her outrage and hoping that "all Europe would express its horror and indignation!" (Weintraub 1996, 603).

The queen became similarly impassioned about the treatment of the "Mohammedans" (Muslims) and other non-Christian peoples of her empire. She felt many were browbeaten into conversion by missionaries with no respect for non-Christian cultures and traditions. She considered it the Crown's duty to set a civilizing, Christian *example* in the colonies, but that was all. Her respect for religious devotion of any persuasion extended to a tendency to favor the followers of Islam, such as the Turks—because they at least "believe most sincerely in a God" (Arnstein 1986, 120)—over and above the Christians of the Eastern Orthodox church, whose religious practice she felt, in Romania in particular, was still too closely bound up with ancient pagan beliefs. After the Indian Rebellion of 1857–1858 the queen, unlike many of her ministers and military leaders, had sided with her viceroy of India, Lord Canning, in advocating reconciliation rather than revenge. She issued a proclamation that disclaimed "the right and desire to impose our convictions on any of our subjects" (120). In 1892, the first Asian member of Parliament—Dadabhai Naoraji—was elected Liberal member for Central Finsbury in London. During the Boer War of 1899–1901 the queen would have liked her loyal Indian troops to be allowed to serve alongside her British troops in South Africa, but she was firmly advised by her prime minister, Lord Salisbury, that such a move would have caused an uproar in Parliament.

The clearest indicator of the queen's lack of racial prejudice came in Jubilee Year 1887, when she introduced the first Indian servants into her own household. She even went to the trouble of learning some Hindustani in order to be able to speak to them. Such an innovation provoked the first distasteful manifestations of the endemic racial prejudice among the members of the queen's entourage. Victoria was incensed by the hostility toward her new personal attendant, Abdul Karim, known as the Munshi, and the refusal of members of the household to kow tow to or to socialize with him. But, as Lutyens observed, such a reaction was as much due to culture shock as it was to racial prejudice, for "there were few English people in those days who would sit down at table with an Indian were he not a prince" (1961, 42). The queen made clear her own feelings, ordering that no one in her court should refer to Indians as "black men" (Longford 1998, 509). When the gentlemen of the household refused to sit at table with the Munshi during her holiday in the south of France in 1897, she openly accused them of "race prejudice" and insisted they should treat him with greater deference. She expected the same respect to be accorded to all the native peoples of the British Empire. As far back as the 1840s she had corresponded with some Yoruban chiefs in Africa, and she felt, as monarch, that she had a duty to protect them. She had, she admitted, a "very strong feeling (and she has few stronger)" (Buckle 1926–1928, 2:361) on the subject. All ethnic groups in the empire "should be treated with every kindness and affection as brothers, not—as alas! Englishmen too often do—as totally different beings to ourselves, fit only to be crushed and shot down!" (2:361).

The queen had wholeheartedly welcomed the emancipation of Britain's slaves in 1833 and, with Prince Albert, had been a staunch advocate of the emancipation of the slaves in the United States. In 1851, she had been fascinated by the presence at the Great Exhibition of a solitary black exhibitor, Josiah Henson. A former slave, Henson was feted as a celebrity during his time in London, meeting the prime minister and the archbishop of Canterbury. He was soon to be the inspiration for the eponymous hero of Harriet Beecher Stowe's classic antislavery novel, *Uncle Tom's Cabin* (1852). Twenty-five years later Henson revisited Britain, at the age of eighty-seven, on a preaching and lecture tour. Having been greatly moved by Stowe's novel, the queen was anxious to meet him and invited Henson and his wife to Windsor on 5 March 1877. Here, they were received with considerable warmth, the queen informing Henson that she "had taken the 'deepest interest'" in his "afflicted people" all her life (Morris 2001, 3).

Another little known story, confirming the queen's personal interest in her African subjects, has recently come to light, thanks to research by Walter Dean Myers. In 1850 Victoria took up the sponsorship of the daughter of an Egbado chieftain, who had been rescued from slavery in the west African kingdom of Dahomey by a British sea captain, Frederick Forbes. King Gezo, whose wealth was built on slavery, had made a gift of the girl to Queen Victoria during a mission to his palace by Forbes, who had brought the girl back to England on his boat the HMS *Bonetta,* hence her adoptive name—Sarah Forbes Bonetta. The queen readily took up the cause of Sally (as she called her), remaining her friend and protector until she was old enough to marry. Sally first visited the queen at Windsor Castle in November and impressed the queen by being "sharp & intelligent" (Dimond and Taylor 1987, 113). After living with the Forbes family for about a year, during which time she visited the queen and royal children at Windsor on several occasions, Sally became particularly attached to Princess Alice. But when she was eight, she was sent back to Africa, in May 1851, to attend a mission school in Sierra Leone (the queen thinking the damp English climate was harmful to her health). Her education continued to be paid for by the queen, with whom Sally corresponded and from whom she received regular gifts of games, toys, and books. But Sally was very unhappy, and in September 1855 the queen agreed to her return to England, recording Sally's visit to her at Windsor: "Saw Sally Forbes, the negro girl whom I have had educated: she is immensely grown and has a lovely figure" (Myers 1999, 72).

Sarah Forbes Bonetta was inevitably the object of considerable curiosity in England, admired for her considerable intelligence and the rapidity with which she learned English. She lived a relatively comfortable life with patrons in Gillingham, Kent, and then in Brighton on the Sussex coast. In January 1858, the queen, as a mark of the high regard in which she held Sally, invited the young woman to attend the wedding of Victoria the Princess Royal. In 1862, Sally reluctantly submitted to marriage to a West African businessman (a widower, James Pinson Labulo Davies), returning to Africa with him. She named her first child, a daughter, after the queen, who agreed to be the child's godmother and presented baby Victoria with a cup, salver, knife, fork, and spoon—all in gold, the cup and salver inscribed "To Victoria Davies, from her godmother, Victoria, Queen of Great Britain and Ireland, 1863" (Myers 1999, 126). In December 1867, on a visit to England, Sally saw the queen for the last time. Victoria again recorded the event in her journal: "Saw Sally, now Mrs. Davies & her dear little child, far blacker than herself, called Victoria & aged 4, a lively intelligent child, with big melancholy eyes" (128). Sally was, however, now sick with tuberculosis; she went to Madeira for her health, where she died in 1880 at the age of about thirty-seven. The queen heard the news on the very day she was expecting a visit from her godchild Victoria, to whom she offered her maternal comfort, later resolving in her journal "I shall give her an annuity" (136).

Related entries:
Boer War; Empress of India; Golden Jubilee; Indian Rebellion; Religion

References and further reading:

Arnstein, Walter L. 1986. "Queen Victoria and Religion." In Gail Malmgreen, ed., *Religion in the Lives of English Women*. London: Croom Helm.

Buckle, George Earl, ed. 1926–1928. *The Letters of Queen Victoria 1862–85*. 2d ser., 3 vols. London: John Murray.

Dimond, Frances, and Ann Taylor. 1987. *Crown and Camera: The Royal Family and Photography*. Harmondsworth, UK: Penguin.

Esher, Viscount, ed. 1912. *The Girlhood of Queen Victoria: A Selection from Her Majesty's Diaries between the Years of 1832 and 1840*. 2 vols. London: John Murray.

Hargrove, W. B. 1918. "The Story of Josiah Henson." *Journal of Negro History* 3 (January): 1–21.

Johnston, Penelope. 1990. "Canada's Uncle Tom." *History Today* 40 (September): 3–4.

Longford, Elizabeth. [1964] 1998. *Victoria R.I.* London: Weidenfeld and Nicolson (352–354, 373–375).

Lutyens, Mary, ed. 1961. *Lady Lytton's Court Diary 1895–1899*. London: Rupert Hart-Davis (38–42).

Morris, Jan. 2001. "The Real Uncle Tom." *Guardian* 21 (April): 3.

Myers, Walter Dean. 1999. *At Her Majesty's Request: An African Princess in Victorian London*. New York: Scholastic Press.

Ramm, Agatha. 1990. *Beloved and Darling Child: Last Letters between Queen Victoria and her Eldest Daughter, 1886–1901*. Stroud, Gloucestershire: Sutton.

St. Aubyn, Giles. 1991. *Queen Victoria: A Portrait*. London: Sinclair Stevenson (354–356, 506).

Sweet, Matthew. 2001. *Inventing the Victorians*. London: Faber and Faber.

Weintraub, Stanley. 1996. *Victoria*. London: John Murray.

Reid, Sir James (1849–1923)

The queen has . . . great confidence in his zeal and unremitting attention and able treatment of herself and family (Reid 1996, 114)

James Reid, the queen's favorite personal physician, resident with her from his appointment in 1881 until her death in 1901, was like John Brown a straightforward, honest Scotsman. Like Brown he uncomplainingly placed himself at the queen's beck and call at all hours of the day and night. His patience, tolerance, and easygoing manner made him naturally approachable, and Reid became the confidant of several members of the royal entourage, who frequently solicited his sympathy and good advice. Like the self-effacing Sir Henry Ponsonby, Reid would tend to hide his own light under a bushel; for this reason his important role in the queen's final years has often, like Ponsonby's, been overlooked.

From a middle-class family in Aberdeenshire, he was born in the town of Ellon, the son of the local doctor. After being an outstanding pupil at Aberdeen Grammar School, Reid studied arts at Aberdeen University until he was old enough to enter Aberdeen Infirmary to train as a doctor. Here he proved to be an exceptional student, graduating top of his class. He then entered medical practice in Paddington, London. In 1874 Reid went to Vienna, a city having then a reputation for its outstanding medical teaching, to undertake further studies in gynecology; diseases of the ear, nose, and throat; dermatology; and syphilis—as well as learning the techniques of the new ophthalmoscope that was pioneering eye surgery. Many of these specialties would later be put to good use in his treatment of members of the royal family and household.

Reid returned to Scotland in 1877 and worked as a country doctor with his father until April 1881, when the queen's commissioner at Balmoral, Dr. Profeit, approached him to take the post of resident medical attendant to the queen and the royal household. Queen Victoria was very impressed with Reid and his exceptional qualifications; after meeting the queen at Balmoral, Reid's appointment was approved by her physician-in-ordinary Sir William Jenner. Reid took up his appointment at Windsor on a salary of £400 per year. His contract would stipulate his constant attendance upon the queen except for six weeks' leave a year; in addition, he was expected to attend any members of the royal family or household in residence with the queen. From now until the queen's death in January 1901 he would accompany her everywhere.

Queen Victoria took very readily to Reid, as an amiable and engaging Scot. His presence in the royal household, as "a man of infinite humour" (Ponsonby 1942, 25) enlivened the dull life at court. Sharp of intellect, he was an entertaining raconteur, in his easy-going nature sharing many qualities with the queen's private secretary, Sir Henry Ponsonby, and his successor, Sir Arthur Bigge. The strict protocol in the royal household, however, meant that Reid, as a middle-class professional and technically only an upper servant, was excluded from the queen's dining table. Reid therefore set about giving his own private dinner parties, which became very popular among the royal household for their humorous and relaxed atmosphere. Lady Lytton, one of the ladies-in-waiting, found his openness most engaging, observing that so many of the household were too *boutonné* ("buttoned up"; Windsor and Bolitho 1927, 81). Stories filtered back to Queen Victoria who, unable to restrain her own curiosity, soon ignored protocol and had Reid dine with her.

Reid acclimatized himself to the queen's demanding nature and her unpredictable moods without complaint. He attended her every morning at 9:30 to check out her latest aches and pains, her most frequently recurring problems being rheumatism and indigestion. He checked her for a final time before she went to bed, any time between 10:30 and midnight, on average consulting on her health between four and eight times a day. In addition, Victoria never hesitated to call on him at all hours of the night, no matter how small her complaint—usually insomnia, for which he prescribed her bromides and other sedatives (although it was her maids and dressers, rather than he himself, who administered them to her). In addition, the queen would fire off daily notes to him, reporting in detail on her headaches, her indigestion, and the workings of her bowels.

Reid's first major medical crisis came with the illness and death of John Brown in 1883 and the task of dealing with the queen's terrible grief. On a happier note, he delivered all four of Princess Beatrice's children, and also the son of Prince Leopold, born after his father had died of hemophilia. The queen by now found Reid invaluable and trusted his discretion absolutely, now asking his advice on family and even political matters. She used him as an intermediary to try and talk her son-in-law, Prince Henry of Battenberg, out of going to Africa in 1895 (he died of fever while there). She candidly discussed with Reid the problem of her son Alfred's alcoholism and her daughter Helena's heavy reliance on laudanum as a painkiller. Reid's confidential and reassuring manner prompted many of the ladies-in-waiting, such as Marie Mallet, to consult him about their own and their children's various ailments, and he also attended the queen's Indian servant, the Munshi, and his family—including his several wives.

In 1887, Reid was called in to consult with the German and English doctors of Victoria's son-in-law Frederick, crown prince of Prussia, when he was seriously ill with throat cancer (see Reid 1996). He was highly critical of what turned out to be the misdiagnosis of the specialist Dr. Morell Mackenzie and greatly annoyed that the queen and her daughter clung to the false hope of some kind of miraculous recovery, remarking that in Victoria's case "the wish being Father to the thought . . . is often the case with Her Majesty" (Reid 1996, 93)—a rare personal criticism. Eventually the queen deferred to his judgment and his sound advice that the doctors should operate; but by then it was too late to save the crown prince.

In January 1894, with the official retirement of Sir William Jenner, Reid was promoted to physician-in-ordinary. He applied for an increase in salary to reflect this senior post, giving a detailed résumé of his duties, which "over the years have steadily become more and more onerous and responsible" (Reid 1996, 112) He was beginning to feel the strain of it all, but such was his loyalty that Reid had dismissed the offer of a medical fellowship in London, in the knowledge that the queen trusted him implicitly and that "it would take years for anyone else to acquire and grow into the necessary knowledge of Her Majesty's health, temperament and constitution" (112). His salary was raised soon after from £800 to £1,500, and in future the queen insisted that his duties should be reduced, with Reid only attending "her *own* personal people" (113). In recognition of his services, in June 1895 Reid was knighted.

The stress levels encountered by Reid in his work nevertheless increased in the 1890s, when he, like other members of the royal household, became exasperated by the queen's obsession with her Indian servant, the Munshi. When things came to a head in 1897 during the queen's holiday at Cimiez in the south of France, Reid acted as mediator between the queen and the household, but became so run down that he took to his bed and seriously entertained the idea of resigning. The queen, anxious not to lose him, for once urged him to rest. That same year she gave Reid a baronetcy.

There were, however, limits to the queen's favoritism where Reid was concerned. She was furious when he committed the cardinal sin of getting engaged in 1899. She would brook no division of his loyalties, especially when he wanted to marry someone above him in social status—Susan Baring, a niece of Sir Henry Ponsonby and maid of honor. For Victoria this was a *most* unwelcome inconvenience; if she had not by then come to rely on Reid so much, she told her daughter Vicky, she would "have let him go" (Reid 1996, 184). Deciding that to do so would be even more disruptive to her routine and far "too tiresome," (ibid.) she kept him on but only offered her grudging congratulations some weeks later—even though Sir James was in attendance on her several times a day. When she did finally accept the inevitable, it was on the understanding that Reid and his wife would do their utmost to "lessen as much as possible the unavoidable inconvenience" (Reid 1996, 186) that this marriage would cause her. She stipulated that Reid must continue living *with* her, wherever she went—thus only being allowed to live at home with his wife when he was on his official leave. Like a school boarder he was instructed that he had to ask the queen's permission if he wanted to go out in the evening, and he had to be back by 11:30 at the latest. The queen also ordained that "his wife should not come up to his room here [Osborne], nor to the Corridor, where some of the Royal Children live. At Windsor she might occasionally come to his room but this must not interfere with his other duties" (ibid.). Reid reacted in the only sane way possible: "The Queen's Regulations" had to be tolerated with the same good humor he enlisted in all his other dealings with her. Duly chastized, he promised that he would not be naughty and do it again.

In the year following Reid's marriage, the queen's health rapidly began to decline; by November 1900 he began getting anxious—as he had never been before—about her frailty and her loss of appetite. By the second week in January 1901, he had come to the conclusion that she was showing the signs of incipient dementia. During the final two weeks of the queen's life, Reid kept an extremely detailed account of her rapid decline and her death at 6:30 P.M. on 22 January (see "Victoria, Queen: Death and Funeral" and Reid 1996, which cites this extensively). Through all his years as her personal physician, Reid had never once been allowed to examine the queen in the manner that is standard practice now—not even to the extent of listening to her chest with a stethoscope. Propriety forbade it. In fact he did not even see her in her own bed until 16 January—six days before her death. And it was only afterward that he was able to make a medical examination of her body, during which he discovered that the queen had not only had a ventral hernia but also a prolapsed womb. The publication in 1996 of a biography of Reid by his granddaughter-in-law provided a moving account of his final devoted duties to the queen and the role Reid had played, in secret, in ensuring that she went to her grave with mementos of John Brown in her coffin. In February 1898 the queen had given Reid private instructions about how her body should be prepared before being sealed in its coffin; after ensuring that her detailed list of jewelry, photographs, garments, and other objects were placed beside her body, he added the queen's final and most secret requests—a lock of John Brown's hair and his photograph.

In December 1901, Reid was formally appointed physician-in-ordinary to King Edward VII's eldest son, the Prince of Wales. He attended the dying King Edward in his final illness in May 1910. Soon afterward, Reid was elected to the Royal College of Physicians. He remained in service to the royal family, as a physician-in-ordinary to King George V, until his death in 1923. He never published his memoirs or letters, many of the latter being destroyed after his death. He kept detailed diaries, on which much of Michaela Reid's biography has been based, but his private notes, made in 1904 when he was asked to negotiate the purchase of some potentially embarrassing letters written by the queen about John Brown, and which might have thrown light on the true nature of that relationship, were destroyed by his son when Reid died.

Reid's crucial role in monitoring the queen's well-being, as doctor, friend, and adviser during the last twenty years of her life, were consistently underrated by her; she has left few comments about him, and her letters to him rarely commend, but only instruct. King Edward VII was, however, prompt in expressing his gratitude after his mother died, telling Reid "I shall never forget all you did for the Queen" (Reid 1996, 212). Like several of Victoria's other ubiquitous servants, notably Sir Henry Ponsonby, Reid's posthumous reputation has suffered by the very fact of his inconspicuousness, although it is now clear that his influence behind the scenes in the royal household was considerable. He is one of several key members of the queen's entourage to be overlooked in the *Dictionary of National Biography.*

Related entries:

Bigge, Lieutenant Colonel Sir Arthur; Brown, John; Clark, Sir James; Jenner, Sir William; The Munshi; Ponsonby, General Sir Henry; Victoria, Queen: Death and Funeral of; Victoria, Queen: Physical Appearance of

References and further reading:

Longford, Elizabeth. 1966. "Queen Victoria's Doctors." In Martin Gilbert, ed., *A Century of Conflict 1850–1950.* London: Hamish Hamilton.

Ponsonby, Arthur. 1942. *Henry Ponsonby, Queen Victoria's Private Secretary: His Life from His Letters.* London: Macmillan.

Ponsonby, Frederick. 1930. *Side Lights on Queen Victoria.* London: Macmillan.

Reid, Michaela. 1996. *Ask Sir James: The Life of Sir James Reid, Personal Physician to Queen Victoria.* London: Eland.

Windsor, Dean of, and Hector Bolitho, eds. 1927. *Letters of Lady Augusta Stanley.* London: Gerald Howe.

Religion

I am nearly a Dissenter, or rather more a Presbyterian (Hibbert 2000, 296)

As head of state, Queen Victoria was also by act of Parliament (1544) Defender of the Faith and (1559) Supreme Governor of the Church of England (also commonly referred to as the Anglican Church). Although conscious of her duties to "preserve her people in wealth, peace and godliness" (St. Aubyn 1991, 313), in private Victoria had her own most decided, and often unconventional, views on religion and religious practice. Although she was a woman of profound conviction, she hated what she called "over-churchiness" and preferred the simpler ceremonials of the Low Church—in particular German and Scottish Protestantism. What Elizabeth Longford has described as the queen's "Protestant militancy" (1998, 402) was characterized by a preference for less ritualistic religious ceremonies, such as those performed at the Scottish Presbyterian Church, at Crathie, near Balmoral. Throughout her life she would prefer the modesties of such small, local churches, favoring also the little, local church at Whippingham, near her home at Osborne on the Isle of Wight. It was only her horror of being gawked at by increasing numbers of curious tourists that eventually led the queen to abandon Whippingham and have her own private chapel built at Osborne in 1880. But she ensured that it was unostentatious and functional, "as simple as a mission-house"—as Marie Corelli described it (Corelli 1901, 16).

Victoria had a strong distaste for the ceremonial of Anglican practice—with its robes and incense. Lytton Strachey has observed somewhat harshly that this was due to a lack of intellectual sophistication on her part, the result of a nature in which "imagination and subtlety held so small a place" and that "made her instinctively recoil from the intricate ecstasies of High Anglicanism" (Strachey 1971, 237). The queen's very particular tastes and distastes marked her own idiosyncratic brand of Christianity, which was an eclectic and contradictory amalgam of both High and Low Church ritual, with an emphasis on the devotional element rather than the traditional fear of God's punishment, coupled with a strong belief in the afterlife—a belief that fueled a considerable interest in the paranormal.

As a girl, Princess Victoria had dutifully learned to recite her catechism, and as queen she upheld the duty of all Christians to regularly attend church. But she and Prince Albert never insisted on their own children's slavishly learning religious doctrine by rote, nor did the queen attend church on every single Sunday. She also ignored the Prayer Book exhortation to take communion at least three times a year, confining herself to the two religious festivals of Easter and Christmas, and she horrified her courtiers by once taking communion, in November 1873, in the Presbyterian church at Crathie. She found the German (Lutheran) communion service "much more impressive and touching than ours" (Fulford 1964, 186) and told her daughter Vicky that she felt neither moved nor strengthened by the Anglican one: "It is so cold—such a repetition of the same prayers again and again, that it quite takes off the effect" (ibid.). She always kept a small crucifix hanging above her bed, as did many Catholics (it was placed in her hands when she was laid out in her coffin). She openly professed a dislike of clerical vestments (particularly bishops in their wigs and aprons) and insisted that all ministers who preached to her should wear only a simple black gown. She personally contested aspects of biblical interpretation—for example, the evangelical fire-and-brimstone insistence on eternal suffering in the fires of hell for all sinners—and challenged clerical controversy over the Bible's stipulation that women should give birth in pain and suffering by opting for chloroform during the birth of her eighth child, Leopold, in 1853.

The queen learned, under Prince Albert's influence, to place an implicit faith in God's will, particularly when it came to an acceptance of the deaths of her nearest and dearest. She liked to recite the prayers for the dead—an aspect of Catholic and Eastern Orthodox rather than Protestant ritual—yet joined Prince Albert in failing to see the necessity that her children, when young, should kneel when saying their daily prayers. Such aspects of subservient ritual did not fit with her understanding of a more simple, down-to-earth faith: "Does not every true Protestant feel the errors of a superstitious religion—full of strange observances repugnant to all the simplicity of our Saviour's teaching?" (Fulford 1976, 104). Closely tied up with her acceptance of divine will with regards to human mortality, Victoria developed a strong belief in the spirit world beyond. Her desire for communion with the dead led her to seek consolation after the death of Albert in the elegiac poetry of Tennyson, which bore the imprint of the poet's abiding belief in the afterlife. The queen also would spend long hours in meditation and prayer in the Royal Mausoleum at Windsor (to the doors of which she carried the key at all times).

As a young woman, the queen had been alarmed by the moralizing vigilantes of the Sabbatarian movement—a campaign embraced by many evangelical and dissenting groups that sought to condemn Sundays to what she regarded as a dismal day of "moping over good books" ([One of Her Majesty's Servants,] 1901, 154). Prince Albert had endorsed this dislike of Sunday's being turned into a dead, dreary day when people were not supposed to visit the theater, galleries, or museums; to dance or play cards; or to enjoy even the simple pleasure of postal deliveries and reading novels. There was, however, a moral if not political subtext to this objection, the queen being of the opinion that enforced idleness among the working classes on Sundays, for whom the Lord's Day was their only day of rest and recreation, might lead them into worse horrors—such as sin and vice. She was, however, obliged to modify these views, as head of the Church, in order not to invite criticism from the powerful moral majority in government and at court. She thus regretfully had to disallow military bands from playing in Kew Gardens on Sundays.

Queen Victoria had a pathological aversion to sanctimoniousness and was, throughout her life, highly critical of what she perceived as the pomposity of church dignitaries. As a young woman, she had particularly disliked being talked at about religion by people with a grim "*Sunday face*" (Hardy 1976, 48). She was impatient with long services and dreary sermons, laying down that none should last longer than twenty minutes. (As she became older, deafer, and increasingly liable to doze off, her private secretary Henry Ponsonby recommended sermons be shortened to five minutes.) A sermon, on the queen's insistence, should be clear and to the point, "a plain exposition of practical truths arising out of some subject of the day" ([One of Her Majesty's Servants,] 1901, 159). Nor should it venture into a commentary on either art, economics, or politics. One of the queen's ladies-in-waiting, Lady Augusta Bruce, records how, at Balmoral in 1861, the queen had been irritated by the fact that two Sundays in a row she had had to endure bad preachers: "She said it is such a disappointment to have a bad Sermon," observed Bruce, for it was the queen's view that "a good one gives one something to think about and do[es] one good all the week" (Windsor and Bolitho 1927, 233). If sermons could be delivered extempore, with a sense of religious inspiration and without reference to notes, then so much the better. When a sermon did become tedious, the queen used a flick of her fan to indicate to the preacher that he should swiftly come to a conclusion.

When she had to appoint a new dean of Windsor in 1882, Victoria made clear her prerequisites: "What the Queen wants is a tolerant, liberal-minded, broad churchman, who at the same time is pleasant socially and is popular with all Members and classes of her Household—who understands her feelings not only in ecclesiastical but also in social matters—a good kind man without price" (Ponsonby 1942, 62). The man she appointed, Randall Davidson, learned to accommodate the queen's idiosyncratic religious views, unlike the inexperienced cleric who in 1861, at the time of the prince consort's death, had suggested, in portentous tones, that "henceforth, you must remember that Christ Himself will be your husband." "*That is what I call twaddle!*" had been Victoria's indignant response (Hardy 1976, 93). In her grief and despair after Albert's death, she would turn increasingly to the simple religious comforts of Crathie Church at Balmoral.

Victoria had first come to enjoy the edifying and frequently extempore sermons of the Glaswegian minister, Dr. Norman Macleod, when she heard him preach at Crathie in October 1854. Macleod, who served as the queen's chaplain-in-ordinary there from 1857 till his death in 1872, epitomized what the queen so admired in the "Scotch Church," which she viewed as a "stronghold of Protestantism, most precious in these realms" (Hibbert 2000, 233). Macleod's fine preaching gave her "a lump in my throat" (Tooley 1896, 208). She had never heard anything finer: "so simple, and yet so eloquent, and so beautifully argued and put" (Duff 1980, 79). She remained close friends with Macleod; at Balmoral he would be in constant attendance, ready to offer the queen consolation, assuring her of God's love and reinforcing her flagging faith, as well as, when asked by her, giving his advice on problems with her children. She found great solace in listening to Macleod read the poetry of Sir Walter Scott and Robert Burns while she sat spinning. When Macleod died, the queen was distraught at losing a "dear, kind, loving, large-hearted friend" (Walsh 1902, 163). There was, she wrote, "no one to whom, in doubts and anxieties about religion, I looked with more trust and confidence" (163).

Much of the queen's personal belief hinged on her conviction that religious observance should be demonstrated not just in Christian piety and acts of religious devotion but in "being and doing good" ([One of Her Majesty's Servants,] 1901, 154). As St. Aubyn observed, the prince consort's influence had also been formative: "Religion, he told her, was chiefly concerned with leading a virtuous life and setting a good example" (1991, 206). The queen therefore frequently visited and commiserated with the poor cottagers on her Balmoral estate, enjoying their homespun, Scottish pieties on matters religious. Her liberal religious outlook and her hatred of bigotry can be traced back to her religious education as a young girl under her principal master, the Rev. George Davys. As early as September 1844, however, the queen had been criticized, during her first visit to Scotland, for attending services at the Church of Scotland. Only the *Sun* newspaper had welcomed her lack of religious prejudice and seen its more significant ramifications, as "set[ting] an example of toleration which is worthy of praise" (Charlot 1991, 236).

During the 1870s this was not, however, the case, when she was dismayed at the signs of Catholic-style ritual creeping back into the English High Church, which she felt was "an undermining of Protestantism" (Fulford 1976, 104). This resurgence had manifested itself in the Tractarian or Oxford Movement of the 1840s, which had attempted to reestablish the Church of England as a branch of the Catholic Church, as it had been before Henry VIII broke with the Catholic Church in 1529. The queen regarded the Tractarians as being "*R[oman] Catholics* at *heart*" and "*very insincere* as to their professions of attachment to the Church" (St. Aubyn 1991, 309). With this in mind she characteristically cast royal impartiality aside (which she always did when it suited her own ends) to ensure the passing of the Public Worship Bill in 1874, which outlawed Catholic practices in the Church of England. Yet in her attitude to Catholicism, as in all things, Victoria was inconsistent: although disliking the Catholic clergy and having a deep mistrust of the papacy and Catholic countries, she was distressed at the "violent abuse of the Catholic religion which is so painful and so cruel towards the many innocent and good Roman Catholics" (Longford 1998, 204), and she had even supported the government grant of funds to a training college for Catholic clergy in Ireland, in the face of criticism in Parliament.

When it came to non-Christian religions, Victoria was exceptionally progressive for her time and defended in particular the rights of Muslims, abhorring their condemnation by some evangelicals to eternal damnation for not being of the Christian faith. She found the work of British missionaries often far too intrusive and believed that they should not impose their beliefs on other religions but learn to respect them. The "Mahommedans" [Muslims] should in her view "be let alone" (Lutyens 1961, 38), and she kept a sharp eye out for manifestations of religious bigotry at court toward her own Muslim Indian servants. Yet such broad-ranging religious tolerance was countered by what St. Aubyn has observed as being the queen's pet hates when it came to "comparatively minor variants" of her own religion (1991, 207). She constantly interfered in the appointment of high churchmen, such as bishops and archbishops; in such cases, her personal preferences always gained the upper hand. She would veto candidates she disliked while promoting those she admired, such as Randall Davidson, who rose through the Church of England hierarchy ahead of other more long-serving clerics.

Perhaps the most telling demonstration of the queen's defense of the religious conscience of the individual came when clergymen lectured her servants on religious observance or when officialdom attempted to interfere. According to Marie Corelli (1901, 17), on hearing that two members of the royal military band had been dismissed because they were Wesleyan Methodists and had refused, as a matter of religious principle, to attend Sunday rehearsals, the queen had immediately had the men reinstated. Similarly, Sarah Tooley related how at Balmoral the queen had once encountered a housemaid weeping on the stairs. Taking the maid into her private sitting room, the queen questioned the girl, who told her that she had been given her notice "because, as a dissenter, she had objected to attending the Established Kirk along with the rest of the Balmoral servants" (1896, 238). Queen Victoria promptly sent for the head of the royal household and had the dismissal withdrawn. In future, she ordered, "no one in her service should be persecuted on account of their religious views" (238).

Related entries:
Davidson, Randall Thomas, Dean of Windsor; The Paranormal; Tennyson, Alfred, Lord; Racial and Religious Prejudice; Victoria, Queen: Personality of

References and further reading:

Arnstein, Walter. 1986. "Queen Victoria and Religion." In Gail Malmgreen, ed., *Religion in the Lives of English Women*. London: Croom Helm.

Bullock, Rev. Charles. 1887. *The Queen's Resolve "I Will Be Good": With Royal Anecdotes and Incidents.* London: "Home Words" Publishing Office.

Charlot, Monica. 1991. *Victoria, the Young Queen.* Cambridge: Polity.

Corelli, Marie. 1901. *The Passing of the Great Queen.* London: Methuen and Co.

Duff, David, ed. 1980. *Queen Victoria's Highland Journals.* London: Webb and Bower.

Fulford, Roger, ed. 1964. *Dearest Child: Letters between Queen Victoria and the Princess Royal, 1856–61.* London: Evans Brothers.

———. 1976. *Darling Child: Private Correspondence of Queen Victoria and the Crown Princess of Prussia, 1871–1878.* London: Evans Brothers.

Hardy, Alan. 1976. *Queen Victoria Was Amused.* London: John Murray.

Hibbert, Christopher. 2000. *Queen Victoria, a Personal History.* London: HarperCollins.

Longford, Elizabeth. [1964] 1998. *Victoria R.I.* London: Weidenfeld and Nicolson.

Lutyens, Mary, ed. 1961. *Lady Lytton's Court Diary 1895–1899.* London: Rupert Hart-Davis.

Martin, Sir Theodore. 1908. *Queen Victoria as I Knew Her.* Edinburgh: William Blackwood and Sons.

[One of Her Majesty's Servants]. 1901. *The Private Life of Queen Victoria.* London: C. Arthur Pearson.

Ponsonby, Arthur. 1942. *Henry Ponsonby: His Life from His Letters.* London: Macmillan.
St. Aubyn, Giles. 1991. *Queen Victoria: A Portrait.* London: Sinclair Stevenson.
Strachey, Lytton. 1971. *Queen Victoria.* Harmondsworth, UK: Penguin.
Tooley, Sarah. 1896. *The Personal Life of Queen Victoria.* London: Hodder and Stoughton.
Walsh, Walter. 1902. *The Religious Life and Influence of Queen Victoria.* London: Swan Sonnenschein.
Windsor, Dean of, and Hector Bolitho, eds. 1927. *Letters of Lady Augusta Stanley: A Young Lady at Court 1849–1863.* London: Gerald Howe.

Rosebery, Archibald Philip Primrose, Fifth Earl of (1847–1929)

He is quite the rising politician of the day and is always very respectful and anxious to please me (Hibbert 1984, 292)

The least known and most reluctant of all Queen Victoria's prime ministers, Liberal politician Lord Rosebery, served in this capacity for a mere fifteen months. Although his political achievements were few, as a great patriot he would be one of the primary architects of the British imperialism that so characterized the last fifteen years of Victoria's reign. In later years Rosebery would probably be as well, if not better, known for the successes of his racing stables.

He was born into the landed aristocracy and was educated at Eton and Christ Church, Oxford. The death of his grandfather, the fourth earl of Rosebery, in 1868 brought the title to nineteen-year-old Archibald (his own father already having died). With it he inherited great wealth and vast estates in Scotland and was entitled to sit in the House of Lords. He entered Parliament in 1869 as a Liberal, having abandoned his degree course when the university authorities objected to his owning and training racehorses. Rosebery's first years in Parliament were unremarkable, although, when he did choose to speak, he proved an effective orator. In 1878 he added to his already considerable wealth by marrying the heiress Hannah de Rothschild. Rosebery's Scottish loyalties drew him naturally into electoral campaigning with Gladstone in Midlothian in 1879 and 1880, a fact that contributed significantly to the Liberal victory in the general election of 1880. He subsequently served as undersecretary for the Home Department (1881–1883) with special responsibility for Scottish affairs, entered the cabinet as the first commissioner of works in 1884, and a year later accepted the post of lord privy seal.

In June 1885 Gladstone's government was returned after a general election, with Rosebery now appointed to the important post of foreign secretary. He protested that he was ill equipped for the role; the queen, from the lofty heights of her fifty years' experience in foreign policy, said she would be only too delighted to assist him. Rosebery attended Queen Victoria at Balmoral in June 1886. She was delighted with him: "Lord Rosebery admires everything here very much. He is certainly a very clever, pleasant man, and very kind" (Hibbert 1984, 299). As foreign secretary he was keen to promote a more regal, imperial image of the queen, as a counter to the reclusive bourgeois, domestic image that had gained the ascendancy during her widowhood. On the opening of an exhibition to celebrate the new Imperial Institute in 1886, he suggested she should wear her full robes of state and crown: "The symbol that unites this vast Empire is a Crown not a bonnet," he averred (Ponsonby 1942, 79). For Rosebery, the Golden Jubilee the following year proved a particularly memorable occasion, with its "proud cavalcade of Princes, its majestic representation of the Sovereignties of the world, and the enthusiastic multitude that hailed its passage" (St. Aubyn 1991, 492). He wrote congratulating the queen: "All was worthy of your Majesty and of the Empire," he told her, and "all has tended to strengthen and to deepen the foundations of a monarchy which overshadows the globe, and represents the union and aspirations of three hundred millions of human beings" (492–493).

Gladstone, meanwhile, had been impressed with Rosebery's surprising performance as foreign secretary and talked of him as "the man of the future," but the Liberals had now fallen from power. During his years out of office, Rosebery vigorously promoted reform of the House of Lords, which he had been advocating since 1884. He was also an early supporter of progressive local government, in 1889 becoming the first chairman of London County Council. But in November 1890 his life was blighted by tragedy when his wife died, leaving him with four young children. He never really recovered from the blow, becoming reclusive and losing all appetite for political life. It was therefore with extreme reluctance that he returned to the cabinet as foreign secretary in 1892, when Gladstone was returned to power, yet despite this, finally establishing his political reputation.

When Gladstone resigned in March 1894 over increases in naval spending, Rosebery found himself thrust into the political limelight. The queen had set her sights on Rosebery as prime minister, but he pleaded that he was ill equipped for the role, particularly as he was also hampered, as a peer, by having to sit in the House of Lords and not the House of Commons. Having bullied Rosebery into taking the premiership, the queen expected things to be a lot less fraught and his policies less radical than those of his predecessor. She soon realized, however, that Rosebery's ministry was precarious and bombarded him with endless directives on how he should conduct the business of government. She took him to task over the quality of his speeches, which she found too flippant, and became seriously alarmed when, in October 1894, Rosebery began campaigning for the long-overdue reform of the House of Lords. The queen was fiercely resistant to any changes to the traditional structure of government. Nor did she like Rosebery's avowed intention of disestablishing the Anglican Church in Scotland and Wales. When he demonstrated his unwillingness to defer to Victoria on every political opinion that he expressed in public, her response was to treat him like a recalcitrant schoolboy.

Rosebery's brief ministry proved to be a largely ineffectual one. His cabinet was irreconcilably divided, particularly over Home Rule for Ireland, and he failed to win the loyalty of many of its members. The only piece of significant legislation was the introduction of death duties and establishment of a British protectorate in Uganda, in pursuance of Rosebery's own imperialist policies. In June 1895, the opportunity to resign, for which Rosebery had been longing, came over a minor issue. For long plagued by insomnia, he had found being prime minister a thankless task. He was glad to go and told the queen that for him it was "an immense relief" (St. Aubyn 1991, 520). Queen Victoria professed that she was not sorry to see Rosebery leave office. She soon found his replacement, Lord Salisbury, even less easy to control, however, and in retrospect would regret the loss of the amiable Rosebery, the most amenable of all her Liberal statesmen.

In private, Rosebery would confess that there had only been two people who had ever frightened him: the queen and Bismarck. He did not fulfill expectations of a return to office, and although he continued to support British imperial policy, he resisted being drawn back into party politics when the Boer War broke out in 1899. His support for British policy in southern Africa isolated him in the Liberal party, and he took an increasingly independent political line. He finally split with the Liberal Party in 1905 over Irish Home Rule, which he opposed. In 1911, on the occasion of the coronation of King George V, Rosebery was created earl of Midlothian. He refused all inducements to return to political office, although he made rousing speeches in support of the British declaration of war in 1914.

In 1918 Rosebery was partially disabled by a stroke and devoted himself thereafter to writing popular biographies of historical figures such as William Pitt (1891), Robert Peel (1899), and Napoleon (1900). In private he was a great conversationalist and wit and enjoyed yachting and horse racing; three of his horses were Derby winners, in 1894, 1895, and 1905. Summing up Rosebery's life, Claud Cockburn remarked that "by marrying a Rothschild, being Prime Minister and winning the Derby, he demonstrated that it was possible to improve one's financial status and run the Empire without neglecting the study of form" (Cockburn 1952, 185).

Related entries:
Boer War; Golden Jubilee; Salisbury, Robert Arthur Talbot Gascoigne-Cecil, Third Marquis of

References and further reading:

Brooks, David. 1986. *The Destruction of Lord Rosebery.* London: Historians Press.
Cockburn, Claud. 1952. *Aspects of English History.* London: MacGibbon and Kee.
Crewe, First Marquess of. 1931. *Lord Rosebery.* 2 vols. London: John Murray.
Hibbert, Christopher. 1984. *Queen Victoria in Her Letters and Journals.* London: Viking.
James, Robert Rhodes. 1963. *Rosebery: A Biography of Archibald Philip, Fifth Earl of Rosebery.* London: Weidenfeld and Nicolson.
Ponsonby, Arthur. 1942. *Henry Ponsonby, Queen Victoria's Private Secretary: His Life from His Letters.* London: Macmillan.
Raymond, E.T. 1923. *The Man of Promise, Lord Rosebery: A Critical Study.* London: T. F. Unwin.
Rhodes, J. R. 1995. *Rosebery.* London: Phoenix.
St. Aubyn, Giles. 1991. *Queen Victoria: A Portrait.* London: Sinclair Stevenson.

Royal Albert Hall

I have to express my great admiration of this beautiful hall and my earnest wishes for its complete success (Nevill 1997, 55)

The Royal Albert Hall, one of the largest auditoriums ever constructed in the Victorian era, was begun in 1867 and formed one of the several buildings located in South Kensington, known as Albertopolis—London's great cultural and scientific center, the brainchild of Prince Albert. Designed by the Irish military engineer Capt. Francis Fowke, the building, originally mooted as a Hall of Arts and Sciences, was constructed at the far end of the Royal Horticultural Society's grounds and faces the Albert Memorial (across the road in Kensington Gardens).

The building of a great hall for the celebration of British culture was conceived by Prince Albert with Sir Henry Cole, with whom he had worked closely in the planning of the Great Exhibition of 1851 and the design and construction of the Victoria and Albert Museum. As chairman of the Society of Arts, Cole had first commissioned Fowke to draw up plans for a concert hall in 1858, but its construction had been sidelined after the prince's premature death in 1861, in favor of the Albert Memorial. Cole, however, continued to lobby for a concert hall in the prince's memory, which would be "the finest in Europe for hearing, seeing and convenience" (Nevill 1997, 53). In 1863 Cole suggested that a contribution to building costs be raised by selling seats to subscribers on a 999-year leasehold. The government endorsed his idea, and 1,300 seats were put on sale at £100 each. Captain Fowke meanwhile came up with a design for the Albert Hall, and construction began in 1866 under Sir Henry Scott, with £50,000 of the profits from the Great Exhibition now having been made over to fund the project (which eventually cost around £200,000).

An emotional Queen Victoria laid the foundation stone of the huge, oval-shaped ampitheater created by Fowke on 20 May 1867. She found having to face an audience of 7,000 people something of an ordeal, having shut herself away in dogged seclusion since the prince's death six years earlier, but, she told them, she had "nerved

The Royal Albert Hall of Arts and Sciences was so named by Queen Victoria to commemorate her late husband's great passion for music, science, and the arts and his lasting legacy, the museums and institutions of South Kensington known as Albertopolis. (Hulton/Archive by Getty Images)

[herself] to a compliance with the wish that I should take part" (Nevill 1997, 53) in deference to her dear husband's memory and promptly surprised everyone by announcing that the hall would be called the Royal Albert Hall of Arts and Sciences. The building that sprang up on the site, which would later irreverently be compared to a wedding cake with its top removed, was constructed in red brick and featured a huge, 135-foot-high dome of glass and iron. It was built between 1867 and 1871 and is 735 feet in circumference. It seats 8,000 in its main auditorium and three tiers of boxes (the imposition of safety regulations has since reduced this to 7,000). The interior and exterior designs comprise elements of Antique, Renaissance, and *Rundbogenstil* architectural style, the most notable of which is the beautiful decorative terracotta frieze in Minto ware—entitled "The Triumph of Arts and Letters"—that encircles the top of its red-brick external wall. Six-feet deep and 800 feet long, it represents a procession of figures and craftsmen from ancient civilization to the modern, steam-driven era of Victorian England.

The design of the hall was and remains much praised, with some likening its grandeur to that of a Roman forum. The auditorium, which boasted the largest organ ever built—weighing 150 tons and comprising 9,000 pipes worked by steam-driven bellows—was constructed by the master craftsman Henry Willis. But it proved to be less than congenial to musical performances, suffering for many years from severe acoustic problems—notably a notorious echo. These were largely resolved in the late 1960s with the installation of special features to improve the sound quality.

The queen was apprehensive about facing what she felt would be a very trying and emotional occasion, when the hall was officially opened on 29 March 1871. It was the first on such a grand scale that she had attended since Albert's death, and she was accompanied to the ceremony by the prince and princess of Wales and several of her other children. Ten thousand people witnessed the ceremony and heard the Prince of Wales read out the queen's address from the dais. It was a highly charged moment, the queen recording in her journal that even Sir Henry Cole had cried with a mixture of joy and emotion. Since then the Royal Albert Hall has become celebrated worldwide as a major cultural venue and concert hall. It is the major home every summer of the famous Promenade Concerts—popularly known as the Proms—a music festival inaugurated in 1895 by the composer and conductor Sir Henry Wood and held mainly in the Royal Albert Hall since 1941, when German bombing during World War II forced the promenade concerts out of the Queen's Hall.

Related entries:
Albert Memorial; Art and Artists; Victoria and Albert Museum

References and further reading:

Darby, Elizabeth, and Nicola Smith. 1983. *The Cult of the Prince Consort.* New Haven: Yale University Press.

Jones, Edward, and Christopher Woodward. 1983. *A Guide to the Architecture of London.* London: Weidenfeld and Nicolson.

Mee, Arthur. [1937] 1960. *The King's England: London, Heart of the Empire and Wonder of the World* [also known under the title *Arthur Mee's London*]. London: Hodder and Stoughton.

Nevill, Barry St. John. 1997. *Life at the Court of Queen Victoria: Selections from the Journals of Queen Victoria.* Stroud, Gloucestershire: Sutton.

Weinreb, Ben, and Christopher Hibbert, eds. 1983. *The London Encyclopedia.* London: Macmillan.

The Royal Household

Civility and consideration for the servants is . . . [a] thing which the Queen is very *particular about* (Stoney and Weltzien 1994, 24)

Throughout her long reign, Queen Victoria enjoyed the services of a massive entourage, who were at her disposal, wherever she went—at home and abroad—and whose various roles brought to each of them a particular code of dress and practice, as part of the complex system of rank and protocol that characterized the royal household. The strict observance of pecking orders was observed not just above but also below stairs, and the queen was a stickler that all members of her household, from the highest to the lowest, should share a common respect for each other.

The system the queen inherited in 1837 was far from efficient, however. In fact, it was downright antiquated and plagued with malpractice and political partisanship. The various and clearly defined functions of a total household of some 445 people were overseen by three different officials, all of them aristocrats and all of their appointments dictated by change of government. The lord chamberlain (the most senior member of the household) dealt with all the staff who worked "above stairs" and who served or officiated at court ceremonies and official functions. The lord steward was in charge of the hundreds of domestic servants who worked "below stairs" in the kitchens, pantries, sculleries, storerooms, and laundries of the palace. The master of the horse ensured the upkeep of the queen's carriages, instructed their drivers, and organized the stabling and care of her horses; the royal equerries also came under his jurisdiction. The maintenance of the fabric of the royal palaces and their grounds was the province of yet another department—the Office of Woods and Forests. Such a division of roles created endless and frustrating anomalies: there was often insufficient supervision of staff above and below stairs; food was frequently purloined from the royal pantries; candles in every room were changed daily whether used or not, and the servants kept the unused ones as a perk; guests lost their way in the badly lit corridors where no one was on duty to help them; and many of the servants themselves simply did not have enough to do.

One of the great absurdities of the system was exposed by the fact that the lord steward, who was responsible for the staff who lay the fires in rooms, did not have suzerainty over the lighting of them. This was the province of the lord chamberlain, in charge of most of the housekeepers, maids, pages, and footmen. Thus whenever anything broke, or needed fixing, the simplest of tasks had to be passed through a chain of command that was often extremely time wasting. Faced with such a clumsy and inefficient system at Buckingham Palace, Prince Albert resolved soon after his marriage to Victoria that "so long as its wheels are not mended there can neither be order nor regularity, comfort, security nor outward dignity, in the Queen's Palace" (Charlot 1991, 220). Backed up by several exhaustive memorandums from his adviser, Baron Stockmar, which set out in great detail the inefficiencies of the existing system, Prince Albert set about tightening up the running of the royal household and attacking "the canker of all"—waste (Martin 1875–1880, 1:160). Costs were rigorously reviewed, and principles of thrift in the preparation of food were put in place. Underemployed staff were dismissed, reducing the wages bill alone by £25,000. Throughout the royal palaces, servants who had been used to working unsupervised now found themselves called to account and bewailed the loss of the perks they had received under the old system. The running of the royal household was now consolidated under the senior authority of a newly created master of the household.

The queen's own immediate entourage of ladies-in-waiting (as they were collectively called when on duty) was composed of three grades. The most senior was that of the ladies of the bedchamber. These women, who were married and usually the wives of peers, received an annual salary of £500; among them, the duchess of Sutherland had taken the most senior post of mistress of the robes on Victoria's accession. The next in rank were the eight women of the bedchamber, who were also drawn from the aristocracy or highly respected families. Finally, there were the eight maids of honor, who were always the unmarried daughters or granddaughters of aristocratic families and who always served in pairs. Both these ranks received £300 a year. But this is not to mention the many dressers and personal maids who also served the queen, to some of whom she became extremely attached. And there were also of course other, male, functionaries upon whose services the queen would call: her private secretary, the gentlemen ushers, equerries, and pages and a range of other military personnel attached to the royal palaces. The personal appointments the queen made for professional services further added to the list: the physicians, surgeons, and apothecaries—extraordinary and in-ordinary—as well as sculptors, painters, chaplains, photographers, musicians, dentists, and even a resident rat killer and chimney sweep.

The smooth workings of the machinery of the royal household were maintained twenty-four hours a day without the queen's notice being drawn, for much of the time, toward those who fulfilled the essential functions that contributed to her comfort. Theirs was, as such, a largely anonymous role: "the staff, never officially acknowledged in the fullness of its functions, had to exercise the most complete self-effacement and become in effect an expansion of the Queen's personal power in action" (Gosse 1901, 84–85). It is for this reason that so few of their names are known to us, despite their long years in service; and only a handful of their stories have been told because the queen forbade her ladies to keep diaries. Their letters (see Stoney and Weltzien 1994; Windsor and Bolitho 1927 and 1929; Lutyens 1961; Ponsonby 1927; Mallet 1968; and Wyndham 1912) have, however, provided valuable insights into life at court during Victoria's reign.

Some of the queen's better-known male servants—her private secretaries such as Gen. Charles Grey, Sir Arthur Bigge, and Sir Henry Ponsonby; the keeper of the Privy Purse (1867–1878), Sir Thomas Biddulph; and her doctors Sir James Clark, Sir William Jenner, and the royal accoucheur, Sir Charles Locock—have at least been accorded entries in the *Dictionary of National Biography.* But we know precious little about the lives in service of the army of royal dressers such as Frieda Arnold, Emilie Dittweiler, Annie MacDonald, and Marianne Skerrett; the nursery staff such as Mrs. Lilly, the monthly nurse; or even of Prince Albert's German valets, Isaac Cart and Rudolf Löhlein. One might imagine from this that the queen cared little about her staff. Although some of her more senior ladies might come and go with greater regularity, as their appointments were part-time, it was rather the reverse when it came to the humbler servants who served the queen all the year round, many of whom stayed in her service for decades. In her journals the queen constantly referred to many of these servants by name—often by their Christian names—suggesting a considerable degree of affection for them. The problem, as Stoney and Weltzien (1994) pointed out, lies in the fact that a distorted view of the queen's attitude to those in her service has come to down us because of the indiscriminate censorship by her daughter, Princess Beatrice, of the journals after Victoria's death. In the process of editing and transcribing them, after which she destroyed the originals, Beatrice deliberately and frequently omitted her mother's specific references to servants by name, thus "rendering their shadowy figures invisible again" (25). The queen's daughter was not alone in objecting to what seemed an unnatural obsession with the lower classes on the queen's part. Many senior members of the royal household were deeply affronted when Victoria's Highland journals were published in 1868 and 1884, containing detailed and loving biographical footnotes by the queen on many of her lowly Scottish servants at Balmoral, whereas their own roles at court were glossed over. A typical example of the subsequent neglect of people who often had the closest contact with the queen is Rudolf Löhlein—Prince Albert's valet—who came with him from Coburg in 1840, at the time of the prince's marriage to Queen Victoria. Löhlein remained in the queen's service long after Albert's death, dying in 1886. Here was a man who was John Brown's de facto superior in the royal household and the only one to whom the notoriously disrespectful Brown would ever deign to defer. Several books have been written about Brown; Löhlein remains a cipher.

One class of servant was particularly close to the queen: her dressers. Being on constant duty in her private rooms, they worked long hours and sometimes suffered ill health as a result of the strain placed on them. Emilie Dittweiler from Baden was in the queen's service from 1857 to 1892, replacing another German, Frieda Arnold (who served from 1854 to 1859), who has left one of the most valuable accounts of the life and duties of a dresser in the royal household (see Stoney and Weltzien 1994). Marianne Skerrett, another of the queen's principal dressers, who entered her service in 1837 and remained till 1862, was effectively her private secretary. To Skerrett devolved the task of writing Queen Victoria's letters to tradespeople, the commissioning of artists and engravers, answering begging letters from old retainers, and paying the bills relating to the making and maintaining of the queen's clothes.

No greater recognition of a dresser's importance to the queen could be found, however, than in her relationship with the Scotswoman, Annie MacDonald, who served her at Balmoral. From a local family, MacDonald had started out as the prince consort's "necessary woman," responsible to him as a general cleaner; she and was then promoted to wardrobe maid to the queen and eventually first wardrobe woman. She took an increasingly central role after Skerrett left the queen in 1862 and is constantly referred to in the queen's Highland journals. The final confirmation of MacDonald's importance to Victoria came in the clearly expressed hope, in the queen's will, that she would be reunited with her faithful Scottish servants John Brown and "good Annie MacDonald" in the next world (Annie had died in 1897). Because they lived in such close proximity to the queen, it was also the dressers who had to bear the brunt of the queen's increasing bouts of insomnia as she grew older. Dr. James Reid, the queen's resident physician, records that "every time she wakes, even for a few minutes, she rings for her maids, who of course don't like it, and naturally call the night a 'bad' one" (Reid 1996, 82). Such stress had caused one of the queen's dressers, Mrs. Tuck, to have a nervous breakdown.

As for the aristocratic ladies who served the queen: one lady-in-waiting and two maids of honor served simultaneously, on a constantly changing roster, for a month at a time, and on three separate occasions during the year. Because the queen regularly moved from one home to another, these ladies had to reside with her, the married ones having to leave their husbands and families behind. The year's roster would be announced every January; the maids of honor would receive most of their orders from the senior woman of the bedchamber, who also acted as a lady secretary to the queen (the appointment of the highest ranking of the queen's ladies, the mistress of the robes, was a political one and changed with each government).

Despite coming from wealthy, aristocratic families, such ladies did not necessarily enjoy preferential treatment and ironically were, if anything, more dispensable, for the queen wrote less about them and showed a decided preference for the simple virtues of her more humble employees. One lady-in-waiting, Lady Charlotte Canning, herself gave out words of warning to newly arrived ladies at court: "You will be delighted with your waiting at Balmoral or at Osborne. You will see the Queen intimately, riding, dancing, playing, dining. You will think she cannot get on without you. And then you will come back one day to Windsor, and somebody else will take your place, and you will have become—a number on the list" (Gosse 1901, 330).

This ever-changing list of ladies-in-waiting contains some names that have become more familiar: the mistress of the robes—the duchess of Sutherland (who proved herself a grande dame at the royal coronation and wedding), Lady Charlotte Canning, Lady Jane Churchill, Lady Augusta Bruce, Lady Constance Lytton, and Marie Adeane (later Mallett)—all of them notable either for the number of times the queen mentions them in her journals or because their letters from court were subsequently published. Despite their often high-born status and the cachet attached to any court appointment, such ladies often found life in service to the queen a thankless task. Life with the aging widow was a dreary round. No one had the freedom to go out until and when the queen herself had done so. Sunday was church, and the only high point of life at Balmoral (although not in the view of most of the ladies and lords-in-waiting) were the rowdy and drunken gillies' balls that they were forced to attend.

Balmoral was undoubtedly the least popular tour of duty for any member of the queen's inner entourage of personal attendants, who moved with her from Osborne—to Balmoral—to Windsor. (The majority of household servants were assigned to different residences and stayed put.) Some said that the monotonous routine was like being in school again; others that it was more like a convent. As Marie Adeane wrote from Balmoral in 1890: "We see nothing of the Queen except at dinner on alternate nights, we have *no* duties to perform to occupy our minds and the weather is horribly cold and wet. We just exist from meal to meal and do our best to kill time" (Mallet 1968, 37). Boredom often descended into idle tittle-tattle and back-biting; a great deal of time was dissipated, as the queen's eyesight failed, in scuttling back and forth communicating her wishes by note to the various members of her household. The only light relief came in the 1880s, when the queen once again allowed the royal household to stage amateur theatricals, and later on the occasional command performance of a play or operetta was enjoyed.

In addition to enduring the excruciating boredom of life at court, the ladies had to take turns in suffering exposure to the elements on daily carriage drives around Balmoral, a fact to which the queen remained supremely indifferent. Of course, when they fell ill with colds and flu or worse still rheumatism, the queen was greatly inconvenienced by their indisposition, their primary function, when it came down to it, being to pander to her comforts. Royal service therefore involved unquestioning loyalty, tolerance of the queen's unpredictable moods, and the acceptance of almost total self-effacement. Maids of honor such as Miss Phipps, Lady Biddulph, and Mary Ponsonby often won the queen's affection, but they never exerted any influence over her. "She accepted their services in a dispassionate, professional way, and she ever, by preserving a quiet tone of decorum, checked any exaggerated expression of personal affection the moment that it was threatened" (Gosse 1901, 329–330).

Because she so hated change, Victoria was a stickler when it came to the selection of any replacements. She would throw up the most trivial reasons for rejecting a candidate, as Sir Henry Ponsonby once observed: "Blow the Lords-in-Waiting. Every one I suggest to Her Majesty is objectionable. One has corns, another is dull, another is a bore" (Longford 1976, 10). The queen felt comforted by having the same familiar faces around her year in, year out. When they retired, the queen let her ladies-in-waiting, her maids, and personal secretaries go with the greatest reluctance, handing out kind words and gifts in appreciation of their service. On their deaths, she made a point of writing her own personal words of condolence to their grieving families, even soliciting photographs of them on their deathbeds, as well as every detail of their funeral service and burial.

Such solicitous tones were, however, never aroused when the queen's staff fell in love or—heaven forfend—announced their intention to marry. Far from offering her congratulations, Queen Victoria was usually extremely annoyed. With this eventuality uppermost in her mind, she interrogated any prospective maids of honor, to ensure that, aside from being able to speak French and German, play the piano, and ride, they were neither engaged nor had any remote intention of becoming so. Once assured that they were not, she determinedly kept them from any possible romantic exploits by banning all male visitors—even relations—from their rooms. The logic behind such strict controls was that, once married, her ladies would, the queen feared, become preoccupied with their husbands and families and less so with her. When the unspeakable did happen, the queen had a brutal instinct for self-preservation. She was furious when Lady Augusta Bruce had the temerity to announce her intention of marrying Dean Stanley in 1863, as she was also when maid of honor Marie Adeane fell in love with Bernard Mallet in 1891. Nor was her disapproval confined solely to her ladies. She was just as averse to male members of her entourage marrying—being of the opinion that husbands might gossip to curious wives about private matters at court. In 1861, when Sir Henry Ponsonby became engaged to one of the queen's maids of honor, Mary Bulteel, the queen remarked: "I highly approve of your choice, but you are taking from me the best of my household" (Tisdall 1961, 45). When Ponsonby's son Frederick (appointed assistant private secretary in 1895 after his father's death) fell in love with a woman of whom the queen disapproved, it took three years of persuasion before she finally agreed to the marriage.

Related entries:
Anson, George Edward; Balmoral Castle; Bedchamber Crisis; Bigge, Lieutenant Colonel Sir Arthur; Brown, John; Bruce, Lady Augusta; Churchill, Lady Jane; Clark, Sir James; Class; Davidson, Randall Thomas, Dean of Windsor; Grey, General Charles; Jenner, Sir William; Lyttleton, Lady; The Munshi; Ponsonby, General Sir Henry; Reid, Sir James; Sutherland, Duchess of

References and further reading:

Auchinloss, Louis. 1979. *Persons of Consequence: Queen Victoria and Her Circle*. London: Weidenfeld and Nicolson.
Charlot, Monica. 1991. *Victoria: The Young Queen*. Cambridge: Polity.
Emden, Paul. 1934. *Behind the Throne*. London: Hodder and Stoughton.
Erskine, Mrs. Stewart, ed. 1916. *Twenty Years at Court: From the Correspondence of the Hon. Eleanor Stanley*. London: Nisbet and Co.
Gosse, Edmund. 1901. "The Character of Queen Victoria." *Quarterly Review* (January–April): 301–307.
Hibbert, Christopher. 2000. *Victoria: A Personal History*. London: HarperCollins.
Hibbert, Christopher. 1979. *The Court of St. James: The Monarch at Work from Victoria to Elizabeth*. London: Weidenfeld and Nicolson.
Longford, Elizabeth, ed. 1976. *Louisa, Lady-in-Waiting: The Personal Diaries and Albums of Louisa, Lady in Waiting to Queen Victoria and Queen Alexandra*. London: Jonathan Cape.
Lutyens, Mary, ed. 1961. *Lady Lytton's Court Diary. 1895–1899*. London: Rupert Hart-Davis.
Mallet, Victor, ed. 1968. *Life with Queen Victoria: Marie Mallett's Letters from Court: 1887–1901*. London: John Murray.
Martin, Sir Theodore. 1875–1880. *The Life of His Royal Highness the Prince Consort*. 5 vols. London: Smith, Elder and Co. (vol. 1).
[One of Her Majesty's Servants]. 1901. *The Private Life of Queen Victoria*. London: C. Arthur Pearson.
Ponsonby, Arthur. 1942. *Henry Ponsonby, Queen Victoria's Private Secretary: His Life from His Letters*. London: Macmillan.
Ponsonby, Magdalen, ed. 1927. *Mary Ponsonby: A Memoir, Some Letters and a Journal*. London: John Murray.
Reid, Michaela. 1996. *Ask Sir James: The Life of Sir James Reid, Personal Physician to Queen Victoria*. London: Eland.
Stoney, Benita and Heinrich C. Weltzien. 1994. *My Mistress the Queen: The Letters of Frieda Arnold, Dresser to Queen Victoria 1854–9*. London: Weidenfeld and Nicolson.
Tisdall, E. E. P. 1961. *Queen Victoria's Private Life*. London: Jarrolds.
Watson, Vera. 1952. *A Queen at Home: An Intimate Account of the Social and Domestic Life at Queen Victoria's Court*. London: W. H. Allen.
Windsor, Dean of, and Hector Bolitho. 1927. *Letters of Lady Augusta Stanley: A Young Lady at Court 1849–1863*. London: Gerald Howe.
———. 1929. *Later Letters of Lady Augusta Stanley 1864–1876*. London: Jonathan Cape.
Wyndham, Hon. Mrs. Hugh, ed. 1912. *Correspondence of Sarah Spencer, Lady Lyttleton 1787–1870*. London: John Murray.

Russell, Lord John, First Earl (1792–1878)

interested in nothing except the Constitution of 1688 and himself (St. Aubyn 1991, 217)

Lord John Russell, best remembered as a liberal reformer in Britain in the 1830s, was a member of the old Whig aristocracy. His physical attributes did not, however, match his skills as a politician: small, scrawny, and timorous and with a thin, reedy voice, Russell lacked the social charms of the more charismatic if controversial politicians of his era, such as Melbourne, Palmerston, and Disraeli. Russell was often the butt of caricaturists; the queen never took to him and thought him a "dreadful old man" (Cecil 1953, 54). Prince Albert also found him difficult to deal with. The royal couple shared an impatience with Russell's lack of resolve; in the queen's view, he seemed at times to be overwhelmed by the events with which he had to deal.

Russell was born in Westminster, London, the son of the duke of Bedford, an old-school parliamentary reformer. He was

Lord John Russell, one the leading Whig politicians of the early years of Queen Victoria's reign, enjoyed a long parliamentary career, from 1813 until his resignation, as prime minister, in 1866. (Library of Congress)

brought up with a strong sense of duty and noble ideals, as a member of the landed aristocracy, to defend the civil and religious freedom of the people. Russell's sickly constitution (the result of his premature birth) affected his schooling, however, and he was educated mainly at home before studying at the University of Edinburgh. He became the Whig member of Parliament for Tavistock in 1813 and from the early 1820s on identified himself with the growing demand for electoral reform among the Whigs as well as with moves toward Catholic emancipation.

During the ministry of Earl Grey, Russell served as paymaster general for the army (1830–1834), as well as, in 1831, becoming a member of the committee that drafted the first Reform Bill. His landmark speech in the House of Commons, in which he introduced the bill, earned him the respect of many as a fine orator but brought also the popular nickname of "Finality Jack," a reference to the fact that Russell insisted that the 1832 legislation would, in his view, mark the full extent of franchise reform. Under the Whig ministry of Lord Melbourne, Russell was home secretary from 1835 to 1839, during which time he introduced the Municipal Corporations Act; established the registration of births, marriages and deaths; and reduced the number of offenses in Britain for which a person could be liable for capital punishment. As secretary for war and the colonies during 1839–1841, he oversaw the Act of Union with Canada in 1840. During the subsequent ministry of Sir Robert Peel, Russell lent his support for repeal of the Corn Laws, abolished in 1846.

Russell's first term as prime minister came after Peel's resignation in 1846 (to 1852). The queen always found it difficult adapting to a new prime minister after the loss of an old favorite, and it is Russell's misfortune that he supplanted a minister whom the queen had grown to love and respect. From the outset, she and Russell were patently never going to get on, for they shared qualities that made conciliation between them impossible—pride and obstinacy. The queen also found Russell physically unattractive, cold and remote, and lacking in social graces (Russell hated court life, preferring the intellectual world of books). In her eyes he seemed weak and ineffectual, for he appeared to have no control over the dealings of his maverick foreign secretary, Lord Palmerston.

Russell's premiership came at a time of considerable social unrest, marked by the Chartist protests in Britain and the potato famine in Ireland and also of disunity in the Whig Party. As a man with a strong social conscience, he did not shirk from attempting to address these issues, introducing a Factory Act in 1847 that reduced the working day to ten hours and pushing through the introduction of local boards of health under the Public Health Act of 1848, as well as initiating reform of the Church of England. But he found the responsibilities of prime minister increasingly onerous and was coming under attack both from the queen and some of his own cabinet, who resisted his plans for reforms.

Russell returned to government in 1852 as foreign secretary in Lord Aberdeen's Peelite-Whig coalition. He tried to introduce a badly timed second Reform Bill in 1854—at a time when Britain was gripped with the crisis in the East and the prospect of war with Russia—a move that was much criticized by his colleagues. He resigned and withdrew from public life, devoting much of his time to writing and literature. Palmerston persuaded him back into government as foreign secretary in 1859, and together they supported the unification of Italy, encountering differences of opinion with the queen, who had a natural antipathy to republican movements of any kind. Created Earl Russell in 1861, on the death of Palmerston he became prime minister again in October 1865 (to 1866). But Russell's attempt to recapture the political successes of his early career, by sanctioning the introduction of a new Reform Bill to extend the franchise, faltered. He resigned after losing the parliamentary vote on the motion in 1866, although the Reform Bill was finally pushed through a year later. His liberal aspirations for reform of education and religious practice did not, however, disappear and found a new advocate in the reformist agenda of William Gladstone in the late 1860s and early 1870s. Russell's remaining years were consumed by grief at the deaths of his eldest son and his daughter-in-law.

Related entries:
Chartism; Gladstone, William Ewart; Palmerston, Henry John Temple, Third Viscount; Peel, Sir Robert

References and further reading:

Cecil, Algernon. 1953. *Queen Victoria and Her Prime Ministers.* London: Eyre and Spottiswoode.
Eccleshall, Robert, and Graham Walker. 1998. *Biographical Dictionary of British Prime Ministers.* London: Routledge.
Longford, Elizabeth. [1964] 1998. *Victoria R.I.* London: Weidenfeld and Nicolson.
Mandler, Peter. 1990. *Aristocratic Government in the Age of Reform: Whigs and Liberals 1830–1852.* Oxford: Clarendon Press.
Newbould, I. 1990. *Whiggery and Reform, 1830–41: The Politics of Government.* London: Macmillan.
Prest, John. 1972. *Lord John Russell.* London: Macmillan.
Walpole, S. 1889. *The Life of Lord John Russell.* 2 vols. London: Longmans.

S

Salisbury, Robert Arthur Talbot Gascoigne-Cecil, Third Marquis of (1830–1903)

What a dreadful thing to lose such as man as Lord Salisbury for the country, the world, and me! (Roberts 1999, 374)

Queen Victoria's last prime minister, the Conservative statesman Lord Salisbury, was, in his courtesy, tolerance, and sense of duty, the last of the old-school, aristocratic prime ministers to come from the House of Lords. In political outlook and temperament he bridged the divide between eighteenth-century Toryism and the new parliamentary democracy of the nineteenth century. The queen had a particular fondness for Salisbury, with whom she had an excellent and relaxed working relationship. His daughter Violet once observed them during the queen's annual holiday in France and wrote: "I never saw two people get on better, their polished manners and deference to and esteem for each other were a delightful sight and one not readily to be forgotten" (Roberts 1999, 793).

Salisbury came from one of Britain's great landed families (his ancestors had been prominent in the court of Queen Elizabeth I) and was born at the ancestral seat, Hatfield House, in Hertfordshire. He had a lonely childhood, his mother's death when he was only ten leaving him solitary by nature and shy. Exceptionally intelligent and cultivated, Salisbury was a natural scholar. He hated sports at school at Eton and developed a passionate interest in science—especially botany. In later years he had his own laboratory built at Hatfield, where he conducted experiments in magnetism and electricity. He was an intensely private and deeply religious man and a devout High Churchman. By nature prone to depression, he was possessed of a streak of ironic, if not cynical, detachment. Eternally mistrustful of the supposed powers of democracy, he tended to a negative attitude in all his political thinking and a desire to play safe by adopting a policy of what has been called "intelligent inaction" (Massingham and Massingham 1932, 475) aimed at preserving the status quo.

Salisbury's studies at Christ Church College, Oxford, were interrupted when his health broke down, after which he made a two-year trip to Australia and New Zealand. Upon his return he became a member of Parliament for Stamford in 1853. During his early political career he also pursued a career in journalism, producing essays and articles on a wide range of topics, mainly for the *Saturday Review* and the *Quarterly Review.* He was a fine, vigorous speaker, not just on politics but also science and communications, demonstrating intellectual power and political foresight,

Queen Victoria deemed Lord Salisbury to be one of her most engaging and amenable prime ministers; she enjoyed a happy working relationship with him and remained deeply fond of him until her death in 1901. (Library of Congress)

which the historian Asa Briggs (1999) has compared favorably with that of Winston Churchill—Salisbury accurately predicting the class struggles and scientific warfare of the twentieth century. Despite family objections to her lower social and economic status, Salisbury had married Georgina Alderson in 1857. Although he had a patent dislike for the shallowness of society, he was a most charming host, together with his wife making Hatfield House, which he inherited in 1868, a welcoming venue for friends and political colleagues.

Salsibury was first appointed to office, as secretary of state for India, in 1866 under Lord Derby, but he resigned a year later over the 1867 Reform Bill. His politics in this respect remained reactionary, and for all his high principles, Salisbury was an implacable opponent of electoral reform. In the end he learned, in the view of Briggs, to "make democracy, which he despised, work for the Conservative Party" (1999, 4). As a High Churchman, Salisbury would also be against ecclesiastical reform, opposing the disestablishment of the Anglican Church in Ireland (1871), the Public Worship Regulation Act of 1874, and reform of ecclesiastical patronage—the latter being the only issue on which he and the queen would ever strongly disagree.

In 1874 Salisbury was appointed secretary of state for India for a second time. In this capacity he accompanied Prime Minister Benjamin Disraeli to the Congress of Berlin in 1878, where he first made his political mark, proving to be an able diplomat behind the scenes in the negotiations to resolve the fraught Eastern Crisis. But it was not until after Disraeli's death (1881) that Salisbury finally began to dominate Conservative politics. At the age of fifty-eight, Salisbury finally became prime minister—in June 1885—also holding the post of foreign secretary, in a minority, caretaker government that lasted only until January 1886. The queen was ecstatic—Salisbury had saved her "from five more years of Gladstone" (Roberts 1999, 318). And for the first time, her prime minister was actually younger than she. When this brief ministry fell, the queen, already impressed with Salisbury, offered him a dukedom, which he declined. She was most put out by the nuisance of a change of government after such a short duration. But what really rankled was losing the good offices of Salisbury himself, a man "who is one of the most intelligent and large minded and unprejudiced statesmen I ever saw, besides being so good, so loyal and so courageous" (Ramm 1990, 28). She kept in close touch with him in the interim, acting unconstitutionally by secretly sending him copies of her official correspondence with Gladstone during the debate over Irish Home Rule (which she and Salisbury both opposed).

The queen was correct in her optimistic prediction that Salisbury would soon be returned to power. Thanks to the support of Liberal Unionists, who joined him to defeat Gladstone's bill on Irish Home Rule, he was back as joint prime minister and foreign secretary in July 1886, remaining in power until 1892 and sanctioning a variety of domestic reform, such as the 1888 Local Government Act, which set up county councils; slum clearance in 1884; free public education in 1891; and compensation for workers in 1897.

In 1892, when Salisbury again lost power to Gladstone, the queen bewailed the removal of "the best government of the century" (Ramm 1990, 147). The imminent return of the dreaded Gladstone in his place, not for the first time provoked highly unconstitutional sentiments in the queen: "It seems to me a defect in our much famed Constitution, to have to part with an admirable government like Lord Salisbury's for no question of any importance, or any particular reason, merely on account of the number of votes" (Longford 1998, 518)! But Salisbury was once again returned for a third, seven-year term in 1895, at the head of a Conservative Liberal–Unionist coalition. Once again, and despite failing health, Salisbury served also as foreign secretary, demonstrating his strengths in the manner in which he sought to maintain the balance of power in Europe, notably by keeping the Russians out of Turkey.

In March 1896, Queen Victoria wrote to tell Salisbury that "every day I feel the blessing of a strong Government in such safe and strong hands as yours" (Hibbert 1984, 333). But from the late 1890s on, she worried about his declining health; he was massively overweight, his legs seemingly unable to bear his weight, exhausted and red eyed. One of the queen's ladies-in-waiting, Marie Mallet, dreaded the loss to the queen and the country should Salisbury be unable to continue. The queen, she remarked, was "very devoted" to Lord Salisbury "and had great confidence in him" (Mallet 1968, 107).

The 1890s were marked by a period of escalating political crisis in Europe, after the death of Bismarck had removed a major, stabilizing influence. The reign of the new kaiser, William II, provoked an increasing estrangement between Britain and Germany, with Salisbury warning of a European alliance of Germany, France, and Russia against Britain. The queen, alarmed by this, wrote to Salisbury, of the opinion that "our *isolation* is dangerous," (Massingham and Massingham 1932, 478) to which Salisbury responded that it was "far less danger than the danger of being dragged into wars which do not concern us" (ibid.). He chose to maintain a negative policy of inaction rather than engagement with Britain's potential adversaries, so long as they did not threaten British imperial power. But the onslaught of the "scramble for Africa" of the 1880s and 1890s was threatening serious conflict among the major European powers, all of whom were competing for territorial gains there. In September 1898, British rivalry with France on the Nile had boiled over into the Fashoda Crisis, at the end of which France had been forced to back down and acknowledge British territorial claims in the Upper Nile. Throughout the crisis Salisbury had endorsed the queen's demand to stand firm against France, without precipitating war, at the end of which the Prince of Wales wrote to his Aunt Vicky: "Mama seems to think her present Government cannot do wrong" (Roberts 1999, 793).

She would, however, become more critical of Salisbury when he did not always take her advice during the Boer War (1899–1902), which dominated the final years of her reign: "I have often told him to put his foot down and I have said over and over again they are too timid," she told Marie Mallet (Mallet 1968, 186). In December 1899, after a string of military disasters during Black Week, Salisbury, now mourning the death of his wife, seemed too old, sick, and mentally exhausted to cope with the protracted campaign. In February of 1900 Mallet described him as "quite played out, I wish to goodness he would retire or resign one or other of his great offices" (177, 188). Shortly afterward Salisbury relinquished the post of foreign secretary.

Shortly before her death on 22 January 1901, Queen Victoria described to the Bishop of Ripon the deep bond that had grown up between her and Salisbury. He held, she asserted, "an equal place with the highest among her ministers, not excepting Disraeli" (Roberts 1999, 795). During his years in office, he retained an amiable and fair-minded manner in his dealings with the queen without ever pandering to her, winning her respect by showing that he could and would resist her hectoring. The key, as he saw it, was to view the queen's reactions and opinions as a barometer for those of the majority of her subjects in middle England. "I have always felt," he remarked, "that when I knew what the Queen thought, I knew pretty certainly what views her subjects would take, and especially the middle class of her subjects" (Longford 1998, 567).

When the queen died, Salisbury recorded his memories of her with great warmth. She was, he said, "always most indulgent to me, both in hours of political difficulty—which in my long service under her were not infrequent—and also in the more trying periods of personal sorrow" (Roberts 1999, 795). He had admired her for her dedication to duty, her statesmanship, and her hard work. The queen had "always displayed a sympathy, a consideration, and a wisdom, which, if my life ran to ten times its probable span, I never could forget" (795). After the queen's death, Salisbury's power within the Conservative party was eroded by his jingoistic colonial secretary, Joseph Chamberlain, with whom he increasingly clashed. By the end of 1901 Salisbury was war weary but determined to see the Boer War through to its conclusion, which came in May 1902. He left Parliament soon after but enjoyed only thirteen months of retirement, dying on 22 August 1903.

The term *splendid isolation* has often been used to describe Salisbury's policies as an international statesman. His was a "do nothing" approach, aimed at preserving the status quo, with Salisbury once observing that "English policy is to float lazily downstream, occasionally putting out a diplomatic boathook to avoid collisions" (Cecil 1921–1932, 2:130). He rejected Chamberlain's advocacy of alliance with Germany, seeing the British Empire going it alone as an enlightened leader of other backward nations. His imperialist political tradition died with him in 1903, setting the final seal on the last days of empire.

Related entries:
Boer War; Disraeli, Benjamin; Gladstone, William Ewart; Ireland; Palmerston, Henry John Temple, Third Viscount; Religion

References and further reading:

Auchincloss, Louis. 1979. *Persons of Consequence: Queen Victoria and Her Circle.* London: Weidenfeld and Nicolson.

Briggs, Asa. 1999. "He Discovered Who the Conservatives Are." *Literary Review* (September): 4–5.

Cecil, Lady Gwendolen. 1921–1932. *Life of Robert, Marquess of Salisbury.* 4 vols. London: Hodder and Stoughton.

Cecil, Lord David. 1973. *The Cecils of Hatfield House.* London: Constable.

Eccleshall, Robert, and Graham Walker. 1998. *Biographical Dictionary of British Prime Ministers.* London: Routledge.

Grenville, J. A. S. 1970. *Lord Salisbury and Foreign Policy: The Close of the Nineteenth Century.* London: Athlone Press.

Hibbert, Christopher. 1984. *Queen Victoria in Her Letters and Journals.* London: Viking.

Kennedy, A. L. 1953. *Salisbury, 1830–1903: Portrait of a Statesman.* London: John Murray.

Longford, Elizabeth. [1964] 1998. *Victoria R.I.* London: Weidenfeld and Nicolson.

Mallet, Victor, ed. 1968. *Life with Queen Victoria: Marie Mallet's Letters from Court, 1887–1901.* London: John Murray.

Massingham, H. J., and H. Massingham, eds. 1932. *The Great Victorians.* London: Ivor Nicholson and Watson.

Ramm, Agatha, ed. 1990. *Beloved and Darling Child: Last Letters between Queen Victoria and her Eldest Daughter, 1886–1901.* Stroud, Gloucestershire: Sutton.

Roberts, Andrew. 1999. *Salisbury: Victorian Titan.* London: Weidenfeld and Nicolson.

Taylor, Robert G. 1975. *Lord Salisbury.* London: Lane.

Saxe-Coburg-Gotha, Royal House of

My Uncle's great wish was that I should marry my cousin Albert. (Esher 1914, 227)

Upon the marriage of Queen Victoria and Prince Albert in 1840, the British royal family adopted the family name of Saxe-Coburg-Gotha, of which Prince Albert was a member. This royal house had been created as the result of a long period of division, loss, and recovery of a succession of ancient Saxon kingdoms in the east central German region of Thuringia. The process had begun in 1485, when they had been shared between the two sons—Ernest and Albert—of elector Frederick II of Saxony.

In 1815, after the fall of Napoleon, these duchies—Saxe-Weimar, Saxe-Coburg, Saxe-Eisenach, Saxe-Altenburg, Saxe-Gotha, Saxe-Meiningen, Saxe-Hildburghausen, and Saxe-Saalfeld—all became sovereign states within the German Confederation, the second part of their names denoting the major city of that particular duchy. In 1826 they were amalgamated into four larger ones, those of Saxe-Weimar-Eisenach, Saxe-Meiningen-Hildburghausen, Saxe-Altenburg, and Saxe-Coburg-Gotha. Of all of them, Saxe-Coburg-Gotha would feature the most prominently in nineteenth- and twentieth-century history, beginning with its union with the British royal house of Hanover in 1840 on the occasion of the marriage of Queen Victoria to Prince Albert. Victoria and Albert's uncle, Leopold, would take the Saxe-Coburg-Saalfed bloodline to Belgium, when he became king in 1831. Other members of the family married into the Portuguese and Bulgarian royal families.

It had always been the intention of Leopold that his niece should retain the close family connection with Coburg by marrying one of her cousins in the Saxe-Coburg line: either Ferdinand or Augustus of Saxe-Coburg-Kohary (a lesser duchy) or one of the brothers—Ernest and Albert—of Saxe-Coburg-Gotha. From the outset Albert had been his favored candidate, and Leopold groomed Albert for the role from an early age.

Throughout their married life together, the queen and Prince Albert would be constantly preoccupied with ensuring that the best interests of Saxe-Coburg-Gotha were served through dynastic marriages, so much so that the German chancellor, Otto von Bismarck, would remark that the duchy had become "the stud farm of Europe" (Aronson 1973, 7).

Saxe-Coburg's capital, Coburg, boasted a splendid medieval castle at Veste and the ducal homes at Callenberg, Ketschendorf, and Reinhardtsbrunn. But Prince Albert's family had lived mainly at their town residence, Castle Ehrenburg (a former monastery), in the winter and during the summer at the charming, country house cum hunting lodge, the Rosenau, located four miles from Coburg, on the edge of the forest. Albert's perpetual nostalgia for this forest home, and the stories he told Victoria of his childhood there, were instrumental in the couple's setting up a residence in the Highlands of Scotland. By all accounts, the Rosenau, despite its modest proportions, was a magical, timeless place, with stepped gables and a romantic, mock-Gothic turret overlooking a valley with a waterfall and "window panes all of coloured glass, decorated with coats of arms" (Bolitho 1964, 3). These and other features would later be copied at Balmoral, which many would remark had more of the German *schloss* about it than a Scottish castle.

In August 1845, Victoria and Albert made their first visit to Coburg together. The queen adored the Rosenau. With its stags' heads on the walls and nearby pine woods, she looked upon it as a home away from home: "I felt as if I should always like to live here with my dearest Albert, and if I was not what I am—this would be my real home. . . . It is like a beautiful dream" (Weintraub 1997, 167). The couple were not able to return to Coburg until fifteen years later, in the autumn of 1860, spending most of their time in quiet retreat at the Rosenau. But although Victoria and Albert might revel in being back there, others in their entourage were less impressed with the castle's modest facilities; lady-in-waiting Mary Ponsonby remarked, "It is a *lovely* spot—but the house, oh so dreary and uncomfortable! What they must think of the *luxe* of our English country houses when they come to us I am at a loss to imagine" (Ponsonby 1927, 43).

When it came time to leave, Albert, by this time already grappling with what he saw as the incontrovertible signs of his own mortality, took a last painful look at his old home. He was convinced that this would be the last time he would see it. He died the following year, still of the firmly held belief that "I Shall never cease *ein treuer Deutscher Coburger, Gothaner zu sein*" [to be a true German Coburger, and Gothaner]" (Strachey 1971, 89).

In 1867 the Saxe-Coburg duchies were incorporated into the North German Confederation. Four years later they were absorbed into the German Empire. During World War I, Victoria's grandson, King George V, issued a royal proclamation that all males in line to the throne would henceforth adopt the surname of Windsor (an act of political expediency to disassociate the British royal family and its German-sounding name from its enemy). At the end of the war, with the abdication in 1918 of Kaiser William, the rulers of all four duchies also abdicated, and the territories were merged into the regions of Thuringia and Bavaria. In 1920 the former duchies of Saxe-Coburg resumed their old, historic association with Thuringia (the mountainous, forested region around Coburg where Prince Albert grew up) by being incorporated into it as a region (*Land*) of Weimar Germany. After World War II, the lands of Thuringia were absorbed into East Germany, until the collapse of the Berlin Wall in 1989. In 1990 Thuringia became a state in a reunified Germany; its former territory in Coburg became part of Bavaria.

Related entries:
"Grandmama of Europe"; Victoria, Queen: Courtship and Marriage of

References and further reading:

Aronson, Theo. 1973. *Grandmama of Europe: The Crowned Descendants of Queen Victoria.* London: Cassell.

Bolitho, Hector. 1964. *Albert, Prince Consort.* London: Max Parrish.

Eilers, Marlene A. 1997. *Queen Victoria's Descendants.* Falkoping, Sweden: Rosvall Royal Books.

Fulford, Roger. 1966. *The Prince Consort.* London: Macmillan.

Grey, Hon. Charles. 1867. *The Early Years of H.R.H. the Prince Consort.* London: Smith, Elder and Co.

Martin, Sir Theodore. 1875–1880. *The Life of His Royal Highness the Prince Consort.* 5 vols. London: Smith Elder and Co.

Ponsonby, Magdalen. 1927. *Mary Ponsonby: A Memoir, Some Letters, and a Journal.* London: John Murray.

Strachey, Lytton. [1921] 1971. *Queen Victoria.* Harmondsworth, UK: Penguin.

Weintraub, Stanley. 1997. *Albert, Uncrowned King.* London: John Murray.

Scott, Sir Walter (1771–1832)

my beau idéal *of a Poet; I do so admire him both in Poetry and Prose!* (Esher 1912, 1:175)

Queen Victoria was born in 1819, the year that the novelist and poet Walter Scott's most popular novel, *Ivanhoe,* was published. As a young girl, one of the few novels she was allowed to read was Scott's *The Bride of Lammermoor.* For ever after Scott would remain a literary constant in the lives not only of the queen but also of Prince Albert, his historical romances serving as a reminder of all that they found lyrical in the Scottish landscape at their home at Balmoral. Although Victoria and Albert's adoration might remain undimmed, Scott's literary contemporaries viewed his artistic talents as limited. He was, in the view of Samuel Taylor Coleridge, a "picturesque tourist" (Drabble 1979, 175): his poetic works would be rapidly eclipsed by Byron and Wordsworth, and the romantic, historical settings of his novels would give way to the great social novels of Dickens, Gaskell, and Eliot. Scott's huge opus is now largely unread, yet in his day he was the world's most famous living author, dubbed "the Scottish Prospero" and "the Wizard of the North" (171).

The son of an Edinburgh solicitor, Scott followed his father into legal training and was called to the bar in 1792. Partially lamed by a withered leg—the result of a childhood illness—he spent time convalescing on his grandfather's farm in the countryside of Roxburghshire, developing a great love for this, the Border region, which he would travel extensively over the following years, becoming conversant with its history, oral traditions, and customs. In 1797, during the Napoleonic Wars, Scott was an enthusiastic military amateur, founding a troop of the Volunteer Light Horse in Edinburgh and serving intermittently with the yeomanry for the next fifteen years; his patriotic and military vigor inspired much of his early poetry. He worshiped the duke of Wellington and, had his wife allowed him, would have joined his Peninsular campaign of 1808.

In 1811 Scott bought a 1,400-acre estate on the River Tweed, in Roxburghshire. He turned down the offer of becoming poet laureate in 1813, content to live the life of a Scottish laird, getting up at 5 A.M. in the morning to write, before spending the day overseeing his estate. Between 1817 and 1824 he built a splendid manor house—Abbotsford—funded on the promise of huge royalties to come.

Sir Walter Scott was one of the first writers whom Victoria had enjoyed as a girl. His poetry and novels, imbued with a celebration of Scotland and of the medieval ideal, remained lifelong favorites both with her and Prince Albert. (Perry-Castaneda Library)

Scott's first published work—*Minstrelsy of the Scottish Border*—was a recreation of traditional Scottish ballads, which he had begun collecting in 1792 and published in three volumes in 1802–1803. His first major success was *The Lay of the Last Minstrel* (1805), a romantic poem based on sixteenth-century legend, set in the Borders. His next work, *Marmion* (1808), set at the time of the battle of Flodden of 1513 and for which Scott received an advance of £1,000 sight unseen, sold 13,000 copies in the first six months. The apogee of his poetic career came in 1810 with the *Lady of the Lake,* another Highland saga of romance and heroism, set in the sixteenth century.

Despite its extremely high retail price of two guineas, it sold more than 30,000 copies in its first year. Scott now had the royal seal of approval: the Prince Regent became so addicted to "dear Walter's" work that on his accession to the throne in 1820 he made Scott a baronet.

Scott's erudition was displayed in his other literary endeavors, which included entries for the *Encyclopaedia Britannica,* as well as the editing of the complete works of Swift and Dryden and translations of Goethe. Like Queen Victoria, he was also a prolific diarist. His heyday as a poet was, however, relatively brief, for he soon found his popularity eclipsed by the rising star of Lord Byron. This prompted Scott to turn to prose writing after 1814, when he published his first novel, *Waverley,* anonymously (apprehensive that it would not garner the same critical acclaim as his poetry). This and subsequent historical romances, many of them set in Scotland, would appear as "by the author of Waverley." In them, Scott set the standard for a new genre of historical writing that would spawn many imitators while exploiting his natural gifts as a consummate storyteller. His use of rural settings and dialect would later inspire the regional novels of the great female novelists who followed him—Charlotte, Emily, and Anne Brontë; Mrs. Gaskell; and George Eliot. Such was the demand for his work that from the mid-century on the "Waverley" novels were made available in cheap popular editions, at three pence each.

The huge income from his novels propelled Scott into massive overspending on his estate, which in turn set him on the treadmill of writing at a ferocious pace in order to keep abreast of his financial commitments. His fortunes came to grief in 1826 when the printing firm that published his books, James Ballantyne and Co., in which he was a partner, folded with debts of £130,000. Scott felt morally obliged to repay the debts and worked himself to exhaustion and premature death in 1832, having paid off £76,000; the remaining money was paid out of the posthumous sale of the copyrights on his work.

Scott met Princess Victoria, on one occasion only, in 1828 when he was invited to dine with her mother, the duchess of Kent, at Kensington Palace. In his journal he later noted how strictly confined the child's upbringing was, remarking that this was not "the best training found for a life destined to be spent among an almost infinite diversity of people" (St. Aubyn 1991, 23). The youthful Victoria eulogized the merits of Scott's narrative poem *Rokeby* (1813)—set in seventeenth-century Yorkshire—in her journal in 1836. His poetry was, she averred, "full of loveliness, sweetness, grace, elegance, and feeling" (Esher 1914, 64). In Victoria's opinion, Scott, the "immortal bard," "never *could* write an *ugly* line" (ibid.).

After her marriage, in 1840, Queen Victoria shared her enthusiasm for Scott with Prince Albert, who found in Scott's descriptive passages strong echoes of the mountains and forests of Thuringia near the prince's home in Coburg. The magical ingredients of romance, heroic deeds, breathtaking landscapes, and, above all, the medieval ethic of chivalry all greatly appealed to the royal couple; when they were first married the queen and Prince Albert would often sit and read Scott together at the end of the queen's working morning.

In the late summer of 1842, Prince Albert and Queen Victoria made their first visit to Scotland, carrying with them a preconceived romantic notion of the country built upon their enjoyment of Scott's writings. In the romantic setting of Drummond Castle, Queen Victoria read to Albert from *The Lay of the Last Minstrel* and *The Lady of the Lake.* Albert endorsed their debt to Scott: "There is . . . no country where historical traditions are preserved with such fidelity. . . . Every spot is connected with some interesting historical fact, and with most of these Sir Walter Scott's accurate descriptions have made us familiar" (Hibbert 2000, 175). It was the beginning of a lifelong love affair with Scotland that would prompt the royal couple to lease a house at Balmoral. In 1853 they began building a new Gothic-style baronial castle as the real-life setting for their own, private Scottish fantasy.

Despite the distance, the difficulty of travel, and the popular perception of Scotland as being a hotbed of Jacobite rebellion, Scott's works, coupled with Victoria and Albert's enthusiasm for them, inspired the birth of the tourist industry in Scotland. As Margaret Drabble remarked, Scott "did for Scotland what Wordsworth had done for the Lakes" (1979, 171). The first trickle of literary pilgrimage would mushroom into an industry when Thomas Cook introduced the first tours there in 1848. And Scott's immortalization of "the noble stag" in *The Lady of the Lake,* which was later captured on canvas by the favorite royal painter Edwin Landseer, was echoed in Prince Albert's almost mystical reverence for the animal. In admiration of the poem's wild and lonely setting, Queen Victoria and Prince Albert took a fancy that Loch Muick near Balmoral resembled the opening landscape of the poem and made an expedition there in September 1850. Whenever she was at Balmoral, the queen ensured that during the often windswept and rainy afternoons her entourage would have ample opportunity of catching up on their Scott. According to Christopher Hibbert (2000, 478), there were thirty-two copies of *Lady of the Lake* and twelve copies of *Rob Roy* to be found in the library there.

The most poignant link with Scott came as Prince Albert lay dying in December 1861. In his final days he was read Scott's 1822 novel *Peveril of the Peak* by Queen Victoria and their daughter Princess Alice. After Albert's death, Scott's writings provided a powerful link for the queen with past idyllic times in Scotland. In 1867, on a tour of the Borders, she finally visited Scott's home at Abbotsford. In the library she was shown the manuscripts of works such as *Ivanhoe*—a tale that, with its twelfth-century setting and thoroughly Anglo-Saxon hero, would be Scott's most enduring work. The queen thought the place "rather gloomy" but after being persuaded to sign her name in Scott's journal (she felt this was presumptuous), she sat, before leaving, and took tea in the dining room in which Scott had died. Two years later, when she toured the Trossachs and Rob Roy country, the queen carried a copy of *The Lady of the Lake* with her, as a guidebook and source of inspiration. Toward the end of her life, when asked who her favorite poet was by a lady-in-waiting, the queen replied without hesitation—"Oh, certainly Scott" (Lutyens 1961, 109).

Related entries:
Balmoral Castle; Landseer, Sir Edwin; *Leaves from the Journal of Our Life in the Highlands*

References and further reading:

Brown, David. 1979. *Walter Scott and the Historical Imagination.* London: Routledge and Kegan Paul.

Drabble, Margaret. 1979. *A Writer's Britain: Landscape in Literature.* London: Thames and Hudson.

Esher, Viscount, ed. 1914. *The Training of a Sovereign.* London: John Murray.

Girouard, Mark. 1981. *The Return to Camelot: Chivalry and the English Gentleman.* New Haven: Yale University Press (chaps. 3 and 4).

Hibbert, Christopher. 2000. *Victoria: A Personal History.* London: HarperCollins.

Johnson, Edgar. 1970. *Sir Walter Scott: The Great Unknown.* 2 vols. London: Hamish Hamilton.

Lutyens, Mary, ed. 1961. *Lady Lytton's Court Diary 1895–1899.* London: Rupert Hart-Davis.

St. Aubyn, Giles. 1991. *Queen Victoria: A Portrait.* London: Sinclair Stevenson.

Sutherland, John. 1988. *The Longman Companion to Victorian Fiction.* London: Longmans.

Sex, Pregnancy, and Childbirth

The Shadow Side (Fulford 1964, 78)

As the archetypal matriarch of her age, Queen Victoria had very decided views on parenthood and the rearing of children. Any assessment of the sexual and emotional relationship within which her children were conceived relies, however, on a considerable amount of conjecture, based on the known facts, of which, in the case of the queen's sexuality, there are few. Many of the most frequently cited views that the queen held about her own experience of pregnancy and childbirth come at some remove from the events themselves. The primary source for these largely retrospective observations on motherhood are the hundreds of letters that Victoria wrote to her eldest daughter, Vicky. In them, the queen volunteered her advice on a wide range of domestic issues, and Roger Fulford's five edited volumes published between 1964 and 1981 are an essential source. They do not, however, present the whole picture.

Of the queen's expurgated journal entries (transcribed and edited by her daughter Beatrice after her death), those written at the time of the births of her first two children indicate the genuine sense of delight that she and her husband shared in the first flush of parenthood. But this joy would be dissipated in the very real anxieties attendant upon any woman enduring her first seven pregnancies in only ten years—as was Victoria's case—at a time when the likelihood of the death of the mother and/or the child during labor was still high. Victoria's pregnancies undoubtedly took considerable emotional and physical tolls on her, which manifested themselves in tensions and rows with Prince Albert. Such tensions are reflected in a hardening of her attitude to maternity, leaving us with a very negative, if not at times despairing, view of the married woman's lot in the nineteenth century. But, as Ward argued, it is likely that the pessimistic views of marriage and motherhood that the queen offered to Vicky and her other daughters "may have been avenues to release long-held repressed memories of the frightening physical aspects of sex and childbirth—which she had had no chance to release previously" (1999, 289).

After their marriage on 10 February 1840, Prince Albert promptly set about molding his young wife in his own image, anxious that she should not fall prey to the emotional excesses of her Hanoverian ancestors. He was greatly preoccupied that his status as husband and future paterfamilias should not be undermined by his technically inferior status to the queen, as her consort rather than king. As a young woman, Victoria had displayed a passionate nature that suggests she had more than inherited the red-blooded sexuality of her forebears. It is thought that she and Albert enjoyed a very fulfilling physical relationship, although biographers have had to rely heavily on only one or two passing and euphemistic remarks in her journals. A veil was necessarily drawn over the details of her sexual life by Victoria, but what *is* clear is that much of her natural physicality and emotional openness seems rapidly to have been stifled by the prince's sexual prudery and his diktats that domestic responsibility should take precedence over personal pleasure.

Like almost all young women marrying at that time, Victoria was naive about sex. But she knew enough of the ordeal of childbirth to remark in her journal that it was "the only thing I dread" (Dewhurst 1980, 169). In the days before reliable methods of contraception, she simply hoped and prayed, as all women did, that each baby would not come too soon after the previous one. In later life the queen would stress to Vicky the importance of the husband and wife having time to build a good relationship when they were first married, before the intrusion of babies made inroads on their precious time together. She herself had become pregnant within a month of her wedding and would later greatly resent the fact.

Prince Albert, in anticipating the birth of their first child and already aware of the queen's histrionic nature, predicted there would be "a great *Rompos*" (rumpus; Longford 1966, 76) when she went into labor. He thought his wife would not be able to endure the pain. As it turned out, Victoria proved exceptionally robust when it came to childbearing, considering her small stature (less than five feet), which must have made the late stages of pregnancy extremely uncomfortable for her. Victoria, the Princess Royal, was born after a ten-hour labor, and without complications, on 22 November 1840. During this and her other eight pregnancies the queen was attended by her personal physician, Dr. James Clark, although his medical examinations would have been of the most superficial kind. Once Victoria went into labor, Clark's role became merely a supervisory one (midwifery not being his strong point). A newly appointed physician-accoucheur, Dr. (later Sir) Charles Locock, had been appointed to deliver the child, with the assistance of a midwife, Mrs. Lilly. Locock also called in two other accoucheurs, Dr. Robert Ferguson and a Mr. Bagden, to attend with him during the delivery. He was paid a generous £1,000 for his services and went on to deliver all the other royal babies with the assistance of Ferguson; this brought him a considerable reputation and the nickname "the Great Deliverer of His Country." Little is known about the equally skilled and devoted Mrs. Lilly, however; she lived to the age of ninety-two, yet her first name has not even come down to us.

Victoria was fortunate during labor to be given considerable support and comfort at her bedside by Albert, in an age when most Victorian fathers stayed well out of range of their wives' suffering. Indeed, she took men to task, in her letters, for not showing sufficient compassion for the agonies their wives endured, such as in an 1841 letter to her Uncle Leopold: "Men never think, at least seldom think what a hard task it is for us women to go through this very often," (Benson and Esher 1911, 2:255) she wrote. But she was resigned to her lot as a woman: "God's will be done, and if He decrees that we are to have a great number of children why we must then try to bring them up as useful and exemplary members of society" (ibid.). Within a couple of months of the birth of Vicky, Victoria was pregnant again. One of the reasons that this happened so soon was probably because Victoria adamantly refused to breast feed. Lactation was known to delay the return of a woman's fertility and was seen by many Victorians as one of the few acceptable methods of birth control. The queen, however, had a very strong aversion to the idea. When the as yet uninitiated Vicky married at the age of only seventeen, expressing high ideals about the joys of maternity, Victoria was quick to disabuse her. "What you say of the pride of giving life to an immortal soul is very fine, dear, but I own I cannot enter into that; I think much more of our being like a cow or a dog at such moments; when our poor nature becomes so very animal and unecstatic" (Fulford 1964, 115). Breast-feeding was thus, for Victoria, part of this debasing and animalistic side of childbirth; it was also, for a woman with her responsibilities, highly inconvenient and placed further limitations on the time she could spend with her beloved Albert. All her children were therefore handed over to a wet nurse as soon as they were born; the first, a doctor's wife from the Isle of Wight, received the huge sum of £1,000 for nurturing Vicky, as well as a pension. When Vicky later announced her decision to breast-feed her own children, the queen tried to dissuade her; she was further incensed when her second daughter, Alice, did the same, promptly naming one of the prize dairy cows at Windsor "Alice" as a snipe at her.

Victoria saw nothing romantic or attractive about the sight of a pregnant woman. Writing in 1859, she observed: "I positively think those ladies who are always *enceinte* [pregnant] quite disgusting; it is more like a rabbit or guinea pig than anything else and really it is not very nice" (Fulford 1964, 195.) She disapproved of the appearance in public of heavily pregnant women, as she did also of their too hasty return to social life after giving birth. Medical practice at that time dictated a long lying-in period (usually two weeks bed rest, followed by four weeks confined to the home), a practice that has long since been rejected by the medical profession as dangerous rather than beneficial to the mother's health. In March 1870, the queen was up in arms about the impropriety of women who had recently given birth choosing "to dance within a fortnight of their confinement and even valse at seven months!!!" (Perkin 1993, 66). "Where is the delicacy of feeling going to?" she wailed; "Sybil St. Albans danced a quadrille!" (ibid). Yet as a young woman she herself had resented not being able to ride and dance when pregnant and had felt imprisoned by the constraints that her condition had placed on her freedom of movement.

In her later letters to Vicky, the queen admitted that having had her first three pregnancies in such quick succession (there would be no significant gap until the three years that elapsed after the birth of Arthur in 1850) had made her feel wretched. "One becomes so worn out and one's nerves so miserable" (Fulford 1964, 195), she remarked. Her second, difficult labor (with the Prince of Wales, born 9 November 1841) had been traumatic; she had taken longer to recover from it, suffering a bout of postnatal depression. By the time she came to her eighth (April 1853) and ninth (April 1857) deliveries, the queen decided that she had had enough of the doctrinal view that women should give birth in pain and suffering—artificial pain relief being regarded in the church as a "decoy of Satan" (Potts and Potts 1995, 40). Ignoring clerical exhortations that doing so would "rob God of the deep earnest cries which arise in time of trouble for help" (40), she gratefully accepted the offer of chloroform, administered to her by Dr. John Snow, a pioneer of anesthetics. She was pleasantly surprised by its effects, which she found "soothing, quieting and delightful beyond measure" (Dewhurst 1980, 178). Her decision to use chloroform legitimized its use by other women seeking pain relief, and despite the debate about its safety going on in the medical press, the procedure, having been given the queen's seal of approval, became popularly known as *Anaesthesia à la Reine* (181).

After Victoria gave birth to Beatrice in 1857, her physician, Dr. James Clark, advised Prince Albert that she should have no more children, fearing that another pregnancy would place too great a strain on Victoria's nerves and bring on another bout of postnatal depression (from which she often suffered). When she heard of Clark's ruling, Victoria supposedly asked him in private: "Can I have no more fun in bed?" (Hibbert 2000, 400)—this question thus forming the basis of subsequent, tenuous discussions of the queen's sex life.

Victoria, lived, of course, at a time when methods for avoiding pregnancy were a taboo subject. Although she never ceased to emphasize how bad it was for a woman to have too many children too fast—because the children suffered, and the young mother rapidly lost her looks—she was utterly horrified when the social reformers Annie Besant and Charles Bradlaugh published a pamphlet on birth control, in which they attempted to help poor working women avoid having endless unwanted pregnancies. The dissemination of contraceptive advice was, in her view, nothing short of an encouragement to immorality and prostitution.

Without recourse to contraception, childbirth remained a bodily experience to which the queen believed her "poor" and "feeble" sex had to resign itself with stoicism. But for those women not blessed with a wonderful husband as she was, but locked in domestic misery with uncaring men, the queen had considerable depths of compassion. Even among her own class, she looked upon marriage as a lottery, where all too often women found "a very doubtful happiness" (Fulford 1964, 99). Her sex had little option, she believed, but to marry or take the risk of growing old, lonely, and embittered. Yet to do so was to submit to the never-ending demands of maternity; women were, she wrote, "born for Man's pleasure and amusement" (205), and this was "a sin from which dear Papa even is not quite exempt though he would not admit it" (205). In a sobering letter to the newly married Vicky in March 1858, the queen warned: "one feels so pinned down—one's wings clipped—in fact, at the best . . . only half oneself. . . . This I call the 'shadow side.' . . . And therefore—I think our sex a most unenviable one" (78).

It is said that throughout her childbearing life the queen was haunted by the stories of the tragic death in 1817 from puerperal fever, after giving birth to a stillborn child, of George IV's heir, Princess Charlotte. It comes as some surprise therefore that she never openly acknowledged her own extreme good fortune in having survived nine pregnancies (at a time when one in every 200 women died in childbirth), without either miscarrying or losing a baby at birth or soon after. Nor did she see any of her infants carried off by the many virulent diseases that contributed to a high mortality rate among children under five years of age. As her children grew up, Victoria became increasingly critical of them. She seemed to take a real pride in them only when they either looked like their father or emulated his high moral and intellectual standards. And she never found consolation in them when Albert was absent on official business. He was her real world, and she was not ashamed to admit it: "*All* the numerous children are as *nothing* to me when *he is away;* it seems as if the whole life of the house and home were gone" (Benson and Esher 1911, 3:240).

Related entries:
Albert of Saxe-Coburg-Gotha; Christmas; "Grandmama of Europe"; Lyttleton, Lady; Women's Rights

References and further reading:

Benson, A. C., and Viscount Esher, eds. 1911. *Letters of Queen Victoria, 1837–1861.* 1st ser., 3 vols. London: John Murray.

Charlot, Monica. 1991. *Victoria, the Young Queen.* Cambridge: Polity.

Dewhurst, Jack. 1980. *Royal Confinements.* London: Weidenfeld and Nicolson.

Fulford, Roger, ed. 1964. *Dearest Child: Letters between Queen Victoria and the Princess Royal, 1858–61.* London: Evans Brothers.

Hibbert, Christopher. 2000. *Queen Victoria, a Personal History.* London: HarperCollins.

Hough, Richard. 1996. *Victoria and Albert: Their Love and Their Tragedies.* London: Richard Cohen.

Jerrold, Clare. 1912. *The Married Life of Queen Victoria.* London: Eveleigh Nash.

Longford, Elizabeth. 1966. "Queen Elizabeth's Doctors." In Martin Gilbert, ed., *A Century of Conflict 1850–1950,* 75–87. London: Hamish Hamilton.

Longford, Elizabeth. [1964] 1998. *Victoria R.I.* London: Weidenfeld and Nicolson.

Perkin, Joan. 1993. *Victorian Women.* London: John Murray.

Potts, D. M., and W. T. W. Potts. 1995. *Queen Victoria's Gene: Haemophilia and the Royal Family.* Stroud, Gloucestershire: Sutton.

Ward, Yvonne M. 1999. "The Womanly Garb of Queen Victoria's Early Motherhood, 1840–1842." *Women's History Review* 8 (2): 277–294.

Warner, Marina. 1979. *Queen Victoria's Sketchbook.* London: Macmillan.

Watson, Vera. 1952. *A Queen at Home: An Intimate Account of the Social and Domestic Life at Queen Victoria's Court.* London: W. H. Allen.

Whittle, Tyler. 1980. *Queen Victoria at Home.* London: Routledge and Kegan Paul.

Smoking

a filthy habit (Nevill 1997, 8)

Smoking was anathema to Queen Victoria: a disgusting vice indulged in by the weak-willed. During her widowhood, however, an exception was always made in the case of her adored John Brown, whom she appears never to have criticized for his own smokestack of a pipe, which he puffed even in her presence. Because she considered smoking an unnecessary and unpleasant habit, the queen consigned those addicted to nicotine to ritual humiliation and confinement in a lepers' colony for smokers, far removed from her own royal apartments. It is unclear whether or not Prince

Albert smoked, the problem arising in her widowhood, by which time all the queen's sons were smokers.

The puritanical atmosphere of the royal residences during the queen's widowhood was heightened by the denial of the creature comforts, not only smoking but also warm fires and convivial evenings staying up late; these denials were accompanied by the imposition of copious draughts of fresh air through every available window. Smoking, for long frowned upon in polite Victorian society during the earlier years of the queen's reign, was something men indulged in along with the port at the end of a meal, and most certainly not in the presence of ladies. But with the mass production of cigarettes from the 1880s in Britain by W. D. & H. O. Wills and Company, smoking was taken up by many courtiers and members of the royal family. For many years, the widowed queen sent those who smoked to an outside room in which to puff away. This proved a torment to heavy smokers such as Bertie, the Prince of Wales; the queen's son-in-law Prince Christian of Schleswig-Holstein; and, on one occasion, the visiting king of Saxony. The latter, feeling this to be an insult to his own rights as a sovereign, became so irritated after two days of imposed abstention that he finally lit up a cigar as he strode up the grand staircase at Windsor. Although kow-towing to his mother's rules on her territory, the Prince of Wales refused to refrain from smoking anywhere else. In 1869, when his club, White's, vetoed the prince's motion that smoking should be permitted in its morning room, he founded a club of his own—the Marlborough—where he could be free to smoke when and where he pleased. One of his first acts of revenge for decades of his mother's domestic despotism came when, shortly after the queen's death in January 1901, Bertie began lighting his fat cigars with alacrity wherever he went at Windsor.

So adamant was the queen that the nonsmoking rule should be observed that she ordered framed notices to be placed in many of the rooms at Windsor, Balmoral, and Osborne—requesting male guests and members of the royal household not to smoke. She could smell tobacco and cigar smoke a mile off and always knew if a piece of correspondence had come from a smoker. Because she dealt with so many documents and official papers daily, Victoria ordered her equerries and private secretaries not to smoke while writing or handling them. Her private secretary, Henry Ponsonby, who had the responsibility of deciphering coded telegrams sent to the queen, was reprimanded for smoking while he did so; the box containing his transcripts reeked of tobacco smoke, the queen complained. Guilty smokers at court all frequently resorted to sucking peppermints in an attempt to disguise the fact that they had been smoking. Others, unwilling to be ghettoized in the designated smoking areas, resorted to desperate measures. A certain Count Hatzfeldt, while staying at Windsor, wished to have a quiet smoke in his room without having to traipse downstairs to the billiard room where it was allowed. So he lay flat on his back, with his head in the fireplace, blowing his cigarette smoke up the chimney. Similarly, lady visitors at court who were secret smokers resorted to sitting on window ledges, blowing their cigarette smoke out of the window.

With her two eldest sons, Bertie and Affie (Alfred), both taking up smoking from an early age, the queen tried hard to prevent her third son, Arthur, her favorite, from doing so. But sooner or later she had to make some concessions. Her daughter Helena married a heavy smoker, Prince Christian of Schleswig-Holstein, in 1866 (he managed to live to the age of eighty-six despite puffing his way through an alarming twenty-four cigars a day). One day, at Balmoral, Christian had the temerity to ask the queen if he could smoke, and she grudgingly allotted him a pokey room in the courtyard of the servants' wing, allowing a chair and table to be placed there for his use. But he was only allowed to do so after Queen Victoria had gone to bed, and then only until midnight. The queen issued a directive that the smoking room be closed at this hour because John Brown complained to her about being kept up late to attend to the gentlemen smokers. A similar outside room was provided at Windsor, and at Osborne a small building attached to the household wing was set aside for the use of the smoking fraternity. There, the confirmed smokers in the royal family would be joined by other male members of the royal household. Such modest little venues became known, rather grandly, as the "gentlemen's smoking room." The queen, of course, looked upon them as little more than opium dens.

The arrival in 1885 of another—and much-loved—son-in-law, Henry of Battenberg, who was also addicted to smoking, increased the pressure on the queen to allow the smokers at court the use of an inside room. Eventually, one was provided at Balmoral, with old sofas and armchairs dragged up from a storeroom. By the end of her reign, the queen had relaxed the rules enough to allow smoking in the billiard rooms at Windsor and Osborne. It is possible that the queen found herself obliged to make these concessions because her Highland servant, John Brown, thought the smell of tobacco smoke was "no a bad thing to have about a hoose" (Tooley 1896, 275) and would not be separated from his pipe. Indeed, such was her devotion to him, that the queen even sent a gift of tobacco to Brown's aunt, when she discovered she was a smoker.

Throughout his life, Bertie, Prince of Wales, had to resort to all kinds of subterfuge in his smoking habits. After the death of Prince Albert (in 1861), a conciliatory Lady Beaconsfield (wife of Benjamin Disraeli) ventured that no doubt the queen found her eldest son a great comfort in her grief, to which the queen retorted: "Comfort! Why I caught him smoking a fortnight after his dear father died" (Collier 1984, 2). On one occasion, while showing his mother round his new home, Marlborough House, Bertie suddenly realized their route would take them straight past the door to the smoking room. He quickly ordered an equerry to post a large sign on the door announcing "Lavatory under Repair." The queen walked on. She never ceased to castigate the prince about his very heavy smoking; behind her back, Bertie observed to a friend that "when H.[er] M.[ajesty] left off her weeds he would leave off his" (Vincent 1978, 219). Prime Minister William Gladstone, despite himself being an antismoker, was however more sympathetic to the prince's addiction; whenever Gladstone was with the prince, he tried to put him at his ease and "always gave his Royal Highness the lead by lighting a cigarette" (Jerrold 1916, 349).

With time the queen grew to be less disapproving of the dreaded weed and mellowed in her attitude toward those who used it. She particularly softened in relation to the needs of her much-loved troops fighting abroad. During the Egyptian campaign of 1882, she heard that her soldiers were complaining about the shortage of tobacco and wrote to her secretary of state, hoping that "something can be done for the purpose of supplying them with this almost necessary of life out there" (Hardie 1935, 223). During the Boer War, when the young Archibald Boyd-Carpenter, son of one of the queen's favorite clergymen, was sent out to South Africa, she asked to see him before he left. To his surprise, she presented him with a cigar-case. "As you are well aware," she said, "I dislike smoking, but I know that when you young men are out on the veldt you will smoke whether I like it or not, so when you do smoke I want you to think of a lonely old woman at Windsor" (Petrie 1960, 54).

Heavy smoking, which killed Prince Alfred in his fifties (he died of cancer of the tongue), would be an addiction of several of the queen's descendants in the Windsor family. Her grandson Edward VIII (who abdicated in 1938) was a chain smoker, succumbing to cancer of the throat when he was seventy-seven. His brother, King George VI, the present queen's father, died of lung cancer in 1952 at the age of only fifty-seven. Smoking, combined with overeating, almost certainly contributed to the death of Edward VII from heart failure when he was sixty-nine, as well as to the death of his son George V, who died of a bronchial infection when he was seventy-one.

Related entries:
Albert Edward, Prince of Wales; Battenberg, Henry Maurice, Prince of; Fresh Air; Helena Augusta Victoria, Princess

References and further reading:

Apperson, G. L. 1914. *The Social History of Smoking.* London: M. Secker.
Collier, Richard. 1984. *The Rainbow People.* London: Weidenfeld and Nicolson.
Hardie, Frank. 1935. *The Political Influence of Queen Victoria.* Oxford: Oxford University Press.
Hardy, Alan. 1976. *Queen Victoria Was Amused.* London: John Murray.
Hibbert, Christopher. 1984. *Queen Victoria in Her Letters and Journals.* London: Viking (206).
Jerrold, Clare. 1916. *The Widowhood of Queen Victoria.* London: Eveleigh Nash.
Lutyens, Mary, ed. 1961. *Lady Lytton's Court Diary 1895–1899.* London: Rupert Hart-Davis.
Packard, Jerrold. 1998. *Victoria's Daughters.* New York: St. Martin's Press.
Petrie, Sir Charles. 1960. *The Victorians.* London: Eyre and Spottiswoode.
Ponsonby, Henry. 1951. *Recollections of Three Reigns.* London: Eyre and Spottiswood.
Tooley, Sarah. 1896. *Personal Life of Queen Victoria.* London: Hodder and Stoughton.
Vincent, John, ed. 1978. *Disraeli, Derby and the Conservative Party: Journals and Memoirs of Edward Henry, Lord Stanley.* Hassocks, Sussex: Harvester Press.

Stockmar, Christian Friedrich von (1787–1863)

(From 1831, Baron Stockmar)

we confided everything *to* Stockmar, *and he was adored in this house* (Buckle, 1926–1928, 1:100)

The subtle, self-effacing Baron Stockmar played the important role as go-between for Leopold, king of the Belgians, and his niece Queen Victoria during the first years of her reign. He also enjoyed a special position of trust as a close friend and adviser of Prince Albert and achieved for himself a unique position of influence at the British court. Such a strong German presence, which Stockmar shared for a while with the queen's former governess Baroness Lehzen, would in itself create problems and a degree of antipathy among British members of the royal household toward the excessive German influences over the young queen.

Stockmar was a master at self-effacement; such was his ability to retreat into the background that he remains an elusive character. For many years he commuted between England and his home in Coburg, ever ready to offer to the royal couple his lengthy deliberations on matters political, bureaucratic, and domestic. For Prince Albert, Stockmar was an indispensable ally. But William Gladstone thought Stockmar "a mischievous old prig" (Fulford 1966, 25). He had the look of a gremlin, a "wizened-looking grim old man with piercing brown eyes," according to one lady-in-waiting (Ponsonby 1927, 6); the shrunken body was also often commented on, down to the inability of his thin legs to hold up his stockings. Some historians have perceived a sinister, Machiavellian side to his personality; others, such as Paul Emden, described him as "that Enquire Within Upon everything" (Emden 1934, 60). Certainly he was a man who could be relied upon to listen to royal anxieties and come up with exhaustively detailed advice on a wealth of subjects, so much so that he clearly pulled the wires behind some crucial royal decisions. As a German, though, he was, like Prince Albert, viewed with suspicion and often resentment by many at court. Lord Melbourne thought differently, however; in his opinion, Stockmar was "one of he cleverest fellows I ever saw, the most discreet man, the most well-judging, and most cool man" (Strachey 1971, 52).

Born in Coburg of Swedish descent, Stockmar was the son of a magistrate and bibliophile. He trained as a doctor and practiced medicine in Coburg with his uncle, before serving as a field doctor during the Napoleonic Wars, after which he was appointed head of a military hospital in Coburg. It was at this time that he came to the attention of Prince Leopold of Saxe-Coburg (Queen Victoria's uncle and future king of the Belgians). Leopold appointed him confidential secretary and personal physician in 1816, at the time of Leopold's departure for England to marry the prince regent's daughter, Princess Charlotte. Charlotte became greatly attached to "Stocky," as she called him, but with his characteristically scrupulous discretion, Stockmar had declined the appointment as Charlotte's physician-in-ordinary. Eighteen months later, therefore, he was forced to look on in horror at the appallingly misguided medical treatment of the pregnant Charlotte and her unnecessary death shortly after childbirth. He had rightly calculated that had he taken the appointment, the English would have taken great pleasure in blaming him, as a foreigner and a German. After Charlotte's death, Stockmar shrewdly advised the widowed Leopold to stay in England and keep careful watch over his financial interests. But Leopold was ambitious, and when he was offered the throne of Belgium early in 1831, it was the trusty Stockmar who conducted the delicate negotiations on his behalf.

With Leopold safely installed in Belgium, Stockmar might well have chosen to retreat back to anonymity in Coburg, but he stayed on in Leopold's service to serve two further, crucial roles. The first was as Leopold's emissary (if not spy) at the British court, keeping watch on the interests of the young Princess Victoria, particularly once the likelihood of her accession to the throne became clear. Once more declining an official post—this time as Queen Victoria's private secretary (as a foreigner he knew this would not be countenanced anyway)—Stockmar remained close by her in an unofficial capacity. On the morning of Queen Victoria's accession, it was Stockmar with whom she chose to take breakfast (not her mother, and this before even seeing her prime minister). At her coronation Stockmar took the parental position alongside the queen in lieu of her dead father and the absent Uncle Leopold. And it was the ubiquitous Stockmar who alerted King Leopold that the reluctant queen should be prevailed upon to marry sooner rather than later, in order to protect her position.

Meanwhile, Stockmar was also in the throes of fulfilling another even more important role—the grooming of Leopold's nephew, Albert of Saxe-Coburg-Gotha, for the role of Victoria's future consort. He spent many years overseeing Albert's and his brother Ernest's education, commuting back and forth between England and Europe. It was Stockmar who suggested the sober schooling in Brussels as more morally edifying than the dissolute atmosphere of Hanoverian Germany. In effect, Stockmar set out with only one great ambition in life and that was to make of Albert his own creature: "I wish for my Prince a great, noble, warm, and true heart, such as shall serve as the richest and surest basis for the noblest views of human nature, and the firmest resolve to give them development" (Martin 1875–1880, 1:92). Once Queen Victoria began entertaining the idea of marriage to Albert, Stockmar reported back to her, as he did to Leopold, on the prince's social and intellectual progress, until the couple married early in 1840.

Stockmar now took up his long-held ambition, shared with King Leopold, that the royal couple—as yet untrained in matters of government—should inaugurate a golden age of constitutional monarchy that would set an example to the crowned heads of Europe. It was Stockmar's fervent desire that a strong Britain would join forces with a Germany united under Prussian leadership. In order to enjoy exclusive access to

Victoria and Albert, Stockmar had, however, to orchestrate the quiet but firm removal of Baroness Lehzen. Her close relationship with the queen and her dictatorial hold over the queen's household infuriated Prince Albert. Stockmar discreetly took the baroness aside and suggested that she might not wish to come between husband and wife in this way. Soon after, she packed her bags and went home to Bückeberg.

Lehzen's departure now cleared the way for Stockmar to further the prince's ambitions of playing a constructive role in government and in promoting their shared vision of constitutional monarchy—in Britain and beyond. There were times in the first months of his new role as royal consort that the prince paled at the onerousness of the task that lay before him, and Stockmar would provide him with the moral impetus by constantly reminding Albert of the great weight of duty he now bore. But even the trusty Stockmar occassionaly overstepped the mark in his desire to expound at length to the royal couple on British constitutional monarchy. His views were fatally flawed by a misguided belief that the monarch (rather than the prime minister) was the permanent head of state and that the prime minister was therefore merely the temporary head of the government—a fact that encouraged Victoria in times of political crisis to override her ministers and attempt to set her own stamp on policymaking. And when it came to the upbringing of the royal family, Stockmar once again meddled in what should have been a matter for Albert and Victoria.

With Teutonic efficiency and dogmatism he drew up a detailed plan for the education of the royal children, just as he had earlier for Albert. The rigid insistence on academic excellence, laid down in tedious detail by Stockmar in his many memorandums to the queen and Prince Albert, worked well with Vicky, the Princess Royal, who was an extremely intelligent and receptive child. But it failed to ignite an intellectual spark in Bertie, the Prince of Wales, who was a slow learner. Instead of acknowledging Bertie's intellectual limitations, Stockmar, the queen, and Prince Albert were all equally unyielding in imposing an educational curriculum with which the heir to the throne could not cope and for which she was constantly punished.

Whenever Stockmar was away from England (he spent half the year back in Coburg), he would continue to fulfill the role of father-confessor to Albert and exchanged long and regular letters with him. Stockmar would remain Albert's one true, unfailing ally, even after 1847, when Stockmar retired to his home in Coburg. He stood for election to the Diet at Frankfurt; from there he continued to nurse his aspirations for a Prussian-led unification of Germany. On a visit to Vicky in Berlin in the summer of 1860, Victoria and Albert visited Stockmar, on which occasion Stockmar registered with alarm how much the prince had prematurely aged and how despondent he seemed. As a doctor, Stockmar had also sensed something ominous in the recurring "stomach problems" alluded to by the prince in his regular letters to him. When Albert died in December 1861, Stockmar was broken hearted—but his despair was not so much at the loss of the *man* but at the demise of his own long-cherished dream: "Here do I see crumbled before my eyes that edifice to whose construction I have devoted twenty years of labour, prompted by a desire to accomplish something great and good, but inspired primarily by a sense of duty" (Crabitès 1937, 259). He outlived Albert by only another eighteen months.

Related entries:
Albert Edward, Prince of Wales; Albert of Saxe-Coburg-Gotha, Prince Consort; Lehzen, Baroness Louise; Leopold I, King of the Belgians; Victoria, Princess Royal; Victoria, Queen: Courtship and Marriage of

References and further reading:
Bolitho, Hector. 1964. *Albert, Prince Consort.* London: Max Parrish.

Buckle, George Earl, ed. 1926–1928. *The Letters of Queen Victoria.* 2d ser., 3 vols. London: John Murray.
Crabitès, Pierre. 1937. *Victoria's Guardian Angel: A Study of Baron Stockmar.* London: Routledge.
Emden, Paul. 1934. *Behind the Throne.* London: Hodder and Stoughton.
Fulford, Roger. 1966. *The Prince Consort.* London: Macmillan.
Grey, Hon. Charles. 1867. *The Early Years of H.R.H. the Prince Consort.* London: Smith, Elder and Co.
Martin, Sir Theodore. 1875–1880. *The Life of His Royal Highness the Prince Consort.* 5 vols. London: Smith, Elder and Co.
Ponsonby, Magdalen. 1927. *Mary Ponsonby: A Memoir, Some Letters and a Journal.* London: John Murray.
Stockmar, Ernst Baron, ed. 1873. *Memoirs of Baron Stockmar.* 2 vols. London: Longman, Green, and Co.
Strachey, Lytton. [1921] 1971. *Queen Victoria.* Harmondsworth, UK: Penguin.
Warner, Marina. 1979. *Queen Victoria's Sketchbook.* London: Macmillan.
Weintraub, Stanley. 1996. *Victoria.* London: John Murray.
Woodham-Smith, Cecil. 1972. *Queen Victoria: Her Life and Times.* Vol. 1: *1819–1861.* London: Hamish Hamilton.

Sutherland, Duchess of (1806–1868)

(Harriet Leveson-Gower)

dearest, kindest, truest friend (St. Aubyn 1991, 414)

Beautiful, gracious, and highly intelligent, "the Great Duchess"—Harriet Leveson-Gower—was much admired at court and was a close confidante of Queen Victoria. Her grandness of manner, which was never less than "princessly" in the opinion of Lord Byron, sometimes struck fear in lesser minions, for Sutherland held the highest office open to a woman—not just in the royal household but also in the state—that of mistress of the robes. She rose to her hallowed role with all the grandeur and self-confidence that her eminent social position dictated, serving the queen from the accession in 1837 until she was forced to resign during the Bedchamber Crisis of 1841.

Lady Harriet Howard was born into the old Whig aristocracy, the third daughter of George Howard, sixth earl of Carlisle. She was the granddaughter of another notable society beauty—the now famous Georgiana, duchess of Devonshire. Lady Harriet married into further wealth and a position of social and political power when in May 1823 she accepted the proposal of her cousin, George Granville Leveson-Gower, Earl Gower, who succeeded to the dukedom of Sutherland in 1833. The couple had eleven children.

According to Prime Minister Lord Melbourne, the duchess of Sutherland appreciated "both the grand and the beautiful" (Benson and Esher 1911, 1:01). She certainly demonstrated this as a doyenne of London high society for forty years, holding court at her grand mansion, Stafford House. A woman of fashion, whose natural beauty and statuesque demeanor lent grace to any social occasion, she moved, according to contemporary accounts, "like a goddess" and looked "like a queen" (Weintraub 1996, 123). Even her aunt, Lady Granville, referred to Sutherland as "that other queen, Harriet the first" (Leveson-Gower 1894, 2:236). But she was also highly intelligent, with many philanthropic, social, and cultural interests, in particular patronizing the Staffordshire potteries, leading to a revival of interest in their work. As a leading social and political hostess of her generation, Sutherland gave great receptions with her husband at Stafford House.

Sutherland took up the appointment of mistress of the robes, and with it a salary of £500 per year, on 1 July 1837, when she was thirty-one and at the height of her beauty. The queen, renowned for her own conspicuous lack of fashion sense, was in thrall to Sutherland's elegance and remarked in her journals that she always looked lovely. It was Sutherland's task to ensure that the queen looked her best on all major occasions, such as balls, dinners, official receptions, and state visits, as well as outings to the theater. The first and most important of these was to attend the queen on 28 June 1838 at her coronation in Westminster Abbey, when Sutherland rose early to help the queen don her elaborate coronation robes. She accompanied the queen in the state coach, rising to the grandeur of the occasion. According to Benjamin Disraeli, "The Duchess of Sutherland . . . full of her situation . . . walked, or rather stalked, up the Abbey . . . like Juno" (Weibe 1982–1999, 3:70), after which she stood close by the queen throughout the long and exhausting ceremony. Two years later, the duchess attended Queen Victoria on her wedding day at the Chapel Royal, St. James's.

On such occasions Sutherland's grandness manifested itself in an excessively deferential manner toward the queen. The obsequious air of ritual she adopted with which to present the queen with her fan or her bouquet after dancing at balls was noted by the American ambassador and was said to have made his Republican hackles rise. With time the queen became not a little jealous of Sutherland's beauty and her close friendship with her adored prime minister, Lord Melbourne. Sutherland would often sit next to him at dinner when at the palace, and the queen often complained in her journal that Sutherland so monopolized his attention that it "made it almost impossible for him to talk to anyone else"—that is, herself (Hibbert 2001, 76).

Although the queen was much in awe of the duchess, she could, nevertheless, effortlessly exert her royal authority over Sutherland when she chose to do so. On one occasion not long after she had joined the queen's service, Sutherland arrived half an hour late for dinner, upon which she received one of the queen's typically acerbic rebukes: "Duchess, you must allow me to present you with my watch, yours evidently does not keep good time" (Howe 1899, 107). So mortified was the duchess that later that evening she sent in her resignation. The queen, "being excessively fond of her," refused to accept it (ibid.). The degree of her affection for Sutherland was made manifest in the Bedchamber Crisis of 1839, when Queen Victoria adamantly refused to give up her Whig ladies of the bedchamber—including the duchess. The need to do so was a political one, with the queen obliged to demonstrate her impartiality by having an equal number of Tory and Whig ladies in her entourage. With Sutherland's brother holding the post of Irish secretary, the queen could be seen as being partisan, but she dug her heels in, insisting that these posts should be a matter for her own personal preference. But at the end of the ensuing crisis the queen was forced to give up three of her ladies—Sutherland, the duchess of Bedford, and Lady Normanby.

The duchess returned to the queen's service on 4 July 1846, remaining until 15 March 1852. But with the queen's marriage, and considerable influence over her now being exerted by Prince Albert, life at court lost much of its gaiety. The duchess found that she and the queen could no longer indulge in gossip in the evenings and at dinner; Prince Albert disapproved. A change of government, when Lord Derby became prime minister in 1852, again forced Sutherland from her post. The queen wrote her a letter expressing how "deeply grieved" she was at having to lose her again: "It has been *ever* a real pleasure to me to have you with me; my affection and esteem for you, my dearest Duchess, are great, and we *both* know what a kind and true friend we have in you" (Benson and Esher 1911, 2:371). Fortunately for the queen, Derby's ministry was short lived, and Sutherland returned as mistress of the robes on 15 January 1853, remaining for five years until 25 February 1858.

Much to the queen's disapproval, during the 1850s the duchess became a close personal friend of the liberal politician William

Gladstone. Nursing an intense dislike for him herself, the queen privately made fun of the duchess's admiration, but the friendship became a close one, with Gladstone becoming a regular visitor to Sutherland's homes at Cliveden and at Chiswick. He found he could talk on an intellectual level with her that he could not share with his wife, and he prized her depth of knowledge and her gifts as a judge of character. He also no doubt admired Sutherland's social conscience. Her philanthropic concerns, particularly her abhorrence of slavery, prompted her, according to Elizabeth Longford, to keep the queen regularly informed, whether she liked it or no, with "the kind of causes which found no place in Melbourne's cynical world" (Longford 1998, 71). The queen certainly disapproved of Sutherland's interest in politics and said as much: "I could not bear women mixing in Politics" (Esher 1914, 273).

Sutherland's nobility of conscience and her natural piety made her greatly sympathetic to the plight of America's slaves (those in the British empire having been liberated in 1833). Her obituary asserts that she was sympathetic to "all that was great and patriotic in the labours of men and women in other countries" ("In Memoriam" 1872, 2). She would not endure "any tone of levity or of indifference in speaking, or in writing of the wrongs of slavery, or of cruelty in any form" (2). During 1852 and 1853, when British readers had been avidly reading Harriet Beecher Stowe's *Uncle Tom's Cabin,* Sutherland allowed Stafford House to be the venue for meetings of women abolitionists. She helped draw up a "Christian Address from the Ladies of England to those of America" in 1853. Aimed at women in the southern states, it was supported by a women's antislavery petition containing 562,848 signatures and expressed "the sorrow and reprobation with which negro slavery was viewed by the greater half of the population of this country" (S. J. Hale, *Cyclopedia of Female Biography,* 1857). When Stowe toured England, Sutherland staged a reception for her at Stafford House.

Sutherland's appointment to the queen was renewed in June 1859, and she remained with the queen as mistress of the robes until 24 April 1861, finally relinquishing the post after her husband died. The queen was kind and solicitous to her in her loss. Sutherland departed, nursing a deep sense of admiration for Prince Albert. It had, she wrote to the queen, "been one of the great pleasures of my life," and she had been forever thankful "that he should be your Majesty's husband. I feel I owe him much" (Benson and Esher 1911, 3:443).

When Prince Albert fell sick in December 1861, the duchess of Sutherland came to Windsor to be near the queen. The morning after the prince's death, the queen took Sutherland into the Blue Room to see Albert laid out on his deathbed. In 1866 the duchess erected a bronze statue of the prince in the grounds of her home at Cliveden. With Lady Augusta Bruce, Sutherland stayed constantly at the queen's side for the first few weeks of her widowhood and later presented her with a Bible, the gift of the "Widows of England" (St. Aubyn 1991, 352).

The queen's subsequent retreat from her public duties worried Sutherland, and she often discussed this with Gladstone, but she herself became ill in 1863 and withdrew substantially from public life. Gladstone deeply mourned her death in 1868, writing in his diary that she had been "the warmest and dearest friend, surely, that ever man had" (Matthew 1978, 6:632). He counted himself very fortunate to have enjoyed such a close relationship with this extraordinary woman. He said he felt "ten years the older for her death" and concluded that "none will fill her place for me: or for many worthier than I" (ibid.). After the duchess's death, the queen visited the Sutherland family seat—Dunrobin Castle in Sutherland—during one of her trips to the Highlands, to inspect the memorial erected to the duchess there.

Related entries:
Bedchamber Crisis; Gladstone, William Ewart; The Royal Household

References and further reading:

Benson, A. C., and Viscount Esher, eds. 1911. *The Letters of Queen Victoria, 1837–1861.* 1st ser., 3 vols. London: John Murray.

Duff, David, ed. 1980. *Queen Victoria's Highland Journals.* London: Webb and Bower.

Esher, Viscount, ed. 1914. *The Training of a Sovereign.* London: John Murray.

Hibbert, Christopher. 2001. *Queen Victoria: A Personal History.* London: HarperCollins.

Howe, Julia Ward. 1899. *Reminiscences, 1819–1899.* Boston: Houghton Mifflin.

"In Memoriam, Harriet Duchess of Sutherland." 1872. Newcastle, UK: C. Hickson.

Leveson-Gower, Frederick. 1894. *Letters of Harriet Countess Granville 1810–1805.* 2 vols. London: Longmans.

———. 1891. *Stafford House Letters.* London: Kegan Paul, Trench, Trübner.

Longford, Elizabeth. [1964] 1998. *Victoria R.I.* London: Weidenfeld and Nicolson.

Matthew, H. C. G., ed. 1978. *The Gladstone Diaries.* Vol. 6: *1861–1868.* Oxford: Clarendon Press.

St. Aubyn, Giles. 1991. *Queen Victoria: A Portrait.* London: Sinclair Stevenson.

Shannon. Richard. 1999. *Gladstone.* Harmondsworth, UK: Penguin.

Weintraub, Stanley. 1996. *Queen Victoria.* London: John Murray.

Weibe, M. G., gen. ed. 1982–1999. *Benjamin Disraeli Letters.* 6 vols. Toronto: University of Toronto Press.

T

Tennyson, Alfred, Lord (1809–1892)

Next to the Bible In Memoriam *is my comfort* (Tennyson 1897, 1:485)

Alfred, Lord Tennyson has long been regarded as one of the Great Victorians, a man whose verse in many respects reflected the moral and religious sentiments of the age. The poet W. H. Auden once remarked that "there was little about melancholia that [Tennyson] didn't know; there was little else that he did" (Auden 1947, x). Like his widowed monarch, Tennyson seemed to make a profession of being melancholy. During the lifetime of the prince consort, the royal couple had both delighted not just in the somber and reflective elements of Tennyson's poetry but also in his celebration of the Romantic medieval past. After the prince's death, Tennyson enjoyed a sustained and personal relationship with the queen, their sympathetic natures drawn close, in the view of the poet's son Hallam, by their shared celebration of death and their fervent hope of ultimate reunion with "Him who is Invisible" (Dyson and Tennyson 1969, 146).

Alfred Tennyson was the son of a clergyman; he was born in Somersby, Lincolnshire. After being educated at grammar school, he studied at Trinity College, Cambridge, where he quickly demonstrated a precocious talent for poetry. He was encouraged by his university friend, Arthur Henry Hallam, to publish his first collection in June 1830 but was deeply disappointed when his *Poems, Chiefly Lyrical,* was not well favored in reviews. For the rest of his life Tennyson would remain highly sensitive to criticism. He left Cambridge in 1831 without sitting for his degree. In 1832 he published a second volume, *Poems,* only to be again devastated by an unjustifiably savage review in the literary journal the *Quarterly Review.* Wounded and discouraged, he would not publish again for eight years.

Meanwhile, tragic news had come in September 1832, which would set its stamp on Tennyson's poetic temperament thereafter. His much-loved friend Hallam had died of a hemorrhage at the age of only twenty-two. A grief-stricken Tennyson had lost not just an irreplaceable friend but also a literary mentor, and to commemorate that friendship he began writing what would become his most enduring work—*In Memoriam.* A long elegy on death, loss, and the will to endure, it would be viewed as his spiritual autobiography, reflecting the highs and lows of Tennyson's changing moods in response to the loss of Hallam, moving from his initial feelings of bitterness, toward acceptance, and finally to the restoration of hope.

Queen Victoria was puzzled and bemused by poet laureate Alfred Tennyson's dishevelled appearance but came to worship him as "the perfect poet of love and loss," in whose work she found great consolation after the death of Albert. (George Eastman House/Getty Images)

It took a considerable amount of persuasion from his friends before Tennyson published a new collection of poetry. By now he had garnered a following in the United States, with admirers such as James Russell Lowell and Henry Wadsworth Longfellow. In 1842 a selection from Tennyson's first two volumes of verse was again tried out on the reading public. It included some new works, notably "Locksley Hall" (written in 1837–1838)—a poem about disappointed love that would become one of Tennyson's most popular works. In 1847 he published *The Princess,* a romantic tale in verse based on an old chronicle and one of his most lyrical pieces of writing.

Tennyson's long engagement to Emily Sellwood, whom he had first met in 1836, finally ended in marriage in 1850. It is suggested that he postponed the wedding because of his sense of shame at his family's impoverishment, but more recent critics have argued that he nursed a much deeper fear—of passing on to his children his own deeply ingrained melancholia. The marriage was a very happy one and would foster a highly productive period of writing. In June 1850 Tennyson finally published *In Memoriam,* which sold 60,000 copies by the year's end. It was much admired by both the queen and Prince Albert. In an age when so many adults died prematurely and the infant mortality rate was particularly high, the poem transformed the universal experience of death into a magnificent mournful celebration, evoking a very personal response in those who read it—the queen and Prince Albert included.

Thanks to the influence of Prince Albert, in 1850 Tennyson was invited to succeed Wordsworth as poet laureate. Shortly before the Great Exhibition the following year, he dedicated the seventh edition of his collected verse to the queen. As laureate, he would find his duties at times irksome and on occasion declined the queen's frequent calls on him, protesting ill health, but in general he succeeded in catering to the royal demand for a supply of public verse brimming with national pride and jingoism—epitomized by "Ode on the Death of the Duke of Wellington" (1852), "The Charge of the Light Brigade" (1854), and "The Relief of Lucknow" (1858).

In 1854 the Tennysons settled at Faringford on the Isle of Wight—not far from the queen's summer home at Osborne. The royal couple were keen to meet their favorite poet, and on 15 May 1856 Prince Albert paid the Tennysons a visit, promising to bring the queen (she never came). Tennyson found the prince "very kind, but very German" (Wheatcroft 1980, 108). Albert, an aficionado of the medieval Gothic tradition, would be a devotee of Tennyson's next poetic offering—the first four of the twelve-poem sequence of Arthurian-style romances, *The Idylls of the King* (1859). Much of the content draws on a mythologized time, including Sir Thomas Malory's *Morte d'Arthur,* about which the prince had a considerable passion. Charles Dickens concluded that *The Idylls* were "absolutely unapproached and unapproachable" (Storey 1997, 112), but the poet Arthur Swinburne irreverently nicknamed the collection "Morte d'Albert, or Idylls of the Prince Consort" (Drabble 1991, 971). *The Idylls* sold 10,000 copies in six weeks. Prince Albert wrote to Tennyson requesting him to autograph the prince's own copy: "You would thus add a peculiar value to the book, containing those beautiful songs, from the perusal of which I derived the greatest enjoyment" (Wheatcroft 1980, 108). The queen enthusiastically sent a copy to her daughter, Vicky, although she struggled for words to describe *The Idylls,* deeming them "so very peculiar, quaint and poetic" (Dyson and Tennyson 1969, 60). Vicky soon knew them by heart. In 1869 Tennyson published four more *Idylls;* the remaining verses in the sequence appeared in 1871, 1872, and 1885.

In December 1861 the death of Prince Albert deprived Tennyson of one of his public champions; it was a terrible personal blow. Within days, a message was passed to him, through Princess Alice, that the queen would like him to write something in the prince's memory. Tennyson did so in the form of a prefatory dedication to the new edition of *The Idylls* published in 1862. The queen was deeply grateful; the lines had "soothed her aching, bleeding heart" (Dyson and Tennyson 1969, 65). One of the first books she reached for in widowhood, in her search for spiritual consolation, was Tennyson's *In Memoriam.* Early in January 1862, as she lingered over these mournful musings, Victoria observed that "only those who have suffered as I do, can understand these beautiful poems" (67). For a while, it would be virtually her only reading, apart from the Bible and religious books. She soon adopted the poem as the literary emblem of her own grief. Tennyson's work, she felt, offered her very personal comfort and the hope that, in the afterlife, she would be reunited with Albert. She later transcribed her favorite passages from *In Memoriam,* heavily underlined, into an album of consolatory words and prayer and annotated her own copy with her personal observations on its Christian arguments. From now on, grief, in all its comforting monotony, would be her everyday companion and, in a perverse way, her solace too.

On 14 April 1862, four months after the death of Prince Albert, Queen Victoria summoned Tennyson to Osborne. She was puzzled by his appearance. Tennyson was legendary for his bohemian style of dress, his unkempt greasy hair, pallid skin, and hollow cheeks. The writer Lewis Carroll talked of him as "a strange, shaggy-looking man" (Wheatcroft 1980, 67), and by middle age the shagginess had taken on an even more eccentric air, with Tennyson himself admitting that he looked like a "dirty monk" (87). The queen was equally disconcerted; he was "very peculiar looking" (Dyson and Tennyson 1969, 69). But she could not help being taken with him: "tall, dark, with a fine head, long black flowing hair and a beard—oddly dressed but there is no affectation about him" (ibid.). She told him how much *In Memoriam* meant to her. The poet responded, his eyes full of tears, by telling the queen how greatly he had admired the prince. Ten days later he published an "Ode Sung at the Opening of the Second International Exhibition," celebrating what would be the prince's last great undertaking (he had been involved in the planning of the exhibition that opened in June 1862). The queen responded by sending Tennyson a copy of Prince Albert's speeches.

Later that summer, Victoria invited the whole Tennyson family to Osborne. Emily Tennyson described in her journal how she and her husband had been surprised by the "breadth and freedom and penetration of her mind" (Dyson and Tennyson 1969, 76), while the queen was struck by "the greatness and largeness" of Tennyson's intellect, albeit "under a certainly rough exterior"

(79). It had been an unforgettable experience for Emily, who would later recall that she and her husband had talked with the queen "of everything in heaven and earth" (Tennyson 1897, 1:491). They came away from their visit the queen's most devoted subjects. She was, Emily averred, "a woman to live and die for" (Dyson and Tennyson 1969, 76). Thereafter, until his death in 1892, the poet exchanged many letters with the queen. He regularly sent her copies of his new collections of verse and had several audiences with her, at Osborne and at Windsor. On one such occasion he even tentatively suggested that she might like to try her own hand at verse, to which she had replied, "No—that I cannot. I never could make two lines meet in my life" (84). She *was* bold enough, however, to send Tennyson a copy of her *Leaves from the Journal of Our Life in the Highlands* in 1868, "trusting he will not criticise it too severely" (85).

Tennyson's considerable output continued with the publication in 1864 of *Enoch Arden and Other Poems*—which marked the peak of his critical acclaim and remained another royal favorite. In 1870, Victoria sent a copy of his *The Holy Grail and Other Poems* (1869) to Vicky. But once again the queen had to admit to finding it a little beyond her: "It is still more unclear than any of his writings and leaves me quite bewildered" (Fulford 1971, 255). She nevertheless reread all four of *The Idylls of the King* in the new Imperial Library Edition presented to her by Tennyson in 1871. Their friendship took on a renewed intimacy, in its more morbid elements, with the death of the queen's favorite prime minister, Benjamin Disraeli, in 1881. Once more Victoria sought consolation in *In Memoriam*. Two years later, at Osborne, she told Tennyson of its continuing comfort to her—for she was now in deep mourning for her devoted servant John Brown, who had died in March. Tennyson with compassion responded to the queen's isolation at that time: "You are so alone on that terrible height" (Tennyson 1897, 2:457), he told her. He thought he might only have a year or two left to live but assured her "I shall be happy to do anything for you I can" (ibid.). The bond between himself and the queen was, he felt, a universal one "which binds human beings together, whether they be kings or cobblers" (2:434). At Victoria's request Tennyson chose some (anonymous) commemorative lines to be inscribed on Brown's statue.

In 1883, as a major establishment figure, Tennyson was the first poet to be honored with a peerage. Michael Thorn has argued that by now Tennyson himself had come to believe in the inflated status with which the laureatship and the queen's admiration had endowed him. He now considered himself to be "a modern prophet" (1993, 479), an oracle to be consulted by the queen on life's greater, impenetrable mysteries. A year later, when the poet's thirty-one-year-old son, Lionel, died of fever while traveling back from India, the queen did her best to console the unconsolable: "You who have written such words of comfort for others will, I feel sure, feel the comfort of them again in yourself. . . . I *feel* for you" (Dyson and Tennyson 1969, 126). But Lionel's death brought down a suffocating pall of gloom on the Tennyson household, provoking the composition of probably Tennyson's most pessimistic poem—"Locksley Hall Sixty Years After"—described by his biographer Michael Thorn as "a work of splenetic isolation and disillusion" (1993, 497).

Tennyson continued to enjoy the status of poet laureate but eventually came to dislike the public glare of fame. In 1889 he urged the writer Marie Corelli to do all she could to avoid it: "Modern fame is too often a crown of thorns, and brings all the vulgarity of the world upon you. I sometimes wish I had never written a line" (Ransom 1999, 49). That year he wrote one of his most inspired and concentrated poems about death—the sixteen-line "Crossing of the Bar." Composed as Tennyson traveled on the ferry from Lymington to the Isle of Wight, the poem is an intensely moving expression of the resignation of a man facing his own imminent death. Tennyson died three years later, 6 October 1892, his hand resting on a copy of Shakespeare, opened at his favorite quotation from Cymbeline: "Hang there like fruit, my soul, / Till the tree dies" (act 5, sc. 5). The same lines, contained in another volume, were buried with him.

As a national poet, Tennyson was accorded a state funeral in Westminster Abbey. On the pavements outside, street vendors sold cheap copies of "The Crossing of the Bar" to the many hundreds of the curious who had come to watch the spectacle and see his coffin, swathed in its white pall (at his specific request; he hated black funerals), embroidered with the final verse of this, the poem that he asked should always be placed last in anthologies of his work:

> "For tho' from out our bourne of Time and Place
> The flood may bear me far.
> I hope to see my Pilot face to face
> When I have crost the bar."
> (Ricks 1990, 52)

Queen Victoria, having listened with great interest to the details of Tennyson's final death throes, as recounted to her by his son Hallam, was convinced his greatness would endure: "A Tennyson we may not see again for a century, or—in all his originality—ever again" (Guedalla 1933, 2:449). It was three years before the vacant post of laureate was filled. Tennyson's popularity, however, rapidly waned after the death of Victoria. He fell out of fashion, as did many other Victorian poets whose high moral tone did not fit in with the dynamic new century.

Related entries:
Corelli, Marie; Dickens, Charles; Oliphant, Margaret; Scott, Sir Walter; "The Widow at Windsor"

References and further reading:
Auden, W. H., ed. 1947. "Introduction." In *A Selection from the Poems of Alfred Lord Tennyson.* Garden City, NY: Doubleday.
Drabble, Margaret, ed. 1991. *The Oxford Companion to English Literature,*.5th ed. Oxford: Oxford University Press.
Dyson, Hope, and Charles Tennyson, eds. 1969. *Dear and Honoured Lady: The Correpsondance between Queen Victoria and Alfred, Lord Tennyson.* London: Macmillan.
Fulford, Roger. 1971. *Your Dear Letter: Letters between Queen Victoria and the Princess Royal, 1863–1871.* London: Evans Brothers.
Guedalla, Philip, ed. 1933. *The Queen and Mr Gladstone.* 2 vols. London: Hodder and Stoughton.
Jump, J. D., ed. 1995. *Tennyson, the Critical Heritage.* London: Routledge.
Martin, Robert B. 1981. *Tennyson: The Unquiet Heart.* Oxford: Clarendon Press.
Ransom, T. 1999. *The Mysterious Miss Marie Corelli.* Stroud, Gloucestershire: Sutton.
Ricks, Christopher, ed. 1990. *The New Oxford Book of Victorian Verse.* Oxford: Oxford University Press.
Storey, Graham, ed. 1997. *Letters of Charles Dickens.* Vol. 9: *1859–61.* Oxford: Clarendon Press.
Tennyson, Hallam. 1897. *Alfred Lord Tennyson: A Memoir by His Son.* 2 vols. London: Macmillan.
Tennyson, Sir Charles. 1949. *Alfred Tennyson.* London: Macmillan.
Thorn, Michael. 1993. *Tennyson.* London: Abacus.
Tucker, Herbert F., ed. 1999. *A Companion to Victorian Literature and Culture. Oxford:* Blackwell.
Wheatcroft, Andrew. 1980. *The Tennyson Album: A Biography in Original Photographs.* London: Routledge and Kegan Paul.

Theater

What *a man Shakespeare was!* (Rowell 1978, 55)

It took some time for the Victorian theater to emerge from the shadows of the dubious reputation that the English stage had acquired for rowdyism and louche behavior during the seventeenth and eighteenth centuries. With the theater being till then associated with the lower classes, it was looked upon as a downmarket form of entertainment. During Victoria's youth, although she would be taken to the theater, it was usually to see innocuous musical performances (mixed bills of opera and ballet), the circus, and the pantomime; her major experience of dramatic performances were those of William Shakespeare. It was during her marriage to Prince Albert that the queen came, with his guidance and vetting, to enjoy a wider range of plays, so much so that they became significant patrons of the theater and contributed to its rise as an important art form in Britain during the nineteenth century.

The first play that the queen claimed ever to have seen—although not in a public theater but in a private performance at Windsor—was in 1828. It was a historical drama, *Charles XII,* by the English playwright James Planché (1795–1880), who enjoyed considerable popularity for his burlesques and pantomimes, turning out 150 plays and opera librettos. From the early 1830s on, the princess also developed an enjoyment of the circus and was so enthralled by performances of Sir Isaac van Ambrugh's circus lions at Drury Lane in 1839 that she went to see them seven times during a six-week period. The Christmas pantomimes at Drury Lane were also a great favorite, and Victoria and Albert maintained the tradition by visiting them with their children.

Throughout her life the queen would show only a limited interest in the more intellectually taxing dramatic work of playwrights such as Shakespeare, preferring French melodrama and light comedy. Although she accorded Shakespeare her respect, the queen found him difficult to comprehend. She had admitted to being deeply impressed by *King John* (one of her first experiences of Shakespeare), and she so admired performances in the title role by both Charles Macready and Charles Kean that this, one of Shakespeare's least performed plays, remained a firm favorite with her. *Richard III* was also, in her estimation, "a fine heart-stirring play" (Esher 1912, 1:272). In contrast, she found *Hamlet* was "a very hard play to understand" (1:266). As for *King Lear,* she "did not like all that madness on the stage" (1:109). She also found the bawdy elements in Shakespeare's *Merry Wives of Windsor* unpalatable—although she admitted "even I have never had courage to go and see it—having always been told how very coarse it was" (Fulford 1964, 178). The young queen's lack of intellectual sophistication would be a talking point among the literati of the day. The poet Elizabeth Barrett Browning was highly critical of the queen's cultural philistinism: "Would that he [Sir Robert Peel] could teach our queen that a man of genius was as worthy of sitting at her table as a post captain or a banker. If Shakespeare were alive now and went to Windsor, he would be admitted by the back stairs" (Kelley and Hudson 1991, 152).

During the 1840s the queen patiently sat through classical French tragedies by Racine and Corneille with Prince Albert, although the standard French fare on offer in London was usually much lighter comic vignettes. With the year of revolutions of 1848 bringing republican upheavals in Paris, it was deemed more politically correct for Victoria and Albert to be seen to support indigenous British theatre, and that year they attended numerous performances by Charles Kean at the Theatre Royal in the Haymarket. Their admiration for him led to regular command performances of English plays at Windsor, many of them staged in the somewhat cramped conditions of the Rubens Room. Here the royal family enjoyed productions of thirteen of Shakespeare's plays, including *The Merchant of Venice, Hamlet, The Tempest,* and *Macbeth* as well as popular comic standbys such as Richard Sheridan's *The Rivals* and *School for Scandal.* So popular were these performances that in the mid-1850s the larger St. George's Hall was made available at Windsor.

During the 1850s the queen developed an appetite for contemporary melodramas, such as works by the Irish playwright Dion Bouccicault—*The Vampire, The Corsican Princess,* and the hugely popular *The Colleen Bawn* (1860)—a play that the queen and Prince Albert saw five times in two months. Another favorite was Wilkie Collins's *The Frozen Deep,* notable for the performance of Charles Dickens in a lead role. But with the death of Prince Albert in December 1861, British theater lost its valued royal patronage overnight. Central to the queen's austere lifestyle after the prince's death was a rejection of worldly pleasures such as the theater. For many years thereafter Windsor became a gloomy place, no longer enlivened by the winter command performances, although evidence suggests that the queen allowed her children to continue to mount occasional theatricals of their own. By the late 1890s, however, court theatricals revived once more, over which the queen began to dictate by censoring the scripts. The younger members of the royal family also now revived the *tableaux vivants* (living pictures) they had enjoyed as children, in which Princess Beatrice's husband, Prince Henry of Battenberg, and members of the household took leading roles.

In October 1881 the Prince of Wales finally persuaded his mother to allow a command performance of A. C. Burnand's play, *The Colonel,* by Edgar Bruce's touring company. Staged at Abergeldie Castle in Scotland, it was greatly enjoyed by the royal party, but it was five years before the queen would agree to another, at Osborne in 1887. In 1889, after enjoying a private command performance by Henry Irving and Ellen Terry of *The Bells* at the Prince of Wales's residence at Sandringham, the queen began requesting similar performances at Windsor Castle, where she enjoyed productions of Tennyson's *Becket* in 1893, starring Henry Irving, and saw the company of the Parisian Comédie Française. In the remaining years of her reign, theatrical command performances became increasingly conservative in tone, although they were enlivened from time to time by the comic operettas of Gilbert and Sullivan. During the final twenty years of Queen Victoria's reign, the British theater enjoyed a spectacular revival, dominated by the works of leading playwrights such as G. B. Shaw, Sir Arthur Pinero, and Oscar Wilde, and dominated by the acting talents of Irving and Terry. The theatrical profession finally achieved respectability with the knighting of Henry Irving in 1895—the first British actor to be so honored.

Related entries:
Dancing; Dickens, Charles; Opera

References and further reading:

Esher, Viscount, ed. 1912. *The Girlhood of Queen Victoria: A Selection from Her Majesty's Diaries between the Years of 1832 and 1840.* 2 vols. London: John Murray.

———. 1914. *The Training of a Sovereign.* London: John Murray.

Fulford, Roger, ed. 1964. *Dearest Child: Letters between Queen Victoria and the Princess Royal, 1858–61.* London: Evans Brothers.

Hardy, Alan. 1976. *Queen Victoria Was Amused.* London: John Murray.

Kelley, Phillip, and Ronald Hudson, eds. 1991. *The Browning's Correspondence.* Vol. 9. Winfield, KS: Wedgestone Press.

Lorne, Marquis of, C. 1901. *V.R.I.: Her Life and Empire.* London: Eyre and Spottiswood.

[One of Her Majesty's Servants]. 1901. *The Private Life of Queen Victoria.* London: C. Arthur Pearson.

Plowden, Alison. 1981. *Young Victoria.* Weidenfeld and Nicolson.

Rowell, George. 1978. *Queen Victoria Goes to the Theatre.* London: Paul Elek.

Vallone, Lynne. 2001. *Becoming Victoria.* New Haven: Yale University Press.

Warner, Marina. 1979. *Queen Victoria's Sketchbook.* London: Macmillan.

V

Victoria, Queen: Accession and Coronation of

my duty to my country is my first and greatest wish and pleasure (Charlot 1991, 112)

King William IV died at twelve minutes past two on the morning of 20 June 1837, having achieved what he had most desired—to live long enough for his heir presumptive, his niece Victoria, to achieve her age of majority and be spared the overbearing ministrations of a regency by her mother, the duchess of Kent.

A small party of officials proceeded directly from the king's deathbed at Windsor Castle to Kensington Palace in order to inform the princess that she was now queen. The preeminence of these dignitaries—the archbishop of Canterbury, Lord Conyngham, and the lord chamberlain—did not prevent them, however, from encountering difficulty in being admitted to Kensington Palace to deliver their momentous news. Having knocked at the gates for some time to rouse the porter, they then found the duchess of Kent reluctant to rouse her daughter: it was barely 6 A.M. and the princess was still asleep. But when she was woken, and despite the early hour, Victoria informed her mother, in no uncertain terms, that she would receive the dignitaries in her sitting room—and would do so alone. This, her first independent act after years of unrelenting scrutiny and parental control, marked an overnight transformation in Victoria's relationship with her mother, for which she had no doubt been privately preparing for some time. Her comprehension of the enormity of the task before her, and the extraordinary composure with which she embraced it, were reflected in her journal: "Since it has pleased Providence to place me in this station, I shall do my utmost to fulfil my duty towards my country; I am very young and perhaps in many, though not in all things, inexperienced, but I am sure, that very few have more real good and more real desire to do what is fit and right than I have" (Benson and Esher 1911, 1:75).

After breakfasting with her adviser, Baron Stockmar, and writing brief notes to her half sister, Feodora, and her Uncle Leopold, king of the Belgians, Victoria found time to send her condolences to "the Queen," as she insisted, out of respect and gratitude, on addressing William's widow Adelaide. Victoria consulted twice with her prime minister, Lord Melbourne, before conducting her first official meeting with the members of the Privy Council, held in the Red Saloon at 11:30 A.M., at which she read out her official declaration upholding the British constitution and the rites of the Church of Scotland. Several of those present would comment on the young queen's astonishing self-possession. It had already

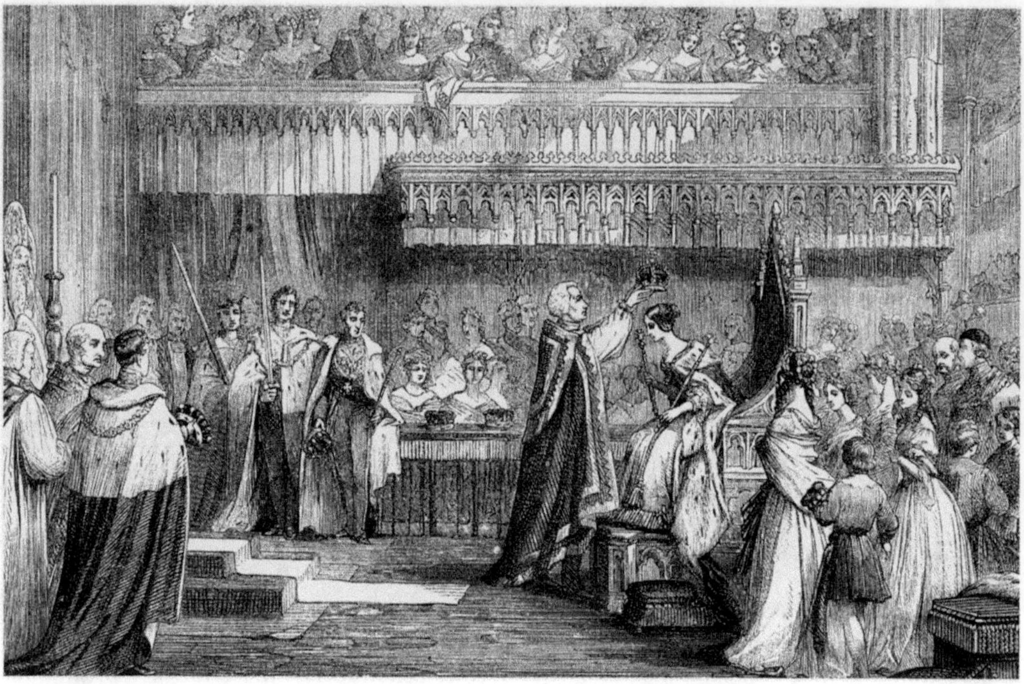

The crowning ceremony during Queen Victoria's coronation, held in Westminster Abbey on 28 June 1838 (Bettmann/CORBIS)

been noted how small and alarmingly young the eighteen-year-old Victoria looked. Yet her physical insubstantiality and her childlike, round face belied an inner strength surprising in one whose whole life until then had been so circumscribed. It had taken many by surprise. As far as the business of government was concerned, Charles Greville would observe, on 25 June, that "everything goes on as if She had been on the throne six years instead of six days" (Strachey and Fulford 1938, 3:376).

Victoria was intoxicated with her newfound regal solitude; for the first time in her life she not only took her dinner alone, but, more important, having had her bed removed from her mother's room, she slept alone also. Nor did she turn to her mother for advice on the challenging task before her. This she received by letter from her Uncle Leopold in the days that followed; with him she would enter into a detailed discourse on statecraft that they would conduct over several months. Advice was also on hand from the discreet and self-effacing Baron Stockmar. But the discordant notes of the duchess's continual bleating about her own peremptory exclusion from the royal presence were politely ignored. "Ma," as Victoria less reverentially referred to her in her journal, would be a thorn in the young queen's side throughout the coming winter, with constant carping about her apartments, her income, and her status.

Deeply wounded by her daughter's rejection, the duchess was now doubly offended that she had been supplanted by the prime minister, Lord Melbourne, who would, from now on, offer the parental advice that she had for so long imposed on her daughter. Victoria's unqualified adoration of Melbourne prompted the duchess to spit with jealousy: "take care that Lord Melbourne is not King!" (Charlot 1991, 52). The elder statesman's presence physically and emotionally reinvigorated the young queen after her previous years of ill-health and nervous strain. With his attentive guidance she threw herself into affairs of state with alacrity, eagerly scrutinizing every official document sent in red dispatch boxes and now signing papers with the name "Victoria." Her baptismal name—Alexandrina—was most firmly and publicly dropped on 21 June, when Victoria, accompanied by Lord Melbourne, went to the official Proclaiming the Sovereign ceremony at St. James's Palace. At the end of the month she gave her royal assent to the first forty new pieces of legislation by Parliament and on 17 July made her first appearance in public as queen, to attend the dissolution of Parliament.

Upon her accession the queen had been anxious to take occupancy of Buckingham Palace, despite its ongoing refurbishment's being incomplete. Undeterred, she announced a date for her move from Kensington Palace and duly arrived in mid-July. Soon after, she held her first drawing room (reception) at the palace—although still dressed in mourning for King William. For so long empty and neglected, the palace was soon enlivened by the music and concerts that Victoria so loved; on her birthday on 24 May 1838 she held her first state ball there, staying up dancing until four in the morning.

Parliament voted £200,000 to cover the cost of the coronation, which, in the event, came to a mere £70,000. This provoked complaints from some members of the aristocracy that this was not grand enough compared to the lavish—but exceedingly expensive—celebrations for George IV. In comparison, it was asserted, the queen's was a mere "Penny Coronation." The ceremony finally took place on 28 June 1838. The government had opted for spending the bulk of the money on a state procession for the benefit of the public at large rather than the usual state banquet for the chosen few at the Palace of Westminster. The day started early for Victoria, who, unable to sleep, was awake at 4 A.M., aware of the gathering crowds outside. London had by now been besieged by some 400,000 visitors in anticipation of the event; the streets were gridlocked with carriages and hackney cabs; Hyde Park and Green Park had been transformed into tent cities of encamped visitors. People with homes along the processional route sold off window and balcony space at a premium; scaffolding with raked seats and festooned with flags had also been erected along the route, to allow the maximum number of people a good view. The noise and bustle had been incessant for weeks, to the annoyance of many residents.

At around 10 A.M. on that fine June morning the queen set off in the state coach drawn by eight cream-colored horses, sitting on a cushion so that she could better be seen through her carriage window and accompanied by her mistress of the robes, the duchess of Sutherland. For the journey, she was dressed in Parliament robes of fine gold tissue, with a hooded crimson velvet mantle decorated with ermine and gold lace. The procession of the queen's carriage, accompanied by the Household Cavalry, military bands, and foreign ambassadors, ministers, and members of the royal family in their various carriages, set off for Westminster Abbey via Hyde Park Corner, Piccadilly, St. James's, Pall Mall, Charing Cross, and Whitehall. The spectacle of the cheering crowds filled Victoria with pride at being "the Queen of *such* a Nation" (Benson and Esher 1911, 1:121). Arriving at the abbey, she faced a grueling five-hour ceremony and two further changes of ceremonial robes.

Attended by eight ladies-in-waiting, Victoria entered the abbey to an anthem, now having been dressed, in the robing room, in her coronation vestments. These consisted of a plain cambric shift trimmed with lace and tied with a thick gold cord with bullion tassels, over which she wore the supertunica or dalmatic robe of cloth of gold, trimmed with gold lace and lined with rose-colored silk. The dalmatic was embroidered in silk with green shamrocks, pink roses, and purple thistles—the national emblems of Ireland, England, and Scotland. Draped around her neck, Victoria wore a five-foot long stole or armill. She processed up the abbey, past the serried ranks of the government and the British aristocracy, many of them accommodated in temporary galleries erected in the aisles, all resplendent in their ceremonial regalia, diamonds glinting. At the altar Victoria knelt in prayer and arose to a chorus of "Vivat Victoria Regina" from the choir of Westminster School.

A distinct lack of rehearsal on the part of the officiating ministers marred the ceremony somewhat, with the bishop of Bath and Wells muddling the sequence of service, and the archbishop of Canterbury violently ramming the ring of state too hard upon Victoria's too large third instead of her fourth finger. Having taken the oath to maintain the established Protestant religion and govern according to the statutes of Parliament, the queen withdrew while the choir sang the anthem "Veni Creator Spiritus." In St. Edward's Chapel she removed her heavy outer robes and her diamond headress, returning to seat herself in St. Edward's Chair, where she was consecrated as sovereign and anointed on the head and hands with holy oil. She then took up the regalia of office—the orb and sceptre and the ruby coronation ring, before putting on the imperial mantle of state. Finally, the crown of state was placed upon her head. This crown had been extensively remodeled to fit Victoria's small head and featured the heart-shaped ruby worn at Agincourt by Henry V—which had been reset, with the addition of pearls and diamonds, over a blue velvet cap, topped by a Maltese cross set with a fine sapphire.

The crowning was, as Victoria later recalled, "a most beautiful and impressive moment" (Benson and Esher 1911, 1:122) and one in which she was joined by the congregation of lords and ladies simultaneously donning their array of coronets, so that the abbey radiated with the light of thousands of reflected diamonds. She was then saluted by cheers of "God save the queen" within the abbey and the ringing of the bells and a reverberation of gun salutes from the Tower of London. After being presented with the Bible and hearing the Te Deum sung by the choir, the queen received formal homage from the royal dukes and the peers of the realm as she sat enthroned. She then took communion at the altar, donned the imperial mantle of state and now processed down the abbey, holding the orb and sceptre and still wearing the crown, before entering her carriage for the slow procession past huge crowds back to Buckingham Palace.

As the queen left the abbey, many of the assembled dignitaries (some of whom had been in their places since 5 A.M.) were by now fainting with hunger and crumpled with exhaustion; others had succumbed to fatigue during the ceremony and nodded off. A few had managed to snatch the wine, sandwiches, and other refreshments laid on (much to the queen's disapproval) in the St. Edward Chapel. As for the queen: far from being exhausted by the physical and emotional strain of the day, on returning to Buckingham Palace, her first thought had been to lift her skirts and scamper upstairs to bathe her pet spaniel, Dash. During dinner that evening she exchanged animated stories about the day with Melbourne, commiserating with him over the heaviness of the ceremonial sword of state that he had had to carry and the weight of the crown that she had had to endure. Melbourne had found the whole experience so enervating that he missed his cabinet meetings for the whole of the following week in order to recuperate.

At 11 P.M. Victoria went out onto the balcony to watch the fireworks display in nearby Green and Hyde Parks. That night, the whole of London was lit up with oil lamps as the public thronged the streets, enjoyed a night at the theater (which admitted the public free that night), or enjoyed the vast fair in Hyde Park. In the smallest of country parishes there were coronation dinners and across the country more bonfires and fireworks; everywhere the nation seemed to have a sense of renewed optimism now that it had crowned a young, pretty, and untainted queen.

The final verdict on the queen's performance that day—or rather the one that most mattered to her—came from a misty-eyed Melbourne. "You did it beautifully," he told her, "every part of it, with so much taste; it's a thing that you can't give a person advice upon" (Benson and Esher 1911, 1:124). Bright and early the following morning the young queen would be enquiring by letter whether her prime minister had "got home safe," announcing that she was "not the least tired" (125).

Related entries:
Bedchamber Crisis; Buckingham Palace; Hastings, Lady Flora; Kent, Marie Louise Victoire, Duchess of; Lablache, Luigi; Melbourne, William Lamb, Second Viscount; Stockmar, Christian Friedrich von; Sutherland, Duchess of

References and further reading:

Benson, A. C., and Vicount Esher, eds. 1911. *Letters of Queen Victoria 1837–1861.* 1st ser., 3 vols. London: John Murray.

Boykin, Edward, ed. 1957. *Victoria, Albert and Mrs. Stevenson.* London: Frederick Muller.

Charlot, Monica. 1991. *Victoria: The Young Queen.* Cambridge: Polity.

Esher, Viscount, ed. 1912. *The Girlhood of Queen Victoria: A Selection from Her Majesty's Diaries between the Years of 1832 and 1840.* 2 vols. London: John Murray.

Lambert, Margaret. 1937. *When Victoria Began to Reign: A Coronation Year Scrapbook.* London: Faber and Faber.

Longford, Elizabeth. [1964] 1998. *Victoria R.I.* London: Weidenfeld and Nicolson.

Lorne, Marquis of. 1901. *VRI: Her Life and Empire.* London: Eyre and Spottiswood.

Strachey, Lytton, and Roger Fulford, eds. 1938. *The Greville Memoirs.* 8 vols. London: Macmillan.

Woodham-Smith, Cecil. *Queen Victoria: Her Life and Times.* Vol. 1: *1819–1861.* London: Hamish Hamilton.

Victoria, Queen: As a Monarch

He [Albert] taught me how to reign. I hope I shall show that I can do it. (Bailey 1927, 1:121)

A regular feature of the many arguments offered up by British feminists in their campaign for women's emancipation and the vote during the nineteenth century was the fact that Queen Victoria's long and successful reign proved that women had a peculiar fitness for governing. The queen, however, violently disagreed; she was convinced that her sex, if they were to be really good women—that is, responsible wives and mothers and paragons of feminine virtue—were not at all suited to the onerous and, in her view, *masculine* responsibilities of government.

The poet Elizabeth Barrett Browning confided her own apprehension about the queen's particular feminine vulnerability in 1837, hoping that her tender heart and natural, womanly sentiments would not be hardened by power and "the coldnesses of state etiquette" (Munich 1996, 19). But even though Victoria's attitude to her position as sovereign would inevitably harden as she contended with the many domestic and international crises that punctuated her sixty-three-year reign, she was never reconciled to what she considered to be her own feminine weakness in the role. There remained something unseemly in a female monarch being consumed by official business at the expense of domestic and wifely duty; in matters political she often adopted the "little woman" role by relying heavily on the "strong arm" first of her husband; later of her ministers, notably Benjamin Disraeli; and finally of her private secretary, Sir Henry Ponsonby, in fulfilling these duties. If

The enduring image of Queen Victoria, as monarch, that was perpetuated during the final years of her reign in popular journals such as the Illustrated London News *(The* Illustrated London News *Picture Library)*

Prince Albert had lived, he would most likely have continued to take much of Victoria's official role from her, as uncrowned king. Instead, after his premature death in 1861, Victoria found herself torn between her desire as a widow to retreat into a half-life of grieving anonymity and the necessity of continuing to fulfill her exacting duties as queen.

At the height of an international crisis in 1877–1878 over the Russo-Turkish War, Victoria wrote that "it is a miserable thing to be a constitutional queen, and to be unable to do what is right" (Longford 1998, 411). The necessity of doing what was right had been ingrained in her by her uncle, Leopold I, King of the Belgians (Victoria's father had died in 1820), as soon as it became clear that Victoria was likely to succeed her uncle, William IV. Leopold, the surrogate father, did not cease to lecture and advise Victoria on her royal duties until his death in 1865, as did her first prime minister, Lord Melbourne, during the period 1837–1841. The eighteen-year-old Queen Victoria had wept with fear and apprehension before presiding over her first meeting with the Privy Council after her accession in June 1837 but rose to the occasion with astonishing self-possession for one so young. King Leopold, however, remained cautious about the future. The following January he warned his niece: "You are too clever not to know, that it is *not* the being *called* Queen or King, which can be of the *least consequence,* when to the title there is not also annexed the power indispensable for the exercise of those functions. All trades must be learned, and nowadays the trade of a *constitutional Sovereign, to do it well, is a very difficult one"* (Benson and Esher 1911, 1:105).

With the help of her uncle and Lord Melbourne, Victoria set out in all earnestness to learn that trade. So conscientious did she become, that by the time she married Prince Albert early in 1840 she allowed time for only a three-day honeymoon. Somehow, in between taking care of business and dealing with an inordinate amount of paperwork and correspondence, the queen also coped with the discomforts of nine pregnancies and the postnatal depression that often followed them. She thus provided the feminists with a strong argument without ever being sympathetic to their agenda, demonstrating her ability to occupy both the domestic and the public spheres simultaneously. The secret of Victoria's unconsciously applied genius as monarch is that her comfortable, domestic familiarity enhanced her credence—embodying as she did a secular trinity of "Mother, Wife, and Queen" (as defined by poet laureate Alfred, Lord Tennyson, in his poem "To the Queen").

Victoria brought to her role a womanly professionalism in the days before it was socially acceptable for women to pursue any career other than matrimony. Her gift as a monarch, as Houston argued, would rest in "the fact that she herself believed in the fiction of royalty and her own representation of it" (1999, 161). It was a belief that she was able to separate from her own innate shyness, if not self-consciousness, as a woman. Many would pass comment on the paradox of the queen's essential ordinariness in this respect, in contrast to the dignified and frequently awesome presence she exuded as monarch.

The traditional basis of the British monarchy, until William IV made the first tentative steps toward a more constitutional form of government, had been a long-held one of the exertion of the monarch's absolute power backed up by the inviolable concept of the divine right of kings. Victoria had long been dismayed by the disreputable history of the Hanoverian kings who had preceded her. By her womanly good example, she set out to restore a high moral tone at court and reestablish the monarchy in a position of respect and authority. But her first years as queen were a public relations disaster. Her constitutional impropriety over the Bedchamber Crisis and her outrageously partisan support for Melbourne, in an attempt to save his Whig government from being ousted by Sir Robert Peel, went hand in hand with a deep distrust of parliamentary reform. Although fearing the power of the mob, she was unwilling to entertain the concept of a constitutional prerogative defined by the will of the people through wider political enfranchisement. In later years, the queen's private secretary, Sir Henry Ponsonby, would observe Victoria's determination to "hand on to her successors the monarchy unimpaired and if possible strengthened" (Ponsonby 1942, 175), and she doggedly opposed any dilution of the sovereign's power. Under Prince Albert's tuition during the 1840s she had begun to absorb his messianic vision of a liberalizing monarchy in Britain that would set a standard for monarchies around the world and stem the rising tide of republicanism, but it was a vision far removed from true democratic government.

In 1867 the historian Walter Bagehot, describing Britain as already being a "disguised republic," produced a classic study, *The English Constitution,* in it outlining the role of constitutional monarchy. He defined the three basic rights of the sovereign as being "the right to be consulted, the right to encourage, the right to warn" (103). As regards her relationships with her ministers, the queen added another prerequisite of her own: the right not be dictated to. She approached her duties with absolute punctiliousness. On one occasion, when Lord Melbourne was pressing her to sign an important state document, she insisted on receiving more information about it before signing. Melbourne pleaded that the document was of paramount importance; to which Victoria replied: "It is with me a matter of paramount importance whether or not I attach my signature to a document with which I am not thoroughly satisfied" (Bullock 1887, 149).

Queen Victoria was not, however, herself innocent of the sin of peremptoriness, at times presenting a determination to break with political precedents when her own very pronounced views and preferences were threatened, particularly when faced with losing her favorite prime ministers, Benjamin Disraeli and Lord Salisbury. She had little understanding of the party political system in Britain and openly complained that the inconvenience to her of a change of government and with it prime minister should not be dictated by a mere matter of the number of votes cast in an election. Having seen her adoring Disraeli fall from power in 1868, she made no attempt ever to disguise her loathing for the Liberal prime minister, William Gladstone, who replaced him. Victoria's turbulent relationship with Gladstone is perhaps the most unpalatable demonstration of how "when political duty clashed with long-cherished prejudice, she allowed her mutinous feelings to become vindictive" (Longford 1998, 151). The queen's stubborn resistance to Gladstone and her relentless character assassination of him did nothing, however, to stem the evolving pattern of constitutional monarchy in Britain after the death of Disraeli in 1881. Philip Magnus has argued that it was triumphantly adopted by the queen's successor, Edward VII, who "transformed the Crown politically into a rubber stamp," in so doing enhancing "to an incalculable degree the force of its moral and emotional appeal" (1995, 427).

That moral and emotional appeal, abandoned to the doldrums by Victoria during her long period of mourning from 1861 to 1874, had largely been rescued by Benjamin Disraeli when he became prime minister again in 1874. He not only restored Queen Victoria to her discontented public but also astutely reinvented her abroad as a powerful, iconic figure—the empress of India. The great showpieces of the queen's Golden and Diamond Jubilees in 1887 and 1897 put on public display a dignified and ceremonial monarchy that was now held in awe around the world while underlining once again the queen's accessibility. Much of Victoria's renewed popularity as monarch in the last twenty years of her reign was due to her shared sympathies with the burgeoning English middle classes, to her plain common sense and her strong sense of family. In her belief in the appropriate subordination of the classes within the existing social order, Victoria, "by a happy intuition . . . was able to interpret and express the spirit and temper of that class which, throughout her reign, was destined to hold the balance of political power in its hands" (Benson and Esher 1911, 1:21).

Victoria frequently bewailed her lot, as well as the exhausting demands that being sovereign made on her nerves and her physique; in 1855 she complained that her ministers had the freedom to resign if things got too much for them, but she never could. She might, in moments of petulance, threaten to abdicate, but none of her ministers paid this any serious attention. For they knew that at heart Victoria never for one moment doubted her indispensability as monarch. She believed implicitly in it and in the duty of obedience owed her by all her subjects. Anything less was tantamount to disloyalty, yet perhaps in this lay Victoria's inability to understand the growing movement for democratic government. Democracy in her book was a threat to the political status quo, and with it, a threat to the very fabric of British society. To the end of her days the queen remained deeply mistrustful of change, clinging to an almost biblical sense of her own omnipotence, her religious adviser Randall Davidson once remarking that she wielded "a personal and domestic influence over the thrones of Europe without precedent in the History of Christendom" (St. Aubyn 1991, 603).

As monarch, Queen Victoria dedicated herself to maintaining the values, virtues, and morals inculcated in her by her late husband—those same standards that, ironically, have often since been derided as hypocritical and "Victorian." One might argue that they were not of her making, but were in effect "Albertian," and that they were sustained not merely by her but by the power invested in the Church, in Parliament, and in the army, as well as by the thrusting energy of industry and expanding empire. It was Victoria's sheer force of character and not her political views that summoned an inglorious monarchy from the dead during the period 1840–1861, revolutinizing the old Regency order and setting new moral standards. She had no agenda, let alone a broad political vision; she simply had the good fortune to occupy the position as sovereign for a long time, reacting to events as and when they unfolded and offering the experience and wisdom of many years. In the words of one commentator, she "didn't drive the Victorian juggernaut—you can't when you're the deity being carried" (Brendon 2001, 40). But she understood the mystique of monarchy and of the act of communion between it and its public, upholding the principles laid down by Bagehot in 1867, that royalty should above all "be reverenced." "If you begin to poke about it," he continued, "you cannot reverence it. . . . Its mystery is its life. We must not let in daylight upon magic" (85–86).

Related entries:

Albert of Saxe-Coburg-Gotha, Prince Consort; Bedchamber Crisis; Chartism; Disraeli, Benjamin; Gladstone, William Ewart; Melbourne, William Lamb, Second Viscount; Ponsonby, Sir Henry; Salisbury, Robert Arthur Talbot Gascoigne-Cecil, Third Marquis of; Sex, Pregnancy, and Childbirth; Victoria, Princess Royal; Women's Rights

References and further reading:

Bagehot, Walter. 1867. *The English Constitution*. London: Chapman and Hall.

Bailey, John, ed. 1927. *The Diary of Lady Frederick Cavendish*. 2 vols. London: John Murray.

Benson, A. C., and Vicount Esher, eds. 1911. *The Letters of Queen Victoria, 1837–61*. 1st ser., 3 vols. London: John Murray.

Brendon, Piers. 2001. "A Nation Painted Black." *The Independent,* 13 January.
Bullock, Rev. Charles. 1887. *The Queen's Resolve "I Will Be Good": With Royal Anecdotes and Incidents.* London: "Home Words" Publishing Office.
Cecil, Algernon. 1953. *Queen Victoria and Prime Ministers.* London: Eyre and Spottiswoode.
Emden, Paul. 1934. *Behind the Throne.* London: Hodder and Stoughton.
Gosse, Edmund. 1901. "The Character of Queen Victoria." *Quarterly Review* (January–April): 301–307.
Hardie, Frank. 1935. *The Political Influence of Queen Victoria 1861–1901.* Oxford: Oxford University Press.
Houston, Gail Turley. 1999. *Royalties: Queen Victoria and Victorian Writers.* Charlottesville: University Press of Virginia.
Longford, Elizabeth. [1964] 1998. *Victoria R.I.* London: Weidenfeld and Nicolson (565–577).
Magnus, Philip M. 1995. *Gladstone.* London: Macmillan.
Munich, Adrienne. 1996. *Queen Victoria's Secrets.* New York: Columbia University Press.
Oliphant, Margaret. 1900. *Queen Victoria: A Personal Sketch.* London: Cassel and Co.
Packard, Jerrold. 1995. *Farewell in Splendour: The Passing of Queen Victoria and Her Age.* Stroud, Gloucestershire: Sutton.
Pearman, Hugh. 2001. "Don't Turn Up Your Nose at Victorian Values." *Sunday Times,* Culture (Section 9), 25 March, 4–5.
Ponsonby, Arthur. 1942. *Henry Ponsonby, Queen Victoria's Private Secretary: His Life from His Letters.* London: Macmillan.
St. Aubyn, Giles. 1991. *Queen Victoria: A Portrait.* London: Sinclair Stevenson (600–608).
Thompson, Dorothy. 1990. *Queen Victoria: Gender and Power.* London: Virago.

Victoria, Queen: Birth of

Take care of her for she will be Queen of England (Edward, Duke of Kent; Woodham-Smith 1972, 32)

Had it not been for the Prince Regent, later George IV's petulant veto of all the names suggested for his niece, on the day of her christening on 24 June 1819, the baby daughter of the duke and duchess of Kent, who indelibly defined her age with her name Victoria, might have become Queen Alexandrina. Fortunately, both public and private preferences over the names given to the baby at her christening ensured that such a foreign-sounding name did not prevail for long.

When Victoire of Saxe-Coburg became pregnant after her marriage to Edward, duke of Kent, in May 1818, it was essential to ensure that her child should be born in England, thus underlining the baby's legitimacy in line to the throne. The Kents had been living somewhat modestly, by royal standards, on the duchess's estate at Amorbach in Bavaria, and the duke, perennially short of money, was obliged to appeal to his friends for loans in order to pay off his debts and make the 427-mile journey to London.

The duke and the eight-months-pregnant duchess set out for England with their entourage on 28 March 1819 in a less than dignified cavalcade of two phaetons, a barouche, a landau, and two postchaises, with servants bringing up the rear in an assortment of vehicles containing the couple's goods and chattels—including a bed, should the duchess require it—and the family plate. The duke himself drove the duchess in the most comfortable of the vehicles—a sprung cane phaeton—to save money on a coachman. The entourage of maids and retainers included, most importantly, a midwife, the renowned Frau Siebold (who was also a qualified doctor). It made the tedious journey across Germany and France at a rate of twenty-five miles a day, at the end of each day the party having to endure the bed bugs and fleas of cheap inns. By 18 April this rattling convoy had arrived at Calais but was forced to wait several days for fair winds for their crossing to Dover, which was effected on St. George's Day, 23 April (according to Longford; other sources say it was the 24), in the yacht the *Royal Sovereign,* grudgingly laid on by the Prince Regent. The journey was rough, with the duchess suffering seasickness.

After another four days on the road to London, the Kents finally took up the ground-floor apartments allotted them at Kensington Palace on 28 April. A lying-in room was prepared for the duchess, and a month later, at 4:15 A.M. on 24 May, she gave birth to a baby girl after a six-hour labor, during which there had been no need for the duke to call upon the services of the Welsh obstetrician Daniel Davis, who had been asked to attend. The duke was delighted with his robust baby daughter and pronounced her "a pretty little Princess, as plump as a partridge" (Stockmar 1873, 1:78). According to the ladies at court, the baby also looked distinctly Hanoverian, bearing a remarkable resemblance to her grandfather, George III. The accomplished midwife Siebold would soon be successfully bringing into the world the baby's future husband, for in August she delivered the son, Albert, of Louise, duchess of Saxe-Coburg-Gotha.

The duke of Kent had been present at the birth while official witnesses—the archbishop of Canterbury, the bishop of London, the chancellor of the Exchequer, the duke of Wellington, and various privy councillors—had hovered in an adjoining anteroom. They had confirmed the new baby's position, under the British law of primogeniture, as fifth in line to the throne—after the Prince Regent, the duke of York, the duke of Clarence, and the duke of Kent—provided of course that none of the duke's royal brothers produced legitimate heirs in the meanwhile.

The Prince Regent designated the time and place of the baby's christening, on 24 June at 3 P.M. in the Cupola Room at Kensington Palace. Forced to recognize his own inability to father a legitimate successor and the likelihood that his brother's child might continue the royal line rather than one of his own, the Prince Regent determined to make the ceremony private and without fanfare. A silver gilt baptismal font, known as the "gold font," which had been used for the christenings of most of George III's children, was brought from the Tower of London, and crimson draperies, hastily borrowed from the Chapel Royal at St. James's, provided the only ornamentation. The archbishop of Canterbury and the bishop of London officiated, but aside from the Prince Regent the baby's other godparents—Tsar Alexander I, the queen dowager of Württemberg, and the duchess dowager of Saxe-Coburg-Saarfeld—were not present, but represented by proxies. When the moment came to name the baby, the parents' carefully chosen names of Victoire Georgiana Alexandrina Charlotte Augusta failed to meet with the Prince Regent's approval. Before the ceremony he had rejected their first choice of Georgiana, which he had insisted could not be placed before the name Alexandrina, given in honor of the primary godparent, the tsar. Nor would he countenance the use of his dead daughter Charlotte's name (for she, indeed, was the much lamented and legitimate heir he had lost). Augusta was considered by the Prince Regent far too "majestic" in tone. With the baby's distressed mother by now in tears and the assembled dignitaries confused and embarrassed, the duke of Kent suggested that the name Elizabeth might follow Alexandrina. The Prince Regent, again resenting the overt regal inference, dismissed this name too, finally conceding that the baby might be named Alexandrina, followed by Victoire—her mother's name.

The baby princess was vaccinated against smallpox two months after her birth—the first in the royal family to receive this new procedure pioneered by Edward Jenner. She bloomed and seemed particularly robust. Much against custom among the upper classes, the duchess chose to breastfeed her baby, an act that emphasized her desire for control over this much-prized child. The Kents soon adopted the habit of making regular outings in an open carriage in order to show off the infant Alexandrina to her potential future public. The baby was even taken to a military review, much to the

Prince Regent's annoyance, who grumbled, "What business has that infant here?" (Creston 1952, 77).

Nobody, however, liked the foreign-sounding name Alexandrina, and for the first nine years of Victoria's life this was shortened to "Drina." Privately, the duchess of Kent and her mainly German entourage spoke nothing but German with the little girl until she was three years old, referring to her in a diminutive form—as Vickelchen. Public dislike of the princess's names persisted for some time, with even the writer Sir Walter Scott hoping that the name Victoria (as Victoire was Anglicized) might prevail in preference to it. In 1831 two members of Parliament even went so far as to suggest that, should she become queen, Princess Victoria ought to assume the title "Queen Elizabeth II." The name Charlotte, too, was suggested as a better alternative to "Queen Victoria." By this time, however, the dogmatic William IV was on the throne; as an ex-navy man he thought the name Victoria would be more popular among his much-loved sailors. He also refused to give Victoria the title "heir apparent," in the faint hopes that his wife, Queen Adelaide, might yet produce a surviving heir. Thus the name Victoria prevailed among the family until shortly after her accession, when the queen renounced the name Alexandrina and declared that henceforth she would be known as Victoria.

Related entries:
Feodora, Princess of Hohenlohe-Langenburg; Hanover, Royal House of; Kent, Edward Augustus, Duke of; Kent, Marie Louise Victoire, Duchess of; Saxe-Coburg-Gotha, Royal House of

References and further reading:

Charlot, Monica. 1991. *Victoria: The Young Queen.* Cambridge: Polity.
Creston, Dormer. 1952. *The Youthful Victoria.* London: Macmillan.
Longford, Elizabeth. [1964] 1998. *Victoria R.I.* London: Weidenfeld and Nicolson.
Lorne, Marquis of. 1901. *VRI: Her Life and Empire.* London: Eyre and Spottiswood.
St. Aubyn, Giles. 1991. *Queen Victoria: A Portrait.* London: Sinclair Stevenson.
Stockmar, Ernst Baron. 1873. *Memoirs of Baron Stockmar.* 2 vols. London: Longman, Green, and Co.
Woodham-Smith, Cecil. 1972. *Queen Victoria: Her Life and Times.* Vol. 1: *1819–1861.* London: Hamish Hamilton.

Victoria, Queen: Courtship and Marriage of

I do not think it possible *for any one in the world to be* happier, *or as happy as I am* (Benson and Esher 1911, 1:217)

In 1836, when Princess Victoria was approaching seventeen, the subject of her marriage became an increasingly important issue, uppermost particularly in the minds of her mother, the duchess of Kent, and her uncle, Leopold, king of the Belgians. Both concurred that the ideal husband would be a German prince—if possible, a Saxe-Coburg one. And they already had their eyes on an ideal candidate: Prince Albert, son of Duke Ernest I of Saxe-Coburg-Gotha. In his teenage years, the young Albert, having been apprised of his mission, had submitted without question to being groomed by King Leopold for the role of husband to the future queen of England.

There were of course many other possible candidates for the hand of this, the most eligible royal bride in Europe. Between the ages of thirteen and eighteen the young Princess Victoria had had several possible suitors paraded for her approval by rival camps within the royal family. It was first suggested that she should marry an English prince, such as Prince George, son of her uncle the duke of Cumberland. In 1828 the duke of Orleans was a candidate; in 1829, the prince of Orange. A serious onslaught of matchmaking came in 1836 when four Coburg cousins and both princes of Orange were all invited to Eng-

First cousins Queen Victoria and Prince Albert of Saxe-Coburg were married at St. James's Palace on 10 February 1840. Theirs had been a brief engagement (the queen had proposed the previous October), but the match had been long sought by their uncle, Leopold king of the Belgians. (The Illustrated London News *Picture Library)*

land to be vetted. In addition, as she entered into society, Victoria herself enjoyed the frisson of brief romantic crushes on Grand Duke Nicholas of Russia; Charles, duke of Brunswick; and Grand Duke Alexander—heir to the Russian throne—on their various state visits to England.

On 17 March 1836 at a grand ball at Windsor Castle, Princess Victoria was finally introduced to her Coburg cousins, Ferdinand and Augustus, sons of Prince Ferdinand. She found them both "dear good young men" (Woodham-Smith 1972, 114). At a series of balls and receptions during the princes' ten-day visit, she became increasingly enamored of their many fine qualities, particularly the good humor of Ferdinand. But after his departure on 27 March, there was a marked shift in her adoration to his younger brother Augustus, who remained in England for another two weeks.

King William IV, however, wanted nothing to do with Victoria's Coburg cousins. Loathing the obsequious and puritanical Leopold and his Coburg family (which he saw as being tainted by Catholicism), he favored the sons of the prince of Orange, a family whose long-standing Protestantism had made them traditional allies of England. While King Leopold and the duchess of Kent had been busily arranging a visit by their favored candidate, Prince Albert, together with his father and brother, King William IV preempted them by inviting the prince of Orange to England with his sons William and Alexander. The party arrived in May 1836, and the princes were introduced to Victoria at a ball at St. James's Palace on the thirteenth. The princess was not impressed and was quick to write and tell Uncle Leopold so: "The boys are both very plain and have a mixture of Kalmuck and Dutch in their faces, moreover they look heavy, dull and frightened and are not at all prepossessing. So much for the *Oranges* dear uncle" (Woodham-Smith 1972, 119).

A few days later, on the eighteenth, an exhausted Prince Albert, still suffering the aftereffects of terrible seasickness, was presented at court soon after arriving from the Continent with his father and his brother, Ernest. Victoria was immediately impressed with the brothers. They were charming and very musical and could draw well. But although she found Albert undoubtedly the handsomer of the two, with his beautiful nose, sweet mouth, and fine teeth, he seemed shy and diffident, and it was the more affable Ernest who initially attracted her. Albert unfortunately seemed to lack the stamina required for the protracted round of receptions, dinners, and balls. Such was his inability for staying up late socializing and dancing—activities that Princess Victoria loved—that he would literally fall asleep wherever he found himself. He could not even rally his energies for a state ball held to celebrate Victoria's seventeenth birthday on 24 May. She noticed he looked "very pale and felt very poorly" and "turned as pale as ashes" and went home early (Woodham-Smith 1972, 120).

Prince Albert recovered his strength to dance with Princess Victoria at a grand ball at Kensington Palace on 30 May, but his powers of endurance were stretched way beyond their limits, with the eager young princess dancing away until half past three in the morning. He rallied sufficiently to enjoy the quieter pursuits of singing and piano playing and occasional rides with the princess until his departure on 10 July, upon which Victoria confided in her journal how much she would miss "these *dearest* beloved Cousins, whom I *do* love so *very, very* dearly, *much more dearly* than any other Cousins in the *world*" (Woodham-Smith 1972, 122).

By this time Princess Victoria had been made aware by her Uncle Leopold and her mother that Albert was their preferred choice of husband. Although her initial preference had been for the more gregarious Ernest, as the visit progressed she shifted her attentions to Albert. But she was still only seventeen and certainly not in love. She dutifully wrote and thanked

Leopold "for the prospect of great happiness you have contributed to give me, in the person of Dear Albert" (Benson and Esher 1911, 1:47). The prince had passed muster and in her view "possesses every quality that could be desired to make me perfectly happy. He is so sensible, so kind and so good and so amiable too. He has besides the most pleasing and delightful exterior and appearance that you could wish to see" (1:47).

King Leopold hoped the marriage would take place when Victoria reached eighteen. But she threw his and the duchess's well-laid plans into confusion when she announced that, much as she liked and admired Albert, she would not consider herself as being bound to him. As a young and vivacious woman, she sensed herself on the brink of many new experiences after the long years of seclusion at Kensington Palace. She thus had no inclination to shackle herself at such an early age to marriage and domesticity. But after her accession in June 1837, King Leopold increased the pressure upon her. He insisted that it was of paramount importance for Victoria to marry and produce an heir to secure her own position. But she refused to be coerced and continued to prevaricate over the decision to marry Albert, denying that she was in any way obligated to him. Marriage seemed a "schocking [*sic*] alternative" (Hibbert 1984, 42). She felt Albert was still too young and his English not yet up to scratch; after discussing it with Lord Melbourne, Victoria announced that she would postpone marrying for another three or four years. Prince Albert was dismayed but obliged to bide his time.

By August 1839, when planning began for another visit to England by the Princes Albert and Ernest, in a concerted attempt to propel the queen into marriage, the mild-mannered Albert had grown increasingly impatient, threatening that he would withdraw altogether if a decision was not made. The Saxe-Coburg brothers arrrived in October, exhausted and unwell after a bad crossing, hours later making their first appearance at Windsor. Queen Victoria could not believe the transformation in her cousin: "It was with some emotion that I beheld Albert—who is *beautiful*" (Hibbert 1984, 55). After dinner she danced a quadrille with him, admiring his handsome figure—the narrow waist and broad shoulders—and his exquisite deportment. The self-conscious frog of 1836 had turned into a handsome prince.

Official channels passed the good news back to Albert that he had made a favorable impression with the queen. By now completely smitten with him, Victoria soon changed her mind about marriage. Five days later, on the morning of 15 October, Prince Albert was summoned to the royal presence. Without the least self-consciousness, and confident in her unique royal prerogative, Victoria announced to (the lower-ranked) Albert "that it would make me *too happy* if he would consent to what I wished (to marry me)" (Woodham-Smith 1972, 184). Albert was overwhelmed by the intensity of her feeling, and was greatly impressed by Victoria's qualities of affection and sincerity. Tired, bewildered, and still struggling to come to terms with the alien English court, its customs, and the climate, he nevertheless enjoyed the remainder of his visit, as the affection between him and Victoria deepened. Sharing similar cultural tastes, they read or sang together, snatching tentative embraces, and exchanging expressions of love in German, as they sat together on the blue sofa in the queen's sitting-room. The wedding was arranged for the following year.

And so it was, that a marriage long planned to consolidate dynastic aspirations fortuitously turned out to be a genuinely happy union, based on love rather than dutiful acquiescence, although the prince was loath to abandon the tranquillity of his beloved home, the Rosenau. He was aware that his new role as prince consort would "have its dark sides," and he feared that it would be "plentifully strewn with thorns" (Bolitho 1949, 59). In January 1840 emissaries from Queen Victoria traveled to Coburg to invest him with the Order of the Garter prior to his departure for England. He was installed in a suite at Buckingham Palace on 8 February, with time to recover from his seasickness for the wedding ceremony, which took place on a wet and windy Monday, 10 February 1840.

On the morning of the wedding the queen defied convention and had a brief, private audience with the prince, before setting off for the Chapel Royal at St. James's Palace where the ceremony was to take place. Her wedding clothes were entirely English made: her dress was of heavy white satin from the looms of Spitalfields, she wore a wedding veil of Honiton lace (an item that had provided 200 needlewomen in Devon with employment) and kid gloves made in London. Her jewelry was a sapphire brooch presented to her by the prince and a Turkish diamond necklace and earrings. On her head she wore a circlet of orange blossom, and in her hand she carried a lace-edged handkerchief and a small bouquet. She was attended by twelve bridesmaids, but an oversight in the design of the queen's short bridal train left all twelve young women struggling to keep hold of it while simultaneously trying not to trip up over their own gowns.

Aware of the widespread antipathy toward her bridegroom in Parliament, the queen had deliberately excluded all but five loyal Tories from the 300-strong guest list at the chapel, with her legendary stubbornness insisting that "It is MY marriage and I will only have those who can sympathize with me" (Creston 1952, 445). To a flourish of trumpets Lord Melbourne preceded the queen down the aisle, carrying the sword of state. The undoubted star of the occasion was, however, Prince Albert, despite the broken English in which he repeated his vows. Contemporary portraits testify to his considerable beauty and his striking physique, set off to such effect by his uniform of a field marshal of the British Army—with its swallow-tailed tunic decorated with white satin bows, and his white knee breeches, topped with the Order of the Garter.

The wedding breakfast was held at Buckingham Palace. The queen then changed into a white silk gown trimmed with swansdown and a bonnet trimmed with orange flowers. At four in the afternoon, in a somewhat shabby looking traveling coach, the couple set off for Windsor, where later that evening the exhausted bride was prostrated by a severe headache. The following morning the couple were up at 8:30 and took the morning air on the terrace. Prince Albert had hoped they would spend at least a week or two out of town on honeymoon, but after only three days Victoria was anxious to get back to the business of government. When he objected, she sent Albert a note, in which, in the most admonitory of tones, she set in stone her lifelong attitude to the duties that lay before them: "You forget, my dearest Love, that I am the Sovereign, and that business can stop and wait for nothing" (Benson and Esher 1911, 1:213).

Related entries:

Albert of Saxe-Coburg-Gotha, Prince Consort; Dancing; Ernest Augustus, Duke of Cumberland; Leopold I, King of the Belgians

References and further reading:

Aronson, Theo. 1991. *Heart of a Queen: Queen Victoria's Romantic Attachments.* London: John Murray.

Benson, A. C., and Viscount Esher, eds. 1911. *Letters of Queen Victoria 1837–1861.* 1st ser., 3 vols. London: John Murray.

Bolitho, Hector. 1949. *The Reign of Queen Victoria.* London: Collins.

Charlot, Monica. 1991. *Victoria: The Young Queen.* Cambridge: Polity.

Creston, Dormer. 1952. *The Youthful Queen Victoria: A Discursive Account.* London: Macmillan and Co.

Esher, Viscount, ed. 1912. *The Girlhood of Queen Victoria: A Selection from Her Majesty's Diaries*

between the Years of 1832 and 1840. 2 vols. London: John Murray.
Hibbert, Christopher. 1984. *Queen Victoria in Her Letters and Journals.* London: Viking.
Hough, Richard. 1996. *Victoria and Albert: Their Love and Their Tragedies.* London: Richard Cohen.
Longford, Elizabeth. [1964] 1998. *Victoria R.I.* London: Weidenfeld and Nicolson.
Lorne, Marquis of. 1901. *VRI: Her Life and Empire.* London: Eyre and Spottiswood.
Weintraub, Stanley. 1996. *Victoria.* London: John Murray.
Woodham-Smith, Cecil. 1972. *Queen Victoria: Her Life and Times.* Vol. 1: *1819–1861.* London: Hamish Hamilton.

Victoria, Queen: Death and Funeral of

like a great three-decker ship sinking (the Marquis of Lorne; Ponsonby 1951, 82)

Throughout 1900 Queen Victoria's health had been visibly failing. She suffered great discomfort from indigestion and her now chronic insomnia made her tire easily during the day, so that she frequently dozed off during her afternoon drives. Her lady-in-waiting, Marie Mallet, had been monitoring the queen's weight loss and fatigue with mounting apprehension, particularly after the outbreak of the Boer War (in October 1899), the setbacks and losses of which greatly distressed her. Victoria's eyesight, now badly affected by cataracts, was so poor that she could no longer read her official correspondence even when copied out for her in large letters and thick black ink. A series of deaths in the family had taken away all her appetite, that of her son Alfred in July being a particularly heavy blow. "All the strain of the last year has told terribly on her, and all about her are really anxious for the first time," Mallet observed in November, adding, "One fears it must be the beginning of the end" (1969, 219).

By the end of the year Victoria was feeling decidedly unwell and taking little food. She did not enjoy Christmas or its usual festive fare and took her meals alone in her room. The loss of her devoted friend and lady-in-waiting, Sarah Churchill, who was found dead in her bed at Osborne on Christmas morning, was more than she could bear. Her spirits were at an all-time low as the new year opened, and in her journal she recorded that she "enter[ed] upon it sadly" (Reid 1996, 199). By mid-January her personal physician, Sir James Reid, noted the first clear signs that the queen's mental faculties were failing, and she was now suffering from bouts of aphasia (the result probably of a slight stroke). The public sensed that something was seriously wrong the day, a fortnight before Victoria's death, that the "Court Circular" was omitted from the morning's papers. As Lady Helier recorded: "All through the Queen's long reign a daily notice of her movements had been published, and when I opened the Times on that particular morning, I felt a great misfortune was impending" (Jeune 1909, 352). By 14 January, Victoria was too weak even to dictate her daily journal entry. The inexorable slide toward death began, with the queen drifting from moments of clarity to bouts of childlike confusion. In the words of Henry James, it was "a simple running down of the old used-up watch" (Edel 1984, 4:181).

The queen's children were called to her bedside on 18 January; Victoria was expected to die at any moment, and on the nineteenth the Prince of Wales allowed a statement to be released, preparing the nation for the worst. No one could mistake the sense of doom underlying the euphemistically bald statement that the queen "has not lately been in her usual health" (St. Aubyn 1991, 594). The fact that the people of Windsor had not seen the queen out for her usual daily drives in itself spoke volumes. But the queen's strong heart and tough constitution allowed her to drift on for four more days, during which she occasionally showed signs of rallying. On the

The funeral cortege of Queen Victoria, her coffin placed on a gun carriage, leaves Windsor Castle on its journey to the Mausoleum at Frogmore on a cold, grey February day, 1901. (Bettmann/CORBIS)

nineteenth she told her personal physician, Sir James Reid, that she should "like to live a little longer, as I have still a few things to settle" (Reid 1996, 205). And for a brief moment Victoria seemed her old self again, when on the morning of the twenty-first, she enquired whether she was better and then asked for her Pomeranian dog, Turi, to be allowed to sit on her bed. In her last moments of recognition, before drifting again into semiconsciousness, she acknowledged her son, Bertie, the prince of Wales, and asked him to kiss her face; she seemed cognisant too, when the dean of Winchester, Randall Davidson, read out her favorite hymn, "Lead Kindly Light."

Reid and the queen's grandson, Kaiser William of Germany, were cradling the queen in their arms during the last hour or so before she died, at 6:30 P.M. on 22 January. The only member of her immediate family who was absent from the deathbed was her daughter Vicky—herself terminally ill with cancer in Berlin. Hordes of journalists were waiting outside the gates to Osborne House when the news came. They immediately made an unseemly scramble for the telegraph office; the writer Marie Corelli later described "a crowd of carriages at the gallop, of bicycles careering down the hill at break-neck speed, of runners bawling 'Queen dead' at the top of their voices" that together sounded like "a babel of voices at a fox-hunt" (Corelli 1901, 30–31).

As a punctilious observer of the protocol of mourning, Queen Victoria had, long before her death, left detailed instructions about her funeral in the care of her dresser, Mrs. Tuck. She surprised the royal family by asking (as had the poet laureate, Tennyson) for a "white funeral," stipulating a white pall over her coffin, and for it to be conveyed on a gun carriage—as befitted a soldier's daughter (her father the duke of Kent had had a long army career). Sir James Reid oversaw the final careful preparations of the queen's tiny body. Swathed in her wedding veil of Honiton lace, the dead queen was a moving sight in her final repose, "like a lovely marble statue, no sign of illness or age" as Reid's wife, Susan, recorded; quite simply, she looked *"the Queen"* (Reid 1996, 214). A delicate watercolor portrait by Sir Hubert Herkomer recorded the image of the queen laid out on her deathbed, surrounded by a drift of snowdrops and lilies of the valley.

After the queen's body was lifted into her coffin by her sons Bertie and Arthur, Reid oversaw the arrangement of the many personal mementos that Victoria had specifically requested be laid in her coffin with her: a profusion of "rings, chains, bracelets, lockets, photographs, shawls, handkerchiefs, casts of hands" (Reid 1996, 216), in addition to the prince consort's dressing gown and a cloak embroidered by Princess Alice (who had died in 1878). In a final, private moment, Reid secretly added a photograph of John Brown with a lock of his hair, at the queen's request, placing them in her hand and concealing them with a posy of flowers.

There was hardly a place on the map that did not record the news of the death of the "Empress of Hearts" and memorialize it in some way. The black-edged columns of the *Times* were filled with condolences from around the empire. Stock exchanges closed; flags flew at half-mast. In Burma the celebration of Ramadan was extended in order that the people could say additional prayers for the queen. In the veldt of southern Africa, a Zulu chief poetically mourned the passing of his "great White Queen," vowing that "then I shall see another star in the sky" (Lorne 1901, 395). All the London theaters were closed, and the pantomime season cut short. In Scotland the traditional celebration of Burns Night on 25 January was canceled. Across Britain's cities, silent crowds gathered on street corners in acts of spontaneous commiseration and mourning. The largest gathering was in the hushed City of London, where the great bell of St. Paul's Cathedral tolled out a lament.

An eight-day lying in state was held for the queen, in the dining room at Osborne House, heavy with the sickening scent of lilies. And then on 1 February, her coffin, surmounted by her crown and royal insignia and accompanied by the sound of bagpipes, was taken to the royal yacht *Alberta,* where it was placed on a crimson dais for the voyage across The Solent to Portsmouth. Its passage, on a fine winter's afternoon, was watched over by a double line of battleships and cruisers: "A quiet, calm sea, the very slow motion of the vessels, which made them seem to glide without visible propelling power, the broad avenue of towering battleships booming out their salutes on either side, the enormous mass of perfectly silent black-clothed crowds covering Southsea Common and the beach" (Bell 1952, 356). It was an intensely moving and memorable occasion, according to the queen's religious adviser, Randall Davidson, who added: "I do not envy the man who could pass through such a scene dry-eyed" (ibid.).

With the country not having witnessed a great, state funeral since the death of the duke of Wellington in 1852, the queen's death had provoked a flurry of diplomatic activity, as court officials pored over the details of royal protocol and rights of precedence, in arranging the funeral procession. Delegations were sent to welcome the arriving royal representatives of the queen's seventy-four living descendants as well as the many diplomats from around the world. Meanwhile the streets of Windsor and London were festooned in purple crape and laurel wreaths in preparation for the funeral procession.

It was sleeting hard on the morning of 2 February, when the coffin was taken by train to Victoria station, where it was greeted by mourners led by King Edward VII and the kaiser. It was then taken in procession on a gun carriage across London—via the Mall, St. James's Street, Piccadilly, Hyde Park, and Marble Arch—to Paddington station for its journey to Windsor. The streets were dense with crowds. Huddling themselves against the bitter cold, the people were eerily silent, the only sound being the muffled drums and the gun salutes fired at regular intervals in Hyde Park. "The most impressive feature of the whole ceremony was the attitude of the crowd: its size, its silence, the universal black," remarked the writer Maurice Baring (1987, 216). "London was like a dead city, and as someone said at the time: 'one went about feeling as if one had cheated at cards'" (216). It was a city mourning not just for its queen but for itself and the end of an era.

People gasped at the sight of the queen's white-palled coffin as it passed—"a mourning groan . . . unconscious, primitive, deep and wild," in the words of writer John Galsworthy (Brendon 2001, 6). "I was fairly taken by surprise which seized me by the throat, when the low gun carriage with its little, little burden hove into sight," wrote another observer, Lady St. Helier. "The tiny coffin draped in softest white satin—the whole thing so pure, so tender, so womanly, so suggestive of her who lay sleeping within—that every heart, one felt, must needs go out to meet her" (Jeune 1909, 280). Everyone agreed that the most imposing figure in the all-male procession (the female members of the family, hidden beneath heavy black veils, followed in closed carriages) was Kaiser William in a great gray cloak and riding a white horse. He was in his element. For once behaving with grace and dignity, rather than his usual bullishness, he had risen to the occasion, determined to ensure that his grandmother's obsequies were fittingly dignified. He would later portentously inform the German nation that he had passed his birthday that year (27 January) "in silent self-communion at the bier of that noble Sovereign" (Hamilton 1964, 3).

The town of Windsor had become jammed with mourners by the time the queen's coffin arrived in the afternoon of the second. A team of artillery horses had been assembled to take the coffin on its final journey up the hill to Windsor Castle and down Long Walk to the Royal Mausoleum. But during the long wait in the cold, the horses had become restless and had broken the traces attaching them to the gun carriage. In their stead, a group of Blue Jackets—sailors from the guard of honor—were hastily organized to drag the heavy gun carriage—the lead-lined coffin alone weighed half a ton—up the hill to St. George's Chapel.

Victoria's constantly reiterated desire throughout her long widowhood had been to be reunited with Albert, the certainty of which he had assured her not long before his own death: "We don't know in what state we shall meet again; but that we shall recognise each other and be together in eternity I am perfectly certain" (Underwood 1982, 202). The queen joined Prince Albert in their own private resting place—the Royal Mausoleum at Frogmore—in a ceremony attended only by close members of the royal family, late on the afternoon of the second. After it was over, the white marble effigy of the queen, carved forty years previously to match a similar, recumbent one of the prince, was rolled into place.

The public expressions of grief over the death of the queen were many but shared a common sentiment, expressed by the social reformer Josephine Butler: "One feels as if one had lost a dear friend. . . . It is a real, *personal* grief. They cannot understand, I am sure, on the Continent, the sorrow we feel" (Jordan 2001, 285). Butler also captured the extraordinary, uplifting atmosphere of those days in January and February, which she said were like an "electric thrill of love & sorrow" (ibid.) that sent its shock waves around the whole of the queen's vast empire. The country was united in its sense of motherlessness; it lamented the loss of the familiarity and security of the long Victorian era. "I mourn the safe and motherly old middle-class queen, who held the nation warm under the fold of her big, hideous Scotch-plaid shawl and whose duration had been so extraordinarily convenient and beneficient," wrote Henry James. "She was a sustaining symbol," he added, and like many, James felt that "the wild waters are upon us now" (Edel 1984, 184). People's thoughts now turned to the new king and expectations for the future. "And so, as the great Victorian epoch rolls away into the deep shadow of the past," wrote Marie Corelli, "the Empire rests as it were on a rainbow edge between storm and sunshine, grief and hope—grief for the Monarch that was, hope for the Monarch that is" (1901, 35). The country had given its queen a fine and emotional send off; as one anonymous person in the crowd remarked to a reporter from the *Manchester Guardian* on 23 January, "she'd have been glad to know we were so sorry."

Related entries:
Brown, John; Reid, Sir James; "The Widow at Windsor"

References and further reading:
Baring, Maurice. [1932] 1987. *The Puppet Show of Memory.* London: Cassell.
Bell, George Kennedy. 1952. *Randall Davidson: Archbishop of Canterbury.* Oxford:Oxford University Press.
Bland, Olivia. 1986. *The Royal Way of Death.* London: Constable (chap. 8).
Brendon, Piers. 2001. "A Nation Painted Black." *The Independent,* Review section, 13 January.
Corelli, Marie. 1901. *The Passing of the Great Queen: A Tribute to the Noble Life of Victoria Regina.* London: Methuen and Co.
Curl, James. 2000. *The Victorian Celebration of Death.* Stroud, Gloucestershire: Sutton.
Edel, Leon, ed. 1984. *The Letters of Henry James.* Vol. 4: *1895–1916.* London: Macmillan.
Hamilton, Gerald. 1964. *Blood Royal.* London: A. Gibbs and Philips.
Jeune, Susan Mary, Baroness St. Helier. 1909. *Memories of Fifty Years.* London: Edward Arnold.
Jordan, Jane. 2001. *Josephine Butler.* London: John Murray.
Lorne, Marquis of. 1901. *VRI: Her Life and Empire.* London: Eyre and Spottiswoode.
Mallet, Victor, ed. 1969. *Life with Queen Victoria: Marie Mallet's Letters from Court, 1887–1901.* London: John Murray.

Packard, Jerrold. 1995. *Farewell in Splendour: The Passing of Queen Victoria and Her Age.* Stoud, Gloucestershire: Sutton.
Ponsonby, Frederick. 1951. *Recollections of Three Reigns.* London: Eyre and Spottiswoode.
Reid, Michaela. 1996. *Ask Sir James: The Life of Sir James Reid, Personal Physician to Queen Victoria.* London: Eland.
Rennell, Tony. 2000. *Last Days of Glory: The Death of Queen Victoria.* London: Viking.
St. Aubyn, Giles. 1991. *Queen Victoria: A Portrait.* London: Sinclair Stevenson.
Underwood, Peter. 1982. *Queen Victoria's Other World.* London: Harrap.

Victoria, Queen: Personality of

If they only knew what I really am like (St. Aubyn 1991, 606)

The public persona of Victoria, queen of Great Britain and empress of India, was one of unity and solidity. Her aura of majesty, when formally portrayed in the robes of state, suggested order, resilience, and continuity and reassured the majority of her subjects that the political institution of the monarchy was safe in her hands. Informally, as mother and grandmother, and surrounded by her family, the matronly ordinariness that Victoria exuded—both comely and unassuming—seemed equally reassuring—like that of any other middle-class woman up and down the land. In these, her two most public incarnations, the queen presented a fascinating dichotomy—for she was, simultaneously, in the words of Elizabeth Longford, "every ounce a bourgeoise and every inch a queen" (1998, 568).

The real and complex woman behind the public figure of the matriarch-monarch has been revealed, by degrees, with the publication of her letters and journals. Elizabeth Longford was one of the first to pinpoint the highly contradictory personality behind the public image—a personality that defies generalization, for a great many of Queen Victoria's good qualities were in fact counterbalanced by their often unpleasant antithesis. Victoria was a woman of unique and laudable strengths, but she was also bedeviled by weaknesses. Her private secretary, Sir Henry Ponsonby, once rightly asserted that attempts at pigeonholing her as a representative of her age were futile, for in many respects she was highly unconventional and held unorthodox views that were often decidedly un-Victorian. Ponsonby believed that Victoria was unique in her own idiosyncrasies, observing that "she bore no resemblance to an aristocratic English lady, she bore no resemblance to a wealthy middle-class Englishwoman, nor to any typical princess of a German court. . . . Never in her life could she be confused with anyone else, nor will she be in history. Such expressions as 'people like Queen Victoria' or 'that sort of woman' could not be used about her" (Ponsonby 1942, 70).

What makes the queen so endlessly fascinating is therefore this *difference*—to be found in the inner conflicts of her character, its inconsistencies and its unconventionality; it was often her unique position as monarch that allowed her to exercise this difference and to at times indulge its extreme and unpalatable elements. The queen's personality, as Giles St. Aubyn (1991) argued, went through several distinct periods of change and adjustment, before she finally settled into the familiar guise of the matriarch of the Jubilee years. As we study her character's progression, the impressionable and impetuous young princess of the 1830s gives way to the stubborn young queen of 1837–1840 and a period of shamefully partisan political behavior, which is followed by the early years of domestic duty, during which Victoria adjusted to marriage and the demands of maternity. A period of consolidation as monarch followed, during which, up to a point, she learned to honor the principles of constitutional monarchy imparted by her husband, Albert.

Victoria's supreme self-confidence and strength of will were exceptional for one so young; her single-mindedness as queen rarely deserted her. She was always impatient to do things in her own way and without contradiction and could be frighteningly dictatorial in this respect, particularly when it came to matters relating to her own children. She could also often be bullying and inconsiderate toward those nearest to her in the royal household who served her with such devotion while, on the other hand, being absurdly sentimental about the treatment of animals. Her outrage, for example, over vivisection was not equaled by the same levels of compassion for Britain's underclasses, nor by a concern for broader social issues such as poor housing and sanitation, dangerous working conditions, and so on. The queen's sentiments were always best milked by individual cases of suffering or hardship, particularly if combined with honesty and self-sacrifice on the part of the sufferer. Sympathetic to the deserving poor, she had no comprehension of what drove the destitute to acts of desperation, in which cases she adhered to established codes of morality and the law; she had no compunctions about signing a death warrant if she thought it was merited.

Yet, when protocol demanded, Queen Victoria could be the most gracious and accommodating hostess to foreign princes and potentates, and her views on religious practice could be surprisingly tolerant and unorthodox. The queen clearly favored the simpler devotions of Presbyterianism and nonconformity above the established Church of England, which as monarch she represented. Sincere and undogmatic in her own religious practices, Victoria hated empty, pious words. With the British aristocracy legendary for its indolence and its ingrained prejudice against Jews, ethnic minorities, and their social inferiors, she confounded her own class by harboring a lifelong admiration for the simple virtues of the lowly and humble and a respect for the dignity of other races and creeds.

Victoria never had any pretensions about her own intellectual shortcomings. Once freed from the straitjacket of the Kensington System under which she was brought up, she read only what appealed to her and Albert and made no excuses if she disliked something. She became quite jealous that she could never aspire to the intellectual plane occupied by her husband and her eldest daughter, Vicky, but worked hard at learning to appreciate the same kind of art and music as her husband and inculcated his views, in so far as her intellect allowed her, on most of the subjects that interested him. There is no disguising the queen's lack of natural curiosity about subjects that were beyond her grasp, yet she had great powers of understanding when it came to complex political affairs, provided things were explained to her with clarity and brevity (an essential quickly grasped by Lord Melbourne but determinedly ignored by the dogmatic Gladstone, who never ceased to lecture). By the end of her reign there was no one to rival Victoria in her years of experience and her grasp of statesmanship and international affairs, but these were acquired rather than innate talents.

Victoria once remarked that she was by nature "too passionate" and felt things too intensely. Mistrusting this aspect of her feminine makeup she had a strong dependency on masculine support and guidance. She clearly mistrusted her own impetuosity and her tendency to neurotic outbursts and felt safe only when they were controlled and subordinated by a man. Thus she became the willing acolyte of a succession of male figures: her Uncle Leopold; her prime minister, Lord Melbourne; her husband; her servant, John Brown; and her favorite prime minister, Benjamin Disraeli. Under Albert's tutelage in particular, the queen rejected her former frivolous lifestyle of riding, dancing, and staying up late. It was his guiding ethos of reason and principle, based on his own very rigid moral philosophy, that was to become the template for his refashioning of the young queen into an Albertian archetype.

Victoria was notoriously fickle in her changing affections for her children, but she never relented in her obsessive, uncritical love for Albert. It was the one great constant in her life both before and after his death. But in many ways this love for Albert, like the love she often professed for others, was inverted. It was, as Jerrold suggests, an "appreciation of the satisfaction it gave to herself [rather] than any realisation of the good it should confer on him. She always stood first, occupying the centre of the picture" (1912, 71). Similarly, the queen's many appreciative comments on John Brown and other members of her household were always made in relation to the assiduousness with which they served *her* needs and comforts.

After the death of Prince Albert in 1861, Victoria entered a new emotional phase. Shutting herself off amid a clutter of memento mori, she became the creator of her own unpopular public image during the 1861–1874 period. The insularity and self-absorption of those lost years saw a hardening of the least attractive traits in her personality, characterized by the mindset of "Balmorality." This, in Longford's view, "implied cold stuffiness, simplicity jellied in convention, all pleasure meretricious, all privations purely tiresome" (Longford 1998, 570). "In its narrower sense," she concluded, "[it] meant little more than the awkwardness of a spoilt old lady" (571). And the awkwardness became more pronounced, at a time when the queen could have been drawing more constructively on the love, compassion, and support of those around her. The once ingenuous, impulsive, and charming monarch had evolved into her own caricature: dour, prudish, humorless, and repressive. The healthy strength of will she had shown since girlhood had mutated into a darker force—of stubborn self-interest bolstered by bouts of extreme neurosis and self-pity, in the worst phases of which the queen could be "maddening, cruel, hateful, pitiful, impossible" (Tisdall 1961,105).

But just at the point where her behavior appeared the most difficult, and the British court languished under the palls both of morbidity and "Balmorality," the queen triumphantly reemerged, with even greater regal dignity, as empress of India and the Victoria Regina of the great Jubilees of 1887 and 1897. With renewed vigor she showed herself to still be possessed of many of the great personal strengths of her youth, in particular her most apparent virtues: her human sympathy, honesty, and downright common sense. Although never ceasing to inspire a "reverential fear" in her own children (Marie, Queen of Roumania 1934, 20), she now mellowed into a softly smiling and doting grandmother, who liked nothing better than hearing the sound of noisy children in the nursery upstairs and seeing them romp with her dogs on the lawn. She learned to be more accommodating to, and forgiving of, other people's shortcomings and even on occasions took time to review her own dogmatic preconceptions. On rare occasions she even allowed herself to be subtly persuaded of the good sense of someone else's point of view; that supreme master of tact, Henry Ponsonby, developed the art of being able to persuade Victoria to admit, by a roundabout way, to being in the wrong, without such concessions ever seeming like a change of heart.

It was probably the queen's complete lack of vanity or affectation that remains her most attractive quality; her religious adviser, Randall Davidson, certainly saw it as being the key to her enduring charm, defining it as "the combination of absolute truthfulness and simplicity with the instinctive recognition and quiet assertion of her position as Queen" (Bell 1952, 2:1216). Lady Lyttleton had observed as much, back in 1842: "There is a transparency in her truth that is very striking—not a shade of exaggeration in describing feelings or facts; like very few other people I ever knew. Many may be as true, but I think it goes often along with some reserve. She talks all out; and just as it is, no more no less" (Wyndham 1912, 331). Inaccuracy was something that always infuriated Victoria. She was greatly annoyed that some of the anecdotes about her life, published at the time of her Jubilees in 1887 and 1897, did not get their facts right. She demanded the same kind of verisimilitude in drawings and paintings of herself and her family and complained if artists were too flattering. Her insistence on accuracy, order, and symmetry in all things meant that having once been introduced to someone, she always ascertained who and what they were and inscribed such facts and faces on the "tenacious tablets of her mind" (Oliphant 1900, 140).

Truth was Queen Victoria's touchstone and the one great constant in her personality. She hated sycophancy and shallowness; nothing annoyed her more than hearing people slavishly echo her own opinions, and she secretly admired the honesty of those who dared to contradict her. (One might argue that, in this respect, she acted inconsistently by allowing the sycophantic attentions of Disraeli, but theirs was a very knowing and elaborate game of manners, of which they were both fully aware.) Queen Victoria's love of truthfulness to the point of bluntness, when exercised in her dealings with her household and her children, often led her to hurt people's feelings and seem uncaring. At times her generally good judgment of character would appear to be maddeningly at odds with this rigorous insistence on the truth, when she either failed to see or turned a blind eye to the shortcomings of those who had won her trust. Nothing caused greater resentment among the members of the royal household than the queen's obliviousness to the faults of her two personal servants, John Brown and the Munshi (Abdul Karim), and her preferential treatment of them. But it is thanks precisely to that instinct for truth that we have such a unique record, in her journals, of the queen's reaction to the people and events that shaped her times. They reveal to us no sanitized view of royalty, no carefully constructed projection of herself as infallible monarch, but an entertaining, full-blooded image of a woman who constantly confounds our perception of her and who, in her moments of humility and her inherent shyness, often inspires the deepest admiration and respect.

Related entries:
Albert of Saxe-Coburg-Gotha, Prince Consort; Animals; Brown, John; Gladstone, William Ewart; "Grandmama of Europe"; The Munshi; Religion; Victoria, Queen: As a Monarch; Victoria, Queen: Physical Appearance of; "We Are Not Amused"; "The Widow at Windsor"

References and further reading:

Aronson, Theo. 1973. *The Heart of a Queen: Queen Victoria's Romantic Attachments.* London: John Murray.

Bell, G. K. A. 1952. *Randall Davidson, Archbishop of Canterbury.* 2 vols. Oxford: Oxford University Press.

Charlot, Monica. 1991. *Victoria: The Young Queen.* Cambridge: Polity.

Gosse, Edmund. 1901. "The Character of Queen Victoria." *Quarterly Review* (January–April): 301–337.

Jerrold, Clare. 1912. *The Married Life of Queen Victoria.* London: Eveleigh Nash.

———. 1916. *The Widowhood of Queen Victoria.* London: Eveleigh Nash.

Lee, Sir Sidney. 1902. *Queen Victoria, A Biography.* London: Smith, Elder and Co.

Longford, Elizabeth. [1964] 1998. *Victoria R.I.* London: Weidenfeld and Nicolson.

Marie, Queen of Roumania. 1934. *The Story of My Life.* Vol. 1. London: Cassell.

Munich, Adrienne. 1996. *Queen Victoria's Secrets.* New York: Columbia University Press.

Oliphant, Margaret. 1900. *Queen Victoria, A Personal Sketch.* London: Cassell and Co.

[One of Her Majesty's Servants]. 1901. *The Private Life of Queen Victoria.* London: C. Arthur Pearson.

Ponsonby, Arthur. 1942. *Henry Ponsonby, Queen Victoria's Private Secretary: His Life from His Letters.* London: Macmillan.

St. Aubyn, Giles. 1991. *Queen Victoria: A Portrait.* London: Sinclair Stevenson.

Strachey, Lytton. [1921] 1971. *Queen Victoria.* Harmondsworth, UK: Penguin.

Thompson, Dorothy. 1990. *Queen Victoria: Gender and Power.* London: Virago.

Tisdall, E. E. P. 1961. *Queen Victoria's Private Life.* London: Jarrolds.

Tooley, Sarah. 1896. *The Personal Life of Queen Victoria.* London: Hodder and Stoughton.

Watson, Vera. 1952. *A Queen at Home: An Intimate Account of the Social and Domestic Life at Queen Victoria's Court.* London: W. H. Allen.
Weintraub, Stanley. 1996. *Victoria.* London: John Murray.
Wyndham, Hon. Mrs Hugh, ed. 1912. *The Correspondence of Sarah Spencer, Lady Lyttleton, 1787–1870.* London: John Murray.

Victoria, Queen: Physical Appearance of

Everyone grows but me! (Weintraub 1996, 4)

When she was born in 1819, Princess Victoria was a fat, robust baby, who as a toddler had the most appealing dimples and fair hair. At age ten she still seemed "fresh and round like a red rosebud with flying curls and large luminous eyes," according to her Uncle Leopold's mistress, Karoline Bauer (Charlot 1991, 43). The diarist Charles Greville, describing Victoria at the same time, however, thought the princess a rather "short vulgar-looking child" (Strachey and Fulford 1938 1:293). The lack of height persisted; two years later she was still short for her age. Uncle Leopold, solicitous about the princess's well-being in his many letters to her, worried that she was not getting enough exercise and the correct diet. But Victoria never grew beyond five feet in height; and nine pregnancies and a lifetime's overeating took their toll on her figure, which spread ever outward rather than upward.

Victoria's childhood prettiness slowly faded; her fair hair became became darker and mousier, and although she had a very good complexion, she tended to high color (her redness of face made worse by an intolerance of the heat). Her mouth was small and rabbity, and when she smiled, the princess displayed small, short teeth "like those of a mouse," according to Princess Marie of Roumania (Woolf 1992, 155), and a decidedly unattractive, gummy smile. Victoria's half sister, Feodora, noted Victoria's habit of keeping her mouth always a little open and advised her to try hard to keep it closed, particularly when having her portrait painted. Unfortunately the mouth, when closed, would often seem pursed and prissy in portraits, and the queen's lovely smile would elude the photographer almost until the end of her life.

With her small, doll-like stature, Victoria also had small hands and short pudgy fingers that swelled and reddened with cold in winter; she was also left-handed. In some of her facial characteristics she shared a likeness with her Hanoverian ancestors—the slightly hooked Coburg nose, and the weak, receding chin were features replicated in several of her children, the queen lamenting the latter in her son, Bertie, Prince of Wales. One particular feature, shared most strikingly by Victoria's sons Leopold and Bertie, was her limpid, china-blue eyes. Although they were protuberant (another Hanoverian feature), they compensated for the weakness in Victoria's other features, in portraits often looking almost as though they were welling with tears. In later life the eyes became even more bulgy, the mouth turned down more decidedly, and the chin disappeared into fleshy jowls—contributing to a public image of the queen as a stony-faced and humorless matriarch that did her a great disservice.

In fact, the queen had a lovely, pealing laugh as well as a habit of shrugging her shoulders when she laughed; her voice was universally admired for its sweet, bell-like tones. Her self-confident delivery in public was noticed from her very first Privy Council meeting, held soon after her accession in 1837. At her first state opening of Parliament later that year, the queen's voice was, according to Sallie Stevenson, the wife of the American ambassador, "sweet as a Virginia nightingale's . . . sweet, yet soft; powerful, yet melodious" (Weintraub 1996, 111). The actress Fanny Kemble considered the young queen's voice to be "exquisite"; she had, Kemble said, "not heard any spoken words more musical" (Hardy 1976, 164). And the voice lost none of its attractiveness in old age; in the 1890s the actress Ellen Terry waxed poetic, remarking that it sounded "like a silver stream flowing over golden stones" (164). Because the queen and Prince Albert conversed among themselves and many of their foreign relatives in German, she had a slight German lilt to her voice; her speech and letters were larded with German words and turns of phrase, and she had the habit of using the German interjection "so." In Scotland she often affected a Highland accent and Scottish speech mannerisms, especially when among the locals on the Balmoral estate.

The young queen might have appeared tiny and unprepossessing, but despite her modest and often undistinguished clothes, she had tremendous presence. Princess Lieven, wife of the Russian ambassador, described Victoria as having "an aplomb, an air of command and dignity that, with her childlike face, her tiny figure and pretty smile create one of the most extraordinary impressions it is possible to imagine" (Creston 1952, 287). From her youth on, Victoria displayed great physical and mental energies; her prodigious powers of endurance remained with her almost to the last. Despite being so small in stature, she had a grace of movement and an extraordinary ability to glide across a room. The historian Thomas Carlyle, describing her when they met in 1869, wrote of how the queen had "sailed out towards [him] as if moving on skates" (Hibbert 2000, 483). Such poise had no doubt been acquired through her youthful enthusiasm for dancing (she remained a nimble dancer into old age, even when suffering from rheumatism).

The queen's diet, however, was a different matter. From her early teens on, it was the subject of much anxiety on the part of her Uncle Leopold, who already in 1833 was noting that his niece "eats too *much,* and almost always a little *too fast*" (Woodham-Smith 1972, 92). Her sister, Feodora, worried about the excessive amount of salt Victoria took with her food; she also tried to prevail on Victoria not to eat so much at lunch and dinner and to take more exercise. By 1838, and now queen, Victoria also received lectures on healthy eating from her prime minister, Lord Melbourne, who was not the only person at court to notice that she was putting on weight. He warned her about her Hanoverian family's propensity for overindulgence, but when he suggested she should take more walks, Victoria complained that she got stones in her shoes and that her feet swelled. Although she would never like to take exercise on foot, Victoria had endless energy for long, fast horse rides as a young woman and when at Balmoral in Scotland would go out for hours on pony treks.

Queen Victoria tried to take Melbourne's warning about her weight to heart but complained that she was always hungry. The logic of sensible diet was something with which she could never come to grips. Soon her dresses had to be let out; by the time Victoria started having babies after her marriage in 1840, her midwife predicted that she would now pile on the weight, so much so that she soon gave up wearing stays. Melbourne failed to persuade her to eat more sparingly and so did her royal doctors. With the queen tucking in to four meals a day, by the time she reached her forties and the menopause she looked decidedly matronly. By the 1880s she weighed almost 168 pounds.

The queen had a rather unfortunate reputation for gobbling her food, and court protocol demanded that all plates should be taken away from those dining once the queen had finished eating. This meant that slower eaters never had time to clear their plates and always went hungry. The queen wondered why she suffered so much from indigestion but never slowed down. She was not a great drinker, disliking beer and champagne and preferring sweet ale and mulled wine—banned by Lord Melbourne as being too sickly. Under the influence of her Highland servant, John Brown, she began taking whiskey in her tea and also enjoyed drinking it with soda water. Her prime minister, William Gladstone, was horrified to observe how she even added whiskey to her claret.

The queen's culinary tastes were simple; she liked traditional "nursery" food, such as porridge at breakfast and comforting Brown Windsor soup (although in its richer form, made with game, shell fish, and a dash of Madeira wine). Loyal to all things Scottish, she loved haggis, and barely a day passed without her consuming roast beef or boiled chicken and potatoes (a particular thrill on her Highland jaunts at Balmoral had been to cook them on a portable stove and eat them by the roadside). But Victoria and her weight were hostages to her sweet tooth: chocolate cake, cranberry tart, trifle, sponge cakes, pralines, chocolate ice creams, and ice puddings—from which she was never able to wean herself.

In widowhood, Victoria's daily mealtimes were strictly adhered to: breakfast at 9:30, lunch at 2:00, afternoon tea at 5:30, and dinner at 8:30. The latter, sometimes held later at nearly nine, was strictly timed to take half an hour. It was, by royal standards, a simple affair as the queen grew older. Meals began with soup, followed by fish, a plate of plain, cold roast beef, and then dessert and fruit, the queen enjoying apples and pears and scooping out oranges with the same dexterity with which she dispatched peas.

When the queen's personal physician, Dr. James Reid, politely suggested that she might perhaps take occasional, lighter meals of Benger's food (a thick, milky gruel often given to invalids and the elderly), Victoria took him at his word, and tucked into Benger's *in addition* to her customary daily fare. "If she would follow a diet and live on Benger's Food and chicken all would be well," lamented her maid of honor, Marie Mallet, "but she clings to roast beef and ices!" (Mallet 1968, 195). The queen's appetite only fell away in the last months of her life, from the autumn of 1900 on, when she developed an aversion to almost everything she was offered and lost a great deal of weight.

Queen Victoria enjoyed a wonderfully robust constitution and had the great good fortune to give birth to strong healthy babies (barring her son, Leopold, to whom she unknowingly transmitted hemophilia). In her youth, the longest period during which Victoria was ill was for five weeks in the summer of 1835—probably a case of severe tonsillitis, put down to typhoid fever at the time. Her only other serious illness, up until her death, came in August and September 1870, when she developed a painful abscess in her arm, which did not respond to treatment and finally had to be lanced by Joseph Lister, the pioneer of antiseptic surgery.

As a girl Victoria had had a tendency to blush and gush, and as she grew older became increasingly distressed when hot. It is possible that this might have been the result of some kind of problem with her metabolism (possibly even a symptom of porphyria—see Röhl, Warren, and Hunt 1998). Her hatred of the heat bred in her a strong resistance to cold and an infuriating tolerance of draughts of cold air. This ensured that all the rest of the royal household shivered in her underheated homes while the queen herself paid the price by developing rheumatism—the complaint that most plagued her in old age.

From 1881 until her death, Queen Victoria was well served by her devoted physician, Dr. James Reid. He patiently listened to her daily reports to him on her every complaint and tolerated being called out at all hours of the day and night, often over very trivial problems. Some might argue that he indulged the queen's hypochondria, as had Sir William Jenner before him, but the monitoring of Victoria's aches and pains was part of her safe and familiar everyday routine. All her life the queen suffered from sick headaches—perhaps a liverishness brought on by too much rich food—for which Reid prescribed Tristam's Liver Pills. She was aggravated too by stomach aches, flatulence, and colic—all digestive complaints that again might well have been eased had she stuck to a more sensible diet. Reid recalled how an earlier royal physician, Sir James Clark, had once told the queen, after an attack of indigestion brought on by her consumption of a copious portion of cranberry tart and cream, that she should not eat it again, a fact that had greatly annoyed her. She might never tire of soliciting her doctor's advice on matters of diet but appeared pathologically incapable of following it.

One aspect of the queen's health had particularly preoccupied royal doctors and that was the state of her nerves. Although the neuroses and hysterical outbursts of the first years of her marriage, made worse by bouts of postnatal depression, slowly abated, the doctors shared the queen's own dread that she would succumb to the "Coburg temperament" and the madness of Hanoverian ancestors such as George III. In the days before there was any understanding of women's gynecological problems, such as premenstrual tension, postnatal depression, and the menopause, it is impossible to gauge to what extent the breakdowns in the queen's mental health were an overexaggeration both by her and her doctors of what in fact were symptoms shared by the majority of women. Victoria certainly suffered a severe nervous collapse after the death of her mother, the duchess of Kent, in the spring of 1861, and after the death of Albert at the end of that year had been expected to have another. Yet somehow she held together, carried along by an obsession with grieving that became a new way of life. There is no question that she often used the precarious state of her "nerves" and her professed ill health as excuses for not resuming her public duties. But by the end of the 1880s the queen's emotional state was on a much more even keel and her sense of humor had returned. Old age now brought with it different physical problems, notably insomnia. For this the queen resorted to a plethora of popular proprietary medicines and sedatives, using camphor lozenges, Dover's Powders, bromides, and tincture of henbane, as well as chloral, to help her to sleep. She also drank Mariani wine, fashionable in the 1880s for its supposed medicinal properties (it was in fact made from the coca plant and contained cocaine).

Victoria surprised the members of the royal household with her renewed vigor in the 1890s. At this time, she was, remarked Marie Mallet, "a marvel of health and strength," and "in excellent spirits" (1968, 108, 171–172). Everyone agreed that the queen now seemed happier than she had been for a very long time. Eventually, however, the bouts of rheumatism, sciatica, and gout in her hands and feet, ankles and shoulders left her permanently lame and needing the help of a stick to walk. She now had often to be carried up and down stairs—and in her final few years was wheeled around in a bath chair or used a small pony chair when out of doors.

The queen might complain endlessly about all her niggling aches and pains, but one thing in particular caused her anxiety—her failing eyesight, which from 1892 on degenerated rapidly. All her life she had suffered from sore eyes but complained that she could not find any spectacles that fit properly. Dr. Reid detected cataracts and tried to palliate the queen's fear that she might go blind like George III. He prescribed eye drops of cocaine solution and belladonna, but to no avail. The queen firmly rejected the suggestion of surgery, but by 1893 could hardly read handwriting at all. Refusing to accept that the fault lay with her own eyes, she complained that it was other people's bad handwriting. In the end, she was not able to see well enough either to read or to write her own documents and letters and had to resort to dictating them.

Related entries:
Clark, Sir James; Fresh Air; Hemophilia; Jenner, Sir William; Reid, Sir James; Sex, Pregnancy, and Childbirth; Smoking; Victoria, Queen: Personality of; "We Are Not Amused"

References and further reading:

Charlot, Monica. 1991. *Victoria: The Young Queen.* Cambridge: Polity.

Creston, Dormer. 1952. *The Youthful Victoria.* London: Macmillan.

Hardy, Alan. 1976. *Queen Victoria Was Amused.* London: John Murray.

Hibbert, Christopher. 2000. *Queen Victoria: A Personal History.* London: Viking (esp. chap. 61, "Dinner Parties," and chap. 64, "Failing Health").

Longford, Elizabeth. 1966. "Queen Victoria's Doctors." In Martin Gilbert, ed., *A Century of Conflict, 1850–1950,* 75–87, London: Hamish Hamilton.

———. [1964] 1998. *Victoria R.I.* London: Weidenfeld and Nicolson.

Mallett, Victor, ed. 1968. *Life with Queen Victoria: Marie Mallet's Letters from Court. 1887–1901.* London: John Murray.

Reid, Michaela. 1996. *Ask Sir James: The Life of Sir James Reid, Personal Physician to Queen Victoria.* London: Eland.

Röhl, John C. G., Martin Warren, and David Hunt. 1998. *Purple Secret: Genes, Madness and the Royal Houses of Europe.* London: Bantam.

Stoney, Benita, and Heinrich C. Weltzien, eds. 1994. *My Mistress the Queen: The Letters of Frieda Arnold, Dresser to Queen Victoria 1854–9.* London: Weidenfeld and Nicolson.

Strachey, Lytton, and Roger Fulford, eds. 1938. *The Grenville Memoirs.* 8 vols. London: Macmillan.

Weintraub, Stanley. 1996. *Victoria.* London: John Murray.

Wise, T. J., and J. A. Symington, eds. 1932. *The Brontës, Their Lives, Friendships, and Correspondence.* 4 vols.: The Shakespeare Head Brontë. Oxford: Shakespeare Head Press.

Woodham-Smith, Cecil. 1972. *Queen Victoria: Her Life and Times.* Vol. 1: *1819–1861.* London: Hamish Hamilton.

Woolf, Virginia. 1992. "Royalty." In *A Woman's Essays,* vol 1. Harmondsworth, UK: Penguin.

Victoria Adelaide Mary Louise, Princess Royal (1841–1901)

("Vicky"; from 1860, Crown Princess Frederick of Prussia and, in 1888, Empress Frederick of Prussia)

My poor, dear persecuted daughter (Jerrold 1916, 368)

The gifted and fiercely intelligent Victoria, Princess Royal, was convinced that she was destined to achieve great things when she married the son of the heir to the throne of Prussia in 1858. As the eldest daughter of Queen Victoria and Prince Albert, and the first of their children to marry, she would forge the most powerful dynastic alliance of all the royal children. At the age of only seventeen, Vicky left England an innocent and inexperienced teenager to find herself thrown into the rigid and hostile Prussian court at Berlin. Here, separated from her adored father and her siblings, much of Vicky's life would, at first, be dominated by her tyrannical in-laws (the Emperor William I and his Empress Augusta), and then by a very public battle of political wills—with the German chancellor, Otto von Bismarck—set against the backdrop of the struggle for German unification. But most tragic of all would be Vicky's fraught relationship with, and alienation from, her own son, the future Kaiser William II.

Christened Victoria Adelaide Mary Louise, Vicky was a large healthy baby. The queen quickly got over her initial disappointment that the child was not a boy; the baby was soon nicknamed "Pussy" (or "Puss" or "Pusette") by her doting parents, who found her an entertaining and amusing child. Of all Victoria and Albert's nine children, Vicky was the most prepossessing, manifesting a strength of will, a stubbornness, and a quick temper to equal her mother's. As the firstborn she was also, inevitably, spoiled and would remain her father's favorite. Her liveliness and quickness

Victoria Adelaide, crown princess of Prussia, grew up a gifted and highly intellectual young woman, much loved by her doting father Prince Albert. In later life she could be as stubborn and intractable as her mother and was tragically alienated from her eldest son, Kaiser William II. (Hulton-Deutsch Collection/CORBIS)

of wit attracted much attention; the superintendent of the royal nursery, Lady Lyttleton, noted, when Vicky was only seven, how she "continue[d] to reflect and observe and reason like a very superior person" (Wyndham 1912, 383).

Among her numerous gifts, Vicky showed herself to be a skilled linguist (at ease with English, French, and German), a fine horsewoman, and a most accomplished artist—superior in talent even to the queen. From Prince Albert she inherited a fine analytical mind; she handled mathematics, chemistry, and Latin with facility and could converse with her father on every topic from art to literature, to politics, to science. At the same time, however, she was possessed of an earnestness and a masculinity of thought that made her seem older and wiser than her years and that would prompt the queen's secretary, Sir Henry Ponsonby, to later observe: "I cannot say that she had the same charm as the Queen: in her great seriousness there was too much of the professor about her" (Ponsonby 1927, 243).

For Prince Albert, Vicky was his much-loved *kleine Mädchen* (little girl). And the more exasperated he became with the intellectual ineptitude of his son Bertie, the Prince of Wales, the more he gravitated toward his eldest daughter for company and intelligent conversation. But he did so not without inspiring considerable jealousy in the queen. When he had first taken note of the twelve-year-old Frederick, son of the future William I of Prussia (from 1860), at a royal christening, Prince Albert had set his sights on a fine dynastic marriage for Vicky. The queen supported her husband's choice of a union with the great Hohenzollern family of Prussia and, with it, shared his underlying political ambition of establishing a constitutional monarchy in Prussia through which a strong alliance could be forged between the thrones of Britain and Prussia (later Germany) that would thwart Russian and French ambitions in Europe. He hoped that Vicky and her husband, Fritz, would exert a liberalizing influence over other European monarchies, particularly after the events of the year of revolutions of 1848 had revealed the uneasiness of "the head that wears the crown."

Vicky had first met the husband her parents intended for her when Prince Frederick had visited England for the Great Exhibition of 1851. He visited again in 1855, when it soon became apparent that the fourteen-year-old Vicky was smitten with the handsome and amiable Prussian prince, and he with her. Before leaving, Fritz asked Prince Albert's permission to propose. Although the royal couple were gratified that this had fortuitously turned out to be a love match, they insisted that no marriage could take place until Vicky was seventeen. Although she never said as much, it was clear that Victoria had apprehensions about submitting her daughter to sexual life and childbirth at such an immature age and felt guilty at sending Vicky away from her siblings. When the Prussian royal family suggested that the marriage should take place in Berlin, the queen exploded with right royal indignation: "The assumption of it's being *too much* for a Prince Royal of Prussia to *come* over to marry the *Princess Royal of Great Britain* IN England is too absurd, to say the least. . . . Whatever may be the usual practice of Prussian Princes, it is not *every* day that one marries the eldest daughter of the Queen of England" (Benson and Esher 1911, 3:253). Instead, Vicky and Fritz were married, with considerable ostentation, in the Chapel Royal, St. James's Palace, on 25 January 1858—the last show of conspicuous royal pomp, as things would turn out, until the queen's Golden Jubilee in 1887. After a short, two-day honeymoon and a few days at Windsor, the childlike Vicky departed for Berlin, in a gale of tears—both her own and her mother's—brokenhearted at leaving her darling papa.

Vicky spent the first months of her married life incarcerated in the great, gloomy, drafty royal palace in Berlin, until refurbishments to their own nearby home—the nearby Kronprinzen Palais—were completed. They moved there in November 1848 after Vicky's eighteenth birthday. But this palace, too, was never held in any great affection by Vicky and Fritz, the home that they most enjoyed for their thirty years of married life being Frederick the Great's 200-room Neues Palais, in the park of Sans Souci at Potsdam—where the Prussian court decamped every summer. Admired as Germany's answer to the great French palace of Versailles, it had fallen into disrepair during the reign of Fritz's father, and together, Vicky and Fritz would restore it to its eighteenth-century rococco grandeur.

The arrival at the stiff and starchy court of Berlin of a daughter of the English queen, as future empress of Prussia, was not universally welcomed. The problem, for Vicky, would be one of assimilation. Bismarck divined correctly that Prussia's new crown princess would have to reconcile her divided loyalties: "If the Princess can leave the Englishwoman at home and become a Prussian, then she may be a blessing to the country" (Fulford 1964, 18). But that is not how things turned out: despite embracing German art and culture, Vicky would often appear to be an opinionated and meddlesome Englishwoman, whereas on visits to England she would often antagonize her own family by praising all things Prussian. Such contradictory behavior would cause Vicky much self-inflicted heartache. From the outset the mission set for her by Prince Albert was stymied; the highly conservative Prussian court disapproved of her emancipated attitudes as a woman, as well as her cultural aspirations, remaining unrepentant in its disinterest in art, philosophy, and history. Nevertheless, Vicky built up a fine library and in her own literary salon courted intellectual interlocutors with whom she maintained her broad interest in politics, religion and economics, history and biography, medicine and political economy.

Shortly after Vicky's marriage, much as her mother had dreaded, the young bride entered into an endless round of pregnancy and childbirth. She produced eight children in rapid succession: William (1859), Charlotte (1860), Henry (1862), Sigismund (1864), Victoria (known as Moretta; 1866), Waldemar (1868), Sophie (1870), and Margaret (1872). The queen monitored Vicky's first pregnancy with particular apprehension, her fears proving well founded when Vicky gave birth to her son William after an agonizing and protracted labor, during which one of William's shoulders was dislocated, leaving him with a withered arm. Of her children, the first three would prove a great disappointment to Vicky, all of them sharing a distaste for their mother's liberalizing mission in Prussia. Tragically, Vicky's two younger and adored sons both would die young: Sigismund of meningitis at only twenty-one months of age and Waldemar of diphtheria at the age of eleven.

The militaristic Prussian state that was Vicky's new home had reinforced itself after a failed revolution in 1848 and was now dominating central Europe. A limited constitution had been reintroduced under Fritz's father, William I, but tentative moves toward a more democratic form of government were cut short with the appointment of Bismarck as minister-president in 1862. Intent on the unification of Germany's thirty-nine states under Prussian domination, he led Prussia on a series of military campaigns—the 1864 war over the Danish duchies of Schleswig and Holstein, the 1866 Seven Weeks' War with Austria, and the Franco-Prussian War of 1870–1871. These combined to crush the reformist liberal tendency under a tide of militarism and with it Fritz and Vicky's aspirations.

Vicky encountered other difficulties in Berlin, many of them stemming from her own difficult personality. Her stubborn streak made it impossible for her to compromise over her own fixed principles, and her impetuosity about saying what she thought would, time and again, offend her adoptive country, particularly when she indulged in tactless criticism of Prussian historical tradition. Brought up with an excess of confidence about her own intellectual superiority, Vicky was incapable of appreciating the opposite point of view, an intolerance accentuated by her often high-handed manner and her sententiousness, particularly when criticizing the undoubted philistinism of the Prussian court. This propensity for tactless criticism would contribute to her extreme isolation in widowhood. Yet, ironically, Vicky was in fact intensely loyal to Prussia. The difficulty, as her niece, Princess Marie Louise, observed, was that she was plagued by a nagging sense of dissatisfaction with both her national identities: "When she was in Berlin, everything in England was perfect: when she was in England, everything German was equally perfect" (Marie Louise 1961, 76).

The deaths of her father in 1861 and her adored baby son Sigismund in 1866 were terrible blows that Vicky tried to mitigate by throwing herself into philanthropic work. Since the Crimean War she had been a great admirer of Florence Nightingale, whom she met in 1868. During the Seven Weeks' War of 1866, Vicky helped set up hospitals for the wounded, raised money for their nursing care, and established a fund for those who were disabled. The bitter Franco-Prussian War of 1870–1871 also provided Vicky with a chance to demonstrate the altruism and compassion at the heart of her abrasive personality, when she set about improving conditions in the hospital at Homburg where many of the wounded were taken. Despite being consumed with anxiety for Fritz at the front, she also appealed for money to support the families of ordinary Prussian soldiers. She was intensely proud when Fritz returned at the end of this conflict crowned with glory. (Germany was unified soon afterward, with the incorporation of the south German states under Bismarck's chancellorship.) In the postwar years, Vicky lobbied for women's higher education and the establishment of nurses' training in Germany, setting up the Victoria House and Nursing School in Berlin (1881), which trained the Victoria nurses named after her. Health care, sanitary reform, and welfare in the community also preoccupied her, and in 1875 she initiated the Society for Promoting Health in the Home, as well as founding many other regional hospitals, workhouses, kindergartens, and schools.

But in the late 1870s tragedy again struck, with the death of Vicky's sister Alice in 1878 (of diphtheria), closely followed by the loss of another of her sons, Waldemar (who died in 1879 of the same disease). Much like her mother after the death of Prince Albert, Vicky was propelled into total nervous collapse by her bereavement, from which she never fully recovered. Such suffering heightened Vicky's fraught relationship with both her mother-in-law and her eldest son and aroused a great deal of compassion in Queen Victoria; it greatly strengthened the bond between the two women as they aged. But during the 1880s, things got worse: Vicky's persistent inability to curb her own outspoken criticisms of Bismarck's absolutist regime isolated her further in Berlin. Her bitterness deepened over the ingratitude of the Prussian court for all she had done, over the accusations that she was a domineering wife, and at the arrogance of her eldest son, who had now become the creature of the much-hated Bismarck. She became dispirited at her persistent demonization: "I am an English woman, suspected of liberal, of free-thinking and artistic tendencies; of cosmopolitan and humanitarian sentiments and the like abominations in the eyes of Bismarck; so I am labelled 'suspicious' and 'dangerous' by the clique who are all-powerful now" (Ponsonby 1927, 259). She laid much of the blame for her alienation from her son William at Bismarck's door; yet her natural intelligence had taught her that Bismarck, despite his xenophobia, was a man of great, if misapplied, gifts. Meanwhile, such was the degree of suspicion in which Bismarck held Vicky, as empress-in-waiting, that she became seriously concerned about the safety of her personal papers from spies at court. In 1887, when they went to England for Queen Victoria's Golden Jubilee celebrations, Vicky and Fritz took many of these papers with them, depositing them for safekeeping at Windsor.

Vicky and Fritz never anticipated having to spend twenty-eight years as emperor and empress-in-waiting, during which time they were kept firmly under the thumb of the soldier-emperor, William I, and his domineering wife, Augusta (who remained legendarily hostile to Vicky). But on 9 March 1888, the ninety-one-year-old William finally died. Queen Victoria could not contain her sense of triumph at her daughter's succession. "My OWN dear *Empress Victoria,*" she wrote to her; "You know *how* little I care for rank or titles, but I cannot *deny* that *after all* that has been done and said, I am *thankful* & *proud* that dear Fritz & you should have come to the throne" (Pakula 1996, 463). The sense of euphoria was, for Vicky and Fritz, muted by profound personal anxieties. His accession had come far too late. "Yes, we are our own masters now," Vicky replied to the queen, "but shall we not have to leave all the work undone which we have so long and so carefully been preparing? Will there be any chance of doing the right thing, any time to carry out useful measures, needful reforms?" (Ponsonby 1928, 293). Vicky's sense of urgency was now heightened by the fact that for months Fritz had been desperately ill with throat cancer. During her husband's short, ninety-ninety-day reign as emperor, Vicky refused to accept the inevitable, grasping at each tiny sign of remission as a false dawn. She rarely left Fritz's side, battling to hide her anguish: "I have to rush away to hide my tears often," she wrote to the queen; "I feel so like a wreck, a sinking ship, so wounded and struck down, so sore of heart, as if I were bleeding from a thousand wounds" (Ponsonby 1928, 315). After Fritz's death on 15 June 1888, Vicky's future without him seemed utterly bleak: "I must stumble on my way alone" (316). The queen saw only too clearly what a terrible personal disaster this was for Vicky: "My poor child's whole future gone, ruined, which they had prepared themselves for nearly thirty years!" (Hibbert 1984, 312).

Now a widow at the age of forty-seven, and her mission in Germany in ruins, Vicky withdrew from affairs of state. Forced to give up the Neues Palais at Potsdam, she could only watch in horror as her son William proceeded to overturn many of her and Fritz's liberal policies. Alone and powerless, she wrote to the queen: "I pass hours of utter listlessness" (Ponsonby 1928, 322). "The future," she told her friend Mary Ponsonby, "has only terrors for me" (Ponsonby 1927, 269). Things were no better a year later: "I feel like a miserable rag of my former self" (275). Vicky was loath to return to the palace in Berlin after Fritz's death but was not particularly well provided for financially. Fortunately, a bequest from a friend enabled her, in 1889, to start building a new home for herself—Friederichshof in the Taunus Mountains. Installing herself in 1894, Vicky made her home, much as her mother had done at Balmoral and Osborne, a memorial to her dead husband and their happy life together. Here she finally enjoyed a degree of release from the machinations at court and found consolation in her three younger daughters and her grandchildren. In her final years, although she became further alienated from her son, Kaiser William, Vicky mellowed in her view of Bismarck, now regarding him as the lesser of the two evils. She and William were a lost cause to each other, Vicky proving stubborn in her refusal to seek out her son's good qualities and seeing only his bad points. Her alarm at William's "chauvinistic megalomania" (Benson 1939, 231) was in some ways justified. In 1899 she was alarmed by the intense anti-British feeling now being whipped up in Germany: "The continual abuse showered on *everything* English *every* day makes me so savage that it scatters all my tolerance, philosophy and patience to the winds, and I long to be a man sometimes and *knock someone down*" (Ponsonby 1927, 286). Vicky's warnings about the dangerous course on which her son had embarked went unheeded. And then she fell sick. She had never enjoyed good health, for many years suffering from a multitude of complaints, some very severe and debilitating. (Recent scholarship [see Röhl, Warren, and Hunt 1998; "Hemophilia"]) suggests that Vicky displayed many of the symptoms of variegate porphyria.) After a bad fall from a horse in the autumn of 1898, a thorough medical examination had revealed that Vicky had breast cancer, which soon spread into her spine; sparing her mother, she euphemistically described her illness as "lumbago." The reality was terrible: Vicky's doctors refused to give her large enough doses of morphia to relieve the excrutiating bouts of pain, which she described as being "like ever so many razors driven into my back" (Packard 1998, 308).

With many of her friends now dead or fallen silent under William's despotic regime, Vicky's final months were lived from one bout of agonizing pain to the next, made worse by her intense loneliness. She now found it unbearable to "open the flood-gates of all the pain and bitterness, the stinging regrets that fill my soul" (Ponsonby 1927, 283–284). "So one lives on—a diminished and crippled existence," (ibid.) she sadly resolved. But she had not lost her faith, or her compassion, and professed herself "still ready to do what is possible for the happiness of others, and still able to rejoice in what is beautiful and great and true and noble; still anxious for ideals to be realised and eager to see the right triumph and truths to be recognised, wrongs redressed, and suffering relieved as much as can be" (284).

As soon as Vicky drew her last breath, only six months after the death of the queen, William ordered the palace to be secured and a search made for her private papers. But in this, at least, she had outwitted him. Neither Bismarck nor Willam had liked the incessant flow of letters between Vicky and friends and family in England and had long wanted to lay hold of Vicky's letters to the queen and suppress their contents, which William knew reflected badly on him. When she lay dying, Vicky asked her brother, the Prince of Wales, when he visited, to ensure that all copies of her letters to the queen be taken to England, where they were eventually published in 1928. The thousands of letters that Vicky had received from Queen Victoria were also carefully preserved by Vicky's daughter Margaret, at her home in Hesse, until World War II, when they were sent to the royal archives at Windsor for safety from bombing.

In 1928 Frederick Ponsonby summed up the tragedy of Vicky's unhappy life in Germany. Despite all her good intentions and her very genuine desire to be of service to her adoptive country, she had remained, for the German people, "*die Englanderin*" (the Englishwoman, 469). If given the opportunity, she might have played a far more significant role in the future security of the German throne: "She was a Cassandra to whom none would listen: an Andromache for whom none had sympathy. Her Liberal counsels, if followed, might have averted the wrath to come" (474). In 1914 her son William would be at war with her nephew, King George V.

Related entries:
Alice Maud Mary, Princess; Bismarck, Prince Otto Edward Leopold von; Crimean War; Frederick William, Crown Prince of Prussia; Hemophilia; Palmerston, Henry John Temple, Third Viscount; William II, Emperor of Germany

References and further reading:
Bennett, Daphne. 1971. *Vicky: Princess Royal of England and German Empress.* New York: St. Martin's Press.

———. 1980 *Queen Victoria's Daughters.* London: Gollancz.
Benson, A. C., and Viscount Esher, eds. 1911. *The Letters of Queen Victoria: A Selection from Her Majesty's Correspondence between the Years 1837 and 1861.* 1st ser., 3 vols. London: John Murray.
Benson, E. F. 1939. *Queen Victoria's Daughters.* London: Cassell.
Corti, Egon Caesar Conte. 1957. *The English Empress: A Study in Relations between Queen Victoria and Her Eldest Daughter, Empress Frederick of Germany.* London: Cassell and Co.
Epton, Nina. 1971. *Victoria and Her Daughters.* London: Weidenfeld and Nicolson.
Fulford, Roger. 1964. *Dearest Child: Letters between Queen Victoria and the Princess Royal, 1858–61.* London: Evans Brothers.
———. 1968. *Dearest Mama: Private Correspondance of Queen Victoria and the Crown Princess of Prussia, 1861–64.* London: Evans Brothers.
———. 1971. *Your Dear Letter: Private Correspondence of Queen Victoria and the Crown Princess of Prussia, 1865–71.* London: Evans Brothers.
———. 1976. *Darling Child: Private Correspondence of Queen Victoria and the Crown Princess of Prussia, 1871–78.* London: Evans Brothers.
———. 1981. *Beloved Mama: Private Correspondence of Queen Victoria and the German Crown Princess, 1878–85.* London: Evans Brothers.
Hibbert, Christopher. 1984. *Queen Victoria in Her Letters and Journals.* London: Viking.
Lee, Arthur Gould, ed. 1955. *The Empress Frederick Writes to Sophie, Her Daughter, Crown Princess and Queen of the Hellenes: Letters 1889–1901.* London: Faber.
Marie Louise, Princess. 1961. *My Memories of Six Reigns.* Harmondsworth, UK: Penguin.
Packard, Jerrold. 1998. *Victoria's Daughters.* New York: St. Martin's Press.
Pakula, Hannah. 1996. *An Uncommon Woman, The Empress Frederick: Daughter of Queen Victoria.* London: Weidenfeld and Nicolson.
Ponsonby, Magdalen. 1927. *Mary Ponsonby: A Memoir, Some Letters and a Journal.* London: John Murray.
Ponsonby, Sir Frederick. 1928. *Letters of the Empress Frederick.* London: Macmillan and Co.
Ramm, Agatha. 1990. *Beloved and Darling Child: Last Letters between Queen Victoria and Her Eldest Daughter, 1886–1901.* Stroud, Gloucestershire: Sutton.
Röhl, John C. G., Martin Warren, and David Hunt. 1998. *Purple Secret: Genes, Madness and the Royal Houses of Europe.* London: Bantam.
Sinclair, Andrew. 1981. *The Other Victoria: The Princess Royal and the Great Game of Europe.* London: Weidenfeld and Nicolson.
Wyndham, Hon. Mrs. Hugh, ed. 1912. *The Correspondence of Sarah Spencer, Lady Lyttleton, 1787–1870.* London: John Murray.

Victoria and Albert Museum

this fine Museum which is to bear the name of my dear Husband and myself (Nevill 1997, 192)

During 1853–1854, the prime minister, William Gladstone, was considering the redevelopment of a twelve-acre site in South Kensington for a vast new army barracks. Local well-to-do residents protested, alarmed at the prospect of having the army, and with it the inevitable attendant problems of prostitution and drinking, on their doorsteps. Prince Albert, however, had his own plans for developing this and the surrounding area (in all an eighty-acre site stretching south from Hyde Park) into one vast complex of colleges and museums—using the profits from the Great Exhibition of 1851. He had plans in particular for a new museum and national art gallery that would promote excellence in design and handicrafts and, it was hoped, go some way toward bolstering British trade in the face of the increasingly competitive European market. Like all Albert's grandiose schemes, it would be a new civic building that would also emphasize the grand sweep of the British Empire.

Parliament allotted £15,000 of the considerable profits from the Great Exhibition for the development of this new museum, which would display many of the artifacts that had been donated to the Crown by exhibitors after the Great Exhibition closed. Prince Albert asked the architect Gottfried Semper to produce some ideas for this new building, along the lines of the Palais Royal (in Paris). He hoped that the building would also house various London art collections (including those of Marlborough House and Somerset House) and include

One of Prince Albert's lasting cultural legacies is the Victoria and Albert Museum at South Kensington in London. (Hulton-Deutsch Collection/CORBIS)

shop units and even living accommodation. A year later Semper produced drawings of an ambitious building of iron and glass (inspired no doubt by the Crystal Palace), but it was rejected on the grounds of expense.

Instead, a rather unappealing and functional, temporary iron structure was erected on the site and opened by Queen Victoria in June 1857, as the South Kensington Museum. Soon nicknamed the "Brompton Boilers" for its unesoteric exterior, it was put under the directorship of Sir Henry Cole, who, over the next twenty years, would invest great energy and enthusiasm in seeing to fruition the creation of Albert's vision. Cole entrusted a team of engineers and artists with the task of constructing a succession of utilitarian courts with their own individual courtyards, as galleries devoted mainly to arts and handicrafts. The earliest is a red-brick picture gallery, the Sheepshanks (1857–1858). Other galleries were added: the Vernon and Turner (1858–1859), the North and South Courts (1861–1862), and the East Court (1868–1873). In this way, the museum was extended piecemeal up until 1884, with designs by a team of Royal Engineers led by Capt. Francis Fowke. The interiors were decorated by leading designers and artists of the day—Frederick Leighton, William Morris, Sir Edward Poynter—who produced murals, stained glass windows, wall hangings, and glazed ceramic tiles.

The core of the museum's original collection was the artifacts from the Museum of Manufactures, which had been opened at Marlborough House in 1852, and the collection of the School of Design, which had been housed at Somerset House. Under Cole's directorship and through the purchase of various collections as well as private donation, a major collection was built up, with the guiding premise that it should "be confined to objects wherein Fine Art is supplied to some purpose of utility" (Weinreb and Hibbert 1983, 914). The increasingly eclectic collection at the South Kensington Museum grew by degrees over a considerable period between 1857 and 1909, eventually becoming an Aladdin's cave of treasures that had outgrown its living space. The uninspiring original iron building had been considered too industrial in appearance to house such a splendid collection, and in 1867 it was dismantled.

The emphasis of the museum's art collection would be postclassical European art, with particularly fine collections of rare Persian and Indian art. It also boasted a collection of tapestries—in particular works of the pre-Raphaelite school by Edward Burne Jones and William Morris. Other notable collections are rare carpets from Central Asia and beyond, Chinese and Japanese laquerwork, Italian sculpture, ivories from ancient Rome and Byzantium, Gothic sandstone carvings, medieval stained glass windows, English and Chinese porcelain, exquisite Georgian and Queen Anne furniture, English needlepoint lace, ecclesiastical silver, Flemish brass, and English watercolors, paintings, and miniatures. The museum also boasts a wonderful costume gallery, a unique library of books on fine and applied art, and a priceless collection of early photographs. It also originally housed scientific exhibits, which were eventually moved to their own site—a new Science Museum—that was expanded between 1913 and 1977.

In 1891, a competition held for a design for the main frontage of the museum received submissions from eight architects. It was won by Sir Aston Webb, who produced a grand Renaissance-style design in terracotta brick. The foundation stone of the new building was laid on 17 May 1899 by Queen Victoria, who, as it turned out, was making her last public appearance at an official ceremony. At her insistence the museum was renamed the Victoria and Albert Museum. This new 700-foot frontage, facing the Cromwell Road, rich in carved historical figures and images of empire, was not completed until 1909, when it was officially opened by King Edward VII and Queen Alexandra.

Related entries:
Art and Artists; Great Exhibition

References and further reading:

Burton, Anthony. 1999. *Vision and Accident: The Story of the Victoria and Albert Museum.* London: Victoria and Albert Publications.

Cocks, Anna Somers. 1980. *The Victoria and Albert Museum, the Making of the Collection.* Leicester, UK: Windward.

Jackson, Anna. 1996. *Victoria and Albert: A Hundred Highlights.* London: Victoria and Albert Museum.

Michael, Kaufman, and Julius Bryant. 1952. *The History of the Victoria and Albert Museum.* London: Her Majesty's Stationery Office.

———. 1991. *The Victoria and Albert Museum.* London: Scala Books.

Weinreb, Ben, and Christopher Hibbert, eds. 1983. *The London Encyclopedia.* London: Macmillan.

Victoria Cross

For Valour (Benson and Esher 1911 3:160)

The Victoria Cross (VC)—the highest honor that can be awarded to a member of the British or Commonwealth forces—was awarded for combatants in all the skirmishes and colonial wars—both large and small—that punctuated Queen Victoria's reign, in countries such as China, Persia, Japan, Abyssinia, South Africa, India, Burma, Tibet, Mesopotamia, and many other outreaches of Britain's vast empire. But there was one military campaign above all in which the number of awards outstripped all others: the Crimean War. It is a mark not just of the heroism of the men who fought there

Queen Victoria, mounted side-saddle, distributes the Victoria Cross to veterans of the Crimean War at a special ceremony held in Hyde Park in the summer of 1857. (The* **Illustrated London News** *Picture Library)

but also a symbol of how terrible that conflict must have been, that 111 were awarded the VC for acts of heroism.

A general Crimean War Medal, for all participants in the war, had been instituted at Prince Albert's suggestion after the queen was deeply moved by the sufferings of her troops there in the first months of the conflict and expressed a wish to reward their courage. In a letter of 30 November 1854, not long after the British victory at the battle of Inkerman, Queen Victoria wrote that "no time should be lost in announcing the intention of the Queen to confer a medal on all those who have been engaged in the arduous and brilliant campaign in the Crimea" (Benson and Esher 1911, 3:56). Her original desire had been for a design similar to the Peninsular Medal awarded during the Napoleonic Wars, which would have accompanying clasps on which the names Alma and Inkerman and any subsequent victories in the Crimea could be inscribed. Officially sanctioned on 15 December 1854, the Crimean War Medal was eventually awarded to 275,000 men, some of these presented to the wounded in hospital by the queen herself, in what was seen as a morale-boosting gesture that would also help recruitment. A Baltic Medal was also instituted for those who had taken part in the naval campaign. But the most coveted British military award would be—and remains to this day—the VC.

Such had been the levels of heroic sacrifice by British troops during what became a protracted and bitter conflict, that on 5 February 1856, just before peace negotiations began, the Victoria Cross was instituted. Prince Albert had been anxious for a more specific award to be made to heroes of the Crimea, and with typical efficiency, in 1855 he had drawn up a five-point memorandum on the subject, detailing the award as being for "officers or men who have served in the presence of the enemy and then shall have performed some signal act of valour or devotion to their country" (Weintraub 1997, 325). What made the award special was that it was given without any consideration of the rank of the person involved—to men in the army and navy, both commissioned and noncommissioned, as well as to private soldiers. The medal would also take precedence over all other British military awards and brought with it, from 1857 on, a pension of £10 per year.

On 29 January 1856 the queen signed the necessary royal warrant instituting the VC, and several of the first awards were made retrospectively (although not posthumously—this did not come into practice until 1920) to men who had performed acts of gallantry in the first days of the war in 1854. In 1867 a Commonwealth VC was introduced for members of the British forces in other parts of the empire.

The medal is of simple design and was traditionally made from the melted-down bronze of Russian guns captured at Sebastopol in September 1855; enough of this original metal remains, apparently, to make another eighty or more VCs. The shape is that of a Maltese Cross with the royal crown, surmounted by a lion, in the center, under which can be seen the words "For Valour," at Queen Victoria's suggestion, written in a scroll (she had rejected the original inscription "For the Brave" as suggesting that only those deemed brave in the war had been given the award). At the time of its unveiling the VC was criticized in the *Times* as being "dull, heavy, tasteless . . . the most shapeless mass that size admits of" (Weintraub 1997, 325). The queen had thought the abbreviation of "V.C." as smacking too much of the term *vice chancellor* and had tried without success to have it changed to B.V.C.—Bearer of the Victoria Cross.

The first person honored with the medal was a seaman—the twenty-year-old ship's mate Charles Lucas of the steam frigate HMS *Hecla*—who, during a naval attack on Russian fortifications at Bomarsund on the Aaland Islands in June 1854, had picked up a shell that had landed on the gun deck, its fuse burning, and thrown it overboard. Lucas was immediately promoted to lieutenant and eventually retired from the navy as a rear admiral. The youngest recipient of the VC would be Arthur Fitzgibbon, aged fifteen, in 1861.

The first VCs, individually made to this day by Hancocks of Burlington Gardens, London, were awarded by the queen on 26 June 1857, on an oppressively hot summer day in Hyde Park. The queen, on horseback, reached down from the saddle to personally pin each medal upon sixty-two men at this special ceremony, in front of 12,000 seated guests. Many of the recipients were veterans of the battles at Inkerman and the assault on the Great Redan at Sebastopol. The queen was greatly moved by the experience:

> "What a *beautiful* and *touching* sight and ceremony (the first of the kind ever witnessed in England) the distribution of the Medals was. From the highest Prince of the Blood to the lowest Private, all received the same distinction for the bravest conduct in the severest actions, and the rough hand of the brave and honest private soldier came for the first time in contact with that of their Sovereign and Queen! Noble fellows! I own I feel as if they were *my own children;* my heart beats for *them* as for my *nearest and dearest.* They were so touched, so pleased; many, I hear, cried. . . . Several came by in a sadly mutilated state" (journal, 26 June 1857).

Although the Crimean War would account for the greatest number of VCs awarded until World War I, the highest number of medals to be awarded for a single action would be the eleven won at Rorke's Drift in 1879 during the Zulu War.

The most recent awards of the Victoria Cross were made to two British soldiers during the 1982 Falklands War.

Related entries:
Crimean War

References and further reading:

Benson, A. C., and Viscount Esher, eds. 1911. *The Letters of Queen Victoria 1837–1861.* 1st ser., 3 vols. London: John Murray.

O'Byrne, Robert. [1880] 1965. *The Victoria Cross; An Official Chronicle of the Deeds of Personal Valour Achieved during the Crimean and Baltic Campaigns, 1856 to 1880.* London: Frederick Muller.

Reid, D. I. 1981. *The Victoria Cross 1856–1981: A Select Bibliography.* London: School of Library and Information Studies.

Smyth, John. 1965. *The Victoria Cross 1856–1964.* London: Frederick Warne.

Weintraub, Stanley. 1997. *Albert: Uncrowned King.* London: John Murray.

W

"We Are Not Amused"

(Popular Expression, Attributed to Queen Victoria)

In his anonymously published tribute to Queen Victoria in the *Quarterly Review* that appeared soon after her death, the writer Edmund Gosse mourned the fact that in all the mass of iconography relating to the queen's life, including the many official photographs taken of her, her smile was nowhere to be seen. "No shadow of it is preserved for posterity in any one of her published likenesses" (1901, 315) he wrote at the time. This is not strictly true, for there were at least two photographs of the queen—one taken in 1886 with her daughter Beatrice, granddaughter Princess Victoria, and great-granddaughter Alice; another taken in an open carriage in 1898—in which the queen is smiling (see Gernsheim and Gernsheim 1954, plates 256 and 313; also in Hardy 1976, plates 19 and 20). But the face in the photographs is strangely unfamiliar, and Gosse is right to observe that, in general, "under the evil spell of the photographic camera" the queen's smile "disappeared altogether" (Gosse 1901, 315).

The prevailing image of the queen that has come down to us is that of a somber monarch in old age, whose fleshy jowls and widow's bonnets did nothing to enhance a facial expression that seemed to be unremittingly miserable. During the long years of the queen's retreat from public view to grieve the loss of Prince Albert, the British public might rightly have believed that their glum queen was incapable of seeing the fun in anything. Nothing, in fact, could be further from the truth. There is plenty of evidence to support an image of the aging queen that is in total contradiction to this.

The phrase "We are not amused," so often attributed to Queen Victoria, is probably apocryphal, although she said something similar on more than one occasion in order to point out the indiscretion of some joke or comment made in the presence of herself and her ladies-in-waiting. When interviewed in 1978, Victoria's granddaughter Princess Alice said that she had once asked the queen about the phrase and was assured by her that she had never said it. But once gaining popular currency, it persisted, no doubt because it so readily fitted the general perception of the queen as having no sense of humor. Since her death, it has become the most overused catchphrase called upon to define not only the queen's personality but also, by association, the staid attitudes of Victorian middle England. As Alan Hardy observed, "this phrase has hung like a millstone round the neck of her reputation. It has damned Victoria as 'Let them eat cake' damned Marie Antoinette" (1976, 1). (In her 2001 biography of the French queen, Antonia Fraser revealed that Marie

Antionette in fact never made that damning remark.)

The catchphrase appears to have originated in 1889 when word got back to Queen Victoria that one of her equerries—probably Alick Yorke—had a talent for mimicking her. The story, already well known in royal circles, was first recounted in the anonymously published *Notebooks of a Spinster Lady* ([Holland] 1909). A fuller version can be found in the memoirs of Lillie Langtry. She related that, one evening at dinner at Buckingham Palace, the queen turned to the equerry and said: "'I understand that you give a very good imitation of me. Will you do it now?' . . . The trembling victim proceeded to give a greatly modified and extremely bad imitation," wrote Langtry, to which the queen said "in a freezing tone '*We* are not amused'" (Langtry 1978, 62–63). The queen's remark was rapidly mistinterpreted as demonstrating her lack of a sense of humor, when in fact she was voicing her disapproval, not of the joke itself but of the manner in which it was told at table. Her objection to the telling of risqué jokes by male members of the royal household, within her earshot, was similar—the queen deemed it indelicate for jokes that might cause ladies embarrassment to be made in their presence. Privately, the queen loved humorous anecdotes; as Hardy asserted: "She personally had a partiality for quite broad jokes"; it was simply that she "always regarded it as her paramount duty to retain decorum at Court" (1976, 8).

The young Princess Victoria has often been described as bright, vivacious, and merry. She enjoyed the collective "mirth" of "gay conversation, music, jokes, dancing, laughter" (Woodham-Smith 1972, 111); she adored parties and fancy dress balls and staying up late, all of which were most welcome diversions in an otherwise dull and often secluded life. The photographer Charles Knight recorded that as a young girl, Victoria's "merry laugh" was "as fearless as the notes of the thrush in the groves around her" (Charlot 1991, 52). Such good humor continued into the early years of her reign; the young queen loved outings to the theater, laughing heartily at farces and pantomime and enjoying pleasantries with her ladies-in-waiting. The diarist Thomas Creevey wrote: "A more homely little being you never beheld when she is at her ease, and she is evidently dying to be always more so. She laughs in real earnest, opening her mouth as wide as it can go, showing not very pretty gums' (Creston 1952, 261). In 1843, on a trip with Prince Albert to France, people observed how gay and happy she was, "as amused as a child could be" (St. Aubyn 1991, 240). Inevitably, this childlike gaiety gave way to more serious preoccupations; marriage and motherhood eroded the queen's natural gaiety, and her husband was influential in weaning Victoria away from her more idle, pleasurable pursuits, advocating a greater air of circumspection and sedateness in public that better befitted a queen of England.

By the time the queen was widowed in 1861, it seemed as though her gaiety had gone forever. Her disappearance from public view into deep mourning established a legend that she had no sense of humor and no tolerance of the enjoyment of simple fun in others. It was not until the darkest years of her widowhood were over that Victoria's childlike delight in things once more began bubbling to the surface. She proved to be as giggly and girlish in her seventies as she had been in her teens, most often at her ladies' dinners, where, in the company of the female members of the royal household, she enjoyed gossip and funny stories that, as Marie Mallet remembers, would make her eyes beam and her face light up with amusement. The enjoyment of a risqué joke would often make her laugh heartily. So uncontrollable could her laughter be at times—particularly when struggling to remain deadpan through absurd foreign ceremonials or when listening to the faux pas of foreign visitors struggling with their bad English—that Victoria would have to stifle it in a napkin or handkerchief, and when no longer able to restrain it, the tears would often roll down the queen's face. She was also a master of the witty riposte, such as on the occasion when, hearing a piece of modern music that she did not like, she had asked "What is that"—"It is a drinking song, Ma'am, by Rubinstein" came the reply. "Nonsense," retorted the queen, "no such thing! Why, you'd not drink a cup of tea to *that!*" (Gosse 1901, 317).

The queen's daughter Princess Helena remarked on her mother's "wonderful capacity for enjoying things" (St. Aubyn 1991, 240)—right to the end of her life. And Ethel Smyth, who met her at Balmoral in 1891, admitted to being quite taken aback by the "the sweetest, most entrancing smile I have ever seen on a human face" (1987, 186). It was a smile by all accounts that lit up the queen's face and showed every nuance of feeling; had we had more photographic evidence of it, the queen's posthumous reputation as a killjoy might never have arisen.

Related entries:
Battenburg, Henry Mauice, Prince of; Dancing; Theater; "The Widow at Windsor"

References and further reading:

Charlot, Monica. 1991. *Victoria: The Young Queen*. Cambridge: Polity.
Creston, Dormer. 1952. *The Youthful Queen Victoria: A Discursive Account*. London: Macmillan and Co.
Crichton, Ronald, ed. 1987. *The Memoirs of Ethel Smyth*. London: Viking.
Gernsheim, Helmut, and Alison Gernsheim. 1959. *Queen Victoria: A Biography in Words and Picture*. London: Longman's Green and Co.
Gosse, Edmund. 1901. "The Character of Queen Victoria." *Quarterly Review* January–April): 301–307.
Hardy, Alan. 1976. *Queen Victoria Was Amused*. London: John Murray.
Hibbert, Christopher. 2000. *Victoria: A Personal History*. London: HarperCollins.
[Holland, Caroline.] 1909. *Notebooks of a Spinster Lady*. London: Cassell.
Langtry, Lillie. 1978. *The Days That I Knew*. London: Futura.
Mallet, Victor, ed. 1968. *Life with Queen Victoria: Marie Mallet's Letters from Court, 1887–1901*. London: John Murray.
Smyth, Ethel. 1987. *The Memoirs of Ethel Smyth*. Abridged and introduced by Ronald Crichton. London: Viking.
St. Aubyn, Giles. 1991. *Queen Victoria: A Portrait*. London: Sinclair Stevenson.
Woodham-Smith, Cecil. 1972. *Queen Victoria: Her Life and Times*. Vol. 1: *1819–1861*. London: Hamish Hamilton.

Wellington, Arthur Wellesley, First Duke of (1769–1852)

the best friend we have (Woodham-Smith 1972, 220)

The man who had become legendary as the nemesis of Napoleon in 1815 at the battle of Waterloo was already, by the time Victoria became queen, probably the most famous person in the land. At public engagements where they appeared together the crowd's enthusiasm was often as much for their great military hero as it was for the queen. Despite their huge age difference (he was sixty-eight in 1837, she nineteen), they shared one fundamental quality that was central to both their characters—an unshakable sense of national duty. Wellington's patriotism had won for him an enduring reputation as a national institution. It also compelled a weary Wellington in later life to take on ill-advised political roles when he no longer felt truly capable of them. The military reputation often covered the cracks in his lack of political acumen and his inability to move with the rapidly changing political climate. A man of the eighteenth century, authoritarian and entrenched in tradition, Wellington found himself forced eventually to accede to that most distasteful of political necessities—reform.

Arthur Wellesley was a man of striking stature and hawkish appearance, his countenance dominated by a long, beaked nose.

The massive and ornate funeral car of the duke of Wellington, designed by Prince Albert and drawn by twelve horses, constructed for this the last great state funeral, held in 1852. (Hulton-Deutsch Collection/CORBIS)

The son of an Irish peer, the first Lord Mornington, he spent little time in Ireland, becoming deeply antipathetic to Catholic emancipation. After completing his education at Eton and military academy in France, Wellington embarked on an army career in 1787, serving as an aide-de-camp in Ireland. Over the next twenty-eight years he had an exemplary career: he was raised to colonel at the age of twenty-four and became duke of Wellington in 1814 and commander in chief of the British Army. He saw battle in Flanders (1794–1795) and India (1797–1804), before becoming revered for his most brilliant command, retrieving British military fortunes during the Peninsular War in Spain and Portugal (1808–1813). His troops affectionately nicknamed him "Old Nosey" during this campaign and under his command were always confident of giving the enemy a "damn'd good thrashing." The Peninsular War brought Wellington not just accolades but also the Order of the Garter and £500,000, together with a handsome estate in Hampshire. The apogee of his military career, as field marshal in command of the combined armies of Britain, Prussia, Holland, and Belgium, came at Waterloo on 18 June 1815.

The duke could now retire to the comfort of his two splendid residences—Apsley House in London and Stratfield Saye in Hampshire. But having served as a Tory member of Parliament in 1806–1809 and as chief secretary for Ireland 1807–1809, he decided to return to politics, in Lord Liverpool's government, 1819–1827, and finally, as a reluctant prime minister, 1828–1830. A rigid and unrepentant Tory, the proud and unbending duke supported the preservation of the old order and the English aristocracy at all costs. He did not mince his words in asserting this unshakable belief—in Parliament, at the dinner table, or in the politest of polite society. As a military man, the duke was fearless about the consequences of what he said and impervious to the sensibility of those to whom his scathing remarks were addressed. When he openly condemned Lord Grey's proposed Reform Bill extending the franchise as "constitutional suicide," the windows of his London home were smashed by demonstrators.

The duke did, however, unbend sufficiently to recognize the political expediency of placating Britain's Irish subjects with a bill for Catholic Emancipation, with the support of Sir Robert Peel. An overriding sense of duty had kept him in politics this long, but finally in 1830, faced with the onslaught of further demands for political reform, he resigned from office. He was now sixty-one and no longer cut the dashing figure of old: his ability as speaker in Parliament was marred by his screeching voice, made worse by the loss of most of his teeth. At official dinners and receptions his extreme deafness also caused him to talk at full volume, and often without discretion. Nevertheless, the duke returned to office in Peel's governments of 1834–1835 (declining the offer of prime minister, he served briefly as foreign secretary) and 1841–1846 (as minister without portfolio). Now a revered elder statesman, he was frequently called on to smooth the troubled waters when conflicts arose between the monarch (William IV) and his ministers, garnering even the respect of the curmudgeonly William IV, who admitted to Wellington in 1835 that he was the only one of his subjects with whom he had ever shaken hands.

When the queen ascended the throne in 1837, she had originally looked upon Wellington much as she did Lord Melbourne—as a father figure and wise counselor. With Wellington's fame preceding him, she had the same reassuring sense of security in his presence, admitting to Wellington that in her duties as queen, the duke was the "one individual for whom I entertain a decided preference" (Bolitho 1949, 31). During the years before her marriage, Victoria enjoyed the somewhat racy anecdotes related by Wellington and relished his repartee. But a cooling off in her affection for the duke ensued at the time of her courtship and wedding in 1839–1840. For, during the Bedchamber Crisis of 1839 that had followed Melbourne's fall from power, she had entertained the unrealistic hope that Wellington might step in and form a government. Now aged seventy and in his own opinion out of touch with contemporary politics, the duke declined. Victoria had been forced to accept Peel, considering the duke's refusal a personal snub. She became further alienated from him when he fired off one of his usual broadsides in Parliament over the reduction in Prince Albert's allowance to a more acceptable £30,000 (rather than the posited £50,000). Wellington then compounded the insult by questioning the purity of the prince's Protestant blood (the Coburg family having intermarried with many Roman Catholics). He also opposed the queen's desire to promote Prince Albert's status above that of all the peers of the realm, including her own uncles. The benign elder statesman now became, to Victoria's mind, "that old rebel"; in retaliation, she decided not to invite him to her wedding. It took considerable persuasion from Melbourne to convince her of the inadvisability of excluding the country's national hero from the ceremony. Wellington eventually relented over the issue of Prince Albert's status, and his relationship with the queen from thereon recovered lost ground, particularly after he supported the passing of a bill to secure Albert's regency in the event of the queen's death in childbirth.

By the time the queen's first child, Victoria, was born on 21 November 1840, the duke was firmly reinstated in her affections; the renewal of their friendship was underlined, in 1850, when he became godfather to Prince Arthur (who was named after him and who called him the "Duke of Wellikon"), by which time he had retired from public life (1846). The duke did, however, make occasional public appearances, such as that, at the age of eighty-two, at the Great Exhibition. Visiting it in October 1851, he was quickly reminded of the public's undimmed adulation. Recognizing him, the crowds began cheering and pressing forward. The duke's entourage, fearing the glass edifice of the Crystal Palace might collapse in the melée, hastily ushered the tottering old duke outside to safety with the aid of police officers.

By the time the duke died at the age of eighty-three on 14 September 1852, the country had run out of superlatives with which to laud its greatest old campaigner. He had, opined the *Times,* "having compressed within the space of his existence the interest of many lives, died as a lamp expires, the oil of which is exhausted." The newspaper set the tone of the duke's mythologization, by concluding that "his career was one unclouded longest day" (*Times,* 18 September 1852, p. 5). Hearing the news while on an expedition to a wild and lonely loch in the Highlands, the queen predicted that "not an eye will be dry in the whole country" (Woodham-Smith 1972, 325). Soon, she too was piling on the superlatives: "He was the pride of this country! He was the GREATEST man this country ever produced, and the most *devoted* and *loyal* subject, and the staunchest supporter the Crown ever had" (Benson and Esher 1911, 2:394).

The duke's funeral equaled that of any monarch—in fact, it would be the last heraldic state funeral held in Britain. The duke's coffin had lain in state at Chelsea Hospital to provide an opportunity for many of Wellington's old soldiers to pay their last respects, as well as 200,000 members of the public. The queen herself had been so overwhelmed with grief at the sight that she had dissolved in tears. The coffin was then conveyed, covered in crimson velvet, with Wellington's cocked hat, sword, and other insignia placed on top, to St. Paul's Cathedral on a lavish, twenty-seven-feet-long funeral car. Designed by Prince Albert and specially constructed for the occasion, the car was embellished with black and gold ornamentation and pulled by six black horses with black trappings and feather plumes. Military bands played funereal music, and muffled drums accompanied the slow march as the hearse progressed through the streets of London

At his death, the duke was a man universally mourned, even by his old political adversaries. For with him died one of the last links with the glorious days of British military might. As the Chartist poet and radical Thomas Cooper recorded: "The great actor in the scenes of the Peninsula and Waterloo—the conqueror of Napoleon—and the chief name in our home political life for many years—had disappeared. I seemed to myself to belong now to another generation of men; for my very childhood was passed amid the noise of Wellington's battles and his name and existence seemed stamped on every year of our time" (Priestley 1972, 106). And Cooper was right: within eighteen months of the duke's death the long forty-year peace in Europe came to an end, with the outbreak of war in the Crimea.

Related entries:
Bedchamber Crisis; Crimean War; Melbourne, William Lamb, Second Viscount

References and further reading:

Benson, A. C., and Viscount Esher, eds. 1911. *The Letters of Queen Victoria: A Selection from Her Majesty's Correspondence between the Years 1837 and 1861.* 1st ser., 3 vols. London: John Murray.

Bolitho, Hector. 1949. *The Reign of Queen Victoria.* London: Collins.

Guedalla, Philip. [1931] 1997. *The Duke.* Ware, UK: Wordsworth Editions.

James, L. 1992. *The Iron Duke: A Military Biography of Wellington.* London: Weidenfeld and Nicolson.

Longford, Elizabeth. 1969. *Wellington.* Vol. 1: *The Years of the Sword.* London: Weidenfeld and Nicolson.

———. 1972. *Wellington.* Vol. 2: *The Pillar of State.* London: Weidenfeld and Nicolson.

Maxwell, Sir Herbert. [1893] 1924. *The Life of Wellington.* London: Hutchinson.

Priestley, J. B. 1972. *Queen Victoria's Heyday.* Harmondsworth, UK: Penguin.

Thompson, N. 1986. *Wellington after Waterloo.* London: Routledge and Kegan Paul.

Woodham-Smith, Cecil. 1972. *Queen Victoria: Her Life and Times.* Vol. 1: *1819–1861.* London: Hamish Hamilton.

"The Widow at Windsor"

the poor fatherless baby of eight months is now the utterly broken-hearted and crushed widow of forty-two (Benson and Esher, 1911, 3:473)

In October 1861, only two months before his tragically premature death, Prince Albert wrote a letter to Queen Victoria in which he expressed his concern at the protracted grieving in which she had been indulging since the death of her mother, the duchess of Kent, that spring. The queen's excessive and often hysterical bouts of weeping had prompted talk at court that she was losing her sanity. Albert found his wife's lack of restraint unhealthy and damaging to her mental stability (today's doctors might well have diagnosed her as having suffered a nervous breakdown). "My advice to be less occupied with yourself and your own feelings is really the kindest I can give," he wrote, "for pain is felt chiefly by dwelling on it and can thereby be heightened to an *unbearable extent*" (Fulford 1966, 249). Had he known it, the prince might well have been describing the extravagant levels to which the queen would go after his own death. In her unceasing ritualization of mourning, the queen would raise herself as an archetype of sober Victorian widowhood, setting in stone her own image in later life as "the Widow at Windsor."

It was clear, from the moment Prince Albert died on 14 December, that the queen's lamentations would be epic in their proportions. She immediately issued a directive "that the mourning for the Prince Consort shall be ordered for the longest time in modern times" (Watson 1952, 156). It was the convention at the time for all widows to wear mourning for a year after their husband's death, followed by a further six months of half mourning (wearing black, lilac, and grey), a ritual also observed by close members of the family. When a master died, his servants also had to go into mourning; in the case of the prince consort, Victoria insisted that no member of the royal household should appear out of mourning in public for a year. She herself rigidly observed the elaborate etiquette with her characteristic punctiliousness. Only women in her closest entourage, such as her daughters and her dressers—as well as the mistress of the robes, the duchess of Sutherland, and her lady-in-waiting Lady Augusta Bruce—were allowed into her private apartments in the first few weeks. Thereafter, Victoria made it a habit to appoint ladies-in-waiting who were also widowed, as Longford observed, making of her court "A Sacred College of Vestal Widows" who must "tend the flame of their sorrow (and of her convenience) forever" (Longford 1998, 310).

The queen soon lengthened her own period of mourning to two years. When rumors began circulating in 1863 that she was about to give up her widow's weeds at long last, she wrote to the *Times* insisting that "this idea cannot be too explicitly contradicted" (Whittle 1980, 129). By now it was evident that her wearing of black was to be indefinite and with it her withdrawal from public view. The queen's refusal to give up the trappings of her sorrow made life difficult for the lady members of her household, who were perpetually limited to the half-mourning colors of lilac, mauve, and gray as well as the ubiquitous black. The queen herself stubbornly resisted any modification to her own swathes of black crape and bombazine, although for her Golden and Diamond Jubilees of 1887 and 1897 she finally allowed a little gray silk, white lace, and feathers.

In her 1896 book, *The Personal Life of Queen Victoria,* Sarah Tooley wistfully remarked that "Her Majesty is a little behind the spirit of the times in regard to regulations for mourning" (270). Like most of the queen's subjects, Tooley could barely disguise her exasperation at the monarch's persistent clinging to "the most lugubrious signs of outward mourning" (ibid.). These had now extended to Victoria's drawing up of a detailed code of etiquette for the arrangement of all royal layings out and funerals, which included specific instructions on the different types of shroud to be used for male and female, married and unmarried. With a succession of deaths in the family to keep her indefinitely preoccupied, Victoria rapidly lost sight of the living. And yet it was precisely this celebration of her own grief that, ironically, kept her alive. It became so much part of the fabric of her daily life that she was most reluctant to abandon it. As Munich observed: "Dwelling on and with the dead cheered her up" (1996, 82).

In the Victorian era, talking about death was not the taboo subject it became in the following century; for death was a far more conspicuous part of life. The interest that the queen had shown in the rituals of mourning prior to the death of Albert had been fairly typical of the times. Indeed, by the time Albert died, the death industry in Victorian Britain had become an extremely lucrative one. And not just for those who made the shrouds and coffins and dug the graves; it also provided work for the fabric makers, notably the firm of Courtaulds, a family of French Hugeunot silk weavers who had settled in Spitalfields and who had, by midcentury, secured a virtual monopoly on the manufacture of the omnipresent black crape worn by widows and their daughters. The company made a fortune from its production in Britain and America as well as on the Continent. Many specialist outlets were opened to cater to the funeral trade, such as Jay's London General Mourning Warehouse in Regent Street, which sold all the familiar paraphernalia: the jet mourning jewelry (it was considered inappropriate to wear gold, silver, or any colored stones), bags and parasols, crape hatbands and arm bands, handkerchiefs, fans, black-edged notepaper, visiting and memorial cards, and even black sealing wax.

After 1861 and until her death the queen retained, without interruption, the heavy half-inch black borders on all her own notepaper; there was always a death in the family somewhere to justify its persistent use. She also had a penchant for presenting members of her entourage with commemorative pieces of mourning jewelry—such as the brooches and pins given to them on the death of John Brown in 1883. Victorian jewelers did a healthy trade in such items of jewelry, particularly those made from the plaited hair of the dead, which was twisted and fashioned into various designs or bunches of flowers and placed inside lockets, rings, bracelets, and brooches. Until the 1880s, when tastes in funerals became less ostentatious, a regular sight would be the great funeral corteges of black ostrich-plumed horses pulling elaborate glass-sided hearses, preceded by top-hatted mutes and other attendants, swathed in crape hatbands. Even the poorest of people spent a lifetime saving for their own funerals; there was nothing more feared than a pauper's burial or, worse still, death in the workhouse (from whence many bodies were sent for medical dissection).

A cornerstone of the Victorian celebration of death was mournful verse, one of its greatest exponents being the poet laureate, Alfred Lord Tennyson, whose long poem, *In Memoriam,* was a great comfort to the queen. In art too, melancholic paintings of churchyards, graves, and bereaved widows—such as those by Frank Holl, another of the queen's favorites—also sold well; even the new medium of photography catered to the most ghoulish of fashions—photographs of the dead, dressed and posed as though still alive. Literature inevitably played its part; the tear-jerking descriptions of beautiful deaths (especially those of innocent children) became a standard of popular novels, most famously enshrined in novels such as Charlotte Brontë's *Jane Eyre* (the death of Jane's tubercular school friend Helen Burns) and those of Dickens (the death of the waiflike crossing-sweeper, Jo, in *Bleak House* or that of Little Nell in *The Old Curiosity Shop*). The Victorian obsession with death led to an increasing interest in the possibility of life on the "other side" and attempts to communicate with the dead, leading to the spread of séances, table rapping, and public demonstrations by spiritualists and mediums—many of them charlatans.

At forty-two, the queen had been relatively young when widowed; there had initially been hope that she might remarry. But she firmly vetoed the idea, adamant that widows should not do so. It was their sacred duty to keep the flame of their dead husband's memory burning; in her own case, she entered into a form of "living suttee," which would involve her in devotion to an elaborate cult of death that was "almost Egyptian in its intensity" (Wood 1976, 25). This can be seen in Queen Victoria's enduring compulsion, like the ancients, to erect great monuments to Albert's memory, their focal point being the great, Gothic-style Albert Memorial in London. In her obsessive interest in the ephemera of mourning, she accumulated busts, statues, photos, and other artifacts, with which she filled her private apartments in all the royal residences. In addition the queen had herself painted and photographed in her devotional widow's weeds, often alongside her equally po-faced daughters, in a variety of poses of nunlike adoration of Albert's portrait, photograph, or marble bust. A hand-colored photograph of Albert on his deathbed became her only nocturnal companion—hung above his (vacant) side of the royal bed in all Victoria's residences. The room in which he had died at Windsor was preserved precisely as it had been during his lifetime, with hot water and clean towels brought in every day and his clothes laid out ready, as though he were about to walk into the room. Eventually, in 1901, Victoria would, like an Egyptian pharoah, join Albert in their own elaborate tomb at Frogmore, her coffin filled with many specific personal items, a list of which she had issued many years before (Reid 1996, 215–217), to accompany her on her final journey.

Even when it came to celebrating the more happy landmarks in the lives of her children, Queen Victoria refused to abandon her unrelenting wearing of black. She cast gloom and despondency over the wedding of her daughter Princess Alice, which took place seven months after Prince Albert's death, when she stood, swathed in black, wearing her widow's headdress—"poor Ma's sad cap," as Princess Beatrice called it (Perkin 1993 ,133)—ensuring that the occasion seemed more like a funeral than a wedding. Things were no better two years later, in March 1863, at the wedding of Bertie, the Prince of Wales, to Princess Alexandra of Denmark. Victoria took no part in the service, choosing instead to secrete herself in a gallery overlooking St. George's Chapel, where the ceremony took place, and not even attending the wedding breakfast afterward.

As she grew older Victoria seemed to derive a strange kind of satisfaction from her obsession with death and mourning. She constantly solicited deathbed portraits and photographs of her extended family and of members of her entourage who died, as well as detailed descriptions of their funerals. She even took a hand in the paraphernalia that was placed in their coffins. As one of her maids of honor, Marie Mallet, observed, the queen clearly came to enjoy such "melancholy entertainments" as pieces of theater (1968, 52), and the more mournful the better. If a ceremony was cheerful, she "always treated [it] with the utmost indifference" (122). Mallet concurred with others that the queen's excessively lugubrious manner was, perhaps, "the dim shade of inherited melancholy from George III" (122). Victoria certainly made much of the funerary rites for Eddy, the duke of Clarence (the Prince of Wales's son, who died in 1892), and of those for her son-in-law, Prince Henry of Battenburg, who died in Africa in 1896 and was brought home for burial. But she also took a close interest in the far more modest obsequies for lesser members of her household. In 1891, when one of the servants who had accompanied her on her holiday to Grasse died, the queen laid down details on the laying out of the corpse, which were followed to the letter. Noting the satisfaction this gave the queen, Mallet found it very curious "to see how the Queen takes the keenest interest in death and all its horrors." "Our whole talk," she wrote home, "has been of coffins and winding sheets" (44). And this interest did not stop at human beings. The queen went to equal lengths over the funerals of her favorite dogs. In the sincere belief that animals, like humans, had souls, she ensured that they were buried with the greatest of ceremony when they died. In some cases—such as her spaniel, Dash; her favorite collie, Noble; and Prince Albert's greyhound, Eos—monuments were erected over the animals' graves.

Such was the queen's determination in widowhood to cut herself off from the world and the capital city, London, that she spent longer and longer periods at Balmoral and Osborne. Life for the royal household during the early years of her widowhood was grim. Windsor especially was cold and silent, like a morgue, with the queen keeping to her rooms for days on end and hardly seeing anyone. The staff crept around on tip-toe and spoke in whispers. The sound of laughter was decidedly absent, and mealtimes with the queen were miserable affairs punctuated by long, agonized silences. Such determined self-immurement made the queen unpopular during the 1860s and 1870s, with people wondering whether there was something wrong with her. Had she become unhinged? Even confirmed monarchists became seriously concerned about the damage this was doing to her public image. In an 1864 edition of the *Saturday Review,* the politician Robert Cecil (later Lord Salisbury) observed that "seclusion is one of the few luxuries in which Royal personages may not indulge. . . . Human affections will not fasten upon abstractions." The British nation could not, he concluded, "live on the loyalty inspired by the Court Circular" (Roberts 1999, 316). Prime Minister William Gladstone resolutely lobbied the queen to appear in public, remarking that she had become "invisible." Victoria made a few brief forays beyond her private apartments, but as such her appearances were low key and informal until she finally capitulated to concerted ministerial pressure and in 1866 and 1867 once more attended the state opening of Parliament. She refused, however, to wear her robes of state and made it clear that the ordeal was like going to her own execution. She could not understand the wish of the public, she told her prime minister, Lord Russell, "to witness the spectacle of a poor, broken-hearted widow, nervous and shrinking, dragged in deep mourning, alone in State as a Show, where she used to go supported by her husband, to be gazed at, without delicacy of feeling" (Hibbert 1984, 193).

The brief first ministry of Benjamin Disraeli went some way to breaking down Victoria's resistance. He enlisted his considerable powers of persuasion in apprising the queen of the importance of her return to public view, however occasional. Victoria continued to protest long and loud about the frailty of her nerves, her precarious state of her health, and the strain of her daily workload on a brain that was "constantly overtaxed" (Hardie 1935, 199). Ironically, it was a succession of family deaths from the late 1870s on that helped restore her popularity, its impetus being the Prince of Wales's near fatal attack of typhoid in 1871. The death of the queen's daughter, Alice, in 1878; the death of the Empress Eugénie's son the Prince Imperial in 1879 (strongly considered as a prospective husband for

Victoria's daughter Beatrice); the passing of Disraeli in 1881 and of John Brown in 1883; and finally, in 1884, the death of another ofVictoria's children—the hemophiliac Leopold—all combined to win back public sympathy for the aging queen. But by now the iconic image of the "Widow at Windsor" was firmly entrenched. The popular phrase had already been in use when the poet Rudyard Kipling immortalized it in his 1892 "Barrack-Room Ballad," although in this, the final decade of her life, the stubborn old widow had at least begun to smile again—thanks, in great part, to the arrival of her many grandchildren, in whom she took a genuine delight.

Related entries:
Albert of Saxe-Coburg-Gotha, Prince Consort; Animals; Frogmore; The Paranormal; Tennyson, Alfred, Lord; Victoria, Queen: Death and Funeral of; "We Are Not Amused"

References and further reading:

Benson, A. C., and Viscount Esher, eds. 1911. *The Letters of Queen Victoria, 1837–1861.* 1st ser., 3 vols. London: John Murray.
Bland, Olivia. 1986. *The Royal Way of Death.* London: Constable.
Curl, James Stevens. 2000. *The Victorian Celebration of Death.* Stroud, Gloucestershire: Sutton.
Fulford, Roger. 1966. *The Prince Consort.* London: Macmillan.
Hardie, Frank. 1935. *The Political Influence of Queen Victoria.* London: Oxford University Press.
Hibbert, Christopher. 1984. *Queen Victoria in Her Letters and Journals.* London: Viking.
Jerrold, Clare. 1916. *The Widowhood of Queen Victoria.* London: Eveleigh Nash.
Longford, Elizabeth. [1964] 1998. *Victoria R.I.* London: Weidenfeld and Nicolson.
Mallet, Victor, ed. 1968. *Life with Queen Victoria: Marie Mallet's Letters from Court, 1887–1901.* London: John Murray.
Morley, John. 1971. *Death, Heaven, and the Victorians.* Pittsburgh: University of Pittsburgh Press.
Munich, Adrienne. 1996. *Queen Victoria's Secrets.* New York: Columbia University Press.
Packard, Jerrold M. 1995. *Farewell in Splendour: The Death of Queen Victoria and Her Age.* Stroud, Gloucestershire: Sutton.
Perkin, Joan. 1993. *Victorian Women.* London: John Murray.
Reid, Michaela. 1996. *Ask Sir James: The Life of Sir James Reid, Personal Physician to Queen Victoria.* London: Eland.
Roberts, Andrew. 1999. *Salisbury: Victorian Titan.* London: Weidenfeld and Nicolson.
Tooley, Sarah. 1896. *The Personal Life of Queen Victoria.* London: Hodder and Stoughton.
Watson, Vera. 1952. *A Queen at Home: An Intimate Account of the Social and Domestic Life of Queen Victoria's Court.* London: W. H. Allen.
Whittle, Tyler. 1980. *Queen Victoria at Home.* London: Routledge and Kegan Paul.
Wood, Christopher. 1976. *Victorian Panorama: Paintings of Victorian Life.* London: Faber and Faber.

William II, Emperor of Germany (1859–1941)

(the "Kaiser")

such a hot-headed, conceited and wrong-headed young man, devoid of all feeling (Magnus 1964, 211)

Queen Victoria's first grandchild, later Emperor William II of Germany, was better known in Britain by the irreverent nickname of "Kaiser Bill"—a name that derided the self-importance of a man who reveled in the grandeur of his German title *kaiser,* derived from the Latin *caesar,* a title formerly used by the head of the Holy Roman Empire. With his waxed moustaches and his fondness for military uniform, William saw himself as a Teutonic hero, the noble figurehead of a great empire. In Britain, however, his overweening manner made him the butt of anti-German feeling. William's personality was complex and difficult and one that too often prompted biased coverage in the British press and led to his demonization as the bogeyman of Europe. But much of this was self-inflicted; posturing and impetuosity frequently antagonizing members of his own extended royal family, particularly after William's highly militaristic style of monarchy set out to raise Germany to a mighty naval and colonial power and set in motion escalating military rivalry with Britain.

It is a miracle that William and his mother, Crown Princess Victoria of Prussia, survived the traumatic circumstances of his

The stiff and stern Teutonic persona of Kaiser William II became the butt of British hostility during the years of mounting political tension between Britain and Germany that marked the end of the queen's reign. (The* Illustrated London News *Picture Library)

birth on 27 January 1859, after a protracted labor and a breech delivery, during which William's left arm was wrenched from its shoulder socket. The damaged limb never grew properly, remaining permanently deformed and virtually useless—for which William never ceased to blame the English doctor who had delivered him. Some commentators suggest that William's disability bred in him an inferiority complex, which would find an outlet later in his personal self-aggrandizement and empire building.

Queen Victoria did not see her first grandchild until September 1860. She was delighted, pronouncing him "a fine fat child with beautiful soft white skin" (Ponsonby 1928, 24). Three years later, she found him still a "sweet, darling, promising child" (Hibbert 1984, 186). But she was quick to advise Vicky: "Bring him [up] simply, plainly, not with that terrible Prussian pride which grieved dear Papa so much" (Pakula 1996, 327). The sin of pride, Victoria believed, would only lead the young child, and Prussia with him, into trouble; it was, she said "unworthy of great Princes—as well as great nations" (ibid.). For a while it seemed that William would remain as affable as he had been as a child. In 1871 Vicky told her mother that William was much like her own brother Bertie, the Prince of Wales, in his "pleasant, amiable ways" (Ponsonby 1928, 11). But as time went on, she found it harder and harder to see her son's good points. From the outset, she had been highly critical of William's intellectual shortcomings: "He is not possessed of brilliant abilities, nor of any strength of character or talents," she wrote to the queen in January 1871; at this point, Vicky still held out hopes that her son would "grow up a useful man" (119).

Vicky's and her husband Fritz's ambitions for their heir were reflected in the highly disciplined academic education they laid down for him. They broke with precedent and sent him to the *gymnasium* (university preparatory school) at Kassel, rather than a military-style high school. Vicky was particularly preoccupied in compensating for William's physical disability by making him take strenuous daily exercise to strengthen him. On his eighteenth birthday, William entered Bonn University. He now began to rebel against his parents, especially his mother. Eschewing the intellectual pursuits she would have wished for him, as well as her desire to see him brought up as an English gentleman and Anglophile, in 1879 William reverted to the much-loved military traditionalism of his grandfather, William I, and entered the army. This training served only to accentuate his worst points—hardening his tendency to be brusque and impolite and alienating him from his gentle but weak-willed father and his domineering mother.

In 1876 Queen Victoria was still referring to her grandson as "dear Willy" and expressing the hope that he might remain amiable and natural. "I shall always take the warmest interest in him," she declared (Hibbert 1984, 243). Even as his displays of bad manners and impetuousness became more pronounced, Victoria continued to make concessions for what she thought was a passing phase. Vicky, meanwhile, was becoming ever more extreme in the words she chose to describe her son; he now infuriated her by being "wrong-headed," "violent," and "arbitrary." His lack of respect for and his neglect of her increased after his marriage (in 1880 to Princess Augusta Victoria of Schleswig-Holstein-Sonderburg-Augustenburg), while Vicky's letters to Queen Victoria frequently complained about his indifference, especially during her bouts of illness: "He is a curious creature! A little civility, kindness and *empressement* go a long way, but I never get them from him" (Ponsonby 1928, 200). Relations between William and his liberal-minded parents now became increasingly strained as he took sides with their implacable enemy, the German chancellor Otto von Bismarck.

In the summer of 1887 William came to England for the celebrations for Queen Victoria's Golden Jubilee. She had been reluctant to invite him, but he insisted upon it as recognition of himself as Germany's future head of state. The queen soon put him in his place, reminding him that his father, now already sick with the cancer that would kill him, was still alive and still in authority over him. It was obvious to Vicky that her son was impatient to be emperor and what is more, in her view, his intention was to be "an absolute and autocratic one!" (Ponsonby 1928, 310). Soon after his accession, on 15 June 1888, after his father's brief reign, William proceeded to offend his uncle, Bertie, the Prince of Wales, by complaining that he did not treat him with the due deference of an imperial majesty—a matter of protocol that William insisted on, even in private among his family. Queen Victoria thought his high-handedness "utter madness" (ibid.). His self-regarding manner was, she exclaimed, "really too *vulgar* and too absurd" (ibid.). "If he has such notions, he [had] better *never* come *here*. The Queen will not swallow this affront" (Magnus 1964, 211). William was thereafter mocked within the royal family as "William the Great." He needed, observed Bertie, "to learn that he is living at the end of the nineteenth century and not in the Middle Ages" (209). His mother, Vicky, agreed: "A little modesty and *Selbsterkenntniss* [self-awareness] would show him that he is not the genius or the Frederick the Great he imagines" (Ponsonby 1928, 412).

As kaiser of Germany, and a firm believer in the divine right of the royal house of Hohenzollern, William inaugurated a new autocratic rule. Now distancing himself from the cautious policies of Bismarck, he advocated domestic reforms in an attempt to buy working-class support—a move that did nothing to stem the rising tide of socialism in Germany. Bismarck resigned in 1890, and William took over control of the government. He had great ambitions, not just to keep Germany in the forefront of European politics but also to establish it as a world leader. In so doing he allowed his political entente with Russia to fall away, in 1890 failing to renew the 1887 Reinsurance Treaty, under which the two nations had agreed to remain neutral in the event of war. In 1897 William appointed Bernhard Fürst von Bülow as foreign secretary, to pursue his expansionist foreign policy, promoting him to chancellor in 1900. Germany now entered a period of aggressive colonial expansion in Africa and the Pacific, coming close to war with France over its territorial claims in Morocco. The kaiser's desire to challenge the age-old British domination of the high seas pushed Germany into a period of rapid industrialization and shipbuilding, masterminded by the secretary of the navy, Admiral Alfred von Tirpitz. Vicky condemned the folly of this arms race with Britain, desolate at her son's abandonment of the mission entrusted in him by herself and his father of bringing liberty, reform, and peace to the German nation.

Now set upon the path, not of progressive reform but of reviving the Prussian macho militarism and ceremonial of his ancestor Frederick the Great (1620–1688), William made Potsdam the showcase for his great military revival. Nevertheless, he was keen to retain his family links in Britain and between 1889 and 1895 made annual visits to Queen Victoria at "dear old Osborne" (St. Aubyn 1991, 542) for the Cowes Regatta. The queen came to dread these visits, which usually ended in William's offending his various relatives. She tried to make concessions and act as peacemaker, but William's brashness and lack of political acumen were beginning to have a disastrous effect on relations with Britain. He manifested a clearly anti-British attitude during the Boer War in South Africa, during which, unable to resist the desire to meddle in the conflict, he was upbraided for his "outrageous" conduct by Queen Victoria.

The public perception of William improved in Britain at the time of the queen's death in January 1901. Although he was inconsistent over many things, William never appeared to vacillate in his devotion to his grandmother. In the summer of 1900 he had shown great concern about Queen Victoria's failing health while simultaneously refusing, however, to pay much attention to his desperately ill mother (who had terminal cancer). On 19 January, when Victoria's death seemed imminent, he traveled to Osborne, where he spent much of the last two days of the queen's life at her bedside. After her death, William expressed his admiration for his grandmother's statesmanship and her grasp of international affairs: "She has been a very great woman," he said. "I have never been with her without feeling that she was in every sense my Grandmama and made me love her as such. And yet the minute we began to talk about political things she made me feel we were equals and could speak as Sovereigns. Nobody had such power as she" (Bell 1952, 353).

Kaiser William's avowed reverence for his grandmother makes painful reading in contrast to his embittered relationship with his mother. The queen's physician, Sir James Reid, was impressed with the profound attachment he showed to the queen. It made him revise his view of the kaiser: "He, more than her own children, displayed finer feelings, behaving impeccably, and with a gentleness and selflessness uncharacteristic of him" (Reid 1996, 213). Such behavior "went some way to mitigating previous misdemeanours" (ibid.) in the view of Reid. Biographer Hesketh Pearson was, however, suspicious of this uncharacteristic behavior. In his view, the kaiser "was all surface" and his manner toward the queen a sham: "He had no discoverable depths. . . . Everyone in this country imagines he was devoted to his grandmother. . . . On the contrary, he hated her for reading him so many lectures" (Pearson 2000, 60).

During the queen's obsequies, William surprised many in the royal family by continuing to behave in a manner that was exemplary for its modesty and restraint; even his uncle, now King Edward VII, was deeply touched. He hoped this marked a change for the better in the family's relationship with William. But, as Reid observed (1996), the kaiser's compassion was nowhere in evidence when his own mother lay dying a few months later. Cruising on his yacht in the North Sea at the time, he arrived in Berlin only thirty-six hours before she died.

Throughout his reign William remained a restless and inconsistent personality, who often found his sense of duty and destiny at odds with his natural sentiments and his familial ties. By turn bombastic and charming, he could be bad tempered and provocative in manner, yet was often well intentioned. Such inner conflict finally broke through in 1908, when he suffered a nervous breakdown. Thereafter he progressively lost control over much of German policymaking, as his behavior became increasingly erratic. When trouble flared in the Balkans in 1914, William dreaded the outbreak of international conflict but felt duty bound to honor Germany's alliance with Austria-Hungary. The declaration of war between Britain and Germany in August brought with it William's systematic portrayal in the British press as an evil, blood-soaked monster.

As the war dragged on, however, William was sidelined to the role of figurehead, particularly after 1916, when Germany's military leaders Paul von Hindenburg and Erich von Ludendorff began to dominate. When Germany was defeated in 1918, William fled to the Netherlands, from where he abdicated. The British had wanted him extradited to face trial as a war criminal, but Queen Wilhelmina had refused to allow this. William spent the next twenty years in exile, remarrying after the death of his wife in 1921 and publishing his *My Memoirs, 1878–1918* (1922) and *My Early Life* (1926). He died at Doorn, near Utrecht, having declined the offer of asylum from Winston Churchill in 1940, as well as the inducement (from Hitler) of returning to Germany to live on one of his former estates.

Related entries:
Albert Edward, Prince of Wales; Bismarck, Prince Otto Edward Leopold von; Boer War; Frederick William, Crown Prince of Prussia; "Grandmama of Europe"; Palmerston, Henry John Temple, Third Viscount; Victoria, Princess Royal

References and further reading:

Balfour, Michael. 1964. *The Kaiser and His Times.* London: Cresset Press.

Bell, George Kennedy. 1952. *Randall Davidson: Archbishop of Canterbury.* Oxford: Oxford University Press.

Cecil, Lamar. 1989–1996. *Wilhelm II.* 2 vols. Chapel Hill: University of North Carolina Press.

Cowles, Virginia. 1963. *The Kaiser.* New York: Harper and Row.

Hibbert, Christopher. 1984. *Queen Victoria in Her Letters and Journals.* London: Viking.

MacDonogh, Giles. 2000. *The Last Kaiser: William the Impetuous.* London: Weidenfeld and Nicolson.

Magnus, Philip. 1964. *King Edward the Seventh.* London: John Murray (chap. 11).

Pakula, Hannah. 1996. *An Uncommon Woman: The Empress Frederick.* London: Weidenfeld and Nicolson.

Palmer, Alan. 1978. *The Kaiser.* New York: Charles Scribner's Sons.

Pearson, Hesketh. 2000. *The Whispering Gallery: Leaves from a Diplomat's Diary.* London: Phoenix Press.

Ponsonby, Frederick, ed. 1928. *The Letters of the Empress Frederick.* London: Macmillan.

Reid, Michaela. 1996. *Ask Sir James: The Life of Sir James Reid, Personal Physician to Queen Victoria.* London: Eland.

Röhl, John. 1998. *Young Wilhelm: The Kaiser's Early Life, 1859–1888.* Cambridge: Cambridge University Press.

Röhl, John, and Nicolaus Sombart, eds. 1982. *Kaiser Wilhem II, New Interpretations.* Cambridge: Cambridge University Press.

St. Aubyn, Giles. 1991. *Queen Victoria, a Portrait* London: Sinclair Stevenson.

Whittle, Tyler. 1977. *The Last Kaiser: A Biography of William II, German Emperor and King of Prussia.* London: Heinemann.

William IV (1765–1837)

(Henry, Duke of Clarence; King of Great Britain 1830–1837)

odd, very odd and singular (Esher 1912, 1:194)

The last and probably the most eccentric of the Hanoverian kings of Britain, William IV, came as a stark contrast to his sybaritic brother, George IV, whom he succeeded in 1830. Unlike him, William was not a man of refined artistic tastes or sensitive intellect. He was brusque and plainspoken, an unsophisticated and diehard navy man, full of bombast, who barked out orders to his subordinates as though he were still in command of the fleet. When he became king, William's popular nicknames of "Silly Billy" and "the Sailor King" underlined this lack of sophistication and the degree of irreverence with which the monarchy was identified in the public mind at that time.

As the third of George III's nine sons and fifteen children, William had seemed unlikely to ever achieve elevation to the throne. He had therefore followed the traditional path of military service, joining the royal navy in 1779, at the age of thirteen. The tough sea-going life of a young midshipman molded his future character. He learned to spit and swear with alacrity (habits that he never abandoned—his habit of spitting from the state coach on official occasions caused much offense). His ingrained, rough-and-ready manner thus had no discernible aristocratic veneer appropriate to a future king. As an unremarkable, lesser royal duke, he lived in relative obscurity for the first sixty-two years of his life, the diarist Charles Greville observing that "if He had been born in a private station, He would have passed unobserved through life like millions of other men, looked upon as possessing a good-natured and affectionate disposition, but without either elevation of mind or brightness of intellect" (Strachey and Fulford 1938, 3:377).

After spending a brief period at the Hanoverian court, where he was sent by his father to learn etiquette (and where he missed "the pretty girls of Westminster" [Tomalin 1994, 104]), William continued his naval career. It culminated in a token elevation to admiral of the fleet in 1811 and was enlivened by a close friendship with Lord Nelson. Although William saw action at the siege of Gibraltar in 1780 and during the American Revolution, his seafaring exploits were probably more notable for the number of women he managed to seduce in every port. In 1789, George III elevated William to duke of Clarence and St. Andrews and granted him an Irish title—earl of Munster. Now back in London, having been recalled at the onset of another bout of his father's supposed "madness," William was captivated by the popular comic actress Mrs. Dora Jordan. He had noted her alluring figure in one of her numerous "breeches roles," as Little Pickle in a production of *The Spoilt Child.* Mrs. Jordan for a while resisted the duke's persistent attentions; when she finally capitulated and entered into an affair with him, they both became the objects of unmerciful caricature in the popular press.

In 1794 Dora Jordan gave birth to the first of the ten illegitimate "Fitzclarences," as they were known, that she and the duke would produce. Despite the irregularity of their twenty-year relationship, they were a devoted couple and loved their children; they lived quietly, and in relative social isolation, at their home on the royal estate of Bushey Park near Richmond, where William had been appointed ranger. Here he proceeded, like all his spendthrift brothers, to bankrupt himself on various home improvement projects. Meanwhile, the generous and warm-hearted Dora, by now one of the country's highest-paid actresses, constantly bailed him out financially, embarking on exhausting provincial tours in between her frequent absences to give birth to yet another offspring.

In 1811, with his brother George now Prince Regent after the king was again incapacitated by illness, William succumbed to mercenary and dynastic pressures. Beset by debts on all sides and having it constantly impressed upon him by official circles that the time had come for him to make a legal marriage and produce legitimate heirs, with ruthless abruptness he separated from Mrs. Jordan. For the next few years he went off in purposeful pursuit of a suitably aristocratic and affluent bride. The twenty-six-year-old Adelaide of Saxe-Meiningen gratefully accepted him in 1818. Despite William's being twice her age, the match turned out to be a surprisingly happy one. The rejected Dora meanwhile responded with great dignity and quietly retreated, only to be evicted from her much-loved home at Bushey—where Adelaide was duly installed—and separated from her adored sons. Eventually, even her daughters deserted her. Ill and dejected, she died in poverty in 1816, having never once said a harsh word against the duke.

In 1817 William's position in the royal accession changed dramatically when the Prince Regent's only legitimate heir, Princess Charlotte, died in childbirth, opening the way for him, or one of his brothers or their heirs to inherit the throne. William now entered an indecorous race with the dukes of Cambridge, Cumberland, Kent, and York to produce legitimate heirs to the throne. Adelaide suffered a succession of miscarriages, stillbirths, and the loss of a three-month-old daughter; the couple would thus live a childless life in a house that had once echoed to the noise of many children.

When William succeeded his brother, George IV, in 1830 at the age of sixty-four, life at court was immediately transformed. Gone was the cultured, but fastidious profligacy of George IV, replaced by the barking commands of the barrack room and, in Greville's words, "a plain, vulgar, hospitable gentleman, opening his doors to all the world . . . with a frightful Queen and a posse of bastards" (Strachey and Fulford 1938, 2:150). William was loud, talkative, and outrageously rude. But he did at least take more interest in affairs of state than his apathetic brother. One of his first acts had been to reject a costly coronation ceremony. He had no inhibitions about going out and about among his public—occasions that were always guaranteed to entertain, such as that witnessed by Thomas Creevey: "Billy 4th at the Opera was everything one could wish . . . his hair five times as full of powder as mine, and his seaman's gold lace cock-and-pinch hat was charming. He slept most part of the opera—never spoke to any one, or took the slightest interest in the concern" (Creevey 1948, 327). Such uncouth behavior inevitably upset the court, especially when William invited all kinds of social undesirables and rowdy naval friends to state occasions. The balls he held at St. James's Palace degenerated into "bear gardens." William and Adelaide's lack of sophistication was such that the royal entourage had to endure endless evenings in the company of a frequently somnolent king and his colorless wife, who, as William himself remarked, "does nothing but embroider flowers after dinner" (Fulford 1975, 25).

William IV managed to live long enough to fend off the ambitions cherished by Princess Victoria's mother, the duchess of Kent, of becoming regent. He had a great deal of affection for his heir, no doubt because he recognized something of his own blazingly honest and forthright manner in the young princess and shared with her a loathing for affectation and hypocrisy. Disapproving of the monarch's rough-and-ready manner, the duchess of Kent kept Princess Victoria away from court—about which King William frequently complained. Much of his reign was consumed by this and other fierce domestic squabbles with the duchess over her demands for status and special preference. William deeply distrusted her, as well as her personal adviser, Sir John Conroy, and constantly tried to thwart their attempts at manipulating the heart and mind of his heir presumptive. He also attempted to block the duchess's and her brother Leopold's long-held plans for Victoria to marry Albert of Saxe-Coburg-Gotha, by deliberately introducing the sons of the prince of Orange to his niece as more suitable bridegrooms. Things came to a head in 1836 after the duchess and Conroy had taken it upon themselves to dragoon the young Victoria into a series of exhausting royal progresses around the country. At a royal banquet to celebrate his birthday in August, William publicly berated the duchess and her "evil advisers." He further antagonized her by making over to Victoria her own annual allowance of £10,000, to which the duchess was not allowed access.

Ironically, for a man who had little truck with the business of kingship, William IV would enter the history books as the monarch who facilitated the passing of the great Reform Bill of 1832. The sweeping electoral changes that followed reduced the power of the old landowning aristocracy, bringing further demands for reform. It all became too much for William, who withdrew in a state of cold panic at the thought of being overtaken by popular revolt, his anxiety heightened by his wife's terror that they would both end up on the scaffold like Louis XVI and Marie Antoinette. He attempted to fend off further trouble by trying to control the appointment of his prime ministers, replacing the Whig, Lord Melbourne, with the Tory, Robert Peel, in 1834. When the Tories were defeated in 1835, William shied away from further political reform.

On King William's accession in 1830, Charles Greville had remarked that, although a buffoon, he would make a "very decent" king (Strachey and Fulford 1938 2:6). Historians have generally concurred that, as a monarch, William had few memorable attributes aside from his warm-heartedness and his blustering honesty—"honest to absurdity," as J. H. Plumb averred (1966, 149). The most significant fact of his reign was the manner in which he conducted it. William's down-to-earth and unpretentious manner narrowed the distance between monarch and people and paved the way for the birth of a more accessible, constitutional British monarchy. Queen Victoria's memory of her uncle underlined the conscientious attitude he had adopted: "Of his kindness to herself, and his wish that she should be duly prepared for the duties to which she was so early called, the Queen can only speak in terms of affectionate gratitude" (Fulford 1975, 36).

Related entries:

Conroy, Sir John; Ernest Augustus, Duke of Cumberland; Hanover, Royal House of; Kent, Marie Louise Victoire, Duchess of; Melbourne, William Lamb, Second Viscount; Peel, Sir Robert

References and further reading:

Allen, Walter Gore. 1960. *King William IV.* London: Cresset Press.

Creevey, Thomas. 1948. *Creevey: Selected and Re-edited by John Gore.* London: John Murray.

Esher, Viscount, ed. 1912. *The Girlhood of Queen Victoria: A Selection from Her Majesty's Diaries between the Years of 1832 and 1840.* 2 vols. London: John Murray.

Fulford, Roger. 1975. *From Hanover to Windsor.* London: Fontana.

———. [1933] 2000. *Royal Dukes.* Harmondsworth, UK: Penguin.

Marples, Morris. 1972. *Wicked Uncles in Love.* London: Michael Joseph.

Plumb, J. H. 1966. *The First Four Georges.* London: Fontana.

Somerset, Anne. 1980. *The Life and Times of William IV.* London: Weidenfeld and Nicolson.

Strachey, Lytton, and Roger Fulford, eds. 1938. *The Greville Memoirs.* 8 vols. London: Macmillan.

Tomalin, Claire. 1994. *Mrs. Jordan's Profession: The Story of a Great Actress and a Future King.* London: Viking.

Ziegler, Philip. 1971. *King William IV.* Newton Abbott, UK: Reader's Union.

Windsor Castle

this fine, old dull place, which please God shall never hold my bones (Fulford 1964, 213)

Windsor Castle has been the home of the British sovereign since the Norman conquest of the eleventh century. Originally a timber structure built on top of earth fortifications made around 1080, the castle was later rebuilt in stone and was much enlarged and refurbished during the reigns of Charles II, George III, and George IV. During the early years of their marriage, before they had established their preferred country residences at Osborne and Balmoral, Queen Victoria and Prince Albert spent much of their time at Windsor, which by the 1840s was only an hour's journey by train from Padddington.

Neither the queen nor Prince Albert had ever been able to look upon Buckingham Palace as a comfortable family home; it was, in any case, too close to the overcrowded and polluted environs of central London for their liking. At Windsor it seemed to them that the cleaner air and the nearby River Thames provided a healthier environment for their children. Unfortunately the castle's rudimentary plumbing and poor sanitation were anything but healthy. And after Prince Albert died here in 1861—some assert as a result of catching typhoid fever from the castle's bad drains—it became a large, cold, and unwelcoming mausoleum: "that castle of the winds," as Prime Minister Benjamin Disraeli described it (Blake 1966, 680). With the Blue Room, in which the prince died, and the Albert Memorial Chapel both dedicated to Albert's memory, Windsor acquired a mournful air that would, in the latter years of the queen's reign, be forever associated with her retreat from public life as "the Widow at Windsor" (see "The Widow at Windsor").

In the last years of her reign, the young Queen Victoria had enjoyed spending time at the castle in the company of her prime minister, Lord Melbourne, with whom she enjoyed going for long gallops in Windsor Great Park after they had completed their work on official papers. She held occasional house parties there for her ministers or visiting relatives; it was also to Windsor that her Coburg cousins, Ernest and Albert, came on an official visit, to be vetted as prospective husbands, in March 1836 and again in October 1839. On 15 October, in the intimate surroundings of her Blue Boudoir at Windsor, the queen proposed to Prince Albert; their three-day honeymoon was spent here. Prince Albert was soon after appointed ranger of Windsor, in which capacity, as an advocate of fresh air and exercise, he set to work redesigning the layout of the footpaths and driveways in the Home Park. He also improved its gardens and farms as well as the facilities there for hunting. But, as such, few alterations were made to the castle during the queen's reign, apart from the reconstruction of the Grand Staircase and the restoration of parts of the Lower Ward. The long-standing problem of the castle's dilapidated drainage system and cesspools was never addressed by Prince Albert, who soon became preoccupied with the construction of new homes at Osborne and Balmoral. Once enamored of the Highlands of Scotland, the royal couple found it increasingly difficult to tear themselves away and make the long journey back to Windsor when duty or protocol demanded. The queen found it ever harder to "reconcile" herself to being at Windsor. In October 1858 she recorded in her journal: "I have no feeling for Windsor—I admire it, I think it a grand, splendid place—but without a particle of anything which causes me to love it" (Hibbert 1964, 107).

The one time that Windsor did come into its own was Christmas, which the royal family traditionally spent there, gathering to exchange gifts and enjoy the pleasures of its decorated Christmas trees, a German tradition revived in Britain by Prince Albert. Like that at Buckingham Palace, however, life at Windsor retained a formality that was not conducive to the intimacy of family life, having no private garden in which the children could safely play. It remained a showcase for state visits and official functions, such as that in 1842, when it was the venue for the first major state visit of the queen's reign—of the King of Prussia—on the occasion of the christening of the Prince of Wales. Similarly, during the state visits of Tsar Nicholas I of Russia in June 1844 and of King Louis-Philippe of France four months later, sumptuous banquets were laid on in the historic Waterloo Chamber—an oak-paneled room that had been designed by Sir Jeffry Wyatville on instructions from George IV to commemorate the personalities involved in the defeat of Napoleon at Waterloo. When the new French king, Louis Napoleon III, visited in 1855, the Waterloo Chamber was discreetly and temporarily renamed the Picture Gallery in order not to offend the emperor's sensitivity to the French defeat at Waterloo. The chamber was also used by the royal family for balls and for command performances of plays, operas, and concerts by the leading stars of the day, including the actor/manager Charles Kean, the "Swedish nightingale" Jenny Lind, and the leading actors Ellen Terry and Henry Irving. Other rooms in the castle—such as the Green and White Drawing Rooms—were used for performances by the legendary Italian actress Eleonora Duse and the Polish concert pianist Ignacy Paderewski—both visiting in the 1890s. The smaller White Drawing Room and Rubens Room were favored for the more intimate family entertainments, *tableaux vivants* (living pictures), and theatricals that were staged from the 1850s on, with the royal children often performing plays in French or German.

But even during the occupancy of the royal family, the vastness of the castle could seem forbidding. In 1855, Frieda Arnold, a newly arrived German dresser to the queen, sent long descriptions home to her family of life at Windsor, in which she recounted that the dark and labyrinthine interior was so quiet that it seemed as though the castle was "quite empty" (Stoney and Weltzien 1994, 41). What little pleasures Windsor had to offer rapidly receded as the queen and Prince Albert grew increasingly besotted with their homes at Balmoral and Osborne. By October 1859 the queen would write to her daughter Vicky in Prussia that such was her homesickness for Balmoral and her "beloved Highlands" that although she could still admire Windsor's splendor, she had grown to dislike spending time there ("I think I dislike it more and more though I am quite aware of its splendour" [Fulford 1964, 213]). When Prince Albert died at Windsor on 14 December 1861, the queen commanded that the Blue Room in which he had breathed his last should be left precisely as it had been during his lifetime—as a lasting memorial to her late husband.

The queen now stayed at Windsor only when she was obliged to be in London on official business. Every year, on Mausoleum Day, the royal family would hold a memorial ceremony in the Blue Room, where a marble bust of Prince Albert by William Theed had been positioned between the two single beds and a memorial wreath placed on the bed on which he died. The castle was still occasionally dusted down for large set-piece state occasions, such as the state visit of the shah of Persia in 1873 and for the Queen's Golden Jubilee in 1887. But by the mid-1880s visits to Windsor had become even more poignant for the queen. For the castle was now associated with two more deaths—that in 1883 of her loyal Highland servant John Brown, whose body was subsequently taken back to Scotland for burial after lying in state in the castle's Clarence Tower, and that in 1884 of Victoria's hemophiliac son Leopold, who was interred in the castle's St. George's Chapel (at his own request—the queen had wanted him to join his father in the mausoleum at Frogmore). For the queen, Windsor had now become "this dreary, gloomy old place" (Hibbert 1964, 287). The atmosphere there was not enlivened until, in 1891, the queen once again requested entertainments to be staged, beginning with a command performance in March by the D'Oyly Carte company of the Gilbert and Sullivan opera *The Gondoliers.*

Prince Albert's death was commemorated at Windsor Castle by the creation of the Albert Memorial Chapel, in the shell of the disused Wolsey Chapel. The financing of the chapel's construction was, however, a problem, and in May 1862 the queen decided to pay for it herself; by the time it was completed in 1875, it had cost far more than the original estimate of £15,000. The renovations, designed and overseen by George Gilbert Scott, were undertaken to compensate for the fact that Prince Albert had not been buried in the centuries-old royal resting place of the nearby St. George's Chapel, but in a private mausoleum in the castle grounds, where the public were denied access.

The suggestion to modify the Wolsey Chapel was first made to Queen Victoria by her eldest daughter, Vicky. Scott added a vaulted Gothic ceiling inlaid with Italian gold mosaic by Antonio Salviati. The stained glass windows displayed images of Prince Albert's ancestors designed by the queen's librarian Hermann Sahl, and the walls were decorated with medallion portraits of the royal family and inlaid marble panels showing scenes from the scriptures. In the center of the chapel an elaborate Gothic cenotaph with a medieval-style recumbent effigy of Prince Albert in armor—a favorite incarnation of the queen's—provided a place of pilgrimage for the public that had all the richness and aura of a medieval shrine. The effigy, by the French sculptor Henri de Triqueti, was put in place in the winter of 1872. It was eventually joined by an equally remarkable one, made by Alfred Gilbert, to contain the body of the queen's grandson the duke of Clarence, who died in 1892. On 1 December 1875 the chapel was opened to visitors.

One of the greatest pleasures enjoyed by Prince Albert at Windsor was to spend time examining the royal collection of 15,000 Old Master drawings and engravings, including works by his favorite artist Raphael, held in the castle's Print Room in the Round Tower. Prince Albert was personally involved in sorting and cataloging much of the collection, making a particular study of the Raphael drawings, which he ordered to be meticulously documented and photographed for the benefit of art scholars of the future. Several members of the royal family, including Prince Albert; the Prince of Wales; his future wife, Princess Alexandra; and Princess Beatrice themselves became keen amateur photographers. The Royal Archives at Windsor would become the repository of a superb collection of photographs either taken for, by, or collected by the royal family, including a fine set of thirty-one prints of the castle and its grounds taken by the eminent Crimean War photographer Roger Fenton in 1860. The Victorian Photographic Collection at Windsor has become one of the most valuable pictorial resources for the queen's life and times. The relatively modest surroundings of the King's Dressing Room at Windsor house the pick of the royal art collection, including three Rembrandts and works by Holbein, Dürer, Rubens, and Van Dyck.

In November 1992 a catastrophic fire at Windsor Castle destroyed or seriously damaged 100 of the castle's rooms, although their priceless artworks had fortunately already been removed to facilitate restoration work being undertaken at the time. Queen Victoria's much-loved Green Drawing Room—the venue for most informal family gatherings, as well as musical and theatrical performances—suffered water damage during the fire but was restored as part of five years of extensive and painstaking renovation carried out by master craftsmen, before the castle was finally reopened to the public in 1997.

Related entries:
Albert Memorial; Balmoral Castle; Buckingham Palace; Christmas; Frogmore; Osborne; Photography; Theater; "The Widow at Windsor"

References and further reading:

Blake, Robert. 1966. *Disraeli*. London: Eyre and Spottiswoode.

Brindle, Steven. 1997. *Windsor Revealed: A New Light on the History of the Castle*. London: English Heritage.

De-La-Noy, Michael. 1990. *Windsor Castle: Past and Present*. London: Headline.

Farndon, John. 1990. *Royal Castle: The Inside Story of Windsor*. London: Viking.

Fulford, Roger. 1964. *Dearest Child: Letters between Queen Victoria and the Princess Royal, 1858–61*. London: Evans Brothers.

Girouard, Mark. 1993. *Windsor: The Most Romantic Castle*. London: Hodder and Stoughton.

Hedley, Olwen. 1994. *Windsor Castle.* London: Hale.
Hibbert, Christopher. 1964. *The Court at Windsor: A Domestic History.* London: Longman.
Robinson, John Martin. 1997. *Windsor: Official Guide.* London: Royal Collection.
Stoney, Benita, and Heinrich C. Weltzien, eds. 1994. *My Mistress the Queen: The Letters of Frieda Arnold, Dresser to Queen Victoria 1854–9.* London: Weidenfeld and Nicolson.

Winterhalter, Franz Xaver (1805–1873)

All these great artists . . . cannot throw life and lightness and animation into a portrait that dear old Winterhalter could (Fulford 1976, 170)

The German court painter Franz Winterhalter, creator of some of the most famous and sophisticated official portraits of Queen Victoria, Prince Albert, and their children, produced over 100 commissions during a twenty-nine-year relationship with the British royal family, lasting from 1842 till his death in 1873.

Born on 20 April 1805 in Menzenschwand in the Black Forest, he was the son of a farmer and was encouraged in his natural talent for drawing by the village priest. Soon the attention of a local textile magnate, Baron Eichtal, was drawn to Winterhalter's potential. Through the baron, the fifteen-year-old Winterhalter gained an apprenticeship at the studio of the artist Karl Ludwig Schuler at Freiburg-im-Breisgau in 1818 but was soon advised by him to study art properly. He did so in Munich, supporting himself by working as a lithographer. In 1828 Winterhalter fortuitously gained the patronage of the royal court of Baden at Karlsruhe, where he obtained an appointment in 1829 as drawing master to Sophie Guillemette, the future grand duchess. In 1834 Grand Duke Leopold of Baden appointed him court painter of Baden at Karlsruhe.

But Winterhalter had by now decided that his future lay in the wider clientele of royalty and courtiers subjects to be found in Paris, where he took an apartment in rue des Petits Augustins late in 1834, retaining his court appointment at Baden. He held his first exhibition in Paris in 1835 and maintained a home in the city for the next thirty-six years, despite regular periods spent in England painting the British royal family. His talent for portrait painting attracted the attention of the French emperor, Louis-Philippe, by whom Winterhalter—in the face of stiff competition from other candidates—was commissioned to paint over thirty formal portraits of the French royal family over the next few years, culminating in a grand set-piece—*The Reception of King Louis-Philippe at Windsor Castle*—painted to commemorate the French state visit to England in 1844.

Winterhalter had already painted Victoria twice before—in 1833 and again on her coronation in 1837—when he finally gained the seal of approval of the royal family in Britain. In 1842, he made the first of his regular, extended summer visits to England, staying at Buckingham Palace and Windsor Castle between July and September to paint members of the queen's family. His paintings of Victoria, Albert, and their rapidly growing brood of children would bring him back for two or three months almost every subsequent year between 1843 and 1850. On this and subsequent visits he remained within the close enclave at court; no doubt here he felt at ease with so many German-speakers around him (the queen and Prince Albert included), aware of the general antipathy to Germans among the public at large. He never really ventured outside this closed world, and few took notice of him, except the superintendent of the nursery, Lady Lyttleton, who recorded somewhat scathingly that Winterhalter was "one of the least agreeable, and most dry and half-sneering mannered men I have ever met" (Whittle 1980, 31). Victoria too

One of the most famous, romanticized images of the royal family, by the court painter, Franz Xaver Winterhalter. In his day, Winterhalter painted members of all the great royal houses of Europe and was much feted for his work. (Stapleton Collection/CORBIS)

found him odd, although after his death she remarked that "with all his peculiarities I liked him so much" (Ormond 1987, 64).

Once she had discovered Winterhalter (whom she later set on a par with that other great British court painter, Van Dyck, who had immortalized the family of Charles I), Victoria rapidly abandoned all other older-established court painters. That is, with the exception of her adored Edwin Landseer, whose animal paintings, especially of dogs and stags, she greatly admired. Winterhalter was a superb craftsman; his high technical skills produced good, accurate likenesses, but they never penetrated below the veneer of regal splendor to suggest the inner person. He romanticized the young and handsome Prince Albert on canvas in a way that delighted the queen, and she applauded what she perceived as the honesty of his likenesses of herself. In 1843 Victoria allowed Winterhalter to paint a surprise present for Albert's twenty-fifth birthday. It is probably the only, and famously, seductive image of her—depicting the queen with head to one side, baring an expanse of tempting white neck and with a long lock of hair meandering down the contours of her shoulder and breast. The mouth is slightly apart and expectant; the eyes those of a young woman full of romantic expectation. Compared to the later stiff and sober images of a rapidly careworn-looking monarch, this image of Victoria in all her youthful fleshiness is richly suggestive of an impressionable and sensuous woman, still very much in love. It was, she averred, "my darling Albert's favourite picture" (Ormond

1987, 191), and he kept it by him in his writing room at Windsor Castle. It had cost Queen Victoria a mere £105.

During his visits to court, Winterhalter also gave the queen lessons in oil painting and helped and advised Prince Albert in extending his own art collections. Albert, in turn, took a hand in the composition of Winterhalter's paintings of the royal family. Winterhalter is little recorded in Victoria's letters and journals, except for mentions of his paintings, his beautiful use of color, and her commendation that he did not flatter his subjects (photographs of herself contemporaneous with paintings he made suggest this was wishful thinking on Victoria's part). The first exhibition of Winterhalter's paintings in London was held at St. James's Palace in 1847, when his portraits of the royal family attracted over 100,000 visitors.

In 1846 he produced one of his most popular images of the royal family, a relaxed image of Victoria and Albert surrounded by five of their pretty, ringleted young children. The portrait would hang in the dining room of Osborne House. The year after Albert's death, on the occasion of a very subdued private wedding held at Osborne for Princess Alice (July 1862), the marriage vows were taken in front of this, the painting that more than any other had summed up for Victoria the happy life she had had with Albert. In her estimation it was Winterhalter's pièce de résistance.

By the end of the 1840s Winterhalter was rich and famous, and his paintings mass produced for circulation among the public brought in huge royalties; but he was now also well and truly caught in the trap of supply and demand. Such popular success led to accusations from his fellow painters and art critics that he had abandoned his artistic integrity to the cause of money and patronage. And although he was rich and famous, Winterhalter now found himself compelled to live a peripatetic existence, traveling from one royal court to another to produce stereotypical portraits of men in military uniform and regalia or ladies with elaborate hairstyles in endless flounces of lace. With characteristic Germanic discipline, aided by his brother Hermann (who conducted the business side of Winterhalter's affairs) and two assistants (who copied many of his paintings), he produced endless, methodical portraits, spending much time every year in Paris painting society figures. As for a private life—little is known except that a brief engagement came and went in 1852 and thereafter Winterhalter gave himself up entirely to his work.

The revolution in Paris in 1848 forced Winterhalter to leave France and spend five months in England. In the early 1850s he painted portraits of the royal children in the Highlands, sketched the queen and other members of the family in watercolors, and completed another famous painting. Entitled *The First of May 1851,* it was executed to commemorate the royal opening of the Great Exhibition at the Crystal Palace. It depicts an elderly duke of Wellington kneeling to offer up a first birthday gift to Prince Arthur sitting on his mother's knee, with Prince Albert behind them holding the plans of the Crystal Palace and the building itself shown in the background.

During the 1850s Winterhalter traveled a great deal on the continent, painting the royal beauties of the day: Queen Isabella of Spain, Empress Eugénie of France, Empress Alexandra Fedorovna of Russia, Queen Sophia of the Netherlands. These elegant images of women adorned with beautiful jewels, fans, gloves, resplendent cascades of hair, and the latest Paris fashions by Worth (carried off to perfection by the Empress Eugénie) set a trend followed by other painters, seeking to cash in on the vogue for Winterhalter. The man himself, however, continued to live a modest, private life. He now dominated a different royal court—France—celebrating in paint the great days of the French Second Empire. Queen Victoria had become so addicted to his work, however, that she had had to ration herself.

In a letter to her daughter Vicky she agonized over whether to commission "three half-lengths of Bertie, Alix and the baby or two full-lengths of Bertie and Alix"—since she could not afford both (Longford 1998, 372).

Ormond asserted that "no portrait painter has every enjoyed such extensive Royal patronage as Winterhalter. One has to go back to the age of Rubens and Van Dyck to find court painters operating in a similar international network of contacts" (1987, 51). By now he had been offered many gifts of appreciation and awarded numerous honors, yet despite enjoying the most eminent patronage, Winterhalter did not put his prices up; in fact he charged much the same as other artists of the genre. He continued to live a relatively modest life, his only indulgence having been the construction of a home, the Villa Trianon, at Baden, in 1859. Never having had time to live there, he had sold it a year later. His last years were spent constantly on the move between Germany, France, Italy, and Switzerland before he settled, after the outbreak of the Franco-Prussian War in 1870, back in Karlsruhe with his brother Hermann. His last official commission in England had been to paint the Prince and Princess of Wales on the occasion of their wedding.

In 1873 Winterhalter contracted typhus during an epidemic in Frankfurt and died shortly after on 8 July. This was yet another blow for the queen—coming only a few months after the death of her other favorite painter, Landseer. Winterhalter's role as British court painter was taken over by Heinrich von Angeli, and Winterhalter rapidly fell out of vogue. A major exhibition of his works was not staged again until 1936—in London and Paris—but interest in his work quickly faded away. A definitive exhibition at London's National Portrait Gallery (October 1987 to January 1988) finally restored interest in Winterhalter's work, coming at a time when much neglected Victorian art was being rediscovered. His paintings are now viewed as an important historical document of many of the great and now defunct monarchies of nineteenth-century Europe.

Related entries:
Art and Artists; Eugénie Marie de Montijo, Empress of France; Landseer, Sir Edwin

References and further reading:
Fulford, Roger, ed. 1976. *Darling Child: Private Correspondence of Queen Victoria and the German Crown Princess of Prussia, 1863–71.* London: Evans Brothers.
Lloyd, Christopher. 1977. *The Queen's Pictures.* London: Chancellor.
———. 1998. *The Quest for Albion: Monarchy and the Patronage of British Painting.* London: Royal Collection.
Longford, Elizabeth. [1964] 1998. *Victoria R.I.* London: Weidenfeld and Nicolson.
Ormond, Richard. 1987. *Franz Xaver Winterhalter and the Courts of Europe 1830–70.* London: National Portrait Gallery.
Whittle, Tyler. 1980. *Victoria and Albert at Home.* London: Routledge and Kegan Paul.

Women's Rights

It is a subject which makes the Queen so furious that she cannot contain herself (Martin 1908, 70)

The writer H. G. Wells, remembering his mother as a fervent admirer of Queen Victoria, took note in his autobiography of "the rise of feminine partisanship in Britain" (Wells 1934, 1:46) that had inexorably gained ground during the queen's long reign. Wells recalled that his mother had "followed the life of Victoria, her acts and utterances, her goings forth and her lyings in, her great sorrow and her other bereavements, with a passionate loyalty" (ibid.). The queen had been "my mother's compensatory personality, her imaginative consolation for all the restrictions and hardships that her sex, her diminutive size, her motherhood and all the endless difficulties of life, imposed upon her" (ibid.). As monarch of a great empire from the age of eighteen on, and the most visible public representative of her sex, Victoria's mere presence on the throne was in itself sufficient to encourage many of her female subjects to call for improved civil and political rights for women.

The slow but steady progress of women's emancipation that was made throughout the queen's reign was, however, achieved without any endorsement from Queen Victoria herself. In fact, she was a great hindrance to the movement, for she constantly reiterated her own opposition to women's rights and her firm belief that her sex belonged in its own separate, domestic sphere. What is more, Victoria frequently averred, as in a letter to her Uncle Leopold in February 1852, that the role of monarch was one that ran counter to everything that was, in her view, womanly: "I am every day more convinced that *we women,* if we are to be *good* women, *feminine* and *amiable* and *domestic,* are not *fitted to reign*" (Benson and Esher 1911, 2:367).

The queen's journals and letters resound with such regularly made protestations of her sex's inferiority and intellectual inadequacy. She constantly reminded her daughters and after them, her granddaughters, of the shortcomings of their own "feeble" sex. Victoria believed that women should defer at all times to their husbands. Writing to her granddaughter Princess Victoria of Hesse in 1884, she emphasized that "the *husband must* be the person to *look up to & obey*—& that a woman can only really be happy & in her right place when she *can* do so" (Hough 1975, 64). Such a statement reflected Victoria's fundamental belief that all women had need of a "strong arm"—male, of course—to guide and support them. In her own case, Victoria found the "strong arm" she craved in prime ministers such as Lord Melbourne and servants such as John Brown. Victoria's attitude to women's role would remain a very narrow one: they should not allow their brains and nervous energy to be overtaxed by things beyond their intellectual and emotional capacity. Throughout her life she made a habit of constantly belittling women's ability to think for themselves (after all, as she once rather proudly observed: "I never bought a dress or bonnet without consulting him [Prince Albert]"[Jerrold 1916, 313]).

The debate over women's rights in Britain had been gathering momentum since the publication by Mary Wollstonecraft of her *A Vindication of the Rights of Woman* in 1792. Campaigning women, such as the members of the Langham Place Circle led by Barbara Bodichon, had garnered support from male radicals, one of whom, the political essayist and member of Parliament John Stuart Mill, first raised the issues of women's enfranchisement in Parliament in 1866. He did so through the presentation to the house of a petition for women's suffrage, the signatures for which had been gathered by members of the Langham Place Circle. A year later the issue of women's franchise was discussed, and rejected, as part of the Reform Bill extending the franchise (see "Disraeli, Benjamin"; "Russell, Lord John, First Earl of").

Despite many other setbacks, and the absence of support from the monarch herself, women in Britain continued to cite the example of the queen as living proof of a woman's fitness to play an important part in public life. The argument was raised even in the United States, in the 1850s, when the dress reformer, Amelia Jenks Bloomer, proposed that "if it is right for Victoria to sit on the throne of England it is right for any American Woman to occupy the Presidential Chair at Washington" (Anderson 2000, 120). Many of the arguments by women reformers in support of their admission to higher education and to public office would run in tandem with the campaign for suffrage that gained momentum in the 1880s. The queen, however, resisted all suggestions of a woman's holding even a token office, such as that of poet laureate; after the death of Alfred Lord Tennyson in 1892, she soundly rejected the suggestion that a popular woman poet, Miss Jean Ingelow, whose 1863 collection of verse had run to thirty editions, should be offered the post. Lord Herschell, who had made the suggestion in good faith, remarked that if the queen was able as a woman to fulfill her own onerous duties as monarch, then surely "another might be trusted to write a royal ode now and then" (Jerrold 1916, 317). The queen, however, did not see things that way.

This is not to say that Victoria's natural compassion was not aroused by the particular cases of individual women; one noteworthy example is the writer Caroline Norton, the victim of a celebrated divorce case in which Lord Melbourne had been cited as corespondent; the case had been thrown out by the judge for lack of evidence. Norton had subsequently left her husband and had lost the custody of her children. She had also been forced, under existing law, to forfeit all rights to her own property, including the royalties from her writing. This had prompted her to set up her own vigorous campaign for the laws on divorce and child custody to be changed. She appealed directly to the queen—as monarch and mother—in March 1855 for support in her cause. In her pamphlet entitled "A Letter to the Queen on Lord Cranworth's Marriage and Divorce Bill," she stressed the "grotesque anomaly which ordains that married women shall be 'non-existent' in a country governed by a female Sovereign" (Norton 1855, 4). Her arguments reiterated those of Barbara Bodichon in her own "A Brief Summary, in Plain Language, of the Most Important Laws Concerning Women" of 1854. A month after the publication of Norton's letter, a bill was introduced on the reform of the marriage and divorce laws. It became law as the Divorce Act of 1857, entitling a deserted wife to retain her own earnings, to claim for maintenance, and to be legally able to bequeath and inherit property. The legislation was a major stepping-stone toward the Married Women's Property Act of 1882. The queen made her own small gesture toward the rights of divorced women during her Golden Jubilee year in 1887, when she did away with Prince Albert's long-standing ruling that divorced women could not be invited to court drawing rooms. Surely, she argued, women who had been the innocent parties in such cases should not be penalized.

In this respect, Victoria seems to have been prepared to accept a modicum of change. What she could not abide was women's attempting to break into areas that she considered socially and sexually improper. She demanded a degree of intelligence and accomplishments in the women whom she appointed to her own royal household, for she could not abide being in the company of dull, socially inept women. But, by the same token, she also had a deep mistrust of women with emancipated attitudes, such as the outspoken Mary Ponsonby, wife of her private secretary. In particular, the queen objected most violently to such women's airing their views in public, an act that she considered "unsexed" them. In 1879, one such high-born woman, Lady Amberley (the mother of the philosopher Bertrand Russell), gave a public speech on suffrage in Stroud, Gloucestershire, for which she was vilified in the press, even though the meeting had been perfectly respectable and peaceable. Victoria queen was incandescent with outrage, launching into a famous and often quoted tirade: "The queen is most anxious to enlist everyone who can speak or write or join in checking this mad, wicked folly of 'Woman's Rights' with all its attendant horrors, on which her poor feeble sex is bent, forgetting every sense of womanly feeling and propriety," (Martin 1908, 70) she wrote. As for the misguided creature who had dared to speak out on the subject, the queen was adamant: "Lady Amberley ought to get a good whipping" (ibid.). These comments, made privately by the queen in a letter to her prime minister William Gladstone—with whom, for once, she concurred on an issue—were in fact suppressed until after Victoria's death. Even then, Lady Amberley's name was for some years styled as "Lady ——." The American suffragist Elizabeth Cady Stanton could not help observing, during one of her several trips to England, how British suffragists continued to refer to the queen with affectionate respect and loyalty in their campaigning speeches while the monarch herself continued to oppose women's rights so adamantly and did absolutely nothing to win their approbation.

Victoria made a point of indoctrinating her five daughters in her own narrow views on women's role, with varying degrees of success. Her eldest two, Vicky and Alice, both of whom had left the fold to marry and settle in Germany and were thus removed from Victoria's immediate ambit, shared an interest in women's education and became passionate supporters of women's training as nurses. The queen, like them, was a great admirer of Florence Nightingale. Whatever apprehensions she may have had about clever women, she could not fail to admire Nightingale's clarity of vision, her overriding sense of social duty, and the tenacity with which she had got things done in the Crimea; Victoria even expressed a wish that they had had a woman like Nightingale to run the War Office. There is no doubt that the queen's patronage of Nightingale did much to make nursing acceptable as a vocation that could be pursued by respectable women. And Nightingale was clever enough to use the high public profile accorded her to forward the things she was really passionate about—her radical plans for sanitary reform and an overhaul of the medical services to the British Army in India.

Victoria's unconventional third daughter, Louise, who moved in Liberal, intellectual circles, would probably have liked to have taken a more active interest in the women's rights campaign had her mother not been so meddlesome. Louise was interested in the work of the medical pioneer, Elizabeth Garrett, who established the New Hospital for Women and Children in 1872, the first in England to offer medical courses for women students. Much to Victoria's annoyance, Louise visited Garrett; she was impressed, for Garrett's work proved that there was "much women can learn, if they put their whole heart, and soul, in what they are about" (Longford 1991, 25). Louise also gave her tacit support to Josephine Butler, who embarked on a long and difficult campaign, in 1868, to repeal the Contagious Diseases Acts.

Under the influence of her antifeminist physician-in-ordinary, Dr. William Jenner, the queen had remained strongly opposed to women's medical training alongside men, although her opposition appears to have been aimed more at its obvious improprieties than at the idea of women receiving medical training of some kind per se. What horrified Victoria was the thought of respectable young women working alongside male medical students in the dissection of corpses in anatomy classes, and—even worse—looking at sexual organs—"things which could not be named before them." Such behavior sought, as she wrote to Gladstone in 1870, "to tear away all the barriers which surround a woman" and would introduce "a total disregard of what must be considered as belonging to the rules & principles of morality" (Guedalla 1933, 1:227). Her strong objections served as yet another opportunity for underlining her fundamental belief: "Let woman be what God intended; a helpmate for a man—but with totally different duties and vocations" (1:227).

A woman as inconsistent as the queen always made exceptions, however, and she certainly did so in the case of women's medical training as obstetricians, having stated that "she always regarded this branch of medicine as not necessarily a male preserve" (Longford 1966, 80). This again was no doubt prompted by the too-awful thought, to Victoria's mind, of women patients having their sexual organs examined by male obstetricians (this may explain why she never ever consulted any of her several, male, doctors about her own prolapsed womb). Victoria made a special case for women's medical training, particularly when its objective was to provide medical help to the poor, oppressed native women of the Indian subcontinent, whose religion forbade them from consulting male doctors. She shared with the philanthropists and Christian missionaries of her era a concern about traditional Hindu and Muslim practices that in their view treated women unfairly. *Sati*—the ritual self-immolation of Hindu widows on their husband's funeral pyres—had been outlawed in 1829 by the British authorities, but it still persisted in many areas. The traditional practices of polygamy, female seclusion, and child marriage also greatly exercised the holier-than-thou outrage of Victorians. Criticism was raised, justifiably so, about the treatment of child widows in India, of which there were many, since girls as young as ten were often married off to much older men. The queen endorsed the campaign to raise the age of consent in India from ten to twelve, achieved under the Age of Consent Act of 1891.

One of the most influential reformist works to attract the queen's attention was Mary Carpenter's *Six Months in India* (1868), a copy of which Carpenter had sent to the queen soon after its publication. This book argued, somewhat simplistically, that child marriage lay at the root of India's social problems. Its practice undoubtedly caused much suffering; not only did it inhibit the mental and emotional development of such young girls, and make grandmothers of many of them by their mid-twenties, but also their subjection to pregnancy at an early age took a severe physical toll on their immature bodies. Carpenter lobbied for improvements to female education in India, in the hope that this would better equip Indian girls to resist early marriage or at least delay it. Like many other women reformers, she advocated the training of women doctors in India, who might exert an influence over changes to traditional practices. The queen was impressed; Carpenter was summoned to Windsor for a private audience in March 1868. She found the queen "so full of quiet dignity, that she instantly inspired me with the feeling that I was in the presence of my *Sovereign*" (Manton 1976, 207). After describing what she had seen in India, in particular the plight of child widows and the "cruel treatment imposed on those who already had the *deepest affliction,*" Carpenter noted that "the Queen's countenance expressed profound commiseration" (207); it was some years, however, before she acted on it.

By the early 1880s women reformers in India and Britain were making representations to the British government to provide funds for the training of women doctors for India. In 1883 Victoria received two of the leading campaigners—Dr. Elizabeth Bielby and Dr. Mary Scharlieb—who were anxious to go out to India and offer their services. As a result of this meeting, Victoria asked Harriet, Lady Dufferin, the wife of the viceroy of India, to look into the matter. In 1885 Lady Dufferin, with Victoria's patronage, established the National Association to Supply Female Medical Aid to the Women of India, a charitable venture that aimed especially to offer medical help to those in purdah. The Dufferin Fund, as it was known, was able to employ British and Indian female doctors, midwives, and nurses to work in hospitals it set up in India.

In the 1880s the queen took a particular interest in the case of an Indian child bride, Rukhmabai, who went to court to have her marriage dissolved. Letters were written to the *Times* in support of Rukhmabai's case;

British and American feminists raised money to pay her legal costs in a case that dragged on for four years. In 1887, after a retrial, Rukhmabai was ordered to return to her husband's home or be sent to prison. She appealed directly to her "Queen-Empress," in this the year of the Golden Jubilee, as a "poor afflicted Hindoo woman" (Burton 1998, 1142). Such subservient tones were guaranteed to pluck the heartstrings of a monarch whom Rukhmabai and many women in India referred to as "the mother." "At such an unusual occasion will the mother listen to an earnest appeal from her millions of Indian daughters," Rukhmabai asked, "and grant them a few simple words of change into the books on Hindoo law" (1141). Queen Victoria soon after signed a special royal decree dissolving Rukhmabai's marriage and preventing her imprisonment. She retained a special interest in Indian women; in the 1890s she met with Cornelia Sorabji, the first Indian woman to study at Oxford as well as the first to be called to the bar.

The Golden Jubilee Year, 1887, was a symbolic moment in the women's rights movement in Britain. In its June issue, the *Englishwoman's Review* declared that the queen had "illustrated once for all the absurdity of the statement that political duties are incompatible with the tender sympathies of a woman's life" (Williams 1997, 145). Barbara Bodichon had argued on similar lines thirty years earlier in her *Women and Work* (1856), saying that the queen had managed to fulfill the "very arduous duties of her calling" while managing also "to be the active mother of many children" (Helsinger, Sheets, and Veeder 1983, 149). In this latter respect, Victoria's reign had indeed been an endorsement of the feminine virtues of domesticity and motherhood. The German feminist, Louise Otto, recorded that during Victoria's visit to Prussia in 1845, she had often been seen "sitting on a garden bench and—knitting stockings for her children." "This," Otto remarked, "seemed a very exaggerated kind of mother love for a queen" (Anderson 2000, 120), but it remained the unchallenged role model for the female monarch as domestic goddess rather than all-powerful autocrat, and one that the queen and Prince Albert had promoted in their own outwardly harmonious family life until his death in 1861.

By the time Victoria died in 1901, women in Britain had achieved a greater role in public life despite her generally virulent opposition to this. As the leader writer in the *Reynold's News* observed on her death: "Her life has had one great use. It has taught us the power we are willfully allowing to go to waste in the womanhood of the nation. If Victoria has been all her flatterers say, then there are many thousands of possible Victorias in the kingdom. No longer can it be argued . . . that women are unfitted for public duties. The feature of the twentieth century probably will be the utilization of this rich reserve of force. If it be so, that will be the greatest result of the reign of Queen Victoria" (Williams 1997, 145)

Related entries:
Alice Maud Mary, Princess; Louise Caroline Alberta, Princess; Nightingale, Florence; Sex, Pregnancy, and Childbirth; Victoria, Princess Royal; Victoria, Queen: As a Monarch

References and further reading:

Anderson, Bonnie S. 2000. *Joyous Greetings: The First International Women's Movement 1830–1860.* Oxford: Oxford University Press.

Benson, A. C., and Viscount Esher, eds. 1911. *The Letters of Queen Victoria, 1837–1861.* 1st ser., 3 vols. London: John Murray.

Burton, Antoinette. 1998. "From 'Child Bride' to 'Hindoo Lady': Rukhmabai and the Debate about Sexual Respectability in Imperial Britain." *American Historical Review* 104 (4): 1,119–1,146.

Guedalla, Philip, ed. 1933. *The Queen and Mr. Gladstone.* 2 vols. London: Hodder and Stoughton.

Helsinger, Elizabeth K., Robin Lauterbach Sheets, and William Veeder. 1983. *The Woman Question: Society and Literature in Britain and*

America, 1837–1883. Vol. 2: *Social Issues, 1837–1883.* Manchester, UK: Manchester University Press.

Hough, Richard, ed. 1975. *Advice to a Granddaughter: Letters from Queen Victoria to Princess Victoria of Hesse.* London: Heinemann.

Jerrold, Clare. 1916. *The Widowhood of Queen Victoria.* London: Eveleigh Nash.

Longford, Elizabeth. 1966. "Queen Elizabeth's Doctors." In Martin Gilbert, ed., *A Century of Conflict 1850–1950.* London: Hamish Hamilton.

———. 1991. *Darling Loosy: Letters to Princess Louise, 1856–1939.* London: Weidenfeld and Nicolson.

Manton, Jo. 1976. *Mary Carpenter and the Children of the Streets.* London: Heinemann.

Martin, Sir Theodore. 1908. *Queen Victoria as I Knew Her.* London: William Blackwood and Son.

Rappaport, Helen. 2001. *An Encyclopedia of Women Social Reformers.* 2 vols. Santa Barbara, CA: ABC-CLIO.

Wells, H. G. 1934. *Experiment in Autobiography: Discoveries and Conclusions of a Very Ordinary Brain (since 1866).* 2 vols. London: Victor Gollancz.

Williams, Richard. 1997. *The Contentious Crown: Public Discussion of the British Monarchy in the Reign of Queen Victoria.* Aldershot, Hampshire: Ashgate.

CHRONOLOGY

1807 Slave trade abolished throughout the British Empire

1815 Napoleon defeated at the battle of Waterloo

1818 Edward, duke of Kent, marries Victoria of Saxe-Coburg-Saalfeld

1819 *24 May:* Birth of Alexandrina Victoria, only child of Edward, duke of Kent

26 August: Birth of Prince Albert at the Castle Rosenau, Coburg

Peterloo Massacre in Manchester

1820 The Prince Regent becomes George IV (to 1830)

1824 Louise Lehzen appointed as Princess Victoria's governess (elevated to baroness 1827)

1825 Trade Unions legalized

First steam locomotive railway opened

1829 Catholic emancipation; establishment of Metropolitan Police

The British government bans the practice of *sati* (ritual immolation of a widow on her husband's funeral pyre) in India

1830 Opening of the Liverpool to Manchester railway

William IV becomes king (to 1837)

1831 Victoria's Uncle Leopold becomes king of the Belgians (to 1856)

1832 First Reform Bill in Britain enfranchises male but not female property holders

1833 Abolition of slavery throughout Britain's colonies

1834 The Poor Law Amendment Act abolishes outdoor relief and extends the workhouse system

1835 William Lamb, Lord Melbourne, is prime minister (Whig) (to 1841)

Princess Victoria dangerously ill for five weeks at Ramsgate

1836–1865 Charles Dickens publishes his major, social novels—promoting an upswing in philanthropy and charitable work in Britain, leading to reform of the Poor Laws and the workhouse system

1836 *May–June:* First visit of Prince Albert to England

1837 *20 June:* Accession of Queen Victoria

1838 *28 June:* Coronation of Queen Victoria

Anti–Corn Law League founded

1838 Chartists launch their "People's charter"

1839 *October:* Prince Albert's second visit to England

15 October: Engaged to Victoria

Lady Flora Hastings Affair

The Bedchamber Crisis

Severe economic depression in England

First Anglo-Chinese Opium War (to 1841)

Development of the daguerreotype

1840 *10 February:* Marriage of Victoria and Albert

10 June: First assassination attempt against queen

November: Birth of the queen's first child, Princess Victoria Adelaide Mary Louise, the Princess Royal

Rowland Hill introduces the Penny Post

1841 *November:* Birth of Albert Edward, Prince of Wales

The satirical magazine *Punch* begins publication

Melbourne's Whig ministry falls; succeeded by the Tory Sir Robert Peel (to 1846)

1842 Chartist riots in England

29 May and 3 July: Second and third assassination attempts

August–September: Queen Victoria and Prince Albert visit Scotland for the first time

Baroness Lehzen retires

1843 *April:* Birth of Princess Alice Maud Mary

Charles Dickens's *A Christmas Carol*

The queen and Prince Albert buy Osborne House on the Isle of Wight

Queen Victoria and Prince Albert visit King Louis Philippe of France at the Chateau of Eu in Normandy

1844 *August:* Birth of Prince Alfred Ernest Albert

Factory Act limits working day of women to twelve hours and that of children aged eight to thirteen to six and a half hours

The first telegraph line is laid in Britain

1845 Benjamin Disraeli publishes *Sybil: Or The Two Nations*

Queen Victoria and Prince Albert visit Coburg

1845–1846 Potato famine in Ireland

1846 Repeal of Corn Laws; free trade

May: Birth of Princess Helena Augusta Victoria

Lord John Russell (Whig) becomes prime minister (to 1852)

1847 Queen Victoria establishes Irish Famine Fund

Cholera epidemic (to 1849)

Charlotte Brontë's *Jane Eyre;* Emily Brontë's *Wuthering Heights*

The queen and Prince Albert buy Balmoral Castle in Scotland

1848 Height of the Chartist Movement and final Chartist petition after mass rally at Kennington Common

Public Health Act

March: Birth of Princess Louise Caroline Alberta

The year of revolutions in France, Germany, Italy, and Austria; major cities—Berlin, Paris, Vienna, Naples, Venice, and Warsaw—are affected

Second Republic in France (to 1852)

Marx and Engels's *Communist Manifesto*

Formation of pre-Raphaelite group of artists

1849 Alfred, Lord Tennyson, becomes poet laureate

The British annex the Punjab in India and acquire the Koh-i-Noor diamond

May: Fourth assassination attempt on the queen

Frances Buss founds the first public day school for girls—The North London Collegiate School

1850 Tennyson's *In Memoriam*

Fifth assassination attempt on the queen

Death of Sir Robert Peel

May: Birth of Prince Arthur William Patrick Albert

1851 *May:* Queen opens the Great Exhibition at the Crystal Palace

John Stuart Mill publishes "On the Enfranchisement of Women"

In France, Louis Napoleon seizes power; proclaimed emperor in 1852

1852 Harriet Beecher Stowe's *Uncle Tom's Cabin*

Lord Derby (Tory) becomes prime minister (February–June); Lord Aberdeen takes over as prime minister of Whig/Peelite coalition (to 1855)

Death of the duke of Wellington; Prince Albert organizes the duke's state funeral

1853 *April:* Birth of Prince Leopold George Duncan Albert

Construction begins of new royal home at Balmoral

1854 British women of the Langham Place Circle begin the campaign for a Married Women's Property Act (not passed until 1882)

1854–1856 *From 25 March:* Crimean War: Florence Nightingale takes charge of the British Army Hospital at Scutari

Battle of the Alma, 20 September 1854

Charge of the Light Brigade at the battle of Balaklava, 25 October 1854

October 1854–September 1855: Siege of Sebastopol

1854 Lord Palmerston (Whig) prime minister (to 1858)

Queen Victoria and Prince Albert make a successful state visit to the emperor and empress of France

David Livingstone discovers the Victoria Falls

1856 *March:* The Peace of Paris ends the Crimean War

The Victoria Cross in instituted

1857 Indian Rebellion (to 1858); *June–November:* Siege of Lucknow

June: Massacre at Cawnpore

Prince Albert is made prince consort by Royal Letters Patent

First Atlantic cable laid

April: Birth of Princess Beatrice Mary Victoria Feodora

Lord Rothschild is the first Jew to become a member of Parliament

Queen awards first Victoria Crosses to soldiers from Crimean War

Second Anglo-Chinese Opium War (to 1858)

1858 Transfer of the British East India Company to the Crown; Victoria becomes direct ruler of India

Lord Derby (Tory) prime minister (to 1859)

Irish Republican Brotherhood (Fenians) founded in New York

1859 Lord Palmerston (Whig) prime minister (to 1865)

Lord Canning becomes first Viceroy of India

Darwin's *The Origin of Species*

John Stuart Mill's *On Liberty*

1859–1860 Mrs. Beeton's *Book of Household Management*

1860 Unification of Italy by Garibaldi; Victor Emmanuel II proclaimed king 1861

1861 Joseph Lister pioneers antiseptic surgery

1861–1865 American Civil War

1861 The *Trent* Affair provokes political crisis between Britain and United States

March: Death of queen's mother, the duchess of Kent

14 December: Death of the prince consort at Windsor Castle

Abolition of serfdom in Russia

1862 Otto von Bismarck becomes premier of Prussia

18 December: Prince consort reburied in the royal mausoleum at Frogmore

1863 Marriage of Prince of Wales to Alexandra of Denmark

First underground rail line opens in London

1864 Albert Memorial begins construction (to 1875)

John Brown is appointed the queen's Highland servant

Austro-Prussian forces invade the duchies of Schleswig and Holstein; at treaty of Vienna, the Danes are forced to concede Schleswig to Prussia and Holstein to Austria

1865 Lord John Russell (Liberal) prime minister (to 1866)

William Booth founds the Christian Mission in the East End (in 1878 it becomes the Salvation Army)

1866 Queen Victoria attends state opening of Parliament—her first public engagement since the death of Prince Albert

Lord Derby (Conservative) prime minister (to 1868)

Austro-Prussian War

1867 Second Reform Bill extends the franchise

Walter Bagehot's *The English Constitution* defines the role of the monarchy

1868 *February–December:* From December William Gladstone (Liberal) prime minister (to 1874)

Benjamin Disraeli's first term as prime minister (Conservative)

Establishment of the Trades Union Congress in Manchester

Queen Victoria publishes *Leaves from the Journal of Our Life in the Highlands*

1869 Opening of Suez Canal in Egypt

J. S. Mill's *The Subjection of Women*

Disestablishment of the Anglican Church in Ireland

Girton College, Cambridge—the first women's college in Britain

1870 Charles Darwin's *The Descent of Man*

Appointment of Henry Ponsonby as queen's private secretary (to 1895)

Foster's Education Act introduces elementary education in England and Wales

Franco-Prussian War (to 1871)

Death of Charles Dickens

1871 Unification of Germany under William I; Bismarck promoted to chancellor

March–May: Paris Commune

Louis Napoleon is dethroned and seeks refuge in England

Third Republic in France (to 1940)

George Eliot's *Middlemarch*

Queen Victoria seriously ill with abscess on her arm; Prince of Wales recovers from a serious attack of typhoid fever

1872 *February:* Sixth assassination attempt against the queen

1873 Foundation of the Irish Home Rule League

State visit of the shah of Persia

1874 Benjamin Disraeli is Conservative prime minister (to 1880)

Sophia Jex-Blake founds the London School of Medicine for Women

1876 Alexander Graham Bell invents the telephone

March: Official unveiling of the Albert Memorial

Sir Henry Morton Stanley explores the Congo River

Queen Victoria is proclaimed empress of India under the Royal Titles Act

Queen Victoria supports passing of the Cruelty to Animals Act—the first attempt in Britain to control the practice of vivisection

1877–1878 Russo-Turkish War

1877 The British annex the Transvaal in southern Africa

Thomas Alva Edison invents the phonograph

1878 Congress of Berlin

Foundation of the Salvation Army

Death of queen's daughter Princess Alice

1879 Irish Land League formed

1879 Zulu War

At age sixty, Queen Victoria becomes a great-grandmother

1880 Gladstone's second ministry (to 1885)

1881 Second Irish Land Act; foundation of Irish National Land League

Death of Benjamin Disraeli

The Mahdi's rebellion in the Sudan (to 1885)

Tsar Alexander II is assassinated

1882 Phoenix Park murders in Dublin

The Triple Alliance of Germany, Austria-Hungary, and Italy is formed

Seventh assassination attempt against the queen

Married Women's Property Act

1883 Death of John Brown

1884 Death of the queen's hemophiliac son, Prince Leopold

Third Reform Act increases the electorate to c. 5 million

Fabian Society and Social Democratic Federation founded

Queen Victoria publishes *More Leaves from the Journal of a Life in the Highlands from 1862–1882*

1885 Death of General Gordon at Khartoum

1886 Gladstone's Home Rule Bill defeated

Lord Salisbury is Conservative prime minister (to 1892)

First Indian National Congress

The "scramble for Africa" begins when gold is discovered in the Transvaal

1887 Queen Victoria's Golden Jubilee

The queen appoints her first Indian servants, including the Munshi

1888 George Eastman develops the Kodak box camera

August–November: Jack the Ripper murders in London's East End

Formation of Independent Labour Party

The queen's eldest daughter, Vicky, becomes empress, but her husband dies of throat cancer after only three months on the throne

The queen's grandson becomes Kaiser William II of Germany

1889 The Paris Exposition

1892 Gladstone's third ministry (to 1894)

1893 Gladstone's second Home Rule Bill is defeated by the House of Lords

Opening of the Imperial Institute

1894 Lord Rosebery (Liberal) is prime minister (to 1895)

Opening of the Manchester Ship Canal by Queen Victoria

Dreyfus Affair (to 1896)

Armenian massacres by the Turks

1895 Lord Salisbury is prime minister (to 1902)

December–January 1896: The Jameson raid in southern Africa

Guglielmo Marconi invents the telegraph

Moving pictures (the cinematograph) are invented by Auguste Lumière

1896 Death of Queen Victoria's favorite son-in-law, Prince Henry of Battenberg

23 September: Queen Victoria is now the longest-reigning monarch in British history

Tsar Nicholas II and his family visit Balmoral

1897 Queen Victoria's Diamond Jubilee

1898 Kitchener defeats the Mahdi and his forces at the battle of Omdurman

Death of Gladstone

The Fashoda Crisis

Rapid expansion of Germany's naval fleet

1899 The Boer War (to 1902)

Edward Elgar's *Enigma Variations*

1900 The sieges at Ladysmith and Mafeking are lifted

The "khaki" election gives Salisbury a Liberal landslide

Emily Hobhouse exposes conditions in British concentration camps in southern Africa

Foundation of the Labour Party

The queen's son Alfred, duke of Edinburgh, is the third of her children to predecease her

1901 *22 January:* Death of Queen Victoria at Osborne House, Isle of Wight

5 August: Death of Queen Victoria's eldest daughter, Vicky

1914–1918 World War I

BIBLIOGRAPHY

Primary Sources

Ackroyd, Peter. 1990. *Dickens.* London: Sinclair Stevenson.

Adkin, Mark. 1996. *The Charge: Why the Light Brigade Was Lost.* London: Leo Cooper.

Albert, Harold. 1967. *The Life and Letters of Princess Feodora: Queen Victoria's Sister.* London: Robert Hale.

Alexander, Michael, and Sushila Anand. 2001. *Queen Victoria's Maharajah.* London: Phoenix.

Alice, Countess of Athlone. 1996. *For My Grandchildren.* London: Evans.

Alice, Grand Duchess of Hesse. 1885. *Letters to Her Majesty the Queen.* London: John Murray.

Allen, Bernard. M. 1931. *Gordon and the Sudan.* London: Macmillan.

Allen, Charles. 1986. *A Glimpse of the Burning Plain: Leaves from the Indian Journals of Charlotte Canning.* London: Michael Joseph.

Allen, Walter Gore. 1960. *King William IV.* London: Cresset Press.

Ames, Winslow. 1968. *Prince Albert and Victorian Taste.* London: Chapman and Hall.

Ansand, Sushila. 1996. *Indian Sahib: Queen Victoria's Dear Abdul.* London: Duckworth.

Arengo-Jones, Peter. 1995. *Queen Victoria in Switzerland.* London: Robery Hale.

Aronson, Theo. 1972. *Queen Victoria and the Buonapartes.* London: Cassell.

———. 1973. *Grandmama of Europe: The Crowned Descendants of Queen Victoria.* London: Cassell.

———. 1977. *Victoria and Disraeli: The Making of a Romantic Partnership.* London: Macmillan.

———. 1991. *Heart of a Queen: Queen Victoria's Romantic Attachments.* London: John Murray.

———. 1994. *Prince Eddy and the Homosexual Underworld.* London: John Murray.

Ashdown, Dulcie. 1974. *Queen Victoria's Mother.* London: Robert Hale.

———. 1975. *Queen Victoria's Family.* London: Robert Hale.

Aston, Sir George. 1929. *HRH The Duke of Connaught and Strathearn.* London: Harrap.

Aubrey, Octave. 1939. *Eugénie, Empress of the French.* London: Cobden & Sanderson.

Auchinloss, Louis. 1979. *Persons of Consequence: Queen Victoria and Her Circle.* London: Weidenfeld and Nicolson.

Auden, W. H., ed. 1947. *A Selection from the Poems of Alfred Lord Tennyson.* Garden City, NY: Doubleday.

Auerbach, Jeffrey A. 1999. *The Great Exhibition of 1851: A Nation on Display.* New Haven: Yale University Press.

Bagehot, Walter. 1867. *The English Constitution.* London: Chapman and Hall.

Balfour, Michael. 1964. *The Kaiser and His Times.* London: Cresset Press.

Ball, T. Frederick. 1886. *Queen Victoria: Scenes and Incidents of Her Life and Reign.* London: S. W. Partridge.

Battiscombe, Georgina. 1969. *Queen Alexandra.* London: Constable.

Bell, G. K. A. 1952. *Randall Davidson, Archbishop of Canterbury.* 2 vols. Oxford: Oxford University Press.

Bennett, Daphne. 1971. *Vicky: Princess Royal of England and German Empress.* New York: St. Martin's Press.

———. 1977. *King without a Crown: Albert Prince Consort of England 1819–1861.* London: Heinemann.

———. 1980 *Queen Victoria's Daughters.* London: Gollancz

———. 1983. *King without a Crown.* London: Heinemann.

Benson, A. C., and Viscount Esher, eds. 1911. *The Letters of Queen Victoria: A Selection from Her Majesty's Correspondence between the Years 1837 and 1861.* 1st ser., 3 vols. London: John Murray.

Benson, E. F. 1939. *Daughters of Queen Victoria.* London: Cassell and Co.

Bigland, Eileen. 1953. *Marie Corelli: The Woman and the Legend.* London: Jarrolds.

Bismarck, Otto von. 1966. *The Memoirs: Being the Reflections and Reminiscences of Otto, Prince von Bismarck.* Edited by A. J. Butler. New York: Howard Fertig.

Blake, Robert. 1966. *Disraeli.* London: Eyre and Spottiswoode.

Bland, Olivia. 1986. *The Royal Way of Death.* London: Constable.

Bolitho, Hector. 1949. *The Reign of Queen Victoria.* London: Collins.

———. 1964. *Albert, Prince Consort.* London: Max Parrish.

Bostridge, Mark. Forthcoming. *Florence Nightingale: The Making of an Icon.* Harmondsworth, UK: Penguin.

Bourne, Kenneth. 1982. *Palmerston: The Early Years, 1781 to 1841.* London: Allen Lane.

Boykin, Edward, ed. 1957. *Victoria, Albert and Mrs. Stevenson.* London: Frederick Muller.

Bradford, Sarah. 1983. *Disraeli.* London: Weidenfeld and Nicolson.

Bresler, Fenton. 1999. *Napoleon III: A Life.* London: HarperCollins.

Brindle, Steven. 1997. *Windsor Revealed: A New Light on the History of the Castle.* London: English Heritage.

Brooks, Chris, ed. 2000. *The Albert Memorial: The Prince Consort National Memorial: Its History, Contests and Conservation.* New Haven: Yale University Press.

Brooks, David. 1986. *The Destruction of Lord Rosebery.* London: Historians Press.

Brook-Shepherd, Gordon. 1975. *Uncle of Europe: The Social and Diplomatic Life of Edward VII.* London: Collins.

Brown, David. 1979. *Walter Scott and the Historical Imagination.* London: Routledge and Keegan Paul.

Brown, Raymond Lamont. 2000. *John Brown: Queen Victoria's Highland Servant.* Stroud, Gloucestershire: Sutton.

Bryant, Arthur. 1961. *English Saga 1840–1940.* London: Fontana.

Buchan, John. *Gordon at Khartoum.* London: P. Davies.

Buchanan, Meriel. 1954. *Queen Victoria's Relations.* London: Cassell.

Buckle, G. E., ed. 1926–1928. *The Letters of Queen Victoria: A Selection from Her Majesty's Correspondence and Journal between the Years 1862 and 1885.* 2d ser., 3 vols. London: John Murray.

Buckle, George Earl, ed. 1930–1932. *Letters of Queen Victoria: A Selection from Her Majesty's Correspondence and Journal between the Years 1886 and 1901.* 3d ser., 3 vols. London: John Murray.

Bullock, Rev. Charles. 1887. *The Queen's Resolve "I Will Be Good": With Royal Anecdotes and Incidents.* London: "Home Words" Publishing Office.

Burton, Anthony. 1999. *Vision and Accident: The Story of the Victoria and Albert Museum.* London:V & A Publications.

Bury, J. P. T. 1964. *Napoleon III and the Second Empire.* London: Hodder and Stoughton.

Campbell, Christy. 2000. *The Maharaja's Box.* London: HarperCollins.

———. 2002. *Fenian Fire: The British Government Plot to Assassinate Queen Victoria.* London: HarperCollins.

Carey, Agnes. 1922. *The Empress Eugénie in Exile.* London: John Lane.

Cecil, Algernon. 1953. *Queen Victoria and Her Prime Ministers.* London: Eyre and Spottiswoode.

Cecil, David. 1954. *Lord M.: Or the Later Life of Lord Melbourne.* London: Constable.

Cecil, Lady Gwendolen. 1921–1932. *Life of Robert, Marquess of Salisbury.* 4 vols. London: Hodder and Stoughton.

Cecil, Lamar. 1989–1996. *Wilhelm II.* 2 vols. Chapel Hill: University of North Carolina Press.

Chamberlain, Muriel E. 1983. *Lord Aberdeen: A Political Biography.* London: Longman.

Chamberlain, Muriel. 1987. *Lord Palmerston.* Cardiff: University of Wales Press.

Chapman, Caroline, and Paul Raban. 1977. *Debrett's Queen Victoria's Jubilees.* London: Debrett.

Charlot, Monica. 1991. *Victoria, the Young Queen.* Cambridge: Polity.

Chaudhuri, Sashi Bhusan. 1979. *English Historical Writings on the Indian Mutiny, 1857–59.* Calcutta: World Press.

Chomet, Seweryn. 1999. *Helena, Princess Reclaimed: The Life and Times of Queen Victoria's Third Daughter.* New York: Begell House.

Churchill, Winston. 1990. *The Boer War.* London: Mandarin.

Clark, Ronald W. 1981. *Balmoral: Queen Victoria's Highland Home.* London: Thames and Hudson.

Conacher, J. 1968. *The Aberdeen Coalition 1852–1855.* Cambridge: Cambridge University Press.

Connell, Brian, ed. 1926. *Regina vs. Palmerston: The Correspondence between Queen Victoria and Her Foreign and Prime Minister, 1837–1865.* London: Evans Brothers.

Corelli, Marie. 1901. *The Passing of the Great Queen.* London: Methuen and Co.

Corti, Count E. 1923. *Leopold of Belgium.* London: Unwin.

Corti, Egon Caesar Conte. 1957. *The English Empress: A Study in Relations between Queen Victoria and Her Eldest Daughter, Empress Frederick of Germany.* London: Cassell and Co.

Cowles, Virginia. 1956. *Edward VII and His Circle.* London: Hamish Hamilton.

———. 1963. *The Kaiser.* New York: Harper and Row.

Crabitès, Pierre. 1937. *Victoria's Guardian Angel: A Study of Baron Stockmar.* London: Routledge.

Craik, D. M. M. 1887. *Fifty Golden Years: Incidents in the Queen's Reign.* London: R. Tuck and Sons.

Crankshaw, Edward. 1981. *Bismarck.* London: Viking.

Creevey, Thomas. 1948. *Creevey: Selected and Re-edited by John Gore.* London: John Murray.

Creston, Dormer. 1952. *The Youthful Queen Victoria: A Discursive Account.* London: Macmillan and Co.

Crewe, First Marquess of. 1931. *Lord Rosebery.* 2 vols. London: John Murray.

Croker, John Wilson. 1967. *The Croker Papers.* London: B. T. Batsford.

Cullen, Tom. 1969. *The Empress Brown: The Story of a Royal Friendship.* London: Bodley Head.

Darby, Elisabeth, and Nicola Smith. 1982. *The Cult of the Prince Consort.* New Haven: Yale University Press.

David, Saul. 2002. *The Indian Mutiny 1857.* London: Viking.

Davis, Richard M. 1976. *Disraeli.* London: Hutchinson.

De-La-Noy, Michael. 1990. *Windsor Castle: Past and Present.* London: Headline.

Dewhurst, Jack. 1980. *Royal Confinements.* London: Weidenfeld and Nicolson.

Dickens, Charles. [1843] 1994. *A Christmas Carol.* Ware, UK: Wordsworth Editions.

Dimond, Frances, and Ann Taylor. 1987. *Crown and Camera: The Royal Family and Photography.* Harmondsworth, UK: Penguin.

Duff, David, ed. 1980. *Queen Victoria's Highland Journals.* London: Webb and Bower.

Duff, David. 1938. *Edward of Kent.* London: S. Paul and Co.

———. 1940. *The Life Story of HRH Princess Louise, Duchess of Argyll.* Bath, UK: Cedric Chivers.

———. 1958. *The Shy Princess: H.R.H. Beatrice. The Enthralling Life Story of a Queen's Daughter and the Mother of a Queen.* London: Evans.

———. 1967. *Hessian Tapestry.* London: Macmillan.

———. 1970. *Victoria Travels: Journeys of Queen Victoria between 1830 and 1900, with Extracts from Her Journal.* London: Frederick Muller.

———. 1980. *Alexandra: Princess and Queen.* London: Collins.

Dyson, Hope, and Charles Tennyson, eds. 1969. *Dear and Honoured Lady: The Correspondence between Queen Victoria and Alfred, Lord Tennyson.* London: Macmillan.

Eccleshall, Robert, and Graham Walker, eds. 1998. *Biographical Dictionary of British Prime Ministers.* London: Routledge.

Eilers, Marlene A. 1997. *Queen Victoria's Descendants.* Falkoping, Sweden: Rosvall Royal Books.

Emden, Paul. 1934. *Behind the Throne.* London: Hodder and Stoughton.

Epton, Nina. 1971. *Victoria and Her Daughters.* London: Weidenfeld and Nicolson.

Erickson, Carolly. 1997. *Her Little Majesty.* London: Robson.

Erskine, Mrs. Stewart, ed. 1916. *Twenty Years at Court: From the Correspondence of the Hon. Eleanor Stanley.* London: Nisbet and Co.

Esher, Viscount, ed. 1912. *The Girlhood of Queen Victoria: A Selection from Her Majesty's Diaries between the Years of 1832 and 1840.* 2 vols. London: John Murray.

———. 1914. *The Training of a Sovereign.* London: John Murray.

Eyck, Frank. 1975. *The Prince Consort: A Political Biography.* Bath, UK: Cedric Chivers.

Fairclough, Melvin. 1992. *The Ripper and the Royals.* London: Gerald Duckworth and Co.

Farndon, John. 1990. *Royal Castle: The Inside Story of Windsor.* London: Viking.

Farwell, Byron. 1999. *Queen Victoria's Little Wars.* Ware, Hertfordshire: Wordsworth Editions.

Fay, Charles Ryle. 1951. *Palace of Industry 1851: A Study of the Great Exhibition and Its Fruits.* Cambridge: Cambridge University Press.

Feuchtwanger, E. J. 1975. *Gladstone.* London: Allen Lane.

Ffrench Blake, R. L. V. 1972. *The Crimean War.* Hamden, CT: Archon Books.

Foot, M. R. D., and H. C. G. Matthews, eds. 1968–1994. *The Gladstone Diaries.* 14 vols. Oxford: Clarendon Press.

Frankland, Noble. 1993. *Witness of a Century: The Life and Times of Prince Arthur, Duke of Connaught.* London: Shepheard-Walwyn.

Frogmore House and the Royal Mausoleum. 2000. Official Guide. London: St. James's Palace.

Fulford, Roger. [1933] 2000. *Royal Dukes.* Harmondsworth, UK: Penguin.

———. 1966. *The Prince Consort.* London: Macmillan.

———. 1975. *From Hanover to Windsor.* London: Fontana.

———. 1981. *Beloved Mama: Private Correspondence of Queen Victoria and the German Crown Princess, 1878–85.* London: Evans Brothers.

———, ed. 1963. *The Greville Memoirs.* London: B. T. Batsford.

———, ed. 1964. *Dearest Child: Letters between Queen Victoria and the Princess Royal, 1858–61.* London: Evans Brothers.

———, ed. 1968. *Dearest Mama: Private Correspondence of Queen Victoria and the Crown Princess of Prussia, 1861–64.* London: Evans Brothers.

———, ed. 1971. *Your Dear Letter: Private Correspondence of Queen Victoria and the Crown Princess of Prussia, 1865–71.* London: Evans Brothers.

———, ed. 1976. *Darling Child: Private Correspondence of Queen Victoria and the Crown Princess of Prussia, 1871–1878.* London: Evans Brothers.

Gall, Lothar. 1986. *Bismarck: The White Revolutionary.* 2 vols. London: Allen and Unwin.

Gash, Norman. 1961. *Mr. Secretary Peel: The Life of Sir Robert Peel to 1830.* London: Longman.

———. 1972. *Sir Robert Peel: The Life of Sir Robert after 1830.* London: Longman.

Gernsheim, Helmut, and A. Gernsheim. 1959. *Queen Victoria: A Biography in Word and Picture.* London: Longman, Green and Co.

Gernsheim, Helmut, and Alison Gernsheim. 1962. *Edward VII and Queen Alexandra.* London: F. Muller.

———.1969. *The History of Photography.* Rev. ed. London: Thames and Hudson.

Gillen, Mollie. 1970. *The Prince and His Lady.* Toronto: Griffin House.

Girouard, Mark. 1993. *Windsor: The Most Romantic Castle.* London: Hodder and Stoughton.

Goldie, Sue M. 1987. *I Have Done My Duty: Florence Nightingale in the Crimean War 1854–1856.* Manchester, UK: Manchester University Press.

Gosse, Edmund. 1901. "The Character of Queen Victoria." *Quarterly Review* (January–April): 301–307.

Green, Vivian H. H. 1963. *The Hanoverians 1714–1815.* London: Arnold.

Grenville, J. A. S. 1970. *Lord Salisbury and Foreign Policy: The Close of the Nineteenth Century.* London: Athlone Press.

Grey, Lieutenant-General, The Hon. Charles. 1867. *The Early Years of H.R.H. the Prince Consort.* London: Smith, Elder and Co.

Guedalla, Philip. 1926. *Palmerston.* London: Ernest Benn.

———. 1933. *The Queen and Mr. Gladstone, 1845–1898.* 2 vols. London: Hodder and Stoughton.

Guest, Ivor. 1952. *Napoleon III in England.* London: British Technical and General Press.

Hamilton, Gerald. 1964. *Blood Royal.* London: A. Gibbs and Philips.

Hardie, Frank. 1935. *The Political Influence of Queen Victoria.* London: Oxford University Press.

Hardy, Alan. 1976. *Queen Victoria Was Amused.* London: John Murray.

Harlow, Barbara, and Mia Carter, eds. 1999. *Imperialism and Orientalism: A Documentary Sourcebook.* Oxford: Blackwell.

Harris, J., G. de Bellaigue, and O. Millar. 1968. *Buckingham Palace.* London: Nelson.

Harrison, Michael. 1965. *Clarence: The Life of the Duke of Clarence and Avondale KG 1864–1892.* London: W. H. Allen.

Hasted, Jane Eliza. 1950. *Unsuccessful Ladies: An Intimate Account of the Aunts (Official and Unofficial) of the Late Queen Victoria.* London: Ayer Publishing.

Healey, Edna. 1997. *The Queen's House: A Social History of Buckingham Palace.* London: Michael Joseph.

Hedley, Olwen. 1994. *Windsor Castle.* London: Hale.

Heffer, Simon. 1998. *Power and Place: The Political Consequences of King Edward VII.* London: Weidenfeld and Nicolson.

Hibbert, Chrisopher. 1964. *The Court at Windsor: A Domestic History.* London: Longman.

———. 1972–1973. *George IV.* 2 vols. London: Longman.

———. 1976. *Edward VII: A Portrait.* London: Allen Lane.

———. 1979. *The Court of St. James: The Monarch at Work from Victoria to Elizabeth II.* London: Weidenfeld and Nicolson.

———. 1980. *The Great Mutiny, India 1857.* Harmondsworth, UK: Penguin.

———. 1984. *Queen Victoria in Her Letters and Journals.* London: Viking.

———. 2000. *Queen Victoria, a Personal History.* London: HarperCollins.

Hilton, Richard. 1957. *The Indian Mutiny: A Centenary History.* London: Hollis and Carter.

Hobhouse, Hermione. 1983. *Prince Albert: His Life and Work.* London: Hamish Hamilton.

Holland, Caroline. 1909. *Notebooks of a Spinster Lady.* London: Cassell.

Homans, Margaret. 1998. *Royal Representations: Queen Victoria and British Culture, 1837–1876.* Chicago: University of Chicago Press.

Hopkirk, Mary. 1946. *Queen Adelaide.* London: John Murray.

Hough, Richard. 1992. *Edward and Alexandra: Their Private and Public Lives.* London: Hodder and Stoughton.

———. 1996. *Victoria and Albert: Their Love and Their Tragedies.* London: Richard Cohen.

———, ed. 1975. *Advice to a Grand-daughter: Letters from Queen Victoria to Princess Victoria of Hesse.* London: Heinemann.

House, Madeline, and Graham Storey. 1965. *The Letters of Charles Dickens.* Pilgrim Edition, vol. 2. Oxford: Clarendon Press.

———. 1998. *The Letters of Charles Dickens.* Pilgrim Edition, vol. 10. Oxford: Clarendon Press.

Housman, Laurence. 1932. "Florence Nightingale." In H. J. Massingham and Hugh Massingham, eds., *The Great Victorians.* London: Ivor Nicholson and Watson.

Houston, Gail Turley. 1999. *Royalties: The Queen and Victorian Writers.* Charlottesville: University Press ofVirginia.

Howarth, Stephen. 1980. *The Koh-i-Noor Diamond: The History and the Legend.* London: Quartet Books.

Hudson, Derek. 1972. *Munby, Man of Two Worlds: The Life and Diaries of Arthur J. Munby.* London: Abacus.

Hudson, Katherine. 1994. *A Royal Conflict: Sir John Conroy and the Young Victoria.* London: Hodder and Stoughton.

Iremonger, Lucille. 1978. *Lord Aberdeen: A Biography of the Fourth Earl of Aberdeen, K. G., K.T., Prime Minister 1852–1855.* London: Collins.

Jagow, Dr. Kurt, ed. 1938. *Letters of the Prince Consort, 1831–1861.* London: John Murray.

James, Robert Rhodes. 1963. *Rosebery: A Biography of Archibald Philip, Fifth Earl of Rosebery.* London: Weidenfeld and Nicolson.

———. 1983. *Albert Prince Consort.* London: Hamish Hamilton.

Jay, Elisabeth. 1999. "'Mrs. Brown' by Windsor's Other Widow." *Women's History Review* 6., no. 2: 191–200.

Jenkins, Roy. 1995. *Gladstone.* London: Macmillan.

Jerrold, Clare. 1912. *The Married Life of Queen Victoria.* London: Eveleigh Nash.

———. 1916. *The Widowhood of Queen Victoria.* London: Eveleigh Nash.

Jeune, Susan Mary, Baroness St. Helier. 1909. *Memories of Fifty Years.* London: Edward Arnold.

Johnson, Edgar. 1970. *Sir Walter Scott: The Great Unknown.* 2 vols. London: Hamish Hamilton.

Jump, J. D., ed. 1995. *Tennyson, the Critical Heritage.* London: Routledge.

Keller, Ulrich. 2001. *The Ultimate Spectacle: A Visual History of the Crimean War.* Amsterdam: Gordon and Breach.

Kennedy, A. L. 1953. *Salisbury, 1830–1903: Portrait of a Statesman.* London: John Murray.

———. 1956. *My Dear Duchess: Social and Political Letters to the Duchess of Manchester.* London: John Murray.

Kent, George O. 1978. *Bismarck and His Times.* Carbondale: Southern Illinois University Press.

Kenyon, Edith C. 1887. *Scenes in the Life of Princess Alice (Grand Duchess of Hesse).* London: W. Nicholson and Sons.

Kerr, John. 1992. *Queen Victoria's Scottish Diaries: Her Dream Days.* Moffat, Scotland: Lochar Publishing.

Kollander, Patricia. 1995. *Frederick III: Germany's Liberal Emperor.* Westport, CT: Greenwood Press.

Kuhn, William. 2002. *Henry and Mary Ponsonby: Life at the Court of Queen Victoria.* London: Duckworth.

Kurtz, Harold. 1964. *Eugenie, Empress, Consort of Napoleon III, Emperor of the French, 1826–1920.* London: Hamish Hamilton.

Lamont-Brown, Raymond. 2000. *John Brown: Queen Victoria's Highland Servant.* Stroud, Gloucestershire: Sutton.

Lant, J. I. 1980. *Insubstantial Pageant: Ceremony and Confusion at Queen Victoria's Court.* New York: Taplinger.

Leapman, Michael. 2001. *The World for a Shilling: How the Great Exhibition of 1851 Shaped a Nation.* London: Headline.

Lee, Arthur Gould, ed. 1955. *The Empress Frederick Writes to Sophie, Her Daughter, Crown Princess and Queen of the Hellenes: Letters 1889–1901.* London: Faber.

Lee, Sir Sidney. 1902. *Queen Victoria, A Biography.* London: Smith, Elder and Co.

———. 1925–1927. *King Edward VII.* 2 vols. London: Macmillan.

Lennie, Campbell. 1976. *Landseer: The Victorian Paragon.* London: Hamish Hamilton.

Levi, Peter. 1993. *Tennyson.* London: Trübner.

Lin, Jain I. 1985. *Death of a Kaiser: A Medical Historical Narrative.* Dayton, OH: Landfall Press.

Lloyd, Christopher. 1977. *The Queen's Pictures.* London: Chancellor.

———. 1998. *The Quest for Albion: Monarchy and the Patronage of British Painting.* London: The Royal Collection.

Lloyd, Christopher. 1991. *The Queen's Pictures.* London: Chancellor.

Longford, Elizabeth. [1964] 1998. *Victoria R.I.* London: Weidenfeld and Nicolson.

———. 1966. "Queen Elizabeth's Doctors." In Martin Gilbert, ed., *A Century of Conflict 1850–1950.* London: Hamish Hamilton.

———. 1972. *Wellington.* Vol. 1: *The Years of the Sword.* London: Weidenfeld and Nicolson.

———. 1972. *Wellington.* Vol. 2: *The Pillar of State.* London: Weidenfeld and Nicolson.

———, ed. 1976. *Louisa, Lady-in-Waiting: The Personal Diaries and Albums of Louisa, Lady in Waiting to Queen Victoria and Queen Alexandra.* London: Jonathan Cape.

———, ed. 1991. *Darling Loosy: Letters to Princess Louise 1858–1939.* London: Weidenfeld and Nicolson.

Lorne, Marquis of. 1901. *V.R.I.: Her Life and Empire.* London: Eyre and Spottiswoode.

Lutyens, Mary, ed. 1961. *Lady Lytton's Court Diary 1895–1899.* London: Rupert Hart Davis.

MacDonogh, Giles. 2000. *The Last Kaiser: William the Impetuous.* London: Weidenfeld and Nicolson.

Magnus, Philip M. 1954. *Gladstone: A Biography.* London: John Murray.

Magnus, Philip. 1964. *King Edward the Seventh.* London: John Murray.

Mallet, Victor, ed. 1968. *Life with Queen Victoria: Marie Mallet's Letters from Court, 1887–1901.* London: John Murray.

Malmesbury, Lord. 1884. *Memoirs of an Ex-Minister.* 2 vols. London: Smith Elder.

Malmgreen, Gail, ed. 1986. *Religion in the Lives of English Women.* London: Croom Helm.

Marie Louise, Princess. 1961. *My Memories of Six Reigns.* Harmondsworth, UK: Penguin.

Marie, Queen of Roumania. 1934. *The Story of My Life.* Vol. 1. London: Cassell.

Marples, Morris. 1972. *Wicked Uncles in Love.* London: Michael Joseph.

Marshall, D. 1975. *Lord Melbourne.* London: Weidenfeld and Nicolson.

Martin, Robert B. 1981. *Tennyson: The Unquiet Heart.* Oxford: Clarendon Press.

Martin, Sir Theodore. 1875–1880. *The Life of His Royal Highness the Prince Consort.* 5 vols. London: Smith, Elder and Co.

———. 1908. *Queen Victoria as I Knew Her.* Edinburgh: William Blackwood and Sons.

Massingham, H. J. and H. Massingham, eds. 1932. *The Great Victorians.* London: Ivor Nicholson and Watson.

Masters, Brian. 1978. *Now Barabbas Was a Rotter: The Extraordinary Life of Marie Corelli.* London: Hamilton.

Matson, John. 1975. *Dear Osborne.* London: Hamish Hamilton.

Matthew, H. C. G. 1986. *Gladstone 1809–1874.* Oxford: Clarendon Press.

———, ed. 1978. *The Gladstone Diaries.* Vol. 6: *1861–1868.* Oxford: Clarendon Press.

Maurois, André. 1937. *Disraeli.* Harmondsworth, UK: Penguin.

May, John. 1983. *Victoria Remembered.* London: Heineman.

McClintock, Mary Howard. 1945. *The Queen Thanks Sir Howard: The Life of Major General Sir Howard Elphinstone.* London: John Murray.

McKinlay, Brian. 1971. *The First Royal Tour. 1867–1868.* London: Robert Hale.

Millar, Delia. 1985. *Queen Victoria's Life in the Scottish Highlands, Depicted by Her Watercolour Artists.* London: Philip Wilson.

Millar, Sir Oliver. 1992. *Victorian Pictures in the Collection of HM Queen Victoria.* Cambridge: Cambridge University Press.

Mitchell, L. G. 1997. *Lord Melbourne, 1779–1848.* Oxford: Oxford University Press.

Moneypenny, William F., and G. E. Buckle. [1910–1920] 1968. *Disraeli, Earl of Beaconsfield.* 6 vols. London: Smith, Elder and Co.

Morley, John. 1905–1906. *The Life of William Ewart Gladstone.* 3 vols. London: Macmillan.

Morris, James. 1992. *Pax Britannica: Farewell the Trumpets—An Imperial Retreat.* London: Folio Society.

Munich, Adrienne. 1996. *Queen Victoria's Secrets.* New York: Columbia University Press.

Nelson, Michael. 2000. *Queen Victoria and the Discovery of the Riviera.* London: I. B. Tauris.

Nevill, Barry St.-John. 1997. *Life at the Court of Queen Victoria: Selections from the Journals of Queen Victoria.* Stroud, Gloucestershire: Sutton.

Nevill, Lady Dorothy. 1910. *Under Five Reigns.* London: Meuthen.

Nichols, J. Alden. 1987. *The Year of Three Kaisers.* Chicago: University of Illinois Press.

Noel, Gerard. 1974. *Princess Alice: Queen Victoria's Forgotten Daughter.* Norwich, Norfolk: Michael Russell.

Nutting, Anthony. 1966. *Gordon of Khartoum: Martyr and Misfit.* London: Reprint Society.

Oliphant, Margaret. 1900. *Queen Victoria, A Personal Sketch.* London: Cassell and Co.

[One of Her Majesty's Servants]. 1901. *The Private Life of Queen Victoria.* London: C. Arthur Pearson.

Ormond, Richard. 1982. *Sir Edwin Landseer.* New York: Rizzoli.

———. 1987. *Franz Xaver Winterhalter and the Courts of Europe 1830–70.* London: National Portrait Gallery.

Packard, Jerrold M. 1995. *Farewell in Splendour: The Passing of Queen Victoria and Her Age.* Stroud, Gloucestershire: Sutton.

———. 1998. *Victoria's Daughters.* New York: St. Martin's Press.

Pakenham, Thomas. 1979. *The Boer War.* London: Weidenfeld and Nicolson.

Pakula, Hannah. 1996. *An Uncommon Woman, The Empress Frederick: Daughter of Queen Victoria.* London: Weidenfeld and Nicolson.

Palmer, Alan. 1976. *Bismarck.* London: Weidenfeld and Nicolson.

———. 1978. *The Kaiser.* New York: Charles Scribner's Sons.

Pearson, Hesketh. 1951. *Dizzy: The Life and Nature of Benjamin Disraeli, Earl of Beaconsfield.* London: Methuen.

———. 2000. *The Whispering Gallery, being Leaves from a Diplomat's Diary.* London: Phoenix.

Pflanze, Otto. 1990. *Bismarck and the Development of Modern Germany.* 2 vols. Princeton, NJ: Princeton University Press.

Plowden, Alison. 1981. *The Young Victoria.* London: Weidenfeld and Nicolson.

Plumb, J. H. 1966. *The First Four Georges.* London: Fontana.

Plumptre, George. 1995. *Edward VII.* London: Pavilion.

Plunkett, John. 1999. "Remembering Victoria: The National Memorial to the 'Great Queen.'" *The Victorian,* no. 1 (August): 4–9.

Ponsonby, Arthur. 1942. *Henry Ponsonby, Queen Victoria's Private Secretary: His Life from His Letters.* London: Macmillan.

Pope-Hennessy, Una. 1945. *Charles Dickens, 1812–1870.* London: Chatto and Windus.

Ponsonby, Frederick, ed. 1928. *The Letters of the Empress Frederick.* London: Macmillan.

———. 1951. *Recollections of Three Reigns.* London: Eyre and Spottiswoode.

Ponsonby, Magadalen. 1927. *Mary Ponsonby: A Memoir, Some Letters and a Journal.* London: John Murray.

Potts, D. M., and W. T. W. Potts. 1995. *Queen Victoria's Gene: Haemophilia and the Royal Family.* Stroud, Gloucestershire: Sutton.

Prest, John. 1972. *Lord John Russell.* London: Macmillan.

Prole, Lozania. 1973. *The Queen's Daughters.* London: Robert Hale.

Ramm, Agatha, ed. 1990. *Beloved and Darling Child: Last Letters between Queen Victoria and Her Eldest Daughter, 1886–1901.* Stroud, Gloucestershire: Sutton.

Ransom, Teresa. 1999. *The Mysterious Miss Marie Corelli: Queen of Victorian Bestsellers.* Stroud, Gloucestershire: Sutton Publishing.

Reed, D. 1987. *Peel and the Victorians.* Oxford: Blackwells.

Reid, D. I. 1981. *The Victoria Cross 1856–1981: A Select Bibliography.* London: School of Library and Information Studies.

Reid, Michaela. 1996. *Ask Sir James: The Life of Sir James Reid, Personal Physician to Queen Victoria.* London: Eland.

Rennell, Tony. 2000. *Last Days of Glory: The Death of Queen Victoria.* London: Viking.

Rhodes, J. R. 1995. *Rosebery.* London: Phoenix.

Rich, Norman. 1985. *Why the Crimean War?* Hanover, NH: Published for Brown University by the University Press of New England.

Richardson, Joanna. 1977. *Victoria and Albert: A Study of a Marriage.* London: Dent.

Ridley, Jasper. 1970. *Lord Palmerston.* London: Constable.

Roberts, Andrew. 1999. *Salisbury: Victorian Titan.* London: Weidenfeld and Nicolson.

Robinson, John Martin. 1997. *Windsor: Official Guide.* London: Royal Collection.

Röhl, John C. G., Martin Warren, and David Hunt. 1998. *Purple Secret: Genes, Madness and the Royal Houses of Europe.* London: Bantam.

Röhl, John, and Nicolaus Sombart, eds. 1982. *Kaiser Wilhem II, New Interpretations.* Cambridge: Cambridge University Press.

Röhl, John. 1998. *Young Wilhelm: The Kaiser's Early Life, 1859–1888.* Cambridge: Cambridge University Press.

Rowell, George. 1978. *Queen Victoria Goes to the Theatre.* London: Paul Elek.

Royle, Trevor. 1999. *Crimea: The Great Crimean War 1854–1856.* London: Little, Brown.

Rushby, Kevin. 1999. *Chasing the Mountain of Light: Across India on the Trail of the Koh-i-Noor Diamond.* London: Flamingo.

Sara, M. E. 1945. *The Life and Times of Princess Beatrice.* London: Stanley Paul.

Sencourt, Robert. 1931. *The Life of the Empress Eugénie.* London: Ernest Benn.

Shannon, Richard. 1982. *Gladstone, Peel's Inheritor: 1809–1865,* vol. 1: *Gladstone, Heroic Minister: 1865–1898,* vol. 2. London: Hamish Hamilton.

Sinclair, Andrew. 1981. *The Other Victoria: The Princess Royal and the Great Game of Europe.* London: Weidenfeld and Nicolson.

Small, Hugh. 1998. *Florence Nightingale: Avenging Angel.* London: Constable.

Smith, E. A. 1999. *George IV.* New Haven: Yale University Press.

Smith, F. B. 1982. *Florence Nightingale: Reputation and Power.* London: Croom Helm.

Smyth, Ethel. 1987. *The Memoirs of Ethel Smyth.* Abridged and introduced by Ronald Crichton. London: Viking.

Smyth, John. 1965. *The Victoria Cross, 1856–1964.* London: F. Muller.

Somerset, Anne. 1980. *The Life and Times of William IV.* London: Weidenfeld and Nicolson.

St. Aubyn, Giles. 1979. *Edward VII, Prince and King.* London: Collins.

———. 1991. *Queen Victoria, a Portrait.* London: Sinclair Stevenson.

Stamp, Robert M. 1988. *Royal Rebels: Princess Louise and the Marquis of Lorne.* Toronto: Dundurn Press.

Stockmar, Ernst Baron, ed. 1873. *Memoirs of Baron Stockmar.* 2 vols. London: Longman, Green and Co.

Stoney, Benita, and Heinrich C. Weltzien, eds. 1994. *My Mistress the Queen: The Letters of Frieda Arnold, Dresser to Queen Victoria 1854–9.* London: Weidenfeld and Nicolson.

Strachey, Lytton. [1918] 1971a. *Eminent Victorians.* Harmondsworth, UK: Penguin;

———. [1921] 1971b. *Queen Victoria.* Harmondsworth, UK: Penguin.

Strachey, Lytton, and Roger Fulford, eds. 1938. *The Greville Memoirs.* 8 vols. London: Macmillan.

Stuart, Dorothy. 1941. *The Mother of Victoria: A Period Piece.* London: Macmillan

Taylor, A. J. P. 1995. *Bismarck: The Man and the Statesman.* Harmondsworth, UK: Penguin.

Taylor, Robert G. 1975. *Lord Salisbury.* London: Lane.

Tennyson, Hallam. 1897. *Alfred Lord Tennyson: A Memoir by His Son.* 2 vols. London: Macmillan.

Tennyson, Sir Charles. 1949. *Alfred Tennyson.* London: Macmillan.

Thompson, Dorothy. 1990. *Queen Victoria: Gender and Power.* London: Virago.
Thomson, Dorothy, and L. Temple Smith. 1984. *The Chartists: Popular Politics in the Industrial Revolution.* Aldershot, UK: Wildwood House.
Thorn, Michael. 1993. *Tennyson.* London: Abacus.
Tisdall, E. E. P. 1953. *Unpredictable Queen: The Intimate Life of Queen Alexandra.* London: S. Paul.
———. 1961. *Queen Victoria's Private Life.* London: Jarrolds.
Tooley, Sarah. 1896. *Personal Life of Queen Victoria.* London: Hodder and Stoughton.
Turner, Michael. 1999. *Osborne House.* Official Guide. London: English Heritage.
Underwood, Peter. 1982. *Queen Victoria's Other World.* London: Harrap.
Vallone, Lynne. 2001. *Becoming Victoria.* New Haven: Yale University Press.
Van der Kiste, John. 1981. *Frederick III: German Emperor 1888.* Stroud, Gloucestershire: Sutton.
———. 1986. *Queen Victoria's Children.* Stroud, Gloucestershire: Sutton.
Van der Kiste, John, and Bee Jordaan. 1984. *Dearest Affie: Alfred, Duke of Edinburgh, Queen Victoria's Second Son, 1844–1900.* Stroud, Gloucestershire: Sutton.
Van Thal, Herbert. 1936. *Ernest Augustus, Duke of Cumberland.* London: A. Barker.
Vicinus, Martha, and Bea Nergaard, eds. 1989. *Ever Yours, Florence Nightingale.* London: Virago.
Victoria, Queen. 1868. *Leaves from the Journal of Our Life in the Highlands from 1848–1861.* Edited by Arthur Helps. London: Smith, Elder and Co..
———. 1884. *More Leaves from the Journal of a Life in the Highlands, from 1862 to 1882.* London: Smith, Elder and Co.
Vincent, John. 1990. *Disraeli.* Oxford: Oxford University Press.
Vyver, Bertha. 1930 *Memoirs of Marie Corelli.* London: A. Rivers.
Wake, Jehanne. 1988. *Princess Louise: Queen Victoria's Unconventional Daughter.* London: Collins.
Waller, John H. 1988. *Gordon of Khartoum: The Saga of a Victorian Hero.* New York: Athenaeum.
Walpole, S. 1889. *The Life of Lord John Russell.* 2 vols. London: Longmans.
Walsh, Walter. 1902. *The Religious Life and Influence of Queen Victoria.* London: Swan Sonnenschein.
Walton, Peter. 2000. *A Celebration of Empire: A Centenary Souvenir of the Diamond Jubilee of Queen Victoria 1837–1937.* Staplehurst, Kent: Spellmount Publishers.
Ward, Andrew. 1996. *Our Bones Are Scattered: The Cawnpore Massacres and the Indian Mutiny of 1857.* London: John Murray.
Wardroper, John. 2001. *Wicked Ernest: An Extraordinary Life Revealed.* London: Shelfmark.
Warner, Marina. 1979. *Queen Victoria's Sketchbook.* London: Macmillan.
Warner, Philip. [1972] 2001. *The Crimean War: A Reappraisal.* Ware, UK: Wordsworth Editions.
Warwick, P. 1980. *The South African War: The Anglo-Boer War.* London: Longman.
Watson, Vera. 1952. *A Queen at Home: An Intimate Account of the Social and Domestic Life at Queen Victoria's Court.* London: W. H. Allen.
Weintraub, Sidney. 1997. *Albert: Uncrowned King.* London: John Murray.
Weintraub, Stanley. 1996. *Victoria.* London: John Murray.
———. 2000. *The Importance of Being Edward: King in Waiting 1841–1901.* London: John Murray.
Whitfield, George. 1982. *Beloved Sir James: The Life of Sir James Clark, Bart, Physician to Queen Victoria, 1788–1870.* London: G. Whitfield.
Whittle, Tyler. 1977. *The Last Kaiser: A Biography of William II, German Emperor and King of Prussia.* London: Heinemann.
———. 1980. *Queen Victoria at Home.* London: Routledge and Kegan Paul.
Williams, Merryn. 1986. *Margaret Oliphant: A Critical Biography.* London: Macmillan.
Williams, Richard. 1997. *The Contentious Crown: Public Discussion of the British Monarchy in the Reign of Queen Victoria.* Aldershot, Hampshire: Ashgate.
Willis, G. M. 1954. *Ernest Augustus, Duke of Cumberland and King of Hanover.* London: A. Barker.
Wilson, Philip Whitwell ed. 1927. *The Greville Diary.* 2 vols. Garden City, NY: Doubleday.
Windsor, Dean of, and Hector Bolitho. 1929. *Later Letters of Lady Augusta Stanley 1864–1876.* London: Jonathan Cape.
———, eds. 1927 *Letters of Lady Augusta Stanley: A Young Lady at Court 1849–1863.* London: Gerald Howe.
Wood, Christopher. 1976. *Victorian Panorama: Paintings of Victorian Life.* London: Faber and Faber.

———. 1999. *Victorian Painting.* London: Cassell.

Woodham-Smith, Cecil. 1950. *Florence Nightingale, 1820–1910.* Edinburgh: Constable.

———. 1957. *The Reason Why.* London: Constable.

———. 1972. *Queen Victoria: Her Life and Times.* Vol. 1: *1819–1861.* London: Hamish Hamilton.

Wright, Patricia. 1992. "Queen Victoria and her Palace." *History Today* 2 (December).

———. 1996. *The Strange History of Buckingham Palace.* Stroud, Gloucestershire: Sutton.

Wyndham, Hon. Mrs. Hugh, ed. 1912. *The Correspondence of Sarah Spencer, Lady Lyttleton, 1787–1870.* London: John Murray.

York, HRH Duchess of, and Benita Stoney. 1991. *Victoria and Albert: Life at Osborne House.* London: Weidenfeld and Nicolson.

Zeepvat, Charlotte. 2000. *Prince Leopold: The Untold Story of Queen Victoria's Youngest Son.* Stroud, Gloucestershire: Sutton.

Ziegler, Philip. 1971. *King William IV.* Newton Abbott, UK: Reader's Union.

———. 1976. *Melbourne.* London: Collins.

Secondary Sources

Aga Khan. 1954. *Memoirs of Aga Kahn.* London: Cassell.

Aldington, Richard. 1948. *Four English Portraits 1801–1851.* London: Evans Brothers.

Anderson, Anne. 2002. "Queen Victoria's Daughters and 'The Tide of Fashionable Philanthropy.'" *Women's History Magazine* 41 (June): 10–15.

Anderson, Bonnie S. 2000. *Joyous Greetings: The First International Women's Movement 1830–1860.* Oxford: Oxford University Press.

Apperson, G. L. 1914. *The Social History of Smoking.* London: M. Secker.

Askwith, Betty. 1975. *The Lyttletons: A Family Chronicle of the Nineteenth Century.* London: Chatto & Windus.

Baird, Diana, ed. 1958. *Victorian Days and a Royal Friendship.* Worcester, UK: Littlebury.

Baring, Maurice. [1932] 1987. *The Puppet Show of Memory.* London: Cassell.

Barratt, Carrie Rebora. 2000. *Queen Victoria and Thomas Sully.* Princeton, NJ: Princeton University Press.

Batty, J. 1990. *Landseer's Animal Illustrations.* Alton: Nimrod.

Begg, Paul, Martin Fido, and Keith Skinner. 1991. *The Jack the Ripper A to Z.* London: Headline.

Boyd, Nancy. 1982. *Three Victorian Women Who Changed Their World.* London: Macmillan.

Brendon, Piers. 2001. "A Nation Painted Black." *The Independent,* 13 January.

Briggs, Asa. 1999. "He Discovered Who the Conservatives Are." *Literary Review* (September): 4–5.

Brown, Craig, and Lesley Cunliffe. 1982. *The Book of Royal Lists.* London: Routledge and Keegan Paul.

Carey, Rosa Nouchette. 1899. *Twelve Notable Good Women.* London: Hutchinson.

Cecil, Lord David. 1973. *The Cecils of Hatfield House.* London: Constable.

Chapman, Caroline. 1984. *Russell of* The Times: *War Dispatches and Diaries.* London: Bell and Hynton.

Chapman, Maria Weston, ed. 1983. *Harriet Martineau's Autobiography.* London: Virago.

Chick, Alfred Noah. 1974. *Annals of the Indian Rebellion.* London: Charles Knight and Co.

Clarke, John. 1977. "The House of Hanover." In Antonia Fraser, ed., *The Lives of the Kings and Queens of England.* London: Futura.

Cockburn, Claud. 1952. *Aspects of English History.* London: MacGibbon and Kee.

Colby, Vineta, and Robert A. Colby. 1966. *The Equivocal Virtue: Margaret Oliphant and the Victorian Literary Market Place.* Hamden, CT: Archon.

Collier, Richard. 1984. *The Rainbow People.* London: Weidenfeld and Nicolson.

Compton, Piers. 1977. *Victorian Vortex: Pleasures and Pecadilloes of an Age.* London: Robert Hale.

Cornwell, Patricia. 2002. *Portrait of a Killer: Jack the Ripper—Case Closed.* London: Little, Brown.

Curl, James Stevens. 2000. *The Victorian Celebration of Death.* Stroud, Gloucestershire: Sutton.

Disraeli, Benjamin. [1845] 1981. *Sybil, or the Two Nations.* Oxford: Oxford University Press

Drabble, Margaret. 1979. *A Writer's Britain: Landscape in Literature.* London: Thames and Hudson.

———, ed. 1991. *The Oxford Companion to English Literature,*.5th ed. Oxford: Oxford University Press.

Eckardstein, Baron von. 1921. *The Years at the Court of St. James.* London: Thornton Butterworth.

Edel, Leon, ed. 1984. *The Letters of Henry James.* Vol. 4: *1895–1916.* London: Macmillan.

Epstein, James, and Dorothy Thompson, eds. 1982. *The Chartist Experience.* London: Macmillan.

Feiling, Keith. 1966. *A History of England: From the Coming of the English to 1918.* London: Macmillan.

Feldman, Paul H. 1997. *Jack the Ripper: The Final Chapter..* London: Virgin.

Fisher, Trevor. 1995. *Scandal: The Sexual Politics of Late Victorian Britain.* Stroud, Gloucestershire: Sutton.

Foley, Daniel J. 1960. *The Christmas Tree.* Philadelphia: Chilton.

Forster, Margaret. 1984. *Significant Sisters: The Grassroots of Active Feminism 1839–1939.* Harmondsworth, UK: Penguin Books.

Gardner, A. G. 1923. *The Life of Sir William Harcourt.* 2 vols. London: Constable and Co.

Girouard, Mark. 1981. *The Return to Camelot: Chivalry and the English Gentleman.* New Haven: Yale University Press.

Golby, J. M., and A. W. Purdue. 1986. *The Making of the Modern Christmas.* London: B. T. Batsford.

Greenhalgh, Paul. 1988. *Ephemeral Vistas: The Expositions Universelles, Great Exhibitions and World's Fairs, 1851–1939.* Manchester, UK: Manchester University Press.

Guedalla, Philip. [1931] 1997. *The Duke.* Ware, UK: Wordsworth Editions.

———. 1932. *The Second Empire.* London: Hodder and Stoughton.

Hargrove, W. B. 1918. "The Story of Josiah Henson." *Journal of Negro History* 3 (January): 1–21.

Helsinger, Elizabeth K., Robin Lauterbach Sheets, and William Veeder. 1983. *The Woman Question: Society and Literature in Britain and America, 1837–1883.* Vol. 2: *Social Issues, 1837–1883.* Manchester, UK: Manchester University Press.

Hobsbawm, Eric. 1975. *The Age of Capital, 1848–1875.* London: Phoenix.

Horn, Pamela. 1999. *Pleasures and Pastimes in Victorian Britain.* Stroud, Gloucestershire: Sutton.

Howe, Julia Ward. 1899. *Reminiscences, 1819–1899.* Boston: Houghton Mifflin.

Hyde, H. Montgomery. 1938. *Princess Lieven.* London: George G. Harrap and Co.

In Memoriam, Harriet Duchess of Sutherland. 1872. Newcastle, Staffordshire: C. Hickson.

James, L. 1992. *The Iron Duke: A Military Biography of Wellington.* London: Weidenfeld and Nicolson.

Jay, Elisabeth, and Francis O'Gorman, guest eds. 1999. *Women's History Review* 6, no. 2.

Johnston, Penelope. 1990. "Canada's Uncle Tom." *History Today* 40 (September): 3–4.

Jones, Edward, and Christopher Woodward. 1983. *A Guide to the Architecture of London.* London: Weidenfeld and Nicolson.

Jones, Steve. 1996. *In the Blood.* London: HarperCollins.

Jones, Wilbur D. 1956. *Lord Derby and Victorian Conservatism.* Oxford: Blackwell.

Jordan, Jane. 2001. *Josephine Butler.* London: John Murray.

Judd, Denis. 2001. "Gilding of the Empire State." *BBC History Magazine,* 18–21 January.

Jullian, Philippe. 1971. *Oscar Wilde.* London: Paladin.

Keating, Peter. 1989. *The Haunted Study: A Social History of the English Novel 1875–1914.* London: Secker and Warburg.

Kelley, Philip, and Ronald Hudson, eds. 1988. *The Brownings' Correspondence.* Vol 6. Winfield, KS: Wedgestone Press.

———, eds. 1991. *The Browning's Correspondence.* Vol. 9. Winfield, KS: Wedgestone Press.

Knight, Stephen. 1977. *Jack the Ripper: The Final Solution.* London: Grafton.

Kreigel, A., ed. 1977. *The Holland House Diaries.* London: Routledge.

Lambert, Margaret. 1937. *When Victoria Began to Reign: A Coronation Year Scrapbook.* London: Faber and Faber.

Langtry, Lillie. 1978. *The Days That I Knew.* London: Futura.

Leveson-Gower, Frederick. 1905. *Bygone Years: Recollection.* London: John Murray.

Leveson-Gower, Ronald. 1891. *Stafford House Letters.* London: Kegan Paul, Trench.

Londonderry, Marchioness of, ed. 1938. *Letters from Benjamin Disraeli to Frances Anne, Marchioness of Londonderry.* London: Macmillan.

MacAlpine, I., and R. Hunter. 1969. *George III and the Mad Business.* Harmonsworth, UK: Penguin.

Macdonald, Gus. 1979. *A Victorian Eyewitness.* London: Batsford.

Mackenzie, J. M. 1984. *Propaganda and Empire: The Manipulation of British Public Opinion, 1880–1961.* Manchester, UK: Manchester University Press.

Mackenzie, Morell. 1888. *The Fatal Illness of Frederick the Noble.* London: Sampson, Low, Marston, Searle, and Rivington.

Mandler, Peter. 1990. *Aristocratic Government in the Age of Reform: Whigs and Liberals 1830–1852.* Oxford: Clarendon Press.

Massie, Robert K. 1968. *Nicholas and Alexandra.* London: Gollancz.

Maxwell, Sir Herbert, ed. 1913. *Life and Letters of the 4th Earl of Clarendon.* London: Arnold.

Maxwell, Sir Herbert. [1893] 1924. *The Life of Wellington.* London: Hutchinson.

Mee, Arthur. [1937] 1960. *The King's England: London, Heart of the Empire and Wonder of the World* [also known under the title *Arthur Mee's London*]. London: Hodder and Stoughton.

Morley, John, 1971. *Death, Heaven, and the Victorians.* Pittsburgh: University of Pittsburgh Press.

Morris, Jan. 2001. "The Real Uncle Tom." *Guardian* 21 April: 3.

Morrow, Ian F. D. 1970. *Bismarck.* New York: Collier Books.

Mundy, Harriot Georgina, ed. 1885. *The Journal of Mary Frampton from the Year 1779 until the Year 1846.* London: Sampson, Low, Marston, Searle, and Rivington.

Myers, Walter Dean.1999. *At Her Majesty's Request: An African Princess in Victorian London.* New York: Scholastic Press.

Newbould, I. 1990. *Whiggery and Reform, 1830–41: The Politics of Government.* London: Macmillan.

Noel, G. 1999. *Ena, Spain's English Queen.* London: Constable.

O'Byrne, Robert. 1965. *The Victoria Cross, an official Chronicle of the deeds of personal valour achieved during the Crimean and Baltic Campaigns, 1856 to 1880.* London: Frederick Muller.

Oliphant, Margaret. [1899] 1990. *The Autobiography of Margaret Oliphant: The Complete Text.* Edited by Elisabeth Jay. Oxford: Oxford University Press.

Pakenhan, Elizabeth. 1960. *Jameson's Raid.* London: Weidenfeld and Nicolson.

Parissien, Steven. 2001. *George IV: The Grand Entertainment.* London: John Murray.

Pauli, Hertah. 1944. *The Story of the Christmas Tree.* Boston: Houghton Mifflin.

Pearman, Hugh. 2001. "Don't Turn Up Your Nose at Victorian Values." *Sunday Times,* Culture (Section 9), 25 March, 4–5.

Pearsall, Ronald. 1969. *The Worm in the Bud: The World of Victorian Sexuality.* London: Weidenfeld and Nicolson.

Pearsall, Ronald. 1972. *The Table Rappers.* London: Michael Joseph.

Perkin, Joan. 1993. *Victorian Women.* London: John Murray.

Perugini, Mark Edward. 1932. *Victorian Days and Ways.* London: Jarrolds.

Peterson, Linda. 1986. *Victorian Autobiography.* New Haven: Yale University Press

Petrie, Sir Charles. 1960. *The Victorians.* London: Eyre and Spottiswoode.

Poschinger, Margarethe von. 1902. *Life of the Emperor Frederick.* London: Chapman and Hall.

Priestley, J. B. 1972. *Queen Victoria's Heyday.* Harmondsworth, UK: Penguin.

Quennell, Pete. 1937. *Victorian Panorama.* London: Batsford.

Radzinsky, Eduard. 1992. *The Last Tsar.* New York: Doubleday.

Randall, David. 2001. "Off with Her Head." *Independent on Sunday,* 29 July.

Rappaport, Helen. 2001. *An Encyclopedia of Women Social Reformers.* 2 vols. Santa Barbara, CA: ABC-CLIO.

Raymond, E. T. 1923. *The Man of Promise, Lord Rosebery: A Critical Study.* London: T. F. Unwin.

Richards, T. 1987. "The Image ofVictoria in the Years of Jubilee." *Victorian Studies* 3 (1): 7–32.

Richardson, Joanna. 1961. *My Dearest Uncle.* London: Jonathan Cape.

Ricks, Christopher, ed. 1990. *The New Oxford Book of Victorian Verse.* Oxford: Oxford University Press.

Robinson, John Martin. 1995. *Buckingham Palace.* Royal Palaces. London: Michael Joseph.

Russell, G. W. E. 1898. *Collections and Recollections.* London: Smith, Elder & Co.

Sanders, Valerie. 1989. *The Private Lives of Victorian Women: Autobiography in Nineteenth-Century England.* New York: St. Martin's Press.

Seton-Watson, R. W. 1937. *Britain in Europe 1789–1914*. Cambridge: Cambridge University Press.

Sewell, Brian. 2001. "Glorious Rummage through Victoria's Drawers" [review of the "Victorian Visions. Exhibition at the V&A]. *Evening Standard,* 27 April, 32–33.

Shattock, Joanne, ed. *The Oxford Guide to British Women Writers.* Oxford: Oxford University Press.

Sitwell, Edith. 1987. *Victoria of England.* London: Cresset.

Smith, F. 1966. *The Making of the Second Reform Bill.* Cambridge: Cambridge University Press.

Souhami, Diana. 1996. *Mrs. Keppel and Her Daughter.* London: Flamingo.

Stamp, Gavin. 1984. *The Changing Metropolis: Earliest Photographs of London 1839–1879.* Harmondsworth, UK: Penguin.

Stanmore, Lord (Sir Arthur Gordon). 1893. *The Earl of Aberdeen.* London: Sampson Low.

Stewart, R. 1971. *The Politics of Protection: Lord Derby and the Protectionist Party, 1841–52.* Cambridge: Cambridge University Press.

Storey, Graham, ed. 1965–2002. *Letters of Charles Dickens.* 12 vols. Oxford: Clarendon Press.

Strachey, Ray. 1970. *The Cause: A Short History of the Women's Movement in Great Britain.* London: Virago.

Stuart, Dorothy Margaret. 1951. *Daughter of England: A New Study of Princess Charlotte of Wales and Her Family.* London: Macmillan.

Surtees, Virginia. 1975. *Charlotte Canning: Lady in Waiting to Queen Victoria and Wife of the First Viceroy of India, 1817–1861.* London: John Murray.

Sutherland, John. 1988. *The Longman Companion to Victorian Fiction.* London: Longman.

Sweet, Matthew. 2001. *Inventing the Victorians.* London: Faber and Faber.

Thompson, N. 1986. *Wellington after Waterloo.* London: Routledge and Kegan Paul.

Tomalin, Claire. 1994. *Mrs. Jordan's Profession: The Story of a Great Actress and a Future King.* London: Viking.

Trow, M. J. 1998. *The Many Faces of Jack the Ripper.* London: Summerdale Publications.

Tucker, Herbert F., ed. 1999. *A Companion to Victorian Literature and Culture.* Oxford: Blackwell.

Uglow, Lynn Jenny. 1993. *Elizabeth Gaskell: A Habit of Stories.* London: Faber and Faber.

Vansittart, Peter. 1988. *Happy & Glorious: An Anthology.* London: Collins.

Vincent, J. R., ed. 1978. *Disraeli, Derby and the Conservative Party: Journals and Memoirs of Edward Henry, Lord Stanley, 1849–1869.* New York: Barnes and Noble.

Ward, Yvonne M. 1999. "The Womanly Garb of Queen Victoria's Early Motherhood, 1840–1842." *Women's History Review* 8 (2): 277–294.

Weibe, M. G., gen. ed. 1982–1999. *Benjamin Disraeli Letters.* 6 vols. Toronto: University of Toronto Press.

Weinreb, Ben, and Christopher Hibbert, eds. 1983. *The London Encyclopedia.* London: Macmillan.

Wells, H. G. 1934. *Experiment in Autobiography: Discoveries and Conclusions of a Very Ordinary Brain (since 1866).* 2 vols. London: Victor Gollancz

Wheatcroft, Andrew. 1980. *The Tennyson Album: A Biography in Original Photographs.* London: Routledge and Kegan Paul.

Wise, T. J., and J. A. Symington, eds. 1932. *The Brontës, Their Lives, Friendships, and Correspondence.* 4 vols.: The Shakespeare Head Brontë. Oxford: Shakespeare Head Press.

Woodham-Smith, Cecil. 1902. *Diaries of the Emperor Frederick during the Campaigns of 1866 and 1870–1871.* London: Chapman and Hall.

Woolf, Virginia. 1992. *A Woman's Essays.* Harmondsworth, UK: Penguin.

Wyndham Lewis, D. B. 1948. *Four Favourites.* London: Evans Brothers.

Zetland, Marquis of. 1929. *The Letters of Disraeli to Lady Chesterfield and Lady Bradford.* 2 vols. London: Ernest Benn.

INDEX

Note: Page numbers in bold type refer to encyclopedia entries covering the topic.

ABOUT THE AUTHOR

Helen Rappaport is a freelance writer, researcher, Russian translator, and historical consultant, specializing in the nineteenth century. In addition to writing two previous books for ABC-CLIO, *Joseph Stalin: A Biographical Companion* and *Encyclopedia of Women Social Reformers,* she has published several articles and has given various conference papers and radio broadcasts on women's and Russian history. She also works in the theater as translator of numerous Russian plays for the National Theatre, Royal Shakespeare Company, and the Donmar Warehouse in London. She is currently developing two biographical projects.

www.ingramcontent.com/pod-product-compliance
Lightning Source LLC
LaVergne TN
LVHW080154100225
803362LV00004B/7